The Life and Adventures of Jack Rann; alias sixteen-string Jack, the ... highwayman ... Illustrated.

James Lindridge

The Life and Adventures of Jack Rann; alias sixteen-string Jack, the ... highwayman ... Illustrated.
Lindridge, James
British Library, Historical Print Editions
British Library
1845?
8°.
12620.e.1.

The BiblioLife Network

This project was made possible in part by the BiblioLife Network (BLN), a project aimed at addressing some of the huge challenges facing book preservationists around the world. The BLN includes libraries, library networks, archives, subject matter experts, online communities and library service providers. We believe every book ever published should be available as a high-quality print reproduction; printed on- demand anywhere in the world. This insures the ongoing accessibility of the content and helps generate sustainable revenue for the libraries and organizations that work to preserve these important materials.

The following book is in the "public domain" and represents an authentic reproduction of the text as printed by the original publisher. While we have attempted to accurately maintain the integrity of the original work, there are sometimes problems with the original book or micro-film from which the books were digitized. This can result in minor errors in reproduction. Possible imperfections include missing and blurred pages, poor pictures, markings and other reproduction issues beyond our control. Because this work is culturally important, we have made it available as part of our commitment to protecting, preserving, and promoting the world's literature.

GUIDE TO FOLD-OUTS, MAPS and OVERSIZED IMAGES

In an online database, page images do not need to conform to the size restrictions found in a printed book. When converting these images back into a printed bound book, the page sizes are standardized in ways that maintain the detail of the original. For large images, such as fold-out maps, the original page image is split into two or more pages.

Guidelines used to determine the split of oversize pages:

- Some images are split vertically; large images require vertical and horizontal splits.
- For horizontal splits, the content is split left to right.
- For vertical splits, the content is split from top to bottom.
- For both vertical and horizontal splits, the image is processed from top left to bottom right.

This Book was
Donated by J. Bartlett
Hare of 1842 to the
Ohio Villa

This Book was
Donated in June 9 1862
to the Ohio Villa

12620.e.1

THE LIFE AND ADVENTURES OF JACK RANN;

ALIAS

SIXTEEN-STRING JACK,

THE NOTORIOUS HIGHWAYMAN.

By James Lindridge, Esq.

BEAUTIFULLY ILLUSTRATED.

LONDON: G. PURKESS, COMPTON STREET, SOHO.

PREFACE.

Twelve months have we journeyed together, gentle reader, and that long pilgrimage has been, I hope, for you as for me, one of happy companionship.

In portraying the life of Sixteen-string Jack, we have abided as closely as possible to the historical facts handed down of him.

The commencement of his career as a costermonger, is a literal fact, there being at the present day aged inhabitants, in the good City of Bath, who well remember the musical voice, handsome face, and persuading eloquence of the young tradesman.

His subsequent career as a servant—his life on the road—connection with Elinor Roche, are all also more or less allied to truth. Whilst, however improbable it may appear, his having a cell full of young ladies to dine with him at almost his last dinner upon earth, is also a verity. Jack Rann throughout his gay career was an especial favourite with the fair sex, and of his acts of gallantry many an exciting page could have been written, but as the work was destined for the main part to fall in youthful hands, it was considered judicious to omit his private amours.

JACK RANN.
ALIAS
SIXTEEN-STRING JACK

By JAMES LINDRIDGE.

Author of "De Lisle," "Tyburn Tree," &c.

LONDON: G. PURKESS, COMPTON STREE, SOHO.

AND SOLD BY ALL BOOKSELLERS.

SIXTEEN-STRING JACK.

CHAPTER I.

JACK RANN COMES IN PROPRIA PERSONÆ BEFORE THE READERS.

The fashionable city of Bath was one glorious November morning aroused by the cries of a vendor of hares, rabbits and vegetables. A slim, slight youth, of scarcely sixteen summers, was leading down the main street a donkey, grown grey and ancient in servitude, across whose back was thrown a couple of hampers, having for contents the edibles before enumerated.

We have said he was slight and slim, and so he was; but had he bared his arm, he would have shown far more muscular power than many a man at twice his age. In appearance he was extremely prepossessing. Dark-chesnut locks, falling in graceful curls (after the fashion of the time) down his back, served only partly to hide a brow which, save from summer labour in the fields, would have been one of snowy whiteness. In addition, and to his further adornation, he possessed a nose perfectly acqueline—none too long—none too short—but being, all in all, as *aquiline* as was originally intended to express—a perfect beauty! And so it was.

Surmounting this nose (as every one *knows* that *knows* anything) were a pair of eyes! And these eyes, black as jet, and dark as midnight, shot forth such lightning in their angry glances, in indignation or in quarrel, that many a spirited man, although possessing double age and double strength, succumbed, ere they would chance a conflict with Bold and Brave Jack Rann!

Yes, Sixteen-String Jack—at once the bravest, most daring, dashing, and intrepid highwayman: whose glorious exploits on the road were unequalled; whose adventures and spirits threw the boasted valour of Dick Turpin and Claude du Val far, far into the rear—was once a peasant boy, and drove a donkey, laden with eatables, through the good city of Bath.

Here's a specimen of his skill as a salesman!

Having led his four-footed attendant to an open space situated near the centre of the city, he placed his hand to his mouth—after the manner of many of our metropolitan hawkers—and then shouted with a tone that made the old place ring again, "Buyers, buyers, buyers!"

The words had not left his lips many seconds, before door after door was opened, and many a damsel, who was more intent on a compliment from handsome Jack than the errand on which she was sent, tripped lightly and blithely towards our hero; followed at a sober, steady pace, by not a few matronly dames who, despising the vain glories of the world, were intent only on a cheap dinner and a good bargain.

"Oh! young bright eyes!" exclaimed Jack, as a pretty girl tripped towards him, "here we are again, young, blooming, and beautiful; with eyes like fire, cheeks like roses, lips like Christmas berries, and hearts as firm"—said Jack, pausing, and then suddenly breaking off, for he was now surrounded by some by whom his flattering speech would have been anything but a compliment—"and hearts as firm," he repeated, diving into a hamper, "as this jolly savoy."

And he drew forth before the admiring eyes of his auditors a fine large cabbage of the species named.

"Here's a specimen of vegetables! Only look! No buyers?" he asked, glancing round. "Well, I *am* glad of that, for I have been watching this fellow's growth for many a day; in fact, set him in a favourite piece of ground on purpose, that he might grow lusty and jolly; and hasn't he, that's all! Fact is, shouldn't have brought him out for sale, having reserved him for my own eating, but father being short of the mopusses—quarter-day coming on ye know—he made me. Poor old codger! I assure you he shed many a tear over it afore he would part with it; for, like his son," said Jack, drawing his cuff over his eyes, with a ludicrous attempt at grief, "he likes good cabbage!"

What, no buyers now?" said Jack. "Yes, by all that's good great generous, beneficent and kind, here comes the tailor's wife, determined to treat her love to that which of all things in this wide world he loveth best namely, a cabb—"

"What's that, you rascal?" exclaimed the lady, whose quick ears caught the phrase just in time to prevent its completion. "What's that you say?"

"What this?" said Jack, lifting the vegetable over his head, and turning the point of conversation from being a personal remark on cabbage to *the* cabbage in his hand. "Why this, ma'am, is the finest specimen—a true specimen—of what a good gardener, on good ground, in old England can produce."

"Lord a massy on the boy's tongue. Why, for talking, he bangs all the women in Bath, I do declare," said the tailor's wife. "Now, Jack—though really—the lowest mite you can possibly take, and perhaps—perhaps I may buy it."

"Sold again, and got the money,' shouted Jack, sure of his customer. Here's a cabbage grown from seed bought of the King of Savoy at a guinea an ounce, going for the insignificant sum of one penny."

The money was paid without a demur, and Jack pocketing the coin with the utmost promptitude, turned to the young lady whom he had first accosted, "Now, my love, what can I do for you?"

"A rabbit," simpered the girl.

"A rare-bit!" replied Jack. "What do I see before me, eh? What else but the rarest bit of feminine loveliness that ever trod in two shoes? And what do I see here?" said Jack, applying himself to his basket, and bringing forth a fine, plump little creature; "what do I see here? why the finest, nimblest little fellow, when alive, that ever run on four feet."

"Come, come, stop this rigmarole," said an old lady, tartly. "If you are going to serve us, don', talk so much about it, but do it, my time is too valuable to be spent in foolery in Bath streets."

Business before pleasure," said Jack, by no means disconcerted or abashed, "an excellent reproof; and, by our lady, in most fitting time. Come, missis, don't be angry with poor Jack!"

"Oh! get out with your foolery," said the woman turning away.

"I will, madam, and to business," said Jack, colouring slightly. "Come, as you are in great haste, it shall be your turn first—this young lady has a lesser distance and lighter legs to carry her over it, so with her usual amiability, I hope she will allow the preference of age before honesty."

"Age before honesty! what the devil does he mean by that?" grunted the old dame; "I am as honest as most folks, I'll warrant, ugh! How much for this?" she said, suddenly seizing a large rabbit, and endeavouring by lifting it up and down to calculate its weight. It was heavy, bony, and, as Jack fancied wiry and tough, "old womanish," he called it, not inaptly, perhaps, but what we, in modern parlance and in milder terms, should pronounce ANCIENT.

"How much?" said the dame; having satisfied herself it was a full weight one

Jack announced the price in a whisper, in confidence, and to enhance the value of the BARGAIN, in her ear.

"You are positive its young?"

"Was at its birth," answered Jack.

"And tender?" said the old woman, fumbling in her pocket for the money.

"As a chicken."

"You are not deceiving me now? eh, you rascal?"

"Judge for yourself," answered Jack, carelessly.

"Here, this will show you it's young," and he adroitly snapped a bone in the creature's foot.

"Oh, you brute, you have broken it's leg," grumbled the old woman.

"He'll run devil a whit the worse for it, marm," answered Jack, drily; "Come, do you buy?"

"Yes, here's the money," said the old woman, seizing her prize and hobbling off.

"Well sold!" exclaimed Jack, triumphantly, "that's dog bite cat with a vengeance! She palmed a leaden sixpence off on me the other day, and now ha! ha! ha!" and his musical laugh rung clear and sharp in the brisk air "she has got my worth for her lead money, ha, ha, ha! and I've some siller to boot."

"What is it, a tough 'un, Jack?" inquired a bystander.

"It's just as," answered Jack, inflated with delight; "something like our old cow we killed the other day, and a rare feast we had, too, over her. My stars, such platefuls, such a tightener. While we were at it tooth and nail, in comes parson. 'Bless me, dear me, God bless me, Rann, what have you got for dinner?' 'Beef, sir,' says my father. 'Beef, sir,' replies parson, 'and can you, sir—you sir, who have ever professed poverty, who have even dared to ask assistance from our impoverished city—can you with the utmost coolness, calmly and with unquivering conscience and unblushing front, sit down in the face of me, to whom you have come for parochial relief, and in the deceitful stillness of your supposed humble home, sit down to the sumptuous fare of roast beef?' I could see dad's face redden at this, and a leer in his eye told me something good was coming. 'Parson,' says dad bluntly and boldly, 'when I 'plied to you I was not only in want of beef, but I was also in want of bread, and so was my kids.' Now, parson, circumstances is a little altered, though I have none too much bread, I have plenty of beef, and all I can say,' says dad, 'as an honest man, is, that if you like to make my dinner an apology for your lunch, you are welcome to a snack.' 'Well, Rann, I will not refuse your invitation; my walk has certainly given me an appetite,' so down he sat.

"Father sawed away at the joint. 'Your knife seems out of sorts,' said parson getting a little impatient at the delay 'why the fact of it is,' said dad, resting a bit, 'I believe the knife has taken a perverse turn, it's like me, parson, it ain't used to beef, and so can't cut it. I am really afraid I shall not be able to digest what I eat—I really am. There,' said dad, cutting off a sliver at last—'there, you are heartily welcome, sir; ask a blessing, and fire away.' Parson mumbled over something, then seizing his knife and fork, he went to work, saw, saw. 'Rann,' said parson, 'you're knives are wretchedly dull. 'Get another, Jack,' father says; I got him another. The same old game, saw, saw, saw. At last he did manage to get a piece into his mouth, and then he found out it was not the knives that were in fault, but the beef. Presently out he spat his mouthful into the fire.'

"What's the matter, sir?" asked father.

"Rann." replied the parson "I asked you for beef' and not mahogany."

"**And** please, father, I asked you for beef," exclaimed my little sister Charlotte.

"And beef I gave you," answered father, sternly.

"Yes, father, but please, father, it is so hard, I think you must have cut it off the horns."

"Didn't I laugh! didn't we all laugh. Parson seemed inclined to melt. "One minute, sir," said father, catching his button as he was going away, "Pray reduce a lesson from this, and learn when you visit a poor man's cottage, that you do so in the sacred capacity of a minister of God; and not as you have done this day, enter his house, to insult his poverty—to wound his feelings—and to trample further down to the earth the care worn man, instead of lifting him, as your duty is, where if performed nearer to

Heaven. Get you gone—and as true as I stand here," said Jack, then dad opened the door, and showed him the way out.

"And sarve him well right," said the old matron, "for a nasty prying sneak as he is; but come, Jack, my dear boy serve us, and let's be going."

"Right, ma'am," said Jack, setting to his work in a business like manner. "I have only to divest this young gentleman of his coat, for the benefit of this young lady, and then I am at your service."

The rabbit was skinned in a twinkling.

"Here he is," said Jack, "and a fine plump little fellow he is, but, if they grumble at your stopping so long, my darling, tell them all I have told you, and so then they'll all want to come and if they do come, I shall have all the more customers, and the more the merrier. Good bye; here, half a minute," said Jack, "perhaps you'll be kind enough to ask Mrs. Thingamay how the rabbit ate I sold her. He was a rare old gentleman and no mistake—great-great-grandfather to the one you hold in your hands, and was to the day of his death, regularly, the oldest inhabitant of the rabbit warren. We should have shot him, but 'pon honour, he grew so childish it was a a mercy to kill him. Good bye, my love—I'll remember you in my dreams," said Jack, then disposing of his wares to one and the other almost like magic, serving all generously, and leaving all well satisfied, both with the goods they had purchased and with him they had purchased of. Jack found himself with empty hampers; and whistling a blythe tune, he turned his donkey's head, as his mission was fulfilled, towards home.

On the road home, Jack fell in with a companion—a dark-haired full-whiskered fellow; glorying in a full round smock, ruddy face, and a rare portly person. This man's name was Jones he was celebrated as a poacher, and on sundry and divers small occasions, such crimes as sheep stealing, horse stealing, and house-breaking were laid to his charge; but no positive proof being obtainable, he had been on all times acquitted, and though he was viewed with a sharp and suspicious eye by the various justices and their minions, the constabulary, he still walked a free man on the king's highway.

On catching sight of our hero, this person broke into the polite exclamation of—

"Strike me ——! and is it yourself, handsome Jack, coming home with your moke, and empty hamper's this time o' day? Strike me! summut must a' happened or you'd never a' show'd your fair skin here yet at this hour, I knows."

"Oh! you was always famous for swearing too much," was all the reply Jack condescended to give him; then striking his donkey with his hand, he trotted beside it to keep pace with the animal's increased speed; his intention was evident—it was to rid himself of an undesirable companion.

"He too, cuss him, like all the rest, treats me like a scurvy hound—like a mangy dog," muttered Jones, with vehement bitterness, between his clenched teeth; "but I'll be even with him; I'll do summut; I'll teach him to respect Luke Jones; I'll tread him under my feet, as I would a snail. I'll crush him to the earth, I will; and by God I will bring him to the GALLOWS. Yes, if I swing

The man's face, ever dark, grew purple as he gave vent to these bitter words, and were, in fact, as disgusting as they were frightful to look upon.

But Jack, happily for him then, though unhappily for him hereafter, trotted on beside his docile companion, pleasantly and quickly, without hearing or heeding the words.

To dismiss from his countenance the angry look and the ominous frown, was, with Luke Jones, the work of but an instant—so great an adept was he in the vile art of dissimulation, that all traces of evil thoughts and malign intent vanished from his face as a summer cloud does before the hurrying winds of heaven.

Jones, by dint of running at considerable speed, speedily overtook our hero, who, upon hearing a footstep behind, immediately stopped and faced about.

"Halloa!" he said to Jones, "what now?"

"Nothing, Jack," was the reply, "but—"

"Oh, if it's nothing," said Jack, "why you are served at once, and are welcome to take it—and go!"

"You're over witty to day, master Jack, sharp as a needle; strike me! as full of pointed replies as a blackthorn is o' prickles. Now pray master Jack, pray don't despise the companionship of poor Luke Jones—did I ever do you any harm?"

"No!" answered Jack, bluntly.

"Then, why spurn me as you would a spitting toad—why treat a fellow-man as you would a 'ojus snake, eh, Jack?"

This appeal was touching Jack in his vulnerable part, for Jack Rann was all generosity—far more prone to good intents and generous deeds, than evil ones

"Dash me down, Luke," said Jack, extending his hand, "but if I've hurt your feelings, I beg your pardon, that I do! But you know, Luke—you must know your character ain't such a one, as one likes to clash against."

"It ain't" answered Luke, with every appearance of openness, "more's the pity. But Jack, lad, if I have done bad to others, has not others done bad to me? and bad as I have been, Jack, I have been always drove to it ; and get a bad name, Jack, be it ever so little, and the devil's own name will cling to you ever after. I speak from experience, Jack ; I speak, to my sorrow, for I've felt and knows what it is to be shunned, hated, and despised ; yes, Jack, and the knowledge that the folks of Bath believed me to be ten times worser than I was—that every tongue around me scoffed and reviled—that every eye meeting mine looked but scorn—that every fellow man around me looked upon me with suspicion, and this contempt has raised the devil in my soul, and has drove me to ten times more sin than I should have committed ; it has hardened my heart, Jack, until I have hated every fellow creature—it has steeled my soul—that aught of evil that was to be done; I've found nerve to do it, Jack ; it has ruined me, body and soul ; it has ruined me!"

As Jones finished these word, tears fell—waters of hypocrisy filled his eyes.

Touched at the sight of this man's distress, a man whom he had but hitherto considered desperately bad, beyond redemption, Jack was moved to his heart's core, and poured forth, in a flood of soothing words, his indignation at the world's treatment, and his pity and sympathy with the object of them; begging in the same breath, again and again, his forgiveness for his ungenerous conduct.

Although Luke's words were clothed in deceit, and spoken with a full intent to the well being of the generous young man, who now in friendly intercourse walked quietly by his side, they yet contained the germ of a sad and dreadful truth.

Every day we have undeniable proofs of the evil to which his words referred; how far a sin, be it ever so light and simple, such is the rule of

No 2.

society, that the person committing that sin is for ever banished, spotted shunned, and an outcast. We do not argue that a man would be acting a discreet part in taking into his service a man who is known to have committed theft, or has been convicted of a crime, be it petty larceny, or, robbery, or what not. We can only regret that, after the first false step, there is not a govermental provision made—that he may have the chance, if he has the inclination, of earning his own bread by the sweat of his brow.

"I feel for you, Luke," exclaimed Jack Rann, "I swear I do, by all's that's good! What else can I say."

"Nothing, Jack," answered Luke, with enthusiasm, "for I now know you are what I always thought you—summat better than the common herd—cuss 'em! You're a brave, generous, sensible fellow."

To say that young Rann did not feel flattered by these words would be to lies, as the mantling blood that then crimsoned his cheek, told he took the words in pride and honour to himself.

"I tell ye what, Luke," said Jack, after a thoughtful pause.—

"What?" queried Jones, anxiously peering into his companion's face.

"That it strikes me, Luke, instead of being, like you are, a poor devil of a poacher—instead of lurking about here as you say you have, half a begger and half a thief, I would have played devil-may-care at once—would have chanced the rope—snapped my finger at the gallows—would have turned—"

"Would have turned," repeated Luke, as Jack in his vehemence, literally paused for breath.—

"A HIGHWAYMAN! Luke—a glorious, dashing highwayman at once!" said Jack, in ecstasy. "Yes, let me but cross the back of a gallant steed—let me but feel want behind my back and a chance before my face, and with mask covered face and pistol in hand, show me the man that dare refuse my STAND AND DELIVER."

Luke absolutely paused in amazement at Jack, as suiting word to the action, and action to the word; the latter stood with firm planted foot, with flashing eye, and with extended hand; in action, thought and look, the very *beau ideal* of a "Knight of the Road."

"Strike me, Jack!" cried Luke, "you've the soul of a man! blast me if I aint struck all of a heap—why who'd a thought it! Here's pluck—here's bottom! almost equal to Dick Turpin hisself."

"Equal to Dick Turpin," cried Jack, with a sneer in the curl of his handsome lip. "Equal! ha, ha, ha! if ever I was driven on the road—and, if I am, Luke, it will be from necessity, not from choice—I never was a thief yet, and I never will be unless I am forced, but if I do, Luke, it shall be to raise a name that shall last in the pages of history as long as the word Highwayman lives in the English language—shall last, ah! until DICK TURPIN'S name, like his body, shall be mouldered and forgotten."

"And," asked Luke, half ironically, "in what name then may future generations hail their hero?"

---

* See note I. at end of book

"Expect! i'faith," answered Jack, "I, a poor hawker-boy, have neither hope or expectation of living in fame or name beyond the term of my natural life; but had I such a thought or intent of figuring in the chronicles of Newgate, I swear to you that the only name that should eclipse that of Dick Turpin for devilry, bravery and adventure, should be that of——"

"Whose?" enquired Luke.

"JACK RANN!"

CHAPTER II.

WHEREIN JACK RANN PROVES HIMSELF POSSESSED OF "PLUCK."

As Jack, accompanied by Luke, proceeded on his journey homeward, they came at length to a wall surrounding a gentleman's mansion and lawn. Luke inquisitively peeped over, and something attractive catching his eye, he called out—

"Strike me sensible, Jack, if old squire aint got a party. My eyes, sich a lot o' gals, and here's some coves a skating and sliding—blow me! who'd a thought it had freezed so hard as that?"

"I should for one," answered Jack, after calling to his moke to stop, "for our cabbages and taters were awful frost bit this day or two past. Hallo!" he shouted, springing upon the wall, in order to view the scene more at his ease. "Old Giles looks as if he found the ice uncommon slippy, don't he. Why, he's going on any how, now he's down! ha, ha, ha!" and Jack being a rare lover of mischief, laughed loudly at the sport.

Luke had by this time joined Jack on the wall, and accompanied our hero's laugh with a loud hurrah!

"Bravo, old 'un," shouted Luke, "that takes the shine out of 'em—there's summut stunning in that—show 'em the same caper agin my wenerable."

We know of nothing worse in the way of sporting punishment than a heavy fall on the ice; a bruised shaken body is bad to bear, and one need have like-Job patience to bear it; but when, in addition you are assailed with contemptuous laughter, then the punishment becomes double—it is un bearable.

The squire, or old Jones, as he was more commonly called, after kicking his legs in all directions, and slipping about in anything but a scientific manner, was at length, by the help of his friends, restored to his feet. Turning his face, scarlet from over-exertion, passion, and excitement, to where young Rann and Jones were seated, he bawled—

"Get off my wall, you villains!"

"You're very kind, old gent'man, but we shan't fall; we're safer here then you are in them skates."

"Aye, that we are, I pound it," said Jones, laughingly; then turning his conversation to the squire, he bid him buckle to and show his agility.

"Oh, you scoundrels," exclaimed the old gentleman, in a towering passion, 'I'll teach you who you are insulting—I'll lock you up, you thieves, I will, for trespassing."

"Who do you call a thief?' said Jack Rann. "I tell you what it is, old fellow, you best be after minding what you are saying, or I'll be down upon you with an action for libel, and no flies."

"Ha, ha, ha!" laughed Luke, tickled at the impudence of the threat. "Bravo, Jack, that's the way to talk to them cantankerous old warmints."

Here was unbearable insolence! The rich squire to be bearded on his own grounds, before a company of visitors, by a mere boy, the son of a poor market gardener, who lived from hand to mouth, by hawking; and to be insulted, in addition, by Luke Jones, the discharged labourer and the reputed theif! The great mans indignation knew no bounds.

"You varlets, you shall pay dearly for this temerity;" and clinching his words with a blasphemous word, he swore he would hunt them with his dogs, if they were not off.

"I say, Jack," said Luke, "the sooner we make ourselves scarce the better I have no fancy of becoming meat for dogs.

"Then go," said Jack, with a sneer. "If he sets his dogs at me, he shall rue it;" and the lad, in his desperate humour, drew a long clasp-knife from his pocket, and opened the formidable blade with his teeth.

"What would you do, Jack?" inquired Luke, with a glistening eye.

"Do," replied Rann, "defend myself, that's all; I won't be called *thief* for nothing If either of his dogs assail me, by the living God they shall taste cold steel."

"Do you mean that, Jack?" inquired Luke.

"You'll see, soon;" was Rann's laconic reply.

"Then by — I'm with you!' exclaimed Jones, flourishing a heavy blackthorn stick he held in his hands; "and if I don't make his dogs cry pen-and-ink, set me down for a cowardly hound!"

"I will," answered Jack, in his determined tone. "See!" he continued, with outstretched fingers and with flashing eyes, "here they come. Mr. Squire is a rare Christian, it strikes me forcibly, to hunt his own fellow man to death with dogs, as he would a ravenous wolf. He's merciless, and so will I be, if he costs me my liberty and life?"

It was true, the squire, giving way to his inordinate passion, and to a naturally cruel and inhuman heart, had given orders for some dogs to be unkennelled, and two ferocious bull-dogs, baying deeply, were following a servant to inflict a summary and bloody chastisement upon the two interlopers.

It may be asked, did not some of the company intercede with the squire to prevent this outrage? Yes, one in particular, the squire's brother-in-law, an elderly gentleman named Malcolm, a rich merchant in the great city of London, used every argument humanity could suggest to dissuade him from his purpose. He might as well have talked to the stones. A squire, in those days, was as great an autocrat as Nicholas of Russia bears the character of being in those of ours. Their will was law. Relying upon their might they feared no evil result from their actions, knowing well, from experience money could buy law or prevent justice to any end they might wish to attain. The servant had now advanced to within fifty yards of the wall, and bending his knees to the ground, was busily employed in untying the leash that bound the two dogs together, when a cry, as of a man in mortal agony, broke upon the ear, and curdled the blood of all who heard it.

The cry arose from the lake, in which the barbarous squire was now fighting for his life!

Not satisfied, it would appear, by the summary vengeance he had planned the wretched man, in order to urge on by his presence the ferocious animals to the attack, had made his way to the edge of the lake. Here the ice being thin and imperfectly frozen, had treacherously broken beneath his feet, and he was hurled into the deep, cold waters!

Both Rann and his companion forgot their danger in the tumult that had arisen, and almost simultaneously they sprang to their feet upon the wall.

"This is something like revenge, Jack," whispered the man Jones between his teeth, his heavy eyes glaring malignantly at the struggling gentleman.

Scarcely heeding the words spoken, Jack exclaimed—

"By Heaven! it is he—it is the squire."

"It is," echoed Luke, with a laugh and a look perfectly fiendish in their expression; "and see the paltroons, his servants, they dare not save their master—they dare not approach the spot. He will die and be d———d! Oh Jack, this is something like revenge!"

"No, no, no, Luke, this is!" exclaimed Jack, dashing his knife to the ground, and springing from the wall. On, on he sped with the speed of the wind; and as the drowning man sunk to rise no more, Jack Rann, with a desperate bound, sprang headlong into the eddying water.

The spectators, who had hitherto remained spell-bound by the frightful and unexpected catastrophe, now broke forth into a shout of applause at the noble intrepidity of the spirited youth—an applause that was followed by a silence as deep as the grave; for they knew not but the accident might even now prove death to both!

"Bravo, bravo!"

Such was the grateful shout that arose from every tongue as our hero rose quickly to the surface of the icy water, bearing in his arms the inanimate body of the squire; and all rushed eagerly forward to drag the brave youth and his burthen from their perilous position. This feat, by means of a rope that was thrown to Rann, was, after some considerable delay, acccomplished; and our noble and brave Jack was, with his insensible burthen, dragged to the shore.

The body of the squire was conveyed to the mansion with the greatest possible speed by the servants, while Jack Rann was also hurried off by the ladies and Mr. Malcolm to the house, that his clothing might be changed, and his exhausted strength might be recruited by cordial refreshments.

After swallowing a bumping glass of brandy that was tendered him by Mr. Malcolmn's daughter, a young lady of surpassing beauty, Jack, without a word, would have left the place, wet as he was, but Mr. Malcolm interposing, insisted upon his changing his wet apparel for dry ones. For a long time Jack absolutely refused to accept their favour, but the kind solicitations of the ladies, the urgent recommendation of the good Mr. Malcolm, and last, but not least, the tearful entreaties of his pretty daughter—following a servant, who led the way for that purpose, Jack found himself in a sumptuously furnished bed-room, where a large fire was cheerfully blazing. He was speedily undressed, and acting upon the commands of the doctor, who was now in attendance, sprang between the warmed blankets of the bed, and from the stupifying effects of the brandy, was soon locked in the arms of Morpheus, the God of sleep.

After a refreshing slumber of two hours' duration, Jack was awoke by voices around his bed. So sweet were the voices—so gentle, so welcome the hours, that Jack would have lain in pretended sleep, ere he would have awoke to dissolve the charms of them!

A small and gentle hand was laid upon his brow, and put aside the ringlets that, in their beautiful disorder, now hid its splendid contour.

"Is he not gloriously handsome, Isabel?" said a rich femenine voice.

"He is, indeed, your ladyship," answered Isabel, in a voice that sounded to Jack Rann, not only surpassingly sweet, but also like the dear tones of the beautiful girl he had heard called Miss Malcolm.

"And, what is better, he is as brave as he is beautiful;" continued her ladyship. "Bella!" she broke forth, abruptly, in tones of bitterness, "I wish to God this boy were my husband instead of the poltroon who now lords over me."

"Your ladyship!" exclaimed Miss Malcolm, in tones of unequivocal surprise, for it was indeed as Jack Rann had surmised, that it was that young lady who had found her way to his bedside; "how can you say so?"

"Because my heart beats with the truth of what I utter. Look!" she exclaimed, drawing back the curtain and exhibiting our hero in all the glories of a calm and happy sleep, "who could lay pressed in such matchless arms as those, and not feel ecstacy! whose lips touching those corals would not taste bliss! whose heart beating beside his noble one, and beloved, too. beyond all, could feel otherwise than brimful of happiness."

"Alas! I know not," said Isabel, sighing at the picture which her ladyship had drawn; "but it does not seem impossible to love him, he is so good, so brave, so beautiful!"

"Never marry, Isabel, unless it be one like him. I swear to you," she went on, vehemently, "the more I gaze upon this boy, the more I love him!" and bending down over our hero, her ladyship pressed her matchless lips—that a king might have resigned a crown to kiss—upon his marble brow, and she paused ere she spoke the words, "and the more I think of my husband the more I hate, despise, and loathe him!" As she spoke these words with withering scorn—with unutterable disgust, Isabel's young soul, frightened and shocked, rose appealingly against her.

"I beseech your ladyship to forbear," she said, shudderingly, "you frighten me with this wicked and unnatural vehemence."

"Then I will cease, Bella, for with all my heart I love you; yes, even as I love myself, and, therefore, will not offend the purity of your fair soul with any thought of my mind. But hear me once again, and then for ever shall silence rest upon this theme. You have called me wicked and unnatural."

"Oh! no! no!" said Isabel, in a beseeching tone, and with eyes glittering with pearly tears. "Indeed, indeed, I meant not that."

"It matters not," returned her ladyship eagerly; "may be in your pure ears my words may seem, but that I am unnatural I deny; for it was enough to create in any soul an intolerable disgust."

'What was, your ladyship?" inquired Miss Malcolm.

"What was? why, the sight we have seen to-night; to see my husband standing shivering like a child, and moving neither hand or foot to save his friend perishing before his eyes, while this poor boy, brave, noble, generous youth, hesitated not, at the imminent hazard of his own life, to save his enemy from the death."

"It was indeed a generous, a noble action," said Isabel, conversingly, advanced a step nearer the sleeping youth, "and I feel assured a blessing will rest upon him for it."

"Ay, there will," replied her ladyship, "but he must look for his reward from heaven, for his matchless heart will never, never find its equal upon earth. But listen, Isabel, I hear footsteps—your door leads to my dressing room, we will take a refuge there. One more kiss at his noble brow, and then farewell."

She bent over the youth as she spoke, and again touched his forehead gently with her lips; unable to resist the temptation and the impulse, guided by the example of her friend, Isabel Malcolm also approached, and with a touch light as a zephyr touched with her beauteous lips the handsome ones of our hero.

A thrill of ecstacy—of passion never before experienced—of delight never before felt—rushed like liquid fire through the veins of Jack Rann. The fruit was too luscious to be resisted—the temptation too overwhelming sweet to be combatted; and the fair young lady to her intense dismay found herself, when their lips met, in receipt of an ardent, burning kiss of love from the supposed sleeper.

"Starting like an affrighted fawn, she sprung towards her friend, and the two beauties immediately left the room.

Before Jack had barely time to congratulate himself on the conquest he had made in thus unexpectedly captivating these two beautiful ladies, the chamber door was quietly opened, and the doctor, accompanied by Mr. Malcolm, entered the room. As Jack had to gain now by counterfeiting sleep, his jetty eyes were very wide awake indeed when the pair advanced towards him.

"Well, my brave boy, how are you getting on?" inquired the doctor, attentively, feeling at the same time Jack's pulse.

"As right as a rivet, sir," answered Jack, gaily; "all I want now is to be up and about. My poor old moke will be out of all patience waiting in the cold such a precious time."

"He is in a good stable and well cared for, never fear. We have not forgotten your friend either, he is feasting merrily in the kitchen."

"My friend!" inquired Jack; "who the deuce is he?" for his head, what with his immersion and the potent effects of the brandy, was somewhat confused.

"Why, the person who was seated on the wall with you when the unfortunate accident took place."

"Oh, ah! I remember, Luke Jones; you don't mean to say he is eating and stuffing down there, though, do ye?"

"I can't swear about eating and stuffing," said the doctor smiling at the strange question, but I mean to say this, he is enjoying himself right merrily."

"Bring my clothes," said Jack, springing out of bed; "I'll make one with them."

Jack was speedily equipped, and was hastening from the room, when Mr. Malcolm laying his hand detainingly upon our hero's shoulder, said

"Before you join their revelries, my young friend, allow me to detain you one moment. The squire is anxiously waiting your presence in the drawing-room to thank you for his preservation."

And taking our hero by the arm, he led him into the presence of the squire.

Pale as a corpse, bowed down, and humbled at his narrow escape from the death, the squire lay propped up with pillows on a magnificent couch whilst his guests were disposed in groups about the room.

A blush of pride, of triumph, mantled to the brow of Jack Rann as his eye, glancing around, fell upon the majestic form of the noble lady who had honoured his bedside with her presence; and more, his bright eyes sparkled with unqualified admiration as they rested for an instant on the transcendant loveliness of Miss Malcolm. Recalled to himself, however, by the voice of the squire, Jack stood and listened—

"You saved my life," commenced the squire, in tones that showed his overbearing haughtiness would not allow a spark of genuine thankfulness to remain in his selfish bosom, "and doubtless expect to be paid for your service; well, it shall be so, you are poor—I am rich, take this purse of gold. Let it make us quits."

Jack took the money in his hand in silence, but his flashing eyes bespoke the indignation in his soul.

"Is the fellow not satisfied?" inquired the squire, raising himself on his elbow. "If not," he said, turning to his valet, "pay him, Smith, and let him go."

"Hear me, you sir," said Jack Rann, in tones of the deepest indignation; "to show you how much I despise your paltry gift; there, take your dirty money back again?" and he dashed it indignantly at the squire's feet. "What!" he exclaimed, turning to the company, who were now grouped around him. "Is it not enough, that this unthankful hound should have treated me like a thief, from the very first—is it not enough that he should have set his bull dogs on me? and now should taunt me with my poverty, and treat me like a beggar?"

"Hush! my dear good fellow," said Mr. Malcolm, soothingly; "he meant not what he said."

No 3.

"It is a lie!" said Jack, passionately, " he did, and does. When he was struggling with death in the heavy water, half his wealth he would have given to save his life—his life I saved! Unfortunate I; for now he accepts the gift—of value, I do declare to God to none in the world, but himself—for to none in the world has it ever been of use—accepts the gift of his life as coming from the hands of a beggar! I looked not for thanks—I looked not for a reward—if I had, knowing his dastardly disposition, I might have expected this insult—but what I did, I did freely. I forgot his scorn—forgot his bull dogs, though they were to have torn me limb from limb; yes, I forgot all but the fact, that he was a fellow-man, perishing before my eyes."

"You acted nobly and generously," said Lady Dashfield, "and are worthy of more generous treatment. Here, take my purse, my brave young man; and, believe me, I shall never forget your gallant exploit."

"Lady," said Jack, in a voice trembling with gratitude, "from my soul, I thank you, for your words. As for your purse, madam, I have done nothing to deserve it at your hands, and will not accept it."

"Will not?" cried her ladyship; "come, Rann, for such I believe is your name, I beg of you to accept it, not as a reward, but as a gift."

"I will have nothing to do with it," said Jack, firmly, "since money is the only reward worthy of being disposed upon the beggar—since not one atom of gratitude is due to him for his exertions; he at the least shows himself as proud as the devil, for he despises the proffered gift."

Speaking these words with a bitter sneer, Jack Rann immediately left the room; and was hurrying from the house, when the noise of Luke bawling forth, with lusty lungs, an old-fashioned ditty fell upon his ear. His brow crimsoned with anger as he listened, that Luke should have so far forgotten his vow of vengeance against the squire, as to make a buffoon of himself for the amusement of some grinning apes of lackeys; and descending towards the kitchen a step or two, he called loudly and angrily for him to come up. For some hidden reason, best known to himself, Luke obeyed the summons; and staggering up the stairs, with a look and step the very reverse of sobriety, he approached our hero, with an inquisitive leer, and asked—

"Did they tip handsome, eh?"

"So handsome," answered Jack, with face of burning scarlet, " that I'd a took your advice had I known it, Luke, and the ungrateful hound should have met the dog's death he was fast hurrying to."

"Sarve him right, too; if I'd my will, blast me," said Luke, " I'd tie all the squires in the country, neck and heels together, and drown 'em, as I would so many blind kittens; it's all they're fit for, cuss 'em! but never mind 'em lad, they're sum o' the right sort below—some rare good fellows, with ale and sack, and whiskey galore. Come and join 'em, man alive, and suffocate re—reflection in a bumper of blue ruin."

Jack turned from his staggering comrade with disgust.

"You may return, if you like; for my own part, I despise their company and am for home."

"So be I, then," said Luke, with an oath, "cuss 'em for a set of idle vagabonds; they set the dogs on us, didn't they? Come on, mate, I am with ye."

Without deigning to answer his inebriated companion, Jack Rann stalked from the house, and having had his donkey delivered over to him, was speedily on his road home.

CHAPTER I

CONTAINS A FURTHER ADVANCE INTO THE LIFE AND ADVENTURES OF OUR MOST ADVENTUROUS HERO.

ANY one who has noticed human life, cannot have failed to perceive how some men, from a most trivial circumstance, spring from their nature, as it were, into a new existence.

There is such a magic in woman's bright eyes, that one glance has oftimes, ere now, made hero's and statesmen. Men, who have heretofore remained mute and inanimate, at a word from the lips of a woman they have loved, have sprung from their habitual lethargy into the world; and fighting with a purpose in it, have bravely won its golden opinions, and shone lustrously in its all-powerful sight.

Woman's love! Why it has reclaimed drunkards—made honest men of thieves—made beggars kings! In good faith, it has done prodigious wonders, and blessings more efficacious than the philosopher's stone itself could have done, even though it were invested with all its boasted powers.

The effects of its all-potent agency was not lost to Jack Rann!

From the time Lady Dashfield and Miss Malcolm's visit to his bedside, his bosom was full of new and almost indefinable sensations. Their words, so heedlessly spoken, had struck upon a chord that had lain sleeping in Jack's breast. The chord thus awakened was *pride*. Rebellious, accursed pride, that has so often, alas! been the cause of man's downfall—of misery, of disgrace, and death!

By a progress gradual, but sure, Jack became in time disgusted with the humble but honest adocation he pursued for a livelihood. The consequence was, that as he grew haughty and careless to his customers; so the once popular salesman, Jack Rann, became indifferent to them, and one by one they withdrew their custom, until the presence of his handsome self and laden donkey no longer produced a posse of eager customers in the city of Bath; but were, the reverse, allowed, on the one part, to pass unheeded, and the weary donkey more than once trudged back again as heavily laden as when he had started. The evil did not rest here—his father was a tenant on the squire's property. Now the squire, ever since the fatal hour of Jack's independence, had viewed our hero with intolerable hatred for the insult he had offered him before Lady Dashfield and his other noble guests, and had determined, by means fair or foul, to work the lad's ruin.

In prosecution of this plan, he had set a narrow watch upon the movements of Luke Jones, this fellow being by far the worst character known about. It was not long before Jones was caught poaching upon Squire Giles's estate, and the latter being a magistrate, he was instantly dragged by the successful gamekeeper before his worship.

A smile of exultation gleamed in the face of Giles as the prisoner was brought before him. The evidence of the witnesses was given, and reduced to writing. Under the pretence of examining the man privately as to his accomplices, and the means by which he had managed so long and so mysteriously to maintain himself, the squire dismissed the constable and his attendants, and was closeted alone with the man Jones for an hour or more.

What transpired at this conference was a profound mystery—the only thing at all certain was, to the astonishment and chagrin of the gamekeepers, that they were recalled to his justice's presence, and after being greeted with various epithets, such as "fools," "asses," "dolts," "idiots," etc., were, to their unbounded astonishment, informed that they were entirely mistaken, and that Jones, instead of being a poacher, was a respectable, steady, quiet man; and was, in fact, merely on the "look-out" for poachers when he was so roughly seized by the gamekeepers.

"But, Lord a massy bless your worship," said the constable, "but may I be squashed as soft as apple sarce if I didn't cotch Luke with the blessed hare in his fist."

"I tell you you're mistaken, sirrah," thundered the magistrate; "the one he had in his hand was a dead one he had found. that some scoundrel had robbed me of."

"I beg your worship's pardon, but it warn't a dead 'un; for blow me if it warn't a kicking in his fist. Didn't we see it, mates?" said the constable, appealing to the gamekeepers.

They jerked their heads in token of acquiescence.

"Alive or dead," said the squire, in a towering rage, "I tell you the man is innocent; and if you dare contradict me in this matter, you shall rue it to the longest day you live."

This, as one classically expressed himself, "bottled them up, and corked them down;" and when the squire formally discharged the prisoner from custody, although they glanced at each other significantly, they spoke not a word.

Luke immediately left the hall, and seemingly bent upon some project, walked towards the cottage inhabited by Rann.

"Is Jack at home?" he asked of our hero's mother, a cleanly, well-looking dame.

"Yes, he is, an upstart, idle loon," the woman answered quickly : " I wish he wasn't."

"What's he bin doin' then, missus?" asked Luke.

"Just nothing, like an idle, good for nothing loon as he is;" replied the woman, angrily. "Ever since that affair at the hall, he hasn't been worth a brass farden."

"Well, I am sorry to hear that, missus; but tell him I want him, will'e, I've summat good to tell him from the lasses at the hall."

"Call him yourself then if you want him," said Mrs. Rann ; " I'll have naught to do with him, the good for nothing dog."

Luke needed no second injunction, but shouted, with lusty lungs—

"Jack Rann there, yo ho ! I want ye !"

"What's up now ?" said our hero, coming forward ; " is Bath 'afire, or is the church tumbled down ?"

"Neither one nor tother, but shove on your castor, I want ye a minit."

Glad of any excuse to get away from home, which his own negligence had rendered an unhappy one, Jack obeyed the invitation.

"Jack," said Luke, when they were out of hearing distance from the house, "I've heard as how the world is going precious queer with you—be it true ?"

"It is," answered Jack, moodily ; "I wish to God I was away from this cursed place."

"Psha ! man, don't go on so—what do ye want to leave for, when there is shiners like these to be picked up in it, without the trouble of hard work ?" and he pulled from his breeches pocket some six or eight golden guineas.

Jack's eyes glistened as they fell upon the glittering coin.

"And are they yours, Luke—all your own, and without work ?"

"They are," answered Jones, triumphantly, "and if you are the game bird I've taken you to be, I'll put you in the way of earning as many this blessed night.

"You will," exclaimed Jack ; "no, damme, Luke, do you mean it ?"

"I do," said Luke, coupling the words with an oath : and at the peril of eternal blindness, he called his Maker to witness his words.

"But how?" cried Jack, impatiently ; "put me in the way, and if I don't earn them, curse me ; why such a sum as that would set my father on his legs for life—would carry me to London, and make a gentleman of me."

"Then if you are the game fellow, I have taken you to be join me tonight, and as a reward for your services—come, you shall run no risk—these yellow boys shall be yours."

"In the devil's name, out with it, man ; tell me what it is," said Jack, with impetuous eagerness.

"You hate the squire? so do I ! You are content with hating him, I have revenge with my hatred too. I'll make him pay for it, and sweetly too. These yeller men came from his estate."

"That will do for the marines," said Jack, with a hearty laugh, "for I'll be shot if you'll make me believe he grows guineas."

"I didn't go for to guess you were so green as that ; no, no, master Jack—

all I say is, he grows hares, and pheasants, and other things that are every bit as good to Luke Jones as gold."

"I see," said Jack, with a whistle. "Whew! that's the way you get your revenge, is it?"

"And a righteous way too, ain't it?" asked Luke, "I tell'e what, Jack. I've the plummiest lot of pusses and birds, that ever lay in a heap, planted to-night in the copse—I've a hoss and cart, too, on the road, to waft 'em off to Lunnon market—wilt mind 'em for me, mate—wilt mind 'em for me, while I tackle the traps?" You shall run no danger, I'll do all that—only whistle when you hear the cart wheels, to tell me the coast is clear."

"And what am I to get by it, eh, Luke?" asked Jack, nervously.

"This gold, mate, every guinea of it," and Jones pressed it as he spoke into his companion's hands.

Jack Rann gazed upon the gold with eager cupidity—the temptation was strong—a vision passed before the boys eyes.

"By this one act, I can leave my father comfortable—can reach London, and once there, I can seek that beautiful lady who loves me, and my fortune will be made; perhaps, too, I may grow rich, and Miss Malcolm may return my love; and to have her for my wife, would be—will be joy, joy unutterable!"

Luke watched the workings of Jack Rann's handsome face, as it was plainly revealed to him in the beauteous moonlight, with a keen and practised eye, and marked with exultation the victory he had gained.

"Come, Jack, my brave fellow, will you do it? 'Tis but a few minutes' work mind you, and no danger."

"And this money is mine?" said Jack, inquiringly.

"Is yours!" replied Luke. "Come, decide quickly, for the night draws on. Will you do it?"

"I will," answered Jack Rann.

* * * * *

Firm and determined as a sentinel on hazardous duty, did our hero guard within the recesses of the copse the pile of game—not game exactly either—for in the heap were many tenants of the farm-yard, *i.e.*, geese, turkeys, and sundry others of its usual two-legged occupants.

Whilst Jack, faithful to his trust, was guarding the gleanings of a supposed successful poaching expedition, Luke Jones, like a treacherous hound as he was, was speeding away to the squire, to inform him their plot was successful—that Jack Rann was "snared," "trapped," and "caught;" that all that was wanted was a constable and a few attendants, and the rest they might safely leave to "providence," so Jones said but we suppose he meant thereby, the tender mercies of a bigoted and merciless country magistrate.

For an hour Jack waited patiently; the moon had risen in all the radiance of its chaste silvery light; but, to tell the truth, the minutes had passed like hours. Presently, however, the sound of carriage wheels broke upon his ear, and then a whistle, peculiarly shrill, broke the stillness of the glorious night.

"Here he comes," said Jack, slapping his gold gilded pocket with ecstasy, "and I've, in one hour's work, enough gold lining in my pocket to carry me to brave old London—and to save dad from his trouble besides. But hark!" he said, as the sound of footsteps rapidly approaching, fell upon his ear; "Luke—Luke Jones, is that you?"

No voice answered, and yet the footsteps evidently, stealthily but rapidly approached him.

He whispered this time—

"Jones, is it you?"

Again silence broke only by the creeping and shuffling of feet in the grass was audible.

Although he had too trustworthy—too brave a heart to know fear—yet Jack Rann's heart beat more rapidly than usual; for a thought had seized him that there was treachery afoot. Still, to the moment we have narrated he had full confidence in Luke Jones, and was determined to preserve the poacher's spoil at any imminent risk. With this belief possessing him, he again shouted—

"Luke—Luke, I say, are you ready?"

There came a rustling in the bushes, such as a tiger might create in springing recklessly upon its prey—the next instant Jack Rann found himself within the grasp of the constable, and a heavy hand most recklessly, and unmercifully placed upon his wind-pipe.

"Yes, I'm ready, you willin'," growled the constable "and we arn't baited our trap without awail. No wonder you could sell poultry so cheap I thought I should have you, and I've got you—what a blessing."

"Is it!" exclaimed Jack, by a sudden whisk, relieving his neck, and leaving only his neckerchief, tied in the usual nautical slip-knot. "A blessing is it, take that then!"

And Jack, like a skilful pugilist as he was, drew up his fist, to the shoulder, and letting fly, with swift and unerring force, knocked the fat head of the adventurous old constable, with one blow into a blackthorn bush.

The fallen man shouted loudly for help—and in less time than our pen could narrate these words, half-a dozen fellows, headed by the squire, sprang upon Jack Rann.

Jack's fist had been industrious—so were his eyes, for the desperate blow the constable had received, had sent him most uncomfortably sharp against the stump of a fallen tree, and his staff of office, by the same unpleasant impetus, had flown from his grasp, into the branches, and meeting with a rebound, had fallen at the feet of our hero. To seize this weapon of defence was the work of an instant, but to apply it might and main upon the skulls of his adversaries, took but barely half a second—one fell, but only as a prelude for another to follow his example; for before the first could recover his feet, a second, by Jack's victorious charge, had reached the ground.

Swift as lightning, Jack Rann now dashed forward, and, leaping the fence that surrounded the copse, and formed a barrier nearly five feet high, at one desperate bound, he alighted safely upon his feet in the road.

With all the activity of a greyhound he sped along, until he reached his father's cottage.

Rann and his wife arose pale and affrighted, as their son came in panting and breathless, and pallid as a corpse.

"My God, Jack, what is the matter?" said the father.

Jack placed his hand upon his heart to still its violent pulsations, ere he answered, gaily and fearlessly—

"Nothing, dad, I swear to you; but I've been caught doing Luke Jones a service, and the squire's men want to lay the blame to me."

"Oh! Jack, what have you done?" said his poor mother, wringing her hands with agony. Then added, by way of soliloquy, "Oh! would the boy had never been born—he's nothing but trouble—nothing but trouble."

"I didn't need them words, mother, to fill up my cup of bitterness," said Jack Rann, in a tone of sorrow, tears the while filling his eyes. "I think you might have found one loving word for our last parting."

"Parting!" cried Rann and his wife, simultaneously.

"That's the word, and that the meaning; and although I arn't no poacher, father, yet I must fly for life, as if I was one. "There," said Jack, "don't you hear the carriage wheels? the bloodhounds are swiftly following their prey. But, if they catch me, dad, depend upon it, they'll have a rare run for it! Farewell!"

"But, one minute, Jack, are you innocent?"

Jack raised himself up proudly, as he answered—

"Yes, father—'fore heaven."

By this time the sound of carriage wheels had caught the quick ears of our hero, and was heard rapidly approaching the house. All a mother's fears were awakened in the breast of Mrs. Rann, as she shrieked, rather than said—

"Fly, Jack, fly!"

"I'm off," answered Jack, "like a shot from a gun—give us a kiss, old lady—there, good bye—good luck to you—keep them in remembrance of me, dad;" and he slipped as he spoke four guineas into the father's hand.

"Jack, where did this money come from?"

"Never you mind, I got it honestly—tell Luke Jones I didn't neglect my part till I was forced. Here they come, I'm off!"

A tumult without could now plainly be heard, and hasty footsteps, it was evident, were rapidly approaching.

"Fly, Jack, fly!" cried his mother.

"Never fear, as soon as old shiver-my-timbers shows his jolly red nose in one door, I'm out at the other. Hallo! here you are then!" said Jack, as the squire, leading the mob, jumped into the cottage, "what the devil do you want?"

"What I shall soon get," exclaimed the squire, springing forward to seize our hero.

"What you have got, fool," said Jack, planting a desperate blow full in the squire's face, from the effects of which his worship measured five feet eight inches on the stone flooring.

"One down," said Jack, "who makes two?"

The constable having received a smarting proof of our hero's fistic superiority, wisely hesitated; Jack hurried towards his pursuers with modest politeness, and said—

"Gentlemen, I'm for London, and have the pleasure of wishing you a jolly good night. If either of you have any inclination to follow me, come on."

These were Jack Rann's farewell words. Springing through the doorway, he scaled a wall at th back, and making for the woods, was speedily lost to view.

No. 4.

CHAPTER IV

JACK RANN FINDS HIMSELF IN LONDON—HE PICKS UP WITH A NEW ACQUAINT-
ANCE, UNDER SOMEWHAT SINGULAR CIRCUMSTANCES; AND AN OLD ACQUAINT-
ANCE BY THE SAME ACT—AND DOES A DEED FOR HIS MASTER, WHICH GEN-
TLEMEN GENERALLY PREFER TO DO FOR THEMSELVES.

A few days after the events narrated in our last chapter, our hero having reached London, was pursuing his way through the old Fleet Market, then thronged with sellers and buyers, in search of a cheap lodging. Whether his country dress made him feel ungainly and awkward amongst the lively genuses among whom he now found himself, or from this reason, to fancy every one was regarding him intently, we cannot say; but certain it is, his face crimsoning from these particular thoughts, soon attracted the attention of some young cockney vagabonds.

"My eyes, Bill," said one, a shoeless, hatless urchin, with breeches that exhibited a torn shirt through each aperture, "here's a yokel full blown!"

The lad, whose attention he now called to our hero, was a smart, active, well-dressed lad, whose quick dark eyes were instantly riveted on the form of Jack Rann.

"So he is, so help me Newgate; let's have a spree with him, Jack."

Jack shook his head, as though they hardly liked the looks of our hero, and considered him capable of resisting any innovation of his dignity, but the taller lad whispered something in his ear, at which the young urchin sprung forward and fell, as if by accident, at the feet of our hero.

Trying to recover his balance, without stepping upon the prostrate boy, Rann fairly staggered for an instant; the next, the other lad adroitly rolled against him, and sent him sprawling over the prostrate boy, head first into an apple stall.

The loud shout of laughter that arose from the bystanders, nettled our hero to the quick, and picking himself up with a face of scarlet from the scattered apples, he turned with looks of anger, to catch the author of this mischievous act. As generally happens, in such scenes, Jack pitched upon the wrong man, for turning to an old butcher, he demanded to know, "what he did that for?"

"Well, I never," answered greasy. "Why, I warn't near ye by a dozen yards."

"It's all gammon, he was," said Bill, the real cause of the mischief. "I saw him push ye. Hit him in the eye, country, I'll hold your hat."

"If I thought he meant to do it," said Jack Rann, looking tremendously fierce, "I'd smash him."

"Well, I don't know," said the butcher, "but that's easier said than done young country; but, although I didn't shove you into the apple basket, I glories in the cove who did, and if you can take THAT out of me, come on—fire away, I'm ready."

"Go it, country," said Bill, jumping round our hero in ecstasy at the point affairs had reached. "Roll into him—give it him—I'll back ye. Hit him hard and often, and a good many times in one place. That's the way to conquer."

"Now, Jack Rann, although, by no means of a quarrelsome disposition, had a strong appreciation of the ridiculous, and feeling himself embroiled in a mess, was determined to clear himself like a man from it. Acting upon this impulse, he struck the ox-like head of the butcher, a blow so swift and resolute, that the latter's teeth fairly chattered again.

From this commenced, as will be readily imagined, a regular shindy. The butcher was strong as a bull, and no mean pugilist, so Jack Rann found, for the first time, a man who could take and receive—could bear punishment as well as deliver it.

The battle, favouring occasionally one and then the other of the combatants, had lasted nearly an hour, and the vast crowd collected around our hero and butcher had prevented by main force the constabulary from stopping it; when a carriage, containing two ladies and a gentleman, and driven by servants in livery, came prancing into the assembly, distributing the crowd in all directions.

"What is the matter?" inquired the gentleman, ordering his servant to pull up, and directing his speech to our hero—

The speaker was a full-whiskered, dark-looking man, of about fifty summers. His hair and whiskers prematurely gray, were carefully dyed and greased, and he looked what he was, the remains of a gay debauchee.

"The matter," answered Jack, with a smile and a bow, "is but little:—my opponent, the butcher there, thought fit to play me a lark because I am fresh from the country, and I have given him a sound drubbing for it. He expected to find a fool, but he found a Bath chap."

"Bath!" echoed the lady in the carriage. "I should know that voice and form. What is your name, my man?"

For Jack's face, from blood and dust, was scarcely distinguishable.

"My name," answered our hero, "is John Rann?"

"It is the same, my Lord Dashfield, whose bravery we admired at Giles's," said the lady, in a whisper, to her husband; for in this relationship they stood.

"Then, by God, he shall make acquaintance with Dashfield House. Here, you sir," he shouted to his footman, "give that butcher a guinea for his gallantry, and tell him to be off about his business. As to you, sir," he said, turning to Rann, "what brings you to London?"

"I am here in search of a situation, my lord."

"Should you like to be a gentleman's servant—valet—groom—eh?" queried his lordship.

Jack answered in the affirmative, that either situation would suit him nicely.

"Then consider yourself engaged. Get up beside the coachman," he said, abruptly; then giving the word "home" to his servant, the carriage, amidst three cheers from the bystanders, dashed into Fleet Street.

Lady Dashfield, whose admiration for our hero has been before mentioned, beheld this occurrence with a strange mixture of pleasure and fear.

"My lord," she said, as they whirled along, "this is a strange proceeding thus to engage a man in the street without a character."

"Without a character, does your ladyship say? Confound my ears, if you didn't give him the best character that any one ever had. Why didn't you tell me he was brave, faithful, and everything—that is—courageous, good and gallant, eh?"

"I did, my lord."

"Then what the devil else do I require? I've got a valet handsome as Adonis, strong as Hercules, and as courageous as a lion—that's all I want; and the comfort is, I've got him," said his lordship, with an exulting smile.

"If you are satisfied, my lord, I AM!" answered her ladyship.

"Then say no more about it," said the earl; "for my own part, I am delighted with the acquisition, and wish I had had him three months ago; then Trevyllen would not have had the audacity—" Here his lordship stopped short, but her ladyship most provokingly finished the phrase with—

"To have given your lordship the ignominious horsewhipping which he did."

The earl muttered an oath between his clenched teeth, but spoke no more until the carriage stopped at the gateway of Dashfield House, Piccadilly.

Dashfield House was one of those gloomy, wall-barred, prison-looking tenements that are to be met with in Piccadilly, and no where else.

The gate being unbarred, and the carriage having been bowed in by the porter, it was speedily rattling over the stone-paved court yard.

By directions of his lordship, Jack was conveyed to the kitchen, where a good meal stood in waiting for the servants; and having refreshed himself with a good wash, he sat down and did ample justice.

The meal over, he was summoned to his lordship's library, where, in addition to the earl's noble self, stood a most worshipful knight of the scissors and thimble, commonly called a "snip," "cabbage," and various other approbious names, who with measure in hand, took the latitude and longitude of our hero, for a valet's suit of genteel sable.

Thus was Jack Rann comfortably installed as the confidential servant of the Earl and Countess of Dashfield.

Jack, by his fistic exploits, soon grew into great friendship with his lordship, and by the amiability of his manners and the respectfulness of his attention, crept into the confidence, and, it must be confessed, into the heart of her ladyship as well.

Now Jack had on various occasions done the amiable, in the shape of vows of love, soft speeches, and other sweets, for one Elinor Roche, the lady's-maid of the Countess of Dashfield. And so strong an impression had Jack's conduct made upon the heart of this pretty servant girl, that she had inbibed a strong and ardent attachment for him, and was transcendantly happy in the belief that she was equally beloved by him in return. This belief, we regret to say, was doomed to bear a shock, and this love, so sanguine and delightful, was doomed to perish with a withering blight.

As she was passing her ladyship's private dressing room, she thought she heard a sigh, and then another; now as she could not by any possibility conceive what could induce Lady Dashfield, possessing a title and unbounded wealth, to be in the least troubled; she was induced, by a curiosity pardonable in a woman, but disgraceful in everybody else, to apply her ear to the key-hole.

Her sense of hearing was indescribably shocked this time, for she heard not a sigh. No, no!—but a sound as of a kiss—a kiss of unusually prolonged time, and of unusually delicious tendency.

She removed her ear from the key-hole, and applied her eye.

If her sense of hearing was shocked, how dire must have been the blow that fell upon her eyesight.

Seated upon a crimson velvet couch, sat her perfidious lover, Jack Rann and her mistress, Lady Dashfield.

Side by side, with his arm around his noble mistress's waist, and his right hand toying with her dislevelled tresses, sat our hero; whilst ever and anon, with looks of burning, most impassioned love, their eyes—their lips met.

From her raven tresses, the valet's wilful wicked fingers wandered beneath the waving satin that hid her matchless bosom; toying with these twin sisters of loveliness, sat Jack Rann, whilst her ladyship, yielding to the strong tide of passion, that lava-like, ran through every vein—forgetting all in the intoxication of that blissful moment—the titled lady forgot her husband—forgot her woman's honour and, in utter abandonment, drooped her head upon our hero's shoulder, and whispered "I CONSENT."

Here we must pause, for if imagination cannot portray, our pen dare not depict!

*   *   *   *   *

Poor Elinor Roche was blighted in her heart's nearest and dearest hopes by the scene she had inadvertently been a witness to. Who can wonder that a strong tide of jealously should be aroused, and that a burning desire for vengeance did from that moment take possession of her soul. For, next to a triumph—vengeance is most sweet to a woman!

Elinor's pretty face contracted, under the influence of these thoughts, until it became the reverse of fascinating; and, in fact, rather a fiendship expression took possession of them than otherwise, as she muttered—

"This shall end in their total ruin—their total ruin."

With this pious adjuration, she betook herself to an escretoire, and wrote a letter to Lord Dashfield.

His lordship, like a gay lothario as he was, after amusing himself with wiling away the greater portion of the afternoon and evening in the company of a favourite mistress, betook himself at length to a fashionable wine establishment, which was a lounge and resort for all the gay nobles of the age, and a select assemblage of gamblers, debauchees, and drunkards.

In such company as this, his lordship was peculiarly at home; for an expert gambler, he knew every trick and device as perfect as any professed blackleg; as a debauchee, he was as successful, and as vain of his exploits as the greatest villain there; and, as a tippler, he stood unequalled. In such congenial and delectable society, therefore, his merits could be fully appreciated, and he felt himself more at home than he did in his princely residence, Dashfield House.

The earl having arrived at the magnificent establishment, stopped his chariot, and bidding his servant wait, advanced into the interior of the house, and mounting a magnificent flight of marble stairs, hurried into an apartment where a number of gentlemen were engaged at gambling.

Nodding familiarly to one or two of the players, the earl advanced to the fire place, before which a couple of officers were standing.

"Captain Smart, as I live—well, captain, how goes it?"

"What's the play?" inquired the captain; then without waiting for an answer, continued, "devilish bad, I assure you, I have lost a cool five hundred, this cursed day."

"Bah! my boy! what of that—you'll win a thousand another time."

"Faith, there is small chance of that," said the Honourable Captain Smart. "I certainly do have luck; but, as regards the dice, it's *all bad* luck."

"Faint heart never won—"

"Fair lady," exclaimed the captain," but excuse my finishing the phrase—but talking of it puts me in mind of the loveliest little adventure in the petticoat line that you ever heard of."

"What was it?" inquired his lordship, eager for the recital.

The other whispered the narrative in the earl's ear; and it must have been of the richest and most entertaining kind, for at its terminus, the three gentlemen burst into a loud and hearty peal of laughter.

"By jingo, it puts me in mind of a little adventure I have coming off of the same sort," said the earl.

"You!" exclaimed the captain, with well-affected incredulity; "'pon honour you are joking, now—why I understood, on your marriage with the incomparable Lady Mary, you had given up for ever all such wicked deeds."

"So I have, Smart—I am tamed down damnably, I do assure you; but, upon my soul, with my warm, gallant disposition, I find it is absolutely necessary to have a sport sometimes."

"And whom may the damsel be who has been so fortunate as to gain your lordship's favour?"

"Now, Smart, be reasonable. Perhaps you would like the name and address of the angel."

"Not I," returned the captain, "I have three ballet girls, one actress, and two milliners on my hands now, quite enough for any poor devil, don't you think so, eh?" he asked, turning from one to the other, and shrugging his shoulders, as though it would be the greatest relief in the world to shift the burthens resting on them.

"But my angel is no ballet girl or milliner. No sir," said the earl, haughtily, "she is the daughter of a *millionaire*, and a particular friend of my wife's."

"Not the beautiful Miss Malcolm, surely, that I saw at Dashfield House, in company with the countess, the last time I was there?"

"Hush!" said the earl "it is the same, I assure you."

"By jingo, what a triumph—but is she—can she be a consenting party?"

"What an absurd question, to imagine one so chaste and beautiful could ever incline to that—no, sir, I shall win her by stratagem—shall conquer her by force, in fact, sir, I mean to run away with her."

"The devil you do," said the captain; "and what will Lady Dashfield say?"

"What she pleases," said the earl, carelessly. "When the deed is done, it cannot be helped. I shall beg her pardon, and promise to be a good boy for the future."

"But, old Malcolm, will he put up with an empty apology for his child's dishonour?"

"My dear captain, you are a perfect baby in such matters."

"The devil I am," said the captain; "I thought I was an oldish hand at them—but go on, perhaps I am innocent in comparison with you."

"These are my plans, as her family are acquainted with my wife, and well aware of the affection existing between the two. I intend calling at Malcolm's for her; any excuse will do; you know the countess is exceedingly ill, and she will enter the carriage without hesitation or suspicion. I have a cottage at Arlington, and an old woman in my pay there, who has more than once aided me in such matters. Once there, my boy, you may conceive the entrancing rest."

"But if she should prove unruly—should refuse to go?"

"Supposing that, yet escape will be impossible. Even if she doubts my honour, I shall have strength enough to keep her in the carriage, and the postillions having their pay, will ride like the devil to Arlington."

"Well, all I can say, my lord, is that I wish you success, and envy you the object of the expedition;" and, extending his hand to the noble earl the Honourable Captain Smart drew on his gloves, put on his hat, and whistling a tune, was leaving the room, when a servant entered with a letter on a gold salver.

"Is that for me?" asked Smart.

"No sir," replied the servant, "it is for my lord, the Earl of Dashfield."

"A letter for me, and lying here? who can it be from?"

"Some lady smitten with your lordship, I dare sware. See, it is rose-coloured, scented, and bound with a silver thread, private, and haste, marked on it, too. By Jove, here's another assignation! 'Pon honour, your lordship is most undoubtedly born to the best of good luck."

"Wait a minute, captain, you shall know the contents," said the earl, taking the missive from the outstretched salver.

"As you like, but mind, I was not inquisitive enough to demand this proof of your confidence."

"You shall have it, nevertheless," answered the earl, as he unfolded the billit. If a viper had sprung from it, he could not have started back with more horror and fear on his countenance. His colour went and came, his breath grew thick and short, he staggered, and sinking into a seat, muttered, convulsively "dishonoured—damnation!"

"Hush, for heaven sake! Do not let all these scoundrels know your business. What is it—are you ill?"

"Ill!" exclaimed the earl. "Read that!"

The captain took the note and read, penned in a neat, lady-like, but evidently a disguised hand, these brief words—

"Lord Dashfield,

Your wife is an adulteress—your valet, John Rann, has dishonoured her and you. If you need proof of this, come home and witness the infamy, and punish it like a man. From a Friend."

"This can never be true," exclaimed the captain—"it is too monstrous to be true! What Lady Dashfield to commit adultery with a low fellow of a footman—I would treat the calumny with the infamy it deserves. Shall I thrust the lying billit into the fire!"

"No, no," exclaimed the earl, hastily; "give it to me, and follow me. If it be false, they shall pay dearly for their temerity. Come on!"

With the speed of a madman, the earl sprang down the marble steps, and from thence to his cabriolet. The servant held the door open until his master and the captain were seated, and springing into his seat, he asked—

"Whereto, my lord."

"Home," said his lordship, bitterly, "and like the wind, you scoundrel, or you shall rue it."

The man, acting upon the impulse, whipped the spirited animal until it sprang forward at a mad gallop.

"My neck is worth nothing, if their's ain't," muttered the man, and again he struck the furious horse. "We shall all go to the devil together, that's one comfort."

It will readily be supposed that this tremendous pace speedily brought the earl and his companion to the gateway of Dashwood House.

The earl sprang up the steps into the hall, and from thence into the drawing-room on the first floor. Here he was met by Elinor Roche.

"Where is your lady?" he demanded, breathlessly.

"In her own chamber, my lord."

"How long has she been there?"

"Ever since your departure, my lord; she desired me not to disturb her."

"Where is Rann?"

"He answered my lady's bell, soon after your lordship left, and I have not seen him since."

"Damnation, it is true! Come on, captain, I will shoot the scoundrel like a dog."

And pistol in hand, he rushed up the stairs to his wife's room, bursting open the door with a vigorous kick, followed by his friend, burst in upon the guilty pair!

Their guilt was at once apparent.

The dishonoured wife, uttering a scream of terror, arose from the couch.

Startled by the scream, Jack Rann was also aroused, and he rose to confront, to his utter confusion and dismay, the man he had so basely injured, his master, Lord Dashfield.

"Villain," muttered the earl, in a hissing whisper, "take that!" and leveling his pistol, he fired.

A scream arose so piercing as to drown the pistol's report, followed by a fall upon the floor

No 5.

The ball missing Jack Rann, had buried itself in the bosom of Lady Dashfield.

"Fly, Jack, fly!" she gasped. "For my sake—for the love of God, fly!"

Gazing with bitter sorrow on the bleeding woman, Jack saw at once the imperative necessity existing that he should obey her dying wish, and thrusting aside the captain, who would have impeded his progress, he hurried from the house.

Without a character and without money, Jack, filled with horror at the scene he had just witnessed, struck into the fields, and wandered heedlessly he knew not—cared not whither.

CHAPTER V.

JACK RANN FALLS IN WITH A NEW ACQUAINTANCE, WHO TAKES THE LIBERTY OF INTRODUCING HIM TO A NEW AND ELEGANT KIND OF LIFE—WHETHER THIS ACQUAINTANCE IS TOTALLY FOR OUR HERO'S BENEFIT WILL BE SHOWN HEREAFTER.

In the parish of Lambeth there is a tract of ground known to this day as Pedlar's Acre. In a particular spot, bordering upon the river Thames, stood at the period of our tale a row of dark, dismal, wooden houses.

Towards these houses, on a dull November night, when the rain falling heavily from the dark murky sky, and the wind blowing in wild and fitful gusts, lent a dismal shading to the otherwise sufficiently dismal scene, two men enveloped in cloaks, and coming from the direction of Westminster bridge, advanced towards the row of houses with rapid steps. Pausing before the centre one, the tallest of the two, a well-built muscular man, muttering an imprecation on the weather, stooped, and placing his mouth to the keyhole, blew through it a significant and peculiarly shrill whistle.

A minute after the sound of the whistle had died upon the ear, a little window was carefully opened from above, and the head of a man, surmounted by a white cotton nightcap, was just discernable in the gloom.

"Who ish it?" queried a voice, tremulous in its tones like that of an old man.

"What do you say, you old fool?" exclaimed the tall man; for a gust of wind had prevented the purport of the words from reaching his ear.

"Who ish dere?" again asked the voice overhead, and this time in a tone sufficiently loud to be heard below.

"Hark at that drivelling old dotard!" exclaimed the man to his companion. "Isn't it enough to make a parson swear to be kept in the wet such a lovely night as this by such an old buffer as he?" Without waiting for his companion's answer to his question, he shouted, at the top of his lungs, "It's me, Mo, Harry Sheppard, wet to the skin like a drowned rat, so tumble yourself together, and come and let us in, d'ye hear?"

"Blesh my life, so 'tish Harry. Well, who'd a thought it, sich a blessed night as this ish, too?"

"Oh, you old sinner!" sung out Sheppard again, 'if you don't tumble down directly and let me and my pal in, I'll shake your life and soul out of you, you precious old bag of bones, I will."

As Harry coupled this speech with the action of shaking his fist at the Israelite, in a manner too vehement and earnest to be disregarded, it was no sort of wonder whatever that the Jew should close the casement, and with all possible speed hasten to let the new arrivals in.

Shading the flickering rushlight he held in one hand, with the other to prevent its being extinguished, after he had withdrawn sundry bolts and bars, the Jew opened the door, and admitted Sheppard and his unknown companion, who was no less a personage than our hero, Jack Rann.

"Strike me sensible, Mo, what an infernal while you kept us at that blackguard door. Did you think we were a couple of prigs, eh, that you wouldn't let us in?"

"O Harries, Harries, my dear, what a boy you ish for the joke. Two prigs! Well, I never," and Moses laughed with delight at the idea—"I declare, 'pon my soul I declare, as soon as I heard your voice, I knew you were two gentlemensh!"

"Then why the devil didn't you imitate the rain, and rattle down a little quicker, eh, Mo?"

"Vy, Henries, my darling, as soon as I knew your voice, I did come down so fast, I vera near break my neck!"

"And a jolly good job if you had quite, Mo, 'twould only have saved Jack Ketch a job."

"Jack Ketch! me no care to talk of him," said the Jew, with a shudder. "But come, gentlemensh's, this way, if you pleas'. We have mooch merry company to-night."

"Shuffle on, then, old stick-in-the-mud," said Sheppard, giving the Jew a probe in the ribs, that nearly bent the old man double—" go on, or by the powers the toes of my boots will be after stripping off the parchment from those yellow old heels of yours."

The Jew went on at the top of his speed, until he reached a landing-place, when throwing open a door, he exhibited to the gaze of the two travellers a well-lit room, in whose grate a large fire was cheerily burning.

Seated around a table, placed in the centre of the room, were four men, each and all holding in their hands some cards, and seemingly deeply intent upon the game; for it was not until Sheppard had advanced and struck one a violent blow upon the shoulder, that they seemed conscious of the presence of any but themselves.

The man thus saluted, sprang instantly to his feet, and extending his hand, exclaimed—

"Blast me, Harry, but I'm devilish glad to see you."

The same opinion, under various forms, having been expressed by the others, and the process of shaking hands having gone round the board, the individual whom Sheppard had first saluted, and who gloried in the name of O'Brien, pointing to the young man who had accompanied Jones, cried—

"And who the divil have you got wid you, eh, boy?"

"Oh, thereby hangs a tale, and a right merry one too, Mike; but as I am devilish hungry, just go on with your game whilst my comrade and I go on with our supper—at the end of which, when we've had a fill over a bumper of brandy and a real cheroot, we'll drink long life and success to our brave companion here, who has consented to-morrow to enrol himself under our banner as a glorious KNIGHT OF THE ROAD."

"Bravo!" cried all four, adding to the uproar their voices created, by beating uproriously on the table with their fists, until they made the glasses dance again.

The young man bowed with the grace of a finished gentleman at the greeting he had received, then immediately following his companion's example, he divested himself of his cloak, and throwing his drenched hat carelessly into a corner, drew a chair to the table, and with the greatest and most admirable coolness, proceeded immediately to help himself to the good things that were set before him. Ample justice having been done to the viands, Sheppard, in reply to the inquiring eyes that were fixed upon him and his companion, commenced his narrative—

The highwaymen, for such will our readers have supposed them to be ere this, sat gazing with evident admiration, and with expectant eagerness.

"Now, lads, as you're all attention," said Jones, "why, here goes. First and foremost then, you must know I was getting infernal short of mopusses, that I bid Dick saddle my mare this afternoon, determined if a canter wouldn't win for me the full purse of some addle-headed fool. For many a mile did I ride, and sorry a soul could I see worth the polite request of 'stand and deliver,' and I was in despair, just about to waste the charge of my pistols on a posse of sparrows, when, to my infinite delight, who should I see coming towards me but this identical cove, our comrade here. To ride up to him was the work of an instant—to level my pistol at his head was the work of half another, and to demand his MONEY, OR HIS LIFE, barely filled up the latter half. I flatter myself," said Sheppard, "when I speak these words, I generally mean them, and am bent on no child's play. But, by jingo, would you believe it? without altering his pace, any further than was necessary to clear himself of my horse, who stood in his path, he coolly walked on, without uttering a word, or taking the slightest notice. I immediately rode after him, and again arresting his progress, swore, if he didn't stand and deliver I would blow his brains out."

"The only effective mode of popping the question, by the powers," said Mike; "what had the spalpeen the conscience to say to that?"

"Say to it, is it? Just these words and no more, upon my soul, their coolness stunned me; he turned round and said, 'you'll get no money out of me, old buffer, so you needn't look so fierce; to tell you the truth, not having any, I can't tip. As to blowing my brains out, if you think they'll be of the least use to you, do so by all manner of means, you are heartily welcome to them, for deuce a bit of good are they ever likely to be to me.'"

"Ha! ha! ha!" laughed O'Brien, with such vehemence, that rolling to and fro in the chair, he suddenly pitched backwards, chair and all, and as might be expected, a hearty roar of laughter followed the ungraceful feat; Picking himself up at length, he blustered out—

"Did you ever now? is it not capital? By the powers, Harry, and what the devil did you say to that?"

"Sorry a word," interrupted Jack Rann, "but he gave me a crack on the pimple with the but-end of his pistol, that made my old cocoa-nut echo again."

"And he in return," said Sheppard, raising and opening his mouth, " gave me such a stinger in the mouth with his fist, that I lay sprawling in the road in something less than no time. Ah! it was no laughing matter, Mike," he continued, as the Irishman again burst into a hearty roar; "lookee here, and then say if you think it was?"

And opening his mouth, he exhibited the loss of three front teeth, while his gums, swollen and inflamed, testified to the strength of the conquering arm that dealt the skilful blow.

"And he knocked them out," said O'Brien. glancing from the giant-like form of Sheppard, to the slim form of Rann; "may the devil admire me! who'd a thought it."

"I didn't for one," said Sheppard, in a tone that showed his lively appreciation of Jack's conquering prowess, "but I felt it, and that a cursed sight worse as I take it. Three teeth knocked down one's throat in a twinkling, and bolted in the confusion, as one would swallow as many peas. It's no joke, I tell you—it's a mystery to me if I don't die of a surfeit of ivory."

"One thing is certain, Harry," said one of the card players, a good looking, well-dressed young fellow, whose name Clayton had more than once figured in the Gazettes of the day, and whose prepossessing person had more than once been confined in the cells of Newgate; "your game as a man of gallantry is entirely played out. What lass in the world will fancy a fellow with such a mug as that—an old fogey without a tooth in his jolly old head."

"You're right I'm afraid, Clay, my boy," said Sheppard, in a desponding tone; "that fact sticks in my gizzard as bad as the teeth; it does, by jingo."

"Well,'pon honour, I am sorry," said Rann, laughing in spite of himself at the rueful countenance of the highwayman, "and if I had known it would have spoilt him in his lady's eyes, I would have struck a little higher—"

"And knocked my eyes out of my head! no thankee, Jack, it's bad enough as it is. I fancy myself dragged by a dog about the streets, my stately person adorned with a card of 'pity the poor blind!'"

"From bad to worse, and no mistake, Harry, my boy," said Clayton, "but go on old Spin-text, you're making your little phrases as long about as a charity sermon on a cold morning."

"The tale's told," said Sheppard: "he had me off my horse with a swinging blow; my pistol from the shock flew from my hand, far beyond my reach, and before I had time to get another from my belt, his hand was on my wizen like a vice—another instant and heaven would have been my doom—dead I must have been, but, thanks to some little mercy in his composition, he released his grasp and let me rise."

"That was all," said Jack, taking up the burden of the narrative in a careless, gay tone; "and when he got on his pins, like a man of sense and a generous fellow as he his, he extended his fist; frankly confessed himself beaten, and offered to stand whatever I choose to take at the first hotel that presented itself; I never bear malice," continued Rann, "'taint in me; I've a good share of the devil, but not that part, so I shook hands with him, with all the pleasure in life; so off we trudged, he on horseback, I on foot, to a public-house, where we drowned all animosity in as good a flagon of ale as ever graced the festal board."

"Bravo!" shouted O'Brien, " by the ten toes of St. Patrick you're a noble fellow, you have the soul of a gentleman. Give me your fist, my boy, you're a friend of mine henceforth, and for ever."

"There you have it, and my heart with it," said Rann, for he had a liking for the Irishman's frank open manner. "Well," he continued, "over the ale we became mighty friends; he told me his adventure, I told him mine, how I had been a gentleman's servant, had lost my character for being too honest, and now without a home for my head, or a penny in my purse—I was an outcast upon the face of the earth. Therefore, like a man as he is, he proposed I should follow his craft—should turn highwayman. Being a spirited, light, easy, and moreover, lucrative trade, the idea liked me well. From being a gentleman's gentleman, I determined to become a GENTLEMAN OF THE ROAD. Following this upshot and my patron, I found myself hither, and now gentlemen, I have to offer my services to you in any way you may require them. You'll find me willing, competent and useful—young, strong and active—I have a arm that can defend a friend or assail an enemy—I have pluck and courage—I fear no danger, until I see it—I am as nimble on my pins as an antelope, and can see as far through a nine-inch brick wall, as most folks. There, you have a catalogue of my perfections, and the question now solely is, shall I do? Will you have me?"

"Yes, yes," broke from the enraptured group, simultaneously.

"It is enough," said Clayton, rising, "call in the Jew—let him administer the oath."

The Jew made his appearance, and having read the contract which bound the robbers together as though they were one man, he with every formality administered the oath.

"Henceforth, then," said Sheppard, seizing our hero's hand with warmth, when the ceremony was finished, and each had drained a goblet of sack or sherry to the health of their new brother, "henceforth, then, London that has so long been startled by the robberies of the five, sha   horror-struck and gaping at the exploits of the BAND OF SIX."

*　*　*　*　*

There was a loud knocking at the street door, as Sheppard finished his exclamation, and the Jew proceeded to reconnoitre, as he had before done, before he ventured to admit the applicant.

Satisfied, it would appear at length by his scrutiny, his step was heard descending the creaking stairs. Peering in upon the highwayman for an instant, he whispered—

"Your masks!" and instantly glided off to admit the visitor.

In the twinkling of an eye, each face was covered with a mask, taken from a cupboard in which a quantity lay, and every person, excepting our hero, was employed in getting on their rapiers.

Seeing him unarmed, Clayton, with a significant gesture, thrust a pistol into the hands of our hero. And thus they stood prepared for friend or foe.

In a few minutes the Jew returned, ushering in a tall man, richly habited.

The stranger glanced for an instant at the masked faces before him, then turning angrily to the Jew, he said—

"You have deceived me, he is not here."

"Oh, is it you, my noble captain," said Clayton, dropping his mask, as he recognised the other's face; "to what unlooked-for cause are we to attribute the honour of this visit?"

Without replying to the question, the captain glanced at the men by whom he was surrounded.

"Are these men to be trusted?" he asked.

"Implicitly, sir," answered Clayton; "we act in common, and have no secrets from each other."

"Enough," said the captain, briefly, and he then proceeded—

"I have to confide to your care, Clayton, a commission of great importance, for which you may hope to reap a golden harvest. Early to morrow evening, a carriage and four will leave London for Arlington, a village the other side of Hounslow. This carriage will contain an old man and a young lady. The old man is a nobleman of great rank; never mind his name—the young girl is the daughter of a merchant in the city of London, and she is exceedingly pretty; this old nobleman is as big a libertine as he is a hoary villain, is smitten with her charms, and is determined to work her ruin. I dare not avow openly my hostility to his proceedings, but with your aid I hope to thwart and nullify them. Listen to me; this is my plan: you will be accompanied by a companion, and at the hazard of your lives, if need be, this carriage must be stopped; your first care will be to rescue this girl from the old scoundrel's fell intent, and one of you must conduct her to this residence," referring to a paper as he spoke,—"it is that of an aunt of her's—she will be safer there than under her own father's roof. For this service, and as an earnest of future reward, I now tender you one hundred guineas," and as he spoke, he placed a bag of gold upon the table, the merry chinking of whose contents sounded wondrously like sweet music to the ears of Jack Rann.

"For the old nobleman, look you, that you spare his life, and for the rest, act as you will. He who remains behind will find sufficient booty in the carriage to repay him for any danger he may incur in the enterprise. Now have I your word this shall be done?"

"You have, captain," answered Clayton.

"It is well," said the captain. "Who will accompany you? I would see the man's face."

Clayton looked around him, and addressing Sheppard, said—

"Will you go?"

"How the devil can I with this mug of mine—my lips are swollen as big as pumpkins already."

"Will you?" turning to O'Brien.

"By all that's good and glorious, nothing on earth would suit my complaint better; but I've a little charmer of my own I promised faithfully to escort to Drury Lane, or by the powers—"

"Will you go, Collier?"

"Well, if I must, I must, but Colledge and I have made up our minds to stop the Dover mail."

"It's a pity to spoil so admirable a plan," said Clayton, thoughtfully, then suddenly looked towards Rann.

Jack caught the glance.

"I offer my services on the lady's behalf."

"Bravo! my fine fellow," said the captain, gleefully, "a volunteer is worth twenty press'd men! I accept your services, and already feel the battle half won."

"It shall be no fault of mine if it be not quite won to-morrow," said Rann.

"Nor mine," echoed Clayton.

"A thousand thanks—Jew, show a light—I wish you, gentlemen, a very good night."

CHAPTER VI.

FREAKS OF LADY DASHFIELD AND LORD DASHFIELD IN THE "MINOR" KEY AND OF OUR HERO, IN THE "MAJOR" KEY.

The shot fired by the depraved Lord Dashfield, that after the principle "of missing the pigeon and shooting the crow," had escaped our hero, but to wound, near unto death, her ladyship, was as disastrous in its end as it was in its delivery.

The unhappy and guilty lady paid dearly for her ill-brought and disgraceful pleasure.

For three months she lay helplessly stretched, not only upon a bed of sickness, but also upon a couch of intense mental and bodily suffering. Death!

awful at all times, yet trebly awful to the guilty soul, would have been a welcome guest to her—such was the agony—such the despair, for her first fatal sin.

Her remorse was so great, her sufferings so terrible at the crime she had almost inadvertently committed, that afte escaping the dangers of the almost deathly wound, she was seized by that terrible disease, the brain fever.

Alas! poor lady! for none who stood around her bedside, who heard her ravings, and beheld her sufferings, could withhold their pity.

"Guilty, guilty, guilty! kill me, oh God, for I deserve the death-shaft—kill me—let me die, and I will bless thee for the stroke. Oh, oh! this raging fever consumes me, and yet I must linger on, to suffer in disgrace, and in black despair to die."

No. 6

Such were the thoughts of Lady Dashfield, as she tossed restlessly upon her couch.

Lord Dashfield was certainly shocked when at first he found his stricken wife weltering in her blood at his feet, but his pity was speedily swallowed in his deep disgust at the infamous wrong she had brought upon him and his proud name. Instigated by these feelings a total separation, ratified by a deed, took place between the unhappy pair, by which contract Lady Dashfield was allowed some five thousand pounds per annum, in consideration that she should transport herself from England, on pain of forfeiting her annuity, and swear never to set foot upon its soil again.

To these terms, at once hard, harsh and imperative, the proud woman, borne down by disease and acute mental suffering, acquiesced, and it was definitely settled, that upon her restoration to a state of sufficient convalescence to merit her removal, she should proceed to France, and from thence whithersoever she pleased, so that she did not again set foot on English ground.

The evening before the one in which the adventure occurred that we are about to narrate, she was sufficiently recovered to be enabled, by being propped up with pillows, to desire a last interview with her lord. For a long time his lordship had kept completely aloof, refusing to see or hold speech with her, but as this interview was to be the last that was to take place on earth, he, after much imploring solicitation, was induced to enter his wife's chamber.

There was no sign of pity upon his face—not one atom of love added lustre to his eye, as he gazed upon the marble and death-like face of his wife, pallid and bloodless to the very lips.

"Well, madam," was his first exclamation, and the words were uttered in cold, chilling tones.

"Alfred," said the lady, in tones yet wavering and feeble from suffering, "I leave England to-morrow, and for ever."

"Your ladyship is heartily welcome to go to the devil, if you please; I care but to get you from my sight, you accursed wretch: and my happiness will rest in the security that you will die miserably abroad, away from home and friends."

"Your malevolence will relentlessly and mercilessly pursue me to the grave, then?"

"To the grave, madam, you have spoken the word."

"Then hear me," said the lady, with sudden vehemence, "and take heed of the last words you will ever hear from Mary Dashfield. That I have sinned, I confess—that I have suffered for that sin, God knows, and he only knoweth to what bitter extent. But of that enough; since nothing will glut your revenge but my inanimate corpse, I will pray that in my death you may speedily have full vengeance. Now listen. Ten years ago this day, accursed be that time!—I, a young girl of eighteen, full of innocence and joy, was sacrificed to you, a man of fifty—disgracefully bartered away through the cupidity of my doting father, who, miserable man! thought happiness was only to be found in golden gee-gaws, and in a high sounding name. Alas, the miserable deception! Alas, knowledge too dearly bought!"

"You may well refer to that sacrifice," said the earl, with a bitter sneer, "since you gained a coronet by it; and I, curses on you! I have gained a w——!"

"For nine years and more, Alfred," continued her ladyship, without noticing the interruption, "although so unsuitably matched in years, thoughts, and wishes, I was to you a faithful and devoted wife; and what was you to me?"

"What was I," inquired the earl—"tell me what I was not?"

"I will," she answered firmly—"you was neither an honest man nor a gentleman! Not ten weeks had we been wedded ere you left your wife's company to indulge in drinking, gambling, and every specious of infamous licentiousness—not ten weeks ere you was seen in houses of ill-fame, and known publicly to be in communication with one of the most depraved procuresses in this crime-filled London."

"It is a lie," exclaimed the earl.

"No," exclaimed her ladyship, "it is the truth I had proof of it, certain proof, of the evidence of my own eyesight confirmed your dastardly and filthy conduct. Now, man, can you wonder that, I being apprised of your infamous proceedings, should have been filled with disgust at you and them? I tell you my indignation has ofttimes near o'ermatched my reason, and I have been at the point of confessing the knowledge of your sin, and my determination of leaving you for ever. Would to God I had done so, for then I should have been spared the pain, the misery, and disgrace of this parting hour!"

"I can only echo your prayer, madam," said his lordship, bitterly, "with all my heart and soul."

"You have reason to do so, Lord Dashfield, for it would have been better to both. Better for both, yet for me in ten times the extent it would yourself, for I should have had a virtuous and fair fame clinging to me, whilst your name, rendered abhorrent by your evil doings and unjust procedings would have been a monument of infamy in the eyes of the world—a plague spot to be loathed and shunned, an evil written register of the damning truth how far it is possible for man to fall."

"I came here, madam," said the earl, white with passion, "not to listen to this tirade against myself, but to find you on your knees at my feet begging for forgiveness."

"Alfred, for the love of God, have mercy on me, pity me; I meant not to upbraid you. Alas, no, guilty wretch as I am, I dare not hope you would listen to censure from my unhallowed lips. Oh, no! but knowing how often you have committed the sin for which I am to suffer and die, I thought you might have mercy on me, and forgive me."

"Forgive you," said the earl in a frenzy of rage, "I swear, by heaven, no! not if it would save from perdition my own soul. Guilty as I am myself, yet guilt in you is hateful. I abhor you, detest and hate you, and loathe your very sight. To h—— with you, perfidious woman!"

He was hurrying from the presence of his wife in a transport of fury, when the door was opened, and Miss Malcolm entered, with all the familiarity of an old acquaintance, her ladyship's room.

We have heard that oil will allay the raging of a tempestuous sea. The influence of her sweet presence in this case was striking and remarkable. Dismissing from his bloated countenance all traces of rage and excitement, he advanced fawningly towards the beautiful maiden, and bade her welcome to Dashfield House.

Bowing politely, but coldly to his profuse compliments, Isabel Malcolm advanced to the invalid's side, and bending with kindly feelings over her, imprinted a warm kiss of love upon the suffering lady's marble brow.

In justice to Miss Malcolm, we must here state that she was entirely unacquainted with her fair friend's infidelity. The earl, to shield his name from the infamy he had so often gloried in himself, yet now so strangely deprecated, had given it out to the world that her ladyship's wound was caused by a pure accident, and kept them in profound ignorance of the sad proceedings which had led to, and produced such fearful and disastrous results.

"My dear, good angel," said Lady Dashfield, tears of joy filling her eyes at the sight of her lovely young friend, "welcome ever, you are a thousand times welcome to-day.' I need the solace of your sweet company to bring me back to thoughts of the happy winsome days of old. Oh, Isabel, my dear, good, beautiful friend, the sight of your sweet face is a whole world of joy."

As her ladyship uttered these words, a flood of pearly tears, betraying in painful beauty the mute signs of a sorrowing and breaking heart, coursed fast and many adown her wasted, yet still enchanting face.

"Your ladyship, I fear, has trouble at heart, or why these tears?"

"Pardon me, sweet friend, this childishness; but my illness, in reducing me, has weakened my strong tide of spirits, dear Isabel. At all events, dear child, I am not so strong nor courageous as I was."

"Never give way, my dear lady," said Isabel, "but keep a brave heart—if patients had but that always, in conjunction with a surgeon, they would nine times out of ten do without the aid of a physician. Do you know," she said, turning in a bantering tone towards the earl, "I can scarce believe his lordship is so kind as usual; I heard his voice in very harsh tones just before I entered your ladyship's boudoir. Fie, upon you, my lord, that you so far-famed for generous gallantry and courtly usages, to behave so badly in the sick room of a beloved wife; why I have scarce patience to think of it. What would your friend, the celebrated Beau Brummell say, if he heard of this laxity of gallantry?"

"My dear Miss Malcolm," said the earl, with singular earnestness, and with such marked emphasis that it did not escape Lady Dashfield's keen eye, "I assure you upon my honour," and his lordship covered his false heart with his wrinkled hand, "I was but performing a service for my lady, by rebuking a froward servant—was it not so, Mary?"

"It will be time to appeal to me, Alfred, when Miss Malcolm doubts your word."

"Quite sufficient," broke in Isabel, with a laugh, that echoed right musically around. "I humbly beg his lordship, to dismiss from his mind the thought that I could ever, in my dear friend's present dangerous state, believe him capable of any but the most kind, most devoted thoughts towards the wife of his bosom."

Every word of this contained a thorn that rankled sore and deeply in his lordship's heart. Muttering an excuse he speedily after left the boudoir of her ladyship.

Descending the staircase, he went to the court-yard, and calling his groom, desired him to order Miss Malcolm's carriage. When the vehicle was driven round to the steps, in anticipation of Miss Malcolm's speedy arrival, he beckoned the coachman to him, saying:

"Miss Malcolm desires you will drive home immediately. Give my compliments to Mr. Malcolm, and tell him Lady Dashfield is so enraptured with Miss Malcolm's sweet companionship, that she had determined upon detaining her for a few days. And, harkee me, my fine fellow, as I am desirous your young lady should not be hurried away, I will give you a guinea if every time you are told to call you forget to do so; and here's the first instalment as a guarantee of the others to follow it."

"Long life to you, my lord. They may tell me a hundred times if they like, but if I am to have a guinea a time for driving in another direction, may the devil admire me, if you catch me near Piccadilly."

"You are a shrewd knave. Now be off, and deliver Lady Dashfield's message. If Miss Malcolm should have a desire to return home shortly, I will, that is, when I am tired of keeping her, drive her home myself."

"God bless your lordship," said the fellow, as he drove away, "he ain't only a lord by name, but selp' me goodness, he's a prince by nature. A rale golden guinea! And I'm to have one every time I'm told to call, and don't leave it alone, that is, to leave it alone, don't go I mean, and in course, they won't catch ME near Dashfield House. Sartinly not! do I look like a fool! not a bit on it, I'll count one with anybody. He's going to bring her home WHEN HE'S TIRED OF HER; rather rum expression that, though there's something wague, arkard, and doubtfully, dubiously questionable, I fancy a few, rayther. But howsomdever, all these lords are gemmen, and what's a gemman but a gemman, damme, that's a clincher; go on, ole hoss! Gee up, Neddy!"

* * * * *

The evening of the day, some of the events of which we have described, was one of extreme beauty, and as the night advanced, and the lustrous stars, in their countless numbers illumined the vast expanse of the heavens, two horsemen coming from the direction of London, pulled up in the front of the old Red Lion, at Brentford.

They were both well mounted, and fashionably attired in the costume of the day—one was Clayton, the highwayman, and the other was no less a personage than our eventful hero.

"House ahoy, there!" shouted Clayton, and in obedience, a jolly and portly person sallied forth, pipe in mouth, and his round rubicund face ornamented with such a brilliant specimen of a " jolly nose," as would leave not a shadow of doubt in the beholders mind, that the tapster had a strong partiality for the liquors he dispensed.

"A good even to you, gentlemen both," said the landlord, bowing; "what can I have the pleasure of serving you with this evening; I have as fine a collection in the larder as any contented man could wish to find—cold fowl, cold ham, cold beef, a splendid veal and ham pasty, tarts, pies, and puddings, fish, flesh, and fowl—yes, gentlemen, I assure you," said the garrulous landlord, "the fowls of air, the fishes of the unfathomable deep, coupled with sundry and divers of the denizens of the farm-yard, the beasts of the field, the fruit of the earth, are there, gentlemen, awaiting. I have also excellent beds downier than down itself; in fact, gentlemen, to take the *summum-bonum*, as my sign board so briefly and pithily expresses it, I have good accomodation for man and beast."

"Will you not dismount, worthy gentlemen? I have a good fire, and a right goodly company."

"What say you, comrade, wilt draw rein for an hour we have time; galore on hand, and who knows but a ticker may be manufactured of some of those yokels within there." This was spoken in a whisper; he then added aloud, "what sayest thee, Jack, wilt dismount?"

"With all my heart," said Jack, springing from his horse, "give me my first lesson in the art of watchmaking."

"I will," answered Clayton; turning to the landlord, he said, "send some one out to mind the horses, will you? my friend's mare is a restless jade."

"Ay, ay! your honour, I'll fetch a man in the twinkling of an eye Jerry, you Jerry there," he shouted, "come along do."

A bullet-headed oastler made his appearance, and yawning as if he had just been awakened from a pleasant nap, sauntered indolently towards the horses' heads.

"Woa mare, woa then," he said, as the animal our hero had bestrode began to show symptoms of a fiery restless nature. "This is a dangy fine horse, and mighty like squire's black Sue."

"She's a fine creature, sure enough," said Jack, as he gazed upon the splendid animal with pride and admiration, "and look that you guard her well, for she's worth her weight in gold."

"I'll mind her, sir, ne'er fear—lor bless you, I've been used to horses all my life, so, mare, gently then."

"That fellow smells a rat, I fancy," whispered Clayton, in our hero's ear; "at all events, he's right in his conjecture, she was the squire's horse."

"The devil," said Jack, "suppose he should chance to come along and claim it?"

"Phaugh, let him, all we should have to do in such a case will be to persuade him he's labouring under a delusion."

"But how did you manage to get possession of her?" inquired Jack.

"By the simple progress that swells wearing a bad hat adopt by going to church and exchanging it for a good one. I was down the road one fine evening, and put up my hack at one of the inns; there was a cove in the bar when after some little confab I discovered to be the veritable squire spoken of; in the course of conversation, I managed to ease him of his watch and purse, then under pretence of going up by the coach, then stopping at the door, I left him, evidently charmed with the gentlemanly personage of your humble servant. While the waiters of the inn were all engaged with the coach and its passengers, I, like a sensible fellow, as I flatter myself I am, quietly went to the rear, and saddling the squire's horse, by mistake of course, quietly rode off with it. The best of the joke was, the squire caught sight of me as I passed, and rushing out like mad, swore I'd got his horse."

"And you?" inquired Jack.

"Coolly took a pinch of snuff, my fine fellow, and begad from his own box, too, respectfully refreshed his memory with a repetition of the phrase that 'exchange is no robbery,' and informing him if he would search the stable, he would find an animal up to his weight, and far more suitable for an elderly gentleman than he was, a 'gemman of the road;' he swore he would not accept my present but as I hate dissatisfied people and grumblers, I left him to the animal and his own blissful meditations."

A rare spree, by jingo," said Jack, with an hearty laugh, "by the powers your CHEEK is inimitable."

"Cheek, my dear fellow, 'pon honour," said Clayton, "I acknowledge to no such debased property."

"What in the name of all that's glorious do you call it then?" inquired Jack.

"Confidence, my dear boy, confidence."

"Ha, ha, ha!" laughed Jack, "but see here, here comes old boniface."

"Gentlemen, I beg to inform you your grog is made, and your cigars only await the lighting," said the landlord, then shouting to his man to keep the 'osses' waiting, he hurried before them into the house.

As he did so, Clayton whispered to our hero, "my name is Clifford, what shall yours be?"

"Allspice," answered Jack, with a laugh.

The landlord now ushered them into the best parlour, and our hero and his companion found themselves in the presence of three gentlemen.

"By the Lord Harry, Jack, that fellow yonder is the squire himself, we are in for it if he recognises either me or your mare."

Then suddenly assuming a swaggering gait, he advanced into the centre of the room, and bowing carelessly as he spoke, said—

"Your servant, gentlemen, your servant."

The three acknowledged the salutation with a bend of the head.

"Landlord, let me see, I ordered brandy, I think—oh, oh yes, I remember perfectly now, it was brandy—"

"And water," suggested the landlord.

Brandy and water—oh, yes, I remember perfectly it was brandy and water," continued Clayton, "but I don't call this brandy and water, sirrah!" he said in a tone of assumed sternness.

"What do you call it then, sir?" stammered the host, sorely perplexed at being carpeted before such worshipful company.

"Why, I call it water and brandy, for the first predominates most infernally over the latter. Come, sir, take these glasses back, and take a little of that filthy water out, d'ye hear?"

"Take some of the water out, sir; it's impossible without taking some of the brandy with it."

"Then I tell you what, and I appeal to these gentlemen, that if it is not effected, that you deserve a good horse-whipping for daring to dispense such disgusting stuff. What say you, Captain Allspice?" said Clayton, turning to our hero.

"I decidedly concur in what you say," answered Jack, catching at the cue, "its well for you, you insulting vagabond, that I havn't yet tasted my grog, or for such an insult I would flog you to within an inch of your life, I would, by God!"

The squire and his friends, supposing that they themselves had been victimised, immediately acquiesced in this suggestion, and suggested that it should immediately and practically be carried into operation.

The panic-stricken landlord, horror-struck at the state of affairs, fell upon his knees and implored mercy.

"Get up, you whining humbug," said Clayton, giving him a gentle jerk in the breech to accelerate his movements, as he spoke, "What you mean?"

The landlord was on his feet in a jiffey.

"Now, sir," said Clayton, in continuation, "to show you how dangerous it is to tamper with gentlemen who may honour your house with their company, I forbear corporeal punishment only upon one condition."

"Damme, don't forgive him," said the squire—"I would cut his life out!"

"Yes, I will forgive him, on condition that he shall bring me in a bottle of Hollands and a bottle of rum."

"Oh, yes, with pleasure I will," and right glad he was to be released from his perilous position.

On these terms, he hurried off, and speedily returned laden with two capacious bottles filled with the liquors named.

Pouring half of the brandy and water from out of each vessel, he deliberately filled them up with an equal admixture of Hollands and rum; then beckoning the landlord, he bade him, on pain of instant flagellation, to drain them instantly to the dregs.

"My good sir, it is impossible—it will make me dead drunk, it will."

"Drink it," said Clayton, giving him a smart lash with the whip.

The ill-fated tapster seized one tumbler of the ardent mixture, and drained it dry.

"Good," said Clayton—"now the other. What, you hesitate?"

Almost consumed by the nauseous draught of ardent spirits he had swallowed, the landlord seized the second tumbler, and was in the act of drinking when his brain reeled, and he fell on the floor, as he himself had predicted, dead drunk!

A burst of laughter greeted the fall of boniface.

"Here, you sir," said Clayton, advancing to the door, "just put your fool of a master to bed."

This was addressed to the boy.

"Please, sir, I can't—I beant strong enough, but I'll tell missus, she wull—she's used to it, I beant."

In obedience to the boy's call, in came the mistress—a powerful, able-bodied, and long-tongued woman.

"The drunken beast—the filthy wretch—the abominable brute!"

Such were the lightest greetings she bestowed upon her insensible husband; then pitching right and left into the urchin, whom she pummelled soundly—not because he deserved it, but because such a display of agility was calculated to tranquillise her excited feelings—after the fashion of the safety-valve of our modern locomotives, to let off the waste steam. When she was out of breath from her exertions, she bade the boy—

"Go and hold the osses, and send Jerry in."

Out went the lad, and in came Jeremiah. The latter's only exclamation was—

"Hollo! what drunk agin!"

Which observation gave the auditors reason to believe that the landlord of the Red Lion, as well as his customers, often bowed at the Shrine of Bacchus. The mistress having seized the head, and Jerry catching hold of his master's legs, they removed the landlord to his bed-room. This was not effected without some difficulty—for putting a tipsy person to bed is very like driving a wayward pig, for they generally go any way but the one you want them to.

Under the pretence of enjoying the fun, but ostensibly with the view of securing the landlady and Jerry up stairs, Clayton followed them up, and adroitly slipping the key from the inner side of the door, quietly retreated, after having locked them in.

On his return to the parlour, he was greeted with a peal of laughter, the squire declaring it was "the richest joke he had ever seen."

"And the beauty of it is, gentlemen, it is not the only spree I intend to have to-night; Jack, guard the door, and the first man that disobeys my orders, shoot him through the head. D'ye hear?"

"I do," answered Jack, "and am prepared to act," and with a pistol in each hand, he looked, in good truth, formidable enough.

"Now, sir squire," said Clayton, "since you perceive that sudden death to you will be the result of any rebellion against our authority, I have to request you will, as a sensible man, deposit your purse, pocket-book, and snuff-box upon that table!"

"I'll see you d——d first!" exclaimed the squire.

"Don't be a fool!" urged one of his friends, "lay them down."

"Your friend argues wisely and well. Come, again I bid you, and be it at your dire peril, if you dare refuse!"

"Let it be so, then," said the squire, doggedly, "I do refuse," and saying so, he drew his sword, and placed himself in an attitude of defence.

"I admire a brave man, but not a fool-hardy one—lay down your trinkets, fool, or I'll spatter your brains upon the wall."

"See, you are playing with a desperate man: for God's sake sheathe your sword, and listen to reason," said his friend.

Cowering—and who would not—before the dreadful death that so menacingly stared him in the face, he advanced to the table, and laid his purse and snuff-box upon it.

"Come, sir—your watch; out with it!"

It had been an heir-loom in the family, and 'twas with a heavy sigh the squire parted with that.

"Now, sir," said Clayton to the second, "your turn has come—I demand all your valuables; but if you have anything upon you which you set great value, for the good advice you gave your friend, and which saved me from bloodshed, you are quite welcome to keep it."

"I thank you for your courtesy, sir," replied the gentleman, "if you will allow me to retain my snuff-box, you are heartily welcome to all besides—in fact, I will give them to you, and regard you in future, not as thieves, but gentlemen."

"Gammon!" sounded Jack's sonorous voice in the rear. It will be understood that our hero still occupied the threatening posture that he, by the captain's directions, first assumed, and having at his finger's end, as it were, by the aid of his levelled pistols, the whole company, he feared not and cared not.

"Do you allow your servant to dictate to you?" said the gentleman, turning to Clayton.

"Sorry a bit of it ; but do you not understand, or must our persuaders teach you leaden-learning ; he dictates not to me, but to you."

"Oh, Lord!" exclaimed the other, emphatically, then nudging Clayton, said, "just tell him to lower his pistol a trifle, will you, they do terrify me so?"

"I cannot lower my pistol's aim from your skull," said Jack Rann, "unless you prefer the bullet to penetrate your heart."

"I've a good thick skull, but I hav'n't a good sound heart," soliloquised the fellow to himself, then turning and speaking aloud to our hero, he said, "thank you, I would prefer you to raise those weapons, and if I am allowed to speak the truth, the higher you do so to the ceiling, the better it will suit my complaint."

"Devilish good!" said the squire, who seemed to have forgotten his own losses in the spectacle presented to him of the robbery of his companions. "A joke worth all the money I'VE lost."

"Ticker and all?" observed Jack, ironically.

"Damme me, you opened a wound there—I bleed afresh."

"If you act as a gentleman, a plaister may be applied to it, in the shape of the very watch itself."

"Do you mean this?" exclaimed the squire, gleefully ; "any time you like to bring it me, I'll give you a good dinner and twenty guineas for it, if I don't, damme."

"I accept the invite, sir. Clayton, my boy, I bespeak that watch."

"It is yours," answered Clayton, " but what dealings have you had with this old buffer, that we need proceed to extremities with him?"

"Dealings I have had none," answered Jack, "but, as a braggart, I have long known him to defy any knight of the road to detect his cunning. In his purse he certainly carries coin, but it is counterfeit—in his pocket-book he has certain documents of the bank note character, but of the criminal stamp, payable not at the Bank of England, but at Newgate—the high road to Tyburn Tree."

"Ho, ho! you snivelling thief," said Clayton, advancing threateningly towards the fellow, "you would deceive us, would you?"

"Don't hurt him," said Jack, "we shall wound his feelings sufficiently through his pocket."

"But the fellow is not fit to live! if he'd rob a highwayman, he'd rob a church. Take that," and he favoured the unfortunate with an impressive kick behind.

"That will do, old fellow," said Jack, "let's now to business." Then turning to their victim, he said, "Come, sir, off with those boots of yours, do you hear."

"My boots," whined the man.

"Ah, your boots, thickhead, and look infernal sharp about it, if you wouldn't have my helping hand to aid you."

The threat having the desired effect, the man nervously drew them from his feet.

"Well, Jack," said Clayton, "what's the use of them now. I've heard there's nothing like leather, but damme, they are worn all on one side."

"If you look closely at the heel of them, you will discover the head of a brass nail."

"Yes, here it is, sure enough."

"Keep your finger tightly on it; that's it, and now see what its contents are."

"Golden guineas, by the lord Harry," said Clayton, gleefully; "who'd have thought the old buffer had a till in each boot."

The process of emptying them having been speedily gone through, Jack next directed his companion's notice to the fellow's hat, in the corner of which neatly folded and secretly hid, they found a roll of bank notes.

"Bravely done," said our hero; then turning to their victim, he said, "let this be a lesson to you—may it teach you the value of prudence, and the folly of making confidents of people you do not know."

"Now, sir," said Clayton, politely to the third gentleman, "may I request the honour of the waste gold you have about you?"

"Gently," said Jack, "one at the time, the other gentleman has not yet surrendered his snuff-box."

"No, more he hasn't, the deceitful spalpeen; come, tip."

"Oh, Lord," said the fellow, as he placed it, with a groan, upon the table, "I'm ruined."

"So Betty said," observed Jack, "and if you live long enough, old stick-in-the-mud, you may, like her, be ruined many a time yet. But time flies: Clay, my boy, just polish off that third swell, and we'll be off down the road."

"Don't let me detain you, gentlemen—I perceive it is useless to deceive you," and saying these words, he placed his watch and purse upon the table; "they are the only valuables I have about me—if you doubt my word, search me."

"I'll be d——d if I do!" said Clayton, "I should hope I know an honest man when I see him; thank you, sir—your'e a gentleman;" and he bowed politely, "much obliged to you."

The other returned the salutation good-humouredly, and by way of a joke, observed that he "hoped soon to have the pleasure of meeting him again," a wish in which both Rann and Clayton joyously concurred.

"We wish we could be always with you," said Clayton, "but the decrees of fate are against it, gentlemen, the best of friends are doomed to part, but before we go, as we have other trifling business to transact down the road, which we cannot well do with any molestation, we must take the liberty of binding you back to back for an hour or so."

"Curse me, if I submit to that," said the squire.

"Curse me, if you don't," said Clayton, and seizing the squire's elbows, he was completely pinioned, without being able to effect the least opposition.

"Now, gentlemen, your turn being next," said Rann, "just oblige me by standing back to back. So, so!" and having stripped them of their long neckerchiefs, Jack tied their elbows and wrists firmly together.

"Safe bind, safe find, an adage good and true, and under the present circumstances, it strikes me particularly applicable to you," said Clayton; "now, Jack, having managed this little affair with neatness and dexterity, 'Hurrah for the Road!'"

"Gentlemen, I have the honour of wishing you a very good night," said Jack, and saying these words, he turned from the room, and locking the door, took the key with him.

CHAPTER VII.

THE ADVENTURE—THE FLIGHT—THE INTERRUPTION—VILLANY PREVENTED.

Returning to his wife's boudoir after having dismissed Mr. Malcolm's carriage, but not until he had given orders for his own to be prepared, and had informed a confidential groom on what mission he was bound, the earl paced restlessly to and fro, nervously anticipating the consummation of his hopes.

Both her ladyship and Isabel noticed his restlessness, but neither imparted it to the atrocious desire animating his breast. Her ladyship conceived it possible that their late conversation might have produced this result. Isabel imputed it to the idea that probably his lordship might be desirous of a private interview with his wife, and being naturally unwilling to be an obstacle, she rose, some hour or so after her time, to take her leave.

"Why this haste, my darling?" said Lady Dashfield, taking her gently by the hand to detain her, "are your visits so imperative, is your time so valuable, that you cannot spare one single hour upon poor me?"

"Why do you wish to detain Miss Malcolm against her will? if she was not urgently wanted elsewhere, she would not exhibit this haste, I'm sure. I am quite surprised at your unreasonable conduct."

These words were spoken by his lordship in cold petulant tones, that added in Isabel's own mind proof to the conjecture that her company, so far as the earl was concerned, could be well dispensed with.

Acting upon these thoughts, and again and again reiterating her sorrow at the shortness of her visit, Miss Malcolm at length was permitted, though with evident reluctance on the part of her ladyship, to take her leave.

The earl, with unaccustomed politeness, insisted upon accompanying the young lady to the carriage, and Lady Dashfield was again alone.

As they passed down the magnificent staircase, and crossed the noble hall, in which stood some choice and antique statues and some flowering shrubs, that lent a fragrant odour and a graceful scene to the place, his lordship hurriedly stopped Miss Malcolm, and asked her in flurried and impatient tones, if she had any objection to his company in the carriage.

"Objection!" answered the artless and unsuspecting girl, with a merry laugh, "how can I esteem it otherwise than as an honour and pleasure?"

"You are flattering me, Miss Malcolm," said the earl.

"Not I, my lord, I do assure you; it is a system I never pursued, and a deception I never practised, I have often been upbraided for my candour—never before for my flattery."

"I am glad to hear you say so my charming lady," exclaimed the earl, his eyes literally gleaming with satisfaction, "and if you will permit me to escort you to the carriage; I will gain leave of absence from her ladyship and rejoin you in one minute."

This feat was performed, and his lordship, bounding with unwonted agility up the staircase, stood again, and for the last time, he was ever doomed to it, in the presence of his wife.

Dismissing, with an imperious wave of the hand, Elinor Roche, who had just entered to wait upon her ladyship, he stood confronting his wife, a smile of malignant—of damnable triumph playing upon his features.

Startled by his frightful look and his extraordinary agitation, her ladyship half rose from the couch. Forcing her back to her seat by main force, his lordship seized her wrist with desperate, and to her, painful energy, and bringing his mouth almost to her ear, he whispered in tones, positively hissing from excitement—

"You love Miss Malcolm?"

"I do dearly," was the reply.

"It would grieve you to the heart's core to see her wronged?"

"I would suffer wrong myself first."

"Woman!" said the earl, tightening his grasp, and in a voice now hoarse from excitement, "if you knew that this night the fair blushing beauty, in all the pride of virgin loveliness, who just now left this chamber, was to be defiled and dishonoured, and that by main force, what would you say— what would you do?"

"Inhuman man, do you want to kill me with this cruel excitement?

Great God! what should I feel—what should I do, my brain—my heart would burst—I should die."

"Die then, accursed one! for what I have conjured to you will literally come to pass; and I, your husband, woman, do you hear? will have the glorious task of ruining this incomparable friend—this model of virtue and beauty!"

"My God!" exclaimed her ladyship, "'tis some frightful delusion; it is too monstrous to be real!"

"It is the truth, jade, the solemn earnest truth—she is now in my carriage, not her own, that I dismissed—in my carriage, and my coachman is in the secret, and will drive her—not to her father's, but to my procuress, as you call her, and to my cottage, or my pandemonian, as you call it, at Arlington!"

"Accursed wretch, this shall not be—weak as I am, I will prevent it!" and almost maddened by the dire villany by which her beloved friend was encompassed, she clung madly to him.

And he, base coward—atrocious scoundrel—Heaven and earth, can it be! can such villany exist?

Yes, twining his hand in her long hair, and forcing back her head so violently till nothing was presented to his maddening gaze but her snowy neck and bosom, he raised his right hand in the air, and—curses on him, for the murderous blow!—struck her fiercely full in the throat.

The struggle was at an end, her fingers loosened their hold, and she fell.

* * * * *

Without regarding the victim of his violence, his lordship seized his hat, and smoothing his ruffled visage as he went, sped down the staircase.

There was one before him though; before he could reach the carriage door—Elinor Roche was at it, and thrusting something into Isabel's hand, bid her "Take it, and keep it, and use it if need be, for her own—for God's sake!"

Terrified at the strange words and visible agitation of the girl, Isabel instinctively shrank from the gift.

"Take it, lady!" said Elinor, in tones of extraordinary earnestness, tones that admitted of no deceit, so earnest, so imploring were they, "in God's name take it! It may save you from a fate worse than death. Quick, lady—he comes, it may be too late!"

Thus abjured, Isabel stretched forth her hand for the gift—

IT WAS A DAGGER!

In one instant Elinor had disappeared, the next his lordship sprang into the carriage.

"I have kept you waiting longer than I anticipated, my dear Miss

Malcolm, but her ladyship, in her unceasing fondness, would scarcely suffer me to depart."

"I do not wish to rob her ladyship of your company, my lord—indeed I should prefer to return home alone—let me, therefore, add my entreaties to hers—let me beg of you to return to her."

"Not I, by our lady! I am too well contented with my present position."

And so saying, his lordship, putting his head through the window, bade the coachman, with an oath, "drive on," then lowering the blinds, he remained with Miss Malcolm in total darkness.

Any person who has ridden over the large stone roading of London, at the present time, may probably form a faint idea of what it was in the last century; at all events, they will have had convincing proof that the pleasure of conversation is extremely curtailed and limited.

Over the rough stones went his lordship's horses at a goodly pace; presently the jolting ceased, and the carriage rolled quietly and swiftly on over sandy road. Startled by the transition from sudden noise to sudden silence, Isabel exclaimed—

"My lord, we are going wrong; this is not London—bid the coachman stop."

"I assure you we are going right, my dear young friend, quite right; but fancying you would like a drive, I bade him go round a little instead of following the direct course—will you not forgive me?"

Appeased by his respectful manner, yet being far from satisfied, Isabel maintained a strict silence, merely expressing her uneasiness, as they rode along, that they were not nearing London.

"My dear Miss Malcolm," said the earl, taking her hand, "forgive me this little ruse, and pray be not weary, for your friends do not expect you home."

"Not expect me home, my lord? explain yourself—I know not what you mean."

"I will speedily explain, Miss Malcolm," said the earl, attempting, as he spoke, to place his arm around her waist.

This innovation Isabel indignantly repulsed, and shrinking from him to the farthest corner of the vehicle, she demanded to know what he meant by such conduct.

"So, so, my gentle one," said his lordship, dropping his assumed character, and exposing his real, "since you are so deeply offended at such a trifle, allow me to explain what my thoughts, wishes, and intentions are."

Poor Isabel's heart beat so violently from apprehension of some approaching evil, of what she knew not, that its pulsations could be plainly heard.

"In the first place, my angel, I have watched your budding charms for many a year, with a jealous eye—jealous, because I sometimes feared your luscious beauties were not reserved for me. Wedded to a woman, for whom my hatred only equals my distaste, your company has been so frequent of late, that the desire to possess you, you charming little creature, as my own, has been uncontrollable, and hence this little deception, and this sant ride."

"You are pleased to be facetious at my expense, Lord Dashfield," said Isabel, in a surpassing tone of cool contempt, "but as I am not in the habit of being a party to deception of any sort, I demand to be taken home."

"'Pon my soul," said his lordship, "having marked for myself a certain line of conduct, it is impossible I can retract. No, sweet angel, the curtain having risen, we must play the play out; and I will commence the first by a few forced kisses at those tempting lips of thine."

And seizing Miss Malcolm, he, by brute force, and in defiance of her struggles to get free, pulled her upon his knees, and commenced a series kisses that were to him delectable—to her wormwood and gall.

Finding all her entreaties were disregarded, and that the hoary villain persisted in his offensive and foul proceedings, she suddenly remembered the dagger, and uttering a cry of joy, she drew it from i's sheath.

No. 8

As she did so, its bright blade flashed in the darkness. The earl himself saw the glare of the glittering weapon, and falling back for an instant, asked, "what was that?"

Pale, breathless, and cruelly agitated, the young girl could not find words to reply.

Aroused by the passion that rushed like a deluge through his veins, carrying thoughts, feelings, moral responsibilities, all and everything in its tide of strong licentiousness, the earl again commenced his work of insult.

Feeling his hand upon her arm, Isabel started as if bitten by a serpent, and rousing herself from her lethargy, she exclaimed in tones so stern, as fully to show her brave determination.

"Touch me not, villain! nay, even so much as lay a finger on me, and, as heaven is my judge, I will strike you dead."

"Damnation!" muttered the earl, "she is armed."

"I am, Lord Dashfield, providentially; and I swear to you, unless you immediately retrace the steps we have come, and restore me to my father's arms, I will stab you to the heart."

"Do you mean this, you she devil?" said the earl, "curses on my foolhardiness for not possessing myself of that accursed poniard; I am a dolt, an idiot! And you think with your heroics to escape me, miss—no, if twenty deaths stood in my way instead of one, I would conquer you."

"Hear me, Lord Dashfield:—Your treachery has aroused the woman in my soul; and if you dare to take the least liberty with me—so much as to lay your hand upon me, that instant shall be your last; for I will plunge this dagger to the hilt in your breast! Cruelly and treacherously entrapped, you thought, in the timid and affrighted girl, to gain a pliant victim to your loathsome, abominable wishes. I thank heaven that I have the means, the strength, and the determination to resist you to the uttermost —to death, if need be!"

"Come, come, Miss Malcolm, I meant not what I said—I did but jest with you. Put up your dagger—let us be friends."

"Friends!" she echoed bitterly—"if this be friendship, I would I had never heard the word. Yet," she said, inspired by a sudden thought, "I will believe it is friendship—I will forgive you this outrage, this insult. Lady Dashfield and my father shall both remain in ignorance of—if——"

"If what?" said the earl.

"You will bid that fellow drive me home."

"And if I do this, you will sheath that dagger and promise, if I return you to your father without further molestation, you will not again threaten me with it?"

"I promise you, my lord."

"Then your request shall be complied with," and throwing open the coach-door, he stepped out, and whispered to the coachman.

The fellow instantly turned his horses' heads towards London; but first dismounting, he approached the carriage-door, and begged to know in what direction her father's house lay.

Whilst she, full of joy at the change in his conduct—full of thankfulness to heaven that the evil that had overshadowed her spotless fame was removed—and giving explicit directions as to her father's residence, the traitor seized her by the wrist, and with an expert and desperate twist, he tore the dagger from her grasp!

"Now's your time, my lord," he exclaimed; "you have nothing to fear from cold steel, so you can recommence your love-making at once!"

His lordship needed no second bidding, but springing into the carriage, he rudely and roughly seized upon Miss Malcolm.

Resisting his rude, unmanly attacks with all her strength did the noble and courageous girl until the very uttermost; until her feeble strength failing beneath the pressure of his continued attacks and a sudden terror at her threatened fate, to her ten thousand times worse than death, that took possession of her soul, she uttered a loud and piercing scream of agony, and her senses forsaking her, she sank powerless and helpless into the libertine's arms!—and with no human soul near to hear that last depairing cry—no human hand to intervene and save her from destruction!

Yes, thank heaven! the cry of distress reverberating through the still air of the night, was heard by our hero and Clayton; yet so faint, it was scarcely to be recognizable as the voice of a human being. Indeed, so low and indistinct was it to the pair, from the long distance between the horsemen and the carriage, that Clayton, turning to our hero said——

"Jack, what was that?"

Rann's quicker ear had distinguished in the sound, borne upon the breeze, the voice of a woman! Zealously intent upon his mission, as much for humanity's sake as in the hope of meeting with a reward, he struck his spurs into his horse's side, exclaiming, in a loud voice—

"Forward, Clayton, my boy, or by heaven we shall be too late—that sound was the voice of a lady, or I never heard woman's voice before."

"Go it, my boy—I am at your heels," and away, under the influence of whip and spur, bounded the two noble animals with the speed of the wind.

It will readily be supposed that their splendid horses speedily brought them within a few paces of Lord Dashfield's carriage. The coachman hearing the sound of the pursuers, lashed the horses with such ungovernable fury, that they dashed on uncontrolled at a mad gallop.

Forward they went, the pursuers and the pursued, Jack's splendid mare gaining upon the carriage at every stride, until he rode side by side with the coachman.

"Stop," shouted Jack, in a voice of thunder.

The man's only reply was a cut at our hero with his heavy whip. Jack saw the movement, and only by a skilful manœuvre escaped the lash.

Turning in his saddle, as he drew a pistol from his belt, he said—

"Stop, villain, or by God I fire!"

Disregarding this threat, or in the impetuosity of the moment, not catching the deadly meaning of the words, the man still continued recklessly to urge on his affrighted beasts.

"Your blood on your own wilful head," said Jack, "you have brought your fate upon yourself, and forced mine upon me. Stop, madman, do you hear me?"

"No, no!" the man, in his desperate obstinacy, still mercilessly lashed on his reeking beasts.

Curbing his horse for an instant, to make sure of his aim, Rann levelled his pistol, and fired. True to its aim, the bullet sped on, and striking the coachman in the right arm, the unfortunate fellow, uttering a cry of mingled rage and anguish, fell headlong from his seat.

On, on sped the horses and the carriage with maddened speed, with redoubled, with terrific energy, for the report of the pistol had only served further to affright the scared animals. And now, at a terrific pace, also went Jack, followed in the rear by Clayton, whose horse, unable to cope with the astonishing swiftness of the beautiful creature our hero bestrode, was left somewhat in the rear.

The horses, left to their own frenzied action, with no arm to curb or controul, sped spiritedly on. To stop them in their headlong career, our hero found would be a task utterly impracticable; and fearing, from their frantic struggles, not only destruction to them, but also death to the occupants of the carriage, unless they were speedily stopped, he drew his remaining pistol from his belt, and levelling, shot the fore horse through the head.

Down went the beast, dragging its companion with it, and the two hinder horses falling over their prostrate companions, went headlong heavily down.

Uttering a shout of triumph, Jack sprang from his horse. She was so admirably trained—so gentle—with all her uncontrollable fiery spirit, that she stood motionless, awaiting her rider's return: Jack rushed to the remaining leader, and cutting the harness which bound him to his dead companion, seized the animal by the head, and thus arrested the further progress of the vehicle.

At this moment his lordship, who, from the alarm created by the pursuit, the report of fire-arms, and the crash of the falling horses, coupled with the abrupt stoppage of the vehicle, which had thrown him flat forward upon his face; he had not until this juncture found himself sufficiently recovered from the panic into which these events had thrown him, to inquire the cause of these murderous proceedings.

Having, with Clayton's help, released the horses from the carriage, and suffered the three animals to wander whithersoever they pleased, nipping as they went the dew-spangled grass, to allay their fearful thirst, Jack Rann turned his attention to the carriage and its occupants: first lowering his mask, however, by way of precaution, ere he did so; an example deemed so worthy of imitation, that it was instantly followed by Clayton.

The earl, having by this time recovered somewhat from his confusion, and also at the same time gained a considerable portion of his haughty tone, inquired what they meant by the outrage; at the same time, with an oath swearing—

"They should both swing at Tyburn for it."

His voice was so thick and guttural from the excitement and fear under which he had laboured, that Jack failed to recognize any resemblance in his tones to those of his late master, Lord Dashfield.

"My Lord," answered Jack, "you have that in your carriage and that in your guilty mind that tells you that you have not been followed from London for nothing."

"What do you mean, villain?"

"This, brother, since we know so properly how to accost each other; that you have in that carriage a young lady, a merchant's daughter of the city of London, who, by fraud and violence, and with most sinister and villainous attempts, you have torn from her home."

"You lie, knave!" said the earl, in tones quivering from rage and excessive passion, "it is a lie, a d—d lie! and scoundrels as you are, you shall pay dearly for this outrage. If I have any favour with the king, I'll have you hung, you villain, I will."

"We will soon see who is the liar," said Jack, putting one foot inside the door of the carriage, and peering anxiously in to get a view of its occupants.

"Yes, you old scoundrel, and if I find you are deceiving me, lord though you be," said Clayton, "you shall pay dearly for your temerity."

At this interval Isabel, whom the shock of the falling horses had awakened from her trance, but who, nevertheless, felt so shocked, affrighted, and confused, as scarce to know what she did, cried in tones of such concentrated grief and fear—of such heart-breaking agony, "Save me! Oh, Heaven, save me!" that our hero was touched to the soul. Seizing the earl, he with one effort dragged him forth into the road, and having confided him to the care of Clayton, he advanced again to the carriage, and bringing Isabel forth with all the gentleness it was possible to exercise, he bid her "look up, she was saved."

Obeying the request with joy, Isabel did indeed raise her pale, bloodless face to that of our hero's; and recognizing, it would appear, the features of him, whom her pure heart had ever worshipped—had ever embalmed with love, she fell upon his neck, and in a flood of joyous tears exclaimed—

"Rann, my dear, dear Rann!"

"Miss Malcolm!" exclaimed Jack, in tones of ecstatic joy, "can it indeed be you whom I have rescued from this old villain's toils? Oh, this is indeed pure bliss! And you, scoundrel," said Jack, turning with flashing eyes to the quaking earl, "who are you, whose villainous audacity, setting aside all justice, happiness, and honour, would find a victim for your hellish arts in this noble and innocent girl?—quick, I say, answer me, who and what are you?"

"One who was once your master—one whom you have wronged as cruelly as I ever could have done that pale-faced girl, even if I had heaped the wrong I meant."

"Speak quickly," answered Jack, himself now pale and trembling with emotion, who are you?"

"I am Alfred, Earl of Dashfield," was the haughty reply, "and I know you, Jack Rann, and now we have met again listen to my vow of vengeance. I swear I would have forgiven you your first offence, if you would have let me had an unimpeded course in this, but since, like a curse, like an evil genius, you cling to me, since yon puny girl has confessed her love for you—since, in every phase of life, you rise to trample down my pride—to blight my wishes—to curse me; I swear to you, and warn you as I swear, that I will never know happiness until I have brought you to the foot of the gallows—never know peace until I have seen you hanged."

This tirade of words was given with such bitter impetuosity, and with an expression of such malignant meaning, that they all stood silent, until he had made an end, literally, as it were, curdled with horror.

"Why, you cantankerous old varmint," said Clayton, giving the earl a vigorous shake as he spoke, "what the devil do you mean? I tell you what it is, my boy, here's a prophecy for you—if your neck escapes the noose, it will be brutal murder if the neck of any loving soul is encircled with an hempen neckerchief—for, by Jove, if ever a cove looked born to be hung, you are that ill-fated individual; and if ever I saw a hang-dog's countenance, yours is that one; all you want to complete your picture in full, is Jack Ketch's frame—Tyburn Tree."

He had scarce done speaking before the sound of horses' feet, advancing rapidly from the direction of Brentford, broke upon the ear.

"Quick, Jack, my gallant fellow, we are pursued. That d—— squire's loose, and, worse luck, like a rare old fox-hunter as he is, has a rare scent for the chase. Off, my brave boy, while there is yet time; there is no time to horse the carriage, so mount, do you hear; she will bear you both, as if you were a couple of feathers. Quick, to your work, the hounds are at our heels."

"This poor girl has fainted—see, she looks like death," said Rann, in despair.

"So much the better, my boy, she isn't alive to the dangers of her situation; quick, lad. be off with you, or it may be too late."

"And what will you do, my friend?" said Rann, "I cannot leave you here to perish alone."

"Perish, be blowed—go on with your gammon. Me and my lord here, mean to give them the double yet. Old Joe (the name of his steed) will have to shake his trotters a little extra to-night, that's all, my boy—I'm safe enough. Get you gone, whilst you have time; see, here they come."

And as he spoke, half-a-dozen horsemen were visible in the distance, who, as soon as they caught sight of our hero, set up a "view halloo."

The time for hesitation was past and gone; springing with a bound into the saddle, Jack laid the insensible form of Miss Malcolm across his horse before him, and giving a shout of derision, applied his spurs, and waving his hat triumphantly over his head, was off with his gallant mare, like a rushing mighty wind.

CHAPTER VIII.

A MEETING OF THE GANG—PROPOSALS, PERFORMANCES, AND THEIR PLAN OF OPERATIONS.

Two or three days after the events occurred, which we have endeavoured to describe in the preceding chapter, Jack Rann having ridden his noble horse to the stables occupied by the gang, and delivered it over to an ostler, made the best of his way on foot to the Old House, in Pedlar's Acre. His application at the door was answered with more alacrity than usual, for without giving our hero need or time to make a second uproar, the Jew gently opened the door, and after gazing quietly round, beckoned our hero, and whispered—

"Come in, mine dear."

Jack, impressed with the cautious manner of the Jew, hesitated not an instant, but stepped within the threshold of the door.

"Up stairs," said the Jew, laconically.

Jack ascended the creaking staircase, followed closely by the Israelite, and was shown by the Jew into the same apartment overlooking the river, where he had first made the acquaintance of the gang.

In the centre of the room, and before the fire, sat a youth, carelessly rocking himself in his chair. This lad had a dark piercing eye, and a certain roguish, leery expression in it, that was calclated to strengthen Jack's opinion that the lad had no small share of the devil in his composition. He was dressed in every way as a man; in point of fact, to such an extreme was this apeishness carried, as to render his appearance, not only peculiar, but also somewhat preposterous. Booted, spurred, and with a brace of pistols in his belt, he looked caparisoned for any emergency; even to an exploit on the road.

Without rising from his chair to accost the new comer—as Jack Rann, having been of late used to courteous company, thought he might have done, without making any breach in his manners—turned to the Israelite, and in a tone of the utmost self-sufficiency, inquired if "that was a new 'un"?

Moses, or Moss—for the sake of brevity, which Bill Shakspeare has somewhere described as "the so   wit"—the Jew was called, answered in the affirmative, and feeling that the task of introduction was left to himself, said—

"Mister Rann"—and then pointing from one to the other, "Young Wide Awake."

"That's me," said the lad, jumping up, "and, damme, if your name's

Rann, I'll be scragged to a lump of dog's meat if you ain't been and done it gloriously—why they've got you in the Gazette already."

"What?" exclaimed Rann.

"Fact, I assure you," said Young Wide Awake, "see here," and drawing a paper from his pocket, he read from the "London Gazette Extraordinary" the following—

"Caution.—Whereas it having been this day sworn before me, Sir John Fielding, one of the justices of the peace for the city of London, that certain portions of the king's highway, to wit, the roads leading from Brentford to Hounslow and thereabouts, are infested by a reckless and daring band of highwaymen, this is to call upon the constabulary of the districts above named, and also upon the other constabulary of London and its environs, to keep diligent ward and watch, in order that these disturbers of the public peace and safety may be apprehended and punished, as the law may direct.

"Given under my hand and seal,

"John Fielding, Knight, justice of the peace for the city aforesaid.

"God save the King."

"Whew!" whistled Rann, thoughtfully.

"Glorious, isn't it," said Young Wide Awake, in tones of the greatest glee. "What a hobby out-an-out blade you must be to wake up the big wigs already; by jingo, I regularly admire you for your pluck, amid here's my fist to prove it."

Jack gazed at the urchin, and then at the hand extended, and bursting into a laugh at the consummate impudence of the boy, said to the Jew—

"Who the devil is this fellow?—he don't look like a man, but by jingo, he has got the cheek of one."

"Are you speaking of me? Why I'll tell you what I am sir," said Wide Awake, with an assumption of supreme pride; "my name's Colledge, sir—alias Young Wide Awake—from being alive to every fakement—down as a hammer to every nail! If nature has given me a manly form, she has given me a man's heart, I hope; and if I thought she hadn't, the b—h, why I'd ollow scripture for once, and 'pluck it out!' You may laugh, sir, but if I'm ittle, I am like a skylark, sirrah, and can mount as high as here and there one—yes, higher than some straw barn yard canaries, who are only game enough to crow on their own dunghill. Ah, you needn't sneer, sir; proud as you think yourself, I am a regularly constituted member of this gang, and your equal any day in the week."

"I don't doubt it, my boy," said Jack, "but, upon my soul, not being used to so great a soul in such a little body, it struck me as being keenly ridiculous at first," and Jack, in spite of his efforts to restrain himself, burst into a loud roar of laughter.

"Are you laughing at me?" said the little man, reddening with anger.

"At you, my dear fellow—how can you think it possible? Ha, ha, ha!"

"I tell you I won't be laughed at by you or any one else—I won't, by G—!" said Colledge.

No more it shan't, then, a pretty little dear—it shan't be vexed; and Jack most provokingly stroked Young Wide Awake down the face.

"I tell you what it is, sir," said Colledge, springing to his feet, "you must be taught your station, if you will not keep it without. I am not to be played and trifled with; I never was yet, and never will be, especially by new coming interlopers."

"Interlopers," repeated Jack, gravely, "what do you mean to say I have forced my services where they are not wanted? If such be the case, the union can be speedily dissolved; and, in faith, I would rather be my own master in any line of life, than be dependant or subservient to any one."

"I didn't exactly mean interloper," said Wide Awake, for he had caught a glance that boded mischief from the old Jew, "but I meant—"

"Nothing," interrupted Jack, in his usual gay careless tone, "and I must be an idiot to think otherwise. Here's my hand, my boy! strong words are

No. 9

always pardonable—always," he added, after a pause, "when they come from a weak stomach."

"Damme," thought Wide Awake, "that's anything but a compliment—but as he seems a John Bull sort of customer—all pluck and no gammon, I suppose I must knuckle down; but, damme, no funcking, notwithstanding."

"Wide Awake, what are you muttering about," said the Jew, sternly.

"Something that would cure your cough, Moses?" answered the youth, pertly, "if it were only swallowed as I'd prescribe it."

"S'help me, what can the brat mean?" said the Jew, lifting up his hands and eyes by one simultaneous movement.

"Mean, Moses," answered the youth, "why that Mr. Rann, after a long ride, would feel none the worse for a gill of good Hollands; and my valient, if that, swallowed in one draught, wouldn't cure your cough as 'aforesaid,' *vide* 'The London Gazette Extraordinary.' Why d—— it, I'd swallow it myself, diluted by water a bit though, Mo."

"S'help me, and would Master Rann like a drop of Dutch? It is vera good, sir—vera nish—very sheap; our 'commodation marchant in Holland often sends us a little drop to drink his health."

"Does he, I'm jolly glad to hear it, for my ride has given me an appetite for aught or anything eatable and drinkable," exclaimed Jack, "and I warrant if I flag, this young shaver here can help me out. Ay! my out-an-out, Young Wide Awake—my nonpariel, that only came into the world once; and then its motive was to prove to the world it was beyond comparison. Ay, my hearty, what do you say?"

"Say," answered young Colledge; "wont I, that's all. Moses," said the youth, in an authoritive tone, as the Jew was leaving the room, "haven't you something that you can furnish a few minutes amusement for a brace of knives and forks?"

"Vy, gen'lemen, had I expected the honour of dis visit, I vould have prepared—I vould, I mean—"

"If you have anything at all toothable, Jew, we will do without preparations," said Jack; "devil take it, friend, if we expected a banquet, we should have sent a long notice; haven't you anything in the house, now? I'm infernally peckish, I do assure you, and will pay what you charge without a murmur."

"Pay," ejaculated the Israelite, his eyes and hands in motion again like clock work, "as if I vould touch the monish! S'help me, I haven't so mooch as nothing in the house."

"Then, s'help me," said Young Wide Awake, imitating the Jew, "you may nibble that for your own supper, Moses. Me and Rann (that is if he be willing) will seek for another elsewhere. But no gammon, Moses," added Colledge, as he buttoned his coat, "haven't you anything in the house, though?"

"Nothing, s'help me Got!"

"Not even a spare bit of cold pork," continued Wide Awake, in a bantering tone; "come, man, unlatch that private cupboard of yours."

The Jew turned and gazed at the youth with eyes that, lit up with malice, gleamed like red hot coals.

"Have done," he muttered, as he scowled furiously at the youngster.

"Oh, I am done, old Israel," answered Colledge, "and as you are in such a pleasant temper, and in such an hospitable humour, instead of showing me your teeth, just show us the door; we'll make ourselves uncommon scarce, eh?" said Wide Awake, appealing to our hero.

"As you like, my boy," answered Rann, "so that I'm in for a supper."

"If that's all you need to make you perfectly happy, rest content, Mr. Rann, I'll guarantee to furnish something worth chewing. Now, Jew, lead on there, will ye?"

"The gentleman said he would have one glass of Schniedam—which am I to obey?" asked the Jew.

"Mr. Rann, of course," said Wide Awake, "but shake your trotters, Moses—don't you know there is a chapel to-night, eh?"

"S'help me, but I forgot!" said the Jew, then hobbling off, muttering as he went, "but one little minute gen'lemen—but one little minute."

"I say, young fellow, your allusion to the pork don't seem to settle on poor Moses's stomach."

"If the word disturbs it, by goles! it's more than the meat itself would. Lord bless you! invite him to dinner over a surloin of pork—give it any name but pork, by-the-bye—and if he don't come, why I'll eat him, tough as he is!"

By this time the Jew had returned with a full-bodied, long-necked, Dutch-built bottle, and filling a large glass for each, he bid them "taste."

Rann did, and being unused to spirits, found a taste sufficient: young Colledge, on the other hand, polished his off with ease and celerity, and, in his own peculiar jaunty manner, turned the glass upside down, to show how conclusive was the last draught.

Our hero looked at him with astonishment, not so the Jew, for as Colledge moved off to light a cigar at the fire, he whispered to Jack:

"Clever youth?"

"VERY!" answered Jack, laconically.

"Up to every blessed move," said the Jew.

"And down to one, at all events," said Jack, pointing to the empty glass.

"Ah! he's a deep young rascal."

"In his cups do you mean?" asked Jack.

"In every blessed pertic'lar thing, sir—I defy you to mention one he ain't up—awake—and fly-to? Look at him, as he stands a lighting that blessed cigar—jist ain't he a model youth? Did ever you see such a manish kid?"

"I never did, that's a fact!" said Rann; "he is a prodigy, and no gammon. Why damme, he's in a man's coat before one could have reasonably expected him to have escaped baby's napkins."

"He is a most 'xprising youth—clever! S'help me, he is clever! Why he'd prig your eye-tooth from your head, sir, if he'd only make up his mind to it."

"Oh, he would, would he?" replied our hero; "well, he MIGHT, I have a wonderful belief in his powers, but upon my honour, I fancy it would be an awful case for him, if he tried that game on me and failed. Why I'd smash him as I would a fly against a wall."

By this time young Colledge having managed to light his cigar, announced himself as being in out-and-out sailing trim, and such being the case, requested to know if Rann was "prepared to vanish?"

The latter acquiescing in his willingness to obey this ghostly invitation, the pair, preceeded by the Jew, descended the staircase, preparatory to departing on their errand.

On reaching the landing, the Jew asked Rann "if he wanted any monish," and upon our hero answering in the affirmative, slipped a leathern bag containing ten golden guineas into his hand.

"Gently, Moses," said Jack, "half of this will do."

"Take all," answered the Israelite, forcing back with his hand the proffered money, " good luck day coming—pay poor Moses then."

"Faith that will I!" answered Rann, shaking the Jew heartily and gratefully by the hand.

When he had said these words, the door was opened, and Rann and Young Wide Awake emerged from the old house in Pedlar's Acre.

Skirting the river's side until they came to the bridge of Westminster, they crossed that fabric of stonework, that has so long and so unworthily spanned the noble Thames.

In a few minutes, the sharp pace at which they were proceeding brought them within the boundaries of the city of Westminster. Passing the abbey by one side, Colledge leading the way, led our hero a pilgrimage through many a dark court and alley, and by many a devious route and mazy turning; until stopping at length before a doorway, whose red blinds and a row of different coloured bottles, which were displayed in the window, denoted it to be a house where "good entertainment could be had for man and beast," he pushed open the door, which, by a mechanical contrivance common unto this day, of a piece of lead and cord, shut-to of its own free will; and beckoning to our hero to follow, and leading the way, the youngster walked straight into the landlord's private and privileged bar-parlour.

The landlord, a bull-headed, rhinoceros-looking vagabond—if we may use the expression, for he seemed rhinoceros-like, perfectly impregnable—rose from his seat, as young Colledge entered, and extending his hand, exclaimed—

"Ha! my daffy-down-dilly, how are you?"

"Tollol, tollolish-like, how are you, Toby?" replied Young Wide Awake.

"How am I, is it, my buoy?" he answered, giving the buo—y a roll with his tongue, that for its unmistakable excellence was preserved in the British Museum, until dragged forth by Paul Bedford, to delight the Adelphi audiences. "How am I, is it? Oh, I'm werry bad—werry, werry, horrid bad."

" Sorry to hear it, Toby," said Colledge ; " what a sufferer you are "

" Ah, you may well say that, kinchin—horrid, werry horrid, ain't I ?"

"You are Toby; more's the pity. But see, here's my friend here, you haven't noticed him."

"More I ain't," answered Toby. "Horrid—awful forgetful, ain't I?" Then turning to Rann, he jerked his huge head and said—"Sarvant, sur!"

"Yours," responded our hero, bowing politely.

"To command," said the giant, with another jerk—then turning to Colledge, he said, in a whisper—loud enough to be heard by our hero, though—"New 'un?'"

"Yes," was the reply.

"Good 'un?'"

Again he was answered in the affirmative.

The giant relapsed into silence; but pulling away at his pipe with a vengeance, and puffing out the smoke like nothing but himself, or a factory chimney. Suddenly breaking the silence, he asked abruptly—

"Want to go down?"

"Any of our folks down there?" asked Wide Awake.

Toby nodded assent.

"Who are they?" inquired Colledge.

"Mike O'Brien," said Toby, in reply.

"Yes," said Wide Awake, "Bill Collier."

"Well?"

"Harry Sheppard."

"All right—any other?" asked Wide Awake.

"Yes; but don't be in such a horrid, hawful hurry—give me time to get my words out, can't you?"

"All right, Toby—go on."

"Well, then, Capt'n Clayton; and—that's all."

"The very man, of all others, I wish to see," said Jack, starting up. "Can I have access to him?"

"What?" said Toby, staring at our hero with looks of profound astonishment.

"Have speech with him," said Jack, impatiently.

"If I didn't think you said have a abcess, shiver me! And Lord, thinks I, what a horrid wish—I had one once!"

"Did you, though," observed Wide Awake.

"I did, my boy—on my starn, too! Warnt it just a teaser, a few, that's all! Why I couldn't nother stand up, sit down, kneel down, nor lay down. Horrid times them—werry!"

"I have no doubt they were," said Jack; "but you mentioned Clayton's name. Can I, my good fellow, have speech with him?"

"Yes—get under that bed."

"Get where?" said Jack.

"Under that ere bed."

"And what am I to do when I get there—be well laughed at?" inquired Rann.

"Hignorant—horrid—awful hignorant!" said Toby, with pious indignation; then turning to Colledge, he said—"Go and show him."

Creeping upon his hands and knees, Wide Awake disappeared under the bed. Not an instant was he under there before he again emerged, and dragging the bed on one side, showed our astonished hero a trap-door; and down it, to the floor beneath, was a ladder of rope.

"Do you see?" asked Colledge, with a smile—"a leery contrivance, aint it?"

"It is," answered Jack, lost in astonishment.

'Come on," said Young Wide Awake; and with the agility of a monkey he sprang down the steps.

Rann followed him.

When they had reached the under floor, Colledge gave the trap-door an impetus, and so excellently was the arrangement of the springs, that it instantly flew up, and was securely clasped overhead.

"What do you think of that, my boy?"

"Excellent, by jingo," answered our hero.

"And what of this?" and unhooking the rope ladder, which was fastened by a hook within a ring, and a second trap-door fell downwards, from what appeared before to be a solid stone paving, exhibiting in so doing a vacancy where it had fallen, as large, as dark, and horrible as a grave.

"Look," said Colledge; Rann did so, and heard at the bottom a sound as of rushing waters. He drew back with a shudder, as he asked—

"What that place was for? It looks like a grave."

"It is a grave," answered Colledge, in a whisper; "and don't you see its use?"

Rann answered in the negative.

"Supposing yourself pursued by the traps, you fly here under the bed, through the trap-door in a twinkling—you know the route well. On reaching the ground, you unclasp the hook—the ladder is no longer firm, but wavering, the trap falls, and if the beak should have the curiosity to follow you, it is to fill a grave already dug for him. Once under this trap," said Colledge, as he raised it with a little exertion, "no mortal man would ever rise again to tell the tale."

"Heaven forbid I should ever live to perform that part," said Rann; "but come, Wide Awake, let's forward, I am all impatience to meet Clayton."

"Wait till I have made the well-trap safe—there, all is right! Now then for our pals."

A long passage, winding and so intricate as to be impossible to any but those having the key of knowledge of its mysteries, and they came to a chamber.

Colledge struck the door with his knuckles three times. No answer. Pausing but for a moment, he struck it with increased force six times consecutively. Still no answer. A lapse of time of the same short duration as the first, and he again struck it, and this time he knocked nine distinct times.

This would appear to be the signal agreed upon, for the door opened, and

Jones, Collier, Sheppard, and Clayton were discovered seated around a table, evidently in the act of glorious enjoyment, for a reeking bowl upon the table threw out a strong scent of that savory compound called punch.

"What," said Clayton, springing to his feet, "can it be? Yes, by the powers, it is—Jack Rann, my brave boy, I give you hearty welcome."

"And I," exclaimed Sheppard, following Clayton's example. "Damme, Jack, I'm right glad to see you—give us your flipper, old boy."

Jack's welcome was extremely hilarious and jolly, and he felt himself at home, and in a more contented frame of mind than he had been for some time past. Naturally of a reckless, gay, free and easy disposition, he caught the happy looks of his companions, and was instantly heart and soul, as free, reckless, and careless as any of them.

"I say, Clayton, how did you get on with the old earl, last night?"

"Before I answer that question, Jack, allow me to ask how you got on with the lass?"

"How I got on," said Jack, triumphantly; "that question is easily answered, my brave comrade, and that right gloriously, too. Springing into my horse's saddle, as you will remember, I laid the insensible form of Miss Malcolm before, and putting spurs to the mare, the gallant Sue was off like a flash of lightning. For five miles I galloped, with the sound of my pursuers and the Squire's voice in a 'hark forward' ringing in my ears. Sometimes they were so closely following upon my heels, I could plainly hear their voices as they shouted to each other in conversation; but my gallant horse bravely increased the space between us, and all sound of them was lost. Then, with all the life blood in my veins boiling with ecstasy at my victory, I would rein in my steed until they were within hearing, and gave them a shout of defiance, and with hat in hand, beckoning them on. Forward they would come, mad with rage, and I coolly giving the mare her head, without using the whip or spur, would distance them at every stride. And so continued the exciting chase for miles further, until Miss Malcolm recovering from the fainting fit into which she had fallen, looked up into my face, and discovering in an instant we were pursued, and fearing the earl and his myrmidons, besought me in earnest tones to hurry on. Guaranteeing her safety with my life, I bid her fear not, and on, on we went, careering at a glorious speed. Suddenly, to my horror and dismay, I came upon a turnpike gate! The gate shut! Shouting, with stentorian lungs, my efforts to awake the gatekeeper were all fruitless—with sudden despair, for the sound of my pursuers approached nearer each instant, I sprang from my horse, and bidding Miss Malcolm sit quiet, I tried with a stone to break the padlock of the gate. Curses on it, and the man who made it! It was impenetrable, resisting all my efforts. And here was I a prisoner, unarmed; for my pistols' shots had been wasted as you are aware—one upon the squire's servant, the other upon his horse. On, on, came the pursuers, and catching sight of the closed gate, they raised a loud shout of triumph—of victory. Springing into the saddle again, I turned in my despair to Miss Malcolm, and bid her be the arbitress of my destiny—bid her direct me what, in my desperate need, to do. Turning her lovely face to mine, her beautiful eyes sparkling again, with courage she said, 'Death before dishonour! Leap the gate, Jack—leap the gate!

LEAP THE GATE!'

Mechanically I took up the cry, and backing with the utmost rapidity my noble mare, I plunged my spurs into her sides, and dashed boldly at the gate. Brave mare! she needed not the cruel spurs! As if gifted with a knowledge of our desperate need, she gathered up her energies, and cleared the gate at one noble and desperate bound."

"Brave Sue," exclaimed Clayton, at this juncture, his eyes flashing with admiration at the glorious spirit of his noble horse. "She is indeed worth her weight in gold."

"She is indeed," said Jack; then continuing his narrative, he went on.

"On reaching the other side, the mare flew forward. Turning, for one last look at the squire and his party, I gave them a farewell shout of derision, and galloped easily on."

"Leaving the squire, fretting, chafing, and as spiteful as a teazed bull, I'll swear," said Clayton.

"You are right in that respect," said Jack, "if ever you was."

"Well, to finish my narrative:—I knew full well now, unless I could find an hostelrie, the exhausted powers of the horse could never by any possibility return with us to town. At all events, it grieved me to test to such extremity the noble beast. I, therefore, inquired of my companion, whose bravery was only exceeded by her loveliness, if, knowing the country thereabouts, she could direct me in this emergency. With a sudden start of joy, she responded in the affirmative, and informed me a friend of her father's lived but a short distance to the right. Taking the bye-road her fair finger indicated, and dismounting from Sue and leading her by the bridle, we came, after a half-hour's walk, to the house. We met with a cordial welcome; and when in most flattering terms, the lady had described the services we had rendered her, no tongue can tell the warmth of their enthusiasm. In short, my boys, they treated me as a gentleman."

"By the powers," said O'Brien, "and is there a spalpeen in this terrestral hemisphere in this eternal world could have the audacity, think you, to trate ye otherwise, man alive? By the powers, if there be, show him to me, that's all, and if black ain't the white of his eye in a jiffey, sorra a bit is my name Mike O'Brien."

"A thousand thanks for your generous thought, believe me, my dear boy,' said Jack Rann, "I shall some day call them into action."

"The sooner the quicker, honey," responed the Irishman.

"Well, Rann," said Clayton, chiming in, "and how finished you your adventure?"

"Right merrily!" answered Rann, "feasted like a prince, and treated like a lord, I stayed with Miss Malcolm's friends the two following days; on the evening of the latter, I accompanied the gentleman and the young lady in a carriage to town, a groom being engaged to follow with my horse. That is all, excepting that I called upon the Jew—that this young effigy of a man—"

"Come, stash it, can't ye?" said Colledge.

"Showed me the way hither, and here I am."

"And right welcome you are, too, old fellow; now for my yarn, which mayhap you will find like a donkey's gallop—short and sweet:—whilst the squire and his followers went dashing by, I managed to throw my lord in the hedge, and gagging him with my hand, muffled the sound of his rebellious old throttle. One of the coveys catching sight of me, it would appear, shouted out, 'there was one on 'em,' and with more bravery than prudence, rode back to the attack. He was armed with a heavy riding whip; being so unequally matched, I disdained to use my barkers, so snatching a cudgel from the hedge, I gave my lord a crack that made his old skull ring again, and down he dropped quiet enough. I was now prepared for my swell, who aiming a blow with the butt-end of his whip, which just happened to miss me, I gave him in return such a stinger, that knocked his hat—and, if there be any truth in appearances—jolly near his head off. Would you believe it, he wasn't actually satisfied with that."

" He wanted one of Jack's gentle reminders," said Sheppard, whose mouth looked still swollen and disfigured from our hero's attack.

" Perhaps he did; at all events, Sheppard, my boy, he had one of mine; for before he had time to rub off the tingling of the first blow, I gave him another on the old spot in a twinkling, that floored him like a shot. Thinking no doubt he was in for his gruel (death), he begged for mercy in most lusty tones, and was right glad, on receiving my bidding, to scamper off as fast as his horse could carry him. No time being now to be lost, I fetched my lord from the ditch, and shoved him head first into the carriage; first, however, taking care to lighten his pockets of all the rhino they contained.

" A thought struck me then about poor coachee, and gazing back to where the poor devil had fallen, I found him lying on the ground, groaning with agony, and in a fainting state from loss of blood."

" Was he much hurt?" inquired Rann, with some concern.

" Not half so much as he deserved, the villain," answered Clayton, "though still decently stung. The fact is, the ball had shattered the bone of his arm. Having been a doctor once, I had some knowledge of surgery; so fetching his neckcloth from his neck, I bandaged up the shattered limb, and leading him to the carriage, put him in beside his master. And a precious pair of rascals they were as ever rode together.

" Keeping a sharp look-out—for I expected, knowing the rattling pace of brave old Sue, that the squire and his gang finding pursuit useless, would return home—I waited until a couple of labourers came along, to whom I gave a crown to catch his lordship's horses, and convey the carriage and its occupants to the Red Lion: this the delighted dogs gleefully promised to do, so wishing them a good night, I struck into a bye-road to avoid the hue and cry of 'a Highwayman!' 'a Highwayman!' and old Joe, cantering on at a merry pace, brought me speedily here. And now, my boy, nought remains for us but to share the mopusses," and Clayton, as he spoke, drew from his capacious pocket a heavy bag of gold, and the watch, snuff-box, and other booty gained by Jack Rann's first exploit upon the road.

Following his example, the others also brought forth the produce of the various robberies in which they had been engaged since the night they were first introduced to the reader.

After an equitable distribution, Jack found himself in possession, for his own share, of upwards of a hundred guineas, a valuable snuff-box set with brilliants, and the watch which he had promised to return to the squire.

CHAPTER IX.

THE SUPPER—A TALE OF A FLOWER-POT—THE PLANNING OF FUTURE ROBBERIES.

AFTER every man was in possession of their money, Clayton proposed that supper should be served—a proposal that met with a joyous concurrence from each and every one there assembled.

"Supper, honey? Long life and many on 'em for that self-same suggestion. Shure it's a meal I enjoy vastly."

"Shall I go and tell old 'werry horrid' to get it ready?" asked Colledge.

"Do you, Wide Awake. He told me he had heard of 'summat good.' Let's hear what his proposal is—so what say you, shall he join us at the supper table, eh, Harry?"

"As you like, my boy—I'm agreeable to anything to night."

"And all the rest of you consent, eh? What say you, Rann?"

"Certainly."

"And you, Mike?"

"Faix! wasn't he always a particular friend of mine? To be shure he was. And is it Mickey O'Brien would be after dooming any individual to cauld mutton, when there is the jolliest round that iver mortal sot eyes on?"

"And as to you, Collier, we can reckon upon you, yon being such a staunch particular of Toby's, eh?"

"The more the merrier," was Collier's reply.

"Since all agree, fetch him down, Wide Awake, and carry your name out for once; and be alive over it, d'ye hear?"

"Catch a weasel asleep! Did you iver know the young spalpeen lose anything?" asked Mike.

With a grin that showed he fully appreciated the truth of the Irishman's saying, and feeling flattered thereby, Young Wide Awake bounced from the place with a hop, skip, and a jump, and speedily returned, ushering in Toby, followed by a couple of waiters, the one carrying a tray with a fine round of beef thereon, flanked with a goodly number of vegetables, and the other with a similar tray laden with bottles, glasses, and a portly punch-bowl.

"Well, Toby, my rare 'un, how goes times with you, old cock?" said Sheppard.

"Werry—horrid—bad!" said Toby; for once in his lifetime giving vent to three words consecutively.

"Horrid bad, eh, Toby," said Clayton. "Sorry to hear that; but how are you in health?—that's the main thing, you know, Toby."

"Bad!" answered Toby, briefly.

"The devil!" said Clayton; "how's your old Dutch clock—your missus, I mean?"

"Wuss!"

"Is she, though," said Clayton—"what's the matter with her?"

"Dun' know."

"Well, what's the matter with you, old fellow?"

"Dun' know."

"Well, you are a rum un', Toby—you are ill, and your wife's 'wuss,' and yet you don't know what's the matter with either of you!"

"No!"

"Well, you are a queer old stick, if ever there was one. I should guess, now, by the look of you, if the truth is known, you've a tolerable good appetite at most meal times, eh?"

"Werry good!"

"And on an emergency—such as the present, now—can drink a trifle, perhaps?"

"You'll see!" was his response, delivered with a broad grin of delight.

"Well, I hope we shall, my friend; for it will be quite disheartening to see you have lost all your appetite. Will you have a glass of Hollands, just to sharpen it, you know?"

Toby nodded assent.

"Pour out a glass of spirits, Wide Awake," said Clayton.

"Let's see," said Colledge, "you've rather an objection to thimble-fulls, hav'n't you, guv'ner?"

"Horrid."

"Thought so, by jingo!" and Colledge, in a chaffing humour, poured into a tumbler more than a quarter of a pint of ardent spirits, which Toby swallowed at a draught, without so much as winking.

"Well done, my hearty, that looks like business!" said Jack. "I say, my swell, do you often indulge in such potations?"

"Allays!" was the reply.

"Then all I can say is, I wish I was a publican, and you my customer."

The supper having by this time been displayed upon the table, they left off talking, and fell to eating.

If Toby was celebrated for "potations pottle deep," he deserved ten times more fame for his prodigious appetite. Plate after plate vanished, until under his heavy and continued attacks the large round of beef began to dwindle with astonishing rapidity into a small one.

As to Jack, he was delighted beyond measure at the fellow's enormous appetite, and nudging Clayton, who was carving, he bid him "give him the whole lot."

"Well, Toby," said Clayton, whose arm, from the continued application, began to tire, "I must say, for an invalid, you have a tolerable appetite."

"Werry good," was Toby's response, as he passed his plate for another slice.

"Another, eh?" said Clayton, in profound astonishment. "Well, damme, but you are a rattler;" and cutting a tremendous slice from the beef, he placed it in the landlord's plate.

"If that don't settle him, Jack, I'll be shot if I know what will."

"God bless you," said Jack, "he has only just found his appetite."

"Think not," said Clayton; "then hang me if he mustn't carve for himself. I'm completely tired of it."

"Phoo! you ain't half a fellow! Pass the dish!" and Jack seized the knife and fork as he spoke, and Toby having by this time disposed of what Clayton had served him with, looked up with his mouthful—

"Any more, my fine fellow? Don't go away with half a supper—don't say no. Come, shall I cut you a piece?"

Toby nodded assent, as he held out his plate.

"Now, my boy," said Jack, "you are just in time for the primest piece in the whole round.

"Werry good!"

"Good! on my honour its my firm and candid opinion you just will find it good," said Jack, using his knife as he spoke, not after the fashion now exhibited in ham and beef shops, but downwards, as a cheesemonger uses a cheese-knife. Amidst the tittering of all assembled, Jack removed from the dish a piece of meat that was, without the least exaggeration, as large as a brick. "There's a plug for your hollow tooth," said Jack. "Pitch into it, my Briton!"

"Want drink, I does," said Toby.

"Pass that jug of ale, you young humbug, do," said Clayton to Colledge; "what, invite a man to supper, and then send him away a hungered and a'thirst; by goles, such conduct is abominable, most reprehensible, not to be borne!"

"Werry horrid, as the venerable would say," said Wide Awake with a grin, as he passed the jug. "Go at it, my invalid; 'pon my soul you look a likely subject for consumption."

"He really does look awful bad," said Sheppard; "why the devil don't you have advice, Toby?" but Toby was too busily engaged to find time to reply. "Don't you think he does, Colly, my boy?"

"Think!" said Collier, "damme, its beyond thinking, got to a dead certainty. If ever there was a fellow that looked as if going into a decline, that unfortunate individual opposite is the very man."

"Poor Toby, we'll all follow him to the grave, won't we?" said Wide Awake, "he'll make such a handsome corpse; I tell you what, though," he added, as Toby, amidst a general burst of laughter, again stretched forth his hand, and, at the same time, not forgetting to hold a plate in it,—

"If he don't look like a deep decline, I can tell you something that does?"

"What's that?" said Clayton.

"The beef," answered Wide Awake, amidst a general roar.

"Yes," said Jack, when the boisterous laughter had sudsided, "we can well exclaim with Hamlet, Prince of Denmark, 'Alas, what a falling off is there!' but never mind, Toby, my boy, let those laugh who win, and if we are not in a fair chance for the victory, devil a one is there round this table likely to, for they have all been furnished this half-hour; you'll have another slap at it, of course?"

"Oh, yes!"

"That's right, my boy; how will you have it, large or small?"

"Small," replied Toby; then bending forward with a smile, that stretched his enormous mouth from ear-to-ear, he added, "but doan't—" and there he stopped.

"Don't what?" said Jack.

"Cut it—" and he paused again.

"Hang it, man, spit it out, what do you mean?" said Clayton.

"Too knify."

Jack threw himself back in his chair, dashing down the knife and fork as he did so, and gave vent to such a peal of laughter, as had not been heard in that place for many a day.

"You will be hung for murder, you dog, you will; I shall crack my precious sides! Oh, Lord—oh, Lord!" and Jack fairly laughed till he cried, and cried till he laughed again. Did you ever hear the like—DON'T CUT IT TOO KNIFEY!"

Such a loud "ha, ha!" burst from every lip, that the old place echoed again.

When they had recovered themselves from the convulsion of merriment into which this incident had thrown them, Jack exclaimed, pushing the dish towards Toby, "no d—— you, I won't cut it too knifey—take the lot."

This proceeding, however, Toby declined to take, "cos he hated gluttons."

A remark, that again, as poor old Yorick is alleged to have done, "Set the table in a roar."

And so loud and long continued was their laughter, that with sides literally aching from its effects, they were glad to change the subject.

Clearing the table of the fragments of their repast, but not before Toby had borrowed a cold carrot from the tray as the waiter passed him, and proceeded to swallow it with every appearance of keen appetite and relish, glasses and mugs, decanters, and jugs strewed the board, and they seemed set in for a merry-making with a vengeance.

Our hero was unanimously voted to the chair, and with a taste that shewed him a proficient in the art, he commenced the concoction of a noble bowl of punch—that liquor so delicious over night, so noxious in the morning.

This preparation having been duly propounded, glasses were filled, the song and jest went round, and these moments passed in the robbers' lives full of pure jollity and happiness, without a cloud or care to dim their lustre.

"Harkee, boys," said O'Brien, at last, "don't ye remimber I tauld ye I was a going to escort my charming little doxy to Drury Lane?"

"I do, for one," said Rann.

"Thank'e, Mr. Chairman, that's quite conclusive and sufficient thin."

"But why?" queried Jack.

"Why is it?" answered Mike; "shure, and didn't I put my foot into it bootifully, that's all."

"How did you manage that, Mike?"

"Shure I did'nt manage it at all, at all, darlint; she managed it for me, the crayture."

"The devil she did, Mike," said Clayton; "she must have been a downy card to get the weather-gage of an Irishman—I can hardly believe it, Mike. What Ireland, the most cunning of all the nations of the earth, and you the most cunning of all her sons—damme, Mike, it is impossible; I can't believe it."

"Listen then, honey, and if you don't say she nailed me to perfection, I ain't the son of the mother who bore me, that's all."

"Spin on, Mr. O'Brien; we love an adventure, especially with the fair sex."

"Shure then don't be after interrupting a gintleman when he's speaking, or you may be after having to tell it yourself. Mister Chairman, will you be so kind, so condescending, so obliging, as to proclaim silence among these rapscallions here?"

"Silence, gentlemen, for Mr. O'Brien's tale. What shall we call it, though, Mike?"

"Call it, faix, it's just directly worth no name at all, but since it's the law o' the land for every gossoon to be christened, suppose we call it then," and the Irisman scratched his head, as if in a brown study—

"What, my, boy?"

"Why—why—a—

TALE OF A FLOWER POT:—

"Boys, when I left the crib, faix I left it in the jolliest of all jolly tempers. Cos why?—why cos when I did leave it, I met (by appointment, mark ye,) with the jolliest, handsomest, loveliest little damsel that iver human eyes iver cast their squinting sheep-eye hoptics at.

"'What my little duck-si-darling, and is it you?' sais I.

"'Ain't it,' sais she, in reply; 'a pretty fellow you are to keep your word—just like you men. No sooner do you leave sight of the object of your affection, than you pick up with some nasty hussies o' the town, you do—you do.'

"An' poor little devil," said Mike, "she actually cried herself into such a pitch of wirtuous indignation, that she sobbed outright. And Lor' bless ye, what could I do?—do, why damme, big as I am, I blubbered like a child, too! Oh, Lor', if you'd heard my blessed apologies—like nothing but the Arabian Nights, so help m' tater!—jist a thousand and one rolled into one; devil a whit more, sorra an atom less. Could she, my boys, refuse me after such a oration?—devil a bit! Faix, no; she threw her little white arms about my precious neck, and declared, betwixt and between a duet of sobs and shrieks, that there were no gemmen in the world but Irishmen, and that I—damme, I—was the gem o' the Imerald Isle!

"A mighty fine compliment, in good truth; and, truth to tell, mighty fine I took it! By St. Patrick! the guardian Saint of good ould Ireland, I gave her such a stunning squeeze, that I heard her blessed whalebone stays go crick-crack, like the ticking of a clock.

"'Ha' done with ye, Mike,' sais she.

"'Ha' done,' sais I; 'what Minny, my darlint, and can it be yourself that sais them self-same cruel words? You'll break me heart intirely—intirely, you will.'

"'It's a piece of cruelty I wouldn't be guilty of, Michael,' sais she, 'for all the blessed universe;' and she sailed the sweet contract on me lips with a glorious kiss. My eyes, my boys, you might have heard it from Charing Cross to Temple Bar!

"'Heaven bless you for that consolation,' sais I, piously; 'and now, Minny, darling,' sais I, extending my arm, 'which, of all the amusements in this mighty city of London, do you choose to go to for intertainment this blessed night?'

"'Whichever place you pick upon, love, I shall be delighted to go with you,' said the delightful leetle lump of simpering modesty.

"'Well, thin,' sais I, 'my darling, what say you to Ranelagh, eh? What say you to a trip on the light fantastic? You've got the build of a dancer, and may the divil admire me, but I can cut a few capers. Lookee here, now,' and I gave her a specimen of my agility at a jig, in half a jiffy.

"'Pon my soul she laughed at me. What the divil she could see amusing in my graceful curvatures, smother me in butter-milk if I can, for the life of me imagine; but laugh she did, and out loud, too. 'Ha, ha, ha!' like that. Perhaps, poor crature, she's only bin used to opera dancing, or something o' that sort; and consequintly, poor little hignoramus, didn't know a good dancer whin she saw him. At all ivints, from some reason or another, she declined to go; and when I pressed her for a reason for declining, she said—

"'Because—'

"'Because what, honey?' said I.

"'People laughs!'

"'Whether she meant to insinnivate thereby that there was anything in me to laugh at, I can't for the life of me conceive; but, notwithstanding, I assured her, time after time, the first spalpeen I caught grinning, I'd smash him to smithereens, do you think she'd make a go of it? Divil a bit!

"'Well thin, honey,' sais I, 'if you wont go to Ranelagh, what do you say to Bagnigge Wells?'

"'Bagnigge Wells!' and she curled up her pretty little nose till it very near touched the crown of her head. 'Michael, I am ashamed of you!'

"'What for, my darling!' sais I, struck into a heap of blessed unkimfortable consternation. 'What the divil do you mean—what have I done now?'

"'It isn't what you've done—it's what you would have done,' said the little angel, allowing one—only one little wrinkle to straiten itself on her fashinating snout.

"'Michael, let me ask you a question.'

"'A dozen, honey, if it plases you,' sais I.

"'Don't you call yourself a gentleman?'

"'Call myself! Faix, its myself that just is that same. If you could only see my astates, the home of my haucestors, the castles of my forefathers, you wouldn't need to ask that question.'

"'And have you much property?' says she.

"'Property,' answers I, 'jist harkee—one of my estates is a thousand miles long by two broad.'

"'Is it, indeed,' said she, lifting up her hands and eyes with astonishment, or admiration, I quite forget which; and shure its little it signifies. 'Then you must be very rich, Michael.'

"'Rich, darlint, jist harkee: if you was to cover every blessed inch of England with guineas, I should jist have five guineas, darlint, to call my own.'

"'Oh, I wish I was your wife, Michael, wouldn't we cut a dash!'

"'Wish you was my wife, do ye? Faix, and don't be languishing long, or wishing for that—I know a priest tw'll join us in two-twos.'

"'Not to-night, Michael, thank you,' she answered; 'but all I have to say is just precisely this: as you are such a gentleman, you ought to be ashamed of yourself to ask me, as a lady, to go to such a common, low, disagreeable place as Bagnigge Wells.'

"'Darling,' commenced I; but she put the kybosh on my clapper, by jist holding up her finger and talking away, like a house a-fire at both ends, herself.

"'And if you was only a million'th part as rich as you pretend to be, you'd take me, as you promised—

"'Where too, honey?' sais I, terrible eager to get the secret.

"'Why to Drury Lane,' sais she.

"'Droory Lane, is it?' sais I; 'faix, an' why the divil didn't ye say so afore? Ain't I willing an' anxious to 'scort you anywhere you please to go to, you precious poppet?'

"'Then call a coach, and let's be off at once—they've begun before this, I know.'

"'Here, jarvey!' shouts I; an' along comes bowling an 'oss and hackney-coach.

"'Yes, sir,' sais jarvey, pulling up. 'Where to, sir?'

"'Droory Lane,' sais I, 'as if old Nick was at your heels;' and arter handing in the lady, away we went, rocking an' jolting. 'Now, my darling,' whispers I, 'which shall it be, pit, boxes, or gallery?'

"'You're a pretty gentleman to ask that question, I don't think—boxes, of course!'

"An' to the boxes we went, as large as life, and in the dress circle, we didn't do it a few spicey! Oh, no, every lady was a staring at us.

"Well, lads, when the play was over (and when it was, if iver I was glad in my life I was then), we adjourned to a oyster-room.

"By St. Patrick it beat the play hollow, to see that little divil bolt the natives! Divil a shadow of a chance did they stand. Regler champion o' England game—one down, t'other come on. Whin she put away about half-a-bushel, in a jiffey, she proposes some brandy; and away we wint, arm-in-arm, as cosey as two turtle doves to a tavern.

"If the oyster affair hadn't opened my blissed optics, it's a pity the brandy job wouldn't, that's all! She bolted glass after glass in sich style—I was reg'lar flabbergasted! However, saying die wasn't directly my game, so we wint to work at some rale poteen, and swigged till I'm blissed if either of us could see a hole through a ladder.

"After a jolly good snooze in the corner, my boys, myself and my doxy came to a bit, lads; and as she proposed home, we went staggering on towards that blissful occupation.

"'Minny, darling,' sais I, (hiccup) 'you won't forsake me till morning, will ye?'

"'Forsake you, Mike—no, cuss me if I do! Come on—as we begun, we'll finish.'

"'That is,' sais I, 'finish the night together, Minny, eh?' I am afraid I hiccupped again.

"'Oh, Michael, and is it yourself can have the heart to ruin a young and helpless and inexperienced female? And can you, after all your protestations of love, wish to deprive me of my virtue, the only gem of price left me in this wide world?'

"'Gim of price,' said I, quite misunderstanding her meaning; 'and shure, Minny, and was it after the treat I've stood to-night, you can have the conscience to be after asking?'

"What do you think her answer to this reasonable quistion was? Oh, crikey, sich a bobbery—sich a flood's tears! Nothing could stop her till the watch came and threatened to lock her up for being drunk and disorderly, whin all of a sudden she seemed intirely to forget she was a highly-respectable lady, whose vartue was as unimpeachable as her morality was refined and cultivated; for, in a jiffey, sir, she pitched into the Charlie with her tongue—she called him all the ugly names that iver I'd heard in all my life, and a good sprinkling I'd never heard before; and not content with that, I'll be squashed if she didn't give him the loveliest spat in the peepers that iver I saw in all my born or unborn days.

"She actilly floored him like a shot; and while Charlie was bawling murder and thieves, she caught hold of my arm, and suddenly leading me up a dark passage, unlocked a door, and shut us inside of a house.

"'Hollo, darling,' said I, 'and what in the divil's-name-place have we got to?'

"'Home, my Trojan,' said she; 'ain't you glad! I say, my hearty,' said she, 'didn't I give that old Charlie a one-er, eh?'

"'You jist did a few,' replies I.

"'If I ain't blastedly mistaken, he'll wake up with a prime pair of mahogany-framed eyes in the morning, eh?'

"'He jist will, my darling,' sais I; 'but where does this lead to?'

"'To bed, of course,' answered modest Minny—'where the dence do you think it leads?'

"'Shure,' thinks I to myself, 'and I'm in luck's way, that's a fact;' but that I was a trifle desaved in the damsel, I must confess, too.

"'Here you are, my broth of a boy,' she said, throwing open a door on the first floor that opened to a room in the front of the house, 'here you are, a ready-furnished apartment—as snug a snuggery as any single gentleman need wish to shove his snug old pimple into!'

"And holding up a lamp that stood burning on the table, she showed me a room with a bed in it.

"'Now, Mike,' she says, 'give us a kiss.'

"Didn't I, that's all. 'Oh, you divel!' says I.

"'I say, do you think so, though?' says she.

"'Shure an' I do,' answers I; 'for ain't you changed from the most modest girl on the face of the blessed earth, to the most daring little divel that iver was?'

"'But did you really think me a modest girl?' she axed.

"'Of course I did, my darling.'

"'Then what a jolly fool you must have been. Look at me now, Mike, is there much modesty about me?'

"Faith, lads, there jist wasn't at that identical moment, I can tell you.

"'I say, Mike, I tell you what, there will be a devil of a rumpus about that old watchman's eyes in the morning, never fear. Blast me! but I wished I'd smashed his conk, don't you, an interfering old s—t!'

"'I jist do,' answers I; 'an' if it hadn't a bin for having to hook it, I'd a give him a game o' two to one, for I'd have given him a twoer for your one.'

"'Bravo, Mike, you've the pluck of a man, as well as the soul of a gentleman. I say, Mike, can you fight?'

"'Blood an' ouns,' sais I, 'show me the spalpeen that wants a licking, and if I don't give it him in such full-blown perfection, that his own mither shouldn't know him! Can I fight is it, honey! Isn't it myself that brain'd a bullock with the butt-end of my fist? Sure it is.'

"'Did you, though; then I tell you what, Mike, as I want to perfect myself in the noble art of self-defence, what do you say, for my instruction, if we have a game of—'

"'What, honey?' sais I.

"'First spat in the cheek for a tizzy,' answers she. 'Come, Mike, mind your eyes—here goes. There's one!'

"And she gave me such a stinger, she made my eyes strike fire.

"'Now again, Mike—look sharp. There, two!'

"And along came another whack without a blissing for poor Mike—my eyes, didn't my cheeks tingle a few!

"'Now, Mike, once more, my boy!'

"'No, no, darling,' sais I; 'I'm perfectly contint.'

"'Why you ain't half a fellow, Mike. Come, come, give us one cuff of the head, or else let me you. Now then!'

"'If you'll believe me, honey,' sais I, 'I am too much of an Irishman and a gentleman to be guilty of such a disgraceful act as striking a lady, 'pon my soul I am.'

"'Ay, that's all very well—all blarney, Mike. The fact of it is, you know you can't!'

"'Can't!' cries I.

"Can't!' sais she, not mincing the matter at all, at all. 'If you think you can, try. There's a one'r to set you going!'

"Oh, mine ears, mine ears! By the bones of good Patrick, how they did burn and tingle!

"To bear such treatment as this, without retaliation, was impossible—I up with my blissed little fist, and gave her such a thwack, that I knocked her from her chair as flat as a flounder.

"She picked herself up, though, as if she'd merely fallen aught by accident, and was already squaring up for another bout.

"'I tell you what, Minny, dear,' sais I, 'this is a piece of experimental philosophy that ain't by no means wholesome, and so the sooner we drop it the better, or—'

"'Or what, Mike?' she axes.

"'Perhaps we may come to blows,' sais I.

"It would have done your heart good to hear the little divel laugh—she declared I was an Irishman every inch o' me, that I was; and mighty proud I felt, to be shure, she had come to that self-same conclusion.

"'Well, Mike, barring all fighting, for fear we should come to blows, what do you say to a drop of blue ruin?'

"'A drap o' blue ruin,' sais I; 'faith, 'twill save me life. I feel so dry after that cursed brandy, that my blissed tongue's all in furrows, like a ploughed field.'

"'So is mine,' she says; 'I feel exactly as if I'd been drinking.

"'Poor divil!' thinks I, 'and more's the pity you hav'n't, that's all!'

"Howsomdiver, lads, she fetched forth in good time a phisying (excellent-prime) bottle o' gin, and there we sat swig, swig, swiggin at this blue ruin till all *was* blue. For my own part, I got so jolly drunk, I couldn't put myself to bed, that's a fact, so the little angel performed that operation for me.

"Quietly tucked inside the sheets, faith I slept like a top, and snoring like a prize pig; but prisintly, however, I got into the land of dreams, and what do you think I dreamt? I'll be shot if I didn't dream I was going to be robbed!

"I was disturbed by this awful anticipation—I positively couldn't sleep one blissed wink the remainder of that night, but lay, three-parts drunk and half asleep, morilising over the demorilised state of society, that a honest man couldn't slape in pace in his bed without fear of midnight marauders, and robbers, and murtherers!

"Prisintly, lads, daylight breaks, Sol shook himself from his slumbers, and, for the matter of that, so did my doxey; for she got from the bed, first shaking me, howiver—

"'You asleep, Mike?'

"Divil an answer, but I snored away like old boots.

"'He's all right, that's one comfort,' she sais—'I thought the gin would do it!'

"'The divil you did,' thinks I; and keeping one eye open as well as one shut, and my nasal organ playing away like a whole regiment of fat pigs, I was jist enabled to take a survey of the room, an', at the same time, to watch marm's movements.

"'Hallo, gently goes it there,' thinks I; for I'll be suffocated if my darling, modest little Minny, hadn't found her way to my breeches, and was emptying my pockets like fun.

"Well, having got all she could, what should she do but come towards me. 'Bless her purty face,' thinks I to myself, 'but she's honest yet, a darling;' for I began to fancy, p'r'aps, she was only taking the liberty of removing it to put it in a place of more security.

"No such luck, by the powers, though; for stooping over me, she said—

"'You snoring, drunken beast, you thought you got a prize in a modest, virtuous little girl, didn't you, you seducing fool of a Greek; but instead of that, my boy, you'll find in your waking moments you had one as sharp as yourself, and perhaps a d—n sight sharper. Snore on, you drunken, Irish hog, do; and while you snores, I'll secure your tin.'

"By the powers, this little exhortation almost induced me to jump from the bed and pitch into her right and left; but Patrick, thinks I agin, 'second thoughts is best—lay still, honey, sleep with one eye open, and if you diskiver where she plants the mopusses, why damme, when you do get up, can't you thrash her till she confesses? To be shure you can.'

"'An' so there,' I says, looking arter marm like a hawk, and snoring on at one and the same time louder and heartier than iver.

"Prisently she approaches the window. 'My stars,' thinks I, 'can she be after throwing my money into the street?' and faix, I listened with all the ears I've got, which counted back'ards or for'ards, make two, divil a one, more or less, to catch the sound of it, if it jingled on the pavement.

"Divil a jingle was there to hear, though, dear innocent Minny! she was a precious sight too artful for that; for arter planting the tin, she comes quietly back to bed, and falls into a comfortable sleep.

"'Hiven bless your pretty face,' thinks I, 'what a thing it is to have an easy conscience, to be shure! but p'r'aps now, marm, you'll allow me to replace in me breeches what you jist now took from 'em.

"An' with this object in view, I was tumbling out o' bed, when up wakes young innocent, and catching hold of me by the tail o' my shirt, says—

"'Hollo, Michael, what are you after—where are you going?'

"Though I am one of 'em, I must confess, I nivir knew an Irishman who hadn't a lie ready made at the tip of his tongue, and I take pride and honour to myself that I am one.

"'Going!' echoes I. 'Oh, by the blessed Virgin, Minny, if you only knew how dry I am, and how long I've bin looking for water widout being able to find it, faith it's yourself would show a little christian feeling, and go and fetch me some.'

"'Oh, that I will, my boy,' she said, jumping out of bed—'why didn't you call me before?'

"'Call you, honey,' sais I; 'by St. Patrick, the greatest gintleman, except myself, iver born in ould Ireland, I've done nothing else but that self-same thing iver since I've been awake.'

"'I never heard, I swear, Mike, or I'd have been up directly. Here goes, my boy—I'll bring you something to wet your whistle.'

"'Long life to you!' sais I; 'but gently a minute, honey, for I was struck with an idea. Can't you get something better than wather?'

"'To be sure I can, my fine fellow, if you like to stand it.'

"'Faith an' its myself is jist game to that same—throw me my coat.'

"She threw it on the bed.

"'There,' sais I, tossing her a brace of shillings which I took from a private pocket, 'take that, and be off with you.'

"I can't help admiring the quick way in which she obeyed my wishes. She was full-dressed, togged out in her gay colours and shiny feathers, like a peacock, in half a minute.

"'Now, darling,' sais I, 'how long shall you be gone?' as most excruciating hurry.

"'Only ten minutes.'

"'Ten minutes, sais I. 'Blood an' 'ouns! and do you think I can wait ten minutes? Why I shall perish with hunger—thirst, I mane.

"'I am very sorry for you, Mike, but there is no help for it,—it's impossible I can get it sooner. Why I have got to go all the way to the Strand for it.'

"'Then vanish, for God's sake—I'm dying by inches.

"'Have a little poteen, man alive,' she said; 'I will be back as quick as I can.'

"Off she went, out of bed gets Mike, and when the sound of her footsteps had died away, I wint to the window. I opened it, and looked out: there was a couple of flower-pots, with a couple of daisies in 'em, but no money, divil a coin.

"'Shure, perhaps, and they're underneath.'

"I lifted up the flower-pots, one after another—divil a sovereign was to be seen.

"Fire and fusee's, Mike O'Brien, and is it the mother's son of ye will suffer hisself to be robbed in this dirty manner, without kicking up a philliloo? Faix and ages, no! and seizing hold of the daisy to chuck 'em in the court, I was, whin the blissed root came out in my hand—devil burn me if I didn't—and I saw at the bottom of the flower-pot not only my own money boy, but three rale shining yellow boys, and a whole pile of silver belonging to her.

"Erin go brach! and did I caper for joy thin, and didn't I speedily walk every blessed farden in o my pocket too, that I did, and planting the daisy agin with a blessing, I pulled on my clothes like mad, and going on tiptoe down stairs, I let mysilf quietly from the house.

"Heaven bliss thim for pots, thinks I, they beat all the money-boxes to squash.

"By the time I got clean out and was well hid up in a doorway opposite, who should I hear come tramping along, but marm herself.

"'Here's a spree,' thinks I; 'I has all to myself, and as you are well paid for enjoying it, Michael, may the divil admire ye if you don't stop and enjoy it.'

"'An' so I did; in goes madam, shuts the door so very quietly, 'fraid of waking poor Mike, perhaps, and away she goes as fast as her precious legs would carry her up stairs.'

"'I guess a few she was rayther stunned at finding the room empty and the bird flown. She waited for a time as if she thought I was engaged in a little business of my own; but presently it would appear, diskivering I had hooked it, she made the best of her way to the window.'

"'Up came the flower, pon my sowl 'twould have done your heart good to have seen the horror, rage, and passion that inflamed her face when she found out instead of duping she'd been duped; instead of robbing she'd been robbed: she positively yelled with passion. I took the money in my double hands, and walking up to the window, sung out 'Minny my darling.'

"She shoved her head out.

"'Lookee here, my stunner,' sais I; jingling the money up and down, 'lookee here!'"

"Did'nt she swear, that's all

"'Here you are,' says I; 'dirt cheap: how much for the other flower-pot, ay my angel?'

"Divil a word did she say, but catching it up she dashed it at my head; I ducked to avoid it, and I'll be shot if it did'nt walk its chalks slap through the window of the opposite house.

"Out came the landlord in a rush, an' in his shirt.

"Before I could answer, down came the other unfortunate flower, and worse luck pot and all agin. I bobbed, and landlord got a bob in the eye, for pon my sowl he just exactly napped it, so down he dropped. He screamed ten thousand murthers, and out rushes his wife in her shift, and by this time too out rushes the gentle Minny: she made a grab at me, but I politely declined the compliment by jest stipping, and by the merest accident in the world, tripped up her heels, and threw her right slap into the landlady's arms.

"Both out an' out fighters, both mad with passion, they spit, and hit, and scratched, and alarmed like nothing but the two Kilkenny cats.

"'Go it,' shouted I, and may the divil admire me, they needed no bidding; they jist did fight! and screamed and swore till the whole place was aroused and in an uproar.

"Having brought things to one satisfactory conclusion—now, Michael, my boy, if you want to escape without a bating—if you want to go home richer than whin you started, now's your time, my boy, to make yourself uncommon scarce.

"And, strange to say, gentlemen all, I followed my own advice, and vanished as fast as my legs would carry me home; and now I have finished, as sweet little Minny did, the article itself—

THE TALE OF A FLOWER-POT."

"Bravo, Mike," shouted Jack, when the laughter had somewhat subsided; for the whimsical manner in which the fellow had described his adventure, acted more on the risible nerves of his auditors than the tale itself. "Bravo! it was dog bite dog, and that to perfection."

"I call it dog bite cat, for my part," said Sheppard—"for he worried the poor little Selina in a style lovely for to see, but most horrid for to hear."

"I calls it werry good!" grunted Toby.

"I ditto ditto Toby's magnanimous sentiments," said young Wide Awake.

"And I," said Clayton, "can only give my opinion that he did his duty only, and no more than he ought to have done; for had he suffered himself to be picked up by a blowen, even though she was arrayed in a little mock-modesty, he would have been a disgrace to the cloth and society of prigs of which, I am proud and happy to say, he forms a creditable and honourable member."

"Miny thanks, gentlemen all, for your kind approbation—I'm glad ye approve of my foresight, d'ye see, 'cause it raly is a blissing to have your labours properly appreciated—but if ye hadn't a liked my perceedings, why you could have lump'd 'em, so 'twould have made no difference at all."

"Werry true," said Toby.

"Jack," said Clayton to our hero, "Toby has something to propose, but his excessive bashfulness won't permit him to do it—poor devil! his bashfulness has been his ruin. Just draw him out a bit."

Jack took the hint.

"Gentlemen all," he said, "charge your glasses—bumpers round."

"Bumpers round!" echoed Clayton, and as Jack rose, they all rose to do honour to the toast—

"I beg to propose, gentlemen, success to Toby's new plant—he will explain himself fully and satisfactorily when the toast is drank."

"Toby's new plant."

And each glass, as the words were re-echoed round the table, were set down inverted, to show that due honour had been paid to the challenge.

No, 12.

"Toby's new plant," said Toby, drily—"that aint so much amiss. What the devil do you know about my new plant, eh?"

"Devil a syllable," answered Jack, "which makes us fidgetty to learn the place of it, for we are eager to make hay whilst the sun shines."

"For with the cloud comes the gallows," said Toby. "True."

"Divil burn me, and what are ye talking about?" said O'Brien, "can't you come into genteel society without making use of thim ugly words? get out wid ye, ye spalpeen, you've given me an ugly crick in my neck."

"Poor child," said Clayton laughingly, "and does the thought of a hempen neckcloth unstring its poor nerves? D—— it Mike, I thought you'd better pluck; every man must die, and never a man will die before his allotted time; for us the glorious death of a public execution is reserved, and what more fitting to expiate a life of sunshine than a gay and sudden exit, eh? Cæsar of old, the old Roman Cæsar I mean, who only had to come and see to conquer, as per motto, *vedi, vidi, vici*, he said the most sudden death was the happiest. What happy dogs we ought to be then, to escape the physicing, blistering, pain and torment, of the infernal doctors with the miserable death that follows it; to leap at once into eternity, wafted thither by the tears, sobs, and prayers of a pitying mob My boy, to the really brave, death can have no terrors. Why an highwayman's life and death are explained in three words—

STRUGGLE! — GUGGLE! — BUBBLE!

"Struggle," exemplifies the vicissitudes of his chequered life: "Guggle," is the only sign he gives of pain in death: and "Bubble," closes the career of the man, as a bubble on a stream of water bursts and leaves no trace behind. Such is one man's death in the stream of life. Now Toby, after this dessertation on death, favour us with your place of proceedure.

Taking, by way of a rouser, a huge draught from the tankard before him, he thus began—

"In the city there lives a marchant—"

"Most uncommon thing that," said Jack. "I should think you might, on a pinch, find one."

"Down Wood-street," went on Toby, without noticing Jack's observation, "is his house. It ain't in Wood-street nether, its part in and part out. There is a drawing on it," and he laid a rough sketch on the table, which they all eagerly crowded round to examine; "here you see is a back door, that's a keyhole, and here's a model on it in wax. Good, ain't it?"

"Werry!" said young Wide Awake, "but it strikes me very forcibly its a great deal of trouble thrown away."

"Why is it, boy?" asked Toby.

"Because one of Mike's old skeleton keys would find a way in without a model in wax."

"So it would, Wide Awake," said O'Brien, encouragingly, "but nevertheless, my leery pal we must promote the arts and sciences, and consequently are in duty bound to lend our countenance to any new invention."

"All right, Mike, if you put Toby's jaw out of place, devil a knowledge of the plant shall we get; spin on my venerable," he continued, turning to Toby.

"Well," continued that worthy, "whether you likes to make use of that model or not, I nather know nor care; there it is, a perfect copy; in fact, as like life as wax-work. If you like to fit a key to it, why do—if you don't—why don't."

"Yours is a glorious mode of argument, Toby, it is so conclusive and satisfactory; but go on old 'un, detail the particulars."

"Well," said Toby, "when you open this ere door, you know, why it will be open."

"That is right!" said Jack Rann.

"Well then, when the door is open, all you have to do will be to walk into the court-yard. There, according to the plan, you'll get a good view of the back premises, which will be very amusing no doubt, but I hope the night will be too dark to let you. At the back of the house there's a little window—look'e here, one on ye brakes a square o' glass, shoves in your fist, and undoes the fastening. T'other one lifts up Young Wide Awake, and shoves him in."

"Oh, yes," said Wide Awake, "I ain't a going to play the boy no longer. No more area sneaking for me, I can tell you. I proposes we crack the crib, and if any on 'em kicks up a bobbery, slice their wizens for 'em, blast 'em."

"Why you sanguinary young ruffian," said Clayton, "you are a pretty fellow to talk as coolly of cutting throats as you would, in any reasonable mind of feeling, an orange. Upon my soul, its awful! Why, man alive, where do you expect to go to, if you harbour such wicked thoughts? No, no Wide Awake, strong as we are, we are not exactly strong enough or mad enough to risk a conflict with a whole household, and abetted at the end with a whole body of Charlies. Quite the other, believe me, my boy. If we pluck the blossom of the plant, it will be done silently and carefully—not by bold violence. In fact it will be done as Toby will represent, if you will only give him time to make his report."

"Proceed, Toby, my brave boy," said Harry Sheppard, "and the first man that opens his mug to interrupt you, shiver me but I'll close it with my fist!"

Thus stimulated and encouraged, Toby again set his jawing tackle in order, and after a lapse of time, exhibited the order to be maintained in this siege, the plan of attack, &c. The sum and substance of which speech were briefly these—

Wide Awake was to enter the house by the window, and from the inside was to withdraw the fastenings of the door, and admit the gang. They were then to proceed noiselessly up stairs to a certain room that contained the family plate chest. This valuable booty they were to secure first. Their next proceeding was to be the lifting of the counting house, where a goodly sum, in gold and silver pieces, was expected to be their booty. With this they were to decamp without doing any violence, disturbing any of the house, or committing any further depredations.

To these articles, all agreeing, lots were drawn as to who should execute them.

Young Wide Awake, from the convenience of his diminutive person, was already set aside as one, he being indispensable to the due furtherance of their scheme, and upon the ballot papers being withdrawn, it was ascertained the lot for this adventure had fallen upon Rann, Sheppard, and O'Brien.

CHAPTER X.

THE EARL'S RETURN HOME—DEATH—THE FURTHERANCE OF REVENGE.

Having left the earl in the disagreeable plight described by Clayton, we are in duty bound to describe his return home—that home that he had left with the blackest and most atrocious feelings animating his guilty breast.

The men, upon being put into possession of Clayton's crown, proceeded gleefully to execute the commission assigned them. They got the three horses together, and having by means of stout cord spliced the harness, they were at length in a position to set out on their journey—first, however, having the curiosity to see how fared the occupants of the carriage.

"Gemmen," said the first fellow, touching a fore lock with his finger, "we've done all the gemmen told us, and now will you be pleased to get out and drive?"

"Drive," whined the coachman, in a tone faint from exhaustion and great loss of blood; "how can I drive with this broken arm of mine? Oh, Lord! oh, dear, the pain is hawful!"

"Poor gemman," said the fellow, pityingly; "but p'r'aps the other gemman would like to try—would you, sur?"

"Me drive, sirrah!" thundered the earl, who was recovering from the effects of Clayton's smart blow, which had produced partial insensibility, and regaining his reason with a racking head, and his heart knawed with bitter disappointment, it may well be conceived he was not in the most amiable of tempers. "Me drive, you scoundrel," he exclaimed, "what do you mean?"

"What I said," replied the man, "axing your honour's pardon, and hoping no offence."

"Me drive!" cried the earl again, "I'll see you d—d first—not while I am able to keep a coachman to do it for me."

"Well, axing your parding, and meaning no offence agin, sir, but where's the coachee to drive?"

"Here he is, a fool," said the earl; "and if it wasn't for his blasted foolhardiness, I shouldn't be in this accursed predicament."

"My Lord," said the coachman, piteously, "it was not my fault—I did all

I could to escape them, but that front one was so well mounted, and such a good shot, I couldn't —— Oh!"

And the sufferer had fainted.

"Why he's stopt short like a full stop," said the man, " in a spelling-book."

"A scoundrel of a highwayman has shot him," said the earl, bitterly, thus comprehending the hopelessness of his situation as he then was, he said to the men, "you see my coachman is insensible, and I myself am sore and suffering, if you will drive us to the Red Lion, at Brentford, you shall be handsomely rewarded."

"What say'st, Tom," said the man to his companion, "can'st drive three in hand?"

"Never druv' aught but a dung-cart in my life, and then I upset it; but, dang it, if he'll stand something, let's try."

And accordingly they mounted the box, for the purpose of driving the hapless earl and his coachman to Brentford.

A couple of greater novices never sat behind a living horse.

"Now, Bill," said one, " catchee tight hold of one rein, I'll steer with t'other—when they ought to go my way, I'll pull, and when they want to go your way, you pull."

"I will," answered Will, seizing the rein with both hands; " but who's to hold the whip?"

"Oh, dang it, I forgot that," said the other, who, like Will, was also engaged with both hands. " Wait a bit—I have it. You gee 'em a cut fust, and then they'll go, I'll warrant."

"You hold on 'em," said Will, seizing the whip—" hold 'em, Tom."

"I've got 'em—hit 'em, Will."

Down came the whip, and forward sprang the beast with such a sudden start, that Will, who was standing up, was thrown flat forward on one of their backs; slipping from whence, with more speed than elegance, he measured his length on the ground.

His companion fearing the beasts would start, tugged so vehemently at the reins, that the tortured beasts reared and plunged to escape the torturing bit. Their endeavours the scared driver imputed to a wish to run away, and he therefore only pulled the harder; and they, as a natural consequence, did but kick and plunge the more desperately.

"You infernal asses," said the chafed earl, thrusting his head from the carriage, "you let the horses go on, can't ye? Oh, you dolts—you idiots, you!" and the earl shook his fist vehemently at them during the torrent of his indignation.

"Get up, Will," said the man to his companion—" come and take t'other rein—we'll manage 'em, sur."

Up Will (who was only frightened, not hurt) got, and after a lapse of time, and after the use of a multitude of " Gee up, old osses," " Mether wuts," and other technical terms, of which there is an established language between whips and their quadrupeds, the horses slowly wandered on as they choose.

The least deviation from the direct route was marked with such energetic precision, that Bill and his companion took instant notice of it, and such a tug at the opposite rein followed as, nine times out of ten, pulled the leader right into the hedge. The cry was then, "Pull him round, Will;" and Will having the opposite rein, would give such an unmerciful jerk, as would indeed pull the poor beast round with vengeance.

These mishaps occurred so often, that Will at length dismounted, and approaching the carriage door, he informed the earl—

"The osses was so hawful obstinate, they wouldn't go no how."

Cursing and swearing as he did so, the earl got out of the carriage, and was about to mount the box to drive himself, when Will made the following proposition—

"Pard'ing, sir, meaning no offence in speaking, hopes no offence from speech, but p'r'aps if I lead the osses they'll be better-tempered, and go then."

"Lead the horses, fool!" replied the angry earl—"if you'd a grain of sense, they wouldn't want leading."

"But as I ain't got a grain, sur, what's to be done then?"

"Oh, lead them, fools!—lead them, but do get on, for God's sake."

"Get down," shouted the fellow to his comrade, "and help me lead 'em."

"That I will," answered the fellow with alacrity, evidently right glad to be released faom his perilous position as coachman. My lord got into the carriage again, and Will and his fellow seizing each a horse by the head, led them with slow and trembling steps forward.

They had not proceeded a hundred yards before another accident occurred; the cord which connected the harness to the carriage, from the unskilful manner in which it was tied, came unfastened, and the vehicle was left in the road, whilst the men and horses went plodding carefully onwards; the latter right glad doubtless to be relieved from the cumbersome machine.

The earl began now to be seriously alarmed that he had fallen again into the hands of the Philistines, and therefore changing his previous haughty tone of command, he begged them, for God's sake, to trifle with him no longer: he pleaded he was ill, his man was dying from loss of blood, and that if they would only take them to Brentford, he swore to reward them beyond their most sanguine expectations.

"Well, I never, I'm struck all of a heap! Why hang it master, you don't suppose we did it for a purpose, I hope? Why Bill ain't we done our best to coax the beastesses on, and yet they won't come no how, the parvarse obstinate brutes"

"O' course we have," answered Will, "and it's werry scurvy of the gemman if he thinks t'otherwise. Hurting our feelings for nothink now; but hang it, mate, I've got an hidear."

It was a thousand pities he couldn't keep it there, for heaven knows his thick cranium was not overburdened with them.

"What is it?" inquired the earl, his testiness returning as his fears of further outrage vanished. "Devil take the man, can't you speak?"

"Yes, I can," answered the fellow, "and I tell ye what, master, it 'ud be a tarnation sight better for you in the long run, if you couldn't speak so many o' them ere oaths; it's horrid hawful."

"At all events you will not have to answer for my sins, so what matters it to you?"

"That's true, it don't matter to me sartinly, only I don't like to hear it like; but what I was agoing to say, master, was this, can you lead osses?"

"Why?" questioned the earl, briefly.

"But can you?" persisted the man; "answer my question, afore you axes another."

"Of course I can," replied the earl; "any fool can do that."

"Then you are just the ticket," said the man; "you lead them ere osses on to Brentf'd, me and my mate 'ull drag the covey inside and carriage arter you."

There was no resource but to obey, for short as the distance, he saw he should never get there without, so Robert, Earl of Dashfield, as he so vauntingly described himself, was compelled to submit to the degradation of leading his own horses.

Tired and weary, and well nigh maddened from disappointment, he reached the town of Brentford, which he found all alive, one and all being up and stirring at the audacious robbery committed at the Red Lion.

"Have they got 'em, sir?" inquired several eager lookers-on, of the earl. "Have they got the highwayman?"

"I know not," said the earl, with vehement bitterness, "but I hope to my soul they will have them, and may I die, if he doesn't hang for this crime."

"What has he robbed you, sir?" inquired a by-stander.

"Robbed!" echoed the earl, "ten thousand curses on the audacious scoundrel; he has not only robbed me, but he has wronged me more grievously and bitterly than tongue can tell."

"As how, sir—as how?" inquired several eager voices, anxious to be in possession of the secret; this indulgence, however, the earl was too prudent to grant them, and uttering a cold and stern—

"It matters not," he strode into the Red Lion.

Here, as may we well imagine, he was again assailed with a host of questions as to "what had become of the highwaymen, whether they were likely to be cotched," and so forth, to none of which the proud nobleman vouchsafed one single syllable in reply.

Turning to the landlady, he said—

"What are all these idiots gaping at? Have they never seen a highwayman before? If they haven't, start them to Tyburn—they are often enough exhibited in due perfection there. And here, you sir," he shouted to Jerry, the oastler, of whom the reader will remember we made mention before, "put my horses in the stable, rub them well down, give them a good feed of corn, d'ye hear?"

"I do, my Lord."

For from being a frequent visitor to Arlington on affairs of gallantry, his lordship had managed to get known on the road.

There was a mighty start of surprise among the loiterers when they found they had been talking to a real lord, and the majority of them, previously all gabble and importance, became extremely quiet, and looked particularly crest-fallen. It needed only a trifle to set them on the alert, though, and this his lordship found from them, in the following words—

"Go to my carriage, some of you fools, and help my servant out; and you boy," to the lad of the inn, whom we also before introduced, "run for a doctor—the man has been shot by one of those scoundrels of highwaymen."

"Shot by the highwaymen!" murmured the listeners, rushing out to the carriage, not so much instigated by pity as by curiosity.

"Yes, shot! I know the man that did the deed, and as sure as I stand here, he'll swing for it."

"Drat 'em," exclaimed the landlady, "I'd hang both, had I my will, athout judge or jury. I am sure it's a marcy that ain't killed my husband;" and being a gullarous dame, she favoured his lordship with a lengthened account, interspersed with numerous invectives of the outrages committed at the inn.

"And was it Squire Thornley and his companions then in pursuit of them for robbery?" inquired the earl.

"It was," answered the dame, "your lordship, and the head-constable, with his staff of office and all to boot; and they swore they'd catch the villains if they rid all night."

"And by God they will," exclaimed the earl, a feeling and hope of revenge animating his words. "I know the squire well as a rare old fox-hunter, and would bet my existence he will not give up the chase. It is bravely done—bravely done!"

By this time the doctor had arrived, and the earl's wounded servant having been conveyed into the house, that functionary was busily occupied in attention upon the wounded man. By the time the ball was extracted, his wounded arm was set and dressed, the squire had returned with his party from their unsuccessful pursuit.

"Have you caught them?" was the simultaneous cry, in which even the earl, in his curiosity, joined.

"No!" exclaimed the squire with an oath, the devil was too well mounted for us; never did I see such a horse in my life. By heavens she cleared the toll bar nobly. She's a gallant mare—as, by God, I ought to know, for she belonged to me—and he is as dashing a rider as ever crossed a horse. By Jove! notwithstanding the scoundrel has robbed me, I am almost glad he has escaped, for his gallant behaviour."

"He leaped the gate, you say?" said the earl, in tones of feverish eagerness, "but he was alone, was he not—pray answer me, was he not alone?"

"The lucky dog, no," answered the squire; "if shape and form can be taken for anything, he had the loveliest damsel in his arms that ever man perilled life for."

"Curses on him," muttered the earl, in tones not loud but deep.

"Ay, my lord," said the squire, "this is an unlooked-for pleasure. Who the devil would have thought of seeing you here? Not I, on my oath. What are you a victim, too?"

"I am," answered the earl, with bitter wrath; "but before these prattling fools this is not a time or place for the revelation. Let us retire, and you shall have the particulars."

"With all my heart, my lord—clear the way, you fellows there;" and arm-in-arm they retired to a private room.

Here his lordship gave a repetition of what the reader is already in possession of from previous pages, wisely omitting, however, anything like reference to the little affair that occurred between Jack Rann and her ladyship.

No. 13

"But how the devil," said the squire, "could this rascal of a servant of yours have found out your intentions towards this young lady, eh?"

"That I would give a thousand pounds to know," exclaimed the earl.

"Cannot you form any idea—damme, recollect yourself. Did you tell any one?"

"Not a soul until I have just now told you."

"Well, its beyond the possibility of doubt that I couldn't have told him; but hang me, he must have heard of it."

"He must—of that I have had bitter galling proof; and I swear to you I would give a thousand pounds if I could but find him."

"I'll tell you for half the money—that fellow that is shot must have told him."

"It is impossible he could have done so, for he himself did not know of my plans an hour before we stated."

"Then that falls to the ground, and the affair still remains wrapped in profound, impenetrable mystery."

"It does," said the earl, moodily.

"Well, my lord, having lost the girl, what the devil do you intend to do? It strikes me you are in a devillish pretty mess! Why you'll have that fiery old father of hers down upon you in something less than no time."

"That I can fight out."

"As how? if I may have the impertinence to ask the question."

"By arresting Rann—that will effectually close her mouth; for, from words that fell from her lips to-night, I am certain that she loves him."

"It's all very well to talk about arresting him. Now I myself had a brave good try to effect that self-same object, and all without effect. I tell you what, I've heard of catching a weasel asleep, and I'll be damned if I don't think catching this Mister Jack Rann, if that's his name, is about as likely an object."

"That he is as nimble, as much on the alert, and as cunning as a fox, I have had proof more than once before this day; but such things as foxes are run to death by hounds, and I'll set the hounds of the law on him."

"The hounds of the law! what sort of animals are they? I've a pack, but damme, they haven't got any knowledge of law, except it is to put their feet to the ground as sharp as possible—that's law with me for them, I can tell you.'

"The hounds that I shall unkennel, sir," with a grin of deep malignancy, "are Bow-street officers."

"Oh, I see—they are the boys to hunt him up. But I say, my lord, in putting him upon Jack Rann's track, wont you also be putting him upon your own? Why the man aint robbed you, has he?"

"Robbed me! has he not? Yes, of that whose loss I lament more bitterly than if he had robbed me of all my riches—had reduced me to beggary itself."

"It's gallows annoying," said the squire, rising and viewing himself in the glass, "but upon my soul, although I am a decided admirer of the fair sex, I don't fancy I should like to give up everything for them, 'pon my soul—decidedly no."

"But not having seen her, you can form no idea of her surpassing loveliness—beautiful as Venus—she is all perfection—she is ravishingly beautiful."

"And so you wanted to ravish her, eh? Oh, you wicked dog, when will you sow your wild oats? Come, come, my lord, take my advice—leave these adventures to younger men, and stick more faithfully to matrimony."

"Matrimony!" echoed his lordship, "is cant fit for plebeians, and are words never made for the aristocracy. Pho! it disgusts me! Would I had never heard its name!"

"Hearing it often enough hasn't tempted me to leap into it," said the squire; "and since it is such a mournful state of life, however could you have been sawney enough to have risked it—more especially a man with your experience and knowledge, too, I am utterly at a loss to conceive?"

"And I am as utterly at a loss to answer, except it be that, like most other men, I have been subject to an occasional silly half-hour. But about this Rann?"

"Well, what about him. How are you going to proceed?—that's the rub," said the squire.

"If I stir in the matter," said his lordship, "it will certainly be with the risk of exposing myself to the world in blacker colours than I care to sport—think you not so?"

"Damme, that I do," answered Squire Thornley. "'Taint I care for a good name in the world, but I certainly should not admire having such a stinger as will cling to you from the publication of this scandal. I really don't see how you can move in it. Fancy going before the judge. 'Well, my man, state your case.' 'Please your worship I was stopped on the king's highway.' 'Well.' 'And robbed.' 'Well, and who did it?' 'The prisoner at the bar, your worship.' 'Oh, the prisoner at the bar—you are positive of his identity?' 'Could pick him out from a thousand.' 'Well, and what did he take from you?—was the property found upon him?' 'Believe not, sir.' 'What was the property, sir?' 'A lady, your worship!' 'Robbed of a lady on the king's highway! Well, in all my experience, I never heard of a more singular case of robbery than this! Can you prove the identity of the lady—can you swear she is your lawful property?' 'No, sir,' says a white-headed old gentleman, 'but I can; and that villain,' pointing to you, not the prisoner; 'robbed me of her with intents foul, criminal, and malicious, according to the statutes of our blessed King George, and that gentleman,' 'pointing to the prisoner, not to you, 'did nobly, generously, and manfully rescue her from his filthy and abominable intents.' 'So, so,' says the judge; then turning to prisoner, 'Sir, you are honourably acquitted.' Exchange of polite bows between late prisoner and judge; then turns to you, 'Officer, seize that man, place him in the felon's dock—he stands charged with the capital crime!' There you are, my noble friend, a picture in little, but from life."

"I am almost afraid it is," said the earl, thoughtfully; then with sudden vehemence, he exclaimed, "I have it, squire—he has robbed you, has he not?"

"He has—there is no mistake about that! The happy dog has at this moment my watch in his pocket, and is sitting astride my mare; and she is as good a horse as any in the wide world."

"And will you not take steps to recover them?"

"I have taken so many steps to-night, that I have almost broken my horse's wind; and damme, after all, it's 'no go!'"

"But will you resign your valued property without another trial for its recovery?"

"Show me a chance, and see if I don't, my lord, that's all."

"Listen to me."

"I am all attention, my lord."

"Go to town to-morrow, seek out Sir John Fielding at Bow-street, lay an information you have been robbed, stating when, where, how, and by whom. Leave the rest to him and his men—if they trace not the lion to his lair, my name's not Dashfield."

"But then the biggest villain will escape. He didn't rob me, although he had my horse and watch—'twas his pal that did it."

"Lay an information against both—surely you can describe the other? I'll give you a never-failing description of that villain Rann, so faithful and correct a portraiture, that go where he will he shall be recognised, and it is hard indeed to me if when he is seen he be not apprehended."

"Upon my soul," said the Squire, "I don't know one from tother, all I know is they're both devillish good looking fellows—polite in their behaviour, and exhibiting in their costume and carriage, the true born gentlemen; they were somewhat energetic in their proceedings, though I remember that, and so on, the fellows that were with me, by Jove you would have laughed to have seen the young 'un fetch off old Cowtons boots, and pour the gold out of their precious heels; it was the best joke I have seen for many a day."

"The younger one did this, you say?"

"He did," answered the squire.

"And how looked he?"

"Pretty well, considering, I thought, that is to say, for only a youngish cove like; he took it pretty cool and comfortable, and pocketed all that came near him without a blush."

"The scoundrel, I doubt him not! No, I'll give him credit for as much audacity and effrontery as any man in the world; but what I mean is this; how looked he in statue, face, form?"

"In statue, I should say at a calculation, he stood at least five feet nine inches; in face, as he stood there pistol in hand, he looked a cove to be avoided; but when he quietly bade us good day, I thought I had seldom, if ever, seen a handsomer one; it was strict and perfect in the richest manly beauty; in form, he was thinly, genteelly, even elegantly, made: that is all I noticed of him; but no, stop! another thing I noticed, and this I could swear to."

"What is it?" inquired the Earl almost breathlessly.

"That he wore at each time the extraordinary number of

"SIXTEEN STRINGS."

"Did any one else notice ? speak, man, speak."

"Yes, all of us, even to the man Jerry."

"Here is evidence enough to hang him where he twice as artful as he his!" cried the Earl, then rising, he rang the bell with violence.

In came Jerry.

"You are the man I meant; you saw those highwaymen, eh? answer fool can't you."

"Yeas all'ays."

"Did you notice anything particular about either of them, come speak up."

"No, I did'nt, Lurd Dashfield," shouted Jeremiah at the top of his lungs.

"Softly fool, can't you speak up without bawling ?"

"Yeas, I'll try."

"Now, on your oath, Jerry, this is very important, and if you answer me correctly, I will give you a guinea."

"What be it," said Jerry with a broad grin of anticipation.

"One of the men was younger and better looking than the other, was he not ?"

"Yeas, and rode a better ass;" and Jerry jerked his finger towards the Squire.

"Now, did you notice anything particular about his breeches ?"

"'Bout his breeches," repeated Jerry, as if he scarce understood the question.

"Yes, about his breeches below the knee, I mean, where they were tied."

"Yeas, I did, Lurd Dashfield, and I thrort as how "

"What, fool," enquired his lordship testily.

"Why I thrort ribban must be monstrous cheap his'n way, he wore such an Almighty lot's o' strings; why he had sixteen aside."

"How do you know he had sixteen aside?" queried the Squire.

"Counted 'em, sur."

"Bravo, Jerry! Those highwaymen have robbed me of every guinea, or I'd give you the one I promised you."

"Won't he lend you one," said Jerry, jerking his thumb towards the squire.

The latter burst into a hearty laugh at their ludicrous situation, as he said:

"By jingo, Jerry, I'm literally cleaned out too; so you must trust."

"Pay to-day, trust to morrow," muttered Jerry; "Bird in hand worth two in bush:" then turning to his lordship, he said:—

"Won't missus ?"

There was no resisting this appeal, the missus was summoned, the money was at once produced, and the man at once paid.

"Now, my dear friend," said the earl to the squire, becoming suddenly on the most intimate and affectionate terms, "all that remains for you as a just man, and as a gentleman, who in the suppression of highway robbery, is doing good to the community at large."

"And yourself in particular," put in the squire, as a parenthesis.

"And myself I confess, in particular," echoed Lord Dashfield, with the blandest of smile, "is to inform against this Rann and his accomplices."

"And get them hanged for the little wrong they have done me, eh?"

"Exactly," said the Earl.

"Then I'm d—d if I do it, I will swear no man's life away for such a thing as highway robbery. Let those who choose to commit legal murder do it, I don't."

"Did I coincide with you about being hanged, my dear friend?"

"You did," answered the squire, bluntly.

"Then, pardon me, I meant it not, in fact, if you will do as I wish you. If they are sentenced to die from any proceedings we may institute against them, I will guarantee to get their pardon from the king."

"Under such circumstances, my Lord Dashfield I consent, for it is self evident if these men are not checked in their career of sin, the gallows will inevitably be their doom, and as a long term of imprisonment may avert such a catastrophe, I will make it my business to see Sir John Fielding tomorrow at Bow-street, and instruct him to arrest these men."

"Thanks my good kind friend, a thousand times," exclaimed the earl.

"Nay, no thanks are due to me for serving you; I consider I am also serving society, and probably saving the men themselves."

From the squires information laid the next day, sprang the insertion of the notice in the "London Gazette," as read by Young Wide Awake, to our hero. And further all the constabulary were supplied with a full, true, and particular account of our hero, even down to his sixteen strings; and the Bow-street runners were on the alert for his capture, Sir John Fielding having issued a warrant for his apprehension, and that of his confederate Captain Clayton.

* * * * *

On the day following his defeat at Hounslow, his lordship, in an hour verging upon midnight, sought his magnificent home, Dashfield House.

He had been drinking deeply throughout the day, as his unsteady footsteps, his rolling gait, and his inflamed face, testified.

The porter having opened the outer gate, his lordship, with an oath upon the man for his tardiness, rolled in—making the best of an extremely zig-zag course towards the mansion, muttering to himself as he went; his lordship at once mounted the steps and entered the house.

Taking from the hands of his valet a candle, and rejecting roughly the man's offered assurance, he bid him "get to; and mind ye fellow, if you hear a noise in the night, pay no attention to it, dost hear, her ladyship and I have a small score to settle."

"God help her," muttered the man, and his eyes filled with tears as he gave vent to the thoughts.

Catching the indistinct words as the man muttered them, his lordship, with a curse, bid the man speak out, to say what he meant!

"My lord, a dreadful catastrophe has happened in your absence, that is all I know; Elinor keeps the rest, a profound secret; she is the only one who knows, the only one who can tell you."

"Is her ladyship worse," inquired his lordship, a flitting thought of their unhappy parting crossing his mind.

"I know not my lord, none have had access to her but Miss Roche, during your absence."

"Was no docter sent for, eh, rascal?"

"No, my lord," replied the valet mournfully, "Miss Roche stated her ladyship has no need for one."

"Did she, by heaven's," said his lordship, in tones husky from excitement and excessive drink, adding in bitter words as he did so, "she shall find need, for I myself will produce the effect that the cause may follow. Yes, I will." and he flourished his fist wildly in the air, "I swear I will."

With these words he staggered up the staircase, and reaching the boudoir of Lady Dashfield, loudly knocked.

The door was opened noiselessly from within, and his lordship was ushered into the exquisite apartment, which save from a night lamp which cast but a wavering and flickering light around, was dark as the grave, in fact the lead-like light was worse to his lordship than total darkness could by any possibility have been.

"Lights, lights!" he shouted.

As the words fell from his lips, Miss Roche started suddenly from a corner and lighting a waxen taper, by the lamp, she placed it upon the table; as she did so, his lordship, even in the disordered state in which he was, noticed the extraordinary, the earthly pallor of the girl's countenance, for her face was white as the driven snow.

Had a spirit (as fables say they so came) clothed in white, have arisen from the grave, her appearance could not have shocked him greater.

"Where, where, is her ladyship?" he stammered; seized by a sudden fear of, he knew not what; but tremulous notwithstanding with thoughts of something terrible and horrible, he held up his hands appealingly to her.

The girl advanced towards him, and seizing him by the arm, pointed to a human form reclining upon a couch; it was covered with a long veil of snow white lace-work: this, with impetuous action more characteristic of a maniac than a man, the Earl tore aside.

Alas! how pale that beauteous face! how motionless that matchless form! The Countess of Dashfield was dead.

"Dead!" how solemn sounds the word; how terribly solemn then is death in all its awful reality!

There she lay, still cold, motionless, and there like the black letters of death stood the evidence of her life's dread bereavements.

Upon her throat—otherwise delicate as Parisian marble—mere marks of violence, cruelty, murder! such marks as Cain bore on his forehead, for they spoke death; that each that looked could know foul injury had been done; black death administered.

Had the Earl been Cain himself who did the first murder, he could not have started back more shocked, more affrighted, more appalled. We have heard of strong frights suddenly sobering drunken men, and here is a record of it.

There she lay, dead, by his hands—for there was the testimony on the dead woman's throat—the irremovable, the damning evidence of his guilt! Grant her frailty, for she was still his wife—yes, the wife of his bosom! Grant her frailty again; and grant him injured, was he justified in dealing her death?

Heaven's record say emphatically, NO! And who dares doubt them?

"Struck as a man is in a fit, the proud and haughty lord fell backwards horror struck at the sad catastrophe: his blood was chilled with horror, with fear, but fear predominated; like most murderers his yearning soul clung to life—his first thought for his own safety.

In this emergency, and in his horror, he turned to Elinor Roche who stood like an avenging angel over him.

"Save me! save me!" was all he could mutter.

"Murdered!" she answered in tones solemn and prophetic. "I will save you."

"Thanks, thanks, oh thanks!" muttered the lord.

"No thanks for me! for her sake who now lies stiff stark cold, and dead; for her sake because I know instead of this dead corpse if there was actual life in her poor bosom, that life would speak and cry for mercy; and you, for her sake, and hers alone, I promise not to divulge your guilt."

"Thanks! oh thanks!"

"And further, I will so arrange the last sad offices for this poor woman, so unmercifully robbed of life, that though the stricken world shall wonder in startled moments "how came she by her death? none but you and I shall know."

"You are my saviour, thanks, thanks!" so muttered the Earl.

"But, man, bear in your mind I will have this lady buried in a leaden coffin, and where you list not, so that at any time whilst flesh and bone can cling together, I can reproduce it to the living world to your terrible and inevitable condemnation; so as you live, let there be this fear on you to guard your life, to render you a better man, that there is one in the world who holds your life in her grasp."

"Think of this, and fear me as you would fear death!"

"I will! I will!" answered the Earl upon his bended knees.

"Up cowardly hound!" said Elinor with flashing eyes, "less I say your craven spirit contaminates the fiery presence of your poor victim."

"What am I to do?" said the Earl.

"Get you to your kennel—I will watch this fair one's head till daybreak—I have given notice of her desperate illness—I will then give notice of her sudden death. Look to it that you make a show of grief, if in reality you hold no sorrow in your heart. It may perhaps tend to the saving of your wife. And now get you gone."

Like a cur whose spirit hath been broken by the lash, the Earl arose from his recumbent position.

"Yet stay, one instant. On so terrible a warning, a repetition may surely be offered. Remember, my lord, you are a murderer, let your actions breathe of repentence, or mind ye these are my final words—mark ye, there is one, who, holding in her hand a secret that will doom you to an ignominious death, will not fail to divulge that secret—will not fail to give that death unless you repent."

"With this, I give you permission my lord, to retire—to sleep, if you can."

CHAPTER XI.

JACK RANN AND HIS PALS STORM THE HOUSE IN WOOD-STREET—A SLIGHT INCIDENT WHEREFROM MAY BE GATHERED SOME OF THE ILLS OF "REPUTATION"—JACK'S CAPTURE AND "A SCENE."

When we last parted from the gang at their jovial meeting at old Toby's, it will be remembered the concoction of a certain robbery was then first on the list of investments, where skill was required, and where capital found itself, and that any veritable hero being a handy man at anything, was about to shift his jacket for the once, from a high-tobyman to a cracksman.

If any reliance may be placed on the pages of history, which are acknowledged on all hands to be facts, *verbatum et literatum*, (there's a bit of Latin for ye, boys), then we have proof conclusive and satisfactory so far as it goes, that Jack Rann was, and no gammon, in modern parlance "a regular stunner." I tell you he was somewhat as a comet is now-a-days, whilst he lasted he set all the worlds of England agog, for everybody in it if they walked abroad expected to be robbed: if they stopped at home expected to be bamboozled—if they rode on horseback, to be stopped *à la mode*, "Your money or your life ?" and when they went to bed at night, for a considerable time every man in our vast metropolis expected to be robbed, and hid their money in all sorts of secret places, sometimes a jewel case or a cash box would find a resting-place on a ledge in the chimney, at other times the valuables were lowered in the bucket to the bottom of the well, (for wells were in vogue in London then, pumps were rarities), and so the wise old inhabitants thought to escape victimization, but Jack was a dead nail, it was a most mysterious thing but "'pon honor," he seemed fated to find valuables wherever they were hid. That there was a mystery attached to this we confess, and to which our readers will have a keystone ere long.

To wind up all, as a short preliminary to the real dashing life of Jack Rann, as it was, we can only say, borrowing modern hands for the purpose again, "he was a devil of a chap for the gals!"

As O'Brien would say, "Divil a woman, old or young, rich or poor—divil a young maid or an old *made*, but expected intirely, night after night, to be ravished by that divil, Jack Rann!"

We let the observation stand as we found it, feeling that any embellishment would spoil it.

On the memorable night in question, as the lads were on the pivot to start on their midnight excursion to the city, who should come driving up to the rendezvous of the gang in Pedlar's Acre but Toby. With a smart little hag (for that time of day), in a smart little cart, he came merely to "ax 'em if they wouldn't prefer riding ?"

A small negociation having taken place between Toby and Moses about the disposal of the proceeds and so forth, Jack at last was called, and he was immediately followed by O'Brien and Young Wide Awake.

"What the divil is this affair for?" said O'Brien, looking at the horse and vehicle. "Are we to have the blessed traps on our heels before we start?"

"Not at all—not at all, my brave boys; but if you succeeds, you will have monish, much monish, more than we can carry."

"And if we fail," said O'Brien, with a whisper in the Jew's ear, "what then? Are we to be blowed upon?"

"By Israel's ——"

Guessing, with an aptness natural in such an old professional, the meaning of the Jew's oath, he said—

"No, Moses, I will trust your word; but remember, sorry will it be for the daylight that brakes over ye, if aught happen to the brave, noble ould Jack."

"Hush!" said the Jew; "we are certainly alone here—only amongst our friends—but if you'se gets lagged, that is, yourself or Mister Rann, or the Wide Awake, why you shall be treated like gentleman's in prison—shall have wines, shall have counsels, shall have witnesses, shall have everytink—everytink!"

"Your word on it, Moses?" asked O'Brien.

"My word, my hand, my soul! my everytink!" answered the Jew, emphatically.

"That's your sorts, my broths of boys! Jump in—jump in, Jack; but damme, 'fore you go, you wont cut off a string or two, bad luck to ye; but from all accounts and from sacret resources I have learnt, them strings of yourn are over dacently celebrated, they are."

"Over celebrated, are they," answered Jack, "well so be it, as Sixteen String Jack in degrading servitude? I have been known for many a day; if Sixteen String Jack suits for the bye-ways, why I ask you, should not the same cognomen suit for the highways? As Sixteen String Jack, I have lived, and come fortune or his accursed eldest daughter Miss Fortune—come fame or infamy, as Sixteen String Jack I will die."

"Bravely spoken—bravely spoken," said the Jew, "but remember the walls have ears—the walls have ears."

"An' by St. Patrick time has wings, or the old fellows most cruelly belied, so hark forward wid the moke, do you hear, or we shall have Oliver looking after us before we know where we are?"

"Werry good advice said Toby, giving the animal an incouraging poke with a sharp pointed stick, then adding immediately after, "go on there can't ye?"

It would appear, if an inference might be drawn, that the animal could go on; for under the goad, it immediately sprang forward.

"Don't forget your promise," shouted Young Wide awake.

"I swear ——"

The words as the Jew would have added, were lost in the distance as the fleet animal rapidly increased the distance between the robbers and their confederate. Following the course of the river they kept on at a smart canter through many a dim lighted and filthy dirty lane, in the delectable borough of Southwark, until they emerged at last into the Boro' Road, then as now, in direct communication with London Bridge. The old bridge crossed, they did not hesitate, but goading the animal on again, passed up the Poultry into Cheapside; pulling round sharply to the left by one of those narrow turnings abutting on Bow Church, the vehicle was brought to a stand still, and Toby placing his hand to his mouth, the better to convey his whisper, said—

"Over the way, I'll wait; be hexpert my hearties, good luck go with ye and here's a dram," and from a long-necked, full bellied, bottle, each man took a hearty draught, not that they needed spirit to nerve them to their daring task, but because the night being chilly it was calculated to arouse and to awaken their spirits. O'Brien and Shephard led the way and were scarcely lost to sight, in Wood Street, before our hero and young Wide Awake, keeping them in view, also followed in their footsteps.

"Hist, quiet," said O'Brien at length, "by all that's good and glorious, here's the identical house. Look around now Wide Awake, ye ghost of a spalpeen, and if ye see the shadow of any individual soul, whistle like blazes."

"Never fear but I'll raise an echo if need be," answered Wide Awake, "and mind you, as Mike would say, 'silent gives consent,' for if all is silent all is well, so fire away my boys, and make yourselves at home, the sooner you do so the quicker and the better. I'll take a survey" and humming a blythe tune as he went, the young rascal started on his errand: first, he directed his steps towards Cheapside, the usually busy street was silent as the very grave, not the echo of a single footstep broke the solemn stillness of the night; young Colledge himself was impressed with the unusual quietude, and as the moon lit up with its heavenly light the tower of St. Mary-le-bow, he muttered to himself:—

"Strike me lucky, what a glorious night for our glorious occupation; nothing stirring at all; no charlies pace their midnight watch; no, devil take me, their all fast enough asleep, I'll warrant; not a lushington is there to be seen, all turned sober I shouldn't wonder; not even a crazy hackney coach with a spavind horse and a lushy driver; all gone! and strike me! but the City, instead of busy London, looks like the City of the dead. All riteous though, the plant's as safe as the Bank, the Bank! I meant Newgate, for once in the stone jug, its mighty good care they take not to part with you there."

With this comfortable reflection, Wide Awake regained his companions, who were impatiently awaiting his arrival ere they commenced practical operations.

"Is it all right, Wide Awake?" asked Rann of the urchin who instantly made reply.

"I should think it was, a few! why there aint a mouse stirring; as to the charlies, they are cosy enough in their boxes as their beds. Wise fellows! they take care of themselves and leave City to take care of itself; and by jingo it ought to be able too, for by all that's good its big enough."

"Hold your cursed jaw, you young thief, do," said Sheppard savagely, "do you think we have nothing else to heed but your cursed gabble? Go to work, Michael, my boy, open the cursed door."

"Divil burn me if I can! here hav' I been poking this half hour, first with Toby's model, next with every blessed skeleton in the bunch, an' without the least effect. Aint it provoking now?"

"Give me the keys," said Sheppard; they were delivered to him; he took them and tried them both persuasively and forcibly, and both without effect, the door remained immovable as though determined to resist all efforts. Jack next tried, but with no better success; suddenly he burst into a hearty laugh, hearty, though not loud or boisterous.

"I tell you what, my boys, the door is unlocked already, no wonder it resisted all our efforts; the fact is, it is fastened in the Bath style, it is barred and bolted, not locked."

"The divil," said O'Brien, "What is to be done?"

"Done," cried Jack; "why we must scale the walls, boys, that's all."

"That's all!" remarked Sheppard, "and a pretty tolerable all too when we see them blasted glass bottles shoving into the air their jagged and ugly edges—used to a quod and in scrapes, that's a fact, but not being a glazier I always abhorred anything like glass in any dealings I have ever had. We had better make ourselves scarce, I think."

"Do you though, then you are just like me, for I don't. Here, hold out your hand;" Sheppard did as he was bid, Jack placing his foot in it, sprang up lightly, "your shoulder, O'Brien, a little lower, that's the ticket:" he now stood balanced upon the shoulders of the pair; he was now on a level with the level of the wall, seizing which with a hand on the extreme edge of either side, he sprang as nimbly as a cat from their shoulders upon the wall; a few pieces of glass as they came in contact with his feet, and dropped on either side, gave notice only of his daring feat. From the wall it was but another spring to the ground, this he took without a moments hesitation, and although the wall was a considerable height from the ground, the spring was effected as marvellously as if a precious cat—those lonely midnight serenaders of the metropolis—itself had taken it. A low secret whistle announced to the anxious listeners his safe descent, and in a few minutes more the door was opened, and the trio with stealthy footsteps stole into the court yard. One glance at the house sufficed to show them it was the same; Toby had so minutely described, and this one glance served to direct their immediate attention to the small window by which means Wide Awake was to make his entry into the house. Lifting the lad on his arms as easily as if he was only an infant, until he was on a level with the window, Jack Rann whispered "Now for it."

The unfastened window flew back on its hinges with a dull grating sound; the next instant Wide Awake crawled stealthily through the aperture. Reaching his feet in safety, he, by means of a phosphoric light, made his way to the door, and with all the ease of a finished locksmith, removed the bolts and bars. The gang once admitted, pushed on right zealously with noiseless but rapid steps to the counting house. Whilst Sheppard, pistol in hand, stood guarding the staircase, Jack, O'Brien, and Wide Awake were busy at work at their spoil. A desk which had long stood against their united efforts, was at length thrown open by Jack's notorious hand, and then in glittering heaps lie piles of gold and silver, and costly merchandise.

A low cry of joy burst from them at the sight of the rare and costly treasures thus thrown open to their avaricious eyes and greedy hands. Unable to contain themselves, they thrust their hands with frantic eagerness amidst the pile of gold, scattering, with their violence, the glittering heaps in all directions. Far more sensible of the value of silence than his companions, Jack seized O'Brien sternly by the arm, and in a loud and authoritative tone, (more so than the others seemed to think the occasion warranted) bidding them desist, adding as he did so with bitter emphasis.

"Fools, would you arouse the house; would you have the Philistine upon us?"

"Not exactly, Master Rann," said O'Brien, restored to himself, "but I'll jest trouble you, my boy, the next time you have an observation to make, do so without using your gripers; by all that's good you have stuck you nails into my arms, an inch an' a half deep."

"Rann is right," said Sheppard, after a pause, "we were fools to be tempted to forget ourselves at the sight of swag which is all our own, if we act but cautiously—come lets finish the work—by Jove here's mopusses enough to make all our fortunes for life." With this they immediately commenced noiselessly and quickly to fill a small leathern bag which Sheppard, in anticipation of valuable booty, had taken the precaution to bring with him. Handful after handful of guineas, found a resting place in this capacious receptacle, until the whole score contained in the desk was safely stowed away.

"If they keep such amount of gold as this upon the premises," said Jack in a whisper to his confederates, "we shall find elsewhere some equally valuable matter in the shape of bank notes—come lads for a rummage," with this they set to work, and what persuasions so disjointed the unhappy desk, that none seeing it as it then stood, would have recognised it as bearing any likeness to the name it bore. Their scrutiny, however, was without avail. Musty parchments, dry deeds, sealed invoices there were in galore, but nothing that bore any resemblance to those flimsy valuables, called per virtue, bank notes. With an imprecation on their non success, Sheppard turned to O'Brien and Jack, and expressed his determination to proceed up stairs, and drawing a crape mask which was concealed under his hat down, so that it entirely covered the upper part of his face, he bid one to follow him. This office Jack, with his usual reckless daring immediately accepted, and the pair crept on tiptoe up the winding staircase, leaving O'Brien and Wide Awake to guard the valuable treasure they had already amassed. To Sheppard's request, "See to your barking irons," Jack immediately responded, by fresh priming his pistols, an example followed instantly by his companions, and with pistol in each hand, they strode with lightened footsteps onwards. The first room they entered they perceived by the dark lantern, which Sheppard carried, was a small drawing room, furnished with all the elegance that the wealth of the period could command.

"Divellish pretty, isn't it?" asked Harry Sheppard.

"It is," answered Jack, "I have seen a more costly room, but never one more chaste or elegant. It has one great fault however."

"What is that, Jack?" asked Harry.

"It is not sufficiently portable to be of any use to us, that is all. Proceed my boy to the upper regions, but gently a moment what is this glittering here?"

Jack held it to the lantern as he spoke, and then perceived it was a diamond ring—small, but of elegant workmanship, and of immense value. Thrusting it carelessly upon his little finger, he observed it was worth finding at all events. With this slight addition to their plunder, they proceeded upon their search. Another flight of stairs ascended—another landing place gained, upon which were two doors at either extremity, Sheppard tried the door of one, pointing to Rann to do the same with the other. The doors opened under the pressure simultaneously, and they both immediately advanced into the apartments. It was Sheppard's fate to find an elderly man and woman peacefully asleep—calm and placid, and beautiful as innocence itself, they looked in that deep slumber. But Sheppard, although possessed of every manly virtue, was, when "business" interspersed its ugly f rm, but little prone to sentimentality, or to admire innocence. Taking the light, which stood burning in the fire-place for safety, and which cast a flickering wavering and uncertain glare around, he brightened it up with the butt-end of his pistol, and advancing to the bedside, held it over the heads of the unconscious pair, who calmly and happily slept on, little thinking—little dreaming of the ominous shadow that cast its sombre and unwelcome shade in the privacy of their chamber. Over their heads, although they were hid from view in bags manufactured for that purpose, as Sheppard could tell from their monotonous ticking, were two watches. To possess himself of these, and to satisfy himself they were gold ones, was his first care. Apparently contented with his scrutiny, he thrust them carefully into his capacious pocket, and approaching the toilet tables, amused himself by removing from them the wigs, gold pins, and other valuables with which they were strewn—whilst he did so, solacing himself with the idea that in taking care of such property merely for the sake of the rightful owners, he was only performing an imperative duty; for if people would lay their valuables about in such a careless mode, they were almost certain to lose it, and he was but performing a religious duty: for how often had less strong temptation lured youths, masculine and feminine from the paths of rectitude and honesty, and honour, to that which led to sin and Newgate. Instigated by these philanthropic and praiseworthy suggestions of his delicate conscience; it will be small matter of wonder to our readers, that Harry Sheppard stripped in something less than no time, the room of all the valuables it contained. Here it would have been as well, perhaps, had his performances ended, but being in a facetious humour at that identical moment, and having found on the lady's toilet table some false ringlets, and a box of rouge, he proceeded to the bedside of the sleeping pair, and succeeded in dexterously arranging the curls about the gentleman's head, at the same time, without awakening him, plentifully bedaubing him with the rouge in question, until he looked, if not like a red Indian, at all events quite as red a specimen of humanity as one would care to meet. Here any reasonable being would suppose his mad vagary would have ended. When, however, thrusting the lady's cap up the chimney, he brought it down crammed with soot; it was dirty in every sense of the word, but little cared Harry for that; taking it pinch by pinch, he so distributed it over the old ladies face, in dabs here and there, that she bore a likeness to nothing earthly, except it be a carriage dog, named from its skin "Spot," or a London made wooden horse. Here he was contented, and stifling, with difficulty, his laughter, with his hand, he stole from the room with the view of joining Jack Rann.

"Now Jack, be it kind even unto all, upon entering the chamber allotted to him for investigation, had found a room beautiful beyond description, and reposing on a bed in which, surrounded by drapery white as driven snow, lay a young lady sleeping. The glance afforded by the flickering night lamp Jack bore in his hand, satisfied our hero that the lady on whom he gazed was surpassingly lonely—was bewitchingly beautiful! And there was something in the exquisite cantaur of her matchless face; something in the sweet smile that played upon her vermillion lips, just opened to show the glittering pearl, they encased, that made Jack Rann's heart beat again; that made his breath come thick and heavy, and brave man as he was, that made his hand to tremble. He had seen that face before; but where, but where? But hush! her slumber is broken; she arouses. Peace be with ye, thou fond and faithful one, it is but a dream!—a *dream!* Yes! but in that dream her thoughts found words, and she murmured—

"Oh dear, dear Jack, my own beloved! and you will love me, will you not, even as I love you?"

Then the voice fell, then silence again reigned—silence broken only by the rapid beating of our hero's heart. But the sleeper awakes again, and clings to her downy pillow as though she clung to some one for sustenance and support. Her heaving bosom, whiter than the snow-white sheets 'gainst which they palpitate, heave and fall in the violence of her emotions.

"Leap the gate—leap the gate!" she almost screams.

Jack started from the curtain, behind which he had hid himself, and gazed with nervous eagerness upon the beauty before him. That voice, once heard, could it ever be forgotten? No! it was her—it was Miss Malcolm. But her voice again murmured—

"Jack, my own beloved Jack Rann—so noble, so generous, so kind, so true! forgive me for my ingratitude—I do love you dearly--dearly!"

Had every word been a dagger, and every dagger plunged into his body, the agony would have been less excessive than the pain that tore his very heart strings, as our hero listened to the ravings of the beautiful girl who lay stretched in beautiful sleep before him. For the first time Jack felt a pang that shivered his whole frame with all the panic and potency of an electric shock, that she should be so deceived—that he should be the despicable thief —the highwayman—the robber that he was: he cursed the strange fatality, that, instead of being in her father's house an honoured guest, he should be there as a disreputable thief! In the bitterness of the moment, he swore to renounce for ever the evil course he was pursuing. These thoughts were speedily dissipated, however, by the entrance of his pal, who observed in a whisper—

"Jack, my leary one, how goes it—how goes the swag?

Aroused from the painful reverie into which he had fallen by these words, Jack beheld his companion making particularly free with the contents of a jewel case.

"A string of pearls, by all that's glorious! A gold repeater—fancy my Sal with this buckled to her side! A locket set with hair—too light to be worth much; but however, every little helps, and so I pockets it. A lady's purse, with a few, a very few golden guineas in it. How fond the women are of gincracks—how foolish it is they don't carry their ochre loose in their pockets like reasonable beings, then they wouldn't stand half the chance of losing it. Pretty purse, though—wont Sal sport it at Bagnigge Wells, that's all. Why Jack, my eagle-eye, you must have been asleep and dreaming to have overlooked this haul. What see I, though—spell-bound by the sleeping beauty! Well, she is handsome, that's a fact, and if it wasn't for disturbing her, may I be shot if I wouldn't have a kiss at her coral lips;" and he advanced to the bed-side as if to carry his sacrilegious thoughts into effect. To prevent this, however, Jack seized him by the arm, and drew him forcibly back.

"Why Jack, what's the matter, man—are you mad?" asked Sheppard.

"Sane or mad, by heavens such insult shall not be! As you value my friendship, Harry—"

"As you like, my boy, and the rest in ha'pence; but see, Jack, what a glorious harvest you overlooked."

"Harry," said Jack, "I know this lady, and had I known it was Malcolm's house we were to rob this night, I swear by heaven I would have had no hand in it."

"Nonsense, chicken-heart, you should always think of your friends, or how can you expect your friends to think of you. You know her, do you? Lucky dog, that you are—I wish to goodness I did."

"You have reminded me of my duty, Harry—I will think of my friends, and with this end in view, I desire you will replace in this casket the pearls you took therefrom, and restore to this table the valuables you took from there."

"Go to blazes with you! Why Jack, you must have taken leave of your senses—you are decidedly mad. Such a loss to our community cannot be submitted to. What do you think Toby and the Jew will say?"

"What they say or do, I care not one pin for. I desire, I command you to replace that property."

"Demand is a word I could never comfortably submit to, yet from better men than yourself, Jack Rann, grand as it seems you fancy yourself, so as I have a little interest in the keeping of this property, I must even decline your wish. And see, our whispering is disturbing your matchless beauty; and having pretty well feathered our nests, it strikes me forcibly the sooner we make ourselves scarce the better."

"Harry, hear me—I have a weighty reason that yon lady should have no reason to think the privacy of her chamber has been disturbed, and I therefore implore, beseech you, by the friendship you have professed for me, to leave this place untouched."

"And go without this string of pearls? No, by the Lord Harry! Come, Jack, you are beside yourself to-night, and would regret having left these beauties behind as much as I myself should to-morrow morning. It is the especial duty of our profession so to manage as to make the night's work bear the morning's reflection; and any reasonable man neglecting such a god-send as this, would cut his throat with envy the next day."

"Your banter is excellent in its way, but it is ill-timed, is misplaced; for I swear to you—knowing, as I do, the least violence will be destruction to us all—that I will wrest them from you by force, unless you resign them peaceably."

"Do you mean that?" asked Sheppard.

"I do," answered Rann; "and if you dare me to the worst, I swear, as a living man, to carry my determination to the very utmost—to death itself, if you dare prolong the quarrel to such odds."

"I have a pistol in my belt, Jack Rann, a rather dangerous fact you seem to have overlooked."

"Not so," answered Jack, undauntedly; "for if the bullet that your pistol holds was this moment to reach my heart, its report, you are well aware, would sound your own death-knell!"

"You speak truth, but Rann, I swear by the living God, were it any other man but you, you should not dare thwart my wishes—I would shoot you like a dog!"

"Were it any other house but this, I would aid you to the end, and glory with yourself in the spoil reaped in this adventure; but a man is surely allowed some private feeling, and will not common honour alone induce him not to rob a friend?"

"Friend," echoed Sheppard, "I like the word. Catch yourself without a stiver in your purse—where would you find a friend then, if you have one in the world, you could rely upon for a sovereign? you are a lucky dog if you could—it's more than I could manage. Business, is business, my boy, and in trade a business man accepts no friendship, unless they tend to his own interests; so man, we are by profession duty bound to take them as they come, and on no consideration to allow business to clash against our interests."

"But in this case it is to my advantage to forebear, and I am determined so to do, once again therefore I command you to replace those pearls."

"If I do, why I do, but if I do, I'm d———d. No, no, Master Jack, because you have lost your wits, I see no reason why I should desert mine; quite tother. Come on lad, lets mizzle; Mike and Wide Awake will wonder where we have got to."

"I tell you Sheppard," said Rann, in a voice which showed his deep determination, " you shall not leave the room."

"Nonsense, Jack, my boy, don't be foolish, why hang it man, this bedroom swag is worth all the guineas down below—come on, I'm off."

Finding Sheppard was as firmly bent on retaining the plunder, as he was in its restoration. Jack, ever averse to violence, and more especially at such a critical time, had no resource to make Sheppard surrender but by main force. He accordingly sprang upon him as he was leaving the room, and dragging him back, Sheppard remembered, on the instant, Jack's skill, and his desperate determination, felt it would be madness to resist.

"Take your hands from my throat he murmured, I resign, you shall have your way."

And as Jack released his grasp instantaneously he advanced to the table, and restored the property piece by piece. The uproar caused in their quarrel, had the effect of waking Miss Malcolm from her deep sleep. A faint sigh gave token of her arousal.

"Your cursed noise has done it," said Sheppard; "we shall be nabbed—its all U P."

"Not so," whispered Jack. "Come on;" and, extinguishing the light, he led his companion through the door, and having, with extraordinary celerity, removed the key from the inside of the door to the outside, he securely locked it, and the pair descended the stairs cautiously and noiselessly. Once arrived at the landing-place, they found O'Brien and Wide Awake eagerly awaiting their arrival; the former of whom accosted our hero with the exclamation of—

"Why, Jack, my stunner, my roaring out an' outer, 'pon honour we thought you had evaporated—mizzled, like a shower of rain! As I am a descendant of Saint Patrick, I declare young Wide Awake exhibited the truth, and nothing but the truth. What the divil detained you, Sheppard?"

"Rann has amused himself by playing the fool above, but if he tries the game below, 'twill be at the risk of a dose of cold steel, or an indigestible leaden pill."

"I am unused to threats," said Jack Rann, haughtily, "and would as leave swallow your steel or lead as your threats; yet mark me, and heed my words, if you heed not your own life, die when I will, I die no coward!"

These words had scarce been spoken before a shrill whistle was heard from the outside of the premises.

"The alarm note, by heaven," said Sheppard. "Jack, what's to be done? the traps are upon us!"

"How know you we are discovered?"

"How know I! Heard you not that signal? By all that's good, we are caged, booked, lost."

"Does that whistle emanate from Toby?" he asked.

"It does," was the startling reply. "I should know it amongst a thousand!"

"We are indeed out-generalled, then; and nothing remains for us but a fight to the death. And hush! already are their feet ascending the accursed stairs—already come their discovering feet nearer and nearer."

"The farce is played out—we are lost!" said O'Brien, mournfully.

"Not so," exclaimed Jack on the instant, a sudden gleam of hope re-animating his darkening soul; "since one is doomed to destruction, why follows it that all should die? Having dared the measure to the end, I am desirous to test death singly, if by that daring the dark fate can be removed from you. Listen to me, therefore—as I guard this door, get you gone, sans hesitation, through yonder window."

"And leave you here to bear the brunt alone, Jack Rann? No, no, curse me if I do!"

"There is no other resource. Begone, I say—delay is death!" and nearer and nearer came the approaching footsteps. "Begone, I say—I will follow you."

"We shall lose all by staying," said Wide Awake, slowly lifting the sash preparatory to leaping through the casement. Quietly and expeditiously, one following the other, O'Brien, Sheppard, and Wide Awake, followed each other through the window, and dropped upon the casement below.

As our hero, laden with all the valuables he could find, was preparing to follow their example, the door was suddenly burst in, and three officers of police sprang with desperate eagerness upon him. One fell like a shot from Jack's skilfully directed blow, and already was the other staggering from the impetus afforded by Jack's vigorous arm, when by a sudden movement the stronger one rushed upon him, and our hero remained kicking his heels in the air, a desperate but hopeless prisoner. For a long time, with frantic eagerness, did Rann struggle to get free, but all was without avail. The chances of war were against him—he was a prisoner. The uproar and noise, created in his desperate capture, was just sufficient to arouse the whole house, and when Jack came to himself, after a period, he found himself confronted by the master of the mansion, and a whole regiment of shivering servants, who, upon the principle of discretion being the better part of valour, had not ventured to make their appearance until the prisoner was safely secured; then, indeed, when no danger was to be apprehended, their actions became bold enough, and their words, heaped in opprobious epithets upon the "atrocious willin," yet bolder still.

Daylight, by this time, came glimmering through the casement, and gilded all with its radiant light, as Jack securely bound, and yet more securely guarded, was conveyed to the presence of Mr. Malcolm. He was a venerable old gentleman, whose benevolent features and silvered hair gave him a benign and attractive appearance.

"And so you would have robbed me, eh?" he said to Jack, "bad man, bad man, you will come to the gallows."

"Robbed you," repeated Jack, undauntedly, "I believe you, old stick in the mud, I just would."

"Calls me old stick in the mud, like his impudence, the d——n scoundrel, the atrocious villain to amuse himself daubing myself and wife with soot and paint; the filthy scoundrel, you deserve to be hung sir, you deserve to be hung."

"It would be the worse for all of us if we had our deserts, old cauliflower; there's but few of us but would learn the Tyburn step of a dance upon nothing, and a kick at less;" said Jack undauntedly.

"And the fellow has the audacity to make a jest of death. Wake up, Mrs. Malcolm, wake up, Isabella, tell 'em to come and look, tell 'em to come, for we have captured a live robber."

"Tell 'em, old frizzle wig, if they want to see an honest man in disguise; now's their time. Why you'd make a precious sight more than you've lost, my old Trojan, if you was to take me to Smithfield and exhibit me as a live highwayman. Walk up, gentlemen, walk up; here you have a young gentleman caught at the fact of robbing an old gentleman, all as natural as to life, all for the small charge of a brown,—walk up, gentlemen, walk up."

"Why don't you invite me to see the raree show, eh! you aint half fly."

"The levity of this man, said Mr. Malcolm, is as ill timed as it is disgraceful, ah, come along me darlings he said as his wife and daughter entered, we have captured the thief, the same scoundrel, we have."

At the sight of the amiable and beautiful Miss Malcolm, Jack's face grew red to white, and from white to red again, whilst she, stricken, as though, felled by a heavy blow, sunk into a seat the very picture of surprise, anguish, and dismay.

"Papa, papa," she stammered, "there is some terrible mistake; this man is as guiltless as I am, he's a gentleman, I know him well."

"Know him, does you, Miss," said one of officers; "more shame for you, then, he's a prig, he is, it aint no credit to be acquainted with high tobymen that's a fact."

"I tell you, father," continued the young lady imploringly, "there is a sad mistake here."

"Not a atom, Miss, not a atom, cotched on the premises, and at the fact; no mistake, oh no, more t'other!"

"You hear what this officer says, my darling child," said Mr. Malcolm, "this man is well known to the constables, and having been caught in the house, there can be no mistake, my child, this man cannot be the one you mean. Take him away, officers, to prison."

"That sounds like business," said one of the men; "bring him on Peter."

"No, no, stop, I beg, I implore you," exclaimed Miss Malcolm, frantically, "I will answer for this man's innocence, with my life."

"He'll answer for it with his life, if he don't look unkimmon sharp," continued the officer, in Newgate dock, too, mayhap.

"Father, dear, dear father, do not let this cruel injustice be done to this brave, good, and generous, gentleman; I am indebted for more than life; it was his generous aid saved me from dishonour; it was his generous aid, his matchless daring intrepidity, that rescued me from the villains toils; he is innocent of this crime, father: he is worthy of your warmest, most devoted thanks! Oh, Rann, dear Jack, for God's sake remove this mystery; convince these men of your innocence, demand your freedom."

"So this is Muster Jack Rann, is it? werry good," continued the officer, "a warrant having been issued by Sir John Fielding for the apprehension of this here indiwiddle, I has great and pecooliar satisfaction in taking him up. Kim along Mister Rann, kim along."

"Father!" exclaimed Miss Malcolm, frantically, "I implore you for the love of God, to let this scene go no further — what, my generous deliverer, my gallant protector, to be dragged to prison like a thief, it is cruel, father— is bitterly unjust. Father, he is innocent, he is innocent!" and wringing her hands in her agony she burst into a flood of tears. But neither that of her father's entreaties joined to hers could induce the officers to forego their duty.

"He is a hinnocent chicken we doubts," said Peter, "but let him gammon us to that at the Old Bailey, that's the place for wirtue."

With this concluding remark, and without a word being spoken by Jack Rann, in support of his innocence so strenously insisted upon by Miss

Malcolm he was conveyed to the City prison, and there confined until morning, when he was conveyed to Bow Street, for examination, before the acute and sagacious magistrate, Sir John Fielding.

A crowded court was awaiting our hero's arrival, for already had the fame of his adventures been blazoned throughout the metropolis. His daring intrepidity also formed no unimportant portion of his fame, and the old police office at Bow-street was crowded with many ladies in fashionable attire.

CHAPTER XI.

JACK RANN FINDS HIMSELF AT BOW STREET.

Two days after the events narrated in the last chapter, Jack Rann heavily ironed, for the constabulary dreaded with awe his wonderous feats of strength, and his singular dexterity, was placed at the bar of the police office, Bow Street, charged in the first instance with the robbery of the Squire of Brentford, and secondly with the burglary at Mr. Malcolm's, Cheapside.

Our hero it was self-evident from his appearance had not been without friend during his short incarceration, for his iron's were decorated with blue ribbons, and at his breast he wore a magnificent nosegay. The matter in fact assumed more the look of a triumph than a trial, thousands of people being in waiting without, who rent the air with shouts of admiration at the appearance of Jack. Bowing composedly to their salutions, Jack was placed in the dock. The first witness called was the squire who both looked and felt unwholsome, the mob having in their admiration of the prisoner and the detestation of prosecutor favoured him with a shower of mud, stale cabbage, an occasional dead kitten, and such concomitants as might be anticipated from the remoteness of Covent Garden. He was called upon at length for his evidence, which was given somewhat after the following fashion—

"Now, sir, having stated you were robbed at Brentford, in a room full of company, by your own statement I suppose you have come fully prepared to swear that the prisoner in the dock is the man who committed the unlawful act?"

"Why, all I say is," said the Squire, "if it was'nt him, it was some one devilishly like him, but he was not the worst; it was the other fellow principally."

"Supposing it was him, as we are led by your statement to suppose, you yet acknowledge him to have criminated himself only in the minor degrees; now are you prepared to swear sir, on your oath, and at his peril, that the prisoner at the bar is the man who robbed you; look at him steadfastly."

"I am doing so with all the eyes I've got."

"What inference do you draw sir, is he or is he not the man."

"Well, pon my soul, now I come to look at him, I think him a devillish sight better looking fellow than the fellow that stopped me."

"A voice in court, in defiance of order and etiquette, here saluted the witness with the words: —

"Had'nt the fellow wot stopped you a pug nose.

"I believe he had," answered the squire, "look at that ere coves beak, do you call that a pug? why its a riglar Roman, no taint, it's a alkinine."

"I presume the fellow means acquiline," said the squire, "and come to look at Mr. Prisoner, 'pon my honour he has a precious sight better looking nose than that scoundrel Jack Rann."

"You forget yourself, sir squire," said Jack, "with a due appreciation of your phisog, I must confess I have never had the pleasure of looking at your ugly mug, and to tell the truth although its before a crowded audience I shouldn't care to look upon his like again. There's Shakespear for you old fellow; and if you can believe a man guilty of petty larceny, who admires natures greatest poet, you will believe anything."

"John Rann," said Sir John Fielding gravely, "I beg to remark that those observations are particularly ill-timed, you are standing now, sir, charged with two serious crimes, that nearly touching your life, demands your gravest attention."

"They shall have them," answered Rann, undauntedly, "for I am innocent of both, and that gentleman yonder, who, charging me with this crime, is making a fool of himself, and, in defiance of all justice, is endeavouring to make a culprit of me; knaves as well as thieves, that I am not the man— that is, the accusation is false."

"Do you think, knowing that, sirrah, I would bemean myself to come here to do you an injury; do you think me so unnatural that I would swear your life away? by heavens, man, you wrong me."

"Sir John Fielding," said Jack, "I desire, I demand, to be released from this charge; it must be evident, even to your worship, that this man is exaggerating, beyond all bounds of truth, his accusation against me. What tangible proof does he bring in court that I am a thief? why I can prove beyond doubt to the contrary that I was ten miles from the spot at the time the robbery was alleged to have been committed."

"Produce your witnesses," said Sir John Fielding.

"Your honour, had I time and opportunity, I could do so with pleasure, I can prove to you, beyond all doubt, my innocence."

"Witnesses not being forthcoming, young man, it will be my imperative duty to commit you to prison—you now stand committed for trial."

"Not so fast, old gentleman, "said a voice at this juncture, and an old man, or at all events old in appearance, placed himself in the space allotted to witnesses. "I am here, sir," and he gave vent to a wheezing cough, as f to prove he was asthmatic to a very desperate and dangerous degree.

"We will endeavour to dispense with your observations if you will but favour us with an explanation of your meaning, sirrah.'

"My meaning is simply this—I declare the prisoner, so ignominiously brought to this bar, was, I swear upon my oath, solemnly before you, that this gentleman was at my house at the time this robbery was stated to have been committed."

"At what time, on your oath, sir, do you allege the prisoner was at your house?"

"What time?—why from three to twelve, o' course he was. Why damme, he's a distant relative of mine, he is. He often drops in for an evening; and sometimes, if I bring out an extra bottle of champagne, the scoundrel makes a night affair of it—he does, by God!"

"And you appear here as an householder—can I rely upon your word?"

No. 16.

"Look at my receipts," said the other—"them's the coveys to teach you what's better nor we, nor worser than us—them's the bona-fide documents, sir, to prove to you, beyond doubt, that I am a respectable member of society. That, in fact, I am a householder—pay the king's taxes, God bless him; and acts, as every honest Englishman ought to act, as an honest man and a gentleman."

"The substantial proofs you here produce weigh greatly in favour of John Rann," said the magistrate, referring, as he spoke, to a bundle of receipts, which, on being handed to him, he cursorily examined to convince himself of the respectability of the witness. Satisfied, it would appear, by his examination, he said, "Rann, you stand absolved from the first charge."

"Thank your worship," said Jack, gaily. "I am much indebted to you, and dispensing with all further bother, will cut my stick at once."

"Not so fast, young gentleman, you have decidedly dropped into the wrong pair of boots," said a voice in the court. "I'm an important witness against you."

"Silence all," said Jack Rann, "for Sir Oracle's declaration."

"Now, witness, your evidence," said the justice. "Speak up."

"Well, sir, to begin at the beginning, as all tales ought to begin, I heard last night an hextraordinary row in our court-yard—fact of it is, your worship, my inside was out of sorts, felt queer like—grumbled like old boots, ached like blazes—I was in bed, your worship, and fast asleep, but this infernal disturbance in my unhappy internals kept grumble, grumble, grumble, until in fact I had no other resource but to hook it, in a style more pecooliar than pleasant, to a small affair, christened after Mrs. Jones, a werry convenient old lady."

A general grin being flying about the court at the fellow's observations, the magistrate peremptorily bid him cease his desultory chat, and enjoining the witness, at the same time, to confine himself to the plain facts of the case.

"Why, your worship, I thought I was a doing so, that's a fact," said the unhappy witness; "I did indeed. I tell you, sir, I seed that chap there," pointing to the prisoner, "clamber over the wall; I seed him help two or three covies over, and I saw him go in the house. As soon as I could, in course I hooked it; and, calling in the Charlies, why we fetched 'em on like old boots, sir, at the very fact."

"And can you swear to the prisoner at the bar is the man?"

"Of course I can," replied the other. "Why I seed him as plain as I ever saw anything in my life."

"Then, without doubt or equivocation of any kind, you are enabled positively and definitely to swear to the person of the prisoner?"

"I am, your worship."

"Nothing then remains for me but to commit you for trial at the Central Criminal Court."

In reply to this pleasant communication, our hero bowed with profound humility. As he was about to be removed from the dock, therefrom to be consigned to prison, a voice was heard demanding an hearing, and an elderly man forced his way into the witness's box, exclaiming, as he did so—

"I appeal against this judgment. I am Mr. Malcolm, in whose house yon gentleman at the bar is reported to have entered violently and forcibly, and with whom my blockhead of a fellow there seems to clash in angry opposition."

"I listen, as is my duty, for your preamble, Mr. Malcolm; but I am nevertheless, at a loss to conceive how you can reverse the evidence with sufficient effect to annul the judgment I have given."

"Having but a duty to perform, I do so my dear Sir John," said Mr. Malcolm who was on terms of friendship with the magistrate, merely to save from the ruin that threatens him, a respectable, reputable, and deserving young man; "I beg to announce to you, sir, without equivocation, and without exaggeration, that Mr. Rann, the gentleman placed at the bar, entered my house with none but honourable feelings, and for the services he has rendered me, I beg here publicly to state he has acted as a man, he has acted as a gentleman, that he has done me a service that to the end of his life will shed honour and lustre upon him; in fact, Sir John, he knows come when he would, he would have been a welcome guest, and coming opportunely as he did, Sir John, he evidently saved property which would have been otherwise wasted and destroyed."

"Your evidence is final and conclusive, and however strong the suspicion, and I confess myself still dubious upon the point, although I dare not doubt your evidence, I have the power, and I exercise it with the greatest imaginable reluctance, John Rann, to pronounce you honourably acquitted; you are free to depart, Sir, but before you do so, pray pardon a few words from an old man to a young man, from your gay appearance here to-day, I am positive, if not actually criminal you are advancing with the companionship of bad men; I beseech you as you have your own fair fame, as you value the purity of your own character, to forsake these bad companions."

"I thank you sincerely and kindly for your words, Sir John, that I will follow them I cannot promise, but that I will not lose sight of them I promise most sincerely, most faithfully."

I trust not, sir," said the magistrate, gravely, "had it not been for Mr. Malcolm's interference, nothing could have saved you from Newgate, and God knows, once in there, the distance is but short to Tyburn.

Profoundly affected by the few words so simply, yet so earnestly spoken, Jack walked from the police office, and to the dismay of Mr. Malcolm who accompanied him to the court, but to his own glorification, was aroused with shouts of, "Long live Jack Rann! Long live Sixteen-String Jack!"

CHAPTER XII.

O'BRIEN'S DITTY DEDICATED TO OUR HERO "WITHOUT HIS PERMISSION," ELICITS UNIVERSAL APPLAUSE.

JACK released from his perilous position, did not fail to avail himself of the first opportunity of making himself scarce; bowing distantly to the cheers of the enraptured throng, as he quitted the place he was borne by the delighted mob to a coach that was in waiting, whilst loud and reiterated bursts of applause greeted him at every step.

Conducted at length to Toby's residence, Jack Rann was there met by a galaxy of gay company, crack_men, hightobymen, in fact every description of prigs were there assembled, from the swell who could boast of the topmost round of fames ladder, to the more humble individual who did not feel above his dignity to gather an occasional stray handkerchief. All were there assembled to celebrate with boisterous joy our hero's safe return.

"Well, strike me," said Clayton, but you have met with a narrow escape Jack, I give you joy my roaring out-an'-outer, that you find yourself a free man once more amonst us. Give us your flipper my hearty,—give us your paw—may the devil admire us but right glad we are to see you."

Rising from the chair in which he sat, Mr. O'Brien making a profound salutation to the company—

"Gemmen, for the benefit of the company following—"

"Why I is jiggered, he's a goin' to give us a song."

"I is my boy, and the beauty of it is after my adventure last night, my composing my mind on the following effusion—"

"Hold your row, quiet you, O'Brien's song," his order for chorus was enchored right vehemently.

"Well, taint much, and what little there is of it I regret to say is borrowed, but howsomdever here we are—

SONG.

A cloudy night, and pretty hard it blow'd,
  'The dashy, splashy, leary little stringer,
  Mounted his roan, and took the—
                        Phililoo!
My Lord Cashall's on the tramp to-night,
Down with the lads, make my lord alight—
  Ran dan row de dow, on we go
      Ran dan, &c.

"You horrid wretch," said my lord to Rann—
    The dashy, splashy, leary little stringer—
"How dare you rob a gentleman?"
                          Phililoo!
Says Jack, says he, with his knowing phiz,
"I ain't werry pertic'lar who it is!"
    Ran dan, row de dow, on we go!
    Ran dan, &c.

Ve collard the blunt, started off for town,
    With the dashy, splashy, leary little stringer,
Horses knock'd up, men knock'd down—
                          Phililoo!
A lady's carriage we next espied,
I collard the blunt, Jack jumped inside.
    Ran dan row de dow, on we go!
    Ran dan, &c.

Jack took of his hat. with a jaunty air—
    The dashy, splashy, leary little stringer—
And he kiss'd the lips of the lady fair—
                          Phililoo!
She sigh'd a sigh, and her looks said plain,
I don't care much if I'm—robb'd again!
    Ran dan row de dow, on we go!
    Ran dan, &c.

"Bravo! Bravo! Bravissimo! I call it phizzing, I do, and show me the man who dare deny it?"

"Well done, my brave boys, but that isn't so well as me and Missus can do," said Sheppard, advancing, "look at us, now why we will actilly turn you off a duet, harkee here goes."

DUET—Sheppard and Sall.

Crissy odsbuds, I'll on with my duds,
    And over the water we'll flare;
Coaches and prads, lasses and lads,
    And fiddlers will be there.
There beauty blushes bright,
    The punch is hot and strong,
And there we'll whisk it, frisk it, whisk it,
    Skip it, and trip it along!

>   There's Charley Rattan, and natty Jack Rann,
>   And giant-like Giles M'Ghee;
>   There's Sidle so slim, and flare-away Tim,
>   And all of them doat on me.
>   Hadelgitha—platonically, Christopher!
>   But Charley, and Jack, and Tim,
>   In vain may exert their wit,
>   For still I'll dance it, prance it, dance it,
>   Flaring away with Kit!
>
>   There's frollicking Kate, and rollicking Bet,
>   And slammerkin Sall so tall,
>   And leary-eyed Poll and blue-eyed Moll—
>   Blow me, I love them all!
>   Christopher—platonically, Hadelgitha!
>   But Winny, nor Jenny, nor Sue,
>   Shall wean this heart from thee—
>   So thus I'll trip it, lip it, trip it,
>   Trip it with Hadelgitha!
>
>   The morning may dawn, as sure as you're born,
>   Will find us dancing alone.
>   I'll get a hack, be off in a crack,
>   An elegant Darby and Joan!
>   How'll the vulgarians stare
>   As they see you sportingly?
>   For none can splash it, dash it, splash it,
>   Crissy }
>   Addy } like you and I!

"Well, I don't think much of that duet," says Wide Awake.

"No more do I," says Toby; "I've heard Jack and his young lady sing a precious sight better than that."

"Well," says Jack, "never mind about that—don't get quarrelling about it, I have got something that will answer our purpose much better. I have been to dine at a club to-day, in the west-end, and have done a little business. The company was very entertaining—"

"And very profitable, I hope," says Wide Awake.

"Of that hereafter," says Jack. "I have left them now, warm with wine, and nobly intent on robbing one another. Here is the list, their routes home are known to ye."

"Charming!" exclaimed Wide Awake "we'll wait on all of them on their return."

"You will find very pretty light work up to two o'clock, and then you will be wanted elsewhere," said Jack, "I have a scheme on hand, gentlemen. Adieu! success attend your endeavours till we meet again!"

"Oh! gentlemen," said Wide Awake, "as the captain says, Adoo! till ve meets again. And jolly good luck. And now my heart of gold, what's the go?—something uncommon slap?"

"You shall hear, Wide Awake," said Jack, "at the fashionable assemblies, I lately met a creature, beautiful as Hebe."

"Them cursed women, Captain, you have but one fault, but that I must say's a wopper—them precious women will be your ruin at last."

"No, no," said Jack "women are like trouts, we tickle 'em only to catch 'em."

"And a werry pretty catch arter all," said young Wide Awake, "well, what of this beauty, number one hundred and thirty-three?"

"She's an heiress," said Jack "and I thought it possible she might have been sentimental enough for a trip to Gretna; but found, that though she was fond of flirtation, she was too wary to be caught that way. Her father, too, hinted at family connexions.

"How disgusting!" said Wide Awake.

"In short, there was no marrying without proving my respectability."

"Vich at the present writing warn't quite——"

"Convenient—true," replied Jack. "Well, the lady's rich, and wont be mine: I have lost some hundreds, and a vast deal of time in the attempt for which I must have compensation."

"Of course; you're not going to give away your valuable time and energies for nothing, as old Mr. Colville—"

"Hush! don't breathe that name," said Rann. "With it comes back the thought of what I was, the sense of what I am."

"Oh, you've much to answer for," said Wide Awake. "You know it was you as seduced me."

"I?" asked Rann.

"Yes, when I cut away from London," said Wide Awake, "because master differed in opinion with me as to what was in the till. I came down to the country, worked hard for my living, and got a sitivation as footman and gardener in Mr. Col— in the old gentleman's service; wasn't I vartuous then?—Then I passed my innocent hours amid marigolds, batchelor's button's, asparagus, and spring onions. Ah! them vos happy days."

"Why, you sentimental rascal, were you not the first in my very boyhood to tell me of the revels of London life; to paint the delights of the "Dog and Duck," and pleasures of "Bagnigge Wells?"

"Werry good, I did so, to warn your young mind agin 'em."

"The nasty creturs!" said Wide Awake.

"I'm grown callous too; gold is the general worship, and gold I must and will have. You are the only man I can trust; for though you take from others what your wishes call for, you still have some heart left."

"Bless you, I am all heart, like a summer cabbage."

"In my assumed character, I visit Manby's house; you must accompany me," said Jack.

"Now don't," said Wide Awake, "If ever I had a failing, it is my cursed modesty;—I could no more swell about, and do as you do, than I could fly; and whether I could fly or not, I ask any reasonable creature to answer.

"You go as my attendant, my footman," said Jack Rann.

"I breathes again; for shoulder-knot elegance I back myself against St. James's Square, and ain't partick'lar if you throw the palace into the bargain," said Young Wide Awake.

"By going to the butler's room," said our hero, "you will learn the depository of the plate."

"Beautiful!" shouted Wide Awake.

"And you may gain guidance to the cash-box. Toby has his instructions; at a given hour you admit him and our pals at the window from the garden; bind and gag the family—you know the rest."

"I do," said Colledge, "elegant gold watches, interesting plate, beautiful half guineas, a bottle or two of the oldest in the cellar, and good morning to your nightcap. There never vos anything half so pretty, since the crack for vich Dick vas topped at Tyburn."

"Your livery is above," said Jack. "You must go as my avant courier, and announce me. Wide Awake, prove your generalship this night, and we are made."

"Captain, I'll stick by you," exclaimed Wide Awake. "I don't know how it is I'm holder, and I think a trifle downier than you; but somehow, I never can go it as you do; but the side o' you, captain—"

"Your spirit is rebuked, as it is said Marc Antony's was by Cæsar!" replied Jack Rann.

"Marc Antony and Cæsar—was they in our line?" asked young Wide Awake.

"Somewhat!" exclaimed our hero. "One lost all the world for a woman—"

"That's exactly like you, captain," shouted young Colledge. "And 'tother chap?—"

"Twice refused a crown."

"That's not like me," said young Wide Awake. "Many bad things has been said of me, but I defies the malice of my enemies to say that I ever refused a crown, or half-a-crown either."

A loud cry of joy burst from the company after they had heard the conversation which transpired between Jack Rann and Young Wide Awake, more especially from Sheppard, who, although possessed of every manly virtue, was, when business interspersed its ugly form, but little prone to sentimentality, or to admire innocence; he then immediately turned the conversation to another robbery which had been planned by Jack Rann.

Is the work done?" says Jack.

"In a workman-like manner. Sich a swag!" said Sheppard.

"Then come away lads, there is more at hand: to their respective homes there are but two roads. Mark me, lads, no violence," exclaimed Jack. "This is a freak as well as a hustle. Dick, plant yourself up the lane, and keep watch. I go on one enterprise, and alone."

"Alone?" asked Sheppard.

"Yes—some one I would meet privately.

"Them cursed women will be your ruin at last! Jack mark my words," said Sheppard.

"There is no woman in the case, this time, Harry, my brave pal, so you are for once out of your reckoning; listen, my boy—after a week's idleness, since my bagatelle at Bow Street, I ventured to-day to a club-room, at the West End, who should I meet there engaged in play, but Brummell, the celebrated Beau, and his friend the bounceable and ferocious Major Hanger. There were several others there, and for barefaced robbery, for consummate impudence, I would match them against any gang of thieves in London. Thinking they had got a flat, they induced me to play, which I did, with well feigned reluctance: they plucked me to the tune of five-hundred pounds."

"Five hundred pounds? phew!" said Sheppard.

"Mister Rann, Mister Rann," said Colledge, "I regret to perceive you carry out the old adage."

"What's that," inquired our hero.

"That fools and their money are soon parted."

"I tell you what it is, young chick," said Rann, seriously, "you were bragging about being older and downier than me, just now."

"Vell, ain't I," said Wide Awake, apologetically, "only knowing you knew old Mr. Colville and his pretty daughter, Mary, I thought there was no harm in a joke."

"Silence!" thundered Rann, "have you dared to desecrate that name in such a place as this ?"

"Miss Mary Colville, who the devil is she ? any one I know," asked Sheppard of our hero, privately.

"No, Harry, she is a lady whom you have never seen, but whom, if fortune be but favourable to us this night we shall all scrape a rich acquaintance with."

"But hang me for a fool if I understand it now," said Sheppard testily; "how the devil is it you have admitted that mimicking conceited young Wide Awake into your confidence, and have excluded myself; damme Jack, as your first friend, it is barely correct. Since your discharge at Bow Street, a whole week has been added to the calendar of old Father Time, and save and excepting young Colledge who seems, by some strange means, to have gained a sovereign hold on your affections; not one of us, up to this blessed night, have had a chance of a confab with you."

"It is explained in a few words, my pal, but this is neither time nor place for the revelation, suffice it when I say I have had a strange and wonderful adventure; that I have picked up a sweetheart, made an offer of marriage, should have been accepted and spliced ere this, but the father, an old magistrate, a shrewd old codger, has insisted upon seeing my title deeds. The night has arrived for me to show them; Wide Awake will make a dashing flunkey, he shall go down and prepare them for my coming: of a hearty welcome I am certain, and, in short, as the old reptile won't give me his daughter, I must content myself, as old Moses would say, with 'hish monish and plate.'"

"And the better bargain of the two, I'll take my oath. Curse the women, say I, with all my heart; you never new a ball at Tyburn but some cursed woman caused the dance."

"I have every faith in the fair sex."

"So have I; faith in their faithlessness, the jades," said Sheppard, bitterly."

"If such be the case, how comes it you cling so steadfastly to your Sal ?"

"Oh she is a stunner, she is," said Sheppard; "if she wasn't, I'd have sliced her wizen long ago."

"I am glad to hear it, for I want her services to-night."

"The devil you do, Mister Jack Rann," said Sheppard, with a knowing leer, and performing certain derisive evolutions with his fingers which are familiarly known as "taking a sight." "You want her, do you, you haven't enough of your own, worse luck, well you shall have her—over the left."

"Listen to my plans, my boy, and if you refuse me her assistance, then why hang it I'll abandon the idea : as I have before stated, 'twas at a club that I played that I lost five hundred pounds, but lost it, lads, only on the certainty of recovering it with probably five thousand to boot."

"Huzza! huzza!" shouted the gang.

"Whilst in their company, you will use moderation, gentlemen," continued Jack. "I represented myself as being the Count Chantrais,—a French gentleman. Our conversation chanced to turn upon highwaymen, and by a singular coincidence, upon the various exploits of your humble servant,—Sixteen-String Jack."

"Well," said I, to them, "I hear dreadful tales of dis robber, but I defy him to rob me, I never shall be rob in my life, dis be such very honest country."

"Oh, very," said Brummell, "very, is it not Major?"

"Decidedly; oh, particularly so," replied Hanger, both bent on fooling me, whilst I, I must confess, had still more unpardonable motives towards them.

"In La Belle Francais," said I, "vhen I travel, if de villens stop de vay, I say to dem I am Count Chantrais; begone vid you, or I vill blow your brain all to letel bit; dey don't stop, dey, vhat you call, run, bolt, mizzle."

"I don't know how they do it in France, but I'll bet that you'll be robbed before you leave England," said Brummell.

"Never! replied I, "I will die first!"

"Then you will die first, and be robbed afterwards," retorted the Beau.

"I'll bet you five hundred pound I'm no robbed to-night," said I.

"Done!" said Brummell.

"Done!" said the Major, adding, "though I agree with the Count, for I never was robbed, and I've been out in the darkest nights on the dreariest roads, in the hope of meeting the rascals.

"In the hopes?—Aye, hope deferred maketh the heart sick," said the witty Beau.

"Mind, having your pocket picked don't go for anything?" said the Major.

"No, certainly. For my part, count, I always carry my notes in my socks —my socks. In a hustle, one of a gang might pick one's pocket. The bet is regularly robbed on the highway."

"I should like to see the man that is bold enough to rob Major Hanger of his boots and socks," said Brummell. "It's my opinion, Count, that you are reckoning without your host. For my part, I am not the man to rush promiscuously into a melee, but I always drive a fast horse, and carry my notes in my left breast pocket."

"This you will believe, my boys, was the very identical information I desired, and am receiving, I made an excuse to leave them for a few hours, and drove down here on purpose to gain your assistance Sheppard—yours O'Brien, and you madam," said Rann bowing politely to Sheppard's Sal.

"I'm good at anything from a wipe to highway robbery, from tooral-loo to manslaughter if Harry's only with me."

"A little acting is all that will be required of you madam," and Jack advanced and whispered a few directions in her ear, at which she laughed heartily. "I leave the rest in confidence to Sheppard and O'Brien. While you are fleecing the major, rely upon it, I shall be waiting with due attention upon Beau Brummell.

"Captain," said Toby, advancing as our hero was about to leave the room, "I axes your parden, but the lades and gemmen present, are axing for a song.

Refusal, Jack knew was in vain, he therefore, tuned his pipes and sang the following."

A HIGHWAYMAN'S LIFE FOR ME.

Let moralists prate that to rob is a crime
That deserves, when it's done, to be punished in time,
You shall find I will prove the reverse in my rhyme.
       And, since robbing's the plan,
       Catch as catch can, and its
       A Highwayman's life for me!

The moon robs the sun of its heat and its light;
The earth robs the moon, which, of course, serves it right;
And mankind rob the earth, such a prig to requite
       Then, since robbing's the plan, &c.

Each cloud robs the sea, all its moisture to drain;
And the earth robs each cloud of it's booty, in rain;
Whilst the sea robs the earth of its treasures again.
       Then, since robbing's the plan, &c.

That the atmosphere's robbed from the flowers, you'll learn—
They depend for their life on its aid, you'll discern;
But the air of their fragrance robs them in return.
       Then since robbing's the plan, &c.

The miser himself robs throughout every clime,
And to heap up his riches robs youth of its prime;
One is robbed of his name and another of time.
       Then, since robbing's the plan, &c.

Death robs us of life in an unpleasant way;
And the grave robs all life of its troubles they say,
But the worms in return rob the grave of it's prey.
       Then since robbing's the plan, &c.

This, I think, is enough angry feelings to smother;
Since here I have proved, without much care to bother,
That throughout all existence we rob one another.
        And, as it's the plan,
        Thus to catch as catch can,
      A HIGHWAYMAN'S LIFE FOR ME!

    *   *   *   *   *

A more glorious moon never had shone from the heavens than that on which this portion of the gang sallied forth to rob the Major and the Beau—Rann having posted Sheppard in a hiding-place, and having instructed Sal in her plan of proceedure, galloped on to intercept Brummell, leaving the ferocious Major Hanger to the tender mercies of his confederates.

They did not wait long before the sound of a heavy footstep could be distinctly heard approaching them with a firm and regular military tread. He was armed with a stout cudgel which he ever and anon kept brandishing in the air with a real Tipperary twirl.

"Well," he muttered, as he came within hearing distance of the hiding places of the gang, "what d—d nonsense people talk, I have been on the heath this half hour; no one meddles with me—perhaps my sceptre frightens 'em, it's all twaddle, no outrages are ever committed in a place like this. Ah! the cry of a woman—hurrah! I'm in a row at last."

As this exclamation escaped him, a shrill scream broke the stillness of the night, and the next instant, Sal, without bonnet or cap, and in well acted terror, rushed completely into the Majors arms, exclaiming as she did so, in tones of heart rending appeal, "Save me! Save me!"

"I will," replied the gallant Major, "my darling, I will, where are the villains, tell me where they are, and if I don't drop this switch upon their cocoa-nuts, my names not George Hanger."

"The villians would have ruined me—have torn me from my aged father's arms and—and, oh villain you are one of them, I know you by that bludgeon—oh, mercy, mercy," and the hapless lady in the violence of her grief and fear, sunk into a heavy swoon.

"The divil take the switch," said the Major, throwing it from him indignantly, a movement O'Brien instantly took advantage of by creeping on his hands and knees from the hedge and securing it himself.

"Poor creature, she has gone clean off, I bear her hence—no, if I meet a body of ruffians whilst she hangs upon my arm, what can I do? best tarry till she recovers; she's very pretty, I am a queer cove myself, and have much to answer for, but it was never said of George Hanger that he insulted the lovely, or oppressed the weak."

"Ha! my brain whirls," exclaims Sal, "recovering, you are my guardian angel sent to save me," and with a movement of violent fondness and gratitude, she pushed his arms to his side, whilst O'Brien and Sheppard springing forward secured him from behind.

"Confusion!" exclaimed Hanger, "ha! you little cockatrice."

"Ha, ha, ha! old gentleman, you are caught at last," said Sal, laughing and brandishing the cudgel gleefully before his face.

"Scoundrels! Death!" cried the Major, struggling frantically to free himself.

"No, old genl'man, said Sheppard, " ve are not in the undertaking line it's no use resisting, 'cause ve has the persuaders. Von't you take a seat?"

"No, I don't want to sit down," roared the Major.

"Vell," said Sheppard, "its very orkard, but as I particularly wants you to sit, vhat's to be done. Show the gentleman to a seat Michael; make yourself contented Major, these ere little disagreeables vill occur in the best regulated families. Your vatch, very good, a tompion I presume. Your purse, vere pretty lose change—handy, very much obliged to you. Your snuff-box, embossed silver inlaid with gold, very good, will you have a pinch of snuff, sir," said Sheppard, presenting the snuff-box as he spoke.

"You villain," said the Major, " is it not enough that you rob me, but you must tantalise me as well. Curse you! every dog has his day, we shall meet again."

"I shall be particularly happy, I am sure, any evening you can make it convenient," said Sheppard.

"Your confounded impudence makes me laugh. Well keep your booty."

"Lor bless your hinnocent hart, vere agoin to it."

"And release me," said the Major.

"No thank you, ve don't do that sort of thing; besides ve ain't quite done vith you, vill you be so good—so kind—so obliging as to remove them ere boots and stockings o' yourn?"

"I'll be d——d if I do," exclaimed the Major, and he bawled loudly for assistance.

"How werry foolish to put yourself out, old gentleman," said Sheppard.

"Mike, wait on that gentleman, and help him off with his boots."

"These here must make it werry uncomfortable valking, Major. Allow me to offer you a drop of mother's milk. You'd better have a drop; it's a raw night, and you might catch cold."

"D——n!" exclaimed Hanger.

"Vell, if you von't you must, Mike steady the Major's nob, vhile I give him a sup of mother's milk. Major, I wishes you a werry pleasant evening, adoo!" and with a polite bow they departed.

"The villains have poisoned me, I suppose," said the Major, "no I'll swear it was cogniac. I'd have given five hundred pounds that this hadn't happened. Um, I was up all last night drinking and feasting of the best the country affords, at Dick Vernon's; to-night on the Heath, dosed with a highwayman's eau de vie. I robbed! I who have licked hundreds, all except Tom Bullock in our Newmarket row, I'll—'pon my life it's laughable—it's —here's good luck to the road; I've lost to the Count—five——"

He had hardly spoke the words before Brummell arrived at the spot in his horse and gig, having from want of knowledge or from the effects of an over dose of wine, lost his way.

"This is an infernal predicament, we are all wrong. I shall catch my death of cold—hallo—somebody—can nobody inform me where to find an Inn?"

At this identical moment our hero gallopped up to the side of the gig.

"Yes, Mr. Brummell," he said, I duly appreciate the honour of putting you on the right road."

"You are a gentleman, sir," said the Beau, with a bow of exquisite grace.

"I am, sir," answered our hero, with equal politeness, "OF THE ROAD, and therefore as a preliminary measure, am under the necessity of demanding your money or your life."

"Eh! oh! what? oh! you are one of those purloining fellows, are you; take away your pistol, I am not partial to bullets: come here's my purse."

"Many thanks, now sir, if you please, your watch!"

"My watch? there you have it, rather out of repair, but still going."

"Very true, now your notes."

"Notes?"

"They are in your left-hand breast pocket," said Jack.

"The fellow's a conjuror, as well as a robber," said the Beau. "There confound you."

"Shall I trouble you for your diamond ring?" said Jack. "I must have it."

"That ring was the gift of a lady, and come what may, freckle me if I part with it!" exclaimed Brummell.

"Enough, sir, a lady's gift is the property of a man's heart, and should be respected," said Jack.

"Sir, the lady and I are alike indebted to you."

"Will you take a pinch?" said Rann, offering a snuff-box.

"Thank you, don't snuff," was the reply.

"Some change, lest you should be inconvenienced at the turnpikes," said our hero.

"Thank you, you are very good."

"You will be polite enough to remain where you are for a quarter of an hour, sir, at the end of which time you are welcome to depart."

"You forget I have no watch."

"You can guess the time; make it a long quarter of an hour."

"But these incipient ruffians," said Brummell, alluding to Mike and Sheppard.

"You are perfectly safe with them. Allow me to assure Mr. Brummell of my profound respect—good night!"

And Jack with a bow was gone.

"The most gentlemanly vagabond I ever met in my life! That rascally groom of mine—this is all through him; the scoundrel ought to be buried alive! This is a most delightful situation! I tell you what it is young fellow," he said, as Mike cooly seated himself on the shaft of the gig, "if your master, or captain, whatever you please to term him, takes liberties with my property, I will suffer no common fellow to approach me" said the

Beau, applying the whip right vigorously, as he spoke, to the sides of O'Brien; "be off with you, you unmannered dog, do."

"All right, my tulip, but by the powers if you'd keep a whole skin on your body, I should advise you not to be so free with your whipcord. Harry?"

"Here I is. my wenerable," answered Sheppard, "jist a looking at this swell of a Major vhat's tied to this tree, he is a object! I say Mike, how dark it is, come here, I'm blow'd if it arn't beginning to rain."

"Vell by the powers then we'd better mizzle, eh, Shep, my stunner."

"Vith all my heart," answered Sheppard; he then advanced to Brummell and bid him "Adoo," with a profound bow, and the same exchange of courtesies took place soon after between himself and the Major. The rain now began to fall in torrents; he rubbed his eyes, yawned, stretched forth his arms, and shouted at the top of his lungs —

"Hallo! hallo! help, here! Hang it, I'm as cold as stone, and wet as a water spout. Hallo! again, help, I say!"

"My friend," said Brummell, dismounting from the gig and advancing to the Major, "do you know where you are?"

"Yes," answered the other rather peevishly, "without hat or boots, tied to a stump of a tree; come, untie us, Brummell, my boy, I see you've got your horse and gig left, and drive us on to some house, upon my soul I'm well nigh perished."

"Thank heaven they overlooked my penknife, or you'd have had a berth for the night, for to untie those knots would have been a moral impossibility. There you are my boy," he said as he severed the last rope, "now crawl into the gig and we'll be off at once.

"I need no second bidding to do that. Oh, Brummell, my friend, this is the demd'est adventure that ever occurred; we shall be the town talk, and yet after all, hang me if I can help laughing."

"The more can I," said Brummell, "the idea of the dashing Major being tied to a tree."

"Faith, its not half so bad as you, stuck like a fool on a heath. Oh, its glorious rich" And laughing in concert at the adventure, and with undisguised merriment, the pair drove on towards London.

Whither our hero had arrived a long time previously: looking round at the assembled gang, he missed the handsome face of his friend Clayton.

"Toby," he said to that worthy, "where is Clay, my boy?"

"Vere is he, cappen. Ay, that's the rub—he is in limbo, he is, sir."

"Good God!" said Jack feelingly.

"Its a lamentable fact, sir, I seed him in St. Giles's Round House not an hour ago with my own blessed hoptics."

"This is most unfortunate, for I wanted his services particularly to-night."

"Then I'm sorry to say, cappen, its quite impossible you can have 'em, but he sent his complements, and said 'if so-be you'd no objection,'" the plant wasn't to be nipped in the bud, I was to go wid you instead.'

"Well, so be it then, but his being lagged is ominous and cursed unlucky. Hold yourselves in readiness, you, Mike, and Sheppard, to start for Richmond directly. I will follow on with Wide Awake."

SIXTEEN-STRING JACK. 137

CHAPTER XIII.

AN ADVENTURER, COLLEDGE PERFORMS THE FLUNKEY, THE ROBBERY.

It may be advisable before commencing a narrative of the forthcoming freak, to give our readers an insight into the means which Jack had taken to ingratiate himself, as he had hinted to Sheppard, into the good grace of the wealthy and accomplished Miss Colville. The facts were briefly these :—

Jack Rann had encountered more adventures within the last few days than are frequently experienced in the course of an entire life, and it may be conceived that his reflections became strangely varied, when, after so much stir and incident, he once more found himself rambling in ease and safety along the high road by broad daylight. The situation appeared quite new to him ; he had recently been so accustomed to peril, pursuit, and excitement of every

No. 18.

description, that he could scarcely believe his senses when he saw himself passed by others without notice, and his appearance viewed with supreme indifference. But the change cast no langour upon his spirits, as few possessed a soul more open to enjoyment of every description than his. Bred to a country life, his heart expanded before every natural beauty he passed, and though the feeling produced was of that calm and almost holy description, which nothing but nature and her charms can impart, it, by a singular process of the mind, made him more in love than ever with the wild adventurous life he had chosen.

Jack continued his ride, leisurely and pleasantly. Now whistling in answer to some robin that hopped from spray to spray along the bushes, and now casting a delighted eye upon the pale and almost silvery sun that brightened without warming the air, and lit up the dazzling frost-work of the trees, while it strewed the ground with mimic pearls. "What would I give," thought he, "if in such a morning as this I could imitate the Free lances of old, and instead of exerting myself for the sake of a few paltry guineas I could lead a brave and devoted band against villages and castles, and free the vassals of the proud from bondage —the fair sufferers under tyranny from imprisonment, and plant the laughing tree of liberty wherever I went, as the cherished memorials of my foot-steps!"

So animated did he become by these reflections, that his volatile fancy insensibly launched itself into the gay regions of romance, and as Sue caught the tone of her master and quickened into a brisker trot, he waved his whip in the air, exactly in the same way that he would have done a good sword, had he really been in the position in which imagination placed him, and was careering along on the high top-gallant of his joy, when a man's hand suddenly grasped the breast of his coat, and his ears were greeted with the electrifying exclamations of "I apprehend you in the King's name!"

When a shot from some approaching enemy falls unexpectedly amid pleasure party, and exploding, spreads death and devastation around—the shock occasioned is not more paralyzing than that which now quickened the blood through every artery of Jack, and sent the burning tide full flush to his head, until it felt as if about to be shattered into atoms. But quick and sensitive as were his feelings, his spirit remained invincible; for though his heart bounded when first startled from its regular play in the cradle of its bosom, it in the same moment resumed that firm action which gave such regular movement to his pulse, and he felt nerved to oppose the most fearful odds. A single blow with the handle of his whip dashed down the arm that held him, and he concentrated his powers to repeat the infliction on the temple of his assailant, when a loud laugh brought him down from the castles he had been building in the air, and he beheld before him not an officer of justice—not any of the men he had robbed, but the laughing, roguish, and irresistible countenance of Colledge.

"Wide Awake!" "Jack!" burst from the twain, and then did the air quiver with a laugh so loud and so mirthful, that the very wind seemed to catch the influence, and rattle more gaily than before amid the branches which here and there struck across the road.

"Vell I never," cried Colledge, as soon as he could get his lungs into a decent subordination. "It von't be a bull-run as 'll ever nab you. A little harder, old feller, and you'd have broken my arm."

"I beg pardon," cried Jack, "but you'll excuse me, I know. A wise man never halts between a question, and when that question is whether to strike or wait to be stricken, you and I know what course to adopt."

"To be sure we does," said Colledge, "and I pardons the whack on account of the wisdom that moved the whacker. But, I say, whither are you bound, old chap!"

"Turn your horse, and accompany me for a mile or two, and I will tell you," said Jack. Colledge obeyed; and as the freebooters rode gaily on, our hero detailed all that happened to his worthy confederates.

"Vell I'm jiggered!" exclaimed the worthy, whose ears had been enlightened by the afore-mentioned account. "And so you are hactually agoing for to face those you have already bearded? I'm blessed if I must be out of this fun; so, vith your good leave, captain, I'll ride along-side of you all the vay, and fudge up some blessed lie as an excuse for getting admitted into the mansion of this Mr. Colledge, with you."

"Not so," returned Jack. "That face of yours is not so easily to be forgotten, and we should meet detection as soon as we entered."

"Vy, bless, you, captain," persisted Kit "no von saw more of my face than the tip of my nose."

"Hold your nonsensical tongue," returned Jack, with a laugh: "I tell you, you could no more keep your countenance, than you could keep your fingers from picking or stealing if you were locked up in the Treasury."

"Oh!" interrupted Wide Awake, clasping his hands, "Oh that the blessed fates would give me such a chance! But, vot makes you speak vith such double distilled positiveness upon the subject? My faculties are at a loss to understand you. Be quiet, you jade," he continued, chiding his beast, which at that moment made a stumble.

"I judge from my own feelings," answered Jack. "You will allow that I'm not a very likely man to open my mouth and cry here I be, when folks shout where's the thief?"

"It arn't probable," cried Kit.

"And yet, I declare to you," returned Jack, "that when I was in the crowd the other day, I heard my name tossed from mouth to mouth, I felt in such a whirl of confusion as to be fifty times on the point of saying it's me you are talking about. Besides which, every eye appeared to recognise me, and I began almost to feel as if there was a perfect understanding between the people and myself,—and that there was, in fact, no secresy about the matter.

"Vy, if i'd felt in that sort of vay," exclaimed Colledge, "I should have popped out summat as I should'nt, as sure as noses is noses."

"No doubt you would," returned Jack, "and it was with the utmost difficulty I forebore from doing so myself, and as you have not the self-command that I have, you would, I think, come off second best in such a dilemna."

By this time our equestrians had arrived within view of the wood crowned heights of Richmond, and Jack suggested that they had better part company lest Colville should happen to be out and see them together. "Yet," added he, "emergencies may arise to render it necesary for us to meet at some given spot, and as I have no knowledge of the place I can't tell how to arrange."

"Oh!" said Wide Awake, "I know the town well, and can easily settle that difficulty, in the new road going near the hill, is an out and out boozing ken where Long Jemmy and the rest on us have had many a roaring night. It's the sign of the Orange Tree, wisited by the Jacks-in-livery about the place, so you'd better make it your practice to go there of an evening and take a cool tankard over the news. You will not only by that means hear all the gossip of the conntry, but be in the way if I come down to bring you any intelligence.

"A capital idea," said Jack. "Alluding to a late feat of Wide Awake's then you will risk meeting the fellow you kicked into the ditch."

Colledge, however, assured his captain that he would so disguise himself as to render discovery impossible, and on the understanding that upon the third ensuing night they were to hold their first meeting at the Orange Tree, they shook hands and parted.

Sixteen string Jack was now once more alone, and having lost more than an hour in conversing with his old pal he made Sue quicken her pace, and in a short time reached Richmond Bridge.

The view around, above and beneath, was beautiful. Parties of pleasure were taking advantage of the fineness of the day, both on land and water, and the river was dotted with boats in every direction. Jack longed to exchange situations with the voyagers, and as he gazed upon a wherry containing a fat old woman and a girl, whose form rivalled in grace the swans that floated past, a barge which at that moment was shooting one of the arches of the bridge, came in contact with the prow of the boat, and by the concussion occasioned, jerked the younger female into the water.

Shrieks and cries of every description followed this accident.

The waterman could not swim, and the drowning girl could not even attempt to do so. The fat old woman threw up her arms, and the watermen threw down their oars, to imitate her example. "She's done for," exclaimed the toll keeper of the bridge, and "Poor thing!" was the exclamation of some gentlemen riding near Jack; but, beyond commiseration, nothing was offered.

Rann, whose whole nature glowed with generous impulses, was however not so apathetic; for, no sooner did he behold the state of affairs, than he once more put the power of his invaluable mare to the test, "Come, old Sue," said he, "now to try your hand at the water;" and with that he took the parapet of the bridge with a flying leap, and to the amazement of all spectators, dashed into the river. Both horse and rider were overwhelmed, and the foam was tossed above their heads, to nearly the height from which they had descended. But the gallant pair lost not their courage, and, on again rising to the surface, Sue laid her nose upon the stream like a water spaniel, and, though she sobbed with the exertion, ploughed her way in splendid style towards the drowning female. Twice did the poor girl disappear before her deliverer got within reach, and she was about to make the third and fatal descent, when Jack caught her by the long hair, which was now united by the wet into one silken web. A convulsive shriek of joy hailed his approach, and the maiden, as she neared the horse, flung her arms round its neck. As if conscious of the value of the life that depended upon him, the animal renewed its efforts, and in spite of the double weight it had to bear, cut across the current like a galley; while Jack sustained the arm of his charge, and in inspiring tones bade her keep a good heart. It seemed also as if the face was a familiar one, but time was to precious too be wasted in idle speculations; so he pushed for shore, and in a few moments had the rapture of holding one of the loveliest of heaven's creations to his breast in safety.

By this time the boat from which she fell had gained the shore, and the fat old woman, whose squalling had been mainly instrumental in attracting the brave fellow's attention, came up puffing and blowing like a grampus, with a waddle that would have done honor to the fattest Alderman who ever graced a banquet.

By the expression of her countenance as she came by, Jack gave himself up for lost: her eyes gleamed like bubbles raised in soapsuds, her mouth was opened like the receiving-box of a penny post office, and her nostrils dilated like the delicate nose of a tom-cat when he encounters a stray scent in his diurnal proportion of cat's meat.

"You hussey!" was her first exclamation, but that was sufficient to alloy the fears of Sixteen-stringed Jack, for it assured him that the fat lady's indignations was addressed against the girl in his arms, and not to himself.

"You jade!" she went on, " what business has a minx in your station of life to give way to airs of this nature, and frighten your betters out of their senses."

"I hope, good sir," she added, addressing Rann, " that you have not torn the tippet round her neck as you pulled her out of the water, for it belongs to me, sir, and I wouldn't lose it for a hundred pounds. I lent it, sir, and very sorry am I that I did it."

"If I have madam," said Jack with becoming gallantry, "I will make you a present of one twice its value. Is there no inn hereabouts, he inquired of the toll-keeper.

"There is no necessity for one," said the lady, "if you will follow me home, you will find everything required, and a hearty welcome! that is my home, sir," pointing to a handsome brick tenement, and my name is Manby; this young lady is Miss Mary Colville—her father is the celebrated lawyer, and she is my niece."

"Mary Colville," echoed Jack, "are you indeed that dear and valued companion of my younger days, who first taught me to read my mother tongue who first taught me what meant love."

"I know not what you mean, sir," answered the young lady, "but hush, for heavens sake, my aunt is absurdly jealous, and will give me no peace if you show more attention to myself than to her."

"I will explain myself anon," said Jack to his lovely companion, " in the mean time, view my exquisite gallantry towards this jolly old antideluvian," and approaching the old lady with the most musing advance possible, he proffered his arm. During this walk his brave Sue, with jetty coat, dripping and glistening with wet, was following her master like a faithful dog. Arrived at the doorway they were immediately admitted, and the ladies having hurried off to their respective chambers to change their dripping habiliments for dry ones. Jack found his way to a dressing chamber, and having had a hot bath, and being now habited in the dress then worn by aristocrats, he looked the very *beau ideal* of a perfect gentleman. There was a whole room full of company, to whom collectively our hero bowed with a grace peculiar to himself. His introduction having been effected, under the assumed title of Count Chambrais, he became an object of especial interest, even of morality, to the whole company for each seemed to strive to outdo the other in heaping praises and honours upon him.

But our hero had cared but for one, and that one was Mary Colville. Mr. Colville, an old inhabitant of Bath, had in Jacks younger days, employed him as an errand boy, occasionally by variation, and by particular favour allowing him to brighten the knives and forks, and to rub up, by dint of bad blacking and elbow grease, a polish upon the various members of the household.

Now Miss Mary Colville was an amiable, pleasing, affectionate young lady, of some dozen years or so, and pitying in her genuine philanthropy; the sad state of ignorance in which our hero had, as it were, been born and bred, she took the opportunity of every leisure hour that presented itself, of teaching him to read and write. In the charity that dictated this action, her father fully considered—indeed he admired his childs perseverence, and finding young Jack Rann a lad of unusual ability, he encouraged him to proceed up learnings steep ladder, by presents of fruit and money. By one single act Jack forfeited this patronage. Mr. Colville entering the study one day, found his daughter and young Rann, not following precisely scholastic pursuits, but indulging in an ardent kiss of love, which his young daughter was returning with childish eagerness and innocence at the time, although the young scapegrace had not at that identical moment either shoe or stockings to hile his precious leg. To dismiss our hero with a sound box on the ear that made his young head ring again, was the first action of the hasty Mr. Colville, to lock his daughter in her chamber was the second. It so happened that young Colledge, or Wide Awake as he was most appropriately christened was in after time a footboy upon the establishment, and carried an occasional note from Mary Colville, the heiress, to the young costermonger, Jack Rann, and *vice versa*. So, as young Wide Awake hinted in a foregoing chapter, Jack Rann and himself were old acquaintances on the ran-dan. It must not be imagined for one moment that Jack, in being re-conducted to his old sweetheart could forget the excellencies, and the luscious moments he had passed in the company of the lovely Miss Malcolm. No, the memory of them is widely impressed upon his soul, but Jack—dead and gone though he is, all honour be to him for it—had too sincere love in his heart for her to endeavour to gain his hand, and gaining her hand, has his own heart foreboded only to doom her to a life of trial and suffering.

Jack, as Count Chantrais, obtained so fine a footing in the house of Mr.

Manby, that he eventually made an offer for her hand. Brilliant as her future prospects looked in being suited to a Count, her guardian was too much a man of the world to suffer her to wed without having fully investigated the character, and fully satisfied himself of the wealth and respectability of the person; this scrutiny, in the present writing, as Wide Awake observed, "warnt quite convenient." Baffled in his aim, and having a mitigated contempt for the Manby's, Jack determined to have revenge, hence the proposal of the robbery. Young Wide Awake, arrayed in a sumptuous livery, having been dispatched to the house to announce his master's arrival it may be as well to follow him there.

As soon as Wide Awake was admitted into the hall, he said, with an air of haughty superiority:—

"I am the representative of the Count Chantrais, so lead the way to the guv'ner, old frizzle."

Now the servant, addressed with this indignified appellative, had been dubbed by his godfathers and godmothers with the interesting name of Theophilus, and in addition to his other excellencies, he was of a literary turn, that is to say, was given to romance and poetry. Ushering Wide Awake into the presence of Mr. Manby, he said:—

"This person comes from ——"

"Werry good," said Wide Awake, interrupting him; "I've the honour of expressing my master's ya—ya—a—respectable respects, and to say, he'll be here as soon as he arrives."

"And how is my valued young friend?" enquired Mr. Manby.

"He's as well as can be expected," replied Wide Awake.

"Well as can be expected!" said Mr. Manby, fancying, "the fellow means to be complimentary about his master's love. What, sighing, eh? can't sleep at nights?"

"Wery seldom does," said Wide Awake, "if you only knew how he suffers."

"His motto's 'All for love,' I presume," said Mr. Manby. "Well, Sir, we are all anxiously awaiting him; his presence will make quite a stir in this dull village."

"Why, he generally creates a sensation go where he may," said Colledge, "and if he don't here, 'tis a wonder."

"No doubt his company is courted, he is much sought after?" said Manby hazarding a question.

"A good deal," replied Wide Awake drily.

"I trust he'll arrive before long. Does he come by the private road?"

"No, sir," answered Colledge, "he prefers the hi'way.

"Well, perhaps he is right," said Manby "and if he used to it—"

"Oh, yes! we're both used to it: I travelled that road myself," said Wide Awake with a grin.

"Theophilus," said Mr. Manby to his footman, "make this person comfortable, and here, sir," he said to Wide Awake "is a guinea to drink mine and your master's health." He added to himself, as Wide Awake pocketed the coin without a blush or a bow, "confound the fellow! he's as stiff as if his master was the Prince of Morocco."

As soon as Mr. Manby was gone, Wide Awake put his hat, cane, and gloves into Theophilus's hands, and leaning familiarly on his shoulder, said "young man."

"Young man! He! he!" laughed Theophilus. "what a joke, what a venerable you is."

"Take me away, young man," said Wide Awake "and make me comfortable."

"Are you for the pantry, or the cellar?" asked Theophilus.

"Ve don't cellar," answered Wide Awake, "ve pantry sometimes, but not just now. That old chap, with the pepper and salt nob—he's the master. What a rummy old guy."

"Old guy! said Theophilus, "what cheek!"

"He's got the rowdy, hey?" queried Wide Awake.

"Rowdy! What's rowdy, I wonder?" asked Theophilus.

"Why, rowdy is," answered Wide Awake, taking out his purse to deposit Manby's guinea, "Rowdy's money."

"Aye, aye, I understand you now. Master's rich as Crœsus; but as the poet says, "What is gold compared to love?" Have you any poetic aspirations?"

"No, no, my perspirations are more in the eating line.

"Haven't you a taste for poetry?"

"Oh! poetry! I see. There's that little poem about a hevening's adventures."

"Evening's adventures! Oh! Young's 'Night Thoughts,' perhaps," queried Theophilus.

"Just so, beginning—" said Wide Awake, bursting into a ditty.

"The sky was all darky, and gloomy the night,
When daring Tom King at the 'Pigeons" did light

"I don't remember the lines; they must be in the last edition.

"Just so—it vos his werry last edition.

"Here comes the company: I'll show you to my room presently," says Theophilus.

"Do, my tulip, and we'll have a snug bottle together," said Wide Awake.

"And something better than a bottle; we'll enjoy, as the poet says, "The feast of reason and the flow of soul," said Theophilus as he left the room.

"How werry amusing that old chap'll be, when he's tied back to back with the cook," said Wide Awake; then examining the articles with the eye of a connoiseur, he continued, "Werry Good. A splendid haul; we are up to our chins in gold; good luck," and saying these words, he left to reconoitre further.

At this moment Sixteen-string Jack, in full dress, with Manby, and followed by two attendants, entered the room.

"My dear Mr. Manby," said our hero, "you do me infinite honour; my rascal has preceded me, of course. I came to take advantage of your hospitality, to throw myself into the arms of friendship, and fling myself at the feet of beauty."

"I am delighted to see you, my dear Count," said Manby, graciously.

"And how is the lovely Mary?—tell me, for I am in excruciating tortures till I know," said Rann.

"What, you are come, I suppose, with all credentials prepared to rob me of her, is it so?" said Manby.

"Exactly!" answered Jack. "To-morrow, when you peruse my old dad's letters, and see the plan of the estates here, and in Demerara, and Nova Scotia, and San Domingo, and Rio, and I really can't tell you where, you'll open your venerable arms, and say, embrace me, my son-in-law!"

No. 19.

"No doubt, no doubt!" said Manby.

By this time Miss Mary Colville was shown into the room, and with a blush that would have put to shame a rose, and with a warmth that showed how full her heart was of gratitude towards our hero, she advanced to welcome him.

"This is indeed a pleasure, my brave preserver," she said, "you are a thousand times welcome."

"I needed but a cordial greeting like that, to make me the happiest dog alive," as he pressed his lips respectfully upon the white hand extended to him.

The company now came pouring in, and having been introduced to our hero, took the station assigned them.

"Who is that tall young man?" asked Jack of his fair companion, pointing out the personage as he spoke.

"He is Captain Manby," answered Miss Colville.

"What, the son of Mr. and Mrs. Manby, here?"

"The same," answered Mary.

"How comes it then, my sweet friend," said Jack, "that in their cupidity of their grasping natures, they have not sat him aside to be the partner of your joys and sorrows?"

"Poor Harry," said Miss Colville, a tear glistening in each eye, "we were betrothed together and I believe he loves me dearly, but the more brilliant prospect of wedding me to you, Count, has induced them to thrust aside their own son."

"Curse them, I say, for their want of feeling. But do *you* love the Captain, Mary? answer me truly," said Jack seriously, "as you value your peace of mind for ever."

"Alas, Count, I did."

"It is enough," said Jack, in a whisper, "he shall be yours; I am not what I seem, Mary, and if in becoming what I am, I can relieve you from the thraldom and tyranny of an ill-assorted marriage, I consider it no less a duty than saving you from the Thames. Mary, darling, you are free."

"Oh my dear, noble, gallant, preserver, if you are not the Count, who are you, that I may know who to thank?"

"That you will know soon enough; I leave you for awhile, but will rejoin you again presently."

And saying these words, Jack left the room, and finding Wide Awake, the following Colloquy took place between them.

"Oh, governor," said Colledge.

"Hush! I've slipped away. Have you reconnoitered here?" said Jack.

"There's not a hole or corner in the premises into which I have not poked my observing nose. Oh! the plate!"

"Good?" asked Rann.

"Luscious! it warmed my heart to touch the wine coolers."

"And the cash?"

"That's the predicament—can't learn where it is no how. But put a brace of pops to the nob of old Tyewig and his dartar, and they'll soon split."

"No! no violence; I feel already some qualms at robbing him whilst enjoying his hospitality—and yet, why should I? It is not me that he welcomes, he worships wealth and rank, and would spurn a beggar from his door. Pity to him were misplaced."

"In course it is. Pity's always misplaced when it stands in the way of the rowdy."

"Caution will be needful; there is one in the house to whom we are known."

"Who?" asked Wide Awake.

"You remember Mary Colville."

"Yes!" said Colledge; "Them cursed women again! What of her?"

"She is here."

"Then we're as good as turned off."

"Not so. She has not recognised me yet; if I can but escape her, the family will retire, and all will go well. Be on your guard, she might remember you."

"No—I thinks not; I never went a philandering arter her as you did. If you'd been said by me—I told you long ago, when she talk'd of virtue and innocence and marriage, that she was arter no good."

"Wide Awake, my brave fellow," continued Rann, "be prudent, be circumspect."

"Lor bless you Captain, I'm as quiet as a mouse and almost as nimble, vy I've been making it righteous with old Shake-his-spear number two that ve've become quite warm friends, and as to the cook I've been walking into her vittles and her affection at the same time, Lor bless you its livery does every thing, I wish that cussed tailor had guv a cove more breathing room though —what with the vittles and drink I'm fit to burst."

"Talking of that," said Jack, "where are my habiliments, I must for the spree of the thing shake off the Count and appear in propria personæ as the play writers say—as Sixteen-stringed Jack the dashing knight of the road."

"Where's the toggery is it? vy Toby's got e'm outside," said Wide Awake.

"Vy I let him into the vash house myself half an hour ago, Sheppard in the copper, and Tobys tucked up in a dry vater butt. My eyes ain't he cramped up for room neither!"

"I will soon release them from their misery."

"Oh don't distress yourself captain" they ain't at all molowcholic, only see one polish the bone of a luscious bit of lamb as iver cried bah! and tothers got some decent pickings at a weal and ham pasty."

"Good" said Jack "there is nothing like attending to the inner man. I must go back or the company will miss me and marvel at my absence."

They'll marvel a precious sight more at your presence presently captain or I'm out of my reckoning, said Wide Awake, "but vy'll you're pitching them the blarneys what shall I be at, can't I do nuffen."

"Yes, said Rann," you know that closet by the drawing, room door?"

"Perfectly well," answered Wide Awake, "I took the liberty of borrowing two or three silver wine labels from there," and he exhibited the plunder as he spoke, "very better trinkets and rayther valuable."

"Can without being dicovered introdnce Toby and Sheppard into that closet."

"Of course I can, they are all busy down below cooking up the vittles; Oh my eyes, such a tightener!"

"Let them take my change of apparel with them," said Rann, "and wait there all three of you, noiselessly and patiently, until I join you, then my boy for a brave harvest, I must now begone—be ye cautious, be ye vigilant."

"Von't I, that's all," said Wide Awake.

Jack Rann now returned to the company he had left.

"My dear Count," said Miss Colville, who, if her welcome before was hearty, now greeted him with a perfect rapture, "we have missed you greatly, where have you been?"

"To settle the preliminaries of a farce, dear Mary, that shall for ever free you from the importunities of the Count Chantrais and other adventurers of his class, and shall place you sooner than you expect in the arms of your loving, pining, moping, poor devil of a lover, there. By-the-bye I should like a word with that self-same Captain Manby."

"Should you Count—I will fetch him to you instantly," and almost as quickly as we have written the words, the gallant young soldier stood beside our hero. "Your hand!" said Jack, frankly extending his as he spoke. "Nay!" he said, as the other hesitated, "I have your happiness nearer at heart than you imagine, therefore, why treat me so churlishly?"

"I beg your pardon Count, pray pardon me my stupidity, I am not myself to-night."

"Listen to me my fine fellow," said Jack, drawing him aside so that they could converse without the danger of being overheard; "you love Miss Colville, nay, never deny it man, she is worthy your attachment were it twenty times as devoted as it is. Now, I do not love her—I am not worthy of her."

"Count, you astonish me!" exclaimed the captain.

"I repeat again, I neither love her nor am worthy of her, and I therefore resign her into your hands unconditionally. I will withdraw in a manner that shall leave you the honourable master of the field, all I require of you is a pledge, that let what will transpire, you will aid and abet neither party; I of course refer to your father and myself. He will doubtless lose money by his grasping cupidity, but what care you if you gain a bride, and one as lovely as Hebe, and as rich as a princess!"

The young man eagerly gave the desired promise, and in addition swore firmly to aid and abet our hero in any design he might have. This conversation had barely terminated before a door opened and an elderly woman muffled in a cloak entered the room.

"Who is this old fellow?" asked Jack, of Manby.

"This is old Mr. Colville, Mary's father, a man who is unnatural enough to confide his only daughter to the care of strangers, and has even promised to give my father twenty thousand pounds if he will get a husband for his daughter; the fact is, he fancies it would be a stepping stone to the peerage."

"Now I perceive the drift of your father's proceedings. Well, hang them for a brace of scoundrels, say I, they both deserve to be bit, and," he added significantly, "both shall be."

Mary had hurried forward to greet her father.

"My dear papa," she said anxiously, "how very very late you are."

"Am I," grunted the old man, "well, I don't suppose I should be so late if I could help it. We have had some important business in town, to-day, very important business, in fact have captured a highwayman."

"A highwayman," cried the listeners in a breath.

"Yes, a highwayman," continued the old lawyer, "and that ain't all we've—that's myself and Sir John Fielding—have found some papers in his possession, that implicate other parties, nearly. You remember reading in the papers of the robbery of the squire, and a whole room full of company, at Hounslow. You remember the rumour of the Robbery of the Earl of Dashfield?"

"Yes," they all answered in the affirmative.

"Well, it appears this fellow we've got, and another calling himself Sixteen-string Jack, the fellow examined and acquitted at Bow Street a few days ago, were the audacious scoundrels who performed both feats."

"Bless my soul," said the fat old lady raising her hands and eyes to the ceiling, "the roads ain't safe at all, are they?"

No notice whatever being taken of this interrogation, the lawyer proceeded with his narration.

"Well, and what think you of the audacity of this Sixteen-string Jack, what feat think you he had performed. Come, you must guess."

Leaving them guessing the most extravagant feats, Jack slipped out, and hurrying to the closet where Sheppard, and Toby, and Wide Awake, were getting impatient and restless, he drew from his boots, wherein they had been hid, the famous Sixteen-strings, and hastily habiting himself in his scarlet riding coat, thrusting a brace of pistols into his belt, he bid his pals follow him, and hurried towards the drawing-room; they reached the door just as Mr. Colville was repeating his question, finishing with "come, they are two of the most celebrated men we have, can none of you guess it, come here's ten guineas for the one who cries correctly."

"I claim the reward," said Jack, throwing the door open, and stalking into the room. The women shrieked from fear and astonishment, the men turned pale and held their breath from the same causes.

"The men on whom Sixteen-stringed Jack did himself the honour of waiting, this evening, are known to the world, as much for their follies and vices as by their respective names, which are, Sir," he said, bowing to Mr. Colville, "Beau Brummell, and Major Hanger."

"You are right, fellow, here is the money, now answer me one question, how came you to hear of this robbery."

"How com'd he to hear on it! Vell that's rich! Vy old Cauliflower vhat a hinfant you is," said Toby sympathetically.

"To tell you the honest truth, I should certainly not have heard of it if I had not been on the spot."

"Who, and what are you then, sirrah, I demand to know?" said Mr. Colville, rising.

"I have the honour to be Sixteen string Jack, your very humble servant, and at your service, Sir."

"Call up the servants, let's capture this audacious robber!" shouted the old man.

"The man who moves one step, dies!" said Jack, sternly, and in a tone that set all the women fainting, and all the men shivering, with fear. "The least noise will prove certain destruction to whoever makes it, we want your money, not your lives, but if the worst comes we will have both, rather than resign our plunder ; therefore you will know how to act. Tobias, wait upon that old gentleman."

"Certney, Captain. Now my wenerable, shake your ancient fakultys together. Shove your hands into your breeches pockets, and show us the colour of the rowdy. Werry good," said Toby, as he complacently received the old gentleman's valuables, and deposited them in his capacious pockets. Much obliged to ye, sir. Adoo!" and he made the old lawyer a profound salutation.

"Now, Sir, if you please, don't hurry marm, don't hurry, I'll wait upon you next," continued Toby, turning to Mr. Manby ; "I'll jest trouble you if you please."

Mr. Manby resigned all the valuables on his person even to his diamond buckles, without a murmur, but with many a groan. From him, Toby, pistol in hand, waited upon Mrs. Manby. This fat old lady seeing the disastrous state of affairs had slipped from her portly waist a diamond brooch of enormous value, and placed it beneath her, forgetting it would appear the article of ornament, was attached to dresses by means of a sharp pointed pin. Certain, however, it is that waddling her porpoised body in her agitation she found the point of the brooch with a latter part of her portly person, and that was'nt all, for the pin it would appear, in a style more sharp than pleasant, also found her, for up she sprang with a bound and a shriek. This movement was carefully noted by Toby who began immediately to moralise over the vanity of womankind, and turning her round to the company previous to remarking the article he requested to be informed vether that vas'nt a pretty place to vear a brooch."

Whilst this little adventure was occupying the attention of one portion of the room, Wide Awake was busily employed removing all the valuables he could lay his hands upon, and, seemingly, not in the least particular where they came from, so that they did come. Alarmed by the shriek of his mistress, Theophilus, the poet, entered the room."

"Vell done old dot-an'-carry-one, the werry cove I've been praying for ; I say, old fellow, do you want your throat cut? eh ;" and Wide Awake drew a knife in a very sanguinary-like style.

"Heevings forbid!" said Theophilus ; "I have'nt got a fancy that way no how ; put up your bleeder, Sir ; I arnt got a fancy for knifes no how, they is so very cutting."

"Werry true," said Wide Awake, has I shall in a few short and easy lessons, exemplify on your wizen if you don't——"

"What?" exclaimed Theophilus, with a start.

"Stow your patter, and toss me the key of the plate chest, old cauliflower."

"Key of the plate chest," cried Theophilus, panting with an amalgamation of fear and astonishment, "what does he mean, oh master, oh missus, I fears we've been a harbouring no genuine gemmen after all, but a common disreputable himposter."

"If you call me an imposter, you vagabond," said Wide Awake, pressing his knuckles deep in the poor wretches throat, "I'll spifflicate—I'll show you I aint an imposter, I will, I'm a gemman of the road—damme!"

Poor Theophilus on hearing these dreadful tidings, sunk down a shivering heap upon the floor, a truly wretched and pitiable object. Administering a sharp kick with his boot in his utter scorn at the fellows cowardice, Wide Awake turned from him with a look of unmitigated contempt, muttering as he did so—

"Oh, Shake-his-spear number twenty-two, vere his thy soul?"

"Curse his soul," said Toby, "vere's the key of the plate chest, that's the article ve vants, eh, my tulips, vere's the key of the plate chest?"

Our hero had, with his usual condescension and politeness, been waiting upon the various individuals present, and having received their cash and jewels with a politeness peculiarly, to his own, he turned to the last couple remaining untouched, which were Captain Manby, and Miss Mary Colville. To the former, addressing himself first, he said, as the latter in his indignation at the despoilation of his fathers home was about to draw his sword and rush upon them.

"Steady young sir, put up your skewer, unless you'd have a bullet from yon fellows pistol, crashing through your brain. Resistance is in vain."

"It is worse than madness, Edward," shrieked his mother, "the villains are armed to the teeth, pray, for heaven's sake desist."

"Your mother counsels well for the first time in her life. Pray put up your sword, sir. In taking these baubles, and purses, and what not, which these good people have resigned to the victorious arm of Sixteen-string Jack, let me congratulate you, sir, that you have saved from the toils of a disreputable adventurer, a young and lovely lady, and by the loss of a few trifling gewgaws, have won for yourself the priceless blessing of a loving and a virtuous wife.

Astonished at the words uttered by our hero, and reminded of the happiness conferred upon himself by the candour and generosity of Sixteen-string Jack, he frankly extended his hand, which Jack frankly received, and a hearty pressure was the result.

Turning from Captain Manby, to Miss Colville, Jack said with a smile—

"Sixteen-string Jack is under the necessity, madam, of requesting a slight token from you, that he swears religiously to prize as a momento of the happy hours passed in your sweet company."

Miss Colville without hesitation, drew a valuable diamond ring from her finger and presenting it to our hero, said, her eyes the while filling with tears as her tongue found the words—

"Take it, beloved friend in welcome, not only indebted to you for life, but also for a life's happiness," and she clung the closer to the gallant young officer whose arm now encircled her waist, "pardon me I pray you, if, as a sister, I give you a few short words of advice."

"A blessing on the kind heart that would dictate the words," exclaimed Rann, "but lady the words would be scattered and wasted as chaff before the wind. Lady, Sixteen-string Jack has entered so far on the path of crimes, loves so dearly the highwayman's adventurous career, that nothing can turn him from the path he is pursuing, can reverse his determinations. Words would be lost upon me, but nevertheless," said Jack, with emotion, "I shall ever hold in my breast a feeling of gratitude for the sisterly kindness that prompted them."

Turning to his pals he said: "Comrades, we will reserve the plate chest for a future occasion, having sufficiently enriched ourselves with gold, thanks to these gentlemen and ladies—we will not burden ourselves with anything so common as silver."

"Werry good," said Toby.

"I can't submit myself to anything like hard work to-night, so I votes old cauliflower there be empowered under our sign manual to take partic'lar care of the plate for us till ve calls agin."

"Yes, you scoundrel, I will," said Mr. Colville in a foaming rage, "I'll take good care to put it in the Bank of England."

"Werry good, our compliments to the Guvner and Board of Directors, and ve'll do ourselves the honour of calling for it this day veek."

"Yes, you scoundrel, and if ever I catch sight of you again, my man, I'll clap you in Newgate," said Mr. Colville.

"Much obliged to you," said Wide Awake, "happy to meet you agin, Sir, only mention time and place, anywheres 'twixt Lombard Street and the Old Bailey vill suit me to a capital T."

"Begone, scoundrels," said Mr. Manby.

"No harsh words, my wenerable, or I'll black the vite o' your eye. Capten, vhats to be done vith this ere interesting congregation; tie 'em neck and heels?"

"If you are the Captain of these men," said young Manby to our hero, "if you will withdraw your men without further violence, I pledge you my word, as a soldier and a gentleman, I will guard this room for one hour, and not suffer any one to leave it during that period with a view of pursuing you."

"I accept your pledge, Sir," cried Rann, "gentlemen and ladies, the high and noble Count Chantrais, alias the infamously celebrated highwayman, Sixteen-string'd Jack, respectfully bids you farewell."

"Adoo! adoo!" said Sheppard, "the best of friends must part, although at such interesting periods as this it is enough to break one's heart."

"Good bye, Theophilus," said Wide Awake to that unfortunate wight, who from lack of courage had not yet risen from his recumbent position, "farewell my blooming cauliflower! If you should write a copy of verses on this here event, don't forget to dedicate it to your friend of the bottle."

"Enough!" said Rann at this juncture, "time flies; that is, *tempus fugit*, as we say in the classics, he added bowing to the company to whom he wished a fair good night, and turning to his comrades as he strode away, shouted gaily and gallantly, "HURRAH FOR THE ROAD."

They were to horse in an instant, and in something better than an hour were safe from pursuit in Toby's stronghold at Westminster.

CHAPTER XIV.

JACK MAKES UP HIS MIND TO VISIT CLAYTON IN NEWGATE.—OUR HERO'S HEROIC DETERMINATION.—A GLORIOUS ESCAPE.

TOBY had announced to our hero that Clayton had fallen a victim to the long and strong arm of the law. Toby had visited him in St. Giles' Round-house. From thence the brave Clayton was conveyed to Bow Street, and examined before that indefatigable magistrate, Sir John Fielding, and was committed to Newgate to take his trial for the robbery of a farmer at Hogsden. This audacious act, committed in broad daylight on the very day Jack had planned the fleecing of Brummell and Hanger, was discovered. Clayton rode for his life, but being mounted on a wretched hack, and the patrol who were pursuing him having splendid horses, he was speedily overtaken and conveyed to St. Giles' Round-house, then the largest and strongest watch-house in London. Here Clayton, after Toby's visit, found himself an object of unprecedented popularity, for immediately after the robbery of Brummell so great was Jack's popularity, that five hundred pounds was offered for his apprehension.

It must be here mentioned, that the joskin wiseheads had, from the moment of their capture of Clayton, considered him to be no other than the renowned hero of the sixteen strings himself; and Clayton, thinking that the mistake might do him some good, and also being proud of the honour of being taken for his leader, never once offered to contradict the rumour.

The city of London, completely staggered at the fresh outbreak of Jack and his gang, whom they considered to have been entirely dismayed, and intimidated by the high rewards they had offered for Jack's apprehension, sent two of the most learned and skilful judges on the criminal bench to try him, in order that he might not escape through any imperfect indictment, or quibble of law. To secure, also, the more peaceful and safe conduct of travellers on the highways throughout the kingdom, a private act of parliament was drawn out, read, and carried in three nights, for the organization of an efficient and vigilant horse patrol throughout England, who were to be well armed, and each man had five miles of road apportioned out to him, with stations where relays of men and horses were kept; so that on immediate alarm of a robbery, a pursuit might be commenced that must end in the capture of the depredators.

The capture of Sixteen-stringed Jack, and his safe lodgment in the jail, which soon found believers, was the topic of conversation in every tap room, coffee-house, hotel, or even private fireside in the kingdom; and the day being fixed for his trial, the town was fast filling to excess. Beds were being let at a guinea a night; apartments of two rooms at ten guineas a week, and seats in the sessions house to the amount of 2,800*l.* were already engaged from five to twenty guineas each, according to the position. And it is a notorious fact, and well worthy of mention here, as a humble evidence of the taste of the aristocracy of that day, that out of the number mentioned above, more than two-thirds were nobles of title, and ladies of high rank and degree!

It was on the morning before the day of trial, that Jack convened a meeting of the gang at the retreat, where he met the whole gang to debate upon the best steps that could be taken to save their companions neck. Jack took the chair, and finding no one ready to come forward with a plan, offered the following:—

"My jolly pals!—one of our number, as brave and as true a bit of stuff as ever snapped a pistol-lock at a traveller's head, has fallen into fingers of the law, and unless we can do something to save him, he will fall a victim to the fate which awaits him, and the road will lose one of its brightest and bravest ornaments. Pity and compliments are of no use here; we are all equally guilty with him, and to rescue him every man of us ought to peril our lives. Of course you are all aware that the guffins take him for me, and think that they have squashed our whole gang because they have caged the leader! But I will soon let them know I have my liberty, and that I fear not periling my life to secure it. As I never yet proposed a thing to any man which I was afraid of doing myself, I am now going to lay down to you the plan I have formed of saving Claytons life. I mean to go down to Newgate this very night, and if gold can pick locks of that jail, as well it can of every other one in England, I will get him from his snare and take his place myself, and leave my life in the hands of fate to seal."

"You Jack; you take Clayton's place!" exclaimed a dozen voices in a breath.

"Aye, me! I have said it; and by all my hopes of fame I will do it."

"Hear, hear!—Bravo, bravo!" was the reply to this patriotic and noble-minded sentiment, by the whole of the gang.

"If I save Claytons life and my own, of course we remain as at present; if I save him and am grabbed myself, why, then he will be your future leader, and I shall die in the esteem and good repute of all true hearts in the world."

The gang finding Jack immoveable in his determination, soon separated for the night.

It was late in the evening when Jack arrived at Newgate jail, and having assumed his favorite disguise of a country gentleman, proceeded to try his luck upon the gullibility of the turnkeys. He knocked at the large iron knocker which hung upon the heavy iron door of the outer entrance, and the door was opened by a bluff-looking fellow, who demanded his business before he would let him put a foot into the prison.

"My business is very important. Can I see the governor of the jail," answered Jack, in a tone of great importance."

"No, you can't; he's out of London, and isn't expected back before to-morrow morning. But what do you want? I'm the head turnkey, perhaps I shall do; tell us your business, and don't keep a fellow standing in the cold all night."

"Well, then, as the governor is not to be seen, and you are the turnkey, I may tell you, you have a person in this prison who is to be tried for his life to-morrow. Can I see him?"

"See a prisoner at this ere time o' night;—no! not if you were the king himself. It's more than my place is worth."

"But there could be no harm; I have been travelling hard all day to reach this place, and to-morrow will be too late. Five minutes would suffice me, and I will pay you handsomely for the danger you incur."

"Humph!—ha! Well, who is it then, you want to see?"

"One John Rann."

"Jack Rann! the cove himself—Sixteen-stringed Jack! Ha! ha! ha! Oh, go home—go home; you've done it now. Why, I couldn't let you see him for the best ten pound note as ever was made. I musn't even open the door to look at him, and hand his victuals—I has to give it him through a little door, and we keep guard over the keyhole, for fear he should jump through it. Ha! ha! ha! a pretty go, truly. Why what the devil would the gov'nor say to me if he knew I was to let any one so much as look at him."

Jack had patiently listened to this long-winded oration of the turnkeys, and was nothing daunted at it, for he knew full well that the golden ointment which he had to rub in would heal up all wounds of conscience; so, waiting till the man had said his say, he replied very coolly—"I am very sorry to hear this; for to tell you the truth, this man is my brother, and I want to see him previous to his trial, to help to provide him with counsel. I think, as I am his brother, I might be admitted to speak to him for five minutes."

"Not even to look at him," replied the turnkey; "so you may as well go and snooze yourself up snug for to-night, and go and see the trial to-morrow. But, take my word for it, he'll be tucked up as safe as dead cod-fish, whether he be your father, brother, or anything else."

"Your words are not very consoling," replied Jack, as he scanned the turnkey's features very closely; "now, I'll tell what I have to propose; you are a very honest fellow, no doubt; and I dare say you don't get more money than you know what to do with. As I have said before, I only want to speak to this person; and if you like to conduct me to his cell, you may keep watch at the door—mind, I only ask for five minutes—and, in return, this note for £100 shall be yours."

Thus concluding, Jack held up the bank note to the turnkey's view, and letting him see that it was no vain boast, waited with anxious expectation for his reply.

"Humph! I hardly know what to say," at length sullenly observed the man, evidently looking at the note with longing eyes, you only want to speak to him for five minutes you say?"

"For five minutes," replied Jack! "and you can keep the door yourself. Come, man! agree to my proposition, and for five minutes of disobedience, make more money than you will get for twenty years of strict vigilance. No one will know it; and you will be as safe as ever."

"Give me the note, and the five minutes chat is yours.

"No, no, I must have the interview first; work for your money, before you receive it."

"May I depend upon your secresy; you won't blab of this?"

"Not a syllable."

"Come in, then."

In answer to this last request, Jack followed the turnkey into the prison, and after groping in darkness through a number of winding passages and staircases, they stopped at a low door, which his guide opening, Jack instantly entered, and found himself in the cell where Clayton was confined. The door was instantly closed; and before his companion could hardly be aware that any one had paid him a visit at all, Jack was before him, and actually clasping him in his arms, exclaimed—

"My chirruper, here is your own leader come to rescue you at last!"

"Ha, so it is, my faithful captain; but what say you—rescue! what do you mean by that, Jack? Your are surely not so mad as——"

"As to come here and pull down the jail, and shoot the governor through the head? No, no, we are not quite so far abroad as that; but this is what I have come to do—and by the hand and help of Fortune, I mean to accomplish. You are here imprisoned in my stead; that is, you will be made to suffer the public odium and spleen on my account—in fact, they take you to be no other than Sixteen-stringed Jack himself; and if you do not allow me to make an exchange of prisoners, and release you by becoming a captive myself, why you are not my pal—you are not the true-hearted covey I took you to be. Come Clayton, words are worth a guinea a-piece here; off with your shakers, and toss on mine—half a minute will do the business. You can slip out and nick 'em all as safe as birds in a cage, while I remain behind, and laugh at them for their cunning."

"What mean you, Jack? take my place in this den, and exchange your chance of life with that of me? You are mad, man! Away, I will not listen to such treason!"

"Nay, nay, but I am resolved," replied Jack, firmly; "I came here with the intention to act, and not to make pretence. Come, off with that coat and waistcoat, and put on mine; or, if you refuse, I will denounce myself at once, and share your fate; and then we shall both be lost to the gang. Besides, the whole squad of them are ready to assist you in any enterprise should my trial go cross, and you can but have a fight for it at last."

Without allowing Clayton time to reply, Jack stripped off his own hat, coat, waistcoat and boots; and as Clayton had done the same without further bidding, the change was very soon made.

"Leave me to myself; be handy, and hear how the trial goes to-morrow, and I shall be at peace. Farewell, the man without is growing impatient."

"Jack, you have bound me to you for life. To snatch you from these hated walls, I will sacrifice every tie upon earth, and will undergo every privation," answered Clayton much affected by his leader's cool determination. The turnkey again appearing, the discourse was again broken off, and pulling Jack's hat closely over his eyes, and disguising his walk and step as much as possible, Clayton passed free from the prison, leaving his leader a captive instead.

Left to himself, Jack made his mind up for the worst, and laughing to himself, pictured the dismay and confusion which would prevail upon his real title and person being discovered. After about an hour's solitary contemplation, Jack tried the door to see if any one was within hearing, and to his great surprise, found it unfastened; and with a slight touch, it opened. He stole on tiptoe into the court-yard, and seeing noone, he made bold to enter the large stone kitchen, where he saw the turnkeys fast asleep, all dead drunk before a large fire. Beside them, on a table, stood bottles of brandy, some ale, tobacco, and pipes; it was very evident to Jack that the money he had given the turnkey as a bribe, had thus terminated their sober moments.

"Well! this alters my plans entirely," exclaimed Jack, as he surveyed the scene around him with cool fortitude. "But I see no harm in my drinking their healths, and long sound sleep." As he thus spoke, he raised the brandy bottle to his lips, and took a hearty draught; then taking up a stout cord, he bound the turnkeys fast to the iron grate, and relieving the man whom he bribed of the remaining part of the unspent money, he took the keys from his belt, and quietly let himself out of prison, taking the keys with him. Jack soon got clear of the town, and proceeded on foot towards Westminster.

CHAPTER XV.

JACK PAYS A VISIT TO THE SQUIRE'S.—A JOLLY RECEPTION, AND A GLORIOUS LEAP BY OLD SUE.

A LULL of profound quietude succeeded the adventures and the escape described in the preceding pages, during which our hero was practising the art of subtraction, which, in their phraseology, meant a few light-fingered tricks, and whose adroitness taught them the art of transferring, without trouble or confusion, the contents of one individuals pockets to their own without trouble or fear of detection. An apt pupil our worthy hero proved himself, beyond doubt, as Clayton and O'Brien were convinced one fine morning on examining their pockets to find they had been cleverly cleaned out by our hero, and without disturbing either of the surprised gentry in the slightest degree; this they voted an exploit, if not unequalled, certainly unsurpassed, by anything in human nature. This pastime being concluded, and each having refreshed himself with a good drop of sherry, they fell to musing and talking as to what should be the next move upon the board.

"You remember that old Squire, out by Hounslow, that tried so hard to cage me once at Bow Street?"

Clayton nodded assentingly.

"Well, my boy, you are also aware I hold a ticker of his, for the safe return of which he promised to give me a good blow out, and twenty guineas now my fine fellows as the ticker is'nt worth, intrinsically, half the value to us, what do you say to give him a friendly look in, to enjoy a feed—doubtless the spread will be a good one—take wine with the old buffer—tip him his twice piece, and claim the stakes."

"It would be a glorious spree, that's a fact," said Clayton, "but I must confess I have misgivings of its practicability. Think you he would not know us?"

"If we went in our dashing habiliments as knights of the road, he would most undoubtedly, as would any fool, from the advertisement and description the newspaper press has lavished upon us; but are there no such things as disguises in the crib, and could we not so equip ourselves that our own mothers, if they mounted spectacles and all, would fail to know us?"

"To be sure we could," exclaimed Clayton, "and I must be blind as a bat not to have seen so: but what disguise would you adopt my boy? what attire would you go in?"

"Attire is it! as a thoroughbred gentleman, his own equal at the least, is own superior if you like, and I vote for the latter. Come Mike, there, if he isn't too bashful to make one of a jovial dinner party."

"Is it myself you are alluding to? Sure I shall be delighted to go," said O'Brien, rubbing his hands with ecstacy, "and if there is any virtue, wont I punish his mutton."

"Well, I propose then, Mike shall be General O'Blunderbuss, yourself Viscount Neverwag, a very aristocratic personage indeed, and I will be my Lord Swipes; a little bit of libertine, and a small, very small admirer of good vintages. We shall each, therefore, have a cue. O'Brien, all bluster, yourself all gentility, and myself all fal de ral, which is about as lovely a character as any fool like myself could wish to pourtray."

"Well, when shall we say go?" asked Clayton.

"Well, to tell you the truth," and Jack yawned, "I am getting so infernally tired of this idle life, that the sooner we go, the better I shall like it. In fact I propose to-morrow."

"To-morrow be it then," they cried with one assent, and immediately betook themselves to a search for the necessary habiliments.

Whilst these gentlemen are thus anticipating their adventure, the reader will please accompany us to the residence of the squire, a manor-house lying to the left of Hounslow, and between that town and the river Thames. The house itself lay nestling in the midst of a large and extensive park; the magnificent lawn that stretches its emerald length before the dining-room upon the grand floor, was edged by a smooth unruffled lake, whose glassy appearance of the waving trees upon its bank, created a picture charming and pleasant to the eye, looking like a cool and luxurious spot, where, lolling full length in a boat, an idle man could dose and dream the live long day, out upon the bosom of the sparkling water; moving in majestic immutable grace, were many snow white swans. In the extreme distance was a boat-house, strongly built of stone, and riding docile within its confines, was an excellent yacht and several pleasure boats. The house stood upon a gentle eminence overlooking from the front the lake and its placid scenery. At the back was a rookery and an extensive garden—horticultural, floricultural, and part dedicated to the still more useful, although less ornamental, task of growing vegetables. The park itself was scattered over with some magnificent specimens of oak, beach, and elm, and that portion adjoining the road, was protected by a high and massive stone wall. The entrance to the house was a fine ornamental gate of bronze, on either side of which were two high towers, also of stone. Why erected, except it were to furnish employment, or to lavish money away, no tongue could tell. They were certainly entirely useless, and by no means over ornamental. The manor-house was built in Elizabethan style, with gable ends, tall chimneys, and diamond shaped windows; in fact it was one of those old primitive particularly attractive edifices, so seldom to be met with in these degenerate days, that seemed to speak of a hearty welcome and a jovial entertainment to all who crossed its threshold. There interior of the house was most beautifully ornamented and decorated.

The rooms were elegantly furnished in the substantial style then in vogue among the wealthy of our forefathers, and everything in point of fact throughout the Mansion, proclaimed the Squire not only a wealthy man but also a person of exqusite taste.

His guests to the number of six arrayed in the gayest, and most fashionable costumes of the day, were laughing in their high backed chairs or pacing the floor, engaged in conversation. Suddenly the eye of one directed towards the entrance of the mansion caught sight of our hero and his pals as they leisurely advanced up the gravel pathway.

"Hallo, Squire" he shouted "who the devil have we here?"

The Squire advancing to the window to reconnoitre, replied "Hang me if I know, but they are three bucks of the first water," which was a fact beyond dispute, for each of these, Rann, Clayton, and O'Brien, were arrayed in the costliest dresses in the very first style of fashion.

Arrived at the entrance to the mansion, they threw the bridles to the grooms who warned by the sound of horses hoofs, had hurried to take charge them, and the trio then strode into the house, quite as free and easy, and as much at home as the Squire himself could by any impossibility have been. Announced in their assumed names they marched into the dining-room without hesitation.

"How dy'e do gentlemen, how dy'e do, I hope I see you in a perfect state of convalescence, and you my old Trojan," said Jack, slapping the Squire familiarly upon the shoulder, " how do you find yourself."

" As hearty as a buck," answered the Squire shaking hands with the new arrivals heartily, " and right glad to see you my lords and gentlemen for I have somewhat of a short dinner party to day, but upon my soul you'll excuse me when I say I don't remember seeing either of you before."

" Don't you remember my face ? said Clayton enquiringly.

"I certainly do not" answered the Squire.

" Nor mine either ?" questioned our hero.

"Nor yours my lord," replied the Squire.

"Elevate your hoptics to my dial plate, my hearty, doant you recollect us now, can't you tell the time of day now, eh, old stick in the mud?"

"I am as much in ignorance, Colonel O'Blunderbuss, as ever, but don't disturb yourselves I beg, you are as heartily welcome as if I'd known you twenty years."

"And do you mean to say you haven't, eh, you spalpeen; do you mean to say you haven't known me iver since I was the height of a bacca-pipe, and about as thick?"

"I mean to say, once again, Sir," answered the Squire, "I have no recollection either of your name or face."

"No recollection of my name!" shouted O'Brien fiercely. "Thunder and

No. 21

turf! Death and the devil! Do you mean to say you never heard of O'Blunderbuss, Gunpowder Hall, Bullettown Blueblazes."

"I mean to say, Sir, I again repeat, I have never heard of you or your birthplace," replied the Squire calmly.

"Oh the ingratitude of human natur! it's enough to make one forswear his own kith and kin, after the battles I've fought, the victories I've won, the divil a hall or cottage, a hut or a house, ought to rear its tiles and bricks in the three kingdoms, but a portrait of myself ought to be stuck upon its walls; and here am I, after fighting the battles of my country, unknown, unrequited, unwelcome."

"Unknown and unrequited I must confess—but unwelcome I do utterly disclaim. You are as welcome to what my poor table affords as the flowers in spring."

"A neat speech, elegantly delivered," whispered Clayton to our hero, "and, thank the Fates, the old buffer don't discover us. Pitch him the soft sawder, Jack, my flamer."

"Gentlemen," said Rann, addressing the Squire and his party, "I fear we have committed a most egregious blunder—have made a most unpardonable mistake."

"How so?" inquired the Squire and his party in a breath.

"By mistaking this house for that of our most particular friend Lord Cashall. Accept, therefore, I beg of you, our humble and sincere apology for the intrusion. We will order our horses and away at once—justly punished for our heedlessness by the loss of a good dinner."

"Jack, you fool," whispered Clayton, whilst O'Brien, shocked beyond power of speech, uttered an involuntary groan.

Jack looked at his confederates and winked knowingly, a hint that convinced them Jack was playing his game with right good policy, merely throwing a sprat to catch a mackerel as the somewhat ancient saying goes, and right gloriously was the bait taken, for not only the Squire but the whole of the company declared they should not leave, and actually laid hands on them to detain them by force.

This of course was scarcely necessary, as our hero and his friends were well content to say.

A glorious banquet was given, to which each and all did ample justice, and when the table was cleared, and wine and fruit were placed upon it, the spirits of the whole company arose, under the exhilarating effects of the golden sherry, free, hearty, and hilarious. Then did our three companions in the tasks allotted themselves, shine forth right brilliantly. O'Briens' tales of wars never thought of, even in romance until that evening, filled the whole company with wonder and astonishment. Clayton's repeated witticisms kept the table in a roar, and our hero shone no less conspicuously, although he confined himself to glowing eulogies on lovely woman.

"Bye the bye, now talking of brave men," said the squire, alluding to O'Brien's conversation; "who think you, now, in my opinion, is the bravest man of the day?"

"A somewhat difficult question to reply to," said our hero, "for amongst such a multitude of brave men now existing, 'twould need an eagle's eye indeed to pick the bravest."

"I tell you, my lord," continued the squire, that where there is one brave man in the world, there are a hundred arrant cowards; but I have one now in my mind's eye, who for real bravery might challenge the world."

"And who is this redoubtable hero?" inquired Rann.

"None other than the renowned highwayman, with whose exploits the world is now ringing. I mean that dashing blade, Sixteen-string Jack."

Our hero having pooh-pooh'd the observation, the squire continued with much warmth—"I tell you he is. Look out, he and that gallant devil, Clayton fleeced a whole room full of us—see how the gallant fellows not only extracted all the valuables from Lord Dashfield's, but actually eloped with his girl—look at their subsequent robbery at Malcolm's and the gallant undaunted bearing of Rann before the magistrate, when the peril of committal to Newgate for trial stared him fully in the face—look again I say at his reckless leap from Richmond Bridge, his gallant rescue of the girl, his love adventures, his audacious robbery of Manby, and of all others in the world, of old Colville. The stoppage of Brummell and Hanger, and their ludicrous plight, is enough to make one crack one's sides. His heroic rescue of his friend Clayton from prison, all pronounce him the king of highwaymen, and I tell you, gentlemen, nothing would give me greater pleasure than to see him and Clayton seated at my table."

"And you mean to say, squire," said Jack, "if this notorious fellow of the Sixteen-strings and his pal Clayton were here at this moment, you would not only treat him like a prince, but would suffer them to depart without molestation."

"I swear I would," responded the Squire, "and if I could have a wish gratified I swear that wish would be to see them before me now."

"Have your wish then," said Jack, throwing his disguise aside and appearing like magic in his habiliments. "Sixteen-stringed Jack stands before you and claims your welcome."

"As does also," said Clayton, following his leader's example, "Charlie, or Kit Clayton, whichever you like to call him."

The Squire advanced and shook them heartily by the hands, "you are brave fellows, and I glory in you, but what has led to the honour of this visit."

"The simple fact that I remain in your debt, and you in mine. I gave you my word I would return you a watch taken from you at Brentford. There, Sir, you have it."

"A thousand thanks," said the Squire, "there's your twenty guineas, and now lay hands on what you like."

Mike was going to work right zealously, but Jack's uplifted hand deterred him.

"We are not here as thieves to-day. No, sir, for once in our lives we can afford to play the gentleman. We thank you heartily for your hospitality, and as we are now straight we'll make our exit." Not so, however; the Squire insisted upon their stopping. A right merrie time was passed, and when at length they parted the whole company declared they should ever look back with pleasure on the hours spent in the company of "Sixteen-string Jack."

* * * * *

On leaving the Squire the three highwaymen parted company, each in search of an adventure.

Gaily and gallantly did our hero pursue his ride: the excitement of the scene in which he had been engaged had given his spirits a stir that made them sparkle through his whole frame; an electric feeling of joy gave lightness to his heart, and animated his head with thoughts of such wild delight, that he involuntary burst into a jovial song, as he breasted the air and galloped swiftly onwards. Lightly and with unslacking pace did his glorious steed continue to hold her course; and such was the pride and rapture which Jack experienced, that his brain actually whirled with extacy.

Between the beast and himself there appeared to be a perfect understanding: for the creature obeyed every movement of her master as if they had been acquainted all their lives. In this respect horses are like women, they show their kindness to many, but fix their affections on one. What secret attraction they are guided by, it is impossible to say; a handsome woman will love a plain man, though surrounded by the finest specimens of manly beauty, and a spirited horse will reject the controul of all strangers till some being suddenly hits its fancy, without an apparent why or wherefore, and it will become more docile in his hands than with its own master. Bucephalus, the renowned charger of Alexander the Great, refused submission to all who approached till the royal conqueror laid his hands upon his mane, and from that moment the noble animal confessed its ruler. It would be an agreable task to trace this sympathy to its source, but, perhaps, like female affection, it is unaccountable; we will therefore confine our attention to Sixteen-string Jack and the glorious animal by which he had become so suddenly beloved.

Onward they flew like spirits of the wind, till they came to Hounslow-heath, when the events in which he had so recently mixed on that spot recurred so forcibly to Jack's memory, that he suddenly stayed his flight and stood still to ponder upon them. He had, however, short time for meditation, for they were soon broken by the distant clatter of an approaching horse, and the taper and flexible ear of old Sue gave instant indication of the fact. "Soho, gentle Sue!" exclaimed Jack. "I find we are to have company along the road. Well, your fleet limbs will carry me out of harm's way, if needed, so I do not care if we encounter twenty." Mademoiselle Sue did not say anything in opposition to this, so her master quietly awaited the advancing comer. This proved to be a single rider, who, from the cautious manner in which he fixed his eyes on Jack, and kept at the greatest possible distance from him, was labouring under no little trepidation. "A fine night, friend," exclaimed Jack, cantering up; "make you for town?"

"Bless my soul!" cried the stranger nervously, "you have brought my heart into my mouth."

"Why, how is that?" said Jack, "who do you take me for?"

"Oh! you are a perfect gentleman, no doubt," returned the other, "but I was startled at seeing you move, for you were standing so still that I positively thought as I came up, that you were merely some scarecrow stuck up to frighten away the crows."

"Indeed!" said Jack, drily. "Is it usual to take such measures for the protection of a heath?"

"Humph! I did not think of that. But who can reflect when they are alarmed? By the bye, however, it would be a good thing for travellers if steps *were* taken for the protection of this place."

"And why so?" said Jack. "There is nothing grown here that I can see."

"No," said the stranger; "but recent circumstances show that there is no safety for those who pass here after dark."

"What circumstances are these?" asked our hero, with seeming carelessness.

"Is it possible that you cannot have heard?" exclaimed the stranger with astonishment. "Why the news is travelling all over the country." With that he launched into a history of the robbery, so interlarded with the embellishments of fancy, that Jack scarcely recognised the circumstances in which he had himself acted. He was, however, gratified at finding that his assumed name struck terror wherever it was uttered.

When the talkative stranger had concluded his account he ran on with his private affairs, being one who would divulge any secret, rather than want a subject for his loquacity. It appeared that he was an attorney; his name was Quire, and he resided in London. He had been to take instructions for the drawing up of a will, and was now returning to the metropolis, with a sum of money which had been entrusted to him for disposal at interest in town.

"I wonder you were not afraid of trusting yourself out with such an amount at this time of night," said Jack.

"Afraid! Bless your heart, I am afraid of nothing;" said the little lawyer, forgetting his display of cowardice half an hour before, "Sixteen-string Jack himself would find it devilish difficult to intimidate me, I can tell you. But, to say the truth, I have a trial comes on to-morrow, at which I am to be a leading witness, and therefore I was forced to set out the moment I got clear of my client, let what would happen on the road."

"Well, business must be attended to," said Jack. "I suppose you took every precaution; you carry pistols, of course?"

"Do you think I am such a fool as to go without?" exclaimed Quire, pointing to the weapons in holsters. "But, I say, mister," he added, "what brings you out such hours? Are you a cockney like myself?"

"By the Lord, there is a sight I have been seeking during the last hour," exclaimed Jack, evading the question, and pointing to a little road-side inn, from the window of which the cheerful light of a lamp reflector betokened that the inmates had not retired to rest. "What say you to a bracing glass of brandy and water? It will comfort the inside this cold night."

"With all my heart," said the lawyer; "I feel quite aguish, and a toothful of spirits and water will do me good." As he said this, both parties turned their horses towards the inn-door, and having committed them to the care of the ostler, dismounted and entered. Jack, however, had been induced by a deeper consideration than mere purposes of refreshment in the proposal he had made, for not being himself armed, he thought it rather impolitic to leave another the advantage which he was without. He consequently watched his opportunity, and speedily rendered the stranger's pistols perfectly useless. He had scarcely achieved this point before two foremen rode up and entered the inn for a similar purpose to that which had ostensibly brought our hero. The talkative lawyer soon drew from the new comers that they were all going the same road, and a proposal was accordingly made and accepted, that they should ride in company. As soon, therefore, as the inspiring glass had been drained, the party, including Rann, remounted in high spirits, and were soon clattering with hoof and tongues along the road—much to the dissatisfaction of Jack. In passing a bye lane a fifth equestrian made his appearance, and begged permission to make one of the cavalcade, as rumours were afloat of highwaymen and cut-throats being abroad.

This gave rise to a renewal of the conversation concerning Sixteen-string Jack, the new highwayman, and marvellous were the tales told concerning him, though only two days had elapsed since his first robbery. Each person outvied the other, and Jack, who was last speaker, painted himself in such terrible colours that his hearers quaked again, and he felt convinced that a single man would find little or no difficulty in dispossessing them of their cash. The only thing that gave him uneasiness was his want of fire-arms, but blindly trusting to his usual luck, he resolved to risk everything and gain his point by the boldness and suddenness of his movements. He felt that to turn round and demand the purses of his companions would be ridiculous, for they had been too familiar with him to fear him now. Besides there was nothing sufficiently formidable in his appearance to lead them to suppose he was in earnest if he took such a step, and as he had no pistol to convince them he did not joke, it became obvious that he must quit them for a time and devise a fitting scheme for his purpose. Accordingly, on passing to his left bridle path, leading to a parallel road on the other side of the pastures, he suddenly bade the company "good night," and saying that his home lay in that direction, gallopped off before the rest had time to utter a word. He had not gone a single furlong ere he leaped the hedge on his right, towards London, and then bringing Sue to a stand, alighted, but passed his arm through her bridle by way of security. He now ripped out the black leather lining to his hat, and with his penknife cut two small holes in it to fit his eyes. With a little more cutting and trimming he thus contrived a very excellent substitute for a mask, which he tied upon his face with a strip torn from his handkerchief. After this he gathered a quantity of tall heath which he stuck in his hat-band, to appear like a plume of feathers; and lastly, he cut from the hedge a short knobbed branch, which had exactly the appearance of a pistol. Thus accoutred he remounted his steed, and though by daylight his appearance would have excited laughter and ridicule, by the uncertain light in which he then stood he cut a most terrifying figure. Thus disguised he scoured across the field and soon regained the high road, considerably in advance of those he had quitted; as, of course, the path he had taken was a short one. He then turned his face towards Maidenhead, and gallopping up to his four friends, brought Sue to a sudden pause, and presenting his mock pistol, exclaimed in startling tones, "Stand all of ye to Sixteen-string Jack! Your money or your lives!"

So startling a salutation, aided by the fierce appearance of Rann as he now stood in a partial flow of moonlight, produced instant obedience, and threw the whole into consternation except the little lawyer; Jack well knew how to account for this, and in order to humour him turned away from him while enforcing the demand just made upon the others. Little Quire absolutely gloated over his fancied advantage, and with as much deliberation as he would have removed a volume from his book-case he drew forth his pistols, and cocked, and presented them at Jack's head. In the next instant he pulled the trigger, and, lo! a few sparks formed all the result.

"Try it again!" cried Jack looking over his shoulder as he spoke with provoking coolness.

The lawyer swore most heartily, but suddenly resuming an appearance of calmness he exclaimed, "Perhaps you are not aware, Mr. String Jack, that what you are now doing is contrary to the statute made and provided against illegal stoppages on the highway?"

"You, however, are aware that snapping a pistol at a man's head is an attempt at murder," said Jack, "and unless you come down with a round sum all the packed juries in the world shall not save you from swinging!"

The man of law was non-plussed and the daring robber taking advantage of the panic, which was now general, very soon put an end to all controversy by completely rifling the four men, notwithstanding the great valour of which they had boasted. As he made free with the lawyer first, the little gentleman had afterwards leisure to once more cock his pistol, and when Jack was about to ride off he repeated his fruitless experiment. Annoyed at his pertinacity, our hero flung his clump of whitethorn at Quire's head, but the adroit lawyer caught it before it reached his temple and at once discovered the stratagem that had been employed.

"What's this? We have been diddled!" exclaimed he in the extreme of passion. "See here, he carries mock weapons! Forward, gentlemen, and overpower the insolent impostor. No second word was needed. On they all dashed as rapidly as their rage could make them spur their horses, and that rage supplied the place of real courage and rendered them truly formidable. Jack heard the words, and heard also the burst of pursuit. He had noted the beasts of his pursuers, and knew them to be mettlesome animals, he felt, therefore, that nothing but the first-rate qualities of his steed could save him, and tender as was his feeling for the horse, he inflicted one lash upon its side sufficient to intimate his temper and wishes, exclaiming at the same moment, " grandfoal of Bess, now is the time to prove yourself!" Stung by the challenge, Sue threw out her limbs with all that grace and freedom which was so inherent to the high-blooded creature, and once more emulated the wind with her pace. But if his flight was hot, the pursuit was hotter, and every step rendered the case more dangerous with Jack. Already was the old-fashioned town of Brentford in view; there was sufficient light in the sky to show him that a number of market people were astir, and he felt that the moment the cries of "Stop thief!" vociferated by the enemy were heard all would be over with him. He cast a desponding gaze on each side, but the glance only added to the hopelessness of his condition. On one side an extensive haw-haw, girt by a row of saplings, too thickly planted in some nursery-ground to allow room for a horse, rendered chance of escape in that direction impossible, and on the other a high wall held out an equally bad temptation. At this anxious moment, also, Quire drew near enough to fling one of his empty pistols with full effect at Jack's head, and still more to madden his bewildered brain. On and on and on he now dashed without being able to properly distinguish the objects before him, when a loud and sudden shout in front restored the perverted sense in one moment, and he beheld before him an array of country fellows armed with pitchforks and other weapons to oppose his progress. Even the door of the Red Lion Inn, which he had now reached, was blocked against entrance had he thrown himself from his horse, for a cart had been drawn up in front, and was half loaded with turnips for Covent-garden market. Earth, in short, seemed to be without hope. Life, dear life—liberty, still dearer liberty—were poised on the risk of a moment, and as if he sought in the skies that succour which the world denied, he dashed spurs rowel deep into his racer and vaulted into the air. Sue's bound was terrific; the dauntless beast fancied that her master wished to clear the turnip cart, and so gallantly did she make the attempt that she gained a momentary footing upon it. A sharp jerk with the rein, a second infliction with the lash, and one more pressure of the spur, urged her to another effort, and she blindly, nay madly, dashed in at the window.

The apartment was filled with people; for it was just at that hour when the roysterers of a place complete their revels, and the honest early-rising caterers for the London markets proceed to take their first morning draughts —a moment in the diurnal course of time which forms the completion of its circle, and renders it without beginning or end. Imagination will easily supply a picture of the consternation produced by the almost incredible incident we have just detailed: the natural idea first entertained was that the house was tumbling in, for the crash occasioned by the smashing of glass was dreadful, but when they beheld Jack on his gallant mare, with his hair hanging wildly round his neck, his bloodshot eyes gleaming through his mask, and his strange attire all disordered by the wind, they fancied that Lucifer himself was before them, and a yell, as fearful as it was dissonant, and which beggars all description, broke from every lip.

"Hurrah! here I am, gentlemen!" shouted Rann, elevated into a sort of superhuman gaiety by the peril over which he had so recklessly triumphed for the moment; then, stooping towards the long table, he snatched up a flagon of hot ale, and drank of its contents, after uttering a wild laugh, and exclaiming—"A greeting to all from Sixteen-String Jack."

The name of terror found an echo from fifty tongues, and the landlord, who was present, looked aghast under the conviction that he was a ruined man; yet so paralysed were the stout hearts of all present, that not a finger was raised to arrest the daring highwayman. Jack saw with eagle glance the dismay of his host, and, fraught as was the moment with danger, he could not forbear giving way to that strange mixture of high feeling with which the commencement of his lawless career had been marked; he therefore drew forth one of the purses which he had just stolen, and flinging it upon the table merrily exclaimed—" Jack always pays for his drink, and will permit no man to suffer damage from him except on the king's highway.

He had scarce concluded ere the clattering of feet was heard on the stairs. His pursuers fancied him now at bay, and were rushing tumultuously up with the certainty of victory. Jack stayed not to reflect; he might be rushing on destruction or he might by some wonderful chance be saved; either way he would avoid the ignominy of capture, and therefore, neck or nothing, he urged forward and dashed through the opposite window to that which had given him entrance.

To scramble in at a window and to jump out of one, it is needless to say, are very different things; and had not the devil taken care of his own, Jack's career and our history must have ended together; but he bore a charmed life, and was saved. While in the act of gallopping across the room, his pursuers had reached the door, and just as he took his harlequin's leap through the glaziery they burst in. All made an instant rush to the window, expecting to see him stretched beneath with a broken neck; but baffled were their humane anticipations, for to their astonishment they saw the robber once more gallop across the fields, and heard him cheerily shout, as he fled, "Jack's alive, and alive still!"

The cause of this phenomenon is easily explained. In the stable-yard flanking the Red Lion there was, in our hero's time, a large well-filled pond, from whence the ostlers, kitchen-maids, scullions, and other officials drew the requisite supplies for watering the horses and washing the place. It was situated about a dozen yards from the house, and served also as a colony for the scores of ducks, drakes, geese and ganders, who patiently awaited that inevitable hour when they should be twisted, plucked, roasted, and served up on that dish to which they were never more to return. The members of this interesting race, summoned by the trumpeter of a neighbouring hen-roost, had just arisen from slumber to take their early excursion upon the lake.

At this momentous period it was that Sixteen-string Jack, with so much temerity, urged Old Sue to burst headlong through the window. Had the distance been measured for the occasion it could not have been more accurately suited to the span of Sue's leap. Down came the undaunted creature into the very centre of the reservoir. Quack! quack, shouted the feathered murmurers, and, simultaneously taking wing, away they flew about the ears of Jack, till he thought himself surrounded by a legion of imps.

For a few seconds both horse and rider were completely engulphed, but no sooner did they rise to the surface than Jack pushed forward, and his horse, at two strokes, crossed the friendly element that had thus saved its rider from a broken neck. Another effort achieved a landing, and in the next instant Jack's cry of "alive, and alive still," announced that he had cleared the dwarf wall dividing the inn yard from the garden, and was once more in flight beyond the reach of pursuers.

The lawyer and his companions vented imprecations and expressions of astonishment in a breath. They had thrown themselves from their steeds with a certainty of having driven the quarry to bay when they entered the long room of the Red Lion; they were consequently not in a condition to renew the chase in sufficient time to render it available, and were obliged to content themselves by declaring that the devil himself had taken care of his own.

CHAPTER XVII.

A WORD OF OUR HERO AND HIS EXPLOITS.—A VISIT IN THE CITY.—A JOURNEY HOME.

NEVER since the days of those immortals, Jack Sheppard and Dick Turpin, had public curiosity been so much awakened, had public interest been so much excited, or public credulity been so much imposed upon. Our hero's adventures following, as they did each other so rapidly, created a perfect terror, and the first glance a man directed to his newspaper, was bent fully upon one object, viz.—to ascertain if there was anything new from Sixteen-string Jack. The whole country, from Land's End to John O'Groat's was ringing with his matchless exploits.

The Earl of Dashfield, at each narrative of his hair-breadth escape, grew well nigh frantic with vexation. He gloated over the papers with the greediness of a miser, in the hopes of discovering tidings that our hero was secured by the arm of the law; he urged the Bow-street runners by bribes and presents to extra exertions; attended meetings of the magistracy and produced a variety of plans, having in their aim the capture of the daring and until now fortunate robber; and as each exploit seemed only the further to set all their concoctions at defiance, like a miser who, instead of gain, has discovered a heavy loss, rage, furious demoniacal rage, was busy at his heart's core. This fever for revenge, for such it had in reality become, coupled with the twinges and misgivings of his conscience for his wife's untimely death, his fear of at length being denounced as her murderer, made the Earl's whole life a curse and a misery to him. Alternately, in the height of his rage, or in an agony of fear he passed his wretched days and sleepless nights; even if he slept, his mind was filled with hideous phantasies, and when he arose he was unrefreshed in mind and body. He was continually being racked with doubts and fears that, taking no definable shape, haunted him, if possible, yet the more severely. Elinor Roche carried her vengeance to the limits she herself had proscribed: the funeral of the Countess took place whilst the Earl was confined to his room by indisposition; and so secretly were all the arrangements conducted, that though all the household saw the hearse and mourning coaches depart, yet none of them, save Elinor, were cognisant where the remains of the once beautiful and high-souled Countess were to lay. The day after the funeral, Elinor packed up what property belonged to her, and left the house, no one knowing for why, or whither she was going. When the Earl came to enquire after her, he was almost staggered by the intelligence of her mysterious departure, and he cursed again and again his own imbecility, in not having decision of mind in sufficiency to have determined on her detention by fair means could it have been so managed, but by force, even by foul means if necessary, so that her escape was prevented. But it was "too late, too late!" and as the maddening conviction forced itself upon him he wrung his hands in his despair and anguish.

A greater contrast in the Earl's feelings could not have been found than was presented in the bosom of the lovely Miss Malcolm. As our hero's name rose in degrading popularity, as larger and larger rewards were offered for his apprehension, and as his danger increased and grew more imminent, so did the maiden's love and devotedness grow the stronger, until her loving heart was like to burst with agony at the danger of her adored Jack Rann, and of the perils which encircled him around and about. The vision of the fatal tree booming in the distance, and, like the Upas tree, casting its sombre deadly shadow over the beloved of her heart, the joy of her whole soul, filled her with indescribable anguish, and in its corroding care so weighed her down at length that illness seized upon her gentle frame, and her very life hung quivering in the scale. Restored at length to health by the physician's skill, a settled melancholy seized her, and living the only hope of her devoted parents, she yet passed on without one hope in life herself, so absorbed was she wholly, heart, mind, and soul, in love with our hero.

And he? methinks our reader questions. Why he, like a thoughtless gallant as he was, wasted his leisure hours in toying with those fair frail ones who, so surely as the butterfly seeks the noblest flame, so surely busy with all the trappings of their enticing art about each daring hero, and win him for themselves, sharing his fame and fortune whilst they last, and as quickly disappearing, like the gaudy insect named, when fortune frowns; as the least symptom of a cloud or shower exhibit themselves to dim life's horizon.

As will have been already gathered from the asseverations vented by Sheppard and Wide Awake and, indeed, such was the feeling of the whole gang, now swollen to a goodly number and entirely under the leadership of Jack Rann, they entirely disapproved of his amorous disposition, acting from experience, bought or taught, that "woman is the devil." Jack, however, he might listen to their remonstrances heeded them no more than he would a passing gust of wind, but continued on in his amorous career with all that unrestrainable impetuosity that marked his character from the very first. It may be readily imagined a disposition "so kindly" was immediately taken advantage of by the reigning belles, and at the period of which we treat, when the dashing highwayman became a darling hero, at least in the eyes of the fair sex, our hero had as many strings to his bow in the shape of lasses, all of whom had a hearty welcome for him come when he would, by night to bed or by day to board, as he had strings at each knee-cap. After his gallant exploits at Brentford, he hastened his noble Sue to the house of a fair inamorata at Kensington. Throwing the bridle of the faithful animal to a groom he strode up stairs and was speedily in the arms of one of his mistresses. Changing his yet damp apparel for dry clothing, and selecting a suit the least likely to attract notice, he, after an hour or two spent in gentle dalliance with his ladye fayre, and in recruiting exhausted nature, sallied forth on foot to Westminster, leaving Sue behind to rest herself until her services should again be required in the field of action.

At the ken he discovered, to his infinite joy, his brave and well-esteemed pals Clayton and Sheppard, who, with O'Brien, Toby, Wide Awake, and the Jew, seemed, from the punch-bowls that lined the table, bent on a glorious night of it. A welcome loud and joyous greeted our hero's entrance into the room.

"What, Jack, my gallant pal, thank heaven you are safe once more amongst us!" said Clayton, fervently pressing our hero's hand with brotherly affection as he gave vent to the words.

"What my natty Sixteen-Stringer," exclaimed Sheppard, springing to his feet, "home again tight and sound! Here, my hearty, we are in for a booze. Tip us your flipper."

"Mister Rann," said Toby, in due time, and, as usual, calmly and thoughtfully, "I has much pleasure in seeing on you, Sir. Sit you down. Make yourself at home."

"Captain," said Wide Awake, "I hope I sees you."

"I hope you do," said Rann, "and if you doubt here's my hand; come and feel," said Jack as he extended his hand. Wide Awake, following this behest, received such a squeeze that he literally yelled with pain, and thought it the happiest moment in his life when, his hand being released, he was suffered to retreat to his seat.

O'Brien now starting up fairly hugged our hero in his arms; Jack stretched out his broad palm to the Israelite, but the latter declined it by a knowing shrug and a leer towards Wide Awake.

"Me mooch obliged—but pleeze—no tankee."

"As you please, Mo," said Rann, carelessly; then directing his conversation to Clayton he continued, "I say Clay, my boy, and you Sheppard, my fine fellow, after leaving you I had the devil's own adventure."

"Not a word of it, I beg," said Clayton, "we are in possession of every particular; for not finding anything the least inviting down the road, Harry Sheppard and myself, Charles Christopher Clayton, or Kit, or Charlie, whichever you please, quietly trotted our nags towards town, laughing heartily with the remembrance of the happy time passed at the squire's—who is a stunner every inch of him—and his singular oversight in not noticing, whilst admiring the horseflesh you bestrode, that you were mounted on the back of his own brave mare."

"Tush, Kit; if he had noticed it he was too much of a gentleman to have robbed our worthy captain of it. I warrant you, rather than deprive Jack Rann of the horse that *can* and *has* saved him in desperate need, he would have put down his stud and walked on foot for the rest of his natural life.' So spoke Sheppard, and never as a surmise were words spoken nearer the truth.

"That, from the specimen of his generosity seen this day, I can readily believe," said Clayton. Then continuing his relation where he had broken off, he went on. "We found ourselves at length before the door of the Old Red Lion at Brentford. Here once more was the devil's own commotion. The place had been taken by storm by Sixteen-string Jack, and the yokels, with wonder-staring eyes, pointed to the window through which you had so desperately leaped. The relation was beyond credence, founded only on words. We dismounted and rushed into the house to find a company extolling the feat to the skies, and what was to us convincing proof, witnessing the imprint of old Sue's hoofs in the sanded floor. The shattered windows confirmed your daring mode of exit, and now, comrades all," said Clayton, filling a glass and rising as he spoke, " here is success and long life to our glorious captain and his brave mare Sue."

The toast was drunk with three times three. When the uproar had somewhat subsided, Toby spoke to the following effect :—

" There was a meeting to-day at the Mansion-hus, by a few select bigwigs to determine what was to be done to capter that ere notorious malefactor, and female factor too for the matter o' that, wiz, yerself," pointing to Jack. " Now, ven sich a lot o' vise heads gits together, it's the awfullest job in the vorld to discover vich is the visest—vich is right and vich is wrong. There is more discussion, an that there, on the pint of fact itself. Just so it vos vith these ere big-vigs. Von proposed von thing, von proposed another, and everybody supposing their motion for captering on you the very identical scheme, no motion was carried at all. Sir John gave it as his hopinion they vere all a parcel of fools, vich being true is comfortable, and left in disquiet, vhich is very consoling, for if he goes a cogitating rely on it there's a rope a weaving for somebody. Now I proposes this ere, as there is to be another meeting to-morrow of only the old fogies—only the old uns—the Lud Mayor, old Colville, and one or two Aldermen—I proposes you, Jack," nodding to Rann, " and you Kit," nodding to Clayton, " and you Harry," to Sheppard, " pay the Lud Mayor a visit at the Mansion-hus."

" Oh yes; that's werry likely that is, you vant to have us lagged I suppose. You don't happen for to have a stray order in your pocket for the guvner of Newgate do ye ?"

" Lagged ! I vouldn't have either of you lagged for all the vorld—no, no, my hearties. I merely vant you to have a spree vith the big vig's to astonish the vorld, and then mizzle into the country and live like gemmen till the storm blows over, for London's getting a precious sight to warm for you all three, and more especially Mister Rann."

" I am afraid a mission to the Mansion-house will have anything but a mission to cool it; but, however, let's hear this notable scheme.'

" The big-vigs, that is the select two or three on 'em, are to meet quietly to-morrow at the hus, and arter dinner this here consultation is to take place. Now if you go in the evening guv your cards to the usher, request a private interview with the Lord Mayor, tell 'em you've something tickler private to communicate about them villains and that ere Jack Rann in particular; they'll admit you at once and no questions asked. Vonce in their august presence play March vith em my boy—bind 'em, gag 'em, and collar the mace if you can. Moses and I has got a few valuables going to Holland in a day or two, and we can just find room for it in the chest."

Incredible as it may appear, this daring scheme, unparalleled in the annals of effrontery and reckless daring, was no sooner broached than it was instantly acceded to by the trip. It was certainly too much like walking into the lion's en, yet what cared they? They feared the exploit no more than Van Amburgh fears to encounter the rulers of the forest, but who, tamed and obedient from rigorous discipline, shrink from his glance, tremble at his frown, an passively obey each movement of his imperious arm.

The morrow evening came, and Jack and his comrades in arms, dressed in the most fashionable attire, wended their way on foot to the Strand, where hailing a coach they were driven with much state to the Mansion-house, and were set down at the private door. One of the Lord Mayor's own footmen saved the Jarvey the trouble of dismounting by opening the coach door. The three alighted and entered his lordship's private door. Clayton and Sheppard were admirably disguised, Jack had on an embroidered white satin vest, a scarlet coat richly edged with lace, whilst his nether garment, ornamented with silver strings and lace adornments, completed his costume and rendered him to perfection's point, the picture of a gallant, gay cavalier. On learning from the three gentlemen they were on a visit to his lordship on private information touching that rascal Jack Rann, and receiving with the information one guinea, the flunkey instantly hurried off to apprise his lordship of the glorious arrival: enhancing its brilliancy by an oratorical display quite unexampled in flunkeydom, and founding his opinion on the gift, expressing his opinion to the worthy chief magistrate that they were princes at least, come in a carriage and six.

The Lord Mayor was actually transfixed with astonishment and delight, muttering, as he huddled on his robes—

"A visit from the Prince of Wales and brothers. I'll be sworn here's knighthood at least; perhaps an earldom! Show them in John; John, show them in."

Now his worthy colleagues said nothing, but their faces expressed as much astonishment and expectation as did their lordly brother cit. Lo and behold the door opened, and in walked not three princes of the blood, but three knights of the road.

But the reality of the new arrivals was to the most worshipful the Lord Mayor and his company a sealed volume, and, supposing the guests to be of royal descent, they bowed humbly and low.

"My dear lord," said Clayton taking upon himself the part of spokesman and comprehending at a glance there was some misconception on the part of the big wigs, although he was entirely in the dark as to what, "it gives me unmistakeable pleasure to salute you."

"My dear Prince—I beg your pardon, your most glorious and royal highness Prince of Wales, I am inconceivably honoured by this visit."

"Here's a spree," whispered Charlie Clayton to our hero, "he mistakes me for the heir apparent. What a jackass! quiet!—see me work the oracle." Then speaking aloud to the head magistrate and his colleagues he said, throwing himself into a chair and speaking the words with vast deliberation—

"My royal father and myself and my august brother here," motioning to our hero as he spoke, "have been much shocked by the audacity of one fellow of a highwayman, who it would appear has up to this day baffled all the endeavours that have been made to overtake him and bring him to justice. Now, my royal sire has desired me to inform you, that in his royal opinion it is gross negligence upon the part of the magistracy and the citizens of London, that this Sixteen-string Jack and his unaccountable gang should have been suffered to go so long undetected, to the peril, as the daily accounts come swelling in, of his Majesty's loyal subjects. He hath, therefore, deputed me to hold conference with you—." Here Clayton paused, for on glancing round he found the flunkey who had admitted them, not having been bidden to depart was listening with greedy ears and open jaws. "But, nevertheless, he did not desire me, I should presume, to deliver my message with such publicity that menials should be listeners thereto."

The Lord Mayor fancied at once he had perceived his error; and yet, could it be possible that princes of the blood would condescend to grant him a private audience! Heavens! such were his magnificent aspirations, he thought the peerage he had hinted at already within his grasp! Turning, therefore, with a ferocity more befitting a mad dog than a sage Christian man, he bade the servant leave the room.

The man vanished like a gust of smoke in a gale of wind—seen for the space of half a second, lost for ever in chaos for the latter half. His lordship arose himself and locked the door, so that no intrusion could by any possibility take place; and bending his knee before Clayton he tendered him the key. Clayton took it and confided it instantly to his pocket.

"The mischief is but half eradicated, my lord. I entered this house as a private gentleman, and as a private gentleman I desire to leave it. Think you we require a city mob hooting and yelling after our carriage with—'Huzza, lads! there go the Princes Royal! Hallo, boys! hallo!' I can assure you if you do, sirrah, you are mistaken—devilishly mistaken!"

"I beseech your royal highness to pardon me. If my scoundrel of a footman dare but breathe a word that you are here, as sure as I am Lord Mayor of London, I'll cut his tongue out."

"And as sure as I am Prince of Wales, I'll hang you at Tyburn for your barbarity," said Clayton with malicious glee. "No, my lord, as I came for a private interview, a private interview I will have, or I leave instantly."

The Lord Mayor started to his feet as his supposed royal guest rose to his. Jack Rann noticed the Mayor's perturbation with undisguised glee, and favoured them with a peal of laughter, if not the loudest, at least as genuine as ever rang throughout the Mansion-house.

His lordship and his guests stared at this unexpected burst of merriment.

"My eyes, what jolly fools you are!" said Jack.

"Fools!" was echoed and re-echoed from mouth to mouth.

"Yes, fools of the first water by all that's good; the jolliest emeralds ever found."

"Can't you perceive, old blind eyes, we require one private confab, eh? you jolly old Greek."

"Had I known it, your royal highness, it should never have occurred."

"Stow your palaver, my out-and-outer," said Jack, giving the Mayor so stunning a whack on the back that he actually writhed again.

"All we want now, my stunner, is a private road out—come!—mind all your hopes of advancement rest on this, have'nt you got one?"

"Yes, prince, we have a private mode of egress from this dwelling, but it runs through the bed room of the lady mayoress, and her ladyship being indisposed is now in the arms of Morpheus."

"Morpheus! lucky dog, that, he is! I envy him the possession of so much loveliness," exclaimed Jack, "but never mind," said Jack, as the mayor and his companions stared with astonishment, "I promise you if you will only allow us to pass that way, neither mayoress or her slumbers shall be in the slightest degree disturbed; come, I claim the promise in my royal daddy's name."

Unable to refuse so flattering a request, the mayor bowed his thanks and his acquiescence at one and the same time.

"So far, so good," exclaimed our hero, gleefully, after the road by which they could depart without knowledge had been pointed out to them. "All alone—all jolly—you do'nt ask us to take wine, old fellow, so suppose I ask myself," and lifting a bottle from a sideboard near, he, without a moments hesitation, drank a copious draught from its inviting and fruitful neck. With the single exclamation of "good," he passed it to his pals, who drank alternately, and by the smacking of their lips seemed to testify it was "good, rayther," finally it was emptied and kicked aside as useless. After this little interlude had been enacted, Jack turned to the Lord Mayor, and said:—

"Now old fellow, about this Jack Rann, what do you promise?"

"If your royal highness will be but pleased to listen, I will read the placard we have compiled."

Clayton expressed his acquiescence with the exclamation of "fire away my hearty," and he forthwith read the following:—

FIVE HUNDRED POUNDS REWARD.—Whereas that notorious malefactor, calling himself SIXTEEN-STRING JACK, having, to the terror and dismay of his majesty's liege subjects, pursued his unlawful calling of highwayman and burglar."

"Callings', not calling, you precious ignoramus," shouted Clayton, "go to school—go to school."

"Callings', I beg your royal highnesses pardon it is in the plural tense I believe."

"I believe it is you precious buffer, but drive on," said Jack.

"We hereby offer a reward of five hundred pounds to any person or persons who will securely lodge in any of his majesty's prisons the body of the said John Rann, or Sixteen-string Jack; and furthermore, promise the said reward together with a free pardon to any of his confederates who will deliver him into the hands of justice."

Here followed a detailed description of our hero, possitively as unlike him as water is unlike earth. At this description the highwaymen unable to restrain their merriment, laughed aloud. When the noise had subsided Jack quietly pulling a pistol from his pocket, placed it upon full cock, and laid it upon the table. This proceeding was eyed with astonishment, mistrust, and fear, by all assembled, except the highwaymen.

"I tell you, you are a parcel of fools," said Jack, " to put yourself to unnecessary trouble and expense to secure me."

"You!" exclaimed the Mayor starting to his feet.

"Yes, me—myself I mean," responded our hero in loud and exulting tones, "no prince of the blood; poor fools that ye are!—but Sixteen-string Jack the highwayman, who, despising your offers of reward, who sneering upon your imbecile efforts to entrap him, who accepting the Lord Mayor's invitation, stands now before him!" And tearing open his coat, Jack Rann stood confessed in all his glorious and celebrated apparel.

"It is he, it is he!" groaned Colville; "we are lost, we are dead men," and he sank as he spoke the words, fainting to the ground.

"You are right, Colville; they are about the only words of truth spoke in this confab, and if his lordship there values his life one pins fee, he will act my bidding or he is a dead man, as you yourself have predicted. I have not stepped my foot in the lion's den, without being so well armed as neither to fear or dread the ensuing consequences. I am here not only to punish your audacity for making a bye word of my name, but I am here also to prove to you, Jack of the Sixteen-strings defies detection, that he will run his gay career so long as it pleases him, and will leave it and England at one and the same time. Now, my lords, and you, gentlemen, will be pleased, at peril of instant death, to obey my orders.

As Jack's brilliant eyes were fixed on theirs, and as moreover to second his threatening frown, the ominous barrels of Jack and his pals pistols were levelled at their heads, they rose like automatons at the bidding.

"Your purses, watches, and trinkets."

They were impassively surrendered as the orders were delivered. When he had stripped them of all they possessed, Jack walked to the Lord Mayor.

"Never turn thief-catcher again, my lord, although devil take me if I doubt that the proverb set a thief to catch a thief holds not good in your case, still, the biter may be bit, as in the present case, and instead of catching a thief, the thief may catch you. You fellows here put me in mind of the foolish gardener, who planting a man trap, was the first to put his foot into it. Now, my lord, adieu, but stay! although you have so kindly favoured us with a quiet and safe mode of exit, and that through the chamber of your sleeping spouse, whose virtues like her slumbers shall remain for us, I give you my word, undefiled and undisturbed, yet it is necessary for our further protection that you should be gagged, lest by any unseemly noise you should disturb the tranquillity of our retreat. Therefore, comrades, silence them."

This was done in a manner, which for business-like dexterity, was certainly admirably expert: my lord learnt a new method of taking snuff, for his handkerchief, well filled with that fashionable powder, was crammed into his mouth. others also were found in mouthfulls if left with empty pockets, for they also were gagged to a nicety.

Taking a profoundly respectful leave of them when this had been accomplished the highwaymen proceeded on their way, in safety, and with exceeding triumph.

CHAPTER XVIII.

JACK'S VISIT HOME.—TREACHERY.—PERILOUS ESCAPE.

THE town—whereby is meant the inhabitants of the leviathan city of London, were thunderstruck and aghast at the audacious daring, exhibited in Jacks visit to the mayor, so much so, it became an object of absolute necessity that Jack should seek safety in flight. He had long had a yearning, a longing, at his heart to visit once again the home of his childhood, to be pressed again to his mother's throbbing heart, to see again his father's glistening eyes in joy fixed upon him.

But to return as an highwayman, on outcast of society, an advertised thief. The thought was agony.

"I'll fly another way," said Jack to himself, "it shall never be said I deserted my father's home, poor though it be, and yet why need they know it? Am I not bound to go so disguised, that my best friend shall fail to know me, and in that disguise, having gold golore at my command, can I not do them essential service? Yes, I will go, it shall be done."

And Jack, attired as a dandy of the first water, took his place inside the Bath coach the next morning. Leaving the vehicle at a village this side of Bath, Jack sauntered towards his father's cottage home. It was a delightful morning, and the familiar scenes that started on every side to greet him, filled his bosom with kindly thoughts of his old home, and with quickened step and beating heart he hurried on his way.

Arrived before the door, he found the garden once teeming with the loveliest of Floras' gifts, with rose, and eglantine, and sweet briar, now overrun with weeds, whilst desolation seemed to have set its corroding mark upon the house, for it was tottering to decay. The wretchedness found an echo in Jacks sympathetic heart, and he hurried from the dismal picture with sorrow in his heart, and with tears in his eyes.

Travelling a few paces further on, he came upon an old man breaking stones by the road side. Jack remembering his features, accosted him, and pointing to the cottage, asked what had become of the Rann's.

"Evil, zur, evil; all be gone wrong-like, Mrs. Rann she be dead, God rest her soul. Her boy Jack, an' a mighty foine lad he was, zur; he be turned highwayman he is, and old Rann he be in prison for debt."

Jack, stunned by this dismal intelligence, gasped for breath, and uttered an involuntary "God help me!"

"I axes your honour's pardon, but come to look at you, sir, you be tarnation like somebody I've seen afore, but terribly like the Rann family, that's a fact; are you any way related to 'em, zur?"

"I am, distantly," said Jack, then changing the conversation, he said "for how long has Rann been incarcerated?"

"Three long months, zur, and there he'll lay and rot if the money is'nt paid, at least, so says Luke Jones."

"Luke Jones what is he? why he was only a poacher or something of that sort when I was here before."

"Oh he be Squire Gile's head man now, zir, he be steward, and gamekeeper, and God only knows what, and what's more sir, he be a scoundrel or he would'nt have persecuted old Rann, when he knew he was broke down with the death of his wife, and he swears he'll have the blood money if Jack ever shows his face in Bath."

"It strikes me no one will have him till they catch him and by all accounts that is not the easiest of jobs," said Jack, "but now old friend you must do me a service for which I will give you a guinea."

"A guinea," exclaimed the old man, joyfully, "it's many a long day since I zeed one. A guinea, by goles."

"Yes, a guinea, if you will place this purse in the hands of Rann, tell him it was given him by a gentleman to effect his liberation. Now hasten off you precious dog do, while Rann's in prison I'm in agony, here take your guinea with you."

The old man sped on his way as fast as his trembling limbs would carry him. The purse contained more than sufficient to satisfy the claim against the elder Rann, who, to the astonishment of himself, of everybody, and of Luke Jones more than any one else, walked from the prison one morning a free man.

For this sudden plenitude of cash, Luke Jones saw at once that Sixteen-string Jack must have furnished the aid, and that he was lurking about the neighbourhood he had not the slightest doubt. Bent upon securing the heavy reward offered for Jack, he immediately began the scent. Now Jack had been living at the best hotel at Bath, but one afternoon, the day before he intended leaving Bath, he took a stroll to an inn near his own home; he surveyed the house and could discover no change in the exterior, so presuming in the safety of his disguise, he made a rush, and swaggered into the parlour. He cast his eyes round the room, and he there recognised the same old pictures; the same chimney ornaments, and well polished high-backed chairs; and being determined to come off with flying colours, he pulled lustily at the bell to bring in the landlord. Being the only occupant of the room, Jack drew a chair before the fire, and seating himself in it, placed a leg on each hob, and a quizzing glass to his eye. "There," he exclaimed, "this will polish them off in out and out Piccadilly style."

The landlord entered, bowed, rubbed his hands, and awaited his guest's orders.

"Let me have a dinner directly, and a bottle of brandy—quick—do you hear?"

"You shall be served in a few minutes, sir," replied the landlord, gazing at Jack with astonishment as he left the room, wondering what great man had honoured his house so far as to visit him.

"Away feeling! away remorse!" shouted Jack, "I'm no longer a country boy now; I'm Sixteen string Jack, the terror of the road—ha, ha, ha! and a jolly life I lead—but here's the brandy."

His dinner was placed before him; he was once more alone, and before he had finished his meal, deep draughts at the brandy bottle had banished all remorse for the peaceful life he had cast away, and he was once more the lion-hearted daring captain of the road.

Guest after guest, visitor after visitor, entered the room; candlelight took the place of daylight; the fire burned briskly and cheerfully, and the old public house parlour presented a very animated and comfortable picture. The newly arrived visitors were all neighbouring farmers and tradesmen, unknown, of course, to Jack, and the conversation for a long time dwelt upon agricultural pursuits, till Jack Rann, nothing dismayed, broke in, and turned it all upon himself.

"If I mistake not," he began, "that notorious disturber of the public peace, that Sixteen-stringed Jack, dwelt somewhere about this spot when a boy? at least, the newspapers hint as much."

"Why, that 'ere be the very identical house as he was borned in, sir," replied a red cheeked jolly looking country farmer, who sat opposite to Rann, at the fireside. "His poor mother only died a short time back with a broken heart, and his father is now a debtor in our gaol."

"Indeed! you surprise me much," replied Jack, opening his lips to give vent to a volume of curling smoke from his pipe.

A long pause now followed; the tankards went their rounds to the various mouths; pipes were re-loaded; the fire stirred, and the candles snuffed, when Jack broke in again.

"This Sixteen-stringed Jack, now I have heard he's a dreadful fellow."

"Oh, very, sir; I dont know how many murders he hasn't committed, and burned down houses out of number; but he'll be nabbed, some day, sir; only you mark my word. He'll be cotched in one of his own nets, and I should much like the job to help take him."

"Ha! ha! ha! you're thinking of the honour and the five hundred guineas," chimed in the red-cheeked farmer; that's what you be driving at, measter coachee."

The conversation was now broken off by the entrance of three strangers, who, seating themselves, looked searchingly round in the faces of all present, and then fell to whispering, winking, and nudging each other. Two of them were dressed as regular travellers, their low-crowned hats tied on with shawls, heavy pea-jackets, and high jack boots completed their outfit, and they carried long heavy mounted riding-whips, a blow from which would have felled an ox. The third was enveloped in a long shaggy cloak, had a tremendous black beard and a slouch hat which rendered his features nearly disguised, except a pair of large, black, piercing, penetrating eyes, which glared forth from beneath his brows with a savage fury. They seemed very repulsive and distant in their manners, drank together, spoke only to each other, and never once ventured a civil commonplace salutation to any one in the room.

Jack had fixed his eyes upon them from their entrance; in truth he did not half like them, and fancied to himself that the pair of wolf-like piercing eyes, just described, had gleamed upon him in fury and in anger once before —he was on the rack to discover them from mere curiosity, and ten times more so, when for the second time he discovered these tiger-like eyes again upon him.

"There's a scent abroad, I'm sure, here," muttered Jack, to himself, as he crossed his arms and leaned carelessly back in his chair, pretending to sleep, though all the time wide awake, and grasping his holster pistols beneath his coat, firmly with his right hand. "I don't half like their looks; they fix their eyes too often upon me; however, here's to see what bait a snore will prove." As he thus concluded, he breathed hard, and sending forth a sonorous sound, gave evident inclination of a sound sleep.

The trick succeeded. The strangers were less reserved; the one who wore the cloak threw it back, lifted his hat for a moment to wipe his brow, which disclosed to the eyes of Rann, his traitorous foe, Luke Jones.

"I know the worst, now," whispered Jack to himself between his teeth—"the old man warned me of this treacherous hound; if I am taken, it shall not be without sending a bullet through his recreant brain—that alone can soothe my own death blow. I must to my wits again; nothing less than a daring stratagem now can save me."

Again the mysterious three were in secret, confidential, conversation—and this time Jack could plainly see Luke point to himself, and touch the butt end of a pistol which hung in his belt. But he was dismayed and confounded to see one of the other travellers go up to the red-cheeked farmer and gentleman's coachman, who both sat side by side at the fire, and after whispering, point to himself, as he sat in his elbow chair in the corner.

"By Jove! this won't do," grumbled Jack to himself. "I shall have the room full on me directly, and then my only chance will be the flue or the window, so here goes, a leap for life."

So saying, Rann started suddenly to his feet, and by the rapidity of his motion, threw back the flowing skirts of his coat, and discovered to all lookers on a couple of holster pistols in his belt, which at least let them know that he was not going to be easily taken. He pulled the bell, and the landlord appearing, he paid his reckoning, wished all a "good night," and to his great surprise, left the room unmolested.

"Clean, by Jove," said Jack to himself, as he closed the door. "Now, a bold stroke for the stable, and once across a horse, they may fire away for honour and glory till doomsday."

Directly Jack left the room, Luke Jones started to his feet, and holding the handle of the door to prevent any egress, denounced their departed guest.

"I am right, I know him, gentlemen, the villain who has just left us, is no other than Jack Rann, or, in plainer words, Sixteen stringed Jack,! he is alone and unaided; five hundred guineas are offered for his head—you who would share the prize, follow and assist us to capture him."

The whole room was instantly up in arms, and in great confusion, and to a man, ten in number, rushed out after Luke to participate in the honour and profit of securing Sixteen-stringed Jack.

Meanwhile our hero bent his steps to the stable; soon forced the door, and by the aid of a dim lantern, selected a horse, and was in the act of buckling on the girth, when the whole posse came pell mell to the stable door, and summoned him to surrender!

"Ha! is it so," replied Jack, "this then must save me;" as he spoke he slammed too the old door, and barricaded it up with poles and boards. Then rushing to the extremity of the stable to try and discover an outlet there, and being disappointed, he drew his pistols, and clenching them firmly in his hands, awaited the next attack. "I am caged by all my hopes of Newgate! not a crevice that I could squeeze my nose through. I am resolved how to act; for my mind is always fixed for my last resource. I have here three bullets for my captors; the fourth shall bury itself deep in my own brain, before I will allow them to take me." Resolved in this dreadful alternative, Jack went up to the door, and anxiously listened for their next appeal.

"Fool! coward! boy; you are known," yelled out a voice which he instantly recognised to be Luke's, "your disguise has failed you; your enemy Luke Jones it is who summons you, and tells you he is come to fulfil his threat, and glut in the reward payable at your capture!"

"Shall I answer him by a bullet," thought Jack to himself as he peeped through a hole in the door; "I could cover him beautifully just now! but it's only wasting a good shot. At that instant his eyes rested on an ostler's suit hanging on a nail in the wall—a flash of thought entered his mind, and he flew to execute it. "Capital! I shall dish them now!" he said, exultingly, as, slipping off his own dress, he put on that of the ostler; then stuffing his own suit out with hay and straw, he tied a white handkerchief up in a round bundle for the head, and putting a rope round it, slung his own effigy up to the beam—a suicide, perishing by hanging! "Ha! ha! ha!— there I am, dangling as neat as at Tyburn!" As yet he had not replied one word; his only thoughts was of escape; and spying an old reaping-hook in a corner he mounted a ladder, and began cutting his way through the thatched roof. "If they are only outside two minutes longer I'll double 'em!" he exclaimed, as he slashed away at the rotten thatch, which cracked and splintered like burnt paper.

"Oh, its no use humbugging like this," said one of Luke's companions, who was no less a personage than the chief runner at Bow-street; "let's crack the crib and go in at once! You know what a slippery cove he is!"

"With all my heart!" replied Luke, "all hands, my boys, to force the door! Who's got a hammer? Bring us a crow-bar! We'll take the rat in his own trap, after all."

All was helter skelter now for implements to force the door with. Some run one way for a hammer, others for a crowbar, poker, pick-axe, or anything that came readiest to hand. In a few minutes the storming party fell to work—banging, hammering, wrenching, bursting, and pushing at the stout old oaken door, which, for some time stood out nobly.

"Ah! ah! go it my Britons," laughed Rann, at this noisy outbreak on the part of his pursuers; "you break in, and I'll break out, and then we shall have come to a settlement." At this moment the thatch gave way, and a hole large enough for him to creep through having been cleared out, he threw down the reaping-hook, and with a spring from the hay-rack, soon managed to drag his body out on to the roof, along which he scrambled, and dropping to the ground from behind, made off through the darkness of the night, across the meadows at the back of the house.

The door at last gave way to the repeated attacks upon it; and Luke Jones, with a yell of savage delight, bounded into the stable.

"He's choused us, by all that's damnable—he's not here," he exclaimed, as he looked round the stable in vain for his victim; even amongst the horses, who, startled from the noise, had turned their heads and cocked their ears at the unwarranted intrusion.

"What's that!" exclaimed one the officers, pointing to the effigy which

Jack had stuffed and hung up by the neck; "curse me if he has'nt hanged himself out of sheer despair."

The whole party now stood aghast and amazed, actually terror stricken and dumb. Luke, never doubting the originality of the figure, clasped his hands with delight, exclaiming, "Have I then run the cunning young fox to earth at last; I thought the old hound would prove too much for him. Somebody run for a doctor, I'll attend to the prisoner; remember, the reward is ours, alive or dead, and as he has given us so much trouble, its safer to take him dead!" Saying this, he dispatched a man for a doctor, locked the stable door, put the key in his pocket, and stood sentry over it, to prevent any one from interfering.

"Let's cut the cove down, and give him a chance for his life," said one of the officers to Jones.

"Yes; to let him slip through our fingers, and get laughed at for our

No. 24.

pains at last," replied Oliver, sullenly. "No, no; the game's in my hands now; he baulked me once before, it's my fault if he does this time."

In a very short space of time the man returned, out of breath, bringing with him a medical man, who was very angry at their not cutting the body down. The door was unlocked for him, and with his lancet in his hand, he rushed in; one hand swayed a sharp knife, and brought the seeming corpse into his arms, as with the other he plunged the lancet into (as he thought) a vein in the arm! but judge of the doctor's surprise, and the captor's chagrin, when with an oath, he pulled the straw from its interior, and cast it at their feet.

CHAPTER XIX.

MEETING OF THE GANG.—JACK PLANS REVENGE.

AFTER the hair breadth escape from Luke Jones, Jack found it his imperative duty, as he studied his own safety, to leave Bath with all speed. But he left it only for a time, for he was determined to wreak a bitter revenge on the head of the traitorous Luke Jones. Acting upon these resolves, he forthwith despatched a letter to Toby, requesting him, and Clayton, and Wide Awake, to join him at a rendezvous where he was staying, at the house of one Master Abel Spiggot. One afternoon there came to this public-house or tavern, three new comers those sort of looking beings on whom, in passing, we will cast a transient glance for some singularity of appearance without being sufficiently struck to pause and stare at them; and who only excite a more lasting notice when their manners or conversation are in keeping with their appearance. The first was a portly substantial looking man of about fifty, hale and florid in complexion, and every line of his countenance marked with eccentricity and good humour. He was evidently a wealthy member of one of the city alleys, for the broadcloth in which he was enveloped was of the best texture, and his watch-chain and seals were of massive gold. He was dressed with that singular mixture of neatness and untidiness, which, time out of mind, has been the characteristic of monied men, although in every point attention has been paid to comfort, from the overalls on the legs to the roquelaire over his shoulders; the ample cravat round his burly throat, to the little neatly curled bob wig and oddly shaped hat which surmounted his " knowledge box." He carried a whip in his hand, and evidently knew himself to be a man of importance, even beyond the sound of Bow bells.

His companion was altogether a different sort of a man, being tall, slender, and cadaverous. His dress bespoke him as belonging to the class termed "quakers," while his manners bespoke him as one of the most rigid of the order. The lines of his face were strongly marked, expressive of a soured disposition, and his long, lank, black hair, by forming a sort of ground relief to his pale, sallow, features, made them look like some sculptured image of austerity, fit only to gleam amid the conventual gleam of the olden churches.

The third of the party was an attendant upon the other two; a neat, dapper black in livery, with teeth as white as pearl, bright lively eyes, and a periwig over his curly pate, equal to snow itself in whiteness, and one that would have graced the chief factotum of an alderman himself.

Abel Spiggot, as before asserted, ushered in his guests with all the respect demanded by their appearance. Their entrance naturally attracted the momentary attraction of all the carousers, while the eyes of the three were only fixed upon one—and that was Sixteen-string Jack. They stared at him as if he had been a spectre, and he stared at them to see what they were staring about. It may be conceived that he did this with some feeling of uneasiness; he thought at first that they might be some of the city connections of Mr. Colville; but the more he scanned them, the stronger was his conviction that he had never seen them before, and so completely did he become engrossed by returning their scrutiny, that he unconsciously continued to hold the hand of the pretty waitress with whom he had been occupied when they came in. What made their regards more unpleasant, was, that their stare was not in the stare of vulgar yet undisguised curiosity, which every one was at liberty to behold, but it was a concealed stare—a stare shot over the shoulders of the bowing landlord, as if only meant to be seen by the party aimed at, and which said, as plainly as a stare could say, "you are known, young man!"

The landlord having bowed them into the centre of the apartment, proceeded to open upon the order of the evening with the customary remark upon the weather. "A fine evening, gentlemen," said he.

"Very," returned the citizen. "Don't you think so, young man at the corner of the table?"

"I've no opinion upon the subject," returned Rann, almost as unconscious of what he was saying as he had been of the import of the question.

Master Abel Spiggot was too good a general to permit what had occurred to ripen into a quarrel, as it was contrary to his interest that either party should be offended, for Jack had spent many a bright dollar in his house, and the appearance of the cockney merchant led him to expect something ample; the wary landlord therefore judiciously stepped between the pair, and solicited to be honoured with the commands of his newly-arrived guests.

"Why, you may bring me a thimble-full of brandy, and a large glass of spring water for my friend with the square toes, here," returned the Cit, with as much importance as if he had ordered the contents of the entire cellar.

Spiggot stared, and pretending not to have understood him, said, "A bottle of the best French cognac with cold water. Very well, sir; you shall have it immediately."

The citizen slapped his hand on the table, and exclaimed, "Harkee, young man!" the landlord was at least sixty, "I said a thimble-full of brandy, and I'll take no more and no less. I'm like the goose in that ere fable what we reads in the spelling books. I'll yield a golden egg a day if I'm properly treated; but if you thinks to get all out o' me at once, you'll find you've made as precious a mistake as the boy did when he ripped up his valuable bird and found *nix*."

At this hint, Spiggot made off with all possible celerity, and returned with the brandy, measured in the smallest glass in the house. He also handed a tumbler of water to the quaker, who took it so awkwardly as to spill more than half of the innocent beverage. The landlord begged pardon, for it is an invariable rule with the monarchs of the tap to take all accidents which engender no expense upon their own shoulders.

"It matters not, friend," said Broadbrim, "for the place of that which is spilt may be more profitably supplied both to thee and to me with something to comfort the inward man. Humph!"

"A good thought, sir," whispered Abel, with a knowing wink. "What say you to a gill of scheedam? It looks as harmless as water, while it warms the veins like running fire. My wife always takes, when the parson pays her a visit, and shams it off as the 'blessed water of the spring.'"

"Verily, there is wisdom in thine advice," answered the quaker; "for though there is no harm in a moderate indulgence in those things which make the heart wax strong, it is not prudent to give the profane an opportunity of passing their jibes upon those whom the spirit moveth."

"No, no," said Abel, with another wink, "or else they might think that the spirit was sometimes distilled."

The quaker was about to reply, when his cockney friend interrupted him by returning his empty glass to the landlord, and smacking his lips in token of high satisfaction.

"That's a drop of the right sort," said he. "I don't care if you now bring me a quart of it."

"Anything to eat?" returned Spiggot; "you will find a snack of something nice and hot a great improvement with the brandy!"

"Methinks I could relish something of the sort. Humph!" suggested the quaker to his companion.

"Relish!" returned the Cit. "Zounds! I could bolt a pair of flat irons, I'm so hungry."

"Then you would do justice to a fine goose that is at this moment ready for roasting in my buttery hatch," said the landlord. "Moll, cook, shall put it down in a twinkling."

"Very good," said the merchant, with an expression about the jaws which betokened that they anticipated the treat. "And harkee, old chap," he added, "let's have your company over the brandy, while the goose is a roasting. I'll throw in something extra for it when I tips the rowdy."

"Your honour has only to command to be obeyed," answered the compliant host, who never refused a glass at the expense of his customers. "Shall I in the meantime show your servant the way into the kitchen?"

"What, blackee?" replied the traveller. "No; he's as good a right here as the white's. Let him take his place near that young man with the dandy knee-strings."

The last expression once more sent a shock through the entire nervous system of Jack, and strange fancies and fears began to agitate his bosom. He had with a hawk's eye scrutinised the travellers from the moment of their entrance, and he felt a conviction that the characters in which they appeared were assumed. He detected, likewise, a false carbuncle on the nose of the merchant that strengthened this opinion, but though filled with apprehensions, he endeavoured to persuade himself that the whole might be a portion of some madcap frolic, such as characterised the times; the allusion, however, to his conspicuous knee-ties at once settled all uncertainty on the matter, and he felt convinced that the officers of justice had by some means found him out, and were now about to take him into custody.

As he arrived at this conclusion, the black footman took his place at the point indicated by his master, and Jack felt the fellow's eyes were upon him with an earnestness that had its hidden meaning; he strove to evade the glance, and as he did so, detected a small patch of white skin behind the man's ear, which proved that the sable complexion that enabled him to enact the negro, was as false as the citizen's nose. This was making "assurance double sure," and he started up with the intention of rushing from the place, and taking flight on Sue's back, if he could reach her before his pursuers came up, but as he rose, the pretended negro caught him by the arm, and exclaimed, "Sit down, massa, sit down. Him hear so long, and him like it very much. Sit down, den, and him stand treat."

On this Jack felt he must trust to artifice more than anything else for his escape, so he turned to Abigail, who was in attendance for orders, and in order to make it appear that his movement had been occasioned by her, he again snatched some of the nectar that lodged on her lips. He then reseated himself, and asked blackee to partake of a flagon of prime Burton ale.

"Ale," said the other with a sneer. "Him been drinking wine, and him nebber put blackguard on genuelman; nebber!"

"What will you please to take, sir?" said the waitress, curtseying rather lower than usual on hearing the boast.

"A bowl of arrack punch," replied the ebony face, "and make him dam trong;—trong enough to play um debel wid 'em all!"

Abigail curtseyed obedience, and in a few moments the pretended black was busily engaged in ladling out the potent beverage he had ordered, to fat Philip, and his associates, and pouring volley after volley of odd things in their ears with such rapidity as to keep them in roars of laughter, unawed by the presence of his master. By this time also the quaker was gravely seated over his hollands and water, while the merchant with "mine host" at his elbow, held his liquor upon his knee with one hand, and supported the stem of his pipe with the other, and launched into a conversation that occasioned Jack to put every listening faculty he possessed into requisition.

"It's a dull place this, Master Spiggot," he began. "Pretty enough, I grant, but Paradise itself would give one the blue devils if there was nothing to keep one alive in it. Now I'd wager all the rowdy I possess— I mean, all my cash, to a penny piece, that you haven't so much as a subject to set your tongues agoing, except of the weather, and the market prices."

"You are not far wrong, your honour," returned Abel, "though at present we have no lack of news to talk about, for the whole town is full of this new thief who is making such a noise—the fellow they call 'Jack with the strings.'"

"Sixteen-string Jack," said the merchant, nodding at Rann with a provoking air of recognition. "Ah! one hears his name everywhere."

"Yea," joined the quaker, "and if he keepeth not close, the man of iniquity will verily be discovered."

"Aye, aye," resumed the cit, puffing forth a complete cloud of smoke, also, "and he will learn the truth of those beautiful lines in Homer's Illiad, where that ere divine poet says:—

"Him as takes what isn't his'n,
Is sure to find his way to prison,
And then Jack Ketch will stretch his wizen."

Having delivered himself of this sublime triplet, he raised the tumbler to his mouth, and emptied it at a single draught, as he thought the recitation deserving of the highest reward. The landlord listened with profound respect with which we always listen to the nonsense of those who pay us well, and then inquired if any real active measures were on foot for entrapping the highwayman.

"To be sure there is," answered the merchant, "and if he shewed his muzzle in London, he would be carried to Newgate as sure as his name is Jack. The whole town is posted with the description of a certain mare that was stolen from a gent, at Hounslow; so closely is she drawn, that any one might recognise her with his elbows if the chap dared to ride down Fleet Street, on her back."

"They do say," observed the landlord, "that the mare has already been recognised by the turnpike-man between Kensington and Hammersmith, and it is more than suspected that Jack is concealed about these parts."

"Let us pray that he is concealed about here," exclaimed the quaker, with an emphasis which Rann could not understand. "Don't think, friend, that the man who standeth at the aforementioned turnpike-gate, hath it in his power to describe the light-fingered villain, who rode the mare?"

"He hath already done so, I'm told," said Spiggot; "and if his description be correct, Sixteen-string Jack must be a sort of half man and half monster, like Orson the man of the woods. Howsomdever an affidavy has been taken about it, so it must be all right, and the consequence is, that every house or shed where a beast may be lodged, is searched morning and evening by government officers, so that if he be hereabouts, he's as unsafe as he would be if he sat where that young gentleman is sitting, and Jack Ketch sat where you do."

"But he'd be more unsafe in Lunnun, cried the traveller, "for the Lord Mayor is so awful angry, that he's put a watch over every livery stable, mews, and inn-yards, within five miles of the Mansion-house. The Bacchanal's at Islington, has been shut up on account of suspicion alighting upon it, and this morning I seed a regular search going for'ard at the 'Cock and Magpie,' Wych-street, so you sees a rat must be smelt somewhere."

Not a word of all this was lost upon Jack. He sat riveted to his seat, like the felon who listens to a condemned sermon; but plucking up his spirit, he turned towards the loquacious traveller with the false carbuncles, and said:—

"I am rather interested in this matter myself, sir—"

"I dare say you are, young man," interrupted the merchant, "Very much so, no doubt."

This again unhinged Jack, and he was obliged to swallow a glass of punch before he could proceed:—"As I was saying, I am at present in the employment of a foreign nobleman who has been robbed by the highwayman you mention, and consequently I am interested in all that concerns him; will you have the goodness, therefore, to explain why so much stir is making to recover this animal, when, as I've heard, the man paid for her before he took possession:—indeed I can vouch for the fact, as I wrote answers yesterday to the magistrates of Bray.

"You are quite correct, young man, and old Boniface, of the 'Nag's Head,' Barbican, was very well satisfied with his bargain, but the common council took it up, willy nilly. There had been so many descriptions given of Sixteen-stringed Jack, and each one so different from t'other, that the look-outs felt fairly bothered; but the moment the grand daughter of Bess was stolen they had a clue to guide 'em. If they could'nt get a description of the rider they could of the horse, and as a hanimal of the specie can't be hid in a mousetrap, or go into an oven for concealment, it is more liable to discovery than we of the two legged gender; Consequently, wherever the mare is seen, tidings may be expected of the man."

"It would have been much better then for the mare to have been left where she was," exclaimed Jack bitterly, and without reflecting how likely the observation was to betray him."

"Not at all," observed the traveller; "for as attention is now more directed to the horse than the thief, he has only to keep the beast where it may now be concealed, and he may walk abroad himself without attracting any notice."

This observation would have given great comfort to Jack, had it been uttered by any other tongue, but being spoken by one he had so much reason to fear he considered it as said purposely to tantalize him and his impatience, and agitation were now greater than ever. As if to increase these yet more, and remove the slight hope he had just held out, the merchant after knocking out the ashes of his pipe, and re-filling, added:—

"But his chance can't last long now, for I heard, as I left town, that lawyer Quire and several gentlemen who were stopped and robbed on the night Jack stole the mare, are coming down to-morrow to have a meeting with this magistrate of yours, and that they are going to compare notes and furnish every necessary particular for leading to his detection."

Had been it the intention of this speaker to put Jack on his gaurd in every possible way, he could not have managed his purpose more effectually, for a

Rann was now acquainted with all he had to dread, he had ample opportunity for taking measures against the coming evil. There was something, too, in the speakers manner, which led our hero to suspect that he would not be inaccessible to the offer of a bribe, so Jack determined to make the experiment before he adopted steps of a more dangerous character. Having made this determination, he gave himself up to unrestrained conversation, which now diverged into more general topics. By this time the punch and other liquors had begun to take effect, and Jack noticed that while the strangers pushed round the glass with increased celerity, they gradually grew more sparing in imbibing their own potations. In short, he plainly saw that it was their determination to make all present drunk.

Nor was it long before the thick heads of the party gave way before the insidious and potent attacks of that enemy before whom so many mighty ones have fallen. The first to fall was fat Phillip the fibber; and oh, what a fall was there! He did not, as some do, slide insensibly from his seat, nor roll gently under the table but rose to make a speech; and in uttering the words "I stand before you gentlemen," his knees bent beneath him, and he fell flat on his face with so stunning an effect, that he was scarcely heard to breath after it. Next to him went his master's valet; and after that the rest sank in succession, either in a profound slumber on the table, or in a torpor of intoxication beneath it. The last to go was Mr. Abel Spiggot, the landord, who at first appeared proof against every attack; but being plied with different sorts of liquor, he at length fell before their combined influence, and sank back in his arm-chair without the slightest consciousness.

Jack had watched these events, and remarked that the travellers also watched them. He likewise perceived that they read his thoughts, and viewed with satisfaction his continuation in a state of sobriety. This rendered conclusive all he had suspected, and feeling that the moment had arrived which had been waited for by the strangers as well as himself, to go through it or die; fixing his eye therefore on the three, who were now drawn in whispering consultation together, he drew a clasp knife from his pocket and bared the blade. Grasping this, dagger fashion, with one hand, he with the other took out a purse, and displaying both with a meaning look, he step by step retreated towards the window, and placing one foot on the sill ready for immediate flight, he muttered in calm but determined tones—

"Now then, my covies, FRIENDS OR FOES?"

"Friends, Jack, friends!" exclaimed the quaker, in a voice scarcely audible, so deeply was it suppressed. "Can it be possible that you do not know us?"

"Know you? no. Why who the devil are you?" returned Rann, withdrawing his foot from its resting-place and advancing a few steps nearer the stranger; but still grasping his knife ready to make deadly use of it if occasion demanded.

"Werry good?" returned the pretended merchant. "We must be safe, Charley, if the captain himself can't recognise us."

"And have I been such an ass!" cried Jack, at once recognising the voice of the speaker, "this is beyond belief! Why, Toby, you look quite like a respectable moral man, and as for you, Charlie, your own mistress would not be able to trace a single feature amid the angular lines into which you have drawn your face. But who the deuce is Smutty Face? I have found out, long ago, that he is no negro!"

"Why, none other than your aide-de-camp, Wide Awake," said Charlie.

Jack felt real pleasure at this intimation, and shook hands with his friends all round.

At this instant the pretty Abigail made her entrance to inform the pretended merchant that the goose was ready, and to inquire whether he would prefer supping where he was, or in a private room—adding, as she glanced significantly round at the liquor-bound sleepers, that she thought the latter would be more comfortable of the two.

"Verily this young damsel adviseth well," observed Charlie in his quaker-

No. 25.

like tones, " for, of a verity, my nostrils hold the breath of these sleepers in abomination."

"Then we had better shake our feathers and toddle; and what say you to this young man supping with us?" interposed Toby. "I may be able to make an advantageous offer to his master concerning the shipping of goods, pretending our hero to be in a merchant's employ, if he has time to give me the information I want, vich he can't by no manner of means if he stays drinking here while we are eating there."

"We are all brothers in the flesh, therefore need we not disdain to sit with him, though he ranketh not so high as ourselves," drawled forth Charlie through his nose.

Abigail curtseyed, and said she would inform the waiters; upon which Toby exclaimed that he should be poisoned if the dishes were to be pawed by a pack of country bumpkins, and that no one else but this black footman should wait at table. Abigail tossed up her head with a "humph!" and, muttering something about the sooty fingers of black East Injins, flounced out of the room in high dudgeon.

"How a touch of red improves the dear creatures!" observed Jack, with reference to the pretty flush that indignation had spread from her neck to her temples.

"You think 'em charming, any how," said Toby. "I shall vear out my blessed tongue in telling you that vomen vill bring you to your latter end. Vy, now, I'd vager if that 'ere young 'oman held a halter in her hand, you'd thrust your neck through, if her lips were on t'other side."

"Oh, no! not while I've such a charmer as the girl whom old Sue and myself fished out of the Thames the other day!" cried Jack. "O Charlie!" he continued, in ecstacy, "such a being!—the rounded plumpness of a woman, and the ærial grace of an angel; and then, Charlie, her lips! Zounds! she wraps her kisses in honey, and seals them with sunshine!"

"I knew a being once, whom I thought the same of," remarked Charlie, with a sigh; then passing his hand rapidly across his forehead, as if to brush away some bitter recollection, he added, "but we have matters of more moment to discuss. Let us leave the women for our own leisure."

The waitress shortly re-entered, to say that all was arranged, and with a curl of disdain upon her lips, asked if she was to awake her master to accompany them.

"Vy, no, poor fellow," answered Toby, "he appears too somnambulant to make any other use of his jaws than to snore. Suppose ve leave him to his nap? Ve'll take care of his silver spoons, and other articles of plate up stairs. Poor fellow! He's as unprotected as a hinfant."

"It would serve him right if old Sixteen-string Jack were to pay him a visit!" exclaimed Abigail, who was a very teetotaller with regard to her admiration of sobriety.

"Ha, ha, ha!" said Toby, rising to follow her as she led the way to the supper-room. "It would be summat like a joke to see him here, would it not, young man?"

"Rather," said Jack, giving his features a twist which none but his comrades understood.

"I'm sure it's an event you needn't pray for," said Abigail, turning sharply round as she spoke.

"And why, girl, why?" he asked, tightening his hold upon the knife which he had not yet restored to his pocket.

"Why," she answered, "because if his robberies were to happen down this way, he'd lick you all as clean as I could lick a platter."

A glance shot between the three, as instantaneously as if propelled from an electric machine, and, as if the look had confirmed a decision in each, stalked after Abigail without another word, closely followed by Wide Awake.

No sooner were they left alone to make their assault upon the goose than Toby, who had already made preparations for carving, laid down his knife and fork, and exclaimed:—

"A voman has pointed the vay out of a scrape for once! The vay to puzzle the beaks, and put all calculation at defiance, is to appear afore this squire in his own house, and rob him on the spot."

"It must be done," said Charlie.

"Gentlemen, it SHALL be done!" exclaimed Rann, fixed with the boldness of the enterprise.

"Think you I mean not what I say?" continued Jack. "I swear I do, by heaven! I tell you, Clayton, my noble friend, and you, Toby, my glorious fellow, and you, young pluck," to Wide Awake, "that had it not have been for the persecution of this man Giles, and his traitorous hound of a gamekeeper, I should not now have stood without the pale of society. No," said Jack, a memory of his mother's early death filling his heart with rancorous bitterness, "but should have remained within its precincts an honest and an honourable man."

"But poor,
Vithout a penny in my purse,
Now tell l vhat in life is worse,"

chaunted Toby, as it where quite unpremeditatedly.

"Devilish true, that's a fact," said Jack, "and so to the devil with the blues, say I."

"Amen!" said Toby, with a cadence so deep, and a look so demure, as would inevitably have immortalised any parish clerk in the world, and was so irresistibly comic to his comrades, that an irrepressible burst of laughter unwittingly escaped their lips.

"Well, old fellows, let feeling and care go together—to the wind with them, say I. We are men—we are highwaymen, man's master! Now mates, I gave you a glimpse of the truth in my letter. I told you I had an old grudge to pay, and besought your assistance to help me pay it in full."

"And it shall be paid in full," cried the trio.

"It shall," said Jack, briefly. "Coming to Bath, my brave lads, I came with a heart full of joyous anticipation, for I had a mother, father, and a home to come to. Picture my disappointment, if you can—my tongue is far too faint to give even an outline of the miserable tale. My home was desolate—my mother dead—my father in prison, and Luke Jones—a man for whom I had sacrificed home and honesty—was, in conjunction with the accursed squire, the cause of it all! Not content with this, even he sought my capture. The facts of my escape you are already aware of."

"Yes," exclaimed Toby, "and if ever I come near him, so help me G—, he is a dead man. Jack, I'll shoot him like a dog."

Without paying heed to this dark threat, our hero continued—

"I am so well acquainted with the squire's mansion, I can introduce you into the kitchen, without disturbing even a watch-dog. Once there—"

"Ve're adjacent to the pantry, heaven be thanked!" said Toby.

"Yes, and that is not all, we are adjacent to the money chest of the apartment. I can tell you, my brave pals, if you will follow my footsteps in this adventure there is little risk, and I may say no danger. I can rob this squire of his massive hoard, if I had but a vehicle, as quickly as I could pick a pocket in Cheapside."

"Talk about wehicles, vhat do you think ve've brought down?"

"I am in no riddle-solving humour to-night, Luke, so don't ask—"

"Vell I vont; but it's a hearse."

"A hearse!"

"Yes, my boy, vith four spanking horses, and relays on the road. The devil himself, if he suspected us, vich he couldn't possibly have cheek enough to do, couldn't by any possibillity catch us if it came to a run. Vonce again, my beloved Sixteen-stringer, all is arranged. If safety lays in flight, ve can fly like vinkin; if it comes to a fight vhat have ve to fear?"

"Precisely nothing," said Clayton; "for if Colledge will be but true to his aim, we are a match for any dozen in Christendom."

"And won't I!" said Colledge, emphatically.

"All is agreed then," said Jack. "The squire shall pay my expenses to Bath and back, and may the devil admire me!"

* * * * *

At midnight, all being in readiness, Jack led his confederates into a road that led directly to the servants' kitchen. To remove a window, and to obtain an entrance was but the work of a few minutes. Once there, Jack's knowing footsteps did the rest. Under his guidance they found their way to the old man's library, and in a chest in this library they found a cash-box heavily laden with gold, a casket of jewels, and divers "law papers, of no value but to any but the owner," but of vast value to Squire Giles, who having obtained surreptitious possession of them, was enjoying a property which belonged rightly to another. Jack, with a keen eye to revenge, secured them privately about his person. The gang, having secured their spoil, returned to the kitchen and did ample justice to a cold supper, invitingly laid open to attack.

It was well attended to, and bottle after bottle of wine having been broached, Jack, under its exhilarating effects, proposed to write a letter apprising the squire of the loss he had sustained, and knowing the road to his bedroom from having once traversed it, he proposed to find his way there alone and place the letter upon the squire's pillow.

"Vell, that vud be out and out slap, shiver my blinkers!" exclaimed Toby, throwing himself back easily in his chair! "only to think now, what the old curmudgeon must think to find a letter close by his nose in the morning, when he emancipates his blessed precious peepers! Post paid too, and no trouble at all! Vy, Jack, my captain, 'twould immortalize you as a man of letters for ever Ha! ha! ha!"

A long and hearty laugh from the half intoxicated burglars re-echoed through the kitchen at this witty remark of Toby's.

"Softly lads, softly;" whispered Rann, as he started to his feet at this outbreak; "we are not at a flash crib remember, I have turned this affair over in my mind, and, by God, I'll do it!" he exclaimed with passionate vehemence. A secret something prompts me once more to see old Giles; and be it for good or evil, I'll go through with it."

"Why you don't mean to say that, captain—you're joking surely," remarked Charlie, in a sort of half-derisive laugh, as he looked inquiringly into the face of his leader. "Go up into the old fellow's bed-room, now! why you are dreaming, sure."

"Then dreams come true," answered Rann, sternly; "for by my soul, I never said anything more serious in all my life. We have no time to patter, lads; so get ready to stow the swag. Come up into the passage, and be ready to bolt over the low wall if anything goes wrong;—you understand me; should I want any assistance I will call for it; but use not a blade or bullet in this house to night, not even if in self-defence. If life is taken here, I am no longer your leader; I will renounce the profession and give myself up to justice, and finally overthrow the whole gang if murder is committed here; as you value me, obey me in this. Am I answered?"

"Faithfully—sacredly," responded his companions.

"Good so far. I now go to take my farewell of the old boy, who treated me like a dog or I should have been better than I am. The devil! Am I moralising now; a toss more brandy, this light, and I'm off presently."

So saying, Rann drained a bumper of brandy at a draught, snatched up a candle, and kicked off his buckle shoes under the table, as he remarked, "these I shall leave to the kitchen wench as a legacy; and if she values famous curiosities, she will store these up for her grandchildren as the very identical shoes of the notorious "Sixteen-stringed Jack," and make their fortunes by them wholesale—now I'm off; don't stop for me."

As he uttered these last words, Rann darted up the kitchen stairs into the passage, and before he mounted the wide oil-clothed stairs of the first floor, he recollected to himself that they might creak most confoundedly, which circumstance had cost him many an oath, but, without being discomforted by this singularity, he climbed on to the balustrades, and by squeezing himself through the wide oaken carved pillars, and holding on tight with his right hand, he managed to reach the bedrooms on the first floor. Listening attentively at the keyhole of the front room, which he knew to be the squire's, and ascertaining that no light was burning within, he tried to open it, and to his surprise, found it fast; a custom that the squire never put in force. This rather startled the adventurous midnight visitor, but his never-failing hope soon restored him to energy and exertion. "I suppose it is my popularity out of doors that has made the old buffer do this," muttered Jack to himself, as he drew an old cork screw from his pocket; "but what can't be helped, must be cured, as the proverb says, so here goes,"

Applying the corkscrew carefully to the inner wards of the lock, it soon gave way, and pressing his knee sharply against a lower panel, the door opened, and he discovered himself in a neatly-attired bedroom, the bedstead enveloped in white curtains, standing in a further corner. Upon glancing round the room Jack was rather surprised to see several articles of female wearing apparel carelessly scattered about, apparently just cast from the person in undressing.

"Surely I am not in the wrong room; this used to be the one, I could swear," he communed softly to himself, as he glanced frequently around him. "But here's to make sure, at all risks."

Thus resolving, he advanced to the bed, and drawing the curtains on one side, he beheld, to his infinite surprise, not the wealthy Squire Giles, but a sleeping beauty of sixteen, a second Hebe, whose snowy arms being extended over the coverlid, Rann could not resist the temptation of carrying her hand to his lips, and imprinting thereon a fervent kiss. This, and the glaring rays of the candle falling full on her face, caused the young lady to turn round in her sleep; and Jack feared he had been to bold; but quickly withdrawing the light, and pausing a few minutes, he had the satisfaction of finding that she had again dropped off into a sound slumber.

"How sweetly and softly she sleeps!" exclaimed Jack to himself, as he now gazed upon her lovely features! "how unconscious of my presence! well, fair beauty, I shall let you know by some token or other, that—Sixteen-string Jack has paid you a visit in your bedroom, which, if not the most dangerous, is the most secret and skilful retreat I ever explored."

Going across the room to a dressing-table Jack perceived a splendid miniature of the sleeping beauty in a drawer; this he transferred to his pocket, and pulling a valuable diamond ring from his own hand, he explained the affair upon a sheet of paper, in the following words:

"Sixteen-string Jack's love to the lady of this apartment, and begs that she will not be uneasy at the absence of the miniature of herself; as the possessor has been so enraptured at the sleeping countenance of the original, that he has sworn to deliver it to no one else; meanwhile, as a pledge of remembrance, he has left this ring in its place, hoping for the favour of its gracing the finger of the lady. And, in so doing, he remains, for ever,

"Her Sincere Admirer,
"SIXTEEN-STRING JACK.

"N.B.—As Jack mixes with the first of company, he does not despair of shortly being able to restore the portrait to its owner."

Leaving this tender epistle with the ring upon the table, Jack advanced once more to the bedside, and, although his peril was at that moment most imminent, he could not refrain from snatching a kiss of the coral, pouting lips of the beauteous maiden, who, slightly startled by the intrusion, buried her fair face deep in the downy pillow, and slept on.

Quitting this apartment as noiselessly as he had entered it, Rann proceeded, with cautious steps, to the floor above, imagining that he must surely be right here. He tried the front door, and it opened at his touch, which convinced him that he was right. The bed stood close by the door, and the round chubby face of old Giles was soon recognised by him, snugly ensconced on his pillow, looking for all the world, as Jack expressed it, " like a red cabbage in a snow-heap."

Rann now proceeded to his task, and laid the letter on the squire's pillow, close under his very nose. His attention was then directed to the room, and perceiving a pair of silver mounted holster pistols laying on the drawers, loaded, he pocketed them. But what was a most valuable prize to Rann was the Squire's banking account book, which he found in the pocket of his great coat; and although banking business was not carried on then as now, yet the more wealthy gentlemen and tradesmen generally had running accounts at a private banking-house; and several cheques were endorsed with Mr. Giles's signature, and the amounts left blank, ready for filling in.

"By Jove! this will pull in a few hundreds," said Jack, with a low whistle to himself, as he tore the leaves out and put them in his pocket; a gold watch, two gold seals, and a brooch followed the cheques; and Jack, turning suddenly round to take a farewell glance at his old enemy, was almost stunned with surprise at beholding that worthy person sitting bolt upright in bed, looking at him. Lowering his mask, and presenting a pistol was the work of but an instant; and for several more both parties spoke not a word.

"Villain! you are robbing me!" said the merchant, in a tone of desponding resolution.

"Move but an inch, and I send a bullet through your brain!" answered Rann, suddenly, in a feigned voice. "I will not willingly harm you; the house is filled with my companions, and if resistance is offered or alarm attempted, you will fall a victim to the rash step; not only yourself, but all those connected with you."

"Robber! I am not so easily intimidated!" screamed the old merchant, in a rage; and leaping from the bed, he closed with Rann and wrested the pistol from him before the latter was aware of the movement. They both struggled fearfully, and Rann's object was to gain the door, shake off his adversary, and, locking him in, take to flight; but the old man was not so easily got rid of. Jack by degrees edged his way to the door; neither speaking a word, the old man had grasped Rann by the shoulder and throat, whilst the latter clutched old Giles firmly by the waist.

"Help! Murder! Thieves!" roared the squire, as they reached the landing.

"Your life will pay for this," growled Jack, as he strained every nerve to hurl the old man back into the bedroom, again. They stood on the edge of the staircase, Jack with his back to the steps; the old man plunged fiercely forward, and, giving Rann a jerk, forced him back a step or two downwards, and he, finding that the old man was resolute, tried to twist him off. In so doing, Rann bent backwards, and pulled Mr. Giles violently towards him, with the idea of throwing him on his back; but there being a turn in the stair at that very spot, Rann lost his balance—the old man grew furious, and in the vain attempt to turn round, they were both precipitated headlong down the gaping chasm.

"Help! help! murder!" roared the old man as he fell.

Bounding, thumping, rolling, and struggling, the two combatants came to the bottom, still clenching the other fiercely. As yet Jack had not spoken a word; neither had Giles seen his face. The thought of murder was farthest from his mind, but still Rann would have shed blood rather than have been taken. At this moment he heard Toby and Charlie in the passage below, and he called out loudly to them for help.

"By Jingo, there's Jack's voice!" said Clayton, as he snatched up a dark lanthorn, and flew up the staircase to where the parties lay kicking and plunging.

Toby was not slow in following him; and perceiving an elderly man foaming with rage, and kneeling upon Rann's breast, he dealt him a violent blow with his fist on the mouth, and sent him reeling backwards.

"The best service you ever did your leader, Toby," exclaimed Jack, as he leaped to his feet. "Now be quick, and give us the rope and the gag; this old buck is too dangerous to be trusted out of harness. He'll raise the city on our heels."

"Villains! villains!" passionately vociferated the old man, as Kit assisted Jack to bind him to the balustrades.

"Peace, you old fool; and be thankful we have not made a window in your wizen," sullenly replied Toby, putting the cord tightly round the merchant's arm.

"You have done worse; you have ruined me," was the dejected answer of the citizen.

"Not so Mr. Giles," replied Jack Rann; "I know you have houses and wharfs enough to keep you snugly; and we are only taking a little because you can spare it."

The report of a pistol interrupted this conversation, and the next instant Wide Awake came bounding into the passage from the backyard, exclaiming, "The watch! the watch!"

"We must bolt then," answered Rann, hastily to this information. "Colledge you assist Toby out at the front door with the swag, while I and Charlie stay to pay our respects to the watch; and then take to your legs."

"Werry wholesome information," exclaimed Toby, assisting Wide Awake to raise a heavy sack on his shoulder, with which they made off.

Three watchmen now entered the house with their huge lanterns and staves from the back door, but before they could put a step in the passage the foremost was hurled down an open trap into a cellar beneath by Rann, who had prepared this receptacle on purpose for him, and the other was stunned by a blow from Charlie's fist.

"Come along, we won't be unhandsome to you, now you have come on purpose to see us," said Rann, collaring the third one; and, assisted by Charlie, they bound him, at the side of the Squire, to the balustrades.

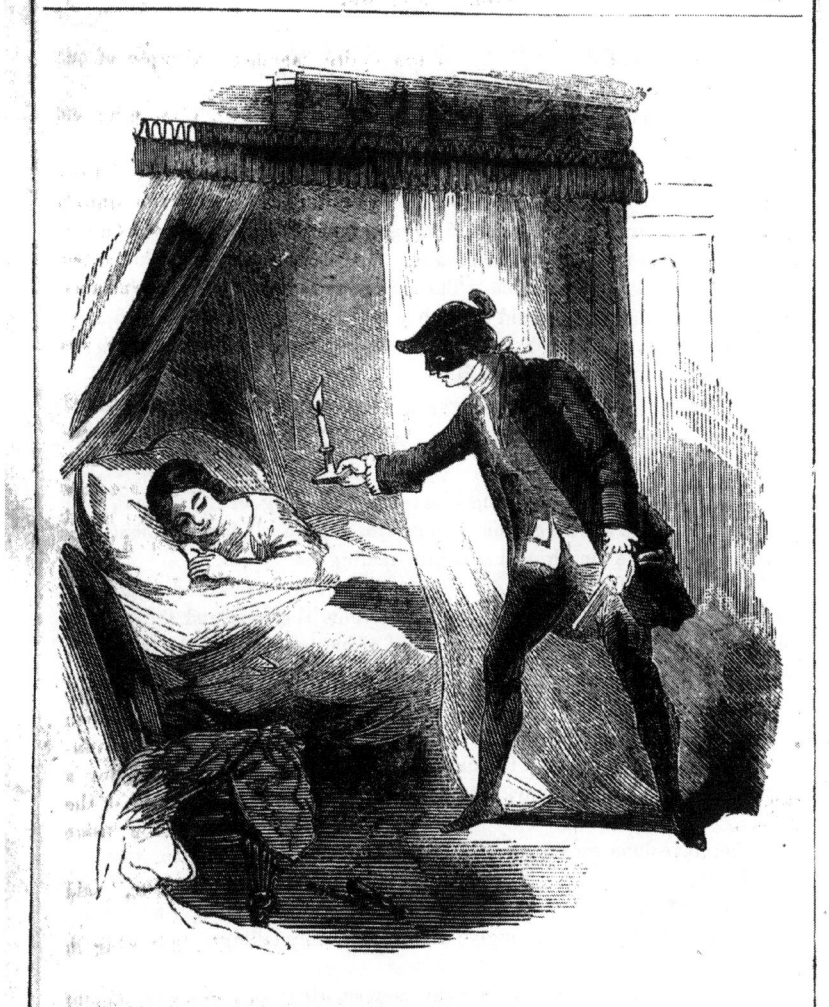

"Now, gentlemen, thanking you for our hospitable reception, Sixteen-string Jack, and his gang are about to wish you good night," exclaimed Jack politely.

"Is it, then, the noted villain I see before me?" remarked the Squire, looking steadfastly on Rann.

"And to think of the five hundred guineas' reward, too!" chimed in the old watchman.

"Come along, Jack," said Charlie, putting his arm within that of his leader's, and swinging him round. But this movement caused Rann's hat and crape to fall off, and unluckily discovered his features.

"'Tis Rann, as I live!" exclaimed the squire, catching a glimpse of our hero's features.

"My letter is not worth reading now," said Jack, as with Charlie he left the house.

"Holloa, my fine fellows, where are you going to?" exclaimed a burly-looking watchman, who, accompanied by two others came up to the squire's door as Jack and Charlie were about leaving it. "We must know who you are before you leave us, there has been " Murder and Thieves," bawled from this house, and some of our men have gone round to effect an entrance at the back—speak out, can't ye?"

Charlie gave it all up for lost, directly; and grasping a pistol which was hid in his bosom, was about to produce it.

"Damn it, Charlie! what are you about?" said Jack, in a low tone, and nudging him at the same time with his elbow; then turning to the watchman, with a most complaisant smile, he resumed,—" You are the very men we are in search of; our master has been robbed, and the thieves are now caught in their own trap by being locked in the kitchen, where we found them eating and drinking; come along—your assistance is just wanted."

"Capital, 'pon my soul!" murmured Charlie to himself, as he saw through the cunning retort of Jack to deceive the watchmen.

The guardians took the bait admirably; "Come along, lads; follow me," said he who looked like the chief of them.

Rann turned quietly round, and by the aid of a picklock opened the door. "After you, gentlemen, if you please," he said, smilingly, as the watchmen strode into the passage. But no sooner was the last man within the threshold, than Jack banged to the door, and shut them in; instantly producing a stout rope from his pocket, with the help of Charlie he tied the handle of the door so tight up to the iron railings outside, that to open it from the inside was impossible.

"There! I think we've boxed the traps up pretty decently, Charlie," said Jack, as he started off at a sharp run.

"It was excellently done, indeed, captain," replied Charlie, following in his leader's wake.

That night, a mourning coach with plumes, and drawn by four splendid horses, set off for London. On the box, as coachman, sat Sheppard, in deep mourning attire, and by his side was Toby in the same sombre garments, he having shifted himself immediately after leaving the squires. Jack, Clayton, and Wide Awake were inside the vehicle, gratings to which were fixed on either side to admit air.

They had proceeded but a few miles, when they were overtaken by a posse of constabulary, who, anxiously scanning the equipage, asked if they had seen any suspicious characters pass that way. Pulling up with every appearance of innocence, Sheppard replied "No," and earnestly inquired if any danger was to be apprehended from marauders upon the road. To this Luke Jones replied that Jack Rann, the highwayman, had committed a burglary at Squire Giles's; that it was impossible he could be far off, that they were seen to take the London road, and he was certain if they of the funeral caravan had been an hour on the road, or more, as they stated they had been, they must have seen them pass. On appealing to the two mounted Bow-street runners as to his correctness in this particular, they immediately expressed their confidence in the correctness of the idea, and one of the two, more suspicious than his confederates, proposed an examination of the hearse itself, which being warmly seconded by Luke and the proposer's brother officer, they dismounted to inspect the vehicle, to this both Toby and Harry Sheppard had a mighty strong objection, such proceeding being naturally calculated to cost them, not only the valuables they had at so much danger secured, but also the liberties, if not the lives of three brothers of the road.

"What is to be done?" whispered Toby to our friend Harry Sheppard.

"Nothing remains but a fight for it," answered Harry, "we are five to two and if we don't o'er match them, the devils in it. Let us dismount. I'll fell the man that opens the door, with the butt end of my whip; let the second taste your oaken cudgel, and if the third shows fight, I'll brain him, by God. Now for it," and saying these words, they dismounted in haste.

"You may be constables, but damme if you arnt a disgrace to the kings livery that ye wear, to stop a corpse on the highway, that's my opinion," said Sheppard.

"Much obliged to you for it, I am sure," said Luke with a grin, "but as these ere gemmen and myself fancy there is something, not only more lively, but also a damned sight more valuable than a box of cold meat in this ere corpse, concealed, p'raps you'll accommodate us with the key in order that we may satisfy ourselves."

"Give the gemmen the key, Peter," said Toby to Sheppard.

The supposed Peter swore with an oath he would throw it to —— first, a place more hot than comfortable. Whether he did consign it to that warm receptacle, remains for ever veiled in mystery, but certain it is that taking it from his pocket, he threw it with all his force into an adjoining copse, and bid them derisively "seek who'd find."

"You dam'd scoundrel," said Luke, scarlet with passion, "that proves your guilt; officers do your duty, wrest the door open by force."

This being a stouter job than was anticipated, resisted their efforts for a long time, but at length the door flying open, Luke Jones peered forward to scrutinise the contents of the hearse, when he suddenly received from within such a thundering thwack from the butt end of Jack's pistol, that he fell as if shot. Simultaneous with his fall, Sheppard brought a runner to the ground by a swinging blow from his lead-laden whip handle; under a sudden blow from Toby's bit of old English oak, the third also lay prostrate. To seize their weapons from their belts, to fling them into a neighbouring pond, was the first feat performed. Jack Rann having sprang from the vehicle, they stood prepared for any emergency that might arise.

A more useful picture could not well be imagined, than Luke Jones and the runners, as with their brains yet bewildered from the smart blows administered on their unfortunate sconces, sat looking at each other with all the vacancy of idiots.

Luke Jones was the first to recollect himself, and catching sight of our hero and springing to his feet muttered an oath and sprang forward to seize him. Our hero was ever an aspirant to a knowledge of the art of self-defence, and frequent practice of late had rendered him a splendid boxer; he therefore viewed Luke's attempt with a contemptuous smile, and stepping aside to avoid Luke's grasp, he instantly, with a strait blow from the shoulder, put Luke's daylights into a mahogany frame—in other words, gave him two terrific black eyes. Following up this advantage with his right, he administered a blow that made Luke's old jaws rattle again. The man staggered from the force: quick as lightning Jack's left hand again descended heavily, and cut him to the ground, on which he lay bleeding and senseless.

Whilst this transpired, some very tolerable skirmishing took place between Sheppard, Toby, and the runners, but the latter having at the outset received a tolerable settler, they gave in, at length, confessing themselves beaten.

As it so happened that these worthies, anticipating the capture of Jack and his pals, had provided themselves not only with handcuffs, but with shackles for the legs, also; the robbers finished the adventure by encasing Luke and the runners in their own irons.

A carrier passing at this time on his way to Bath, our hero hailed him, and asked, if he was well paid for the accommodation, if he would find room for three drunken men—for the men, cut, bleeding, and insensible, really had that appearance.

After a long confab, the amount was settled; the unhappy wights were thrown headlong into the cart, and the man cracking his whip, moved steadily on his way.

Preferring the outside of a horse to the inside of a hearse, Clayton and Sheppard mounted the runners horses; the horses attached to the hearse set off at a gallop, and the whole party merrily jogged on towards London, whither they arrived in safety, without further trouble or mishap: but as Toby's hostelrie was becoming too warm for a safe accomodation to our hero, Clayton sought out for him a fresh habitation; a description of which follows in the next chapter.

CHAPTER XX.

THE SWELL MOBSMAN'S CRIB—SENTIMENTALITY, HOSPITALITY, AND JOVIALITY—A YOUNG LADY'S BALLAD, AND AN UNEXPECTED ENTRY.

ONE of the most noted places of resort for thieves, at this period, was the "Cock and Magpie" tavern, above alluded to; with its quaint, old-fashioned gables and bay windows jutting over the pavement below, and threatening the heads of all passers underneath with its unpleasant proximity. The sign itself—lately revived, by the way, in fresher colours—was emblematical of the high-spiced toby-men who frequented the place, chanticleer betokening one of the principal instruments used in a burglary—the *crow*-bar—and the magpie indicating the freedom with which talking was indulged in by the parties present. But it is not with the exterior of the house that we have on the present occasion aught to do—our business is to glance into the interior; and here we might find enough to employ our pen in depicting; but not wishing to exhaust our readers' patience or our own powers upon objects irrelevant to the interest of this tale we shall at once introduce them to the particular apartment in which the chief characters will be found.

In the centre of a long room, illuminated by dingy oil-lamps, and shrouded in tobacco-smoke, the redolent fumes arising from which blended most unfragrantly with the reeking steam of gin-and-water and other liquors, stretched athwart the apartment a long greasy table, covered with broken glasses and fragmentary pipes, and surrounded by several personages who will hereafter have to play not unimportant parts in our history. At the further end, and officiating as chairman, was an elongated specimen of humanity, with a pipe of corresponding longitudinal dimensions inserted between his thick lips. The real name of this singular being was unknown; but his appropriate title of "Long Jemmy" served to distinguish him from the rest of his pals. At his side were some of the most notorious cracksmen of the period, busily engaged in fathoming the depth of sundry glasses of purl and tankards of hot ale that smoked along the board; nor was the presence of the weaker sex wanting to complete the social aspect of the place—for, edged in between the male portion of the visitors, were some particularly sinister-looking damsels, bedecked in flaunting caps and ribbons, who accompanied the utterance of each sentence with an illustrative laugh or a contraction of the dexter eyelid, which a casual visitor might have had the impoliteness to denominate —a wink.

"Kim up yer varmints," breathed forth the lanky chairman at the further end. "Stash business for the nonce, and let's have a song; I'm a sticker up for humanity, and I hates to have a man continually a talkin' of knockin' people on the head. It's uncommonly unpleasant, to say the least of it. So, come, Nan, flare up and rig your roarers."

After a great deal of hesitation, this polite call was responded to by one Miss Nancy Brown, a young lady tastefully clad in a sky-blue scarf, a pink cotton dress, and with a gentleman's hat, facetiously usurping the place of her own beaver bonnet (which, for want, doubtless, of a peg, had been hung upon the wiry head of "Long Jemmy,") "obliged" the company with a song, which, as an illustration of the sentimental style of ballad-singing, then so much in vogue at that period, we have given entire. An extemporaneous prelude on the bowl of a tobacco-pipe, played by the teeth of "Long Jemmy," having received the unanimous applause of the company assembled, Miss Nancy Brown warbled forth the following ditty, to a tune somewhat similar to the one so immortalised nearly a century afterwards by Tom Moore, under the title of "The lass I've left behind me."

From prigs that squabble the praucer's strong,
  To you of the peter-lay, o,
I pray now listen awhile to my song,
  How my bowman he snivelled avay, o.
How he broke off all the dubbs in the whitt,
  And chivied the darbies in twain, o ;
But through filing of a rumbo-kit,
  My *lovyer* is gabbled again, o.
    With his ran diddle dan, oh! he was the man,
      With his quips and cranks so leary ;
    And he won me o'er with his ran dan dan,
      To be his only deary.

My first love he was a prancing cove,
  And he tipped the ogles roundly ;
And a fighting chap was my second love,
  And he vhopped my first von soundly ;
My third he vos a Beefeater,
  As tough as any leather—
So he set to vork and he pummelled the pair,
  Till he vhopped 'em both together.
    With his ran diddle, &c.

So now I'm on the boozing rig,
  As I dare say you suppose it ;
I duzzn't mind the beaks a fig,
  And I duzzn't care who knows it.
For I am the gal for a fake and a cly,
  And I lush till the dew is falling;
To every move on the board I'm fly,
  And I'm not above my calling.
    Singing ran diddle, Oh! Snooks vos the man,
      With his quips and cranks so leary ;
    And he von me o'er with his ran dan dan,
      To be his only deary.

Which qualification Mr. Snooks possessed, that was alluded to by Miss Nancy Brown, under the title of his "ran-dan-dan," we cannot possibly conjecture ; and doubtless a metaphysical discussion on this subject would have immediately arisen, had not three significant knocks at that instant been given at the door; and in another instant Clayton and Jack Rann stood in the midst of the assembly.

A loud shout of triumph followed our hero's recognition, for, from his late dashing exploits, he was looked up to by his brother highwaymen like a god. Clayton silencing the uproar by a movement of the hand gave the company to understand as our hero was playing at hide and seek, that silence was wisdom.

"Werry good, Kit, my leary one, not so much of that Rann gemmen, *if you please.*"

From these words and following the advice therein given, the conversation from being personal became strictly of a professional nature.

Speaking of the badness of trade in general—

"It's perfectly heart-breaking!" said a thin gaunt-looking fellow with one eye, and who rejoiced in the appellation of "One-Peeper-Tom." "They von't give us a chance. Ve've been so long in the beat that they knows the very cut of our little fingers, and watches us like cats does warmint."

"Yes," said another, "and if we do get a spicy young hand to assist in reviving trade, the beaks won't give him the fair swing that was allowed to the old 'uns of the 'way, for they nails him at once and gets him scragg'd as soon as possible for the sake of his blood-money."

"Ah! the hevils of havarice!" interjected One-Peeper-Tom. "It renders people quite dishonourable. One of the old runners would have scorned such baseness, and never thought o' giving a beginner less than three years for fear of intimidating him."

"Well, catch as catch can," cried a handsome and somewhat foppish member of the junta, whose singing qualities had gained for him the name of "Chirruping Charlie." "I'm a believer in fate, and will hazard all chances. He must have a tight grasp that would hold so slippery an eel as myself; and if I *am* to show my pluck on the scaffold, I'll die game with the words of the old song in my mouth:—

> What matters a death like this to me!
> Luddi fuddi! Ah, poor Luddi, heigho!
> What matters a death like this to me?
> Why, it is but a leap from a leafless tree,
> Luddi, fuddi! Ah, poor Luddi, heigho!

"Neat ditty that, but somewhat of an unhappy theme to practise upon," said Clayton; "but, however, there is pluck at its basis. Well, Charlie, my chirruper, what are you doing?"

"Just precisely nothing," answered the Chirruper, "how fares business with you, Kit, which was the technical term by which he was known to the prigs of London—"

"Oh! bobbish-like; me and my friend Rann, have been doing pretty tidy pickings here lately; but, hallo! as I live here is my old friend Jared Steele, the gypsey—how are you, old fellow?" and Clayton advanced with outstretched palm to greet his old pal. While this pair of worthies remained in conversation, our hero nudging one Peeper-Tom who sat beside him, enquired who that Jared Steele was.

"A tobyman of the first water—a stunner every inch of him—and faithful in nature as in name—he is as true as steel itself. I'll tell you a rare anecdote of those two fellows," pointing to Clayton and Steele—

"Let us have it. I'm all attention," said Jack.

"Here goes, then," said Tom, taking a pull at the tankard.

One evening as those two cracksmen were taking a range, they were accosted by a country joskin of a fellow, near Pall-mall, who, taking them for a pair of country nobs thus accosted them:—

"I say, measters, ye'll excuse me, but as I always likes to ax respectable persons about my affairs, I jist want to ax you where I can get a comfortable and decent lodging to-night. There be so many thieves and vagabonds in this ere 'nation great town, that I be afeard to ax some people, lest I be robbed. Feyther told I, when I left home, to take great care of my money, eh, eh, and so I means to't; danged if any of the London sharps will rob I; look'ee gentlemen, I've just taken the liberty of popping a guinea into my mouth, and if any of them can get that out without my knowing it, my name is not Simon Beanstalk, that be all."

"My friend, I am very glad you spoke to us," answered Kit Clayton, tipping Jared a wink, "as you might be imposed upon. Here is a card, and you will find an excellent night's lodging there, I can assure you." As Kit replied, the countryman's eyes brightened up, and bowing low he was about to depart.

"Where have you sent him to, Kit?" whispered Jared.

"Why, to the snoozing ken, in Drury-lane, to be sure; where he'll get stripped of everything down to his bare stockings, and he may think himself well off if he gets out alive. But I means to have that guinea out of his mouth if I swings for it, if it's only to revenge the insult he passed upon us, by speaking so lightly of the profession."

"Don't be a fool, Kit," replied Jared, whispering low, "consider the risk we run in the job. Come along, let's leave him."

"Well, gentlemen, this be my way then, so good night," said the countryman to the sharpers, as he turned on his heel and left them.

"Now then, here's after him, to twig that ere shiner out of his blessed jaws," said Kit, as he prepared to follow the joskin.

"What are you about, Kit," said Steele pettishly, "surely you don't mean to endanger your own safety and mine by attempting to rob a joskin of a paltry guinea!"

"Rob him! vy you thinks I'm a pickpocket, I suppose," replied Kit, laughing, "no, I means to do him out of it clean, and if you want to see the trick come along," and away he bolted in the way the countryman had taken.

Jared finding all remonstrance in vain, started after his companion, resolving, at all events, to share the danger, and coming up with him was eye-witness to the following adventure:—Taking a purse from his pocket, Kit swaggered nimbly past the countryman, and directly he got before him he shook his purse, and a shilling and some half-pence rattled loudly on the stone pavement. Kit started instantly, all eyes and fingers were at the spot, and the unsuspecting countryman was the first to drop on his knees, and offer to pick them up for the gentleman.

"Confound the purse," exclaimed Kit in a swaggering tone, "give the coppers to the boys, where's the guinea though?" and turning his purse over in his hand, he pretended to search for it.

"What! and hast lost a guinea, sir," exclaimed the wondering chawbacon, staring with both his eyes open; "I'ze very sorry, sir, to be sure!"

"Very sorry! why, you cheating vagabond," roared Kit, "you have the guinea in your mouth there; I suspected you was no good when you stopped me just now. Where's an officer! fetch a constable!"

"O! crikey, here's a go!" shouted the boys who had gathered round.

"Well, I never did!" roared out Simon Beanstalk, lifting up his hands in astonishment.

"What's the row?" enquired one of the Bow-street traps, who had just before passed Kit and his companion. "What's all this shindy about?"

"Why, only look," said Kit, in corroboration of his evidence. "he has actually got my guinea between his teeth."

"Give the gentleman his money directly, you thieving hound!" exclaimed the officer, collaring him; and the shock causing Simon to open his mouth rather wide, the guinea rolled out on to the pavement, and Kit instantly snatching it up, thanked the officer, and accompanied by Steele, hastily withdrew.

"Come, young fellow, I shall take you along with me," said the officer, "you must be one of Toby's lot in disguise; nobody else would have the impudence to commit such a barefaced robbery in the open street; what have you got here?" as he spoke, the officer pulled the card that Kit had just given

No. 27.

him, out of the countryman's waistcoat pocket and read it—"Good accommodation at the 'Cock and Bottle,' Drury-lane!—why now this convinces me you are one of his gang; for I know this is one of his houses."

"Noa, I bean't sir! I bean't indeed, sir. I be Simon Beanstalk, all the way from Somerzetshire, sir."

"I don't believe you, you prigs can imitate anybody, and I believe you are only imitating now; so come along with me to the round-house," and away the poor countryman was dragged to the watch-house.

"Not so bad a spree I must confess; but your friend Jared seems to have played but a minor part in it. Why, my esteemed pal, Clayton, deserved all the credit for his surpassing impudence," said Jack.

"Ay, I agree with you, a few, in course he did, but the spree did'nt end there, for Jared Steele, although he gloried in Kit Clayton for plucking the countryman, did not like to see the yokel lagged on a false charge, so turning up the collar of his coat to hide his face, and pulling his hat over his eyes for ditto ditto reason, he bid Kit wait, and turning up a street that would bring them face to face with the watchman and his charge, he, as soon as he caught sight of them, assumed the swagger of a cove a few sheets in the wind, in fact, with more brandy than brains in his noddle, he run against the watchman vith sich premeditated fury, that the unfortunate watchy was pitched backwards on his cocoa nut. Vether the outside shell was cracked or not I can't pertend to assert, but shiver my blinkers if he didn't lay there with his mouth wide open, and as silent as a jolly mummy. As to Simon, like a Simon as he vas, he stood like a stuck pig, and it was not until Jared had requested him over and over again, to bolt, to mizzle, hook it, namhus, kut his lucky, shake his trotters, waggle his extenders, that he could see the policy of mizzling, but when he did get in motion, Jared says, to see his long legs in motion, was worth a fortin."

"If Jared Steele was not good, brave, and true, he would not have acted so," said Rann, "come, Sam, I claim an introduction from you—I must make his acquaintance."

His acquaintance made that night and sealed in bumpers of sherry, commenced a friendship to be ended only by the death, for from that time forward, Jack Rann and Jared Steele were steadfast friends.

CHAPTER XXI.

A SCENE AT THE COCK AND MAGPIE.

In the hiding place offered him by the walls of the "Cock and Magpie," our hero continued to lurk for some time, until at length he became so eat up with ennui, as to beg of Jared and Kit Clayton for God's sake to find him some employment.

"I tell you what," said Jared, "I have a glorious swag in my eye, that beats everything ever done—even by you, captain," and he bowed respectfully to our hero.

"What is it, Steele—come, curse it man, don't hang fire—spit it out."

"I have heard, through the medium of a gang of gypsies, to which I formerly had the honour of belonging, that a French marquis, excessively rich, and positively laden with jewels and gold, leaves Dover for London to-morrow. Now, if we could but waylay him, a magnificent spoil would be ours, enough, so said the hag from whom I had the story, to make the fortune of a dozen such as us."

"It is enough, by heaven," said Jack, I am game to try—"

"If you say you'll do it, captain, its as good as done, say but the word, if I raise the storming party, as this marquis travels well guarded with armed attendants, more will be required than us three, will you be our leader?"

"I should have no objection, but I am almost unknown to the gang here; and they, being older hands on the road, might look upon any assumption upon my part as an infringement of their liberties—might look upon me in fact with a jealous eye."

"Stuff and nonsense," said Jared. "I can set that aside at once; is there not already those who acknowledge you as their captain. There is old Toby, Harry Sheppard, Clayton, here, young Colledge and myself—and the rest that I shall provide will be merely supernumeraries, bound to obey you—"

"Sheppard and Wide Awake are not eligible, both being in the country, not only for a professional tour, but also to recruit their health and strength."

"Combining pleasure with profit, I presume," said Jared.

"Exactly," answered our hero.

"Well, never mind, we can do without them. I'll find a gang, I tell you, who will obey you."

"They *shall*," said Jack in a determined tone, "if the command is placed in my hands."

"Well, they 'shall' then, if it likes you better," said Jared, so captain—don't hesitate—say the word—you will head us, won't you?"

Jack looked appealingly to his friend Clayton: Kit nodded assentingly.

Yes, I will take the command," said Jack.

* * * * *

On the following evening, Jack, accompanied by Toby and Clayton, set out for the spot assigned by Jared Steele for the meeting. They reached it, and having been joined by Jared, who informed our hero that half a dozen trusty fellows were lying in ambush close at hand. He had hardly spoken, before Rann, raising his hand for silence, said—" Hist lads—I hear the sound of wheels."

At these words every rein was tightened, and the cavalcade brought to as sudden a check as if a wall had risen before it—each ear was attentively stretched to catch the welcome sound, and a moment of the deepest interest succeeded. Rann was right, for not only was heard the sound of carriage-wheels as they grazed the heavy road, but the quick eyes of the gang even discerned the occasional jets of sparks which the hoofs of the horses drew from the flints that were strewn along the ground.

"We're upon 'em, by jingo!" exclaimed Kit Clayton.

"And in good time too!" remarked Jared. "We shall just meet at a spot from whence no cry for assistance can be heard."

"But, gentlemen," said Steele, "you forget that in standing here we shall expose ourselves to the view of the enemy directly he makes the turning, a quarter of a mile beyond the sign-post, yonder."

"On, then!" cried Jack. "Let us take them by surprise," and he was just about to lash his steed into activity, when a sudden action of Clayton's arrested his arm.

"Zounds!" cried Clayton, "you would spoil everything. "Don't you see that the carriage is guarded by at least a dozen lacqueys? Why, if they caught sight of us, they would dispatch a courier for assistance, and then, perhaps, thrash us before it arrived."

"What must I do, then?" asked Jack; "my blood is up, and I care not what danger I tempt!'

"Very likely," said Toby; consequently, there's more 'casion for the hex-ercise hof phylosification."

"Our aids wait us behind yonder bank of furze," interposed Jared; "and as that will not only screen us from observation, but give us an opportunity of laying our plans according to the disposition of the enemy, we had better make for it at once. The rest depends upon your discretion; and now, captain, we await your orders." So saying the gallant fellow raised his hat to his young leader, an action that was imitated by the rest, and awaited a reply.

"On, then, to the covert!" cried Rann. "We will there hold a council for two minutes, and then proceed to enterprise." With these words, our hero clapped spurs to his horse, and, with one leap, gained the foot of the bank to which his attention had been called, and which overhung the road. The rest followed, and away they went like squirrels up the rise, behind which was a hollow, wherein they alighted upon five or six fellows round a turf fire, most of whom Jack recognised as the worthies he had been in the habit of associating with at the "Cock and Magpie." One stranger, however, struck him as particularly repulsive in appearance. This was a fellow, known by the name of "Night-owl Oliver," and carried the character of a desperate, black-hearted villain upon his countenance. To this ruffian Charlie introduced Jack as their new leader, and the fellow, after a surly, insulting stare, exclaimed,

"Things are come to a fine pass, when an old dog like me is forced to run in the same leash, with a whelp that has scarcely come to his eyesight."

"None of your insults!" cried Jack, "or you will find the young bull-dog a match for the mastiff! Either part company, or behave with proper respect to your leader!"

This little conversation might have been followed by an equally inflammatory response, had not Long Jemmy and One-Peeper Tom interposed for th restoration of order, and pointed out the necessity for promptness, on account of the near approach of the carriage, which was now not half a mile off. Jack, with admirable temper, immediately turned his thoughts to the main purpose. "Let our foot forces," he said, "throw themselves on their faces behind any favouring tufts, which may girt the road on each side; and the instant the outriders have passed, let a rope be thrown across the highway; so that, if they return to learn why the carriage stops, their horses may be flung. We shall thus divide their numbers and throw them into confusion. I, myself, will have an eye everywhere, and be wherever I'm most wanted !"

Not a word of opposition was offered to these orders, and even Night-Owl Oliver drew off his gang to obey the high spirited Captain in silence. Rann watched them till he saw that all had been attended to; and then, turning suddenly to his mounted followers, continued, "We must creep down the bank, and make our steeds crouch in the shade at foot. Whatever I do, stir none of you till I give the word 'advance!' Let each man, then, pick his customer, and act at discretion !"

"Trust to obedience," answered Steele.

"But, understand this, all of ye," said Jack, "the man who presumes to discharge his piece at a fellow-creature, while I am his leader, will receive my bullet through his brain."

Jack uttered these words in a tone of sternness that bespoke him to be in earnest, and as his colleagues followed him down the slope, they whispered to each other that they had "caught a tartar." Having reached the foot, they arranged themselves according to Jack's instructions, and remained lurking, in shade and silence, like the explosive elements of a mine—only lacking the necessary impetus to spread dismay and mischief. The hollow rumbling of carriage wheels that had hitherto rather been felt than heard, had by this time increased to that sharp, snapping 'whizz!' which forms the peculiar indication of the near approach of a vehicle in rapid motion. The whistles of the postillions, the cracking of their whips, the snorting of horses, and even the creaking of the crazy old carriage, could be distinctly heard, while the more muffled sound of the horsemen in advance would have been almost inaudible, but for the regularity with which they galloped. Sixteen-string Jack looked and listened with breathless interest.

On came the cortege, and Jack's blood mounted as the advance-guard passed close enough to fan his forehead with the commotion they raised in the air. The carriage followed closely, and he was preparing to ride forward, when he saw that, besides the postillion, there was a guard on the box with a brass-mounted implement, which the tell-tale moon revealed to be a blunderbuss. Jack's resolution was instantly taken; he knew that to ride within range of so dangerous a weapon would be madness; he, therefore, determined upon an experiment as daring as it was well-conceived. He drew up his feet to the saddle of his horse, and remained doubled up in readiness for a spring, like the tiger in its native jungle. The postillions drove by, little dreaming of what was about to happen, and the tails of the rear horses were just whisking before Jack's eyes, when, with one elastic bound, he leaped into the air, and alighted upon the splashing-board, as if he had dropped from the skies. With one hand he seized the blunderbuss, and, with the other, grasped the throat of its owner.

"Not a word, you dog, or you are lost!" exclaimed he, giving the fellow a hearty shake. He then flung the weapon at least twenty yards from him, and having thus prevented the most formidable species of resistance, he gave the longed-for signal of "Advance!"

At the word, his five confederates dashed into the road. One-Peeper Tom and another checked the progress of the coach-horses, with a suddenness that almost threw them upon their haunches, and presenting a pistol at the head of each postillion, commanded them to "Halt!" Chirruping Charlie pricked round to one window of the carriage, while a fourth highwayman, Clayton, rode up to the opposite one. Toby had assumed the charge of his leader's nag, and consequently stood in waiting for further orders. These were given almost as soon as he came up, for Rann lost no time in thrusting his unwieldy antagonist to the ground. upon which he feel like a heavy lump of dough. "There, Jared," cried Jack, as soon as he had performed the action, "pick that bone if you like, and remember you can't do him much mischief if you thump him ever so soundly."

"Cot dam! what is all dis?" exclaimed the chief occupant of the carriage, thrusting a thin sallow visage through the window, and peering round with astonishment.

"We are immortals, in disguise, come from above to visit the earth; and we want some rhino to help us on the way," replied Jack, stretching himself full length across the roof of the carriage, and looking down upon the face that was now upturned in astonishment at the sound of his voice.

"Den, by gar, you are von dam silly nincompoop to expect it from me," said the other, who was a French marquis, notorious for the sums he won at the gaming table. "Me no have von guinea to jingle against anoder."

"I don't doubt it in the least," said Jack, "but by my magic art I intend to conjure a sufficient supply for us both." So saying, he unceremoniously caught hold of the sharp nose of the marquis, and, after giving it a dexterous tweak, used it as a handle to assist him in jumping to the ground.

"*Parbleu!*" cried the marquis, twinging with pain. "Do you tink noses have no feeling?"

"I leave that question to be decided by yourself," said Jack, opening the carriage door. "At present I have other matters to inquire into." So saying, he stepped into the vehicle, and seated himself on the opposite seat to that occupied by the marquis. He now found that the place had two other inmates; one, an old harridan, shining in all the varieties of blue, red, and yellow, while the other was a pale interesting girl, attired in a plain pelisse, that set off to advantage a form which might have tempted a less ardent eye than the one that now gazed upon it. Our hero was received with shrieks, but, with a voice which he had the power of attuning to the sweetest tones of tenderness, he sufficiently calmed their fears to render them silent, and then betook himself to business. "Bring a carriage lamp this way," said he to one of his gang, "and let us see how the land lies." "Aha!" he added, as the order was obeyed and a blaze of jewellery became revealed to his sight, "That watch, madam, has a sparkle that is irresistible. Real brilliants, as I live! You *must* present me with the bauble by way of keepsake. It will enable me to keep any future assignation I may make with you. Those rings, too! Really you ought not to travel with such valuables in your possession; nothing more tempting to a highwayman; lest, therefore, you should unfortunately be robbed, I will take charge of them myself, and you may depend upon their safe keeping."

"But, sir, fellow! knave!" cried the old woman in a passion, as Jack dispossessed her of the articles in question—"You are robbing me yourself."

"Oh, fie, Madam!" said Jack, "I wouldn't do such a thing for the world! Let us consider it as a simple matter of exchange. What can I give you in return? Oh! I have it. You shall receive a salute from lips that are destined to make every hearer tremble!" He then raised his hat, and, with an air of the deepest devotion, he impressed a kiss upon a cheek that, in hue and plumpness, exactly resembled a pulpit cushion.

"Well, young man," said the gratified old lady, "I must confess that your manners are far better than your morals."

"You make me blush, madam," returned Rann, with a bow. "But let us see what the younger fair one has to sell for a salute."

"Nothing! indeed, nothing!" exclaimed the agitated girl, bursting into tears. "Although you find me here, I am poor and friendless, with but one thing in the world that I prize. It is this ring," and she drew a ring from her finger, and tremblingly placed it in the hand of Jack. He took it and examined it attentively.

"So, so!" said he. "A ruby, an emerald, a garnet, an amethyst, another ruby, and a diamond. Take the initial letters and they form the word 'REGARD.' Take it back, maiden; the gift of friendship is too sacred to be profaned." So saying he returned the ring.

"She's an artful hussy, Mr. Freebooter," cried the old woman, "and has as much right to be robbed as I have. The ring is very valuable, though, to be sure; she only prizes it because she had it from some old lover, and one would think it was a bit of her own heart."

"Since I cannot rob the hand without the heart," said Jack, "I will remain content. But lest you should think I show favour, I am determined to steal something—a tress of hair! It shall be woven into a chain for your watch." Suiting the action to the word, he handed a knife to the poor girl, who, sensible of the folly of resistance, and grateful for his generosity, proceeded to denude her brow of a rich glossy lock, black as the jettiest plume of the raven's wing. Rann took it with more real pleasure than he would have done the ring, and exclaimed, " And now, sweet one, for payment." He then once more raised his hat, and bent towards the lovely being before him. She shrunk back, but he pointed impressively to the circlet on her finger, and he was suffered to take the kiss, although her ripe and rosy lip instinctively recoiled as he approached it.

"You are a brazen-faced hussey, Madam!" exclaimed the old woman, ready to burst with envy. All this time the little French marquis had sat paralyzed in the corner of his carriage, expecting to have his throat cut.

Jack now turned to him and said, " Now, monsieur Yellow-jaundice! just let's have a shy at your rattle-traps."

" Me no understan—*je ne sais pas*," cried the marquis.

" Don't talk to me of your pa," said Jack, " I'd serve him and your ma in the same way, were they here. Come," he added, presenting the muzzle of his pistol at the Frenchman's head—" Deliver, or pop goes the trigger."

This hint was too intelligible to be mistaken, and, with a groan, a shrug, and a contortion that was meant to be a grimace of politeness, gave up his gold snuff-box and jewellery; he next delivered his sword, and an ample box, filled with hard cash, and then uttering another groan, declared that he had nothing left. Jack, however, had learnt enough at Lord Dashfield's to know the secret receptacles of a carriage, and, availing himself of this knowledge, he speedily ransacked every hole and corner, and brought to light a store of notes and acceptances to an immense amount. As soon as everything worth taking had been thus cleared away, Jack prepared to take his leave, when the Frenchman, with another shrug, exclaimed—

" And sal you leave me so, monsieur? Vil you no make exchange vith me as vell as the ladies?"

" It would give the affair a more mercantile appearance, certainly," said Jack; but I am at a loss to know what to offer. You would not have me kiss you, as I did the ladies?"

" *Non, non*," said the marquis; " suppose you let me have your pistol. It vill remind me of dis pleasant adventure, and de acquaintance me have formed."

" Oh, with all my heart," said Jack, without for a moment reflecting upon the probable consequences of the act. " I would turn dealer in fire-arms at once, if I could dispose of all my weapons to equal advantage."

He then laughingly gave the pistol, which was only on half-cock, to the marquis, who, cocking the piece with the speed of thought, presented it at Jack's ear, and, with desperate vehemence, exclaimed:—

" Now, villain! restore my property, and order your gang to disperse, or I will bespatter them with your d—d rascally brains."

The moment was fraught with peril, and Jack felt himself to be on the brink of a dreadful eternity, but his presence of mind—the mightiest quality with which we are gifted—did not forsake him. The smile on his countenance remained unchanged—it even brightened, and his manners were unruffled as he replied—

" Fire away, my Lord Marquis! The pistol contains nothing but a little harmless gunpowder to frighten fools and Frenchmen. I never have shed blood, upon my honour!"

The *ruse* succeeded, and the Frenchman with a " sacre!" flung the pistol at his feet. Jack instantly jumped out, and, springing into his saddle, raised a cry of triumph, and exclaimed,

"Farewell, your lordship; and, when asked by whom you were robbed, answer, ' JACK, WITH THE SIXTEEN STRINGS!' "

CHAPTER XXII.

ATTEMPTED RESCUE—JACK FINDS THAT A WISE HEAD IS SOMETIMES BETTER THAN A STRONG HAND—THE FIGHT—THE VICTORY.

THE events concluding our last chapter, from the stopping of the carriage to the escape of Rann from an almost certain death, did not occupy more than five minutes, so rapidly did everything transpire. Our hero was received with a cheer by his comrades, and Jack was already felicitating himself upon having baffled the Frenchman, and escaped the slugs with which the pistol was, in reality, loaded, when a new call was made upon his energies.

This was occasioned by the sudden return of the out-guard. They had ridden on for some minutes without missing the lumbering of the carriage at their heels, when the shouts of the thoughtless robbers were wafted to their ears. They turned round, and the moon at that moment shining out in full splendour, beheld the true state of affairs.

"The marquis is attacked," cried the chief. "Back, lads! back to the rescue!"

With one burst the whole returned, and came full swoop upon Jack and his devoted companions.

The ominous clatter was heard by every member of the gang, and all looked aghast at our hero.

"Oughtn't we to be off?" said Clayton.

"No!" replied Rann. "Let us gain a character for high daring; and country folks will, on future occasions, be afraid to pursue us. A poor sneak is soon hunted up and caught, but men like Dick Turpin, and Claude Du Val are suffered to escape through the very terror of their names."

"You are as good as a general, Jack," said Toby, "and ven you've finished your freaks by dancing on the tight rope, wot proves so fatal to us all, them ere chaps as fills their bellies by hemptying their brains will get writing romances about you."

"That would be glorious!" cried Jack. "And may I come to the tree before my time, if I don't prove a hero of the first water!"

"Then you won't leave much to their hinwentive faculties!" returned Toby

"No, the numsculls," cried Jack; "they'd only spoil the work. Let 'em stick to truth, and I'll furnish 'em with incidents for the best romance ever written. But, see! the horsemen are within three hundred yards of our ambush. When I give the signal, fire into such steeds as may not have fallen but take care you don't hit the riders. My lord marquis," he continued, elevating his voice, so as to be heard by those occupying the carriage, "remain passive, and you are safe; stir, and you are a dead man!"

"The post boys?" exclaimed Clayton, in a breathless tone of inquiry.

"Let One-Peeper Tom knock 'em gently on the head, to keep 'em from mischief," cried Jack: then turning suddenly to Toby, he added, "What have you done with the fat fellow who sat on the coach-box?"

"Oh, he was the most obstinate hanimal as ever I seed!" said Toby. "I hargued vith him, and I vallopped him; but wisdom and walour was alike thrown avay upon him. I even gived him a kick or two, but the more I kicked the more dissatisfied he was, so, at last, I vos obligated to—"

Here a stop was put to Toby's story by a loud shout that burst from the cavalcade in pursuit, as the infuriated men swept like wolves round a projecting bank, and dashed up to the gang. In mid career, however, the picquets, under Night Owl Oliver, elevated the rope that had been stretched across the road, and the legs of the three foremost horses were instantaneously tripped up, and the animals thrown. The shock jerked the holders of the rope into the middle of the highway, and their sudden appearance had the effect of so completely stunning the faculties of the remaining nine horsemen, that they rode without precaution against the fallen steeds of their companions, and four men were precipitated to the ground.

"On to 'em, lads. Fire!" cried Jack, galloping forward. The rest obeyed, and such was the nicety with which the five weapons were aimed, that each brought a horse with its rider to the ground. Not a moment was now lost. Every member of the gang pounced upon its prey, according to previous orders, and a struggle took place, in which each man fought for his life. Jack encountered a desperate fellow who was built like a bull, but the thews and sinews of our hero had been too much hardened by country exercise to render him an easy conquest; his activity also was such, that he was enabled to elude the dangerous hugs of his antagonist, like a will-o'-the-wisp, and though they repeatedly rolled over and over upon the earth, locked in each other's arms, Jack always managed to slip like an eel from the embrace, and then to renew the struggle with fresh advantage. In a few minutes he had beaten the fellow to submission, and, starting up for fresh employment, he beheld Toby flying for his life, followed by a man who had picked up the blunderbuss that Jack had thrown from the coach-box. No sooner had the pursuer got within range of the fugitive than he raised the weapon and fired, but Jack, although on foot, had got up to him in time to dash it aside, and consequently the charge rattled harmlessly over the heath, with the exception of one shot, which glanced more than skin deep across the temple of our hero, and suffused his features with blood. The undaunted highwayman repaid the wound with a blow that felled the man to the dust.

"Very good, muster Jack," exclaimed Kit, who had turned to face his assailant directly the blunderbuss had been discharged. "I'm not much of a scholar, but whenever I looks at the scar of that there gash, I shall read a better sarmon about gratitude than ever was spun by our parson."

"Pish, man!" said Jack, "you would have done as much for me." So saying, he immediately turned upon his heel, and once more made for the field of action. He there found that the fight had been brought to a close by the capture of the enemy, who were all tied back to back, in as woeful a plight as black eyes and bloody noses could reduce them to. The victors met Jack with congratulations, which he modestly acknowledged, and then gave orders for the disposal of the vanquished. These were simple and to the purpose: the poor devils were first rifled of everything they possessed in the shape of money or valuables, and then fastened to the splinter-bar of the carriage, from which the horses had been previously removed. The fat occupant of the coach-box was also sought, and found in a shallow pit of sand, into which Toby had kicked him, and he was once more elevated, in shackles, to the post he had occupied. This done, our hero remounted his horse, and riding up to the carriage window, exclaimed, "Your lordship must pardon the substitution of a team of bipeds for the prancers by which you were drawn hither; but if I did not take that precaution, you might probably return with a fresh force more speedily than was convenient to me. And now, may I intrude upon your politeness, for the pistol that you dropt a few minutes back?"

The marquis, who, as well as the females, was almost dead with terror, complied. Jack thanked him, and added, "And now, my lord, take a word of advice, when next you are told that a pistol is unloaded, pull the trigger and try!" With that he slightly touched the quadruped on which he was mounted with the spur, and coming up to the foremost of the domestics, gave him a smart swish with his riding whip, and ordered him to proceed. The poor fellow, with his companions, strained every nerve, and commenced toiling along the road in prosecution of their laborious journey, amid the jeers and shouts of all the robbers.

Jack now turned to the postboys, and said, pointing to the beasts that had been detached from the carriage—"To whom do these cattle belong?"

"To Giles Doubledo, of the Little Bush Inn, on the borders of the heath yonder," answered the head postillion, in anticipation of another crack on his sconce.

"Very well," said our hero: "then give the compliments of Sixteen-string Jack (you will not forget the name I dare say), to Mr. Giles Doubledo, and tell him that I return him his animals unhurt, as I am determined that no innkeeper on any road in England shall ever suffer a loss at my hands, unless he first provoke me. Tell him, also, that, in return, I shall expect him never to refuse shelter to one who asks it in my name. Should he think it worth while to turn informer, and send the hounds of the law in pursuit of me, he will provoke my revenge, and lose his labour, for I defy every constable in the land to take me alive, and the keenest nose to scent my retreat. Your master may repeat this to whoever he pleases, for I wish the country to know that a man has at length arisen to rescue the Fancy from the present downfallen condition, and to walk in the footsteps of DICK TURPIN!"

Jack purposely uttered all this fustian in a theatrical tone, so as to produce an impression, and, having concluded this harangue, he gave the postboys a guinea each, and bade them mount and depart. Thus ended an exploit which rung through all England for many a day afterwards.

The gang, careless of pursuit, now retired to the hollow behind the hill which had formed their rendezvous. A fire was speedily lit—flasks of spirits were produced, and all gave loose to jest, glee, and encomiums upon Jack. Chirruping-Charlie was in ecstacies, and vowed that Rann deserved to be immortalized. "You have done more," said he to our hero, "than the oldest hand on the highway would have dared to attempt, and the message you sent to old Doubledo will prove as serviceable as if you had given each of us a three years' lease of our lives."

"I acted upon an idea that the Bow-street officers generally spare the most notorious offenders longest," said Jack.

"And you were right," said One-peeper Tom. "They's got their own interests to look arter as well as we has, and, in course, if our trade was to fail, theirs would also."

"To be sure it would," said Charlie—"just the same as the parsons would drop if the devil was got under. Our only plan now is to follow up to-night's work, and make ourselves worth being spared. Just get a name, and half the robberies that are in future committed will be laid to your charge."

"That's an odd sort of an inducement to hold out to a fellow,' said Rann, passing a flask of brandy to his associate.

"But a very valuable one, for all that," said the other. "Look here. Whenever a man now loses his purse, off he goes to Bow-street, and tells the beaks that he has been robbed by Sixteen-string Jack."

"Well!" said Rann.

"Well!" returned Charlie. "Don't you see that the trap will then receive a fee to look after Sixteen-string Jack; and these fees will keep tumbling in as long as Sixteen-string Jack is at large; whereas, if Sixteen-string Jack got lagged, there would no longer be a mark to point at, so that when a man lost his rhino, he would hold his tongue, thinking that his stuff had been stolen by some obscure nobody, whom it would be useless to look after. The officer would thus remain unemployed; the magistrates would shut up shop, and all would go to wreck and ruin, until some new Toby-man of spirit started up to revive the game."

"Such was my own view of the subject," returned Rann. "I have heard that, on the same principle, the life of a brave general is never sought by the enemy, lest his death should put an end to the war, and reduce the army to half-pay.

"Vell, I must say," said Toby, "that this sort of logic makes a man's neck sit unkimmon easy upon his shoulders. But take care, Jack, how you trusts yourself too near them, for though they has a capital knack of shutting their eyes at times, it don't do to run under their very noses."

"I'll do that, and they shan't smell me," said Jack. "But fear not, as long as a guinea is to be got by chasing me, I shall always have a headway."

"You are born to restore to us the golden age," cried Charlie. "Come, lads!" he continued with enthusiasm, "Let us proceed to elect him our chief at once!"

To this they all unanimously agreed, and our hero having been elected, with bumpers round, and with cheers, nine times nine, they arose for home, where their jollifications were continued until a streak of light in the distant horizon announced the approach of day.

CHAPTER XXIII.

OUR HERO STARTS UPON A QUIET JOURNEY, BUT IN EXERCISING A LITTLE PROFESSIONAL ECCENTRICITY, MEETS WITH A REBUFF AND AN ADVENTURE UPON WHICH HE HAD NOT CALCULATED.

THE day, after the robbery of the marquis, was spent in carouse by Jack and the whole party engaged in the enterprise; and what added to their merriment, was the fact that the marquis had laid immediate complaints of his robbery, and the consequences resulting from this information, were, that every dead wall and hoarding throughout London, was literally covered with bills offering rewards for the apprehension of Sixteen-string Jack, and his audacious gang.

Tired and, perhaps beaten by the reckless revelry, Jack parted from the crew assembled, and started, as he expressed himself, for a ride in the country.

He then started for the coach-office, but recollecting that the stage did not start till later in the evening, he changed his mind, and being fond of a walk, determined to foot it as far as the "Pack-horse," at Turnham-green, and there wait its arrival. He had taken care to consign the produce of his robbery, to the custody of his comrades, so that he had nothing to encumber him but his cloak. Jack, however, had miscalculated the hour, for the coach overtook him before he had walked a mile. He hailed it, and got in without another word, and as the night was dark, unrecognised.

There were only two passengers besides himself—an old militia captain and a quaker. The conversation speedily turned upon the great highwayman.

"He beats Turpin by chalks, and leaves him nothing to brag of," said the captain. "By heavens I never heard or read of such an audacious scoundrel, such a daring devil in the whole course of my existence. But his repeated robberies have finished him; his robbery of the marquis has completely put his neck in the halter, why, the Frenchman—and, damme, as an Englishman, I hate all the accursed crew, and yet as an honest man, I must glory in his perseverance—has set such measures on foot, that the capture of Sixteen-string Jack is inevitable. His own guilty conscience has given him warning of it, too, for he has flown from London, as he would from Tyburn Tree."

Jack muffled his face in his cloak, and contrived to fix on his mask as he said, "It's my belief he cares no more for the gallows than I do," he exclaimed, disguising his voice.

"Let him come and prove it," said the militia-man; "but its more than he dare do."

"There you are mistaken," said Jack; "I know for a fact that he is back already."

"Pooh! what's the use of telling lies like that? Can you prove it?"

"Yes!"

"How?"

"Thus!" cried Jack, suddenly dropping his cloak, and collaring the quaker with his left hand, he presented a pistol with his right, to the captain, and cried, "Deliver, on your lives! deliver to Sixteen-string Jack!"

The travellers started back, and it is impossible to say whether doubt, astonishment, or dismay, was predominant in the expression of their looks. Their first impression was, that the young man was playing off some practical joke in revenge for being disbelieved, but his determined manner rendered them dubious on the point. Jack, on his part, had no sooner uttered the words than he repented them. He had been piqued at their incredulity, and acted more in revenge of the slight cast upon his reputation than from any other impulse. Had he given a single moment to reflection, the impolicy of his rashness would have struck him, for it was certainly an unwise action to give intimation of his return to the metropolis. Jack, however, unlike the majority of those who go slap-dash to work, as the maggot bites, never flinched from consequences; and when once he began a thing, went through with it. Would that his habit was more prevalent.

The pause succeeding his attack lasted hardly two seconds, and the first to break silence was the captain of militia:—

"Why, you audacious young scoundrel," exclaimed he, blinking like an owl at sunshine, as the muzzle of Jack's pistol peeped into his eye. "How dare you behave in this manner to strangers and gentlemen?—Take that d—d thing away, sirrah: it may go off! Take it away, I say, I'll indict you!"

"Verily, friend, the man of war adviseth well," said the quaker, now beginning to turn black in the face, from the effects of Jack's gripe. "This is a foolish jest, and if—'

"Peace?" roared Jack, cutting short the quaker's speech without ceremony, "I mean what I say, and stand no parleying. It is Sixteen-string Jack who speaks, and unless you obey me, I'll blow the brains out of both with one shot."

"Of a verity they will be useful to thee, for they are a commodity thou seemest to lack, young springald," exclaimed the quaker, who still conceived that our hero merely intended to frighten them.

Jack, who grew more anxious each moment, fancying, though not fearing, that the coach might stop to take up other passengers, now tightened his hold on the throat of the poor quaker, and with an imprecation that betrayed much ferocity, again swore, that if they did not deliver on the instant, he would fire; and to enforce his demand, he struck the captain of the militia a smart blow on the temple with his pistol, not sufficient to do him any damage, but still with enough force to draw blood.

It was now evident that no child's play was going forward, and the travellers, with an expression of reluctance that would have been ludicrous under less serious circumstances, drew forth their watches, purses, and rings. Jack eyed the booty, and received it with glistening eyes; but even while thrusting it into his pockets, his mind was diverted by considerations for his own safety. This mad-headed act had got him into a scrape, and the question was how he was to get out of it. To quit the coach would be dangerous to stay, still more so. Little time, however, was given him for reflection, for in an unguarded moment, when the necessity for using both hands, obliged him to lower his pistol, the quaker suddenly dealt him a buffet under the ear, that struck fire from his eyes, and made his brain reel like a top.

"Now, friend, do thy part," exclaimed the disciple of the broadcloth; and, in nowise behind-hand, the captain followed his example with interest, giving Rann a fisty-cuff under the other ear, in the throat, and in the region of the stomach. Jack was doubled up by these inflictions, and his assailants took advantage of his momentary weakness, by dashing the pistol from his hand, and seizing him on each side by the arm and throat.

Jack gave all up for lost. He struggled violently, but could not release himself, nor, from his arms being pinioned to his sides by the grasp of his assailants, could he even repay the blows which they continued to deal him with their unoccupied hands.

"Gentlemen, gentlemen!" at length he exclaimed, "Quit your hold, I did but jest!"

"You carried the jest too far," cried the militia officer, "and it's our intention to pursue it in earnest now. Tear off his mask, friend Peaceable, and assist me to raise an alarm. Hallo! Hallo, here!—We've Sixteen-string Jack, the highwayman, in the coach!"

The quaker joined in the outcry, and matters assumed a terrible appearance. The scene was altogether as singular as it was terrific. Here were three men cooped up in the narrowest possible limits, and engaged in hostile encounter; while the cramped apartment in which they maintained their deadly strife, was being whirled along a dark road with unceasing motion, as if to debar all parties from the possibility of escape. Infuriated with his own folly, and desperate at the consequences, Jack struggled like a madman, for fight he could not: he kicked, he plunged, he butted his head like a wild bull against his assailants; but all he had power to effect was to preserve the mask from being torn from his face. Meanwhile the quaker had managed to get one of the windows down, and, thrusting out his head, shouted for assistance as loud as possible. It was a considerable time before he could make himself heard; but, at length, one cry louder than the rest, attracted the dull ear of the driver, and he pulled up.

"Now, then, what's the matter?" inquired coachy—not exactly in the tones in which he would have made love, or asked credit for a pint of purl.

"We have gotten the man of abomination—the man of the highway—within," returned the quaker, "and crave thine assistance to help us out of peril."

"Eh! what!—speak English. Are you murdering each other, or only quarrelling?"

"I charge you, come down directly," cried he of the militia, delighted at his conquest. "I have apprehended Jack, the highwayman—Jack with the Sixteen Strings!"

"Sessions!" shouted the coachman, and down he jumped in a moment, as did also the outside passengers, and the guard. But notwithstanding their numbers, they huddled together like children, when a strange dog invades their circles, and moved as if about to attack a giant.

"Now, then, show him to us—let's see him!" vociferated the passengers, brandishing their sticks and umbrellas in readiness for defence.

"Not so fast;" cried the guard. "He goes armed to his teeth, and he can hit the eye of a needle with his own eyes shut."

"Never fear," called out the captain; "we have taken his artillery, and secured a whole waggon-load of ammunition."

"That alters the case," returned the guard. "Then you may open the door, and turn him out—and if he don't nap it, my name ain't Ben Bingo. I've got a blunderbus here, charged to the muzzle, and the moment I get a peep at Jack's sconce, pop she goes."

"Hurra!" shouted the rest. Turn him out—turn him out."

"Hold your noise!" cried the Captain; "and you, master guard, keep your d—d blunderbuss quiet, unless you wish to hit friends as well as foes."

"But what's to be done?" said the quaker. "I like not the looks of the robber well enough to remain with him, and it would not be safe to leave him in the coach alone."

"If I might put in my verdic," exclaimed the coachman, "I'd sarve him out as we did the Jew crimps at Portsmouth, when I was a publican there."

"And how was that, Samivel?" asked Ben Bingo.

"Vy, we used to gather a mob round the door of the offender, and have his wile carcase pitched out amongst 'em, to be beaten into decorum. Every man as hadn't a stick had his fists, and we continued to larrup away with these natural and artificial veapons until he consented to valk quietly and be ducked."

"Ca-pi-tal!" shouted a tailor's shopman, in shrill tones. "Commit the horwible barbawian to our wengeance. We'll teach him how to go about picking pockets and cutting children's thwoats."

No. 29.

"Aye!" responded the coachman. "Men as don't leave travellers enough to pay their coachman's fees, don't deserve no mercy."

"Turn him out, turn him out," again burst from every lip, and the quaker, though inwardly pitying the offender for the fate that awaited him, threw open the coach door.

"Now, then, my old 'un," cried the captain to his sullen prisoner, "put your springs into action and let us see how far you can jump!"

As he said this, with the spitefulness of a coward, he gave Jack a kick, and and struck him also on the side of the head. The indignity caused a flow of blood to Rann's heart which renewed all his wonted spirit: he shook himself furiously, and dashed his head with such violence into the captain's face as to flatten his nose, ram four front teeth down his throat, and bathe every feature in blood. "Take that, you ruffianly cur," he shouted, following up his attack with a blow that freed him from the other's hold, and with a third desperate effort he pitched the unfortunate captain out of the coach. In an instant all were upon the prostrate man—coachy, guard, tailor's shopman, male and female passengers—even the quaker, who in the confusion could not recognise the right man from the wrong—and amid yells and shouts of triumph the unfortunate captain was belaboured within an inch of his life. As for Jack, he was too much excited at the peril in which he stood, to be conscious of the advantage he had gained, and as the furious cries of those outside met his ears, he fancied they were rushing into the coach to tear him to piecemeal; he, therefore, started instinctively back, and whether the opposite door had been insecurely fastened, or whether the mortice of the lock was decayed, we know not, but it flew open as he struck against it, and he fell into the road.

It was "touch earth and up again!" The next instant saw him on his feet and in flight through the darkness; but not heeding his way, he went violently against the hedge that girted the wayside, and fell with his head and shoulders on the top. In boyhood he had often done a similar thing in sport, and by throwing up his heels, contrived to roll himself from one field into another, so that it was a natural impulse to do so now, and a very slight exertion of his former dexterity was sufficient to lay him safely in a dry ditch on the other side of the hedge.

"St. Nicholas be praised!" he exclaimed, stopping for breath; "how the dogs keep on shouting; they'll attract every cottager within a mile of the place. Ten minutes of Old Sue's company would now be worth her weight in gold."

The words were scarcely out of his mouth before his quick ear was attracted by a low neigh within a yard of where he was resting. He raised his hands and caught hold of a pair of long ears, which he knew to belong to a horse of some sort that bent its head close by him for the purpose of cropping a mouthful of clover. Jack joyfully sprung to his feet.

"May your shaddow never be less, old chap!" he exclaimed. "I bear a charmed life. Come along, my unknown friend; I'll make free to borrow you of your owner."

He took off his neckerchief, and twisting it as tightly as he possibly could, without letting the horse go, slipt it into the animal's mouth, as a substitute for bit and bridle, and then vaulted upon his back. "Huzza!" he exclaimed; "if I keep due east on this side of the hedge, I shall get safely to the Old Pack Horse before the coach; and now, gentlemen, owners of parks, plantations, and gardens, have the goodness to allow Sixteen-string Jack, the highwayman, to make a path across your private property."

So saying, he struck the horse with his switch, who, administering a hearty kick or two, bounded off in the direction he wished. Fortunately for Jack, the animal was a pet pony, accustomed to the rough usage of a parcel of schoolboys, so that his present usage was nothing new to him, and he gambolled along with a notion that he was engaged in one of his accustomed frolics. Jack had some difficulty in keeping his seat, and was obliged to hold on by mane and handkerchief, while the back bone of the animal galled him not a little; but he treated these inconveniences with indifference:—every yard he gained gave him a wider scope of liberty, and had he bestrode the edge of a saw, he would have deemed the seat an easy one.

Never had he felt more light-hearted. The peril he had been in was forgotten, and he only remembered the humours of the scene: he thought of the dismay of the Quaker and the captain, and chuckled as he fancied how the latter might still be receiving the drubbing intended for his own hide: he would have given a guinea for a peep, and was so elated at the retaliation he had been enabled to procure for his enemy, that he thumped his courser at the idea, and made him gallop along like wildfire. His flight was a headlong one: he made no attempt to avoid flower beds, cucumber frames, or other choice places; but dashed sturdily through them all, without remorse at the damage he might inflict. At length, a faint reflection of light against the sky, informed him that he was in the vicinity of Turnham Green, and having gained a convenient spot for alighting, he reined up his steed.

"Thank you, old fellow!" he exclaimed gaily, as he quitted his steed; "if ever you and I meet again, and you tell me of this, I will pay you for it. Stop! stop! give me back my handkerchief! There—that will do—now then, you may find your way home agaid!"

He gave the animal a hearty lash as he spoke, and, finding itself freed from restraint, it pointed its nose towards its own paddock, and set off at full speed. "I owe a good turn to the owner," said Jack, and then regaining the highroad, he made as fast as he could for the hostel of the Old Pack Horse.

Of old Enoch Finings, the landlord, Jack had some knowledge, from having met him on various occasions at Richmond. He was one of those quaint, old-fashioned characters who are generally to be found conspicuous in similar localities. He was a tall solemn-looking man, with a grave squint, and an oracular mouth twisted a little on one side. He was the repository and dispenser of all the news in the neighbourhood, and was not a little looked up to by those of the village. Maugre his importance, he was one of the most inoffensive men alive, and as innocent as a sucking pig. He swallowed everything that was offered him, from the thimblefull of "daffy" to the flagon of "stingo"—from the dish of harmless gossip to the most outrageous Munchausen ever invented; yet was he never intoxicated either with drink, or the magnitude of his exclusive intelligence. Folks, however, gave him credit for knowing more than he really did; but this may be attributable to the sagacious expression his countenance maintained, for even when totally ignorant of a subject that was broached, he would wink with his squinting eye, and nod his head, as much as to say, " I know all about it."

He was leaning against his sign-post, with a short pipe in his mouth, when our hero approached; but the appearance of one whom he knew to maintain an important position amid the councils of the great, caused him to assume a more erect attitude. He had formerly been a military man, and could stand as upright as the monument, when in the presence of a superior; and this, by the bye, is the only redeeming feature in the slavishness of the army. Civilians bend the body, and cringe before the great—but the soldier holds up his head even in the presence of royalty.

"Good evening, Mr. Finings," said Jack, as he came up. "Has the 'Regulator' passed yet?"

"No, your honour—not yet," replied the host.

"Then I am in time. When do you expect it up?'

"Can't say. The 'Regulator' is the most irregular coach going. It should have been here by this time."

"Well, the sooner the better, for I have walked from Richmond, and am tired. What have you in the house?"

"Everything, Sir, from an elephant's tusk to a horse-shoe."

"These are rather indigestible matters," said Jack, with a smile. "Could you not furnish something in the shape of a round of beef?"

"I might, your honour," said Enoch, with a wink and a grin, "but I am afraid you would spoil its shape for me."

"Well, if I spoil the *round*, I'll make all *square* in return," exclaimed Rann.

The landlord gave a broader grin than before, and with another wink marshalled his customer into the best parlour. This was already occupied by a young man of gentlemanly appearance, who was enjoying a Welch rabbit and a small tankard of mulled sack. The usual salutation passed between the travellers; and when the landlord retired to execute Jack's order anent the round of beef, they speedily fell into a sociable chat. Finings soon returned with as glorious a buttock as ever tempted the grinders of a hungry man, and a measure of the best ale in his cellar. Jack fell to with a good appetite, but could not help remarking that the host kept popping in and out of the room, as if anxious for an opportunity of addressing him; he therefore, when pushing his plate from before him, after its third replenishment, said, "Now, then, old friend, what is it?"

"I beg pardon, your honour," returned Finings, stooping towards Jack's ear, and speaking in a mysterious whisper, "but has you heerd anythink of that terrible willain?"

"Of what villain do you speak?" exclaimed Rann, leaning back, and picking his teeth, "You know there are more villains than one in the world."

"Aye, aye; you may well say that," returned the host; "but I am speaking of the villain with the sixteen halters round his throat. You know who I mean—Sixteen-string Tom—or Peter—or Jack, or whatever else his godfathers or godmothers thought proper to call him."

"What, the famous highwayman?" said Jack. "Oh, yes, I hear that he has returned towards town, and intends to give this neighbourhood the benefit of his abilities."

"No," exclaimed the landlord, "and have you really heard such a thing?"

Jack's object was to set a rumour afloat that might draw the attention of justice from London; he therefore repeated his assertion, and added a pretended conviction that the robber might make an appearance in the adjacent towns and villages, but would not dare to show his face in town for several months to come.

The landlord gave one of his wise looks, and bringing his mouth still closer to Jack's ear, and taking hold of his arm, whispered—

"You are right, but he is nearer than he would like it to be known. Nay, he is not many inches distant this moment"

Jack started to his feet, instinctively feeling in his breast for the pistol of which he had been deprived during his struggle in the coach, cried, "How know you that—Who do you suspect?"

The solemn host uttered no reply, but nodding significantly towards the stranger, he tucked the table-cloth under his arm, and made his retreat with the remains of the round of beef, leaving Jack to draw his own conclusions. Our hero sank into his seat again, and burst into a fit of loud laughter.

"May I ask the occasion of your merriment?" inquired the stranger, who had been occupying himself with a newspaper while Jack was at supper.

"You have a right," exclaimed Rann, scarcely able to speak for the excess of his laughter, "Why, who do you suppose you are taken to be by our wise landlord?"

"I cannot imagine, an honest man, I hope."

"Quite the reverse. He thinks you are none other than the famous Sixteen-string Jack!"

"Preposterous!" cried the stranger. "Yet now I think of it—Ha! ha! ha!—the good man is not without cause for his suspicions."

"Indeed!" said Jack, "you excite my curiosity."

"It shall be gratified returned the other. "You must know that I am contemplating a trip with a fair lady to Gretna, and, as I expect a hot pursuit and powerful opposition, I have been making arrangements with my servant, such as the providing of pistols, relays, and so forth—which have, no doubt, sounded suspiciously in our host's ear. Egad, I've a good mind to carry on the joke, and adopt the highwayman's name for an hour or two."

"Take my advice, and do nothing of the sort," said Jack. "You don't know what trouble it may get you into; and, besides, it might hinder you from carrying on the design you were speaking of with your *cher amie*."

"True," said the stranger, and I thank you for the hint; but what a noise this fellow has been making in the world."

"He must be a consummate rascal," said Jack.

"I cannot think so," observed Captain Heyman, which was the name of the gentleman. "He seems to soar above the common run of thieves, and has a dash of genius and enterprise in his character, that fit him for better things."

"But his talents, whatever they may be, are no vouchers for his morality," said Jack, not displeased to hear Heyman's opinion.

"I have my own sentiments on that point," resumed Heyman. "It may be presumed that men of ability know right from wrong better than the rest of the world, and I cannot help thinking they would in most instances prefer the safer and more honourable path, if the injustice of others did not drive them into vicious practices."

"Never did man speak truer," said Jack; "what a mournful thing it is to see abilities perverted.

"It is, indeed. This highwayman now—what a head for scheming; what power to execute he has displayed. Such a man would be invaluable at the head of a regiment; and if I would go a mile to see him hanged, I would walk fifty to see him placed in that position, for which nature has evidently qualified him."

"I admire the liberality of your disposition, said Jack, "but do you think he might be trusted?"

"And why not? any man who is clever would rather shine in a just than an unjust cause. You may depend upon it, that if the rulers of a country made an invariable practice of promoting every man according to the peculiar gifts with which he was endowed, we should have few living on their wits in a roguish course."

"But the bent of a man's powers are not always to be discovered," remarked Jack, who felt a deep interest in the conversation. "There are many in obscurity who do not know themselves until some accident calls into display the darling passions of their souls. Sixteen-string Jack, for instance, may have contentedly passed his early years in some hum-drum occupation, and never thought of change, until some peculiar event sent him on the highway. Now, had you a voice in the government of things, what would you advise to be done in his case, seeing that he had never given an intimation of talent before going wrong?"

"You will think me singular when I say I would send to him with an offer of honourable employment. I would say, 'Jack, my boy, you are a clever fellow, but are turning your talents to a bad purpose. Now if you like to annoy our enemies instead of your own countrymen, I'll give you an opportunity of distinguishing yourself—deny me, and I'll have you hanged.'"

"He would jump at the offer," said Jack.

"To be sure he would, and I should thus reclaim a lost man, give society a new member, save the hangman's fee, and enable travellers to pursue their routes in security."

"Would to heaven you were prime minister," exclaimed Jack, grasping Heyman's hand with much emotion. The conversation was prevented from proceeding further by the sudden arrival of the Richmond coach, and in another moment a confusion of tongues outside announced that the passengers were making their way into the Pack-horse. The door burst open and

Samuel, the coachman, and Ben Bingo made their appearance, bearing between them the redoubtable captain, with his head bound up. They were followed by Zachary Smith, the quaker, and the remainder of the travellers, male and female, who all appeared to be eager to be first to communicate what had occurred.

"What can have happened?" exclaimed the landlord, as they burst in.

A dozen voices were raised to unfold the new outrage of Sixteen-string Jack. The men swore that they had all been murdered, and the women that they had been ravished; and it was with the utmost difficulty those present could gather what had really occurred. Jack was almost ready to betray himself with laughter, at some of the embellishments which the story received; but the impulse grew still stronger when he learnt that the poor captain had been mistaken for him, and in consequence been pummelled within an inch of his life the instant he was thrown from the coach to the ground. He, however, could not help pitying the deplorable condition to which the unlucky militia-man had been reduced, and on hearing that he had not a coin left to pay his expences to London, Jack very generously presented him with a couple of guineas.

Mine host stood confounded. He had expected to have seen Heyman draw forth a couple of horse pistols, and rush through the party as it entered, instead of which, the young man preserved the utmost composure, and appeared more amused than alarmed at what was passing. Human nature could endure this no longer, and Finings, exasperated beyond all wonted forbearance, seized Heyman by the throat, and, shaking him as a mastiff would a young kitten, exclaimed :—

"E'nt you ready to drop into the very earth, you brazened sinner you, or do you think that all these smooth looks will have any effect upon an old soldier like me."

"Come, I say, hands off, old chap!" exclaimed the young man, turning almost black in the face; "Who the deuce do you take me for?"

"Why, for Sixteen-string Jack himself, and I claim the reward for apprehending you."

"Pooh!" said our hero, knocking the landlord aside; "how could that gentleman be the highwayman, when I found him here on my arrival, which must have been about the very moment at which the robber made his assault upon this company, and by the bye, he continued turning to Samuel, which was the name of the Jarvey, how came he in your coach? It is a very suspicious circumstance, Mr. Samuel, and, as one determined to investigate the affair, it is right I should learn how your acquaintance with so bad a character commenced."

"Vy," said Sam, "he made his appearance afore the drag all of a sudden, like a Will o' the Wisp, and said three times, "Samivel, Samivel, Samivel!" "Here am I, your honour," siz I ; "guv us a lift," siz he, "and I pulls up, and lets him in, for seeing as how he looked most indicatively sowspicious, it occurred to me that it might be as vell to secure him."

"Then you had some idea of what sort of a character you were harbouring," interrupted our hero.

"To be sure I had! Vy, as soon as I seed his cocked hat and whiskers, I said to myself, as sure as osses is osses," siz I, "that e're covey is the great highwayman hisself."

"Then I think, friend," exclaimed the quaker, with great indignation, "thou didst not act like a faithful shepherd to the coach, in thus turning the wolf amid the sheep which were in fold."

"Vy you sees," said Jarvey, a little perplexed, "I seed nuffen of his pistols, so I didn't apprehend not no danger; but ven I heerd 'em fired off, I says to a gemman as sot on the box, I says to him, says I, that means mischief."

"Oh!—he fired, did he," said Jack.

"Either he or his comrades did—that I'll be upon my oath."

"I thought you said he entered the coach alone."

"Vell, so he did, Muster Rann, but he was surrounded by the rest of his Sixteeners ven he first riz from the ground; and I'll be upon my davy that they had at least sixteen six-pounders, all loaded and pointed at the drag, ready to blow me and it into small pieces, in the event of our refusing to give Jack a lift."

This was too much for our hero, and but for the impolicy of the act, he must have forgotten his gravity, had he not put a stop to the exaggerations of the worthy coachman. He, however, pretended to believe all, though with some difficulty, and suggested that special messengers should be dispatched on horseback, to scour the intervening grounds between the Pack Horse and Richmond. By this measure, he knew that the ground would get sufficiently trampled up, to obliterate all trace that might have been afforded by the foot marks of the beast he had so unceremoniously borrowed to convey him to his present resting place.

"I sanctions and approves of all you have suggested, sur," exclaimed the coachman; "and it only shows that them as set you to sift these here sort of matters knowed vot they vos about; and now I considers as how ve had better think of going to go."

"Prythee don't think of stirring," groaned the captain of militia, trembling at the bare chance of again encountering the highwayman—" My bones are in such a condition that I shall not be able to move for a month."

"In that case you had better be put to bed, while we proceed to town, and spread the intelligence," returned Rann. Then, addressing Heyman, he added, "Do you go to town, or do your arrangements force you to remain where you are?"

"My arrangements force me to ride with you," replied the young man, "and I shall be happy to travel in such good company."

"Then, let's be off," cried Jack; "but in the first place, let me have the highwayman's pistol; it will not only be of service, should we again be attacked, but must be preserved as evidence against the rascal when he is taken."

"Here it is," said Ben Bingo, and he forthwith again put Jack in the possession of that weapon which had so often served him without shedding blood.

Jack welcomed it in his own heart as he would have done the presence of an old friend; then thrusting it once more into his breast pocket, exclaimed, "Now, I have nothing to fear. Let's be off as soon as you like, Master Sam."

"Doesn't you think as how a drop within would fortify us agin all without, provided we had the precaution to take it afore we wentured into the open air?" said Samuel, with that bland, insinuating smile, with which a clown is seen to ogle Columbine in a pantomime.

"You may do as you like," exclaimed Jack, "only make haste."

The grog was called for and dispatched. A pause then ensued, during which the landlord was seen to scratch his head.

"Why are we waiting?" said Jack, now growing impatient; "Are we to reach London to-night?"

"As soon as your honour pleases, I'm ready to take the ribands this wery instant," returned Sam.

"Then pay for what you have had, and lose no more time," said our hero.

"Pay!" said Sam, then smacking his lips, he shook his head with an expression that seemed to make payment a doubtful matter. Ben Bingo, who had partaken of the liquor, shook his head also, and then both looked as grave as undertakers.

"Why, is there any objection to paying?" asked Rann, not fathoming their meaning.

"A wery great deal," said Sam, with solemnity. "It vos I as started the notion, and no man should pay for his own ideas."

"Stuff!" exclaimed Rann.

"It vos stuff!—It was THE stuff! and glorious stuff it vos."

"No doubt; consequently there should be no hesitation about paying for it."

"None, sur, none; but did you ever read or hear tell of a poem called Milton's loss of a pair o' dice?"

"Something of the kind," replied Rann, with a smile.

"Vell, and who found the tin to publish it, do you suppose? Vy, the bookseller who approved of the work, of course. Milton guved the hidea, and the 'tother tipped the browns; and by a logical coincidence of comparative hargument, if I vos the hauthor of the hidea about the grog, you as the encourager of the hidea, is bound in common justice to tip for the same."

"Oh, is that what you are driving at?" said Rann. "Why didn't you say so at once? There, master landlord, take your charges, and now farewell. Do not be under any apprehensions concerning Sixteen-string Jack, for, depend on it, he'll now not dare to shew his face before you see me again."

With these words he departed, and the rest of the company followed Rann rode in the basket, and young Heyman placed himself by his side They were soon in full motion, and, as is generally the case with travellers their tongues were equally soon in full wag.

"It somewhat puzzles me," exclaimed Rann, "what can be your business in town, when your arrangements at the Pack Horse would appear to render your presence so necessary!"

"I wish to be seen there as little as possible until the proper time," replied the young stranger. "I shall, however, return in the morning, and hope by this time two days to have crossed the borders."

"I suppose, from what you tell me, that your courtship would form quite a romance."

"It is one often told in real life. I love the daughter of a rich man, but although I sprang from a good family, my whole fortune is limited to my commission in his majesty's service—no crime is so heinous as poverty in his eyes, and, therefore, my application to be accepted as a suitor, was rejected by him with scorn and contumely—"

"And the lady?" queried Jack.

"Heaven bless her!" said the young soldier, fervently, "the impediment thus raised to bar our road to happiness, served only to awaken in her heart as in my own, the desire to cast aside the fetters her sire would weave about us, and to show our independence of the world by following our own inclinations."

"Of course without the knowledge of her father," said Jack.

"I need not say, yes," replied Heyman. "The old man, who is an usurer and a miser, was all along too deeply engaged in his devotions to Plutus to detect the entrance of Cupid into his house, so that I made advances to his daughter, as it were under his very nose without detection. Neither of us had, however, made up our minds to anything decisive, when a crony and schoolfellow of the old dad made his appearance in the character of a suitor.'

"Which circumstance made you begin to think of looking about you."

"It did, for the old fellow knowing the uncertainty of life, insisted upon having the ceremony performed forthwith. They would have had a special licence, but for the cost, and, in order to save that expense, it was agreed that the ceremony should take place by banns. This was salvation to us, as it gave us three weeks to make our arrangements in."

"Has the young lady any tin? I beg pardon, I mean, is she possessed of any fortune?" enquired Rann.

"Thirty thousand pounds in her own right, my boy," exclaimed the lover, with elation.

Jack gave a long whistle at hearing this, and exclaimed, "Why, if old mother Shipton was to come to life, and possessed of such a fortune, I would marry her."

"How much stronger would be the incentive were you tempted as I am, by loveliness, virtue, and accomplishments?" said Heyman. "But I can scarcely dream of success. It appears a piece of fortune too glorious for a mortal in my position to achieve!"

"Never despair," said Rann, "all things are possible to the adventurous; and he who plays the most desperate game is generally the winner; but how is it that you are not now with your lady-love.

"For this reason: it is proposed that the parties should be married in London, and they will put up at the old "Pack Horse," on their way thither. I have prepared post-horses, and everything requisite, so that when the young lady retires to her chamber in the evening, she will be enabled to slip down to me, and start with me in the chaise at once."

"Then you will gain a night in advance of them. Why, that will be glorious," said Jack.

In conversation of this nature, the pair whiled away the time until the crazy vehicle on which they rode, made its way without further adventure to the old "White Horse" cellar in Piccadilly. As it drove up, Rann's attention was arrested by an appearance of great confusion, amid a crowd that had congregated near the door of the inn, while loud clamours of contention were plainly to be heard. He would have thought little of an occurrence so common, had he not heard amidst the confusion of sounds a voice that sounded familiar to his ears. He strained his eyes to recognise the party, and at once beheld his old friend Clayton in the hands of constables, from whom he was striving to escape. Jack leaped to the ground in an instant, and knocking aside all who impeded him, he jostled his way into the heart of the crowd, and striking down the captors, released Clayton with scarcely an effort. The difficulty now was to get him clear of the crowd but this he might have effected with ease, had not the officers been too quick for him. They regained their feet without loss of time, and, calling on the bystanders in the King's name to assist, they fell upon Jack, and a regular battle royal took place. Twice was our hero knocked down, and twice he sprung up as undaunted as ever, and returned to the scratch. At length a blow on the back of the head not only felled, but stunned him, and his assailants were dragging him along the ground in triumph, when young Heyman, who had conceived an extraordinary liking for Jack, resolving that his new friend should not suffer in his attempt to serve a friend in distress, flung a portmanteau at the head of one of the officers, and then seizing the coachman's whip, jumped into the midst of the throng, and laid about him so effectually, that he cleared a tolerably wide space. By this time Rann had again come to himself, and seizing Clayton's arm, exclaimed to his preserver "Now then, my boy, let's make a bolt of it."

So saying he darted forward and was followed by his ally. In the present time the bude lights and gas gives little chance for escape unseen down so crowded a thoroughfare as Piccadilly, but in the nights of which we write, the most illuminated part of London was too dark to enable one to see a yard beyond his nose; it was therefore no difficult matter for Jack to penetrate the gloom, and get out of sight of his pursuers. He made his way to the park, and when there, threw himself upon the sward, and invited his companions to do the same. Heyman declined, as his business was too urgent to admit of a moment's delay, and he apologized for leaving so abruptly.

"You have served one," said Jack, grasping his hand. "who never forgets a kindness, and who may have it in his power to serve you more deeply than you imagine."

"I hope in a few days to be placed beyond the need of aid," exclaimed Heyman; "however, I appreciate your expressions of gratitude, and trust that we shall meet again." So saying, he shook hands with Jack and departed.

CHAPTER XXIV.

THE MEETING—JACK'S PROPOSITION—THE PROCLAMATION.

Jack's return to the metropolis was duly notified to the authorities, who from that moment became still more eager to obtain possession of the highwayman, who laughing at all their efforts to entrap him—who setting all attempts at defiance, had made them the laughing-stock of every intelligent person in the kingdom, from one end to the other.

Not only Toby's hostelrie, and the "Cock and Magpie," but also every other inn bearing the least taint upon its wordly frame, was watched by night and day, and so strenuous where their endeavours to entrap our hero, that dozens of innocent persons, supposed to bear a resemblance to him, were arrested and conveyed before the magistrates, where proof being forthcoming that they were severally and individually respectable members of society, they were, of course, discharged.

"Now Jack and his pals, after a rest from their labours, began to knock their precious brains together, for since they were gaining so vast a popularity for what Toby described as "not nothing," they were desirous by one unexampled feat to set the world agog.

Several schemes were mooted, all of which were pronounced "humbugs," "no goes," and so forth, until Jack, at length clearing his throat with an ahem! and swallowing a hearty draught of brandy, rose and said:—

"Gentlemen, our chief aim must be to put the enemy on a false scent, and enable us to remain on this spot until pursuit is at such a distance that we may show our faces in London without dread."

A nod from the rest assented to this, for all were too interested to speak, and Jack continued—

"I have thought of a scheme for effecting this. It is one which failure would render absurd, but success glorious. It will require all my own presence of mind; all your wisdom, Kit; all Harry's bravery and enterprise; and all my friend Jared's sagacity, cunning, and activity."

"Out with it then!" cried Clayton. "D—n it, you set a chap longing like a breeding woman, to hear you talk."

"Listen then. Who here is not aware of Turpin's ride from London to York?"

"Not one of us! That unequalled feat has rendered him King of the Tobymen."

"And I will perform another that shall crown me their Emperor!"

"What is it? what is it?" asked all in a breath, and as Jack leant forward to reply, the most intense anxiety made every heart pant.

"Prepare yourselves for something that will make you disbelieve your own ears," said Jack. "In short, gentlemen, since Richard Turpin rode from London to York in one night, on the back of Black Bess, it is my intention to make old Sue go on to Newcastle-upon-Tyne in the same period. If that won't be taking the shine out of Dick, I don't know a mare from a donkey."

The hope-illumined countenances of the gang became blank at this astounding proposition, and instead of the enthusiastic glance of delight with which his propositions were wont to be received, Jack only saw the cold looks of vexation and disappointment. At length, Kit Clayton gave a nod, as if in approval of the good intentions of the captain, and said—

"I honour your pluck, Jack; none but the gamest cock alive would have ventured sich an out-and-out proposal, but the thing's impossible."

"It must be done, nevertheless," said Jack.

"But it can't be done," said Sheppard. "Newcastle is a hundred miles beyond York, and, remember, Turpin had scarcely won that city before his matchless charger paid the forfeit with her life."

"It must be done, nevertheless," repeated Jack, in a still more determined voice than before.

Jared Steele shook his head, and a sigh swelled his breast, as he exclaimed with interceding look—

"But that beautiful creature! an animal in whose veins both fire and milk seem to flow. And are you indeed resolved upon sacrificing her life?"

"No! but it must be done, nevertheless," reiterated our hero. "Come," he added, with a laugh, "I'll keep you no longer in suspense. I am quite as conscious as you are, gentlemen, that none but a madman, or fool-hardy idiot, would attempt what I have proposed. But, by artifice and stratagem, we may contrive to make it appear as if the act was performed, without "Sue's" lifting a leg!"

"The deluded arts of that 'ere hangelic captain of ours," exclaimed Toby, pretending to faint with extacy. "But go on," he continued: "unfold your plans, and kill us vith rapture at vonce."

"The scheme is a complicated one, and could only be executed by clever fellows like ourselves—"

"You says right," interrupted Clayton. "We are clever fellows, Jack."

"I know it," resumed Rann; "and therefore I feel no doubt of success. My plan is as follows:—you, Jared, must hire a black mare as like old Sue as possible, and post yourself, by the time we shall hereafter fix, on the road, about midway between London and York. I need not ask if you comprehend me?"

"Perfectly, captain," answered Jared; "and I presume it to be your wish that I should represent you as closely as possible."

"You are quicker witted than I thought you," said Jack; "such is, indeed, my wish. You Sheppard, must also provide yourself with a similar horse to mine, and place yourself in some sequestered spot near York, on the same evening."

"I am all attention," said Sheppard.

"And you, Clayton," resumed Rann, "must also get yourself a black mare, and carry her a hundred miles beyond Harry's.

"Close by Newcastle," said Kit.

"Yes," answered his Captain; "we shall then be seperated in four different places at the same moment, and each provided with a black mare."

"I now begin to see your drift," said Clayton, with delight.

"You wish us each to rob our man on the same evening, and want the world to think that Sixteen-string Jack did it all?"

"Exactly so," cried Rann—"What think you, gentlemen, of the idea?"

"Enchanting!" exclaimed all. "It will immortalize you."

"I hope so," returned our hero. "But in order to succeed, everything must be arranged like clock-work. I must burst upon the road in a terrific disguise at a certain hour. The gypsy in a similar disguise must cry, stand; to the first man he meets, in a given time from that hour fixed upon for my attempt. In a certain number of hours from that, Charlie must rob his man near York, and in a further number of hours from that, Kit must do the same at Newcastle."

"Vell," exclaimed Toby, relieving with a deep sigh the intensity with which he had listened—"arter this, they have only to place you at the head of the ministry, for old England to flourish! Vy, a thing like this will puzzle every wise acre in the nation, and if we each tells our man that he has the honour of being robbed by Sixteen-string Jack, the country, in spite of common sense, will be obliged to believe that you have gone on one horse from London to Newcastle in a single night."

Kit's commendations were echoed by all with expressions of delight, and many excellent hints were suggested for perfecting the plan. Amid these, one by Jared, the gypsy, was unanimously adopted. He proposed that instead of at once taking his station midway between London and York, he should lurk near the mansion of the marquis, ready mounted, while Jack put his enterprise into effect—for Rann had promised the marquis a visit at his house, and was determined, at all risk, to pay it—and that the moment Rann disappeared from the apartment, Jared should dart off and invite pursuit.

"I will take care to provide myself with a beast that has some blood in her," continued Steele, "and will undertake to outstrip all who follow. You, sir, can yourself lead the pursuit, and by so doing, not only strengthen your own security, but keep those who give chase from coming too near me."

"Upon my soul it will be an impudent affair altogether!" exclaimed Jack laughing at the proposal.

"However, it will prevent the possibility of suspicion falling upon me therefore if you have no objection to a long and hard ride, so be it. Egad' I wish we had confederates enough to carry me all round the island in this manner!"

The conference was now broke up. It was arranged that Clayton, Charlie, and Jared, should take beds at the tavern, and that on the following morning, Clayton should dispatch the gipsy on some pretended message to town, in order that, as he was not known in London, he might go in search of three black mares with safety. He required almost the entire capital of the gang to put him in a condition for making the purchases, but it was subscribed without a murmur, and having made arrangements for their next meeting, the friends separated for the night.

According to promise, the two chief confederates of our hero dispatched Steele, the gipsey. He assumed the disguise of a West Indian gentleman as that best suited to his complexion. Nor was his gait ill-suited for his part' as his figure was too shapely and genteel for any to suspect him, but the extremely critical in matters of high life. With a suit of good clothes and well-lined pockets, a man has to wait for little in London; Jared had not, therefore, been many hours in town before he had purchased the animals for which he had been despatched, and seen them safely stabled. He then strolled into the City towards the Minories, in order to purchase three disguises resembling Jack's dress, in readiness for the plot which had been projected the previous evening. From prudential motives he waited until it was dark before he took this step, and as the night had again set coldly in, he found the streets comparatively deserted as early as seven o'clock. To Steele this was rather a desirable circumstance than otherwise, and he sauntered carelessly along until he reached the Mansion-House, on the roof of which he saw a fire burning. This was on account of some plumbers having been employed to sit up all night to repair the damages occasioned by a recent storm, which it appeared had made sad havoc among the City pantiles, and spread destruction in all quarters. The effect of this nocturnal labour was singular and pleasing. The base of the edifice was just rendered visible by the dim oil lamps which in those days served to illuminate the streets, while the summit was crowned with a glowing ruddy fire for heating the solder, leaving the main mass of building in darkness that was rendered more profound by contrast with the lights above and below.

Jared looked upon all this with an eye of common curiosity and was passing along, when he stumbled against a ladder, which was placed against the Mansion-House, but which he had not perceived on account of its skeleton becoming lost in the utter darkness. Quick as lightning it struck him how this might be improved to advantage. He felt assured that a man might stand, against the facade of the building without being noticed from the the street and he felt at the same time how admirable was the opportunity of following up Jack's former defiance to the authorities by some announcement of an equally bold nature.

While he was pondering on the means of carrying this into effect, a man as if sent by destiny, passed by with a board on his head containing a number of paint pots and brushes of all sizes. This man, who was a painter and glazier, was stopped at the corner of Mansion House-street, by an acquaintance and they stood still to converse together. Without losing a moment's time Jared whipped a small pot of white paint from the man's head without being noticed, and darted up the ladder in an instant—when he had arrived midway he swung himself to the under side of the ladder, and stretching out his foot, rested it securely on a window sill—the other one remaining on the step of the ladder. He now took his brush and painted the following words on the front of the building:—

"SIXTEEN-STRING JACK

INTENDS TO RIDE

FROM LONDON TO NEWCASTLE-UPON-TYNE,

IN A SINGLE NIGHT,

ON THE BACK OF HIS MATCHLESS STEED,

OLD SUE.

STOP HIM WHO CAN!"

The bold act was performed with a coolness and intrepidity worthy a better cause. Twice while the gipsey was engaged in his work was he disturbed; once by one of the plumbers descending the ladder, and a second time by the same man. On each occasion, however, the shaking of the ladder gave him timely warning, so as to enable him to crouch against one of the windows of the building, preserving his equilibrium on its narrow ledge with all the dexterity of a rope-vaulter. The labourer was thus kept in ignorance of Jared's presence, for the man passed too rapidly for the scanning of objects, even in daylight, much less than when wrapped in the obscurity of total darkness. To those who can now, by the blaze of gas trace the smallest mark in front of the Mansion-house at midnight, the adventure may be a little inconceivable, but when it is remembered that Jared stood so high beyond the reach of light as to become actually invisible to the passers by, all appearance of improbability disappears. His own close propinquity to the building, of course, enabled him to see sufficiently for the guidance of his hand.

The whole process did not occupy ten minutes, and no sooner was it completed than the gipsey, watching a favourable opportunity, descended as rapidly and as stealthily as he had made his ascent. He found the painter still in conversation, having deposited his burden upon a resting place, the adroit gipsey, therefore, ran little risk in nimbly returning the loan he had borrowed with so little ceremony, and having thus got rid of his paint pot without inconvenience, he girded up his loins and went his way with a light heart.

He speedily suited himself with the required disguises, and on returning, naturally cast a glance towards the Mansion-House. It was now deserted, for the men had finished their job earlier than they expected, and had consequently extinguished the fire on the roof, and departed with the ladder that that had been of such singular service to our gipsey highwayman. He could not help laughing as he thought of the adventure, and fixing his keen eye upon the edifice, wondered within himself whether the writing still existed. Gradually his vision became sufficiently accustomed to the darkness to penetrate it, and distinguish the faint evidence of his handiwork, but it appeared so imperfect and confused that the most zealous watcher could not have made it out. Satisfied with the inspection, he again shook the dust from his shoes, and resumed his walk. He soon was again beneath the roof of the "Cock and Magpie," whence he despatched One-peeper Tom and another of the gang (whom, however, he kept in ignorance of the intentions at head quarters) each to convey one of the horses he had purchased, by different routes to a locality that appeared to suit his design.

CHAPTER XXV.

JACK'S PLANS PROCEED—A ROBBERY—JARED'S RIDE.

Now Jack, pursuing the plans on which his heart and mind was bent, and which, from experience, he felt fully assured would set the wonder-mongers on the *qui vive*, and would gain him a notoriety time could never efface, despatched his two comrades, Clayton and Sheppard, to pursue their journeys to the appointed stations, and then and there, simultaneously, to rob their man as had been already proposed.

After Clayton and Sheppard's departure, the time speedily arrived for Jack and Jared to fulfil the mission they had themselves appointed, which was, that Jack should travel on foot some distance down the road—should commit a robbery sufficiently daring to arouse for the pursuit—that he should return quietly to town on foot, as he had left it, and that Jared being enabled to place sufficient reliance on the steed he bestrode, to laugh at any attempt that could be made to capture him.

Jack started a few hours before Jared, but being overtaken by the latter, they, under cover of the twilight, proceeded on their journeys, Jack occasionally hiding in the hedge as passengers approached, that they might not be seen in company.

"Why, captain," said Jared, " on leaving town to-night, I'll be hanged if you were not the theme of every tongue. What hadst thou been doing ?"

"Doing !" cried Jack, with a hearty laugh, "that which will set a whole posse staring. and set every constable in London on the alert, and hang them for sleepy fools, say I, or they'd have nabbed me ere this. Well, Jared, to shorten a long tale, I came to an inn, before which a few farmers were sitting, talking of my promised ride to Newcastle." "He must pass by this way if he does ride," said one, "but hang me I arn't seen him yet." "He won't ride," said another. "Damme, it be more than his neck's worth; why, arter the long notice my Lord Mayor's had, d'ye think he'll be such a tarnation fool not to post men all down th' road ?" "Hang'd if it don't 'ppear like it anyhow," quoth another, "for sorry a tipstaff ha' we got this end o' town, save and 'cepting old Stocks, and a rare cove he'd be to catch the Sixteen-stringer, wouldn't he—why, he's blind of one eye, and can't see out of t'other."

"Now, I listened to all this conversation until an old farmer came up, well mounted, and swore " his horse could do any mortal thing that bees could do, but damme, if it could manage London to Newcastle, not a bit on it, nor more couldn't any other creater in the world.' And the old infidel, warmed up by expressing his opinion, the magistrate would be mad to take any notice of such a " werry ridiculous hidea."

Unbuttoning my long outer coat, excepting the two top buttons, so that I could, in an instant, tear it open, and show them my habiliments with pistols in belt, and all the formidable concomitants attending me, I advanced to the horse the farmer had just left, for he had dismounted, and patting the noble animal, I said quietly, "she is a noble horse, and shall this night do a deed for herself that shall earn her a noble name." In an instant I was in the saddle, and tearing open my coat, shouted, " Sixteen-string Jack will ride to Newcastle, and that, too, on the back of a borrowed horse !" and striking the animal with my spurs, she was off like the wind. Looking back, I had the pleasure of seeing the old farmer amidst the laughter and jeers of the populace, hurry off towards London as fast as his legs could carry him, in search of assistance.

"A laughable freak I confess, captain, but one calculated to bring an hornet's nest about your friend's ears. I value not my own safety one jot, Captain Rann; but, nevertheless, you might still have borne in mind, Jared Steele was flesh and blood as well as yourself."

" And think you I could forget you, Jared ? no, by heaven," said Jack, indignantly. "And if you think I am forcing you into any danger, return at once, I abandon the expedition."

Jared shook his head dissentingly, " but explain, Jack, explain—I am quite content with the danger likely to be incurred in *my* part of the farce, so proceed."

" I gallopped on half a mile, not further, and here I paused, bethinking me what was to be done. I was quickly decided. Springing from the mare's back, I hid myself in the clustering branches of a thick oak, in an adjoining road, whence I could see the road without fear of being detected from it. In a short time I had the pleasure of seeing the old farmer and a troop of horsemen ride up to the spot, where, instead of Sixteen-string Jack, pistol in hand, awaiting their advance, they found the farmer's horse quietly nipping the grass by the road-side. Fancying some wag or other had been playing a practical joke with the farmer, they retraced their steps, laughing right heartily.

The travellers had now come to the walls of a large mansion.

"Hush!" said Jared, "I hear voices, and by heavens that of our old friend the Marquis de'Vauxrien."

"So it is, by jingo," said Jack, quietly, yet gleefully. "I promised the old swell we should meet again, and here's a glorious opportunity! Take your horse to the end of the shrubbery, and stir not from thence, hand or foot, till you have my bidding."

"Let me accompany you, Jack," said Jared. "I cannot bear you to run singly into danger, unless I accompany you."

"Silence, Steele, my brave friend, I run no risk—that is all reserved for you, my share will be only sport. So, so, where are the stables?"

"By the side of the house; but what want you there?"

"You'll find out anon, I've a scheme in my head," and with bent back and stealthy footsteps, he advanced towards the range of stabling. The door stood slightly opened, sufficiently so to show Jack, by the light of a lantern, which hung from the ceiling, that save and excepting several horses, the place was tenantless. Jack entered, and finding a box of farrier's tools, he speedily removed a shoe from each of the horses. This done, he withdrew from the stable as noiselessly as he had entered it, and picking his way, he carefully, but fearlessly entered the house. Here he came at once full butt upon the company in the drawing-room, for they had returned from the garden to that apartment. Jack mixed with them, but for several minutes, so numerous was the party, not one of them noticed there was a stranger in the room. The few minutes so occupied was not spent idly by Jack. Several watches, purses, and snuff-boxes found their way by some magic process into his pocket. He was in the act of transplanting a snuff-box, when the owner, feeling it in a most insinuating manner, taking french leave of him, suddenly placed his hand upon it, and exclaimed, "After me is manners, if you please." This exclamation, as may be imagined, drew all eyes upon our hero, who bore the gaze undauntedly.

"Why, who have we here?' said the marquis, scanning the intruder from head to toe, and from toe to head again, "who are you, sare, I say, that you dare intrude yourself here, in my house?"

"Who and what I am," said Jack, throwing open his coat, and pulling his mask lower down (it being at the time, partly lowered), "you can not, perhaps, my lord marquis, determine."

"*Sacre dieu!* I hav no recollection of your cursed face, before, but you be one thief, dat be certain, dat be certain, and dat be quite enough; I shall arrest you on suspicion."

"Perhaps he is Sixteen-string Jack, of whom we have heard such talk," said one.

"I am Sixteen-string Jack," said Rann, drawing himself to his full height, and levelling his pistols as he spoke—a proceeding whereat the men started and the women screamed, "and in duty bound to express my gratitude for the marquis's late act of generosity to myself and companions. I have deviated from my journey to Newcastle to pay this visit, and having gleaned sufficient in this assembly to pay me my expenses to that town, I have the honour of wishing you a very good night, Marquis. I am your most obedient, madam,"—to the old lady—"yours ever, whilst you wear such lovely watches. Jack Rann, or Sixteen-string Jack bids 'each and all a fair good night.'"

"Forward, and seize the scoundrel," shouted several, simultaneously, but none advanced one step.

"If there is a man among you fancies himself capable of arresting me let him now do it;" and Jack, with a firm step returned from the glass door to which he had flown, into the centre of the room. The men fell back, the women's shrieks echoed again and again.

"By the noose! this will never do, they will alarm the household," though Jack, then springing forward he seized a bottle, and pouring himself out a goblet, he exclaimed "Health to all—I'm now for Newcastle, follow me who dares, who can, and will!"

And saying these words, he sprang through the glass door, clearing the terrace parapet at a bound, and was lost to sight.

Jack ran along with unabated swiftness, until he reached the ambush in which his gipsy assistant was hidden, and as this was a portion of the part that lay concealed in the shade of several ancient chestnuts which stretched their gnarled limbs across the cultivated grounds. Jared then rode forward in the open moonlight, at a gentle pace, to attract the attention of the visitors while Jack skulked secretly round to the back of the house, and, having given Jared his directions, made his way across country towards London.

In a moment all the servants were aroused by the confusion that broke out above, and communicated itself like wild-fire through the house as soon as the first stupor of astonishment had given way to more active feelings. The cry of "To horse, to horse!" now became general. The

"—summons dread brooks no delay;
Stretch to the race—away, away!"

Excitement often supplies the place of courage, and thus may be accounted for the fact that, after the word to mount had been given, not five minutes elapsed before every male in the place, from the foot-boy to the marquis, was in his saddle. He who could not get a hunter mounted a coach-horse, and those who could not procure either, were content with mules or asses. "Off" was the word in the following moment, and away started the squadron in pursuit of Steele.

The gipsey, in his disguise, as Sixteen-string Jack, made direct for the great North Road, and was followed with "many a whoop and wild halloo!" until the effects of Jack's foresight in removing a shoe from each of the horses became manifest. First one stumbled, and then another, until the hunt became fairly up; the party of pursuers dead beaten; and Jared Steele was left to pursue his route without further molestation.

"Alone, but with unbated zeal
That horseman plied the scourge and steel!
All jaded now, and spent with toil,
Embossed with foam, and dark with soil,
While every gasp with sobs he drew,
The labouring steed strained full in view."

Not long, however, did he remain "full in view;" for his pursuers having dropped off, one by one, he was completely out of sight. Having thus pleasantly accomplished the hazardous beginning of his adventure, he struck into an easy trot, and pursued his way to its accomplishment.

Outstripped and foiled, the party of pursuers breathed nothing but imprecations on the head of Sixteen-stringed Jack, and were put to the most laughable shifts to make their way back to the chateau. In some places there were no horses, and in others no blacksmiths, so that, eventually, the greater portion of the pursuers were obliged to return on foot.

Meanwhile Jared pursued his way alone until after several hours' hard riding he reached the point of road which had been mentioned by one of the magistracy, Mr. Tykespeech, at a meeting, as the place passed by him on horseback every day at a certain hour. The gipsey felt no hesitation about the matter, for his wandering life had rendered him so familiar with the country, that he knew every highway and byeway of the nation as well as a schoolboy does the lanes and alleys about his own parish. Having thrown a precautionary glance around him, he once more adjusted the mask to his face, and, resuming the rest of the disguise, he rode anxiously forward, burning for the coming adventure, yet almost fearing that something would happen to disarrange it.

"We have got on gloriously thus far," thought he, "and it would indeed be a pity if the devil were now to put in his hoof, and spoil sport. But the devil is too fond of his own." As he thus soliloquized, the prevailing stillness became suddenly interrupted by a loud, but not unmusical voice, which, in tones more remarkable for energy than attention, time, or key, sang the following chorus to an old song, of the coarse description, with which the Bacchantees of modern times are wont to illuminate the hours devoted to carousal:—

> "Beans, peas, and cabbages,
> Beans, peas, and cabbages.
> Oh, the old day when we frolicked away
> Over beans, peas, and cabbages!"

"This is my man, for a thousand pounds," exclaimed Jared with delight, and he gave the representation of "Old Sue" an immediate hint to resemble the mare it imitated in celerity. The animal was neither a dullard nor a laggard; it took the hint like a well-bred creature, and obeyed it like an obedient one. The sound of her hoofs, as they now clang briskly along the road, evidently attracted the notice of the approaching stranger. He paused for a moment, and Jared did the same; upon which the former, under the impression that he had only heard the echo of his own trot, resumed his journey, and singing as follows:—

> "A Flea, a Fly, and a Flitch,
> Be Yorkshireman's heraldry,
> And he's a son of a bitch
> Who knows not the reason why—

> Your Flea bite's all he come nigh,
> A Yorkshireman does the same,
> Sup wi', all will the fly;—
> And Yorkshire lads follow the game.
>   Too ral, loo ral, loo,
>   Too ral, loo ral, lay."

At this point of his most exquisite distich, the horseman turned a clump of trees which had hitherto concealed him, and Jared became enabled to take a view of him as he approached. His burly figure was not to be mistaken; it was Martin Tykespeech himself. He wore a stout broad-brimmed hat, with a low crown, possessing the strength of a helmet. His frame was enveloped in an ample grey coat, with mother-o'-pearl buttons, and enough capes to have formed a bulwark for Cape Horn.

Jared did not much relish the stalwart appearance of his adversary, but he resolved to trust to his own activity, and abide the result. Tykespeech had evidently been imbibing more of the juice of the grape than was altogether prudent, but still he was quite sensible enough to know what he was about. He came on singing the conclusion of the song he had already commenced:—

> "But the Flitch it comes closer home,
>   And to guess why needs no wizard;
> —Though, when abroad we roam,
>   The fact speaks in each gizzard.
> The heralds they been't mistaken,
>   Although they deserve to be hanged,
> For neither us nor the bacon
>   Are fit for a fig-tree we're all hanged.
>   Too ral, loo ral, loo,
>   Too ral, loo ral, lay."

In concluding his chorus, our merry Yorkshireman was disturbed by Jared, who, spurring suddenly in front, clapped his pistol to the ear of Tykespeech, and sternly asked the way to York.

"Thee means't York Castle," exclaimed the Yorkshireman, moved, but not disconcerted, by this unexpected salutation—"Why, thee'lt find the way easily enow, if thee repeats thy present action when thee gets within limits o' the county."

"You are as fond of a joke as ever, Tykespeech," said Steele, still holding his weapon within earshot of the oracular organs of his friend.

"And how the dickens does thee know that my name be Tykespeech, measter? Aye, and what hast thee sootened thy face for? Art thee a chimney sweep?"

"All in good time," said Jared. "Are you married?"

"What's that to thee?" exclaimed the honest grazier.

"Not much; only if you possessed a wife and children, I might be merciful, and not shoot the whole of your brains out."

"Ecod, thee bee'st a funny chap, howsumdever. But before I answer any o' thy questions, let me ax two or three of thee. I' the first place, what be thy name?"

"Sixteen-string Jack, the highwayman."

"What—say that again—do; but dom thee, if its a lee, I'll knock thee down arterards."

"I repeat it," said the gypsy. "I am him of the Sixteen-strings."

"Tal lal de riddle liddle!" sung the Yorkshireman. "I telled 'em it would be so, I kenned it would. Lord love thee, man, how is't thee?" So saying, he grasped Jared's hand, and shook it with an earnestness that proved the cordiality with which the action was performed.

Steele, who had a kindly nature, felt considerable compunction at the idea of rifling the pockets of a man whose heart and hand were so open, and he would at once have abandoned his purpose could he have done so without demolishing a scheme which had cost so much to set a foot; and as this consideration crossed his mind, he steeled himself against his own feelings, and once more presenting his pistol, he exclaimed—

"Your shake of the hand is ill bestowed. I am here to bid you stand and deliver."

"I ken that weel enuf," exclaimed Tykespeech, in return. "To be sure thee ort! I tell'd all t' chaps within ten miles of Stilton to expect thee, and I han't missed a night this fortnight to cum, in expectation o' meeting thee."

"Nonsense!" cried Steele, who could not believe his own ears. "Impossible!"

"But I tell thee we have, mun. And what be mair than that, here be a purse well-filled wi' brass, which I ha' brought we me on purpose for thee to steal."

"Oh! you are fooling me!" cried the fictitious Jack, enraged. "You are creating time for the arrival of assistance."

"If I be, I'm dom'd!" said Tykespeech, "no, no; we lads o' the North like a chap o' spirit, and as soon as I telled 'em how you promised to beat Dick Turpin, and ride from London to Newcassel, they all tuk a liking to thee. We agreed to wait a month;—if thee failed, we could na' help it, but if thee com'd, as thee hast, we agreed to gie thee a jolly good welcome, and make thee empty a bottle on t' road. So cum along, lad; they're at an inn hard by, and will be as glad to see thee as if thee wert their ain brather."

"You must be mad, or take me to be so," cried Jared, who, however, could not help laughing at the whimsicality of the proposal. "I suppose the first of your friends to whom I should be introduced, would be the parish beadle!"

"Hum," said Tykespeech, scratching his shaggy head. "It be natteral enuf that thee should think so, but I did hope that Sixteen-string Jack wur a chap o' too much pluck himself to suspect such a cowardly act in another. But see here, mun; I'll get off my beast and walk a foot. Thee shan't be asked to alight unless thee first likest thy company, and if thou seest a symptom o' foul play, thee canst ride off afore hand o' man can be raised against thee."

Steele mused on the offer; at length, a thought crossed him, and he said —"I see how it is: this is a manœuvre to avoid losing your money."

"How can that be, mun?" said the other in evident surprise, and taking out a purse containing a handsome sum in gold. "Does the lad think I'd let him ride three hundred miles at a stretch, without encouragement! Nay, nay; not so shabby as that, either," so saying, he thrust the purse into Jared's hand, and instantly alighted.

The gipsy could hardly credit the evidence of his senses, and he tossed, jingled, and weighed the purse in his hand, to satisfy himself that it really was what it appeared. The grazier, fancying that he was discontented with the amount, exclaimed—" Thee'll get more at York. Brother is on the look out for thee there the same as I was here ; but thee won't get a brass farden out of him unless thee showest him a certificate from me that I ha' been robbed in the same night, and that thee hast committed a robbery in Lunnon aforehand."

"I have not only committed a robbery in London, but at the chateau of the Marquis de Vauxrein," was Jared's reply.

No. 32.

"Better and better!" cried Tykespeech. "Give us thy fist again, mun. And so thee robbed the old markiss's? Well, that were dom'd clever. Ha ha, ha!"

In this sort of conversation, the pair proceeded nearly two hundred yards along the road towards Yorkshire; at the termination of which they came to an ale house. Jared was not altogether devoid of uneasiness, as he saw his conductor knock at the door, and he looked around to see if all was clear for escape. There was no visible obstacle, and he now directed his attention towards the door. This was opened by a runt square-built fellow, with as much hair on his face as on the top of his head. Tykespeech addressed something to him in a whisper. The man appeared thunderstruck, and gazed upon the gipsy as if he saw a spectre; then suddenly retreating, slammed to the door with a violence that made every beam of the house vibrate. A confused sound of human voices now emanated from within, and Steele distinctly heard the words "Sixteen-string Jack," repeated by twenty different tongues. Before he had time to draw any conclusion from this, the door was again opened, and out burst a whole crowd of men, of all grades and ages, who immediately surrounded the gipsey and made captive of his horse in a moment, a loud hurrah testifying their delight as they did so.

He now thought it high time to use his weapons; but a glance at the looks of admiration which were cast upon him from every eye, at once removed his fears, and returning his pistol to its holster, he raised his plumed hat and courteously bowed an acknowledgment of the friendly greeting he had received. A second cheer announced the satisfaction this occasioned, and an honest Huntingdonshire farmer rushed forward with the utmost enthusiasm, and exclaimed:—

"I shall boast of this hour when I am an old man. Pray come in, my hearty. There's no one here who would raise a finger to do you harm and we will not even ask you to unmask."

"I would not hesitate a moment," said Steele, "but unless I reach York immediately, I shall forfeit my pledge."

"And dost thou really affirm that thou hast ridden from Richmond in Surrey, within the last eight hours?" said the farmer.

"Here is my voucher," replied Steele, displaying the certificate that had already been prepared. "And what is more, I will not dismount till I have gone two hundred miles further."

"The beast will never stand it," exclaimed Tykespeech, viewing the exhausted condition of Jared's mare with real concern.

"Old Sue never failed me yet,!" returned Jared gaily, "and I'm determined not to lose faith in her. Come, gentlemen, as you would scorn to detain me against my will, do not do so against my interest—time wears—and—"

"Brother waits for thee, I know that," exclaimed Tykespeech. "Let me sign the certificate, and while I do, drink to the health of all of us."

"Right willingly," said Jared, and he handed the paper to his eccentric friend. A bowl of hot punch was now brought out, and speedily drank to the toast proposed. Meanwhile the pretended Old Sue was honoured with the caresses and compliments of all who could get near her! but not possessing the docility of her prototype, she unceremoniously shied and bestowed sundry kicks upon those around her. This was construed into the evidence of a spirit undiminished by her long run, and new encomiums were being poured upon her in consequence, when Tykespeech approached, and desired them to listen while he read the certificate he had signed beneath that borne by Steele. He then read aloud—" I, the undersigned, do hereby certify that I was stopped on the King's highway by Sixteen-string Jack, who, having put me in great bodily fear—" here he interrupted himself with a loud laugh in which his friends, and even Jared, joined, and then concluded by reading how he had been " robbed and plundered by force and arms, of a certain sum," &c., &c.

" There, friend Jack," said he, when he had concluded " show this at York in eight hours, and they'll mortalize thee."

Steele thrust the paper in his bosom, and throwing down ten guineas, from the purse of which Tykespeech had so willingly allowed himself to be robbed, and having taken a farewell draught, he rode off on the road to York, followed by hurrahs that made the welkin ring again. No sooner, however, was he enabled to avail himself of a turn in the road, than he selected the first thicket he came near to enter. Being satisfied that he was concealed from all eyes, he divested himself of his disguise, and thrusting it into a wallet which he had provided, buried it beneath the root of a tree. He then adjusted his own attire, and by rubbing down his mare with some grass and leaves, he deprived some portions of her body of certain patches of colour with which he had plastered several white spots on her skin, to render it marked as Sue was,

Horse and rider being thus transformed, Jared, turning towards London, took a sweep that compassed the rear of the inn, and brought him once more into the highroad. He then again turned northward, and, in a few minutes stopped at the very inn he had just quitted, and so completely was he altered that not a soul knew him.

He found the entire conversation engrossed by the recent adventure, and bets were being laid on all sides as to the result. It was a great puzzler to the knowing in horseflesh. Their wishes and love of the marvellous, inclined them to encourage the notion that the famous highwayman would accomplish his feat, and yet their practical knowledge convinced them, that no powers of endurance could carry a horse through a single ride of nearly three hundred miles; and the more the subject was canvassed, the greater was the interest it excited.

Jared was eagerly questioned which road he had come, and whether he had witnessed anything remarkable on the way.

"Not very," said he. " I started from Eaton-Socon about three hours since, and when I had got about a mile this side of Weston, I was passed by a chap with a black face, and a bunch of strings at each knee, and who gallopped more like the devil in a high wind than any human being."

When they acquainted him, in return for his information, that the person encountered was the robber whose name filled every mouth, the gipsy of course joined in the general expression of astonishment, and then proposed a bumper to the achievement of the feat. This was drank with a heartiness that proved the popularity of Jack, and many a bowl was drained to the same toast, until the morning had far advanced.

The gipsy, finding himself so completely unsuspected, thought that he could not do better than take up his quarters at the inn, which bore the sensible sign of the "Cat and Candlestick," until he received further orders from his captain.

Pretending, therefore, to have an appointment with some one from Berwick-upon-Tweed, he engaged a bed for the period of his expected stay, and ensconced himself in the chimney corner, well pleased with what he had done, and in anticipation of what was to follow.

CHAPTER XXVI.

SHEPPARD'S RIDE.

HARRY SHEPPARD was equally successful in accomplishing his part. Disguised as a trinket-maker, he had taken lodging in York, and regularly ridden out by break of day, as if to dispose of his wares—and he even took the precaution of calling at the shops of many country dealers with some specimens of his art, in order that no suspicion might afterwards arise. His evenings were spent at the different taverns in the city, so that he might gather from the prevailing gossip everything affecting the cause in which he was engaged. This was a fortunate stroke of policy, for he thereby became acquainted with the elder Tykespeech, and soon ferretted out the feelings that existed in favour of Jack, and the determination that had been made to aid his exploit as much as possible. To carry the joke to the utmost extent, he would sometimes ride out with the Yorkshireman, and by this means acquired a knowledge of the exact locality traversed by Tykespeech, which generally terminated near an enclosure on which the Dring-houses are now standing, about two miles from York, and where an ale-house then stood, to turn the thirsty traveller from the high road.

In the meantime he wrote to Clayton, to put him on his guard, and Harry judged that the same feeling would prevail in favour of Jack along the entire line of road. The intimation was a timely one, as will be seen anon.

As the night of action approached, Harry discontinued his usual trip with his new friend—giving as a reason, the probability of Jack's being deterred from attacking Tykespeech at all, were another in his company.

"Ecod, mon," said the Yorkshireman, "that wouldn't do at any price. I wouldn't miss him for a ten-pound note—so thee see'st, lad, I had better ride alone, and then if he cums past, he may be tempted to bide a bit, and have a chat wi' me along the road. I know that the Lord Mayor be hatching mischief against the poor lad, and I'd rather lose a year's income than a chap wi' so much pluck in him should come to any harm."

Harry of course acquiesed, as he had himself originated the suggestion, and the twain separated, well pleased with each other.

But a scene awaited Harry, which he had not anticipated—a scene of powerful excitement, and one which might have tried the intrepidity of Jack himself. Mr. Richard Tykespeech, or as he was commonly denominated Dick Tyke, entrusted his intentions to so many persons, that as the day drew near, the city each day seemed to empty itself of half its contents, while the roadside was thronged with whole multitudes of eager expectants, all desirous of catching a glimpse of the redoubtable Jack. But the affair got farther wind than was intended; and amongst the most interested of the spectators was a large body of the constabulary force in disguise, the members of which received from the Lord Mayor orders to lay hands upon the first suspicious looking personage who might appear. At length, the appointed hour arrived. As the announcement published concerning the ride, had made no intimation of an intention, on the highwayman's part, to commit any robberies as he rode, the preparations made by Dick Tyke to be voluntarily robbed, might have confounded Harry, and rendered him fearful of perplexing the operations of the whole scheme, had he not learned that Martin Tykespeech intended, as well as his brother, to insist upon having the honour of being robbed by Sixteen-string Jack. From this circumstance, Harry inferred that the certificate which Jared procured would be couched in some whimsical terms. In preparing the counter pair, therefore, our shrewd knave endeavoured to anticipate, as nearly as possible, the language he expected to be employed, and happily hit upon a sufficient degree of similarity to give it an air of genuineness.

The hour being at hand, and all ready, Harry rode quietly out of York with his pack behind him—not, as usual, filled with trinkets for sale, but stuffed with his disguise. As he pursued his road at an easy amble, he could not but reflect on the danger he was about to incur, for though he did not dream of its extent, he felt that it must prove great. To have executed their manœuvre, and then have boasted of it afterwards, would have been a certain mode of securing safety; but having so publicly announced what was to take place, the contrary had been rendered as certain, and Harry felt that the only loophole for safety existed in the ignorance of the people, of the hour and day to be selected for the enterprize.

"However," said he to himself, "Come what, come may, I'll not disgrace Jack while representing him."

He was by this time pretty close upon Tadcaster, and he sought a sheltered spot, where he might disguise himself unobserved. To the right he saw a dressing room, of nature's own building; furnished, too, with a mirror fit for use. It was a small dell, of about twenty feet in depth, overhung with willows, so thickly planted that their branches interlaced, and formed an almost impenetrable screen from the eye of the observer. A glassy stream, that ran to the edge of one of the surrounding hills, took an uninterrupted leap to a cavity below, and presented a surface so smooth and unbroken, that no cheval glass could have been better suited for the purposes of the toiletto.

Down the slopes of this charming place there grew a quantity of nuts and

wild fruits, so that Harry, as he descended, could not help exclaiming—
"Board, washing, and lodging, gratuitously."

He was soon equipped. He then stuck the certificate conspicuously in front of his cap, and having peeped forth to ascertain that no one was nigh, he gallopped fearlessly into the road, pistol in hand. In about half a mile in advance of him he descried two horsemen proceeding at an easy trot towards York. He saw that they were not to be apprehended, being plain country gentlemen in their appearance, so he resolved to secure their testimony that he had passed along the road; and to direct their attention, he raised his pistol and fired. They looked round immediately, and he galloped furiously up. "Make way, make way!" he cried.—"Sixteen-stringed Jack is on his way through York to Newcastle!" So saying, he dashed between his astonished hearers, and was almost out of sight before they could recover themselves. When, however, they did regain the senses which had been thus steeped in astonishment, they put spurs to their steeds, and galloped off in pursuit.

Harry was now "in for it:" he had nothing now to depend upon but luck, courage, dexterity, and a brilliant impression upon the people. His animal, fresh and in high spirits, flew along the ground like a cricket ball, and though the horsemen behind were enabled to keep him in view, they had no chance of gaining upon him. In a very short time he was within the vicinity of York, and his heart beat high as he saw Mr. Dick Tyke riding along in pursuance of his daily quest for adventures. The clattering of hoofs aroused the Yorkshireman immediately, and he waked up with as much eagerness as if he had expected to meet an old and long absent friend.

"Heigh, man—heigh!" he shouted, the instant he beheld Charley. "Bide a bit. Hollo! Sixteen-stringed Jack! stop!"

"Stop you!" shouted Sheppard, presenting an empty pistol, for he knew that he had nothing to fear. "Stand and deliver, or you are a dead man."

"Doan't ye, Jack, doan't! thee'll brusten I wi' laughter. Ecod, I shall get a foine neame i' the history books when thee art hanged, and they print all about thy famous ride, and how thee robbed I as thee went."

"Silence, miscreant!" roared Sheppard, as much to smother his laughter as anything else. "Deliver immediately!"

"Dinna be in such a dom'd hurry, Jack—I'm all ready for thee, lad. Hast thee cried 'deliver' to ony one else on the road?"

"Aye, or I should not have been able to have proved my ride. See here,' added Harry, pointing to the paper in his hat—"Within the last eighteen hours I have rifled one man in London, one man at Richmond in Surrey, and another at Stilton in Huntingdon."

"And here thee art where Turpin finished his journey," cried Tyke, hauling out a purse, and presenting it.

"Whilst I have a hundred miles further to go," returned Harry, giving Dick the certificate to sign.

"Fal lal de lal!" sung Dick, as soon as he recognised the pretended signature of Martin. "This be brother's writing sure enuf. Ha, ha, ha! We shall cut a fine figure in company wi' a Markiss. But gies thy pen. There,

R. O. B., with a little t at the top. Capital T. and a Y. K. E. S. P. E. E. C. H; Robert Tykespeech. The signature be known to half Northumberland; and if thee send it to the Mayor of Newcassel, he'll make an affidavit of the fact. Which road dost thee take there?"

"Through Pickering to Whitby; thence to Durham, and so on to Gateshead," replied Sheppard.

"It's an open road, and may expose thee to danger; but I'll not detain thee. Long life to thee and thy canny mare; and if thee should'st be hanged in these parts, Jack, I'll come and shake hands with thee on the scaffold, though I miss a day's market through it. But I say, lad, dinna thee go spreading abroad that I aided and abetted a thief on his journey, instead of apprehending him, as is the duty of a liege subject."

"I leave you to betray your own secret," said Sheppard; and so saying, he made the air crack with his whipcord, and started off. He was already congratulating himself upon having a clear field for escape, when turning an angle of the road, he reined up with positive terror, at seeing the wayside lined with thousands of people.

A shout—loud, hearty, and prolonged—rent the very skies the instant he was seen, for the good people of York had so completely made up their minds to witness the feat of horsemanship which had been promised them, that they had assembled in multitudes, day by day, to give the modern Turpin a welcome as he passed; and were naturally impressed with the conviction that a masked horseman, wearing so remarkable a dress as that assumed by Harry, must be the object they had come to greet. Their shouts reassured the highwayman, and with graceful action he waved his plumed hat to the crowd, and urging his courser into a gentle amble, he proceeded through the midst, bowing on each side, as if he had been a prince receiving the homage of his subjects.

"Huzza! huzza!" was the cry that again broke the still heavens, and the popular feeling became roused to positive enthusiasm. "Look at 'un! look at 'un! look at tid mare," cried several. "She looks as fresh as if she had just left the stable." This called forth new encomiums from other lips, and Harry's own appearance, as well as that of his steed, came in for its share of praise. He, however, rode on warily and watchfully; he felt that there was danger, and he knew that nothing but the most consummate nerve and address could carry him through. Without betraying, therefore, the slightest mark of fear, he now coolly reloaded his pistol—looked well to the priming, and placed it in the holster, where another weapon of the same description was awaiting, like a good soldier, to be ordered into action.

This evidence of determined daring produced an effect that saved him. The constables, who were mostly raw young men of little practice, were thunderstruck at beholding it. Amazement, admiration, and some portion of fear, tended to paralyze them, as Harry passed within very arm's length of them, and they allowed him to gain an advance of some yards, before they sufficiently recovered from their astonishment to make attempts at apprehending him. Another feeling operated also in his favour: in their hearts they hoped that he WOULD accomplish his purpose, and felt as if it would be a crime to prevent the fulfilment of an exploit which might prove the boast of Yorkshire for the next hundred years to come; for, as OLD SUB, like BLACK BESS, had been foaled in that county, they imagined that their supremacy in horseflesh would be established by the result. It was thus that the entire progress of this far-famed hoax became marked with incidents, which attached to it a deserved celebrity, that would scarcely have been exceeded by the actual execution of an uninterrupted ride from London to Newcastle.

Sheppard now quickened his pace; but things were not destined to go on so smooth and uninterruptedly as they had done. The favourable sentiments of the constables were as transient as the passage of the individual who had excited them, and scarcely had he got a head of these men before they were recalled to a sense of duty, and shouted to him to surrender. The summons, of course, produced an opposite effect to that intended; the robber spurred his mare to the top of her speed, and flew off like some projectile armed with superior powers of swiftness; but his pursuers were well mounted also, and he soon found that, when the strength of his steed was exhausted, he should stand every chance of being taken.

"But my beast shall drop dead before that happens," he exclaimed, gnashing his teeth as the conviction struck him; then once more applying cord and steel, he took a detour, and urged his flying pace across a track of country to the right of the city, and which he thought would be less dangerous than pursuing a route, where every man he passed might prove a foe. The officers followed, and in a short time the pursuers and the pursued had left the hallooing mob some miles behind them. Harry cast an eagle's glance around. There was not a single rider before him, to impede his progress, and those behind were raw countrymen, whom he had no doubt of intimidating. He thought, therefore, there was no danger in a momentary pause, and that it might prove good policy to endeavour to operate upon the fears of the constables before his mare was thoroughly blown, than leave himself at their mercy afterwards.

Acting upon this decision, he reined up, and turning round in his saddle, he shouted "a parley."

The men instinctively reined up also, for the force of example was stronger than their presence of mind, which should at that moment have urged them to dash on, and effect his capture at once. No sooner did he see them at a stand, than he drew forth both pistols.

"Now, my merry men," said he, "in the first place, let me know what you mean by running after me in this manner?"

"Whoy, that be clear enuf, lad," said the chief of the constables. "We wants to make thee our prisoner."

"And for what? Cannot a man ride along the highway without being deprived of his liberty?"

"Ees, ees, when he be riding in an honest way," returned the constable.

"And am I pursuing an unlawful ride? What have I done, sirrahs? What crime committed?"

"Eh!—thees't done summat, I know, but I canna exactly tell what."

"Here's a pretty fellow," cried Harry "and so you would lay a man by the heels without cause! Perhaps there is something in my name that has offended the laws. Who were you desired to apprehend?"

"Eh!—Dom'd if I know. They call thee Jack with the Sixteen-strings."

"But that won't do for an indictment. Have the goodness to ride singly up, Mr. Constable, and let me see how the warrant is worded, by which you are empowered to take me."

"Eh! I have no warrant: his lordship forgot that: he only bid us to take up the first suspicious character we met wi."

"Very well, then, gentlemen," returned Sheppard; "I need'nt now tell you that you are in the wrong box, and that unless you have a properly signed warrant, Sixteen-stringed Jack has a right to pursue his little trip to the colleries without molestation."

No. 33.

"The constables looked at each other with a stupid expression of indicision. Each

> "Scratched his ear;—the infallible resource
> To which embarrassed people have recourse."

"Robert," said the head constable, to the man that was nearest him.

"Tummas!" exclaimed the other. "I thinks as how 'tid honest chap be roight. We must'nt do anything contrary to law."

Tummas again scratched his head; and then brightening up, exclaimed, "But it rests wi' his right worshipful lordship to say what be law, and what be not. So don't let us bide any longer. Grip him, lads."

"Hold!" shouted Harry, "I'm on the king's highway, and will resist all efforts to arrest me without a cause. Approach, and I fire."

At this moment the animal bestrode by Harry made a sudden curvet, as if the bridle had been roughly seized, and he felt his coat grasped by a band equally muscular, while a hoarse voice exultingly exclaimed—

"Forward, men, to your duty—Sixteen-stringed Jack is captured!"

Harry turned round without loss of time, and to his indignation beheld in the speaker no other person than Luke Jones, who, on meeting the eyes that glanced fiercely at him through the mask, exclaimed—

"You are pinned at last; and now, friend Jack, we shall soon be quits."

"Traitor!" shouted Sheppard, and raising his pistol, lodged its contents in the miscreant's shoulder. With a cry of pain, the villain dropped immediately; and the constables, though aghast at the scene, rode promptly up.

"I warn ye back," cried the representative of our hero. "Back or I will not answer for your lives!"

"They still, however, approached, for the sight of blood only served to exasperate them, and Harry was reluctantly compelled to level his remaining weapon at the foremost man. He fired, but the ball only inflicted a slight wound. It, however, sufficed to throw the enemy into confusion; and the gallant young man once more resumed his terrible flight.

The natural feelings of humanity prompted the constables to surround their wounded brother, for they were too unaccustomed to scenes such as this, not to be horror-stricken at his disaster; but he motioned them back.

"Never mind I," he exclaimed: "I'm not much hurt, and have strength enuf to 'tid poor chap as is.—Do thee take the command, Robie, and revenge what has been done to us. Not another moment—Away!"

Stimulated by these words, they started anew, and many who witnessed the race that followed were reminded of the glories of Newmarket and Doncaster; while the scene before them possessed a superior interest through the nature of the prize that was sought to be won. Harry kept up manfully, and now pushed for the high-road. Having gained this, he still kept a northerly course, for he did not once entertain a thought of abandoning his design. But there are limits to the endurance of beast, as well as men: his mare became now embossed with foam; her sides trickled with blood; her foot was tremulous when it touched the ground; her withers shrunk with every motion, and her eye became fiery, and her tongue parched.

"This will never do," thought Harry. "One effort, and I must take shelter, though it be like King Charles, in the branches of an oak."

While he was yet speaking, he descried an inn. His pursuers were about three miles behind him; and had his beast been as well calculated for speed as she was for distance, he would have endeavoured to have outridden them, but he felt that a pause was necessary, and was debating within himself whether to take it where he stood, or risk it at the inn, when he perceived a posse of mounted men before him, who were conveying a number of criminals to York Castle. This decided him; he knew that they would not suffer a man, whose dress announced the highway-robber, to pass unquesoned, and he was not yet sufficiently near for them to distinguish anything remarkable. The inn, also, was close by, and thus everything favoured the plan of seeking concealment, which he now followed, without further loss of time.

He turned so suddenly into the stable, that those in the distance did not at first notice his disappearance; and as a postboy happened to be going the same road, some yards beyond its first curviture, they kept their eyes fixed upon him, thinking that it was Jack, who was momentarily lost to sight through the aforesaid curve. In this delusion they passed the inn, and were delighted to find that they gained considerably upon the horseman in advance. A mad career along a dusty road does not greatly clear the eyesight, and it is not to be wondered at that their mistake continued for some time, and such was the speed at which they now rushed to consummate their victory, that the javelin men and their prisoners, whom Sheppard had noticed, were obliged to make way for them, to avoid being ridden down.

"Now, my lads," cried Robert, much elated; "one more push, and we've done for him."

The one more push was made, and great, indeed, was the disappointment which all felt when, on making a simultaneous sally to surround their victim, they discovered that the man whom they had been following was an honest, inoffensive character, whom they all knew.

"Hallo! hallo!" cried he, on being surrounded, and called upon to surrender. "Ha' ye been dining off March hares, ye fools? Who the devil do you take me for?"

This was the first intimation they had of their blunder, and their consternation may easily be imagined. Each jaw dropped, and each eye rolled. For an instant they fancied that Jack had by some inconceivable dexterity, disguised his person; but the features of little Joe Robson, the elderly postboy, were not to be mistaken; and Rob Copping, the constable, with awe as well as wonder, said—

"What has thee done wi' him, Joe? hast thee given him in tid custody of Old Nick?"

"Why, L—d deliver us, thee art drunk, mon," said the elderly postboy. "Oh, Robie, Robie! What'll thy mother say?"

"Never mind t'ould woman. What'll the Lord Mayor say? We wouldn't ha' let him slip for ever so much."

"Let who slip, Rob," said the elderly postboy. Copping, in reply, contrived to make Robson understand what had occurred, and his awe increased to terror, when the little man assured him most solemnly, that he had not been passed in that direction by a creature during the last half hour.

"Then take my word for it, Joe," said Robin, his very teeth chattering with affright, "that half his journey will be taken under ground, and that he can mak' earth swallow him up whenever he pleases."

"Be there no possibility of his having turned back?" inquired one of the constables, who was rather sceptical on matters of witchcraft.

"Eh, by gum!" exclaimed the little elderly postboy, slapping the polished surface of his leather un-breathables; "I ken all aboot it noo. I seed Jack Pritchard, and three or four other chaps belonging 'tid Castle just noo, and in passing they said they had got some prisoners in charge."

"Then Jack be among 'em," said Rob Copping. "Dang it, lads, let's claim him afore they reach York, or we shall lose the prize!"

Turning their horses' heads, they now retraced their steps, and after once more passing the inn which Harry had entered, they came in sight of their brother functionaries of the law; but wishing to spare their horses, which had now been on full gallop for some hours, they bawled lustily for the officers to stop. A new and ridiculous blunder, however, now arose, for it having been intimated that it was probable that an attempt at rescue would be made, the man with the prisoners fancied that it was now about to be realized. They had wondered at the uncommon speed with which the party of horsemen, whom they had not time to recognise, had passed them a short while previous; and thinking that the parties were now about to make up for having let them go by unmolested, they gallopped off, in order to avoid an attack. This increased the clamor and the speed of those behind, and the faster the first party of constables went, the faster they were followed by the second; so that in a short time a convenient distance became placed between Harry and his enemies.

Not until they had reached York gates did the two parties of officers discover their egregious blunder. Jack Pritchard, the man who was conducting the convoy of prisoners to the castle, no sooner found himself in the neighbourhood of succour, than he waxed valiant, and ordered his assistants to look to their carbines, and face the enemy. He was obeyed, but the prisoners grumbled terribly. They had been jolted along at this rapid rate till they were chafed and galled in all directions.

"I'll complain to'd governor," said one of the fellows, who had long been infesting the country as a poacher. "Dost think we wear cast-iron breeches, that thee jogs us against the saddles at such an infernal rate?"

Pritchard had no time for reply, for the pursuing party was now hard upon them. He looked to his priming, and had already raised his piece to his shoulder, with the intention of firing, when he heard his own name shouted by Rob Copping.

"Jack. Hoy! hoy!" cried the police-officer. "Only a single word."

"Dang it all!" said Pritchard to his brother constable; "we ha' been riding at this rate for nought. What be it, lad?" he added, as the other came up.

"I only put it to thee in common fairness. It was we runned game down, and if thee picked him up without trouble, thee hast no claim to him."

"No claim to a man whose mittamus were put into my awn hands? Go, and hang thysel', Rob."

"Mittamus? Sixteen-string Jack's mittamus?"

An explanation now followed, and great was the laughter of the by-standers, who had been attracted by the rencontre.

"Why thee born fool, thee!" exclaimed Pritchard, in a passion. "Why didn't thee shoot oot?"

"Shoot!" repeated Rob; "so I did till my lungs were sore; but the more I shooted, the more thee wouldn't hear."

"Then thee should'st have run faster," said Pritchard.

"Odd's daisy, mun," said the other; "the more faster I runned, the more thee wouldn't stop."

Finding that the progress of the argument only amused the spectators, the officers, very prudently, reserved their further discussion for a more private moment. A hasty parley sufficed to show how matters stood; the highwayman had contrived to slip all parties, and was now, as they imagined, on his road to Newcastle. With this intelligence they proceeded, with elongated faces, to the authorities, whose indignation, at being thus outdone, vented itself in thunders of threats towards the offender, whom they now vowed to hang, draw, and quarter, if they could catch him.

Meanwhile the adventurous Harry was undergoing as many hair-breadth escapes as Charles II. No sooner had he entered the stable than he leaped from his mare, and crouched beneath a heap of straw. So sudden had been his entrance, that no one belonging to the establishment had noticed him. The stable was entirely empty, and from all appearances was seldom used; Sheppard, therefore, lay without interruption. His quick ear caught the sound of the pursuing horsemen as they passed the inn, and he was already congratulating himself upon his escape, when the clatter of the returning hoofs struck consternation to his heart. He thought that they had, of course, learned the place of his concealment, and were coming to put an inglorious termination to his career. Fired with desperation, he sprung from his concealment, and drew forth his pistols, forgetting that they had already been discharged—his determination being to sell his life as dearly as possible.

To his utter astonishment, the cavalcade gallopped past, and he cautiously crept to an open chink in the building, which enabled him to observe what was passing without. He there beheld the constables following the body of horsemen he had seen advancing towards him, and for a moment was puzzled to guess what the meaning of the scene could possibly be. The loud shouts, however, of those in the rear, and the consequent quickening of the pace of the party in the advance, let him at once in the secret, and he burst into a hearty fit of laughter. Determined to profit by the mistake, while there was yet time, he divested himself, with the utmost celerity, of all the outward habiliments and trappings, which had given him the requisite appearance for playing his part in character, and he now once more stood the quiet trader, for which he had passed in York. He then deprived his mare of everything that gave her a suspicious look; and, having made the whole up into a bundle, he hid it in the most obscure part of the stable. This done, he loaded his pistols, and concealed them about his person; he now again peeped through the chink, and to his satisfaction found that not a being was in view. The house, in fact, was little better than a hedge ale-tap; and at the time Harry had sought the friendly shelter of its walls, there was literally not a single person in it. The landlord and his man, who acted in the triple capacity of waiter, ostler, and chambermaid, were engaged in a solemn game of skittles in the back-grounds. The landlady and her two daughters were out on a visit, and thus the entire establishment were as conveniently disposed of as if Harry himself had the whole arrangement of the matter. Our adventurer, however, was not himself aware of this favourable disposition of matters; it was, therefore, with no small degree of anxiety that he crept forth, leading his courser again into the open air, as he knew, that to be seen, would subject him to some awkward questioning. Emboldened by the reigning solitude, he mounted his mare, and then began to bawl most lustily for the ostler, as it was not his intention to proceed one way or the other, until the animal had been well rested. It was some minutes ere his summons was obeyed, and even then, both landlord and waiter seemed to growl at having their game interrupted.

Harry's gay and pleasant manners, however, speedily restored them to good humour, especially when he offered to groom his own horse, in order to give them an opportunity of finishing their game, and to join himself in the pastime when he had done. This was giving them a treat, and paying them for accepting it. It will not, therefore, be doubted, that they gave a most gracious acquiescence. Accordingly Sheppard re-entered the stable, and the host returned to his game with the ostler. Soon afterwards Harry joined them, and though he played with spirit, he still could not entirely quell his anxiety to hear news from York, for the complete silence, which had succeeded the excitement of the morning, seemed as if it augured secret mischief.

In the afternoon the landlady and her daughter returned, and then for the first time did the apathetic host learn the great event of the day. His grief at the tidings was mighty: he exclaimed that he should never sleep easy for the reflection that Sixteen-string Jack had ridden past his house without stopping to drink, and in order to console himself, he swallowed a full goblet of brandy and water, without drawing breath.

The afternoon customers brought new additions to the tidings, and Harry Sheppard had soon the satisfaction of learning that all was safe, and that his portion of the exploit had been performed with the fullest success. In the evening he returned to York, where he met Dick Tyke, who favoured him with an account of his adventure, and occupied nearly two hours in the relation. He then invited Harry to accompany him next day on a visit to his brother, at Stilton, that he might learn every particular connected with the affair.

Our highwayman accepted the invitation; and on putting up at the "Cat and Candlestick," encountered Steele. They, however, betrayed not the slightest symptoms of recognition; and thus, by an odd conjunction of events, the two conspirators were once more thrown into a position for communicating with each other. We shall now pursue the adventures of Mr. Kit Clayton.

CHAPTER XXVII.

CLAYTON'S RIDE.

AND now, Momus, approach; bring Euphrosyne, laughing, on thine arm, and let Bacchus and Silenus follow in thy train, that we may invoke the inspiration of your combined mirth, while detailing the pranks of Mr. Charles Clayton in putting a finishing stroke to the mock ride from London to the North. It seemed destined that the affair was to be marked with every variety that could occur: Jared, the gipsey, had to bring all his wit and dexterity into play; Harry encountered terrors which tasked all his courage and invention, while it was left to Clayton to wind up the adventure in as humourous a manner as suited his jocose temperament.

He had put up at the Old Elvet Inn, just above the arched gateway, at the top of Sadler-street, in the quiet and ancient city of Durham. Up to the period of receiving the letter written by Harry, at York, his heart, to use his own expression, bumped in his breast like a dumpling in a kettle of hot water. But when he received the intimation that he need not anticipate any serious attempt at capture, or even resistance, he resolved to prosecute the plan in a way that should put John Bull into a good humour, in addition to astonishing him. "I'll cram them with as many lies as was ever told by Gulliver himself," said he; "and if I don't make 'em think Sixteen-stringed Jack somebody, I'll give 'em leave to stick me in a barley field to fright away the crows."

With this determination he remained quiet, until the hour arrived for starting. He passed his days in the ordinary manner of a stranger, viewing the curiosities of the place, and watching the little boys "plodging" across the river. Of an evening he mixed with the guests, and he took every opportunity of introducing the reigning topic of conversation. In that dull, quiet city there were few who knew that such an adventure was contemplated; and those whom he informed of it ridiculed the notion of a man accomplishing such a feat within twenty-four hours. The affair, however, had got wind at the termination of the intended journey, and the "canny Newcassel" lads were on the alert, as he learnt from those travellers from that town, who happened to put up at the "Old Elvet." The characteristic remarks that passed between our merry friends and the northerns on these occasions would suffice to fill a jest book; but as we cannot afford to depart for so long a time from the main current of our romance as would be required to convey any impression of them to the reader, we must leave that task to some future Joe Miller, who may be anxious to furnish the world with a new edition of the best jokes.

It is as much a national characteristic of Englishmen to desire to witness the first and last of everything as it is for them to blindly take the part of the weak against the strong, without diving into the merits of the case; and Englishmen generally are as much operated upon by the latter prejudice as the former one. They felt a generous impulse towards the man who seemed hunted by all his fellow-creatures, and from first resolving to avoid the active measures they had made for apprehending our hero, they insensibly fell into the opposite determination of doing all they could to shelter him.

On the day previous to that on which Charlie was to start, he heard loud sounds of merriment below, and being a lover of fun in every shape, he descended into the kitchen, to learn the cause. He there found an old pur-blind man, seated upon a bundle of brooms, and presenting an appearance at once comical and interesting. He was bald, with the exception of a few wintry locks on each side of his head. His brow had a hundred wrinkles, which, when he laughed, were increased fourfold, and gave his forehead an appearance resembling the rind of a Dutch cheese chopped up. One eye was completely closed, and the other turned upon a swivel, so that he seemed to be perpetually cocking it and winking at every one in the room. He wore three red waistcoats, but they were all open, and displayed his bare chest in broad proportion. He had on also a pair of long blue trousers, and over them a pair of corduroy breeches, patched with all manner of colours. An eternal restlessness seemed to animate him, for he was continually slapping his knees, sides, and different parts of his person, as if determined not to let a moment elapse without ascertaining whether time had left his old trunk as sound as ever.

This was a remarkable character, who wandered about the Northern counties, and well known by the appellation of "DAFT WILLEY." He had been collier, soldier, sailor, and ballad singer; but having been whipped for vagrancy, had for some years past sheltered himself beneath the ostensible trade of a broom vendor.

"Bravo! Willey, bravo!" exclaimed several of the idlers, as Clayton entered; "gies anither sang, lad."

"Aw'll gie thee yen aw' meyde mysel'," returned the old man, and beating time with his hands upon his knees, he struck into the following words, to the tune of "Lunnen is the Devil."

DAFT WILLEY'S SONG.

Aw wish aw had a fiddle,
  Wish aw'd wishes three,
Life may be a riddle;
  'Twould na' poozle me.
    Buy besoms, buy;
    Buy them when they're new.
    Better new than au'd,
    The best that ever grew.

Aw wish aw had an axe,
  Aw wad chop a tree;
Aw wad build a ship,
  And send it out to sea.
    Buy besoms, buy, &c.

Aw wish aw had a wife,
  Aw care na' what she be;
So she be a woman,
  That'll do for me.
          Buy besoms, buy, &c.

Aw wish aw had some bairns—
  One, two, or three—
Aw'd set the deils to wark,
  Tiv earn the brass for me.
          Buy besoms, buy, &c.

Aw wish aw was a king,
  On a throne to be,
All my foes should swing,
  And that wad do for me.
          Buy besoms, buy,
            Buy them while they're new.
          Better new than au'd,
            The best that ever grew

"Brey-vo, old feller!" exclaimed Clayton, as soon as the more loudly-expressed applause had subsided.

"Smash marrow! what a cliver chep thee must be to feynd that oot; and having done so, what a daft fail thee must feynd thysel' to be capable o' sic a bloonder?" So saying, Old Willy, amidst roars of laughter, commenced slapping his sides and hams to the chorus of—

"Buy besoms, buy, &c."

"Nay," said Kit, "since the wisest man made the greatest fool of himself it is not so very unreasonable to expect wit from idiots."

"Sae bekase the fountain tumbles into a muddy channel, thee thinks to feynd clear water in the ditch."

"Why, yes, when filtered through such a head as thine, Willey," said Clayton, amused by the shrewdness of the old man. "But I cannot help thinking that you are not such a fool as you look."

"Do I look as if I would say nay to a crown-piece when offered? vor if I do, I'll luik wiser next minnit."

"A good hint, but crowns are not so plentiful, except cracked ones, like thine. But, for your wit, I dont mind buying a birch-broom of you."

"No, thee won't."

"And why not?"

"Keaso they're a' selled to the Mayor of Newcassel. He sent me to Durham Moor to make 'em, but I didn't make enuff to clear the town of such chaps as thysel', who either laugh at other folks nonsense, or else their ain—

Buy besoms, buy,
  Buy them while they're new;
Better new than au'd,
  The best that ever grew

Although Daft Willey had made this answer the vehicle of a sally at

Charlie's self-sufficient tone and manners, the information it contained was true enough. Daft Willey frequently became exceedingly troublesome to his best patrons, and, on such occasions, they were in the habit of dispatching him to some neighbouring town, to make a set of besoms for them. This always succeeded in keeping him away for some weeks; but yet he was as sure as clock-work, for when he did return, it was always found that he had executed his mission with the utmost fidelity.

Clayton, though entertained by his answers, felt that the laugh was against him, and, in hopes of turning the tables, exclaimed—

"Well, since your besoms are so very efficacious in clearing away disagreeable things, you had better sell me that large one in the centre of the bundle, that I may try its effects in clearing away you."

"Ho, smash!" cried Willey, "the chep wants tiv be the ownly full in the company. But I canna indoolge thee, bairn. Why, who dost thou think that besom be for?"

"Who?" asked Clayton.

"The mayor himself, to use when thou gangst to dine with him."

There was a general shout at this witticism, and Charlie, with some heat, endeavoured to wriggle out of the scrape he had got himself into, by saying that some were termed fools from always speaking the truth, but that Willey proved his folly by the opposite course. The old broom-seller retorted that it was Clayton who did that, and, to prove his own veracity, invited our disguised highwayman to meet him at the mayor's house, by eleven, the next evening. "I always gang at night," continued the old man, "as I come in for the day's scraps of the kitchen."

"Do you deliver your work into the hands of your employer yourself?" asked Kit, struck with a sudden thought.

Willey answered in the affirmative, for he was cunning enough to have established it as a rule never to do business with an intermediate party. He knew the effect and value of his jokes, and was, of course, aware that such commodities never benefitted the author when delivered at second hand.

The moment Clayton ascertained that such was really the case, he contrived to slip away, and scribbled the following words on a scrap of paper:—

'Sixteen-string Jack presents his compliments to the Mayor of Newcastle, and having arrived in that ancient borough on the back of another mayor (mare), named "Old Sue," within twenty-four hours from Richmond, he begs his mayorship to certify that fact to the Lord Mayor of London with all convenient speed. Having thus proved the fruitlessness of pursuit, Sixteen-string Jack hopes that no one will, in future, be fool enough to attempt to take him when on horseback."

Having drawn a piece of twine through this with a needle, Charlie returnes and, pretending that he had been to his room to get half-a-crown, he seated himself by Daft Willey, on the brooms, and offered him the amount to sing another of his songs. Willey, of course, complied, and, while he did so, Kit contrived to insinuate his letter in the midst of the heath which formed the mayor's brom, trusting to luck and circumstance for bringing it to hand.

Shortly after this the old man departed, and on the following evening Kit mounted his mare to return, as he said, to London; but, after going southward about a couple of miles, he turned into a bye-road that conducted him a little beyond Paulsworth, on the way to Chester-le-street. He here waited till nightfall, and then, making the necessary alteration in his appearance, and, taking his mask in hand, ready to hold before his face at the proper opportunity, he dashed forward, as if urged by something of the utmost importance. The country people viewed the fleeting horseman with astonishment, and were convinced that he was some courier from the metropolis; but he contrived by certain exclamations, as he went along, to excite other suspicions, and prepare them for feeling the necessary conviction that they had seen the much-talked-of highwayman, on his long promised career. In this manner he proceeded, until he came in view of the Windmill Hills, which stretch, in undulating beauty, in the vicinity of Gateshead.

In a snug little domus in the vicinity mentioned, a Mr. Teddy Coleman had taken up his residence to lay wait for the appearance of Jack, until the expiration of the period within which he had pledged himself to take his ride. This worthy Northumbrian had chosen his station—at a point which commanded a sufficient view of distance to enable him to mount, before any suspicious character could reach the door, and he took the precaution to have a steed ready-saddled, that he might start at a moment's notice. In addition to this he fee'd a lad to play the scout for him, and give notice of all approaching equestrians.

The advance of the mock Jack, was, in consequence of these arrangements, duly heralded to the expectant, as soon almost as Kit appeared in sight, and Coleman immediately clapped a night-telescope to his eye.

"By the hookey! exclaimed he, "gin that bean't Jock it's yean iv his bruthers," and dashing down the night-glass, he turned out in an instant, and was riding towards Kit before many could have got rein in hand.

It was not very light, as a mist hung over the room; yet Kit recognised an adversary at once, and, with a loud shout, pushed forward at increased speed. Mr. Coleman threw himself directly in his way, and exclaimed—"Stand!"

"Ditto!" cried Clayton, presenting a pistol.

"Double ditto!" snouted Coleman, pulling out a flask of brandy, and imitating the action of Kit. The effect was so ludicrous that each burst into a loud fit of laughter, and it was some moments before either could speak.

"You are the rummiest cove I ever encountered," at length exclaimed Clayton. "Do you know who you are speaking to?"

"No, dost thou?" said Coleman.

"Above a bit," returned the other; "but that's no reason I should tell you."

"Smash, but thou must!—What's thou called?"

"By some a gentleman, and by others otherwise."

"But aw mean *how* is't thou called?"

"Sometimes loudly, and sometimes in an undertone."

"Odd smash!" shouted Coleman. "Canna thee tell what thy neame be?"

"Of course I can, but I won't. Go and ask my godfathers and godmothers."

"Aw'd rather ask their godson. Is't thou ca'd Sixteen-string Jack!"

"I wasn't christened so."

"By gum I believe thee, unless au'd Nick stood sponsor."

"Why, if I'm ca'd so at all, it is a Nick-name," retorted Clayton. "But what if I'm Sixteen-string Jack?"

"Wey then, aw wad like nought better than to have yen or twee hours crack with thou, ower a jug o' ale, afore thou gang'st across the water, yonder."

"A kind invitation," said Kit, "certainly, but you must stretch your liberality further this reckoning. I'm the great King Mustemthrustem, and have come to levy taxes upon all who travel by the highway."

"Oh, I'm agreeable to that," exclaimed Coleman. "Here's a five-pund note, and if that winna satisfy thou, here's another."

"I'll answer your last note another time," said Kit, pocketing the te pounds. "And now, what's your name, and where do you live?"

"Ted Coleman, in Pudding Chare," answered the other, laconically.

"Pudding Chair," reiterated the other. "You must have soft seats in the north. I suppose then you use dumpling stools?"

The shout with which this was responded to, made Clayton fear that it would alarm the neighbourhood.

"Why, mon!" exclaimed Coleman, "Pudding Chare's the name of a street, where thou shalt be as welcome as the flowers of May, if thou'lt take pot luck wi' me.

"Oddsheart! I've a good mind to take thee at thy word," said Clayton; "but I must first finish my ride to Newcastle, and before I am duly qualified to do so, you must give me a certificate of the robbery I have just committed."

"Then thee must step inside, for I canna see without a light," answered Coleman. And as Clayton felt no little thirst at the moment, and had moreover been apprized of how little he had to fear, he boldly consented, and they entered the house together which Coleman had but a few moments before quitted.

On reaching the long room, Kit thought that he had reached the interior of Mount Vesuvius, and was surrounded by the Cyclops. A sturdy race of swarthy colliers, grimed in coal-dust, were seated around an ample table covered with every liquor, from humble malt to imperial Jacky, and, from the loudness of their mirth, and the merriment seated upon their features, it would never have been supposed that half their hours were passed in the darkness and gloom of a coal-mine.

All eyes fell upon Clayton, and one fellow, after gazing like a stuck pig at the black mask Clayton wore, exclaimed to Coleman:

"I say, skipper—be that chap one of the black beggars that fight?"

A loud laugh rewarded the blunder of Dick. He had seen a prize fight some days previously, in which one of the combatants had been a negro; and to his uninitiated eyes, the silken cover to the visage of Kit, looked every bit as natural as thin sable skin, which had struck him with so much surprise;

for till the moment of clapping eyes upon the pugilist, the only black faces he had ever witnessed were the grim countenances of his fellow pitmen.

Coleman was infinitely amused at the mistake, but he answered, "No, no, honest Dick. This be a canny lad o' the Robin-Hood breed. The poor chep has ridden nearly three hundred miles in a day and a night, and he wants to gang on tiv Newcassel; but the bodies up at the Mansion House winna let him be at peace, and he's afeared to show his nose there, and is maist likely to lose a great wager in consequence."

"Smash!" cried Roaring Dick, "but we'll carry him there, eh, lads, and may the devil ha' my buttons gin we don't crack the jaws of ony that lays fingers upon him. How art thee called, my lad?"

"It's so long since I was christened that I forget," said Kit; "so you may call me Mister Anybody, or Mister Nobody, if you like."

"Ho, ho!" shouted Dick. "But thee cans't tell us where thee wast born?"

"Oh, yes; in Old England."

"Marrow! so was mysen; but in what part?"

"In what part? Oh, just down yonder, where the old woman kept a one-eyed blackbird, and gave it snuff to make it sing."

"And where was that?"

"Why, just on the spot where a one-eyed blackbird was kept by the old woman."

"Gie o'er, Dick, gie o'er," cried Coleman, laughing. "The gentleman has na' stoodied geography enuff to answer thy questions."

"Then he'd better gang to school again. What for should I put mysel' oot o' my way to serve him, if I don't know he deserves it?"

"Never fear!" exclaimed Kit. "I'm a greater man than you imagine. I'm grandson to Hoki-poki, the king of all the seven Russias. I have travelled three times round the world, and gone so near the edge of it, that if I had taken one step more, I should have trod upon nothing."

"Didst ever gang doon a coal pit?"

"Aye, and came out at a copper mine in America. I've travelled into unknown countries, where the inhabitants live in the sea, and the fishes upon land. I've gone from Nova Scotia to the Cannibal Islands, on the back of a comet, and once went so high in a balloon that I darkened the sun, and made everybody think there was an eclipse."

"Then thee wast in a fair way of going to hell!" exclaimed one of the colliers, with a shout. This was highly relished by the rest, for such was the ignorance of these men, who passed the chief part of their lives in the bowels of the earth, that is was a prevalent opinion amongst them, that the fiery orb of day was neither more nor less than the infernal regions. Kit knew nothing of this; but seeing that a joke of some sort or other had been uttered, though he did not comprehend it, he nodded assent, and joined in the laugh.

"And what fashioned pleace did it seem?" asked Roaring Dick.

"Just like the furnace of a glasshouse," returned Kit; "but you'll see yourself some day or other, for you are sure to go there."

This raised another laugh; but Coleman saw that Dick was not over pleased; so to turn the conversation, he asked Clayton "if he had ever seen the man in the moon during his travels?"

"To be sure I have," said Charlie, "and supped with him off cream cheese. We had a maggot race afterwards, for five pounds aside, and spent the rest of the night in singing such jolly songs. There was one I remember, that made me nearly split my sides with laughter. It began thus—

"Let us be off, and tool to Greenwich,
And have a good dinner of gammon and spinach."

"But how came he to know that there was such a place as Greenwich?" cried Coleman, who, though he knew that Charlie was running his lengths, determined to encourage him, perceiving that the wonderful crammers of his guest were just to the taste of the auditors."

"Why," replied Kit, "doesn't the moon set every night behind Greenwich Hospital?"

"Aye, aye, to be sure," returned Coleman, "and na doot he knew a few of the inhabitants."

"Bless you, he used to assist the chief astrologer every night to make out the almanacks," cried Clayton.

At this moment an incongruous sound was heard without, as though Noah's ark had broken loose, and in another minute the apartment received the acquisition of a new guest, in the person of a travelling showman, who intended on the morrow to give an exhibition of wild beasts in the field, which at that period skirted the "Forth." The circumstance itself had nothing remarkable in it; but its effects, owing to the almost barbarous ignorance of the colliers, were ludicrous in the extreme. The man carried in his arms a large baboon, which he had dressed up in a scarlet coat, with hat and feathers, so that to an unscrutinizing eve it seemed like a miniature resemblance of wild Kit Clayton.

The likeness struck Roaring Dick the instant that the showman placed his grinning charge upon the table, where it squatted like the grand Turk, and he immediately exclaimed to Kit, "Lad! lad! luik here. Smash if thee hasn't been getting a bairn in the sun, and here he be dropt down amang us to swear to his feyther."

"Why, luik at his jaws," cried another. "He's many a hundred years old if he's a day."

"Smash, marrow, how he grins," cried Dick, who began to be really terrified at the apparition. "Lord send it an't Belzebub."

"Belzebub!" said another, with contempt. "He's nothing but a hairy-faced jew."

"Duck him, then. Hey, life! "we'll shave him in tarry watter," exclaimed several voices at once. The showman interposed; but Kit, who enjoyed the fun, drowned his voice, and shouted—

"You had better defend yourselves, gentlemen. "It's my belief he is either a Russian or a Cossack."

These words threw all into consternation. Every man jumped up, save

Kit, who, after emptying a glass of ale, filled it up again, and handed it to the monkey. The animal, following the imitative habits of its tribe, nodded gravely to Clayton, and drained the measure of its contents.

"Ho!" shouted Dick, indignantly. "Is he thus to sup afore our faces? What next will he do? Mayhap the'll steel the pipe from our jaws;" and, in the anger of the moment, he tauntingly held his pipe towards the animal. The creature, who was accustomed to things of that sort, received it with the utmost composure, and sticking the end between his lips, puffed a volume of smoke into Dick's face. The rage of the pitman now knew no bounds, and catching up a gill of liquor, he threw its contents into the monkey's face; whereupon the assailed party began to show his teeth, and chatter in a manner that made his assailant's hair stand on end! and, to crown all, serving up a creaming jug by its side, showered a torrent of liquor on the coal-begrimed countenance of the collier, and with a nimble spring leaped upon a shelf that overhung the company, where he sat grinning and chattering with all his might. Some of the pitmen, upon this, really fancied that the evil one was amongst them, and in endeavouring to rush from the place, upset chairs and tables, and fell over them, with a force that sent the legs and backs upon voyages of discovery into different quarters of the room; while others, rendered courageous by passion, gathered pipes, jugs, and all sorts of missiles, and flung them at the monkey, who, catching the ammunition, returned it with such precision, that there was scarcely a head which did not show blood. At length the assailants fairly turned tail, and evacuated the place roaring that the grinning Cossack was a match for all Newcastle.

Clayton now mounted a table, and suddenly seizing Jocko by the collar, brought him from his elevated position, and displaying him at the window, called out that the enemy was captured. This at once established him in favour of the pitmen, who received the intelligence with a shout, and vowed to stand by him through thick and thin. Clayton smiled, and turning to Coleman, observed, that in case it was attempted to take him, he did not expect much aid from their valour; but Coleman told him that he formed a wrong estimate of the canny colliers.

"You may frighten them wi' a squib, if they are not used to it," said the worthy skipper; "but only give them an enemy they ken, and they'll tackle two to one any day. The only thing to fear, Jack," he continued, "is that when you reach town, you'll not be able to get shot o' them. They all long to see your face, and I cannot see how it's to be avoided. But come, au'd Sue ha' got a rest by this time, and we'd better be ganging."

"With all my heart," said Kit. "But first sign this certificate." As he said this, he handed the paper he had prepared to Coleman, and struck by a sudden thought, he contrived, while the skipper was signing it, to whip the monkey unperceived under his coat, and muffle its head in a handkerchief. The showman was not present to prevent this manœvre, for fearing an attack upon his caravan, he had rushed out, and was now employed in using his eloquence to prevent the colliers from giving liberty to two she bears, a Russian wolf, and a Bengal tiger.

"There, lad," said Coleman, handing his specimen of penmanship to Kit, "last time I spelt my name, it was with an undertaking to lay you by the heels."

"And now," exclaimed Kit, "it is placed to a certificate, as 'll prove to the rum 'uns that I'm not to be had. But let's mount our beasts. Old Sue will get stiff in the joints if she stands much longer."

They now sallied forth, and to Kit's infinite amusement, he saw that at least a dozen of the pitmen were mounted on one kind of animal or other. Some had dragged two or three half-blind cart-horses from their stables, others had procured donkeys, and a few had managed to get hold of beasts of mettle. Amid these was Roaring Dick, who sat grasping the mane of his Bucephalus, and with his knees digging into its sides as if he expected the first motion to lay him sprawling; yet he nevertheless appeared determined that nothing should prevent him from proceeding

Kit and his humourous friend exchanged glances, but mounted without a word. "Now then," said Clayton, "to finish a ride such as never was run in the world before."

'And aw'll be in at the death," cried Dick, pushing forward and starting off side by side with the highwayman. Kit, for a moment, endeavoured to outride him, but Dick was an old equestrian after his own fashion, and being well mounted, rendered abortive all Clayton's efforts to get ahead. Perceiving this, Kit gave up the attempt for the present, and slackening into a trot, began to enter into conversation with the master collier. Dick aimed at nothing else, and wishing to "show off" in presence of a man who had visited the moon, and caused a total eclipse of the sun, he began to brag of his own feats—real and fictitious—amid the collieries. Kit listened with profound attention, and, encouraged by this, the pitman became more and more marvellous in his narrations, until he even had the temerity to begin to talk of apparitions and evil spirits which he had seen, when an ominous sound, resembling the cry of "Hoo! hoo!" was heard from a direction of a hollow oak tree on the road side, and startled both speaker and listener.

Thinking that it was Kit expressing disbelief, the pitman angrily exclaimed, "Whet dis thou 'hoo, hoo!' for, man? Dost think I lie?"

"I didn't speak," said Kit, looking round

"Who makes game of us?" shouted the pitman, not without alarm. "I say it again that I saw Jenny Dawson's gaist myself. It was four nights arter she drooned herself."

"Hoo, hoo!"

"Hoo, hoo, again! God smash aw'll 'hoo, hoo,' thee, thou imp of hell," cried Dick, who thinking it to be one of its companions endeavouring to bring his ghost stories into ridicule, spurred up to the place from whence the sound proceeded, with the intention of inflicting summary vengeance upon the offender. Kit paused to witness the result, and the rest reined up also, for the sounds had occasioned no little consternation amongst them.

"Dare say au'd Nick has summat to say to him," said one of the men to another.

"Aye, aye, I thought his time was near hand," said the other.

At this moment Roaring Dick was heard to utter one of those stentorian laughs, which never failed to produce a sort of air-quake, and awaken every echo within five miles of him. "Ho smash!" cried he, riding back in a convulsion of merriment; "whe dis think 'hoo, hoo,' be?"

"Why? Jenny Dawson's ghaist?"

"Nay, begox! it's nout else but a Jenny Owl."

The mirthful host received this intimation with a shout, but as they resumed their ride, they began to reflect more deeply upon the circumstance, and view it with suspicion. For some time past they had been casting uneasy glances at Clayton. His singular appearance; his outrageous adventures of which he had boasted; the almost incredible ride which they considered him to be now concluding; the strange apparition of the monkey, an animal which few of them had ever seen before, and the last alarming event of the owl, conjoined to make them think that our highwayman was not altogether "canny," as they termed it, and a few of the boldest resolved to lay hands upon him, With this view, an elder brother of Roaring Dick's rode up to his side and said :—

"I say, hinny, what wad a man get for catching hold o' the scruff o' thy neck.'

"The contents of this in his head," returned Kit, pointing a pistol at the other.

Daresay!" said Dick, who was ignorant of the impressions under which his companions laboured, " but brother wants to ken what he should get in cash?"

Oh!" exclaimed Kit, putting up his weapon, "a hundred pounds, at least."

"And the contempt of all who knew thee," cried Coleman.

Contempt never broke a man's head," returned the first questioner. "And what—I only ax from curiosity—what wad be the best manner of catching thee without having an ounce of lead by way of a stopper?"

"What would be the best way of catching me," reiterated Kit, pushing a little in advance, and turning towards his questioner.

"Aye. Thee seem'st so clever, that I'd like to ken."

"It's the easiest thing imaginable," said Kit. "Do as the little boys do when they want to catch little fishes?"

"And what be that?"

"Put salt on my tail!" And with these words Kit plied thong and steel in the same moment, and gallopped forward at the greatest speed to which he could urge his courser. The pitmen floundered after him, but impeded each others efforts; while Coleman did his best to heighten their confusion. Kit therefore kept gallantly a-head, and increased the distance between himself and pursuers at every stroke. But he saw that the alarm once being raised it would be impossible to avoid capture unless by the aid of stratagem, and with that weapon he was prepared to fight. Availing himself of the first turn of the road, he took the muffle from the head of poor Jocko, and placed the animal before him on the saddle. The ape instinctively caught hold of the pommel, and thus secured to itself a firm seat. "Now, then, Jocko," said Clayton, " you are a light weight, and bid fair to give them the slip. You'll do in the distance for Sixteen-stringed Jack as well as myself—and so good-bye; The mare has answered my purpose, and I'd better lose her than my own liberty." With these words he slid quietly off, and jumped into a dry ditch that opportunely presented itself beneath the shade of a hedge. Freed from his weight, the representative of Sue, redoubled her pace; and the hue and cry having by this time turned the corner, the flying form of the monkey was caught sight of, and occasioned the pursuers to think that their prey must have escaped in a whirlwind, to become diminished by distance in so short a time. No one was more surprised than Coleman, who inadvertently exclaimed, in his admiration—" Smash if Sixteen-stringed Jack can't ride like a bullet?"

"Ho, begox—be it he?" roared Dick. "Give it him, lads,—give it him!" And thus urged, the whole train clattered forward to Gateshead.

Well," exclaimed Clayton, as the motley crew swept past him; "they may talk of the cockneys being monkey-led after this, but I'll be shot if I h'ant made the 'cute northern lads follow the same game. The miners are counter-mined anyhow, and though they don't think jack-an-ape is, I made 'em think an ape was Jack. Whew! there was a burst, they'll be coming to a wind-up presently, without the aid of a windlass!"

The last part of this speech referred to a new accession of force to the riders in the persons of a large body of keel-men, who having seen Jocko flying before his enemies, naturally thought that some fun was a-foot, and followed as fast as their heels could carry them, with a shout that reached even the ears of Clayton. This shout was immediately caught up and echoed by the equestrian pitmen, and what with the ardour of the pursuers, and the new speed to which they incited the pursued, the celebrated lines of Burn's were fully realized :—

> "As bees bizz out wi' angry fyke,
> When plundering herds assail their byke;
> As open pussy's mortal foes,
> When pop! she starts before their nose;
> As eager runs the market crowd,
> When 'catch the thief,' resounds aloud,
> So Maggie runs, the witches follow,
> Wi' many an eldritch shriek and halloo !"

The inhabitants of Gateshead, then confined to the narrow streets which still descends towards the bridge, were startled from their slumbers, and many a night-capped head might be seen protruding from cautious opened windows to see what so much noise was about; to their great subsequent satisfaction when the name of Sixteen-string Jack was afterwards bruited abroad as the hero of the hunt, and thus enabled them to boast of having seen him. Jacko, in nowise disliking his ride, though in the begining he had been somewhat alarmed at it, continued to maintain his seat with a steadiness that might have elicited the envy of a Ducrow or a young Hernandez, while the mare, being left entirely to its own guidance, and, moreover, urged on by the monkey, who plied the whip with the true frequency of a jockey followed its outstretched nose right through Gateshead, and over the old bridge. The last feat was a dangerous one, for the adventure we are recording occurred but a short period after the great flood, which in the eighteenth century, swept away four entire arches of the bridge, which at that time was covered with houses, and the gap had only been hastily patched up with rotten plank-work. Jocko being a light weight, however, passed with safety ; but the sturdy colliers caused so many fractures and laughable accidents, such as horses being rendered immovable by their hoofs getting stuck in some hole in the flooring, that the heroes of the race were entirely absolved from the charge of ingratitude, when they afterwards spoke ill of the bridge that had carried them over.

Those whose good fortune enabled them to avoid these misadventures kept up the chase, with an obstinacy that nothing could resist; and in a few moments the major part were sweeping along the quay side. From this place the hunt took a zig-zag direction. Ascended the steep of Silver-street, and leaving All Saints's church on the left, crossed a place called "Pudding Chare," and then got into Pilgrim-street. From there the monkey and its steed took another turn, and found their way into a large piece of muddy ground called the "Croft;" and then on they both went splashing at every step, and making direct for the open country.

"Odds life!" cried Roaring Dick, "if he gets out by the coal-pit, I'll gie him a stock for his winter firing, for I'll pelt him till he drops."

"You must be very rich, if you are so ready to post the cole," said Coleman, who still kept his place in the hunt.

"Nay, nay, the post sometimes miscarries, so I'll send it by hand," exclaimed Dick, unconscious of a jest.

What further might have been said is uncertain, for at this moment every man-jack amongst the riders were suddenly precipitated head formost into the mire, where they stuck heels upwards, like so many stumps. In short, this was occasioned by their coming to an abrupt steep in the grounds which they overlooked in the darkness, and caused every horse to stumble at the same moment. It was a regular stick in the mud concern, and roaring Dick was heard to exclaim, as he tumbled:—"Ho, smash! I'm going to h—!"

The monkey's steed fared no better, but the rider being more expert than the pursuers, regained his feet in a twinkling, and in another moment the astonished pitmen beheld him scouring over the morass like a shadow; and Coleman, with new astonishment, exclaimed:—"Now to think he could walk over water itself."

It is needless to say that the ape soon got out of sight, and the discomfited colliers returned to Newcastle, to swear they had been running after the eldest grandson of the devil.

Of the further adventures of the ape little is known, save what is gathered at the time from the exaggerated reports of those who afterwards encountered him, and imagined they had won the honour of an interview with Sixteen-string Jack. At one place an honest ditcher, who had been spending a little of his wife's earnings at the ale-house, and was returning rather later than usual, saw something hopping forward before him like a kangaroo. Our sober reveller, who by the variety of his visits across the road, appeared to have business on each side of the way.

"Ho, faggots! who goes yonder?" he exclaimed, and holding up his lantern, endeavoured to ascertain the appearance of the wayfarer.

Jocko at that moment turned round, and having been accustomed to see his supper of chesnuts roasted nightly at a fire, conceived that the long delayed operation was at length about to be performed, and sprung towards the fancied furnace with the greatest agility. Simon roared like a full-grown rhinoceros, and flung himself, on his face, in the mire, bellowing that Death or Doctor Faustus had come to claim him. The monkey, frightened by the outcry, kicked and scratched with a vengeance, until a blow from its victim dispatched it from the perch it had taken on the old man's breast, and snatching up the lantern, it now hopped off again, and was soon far enough from harm in that quarter.

Jocko next alighted on an encampment of gipsies, where the chief was thrashing his wife with a stick. The monkey, thinking the sport an amusing one, caught up a bludgeon, and jumping on the gipsey's back, commenced paying off the fellow in his own coin, belabouring his lusty shoulders with a vigour that might hardly have been expected.

"Thou insolent dwarf," exclaimed the wife, who, like a true woman, would suffer no one to punish her husband for his barbarity but herself, and catching the interloper by the collar, commenced shaking and punching him for dear life. This made Jocko thump all the harder, and that gave a new vigour to the husband's arm; so there they were paying and receiving all round: the man pummilling the woman, the woman wiping off the score at the monkey's expense, and the monkey retaliating upon the husband. By and by, however, the uproar collected several of the gang, and they immediately cried out that their ruler and his mistress, after playing the devil together, had at length raised him to take a lead in the game. Some made off at the supposed discovery, and others remained to pelt the intruder, who, finding that he gained more kicks than halfpence in the affair, once more took to his heels.

His next visit was at the open window of a mansion belonging to a justice of the peace. The worthy magistrate was a noted miser, whose constant practice was to waste his midnight oil while he counted over his bulging money bags. His whole life had been spent in the acquirement of coin; and the only use he made of it was to spread it night after night before his eyes, and gloat upon the treasure. Gold, in short, was so much his idol, that it seemed to have entered into his composition, for his jaundiced skin and bilious habit, gave him the appearance of having been plated with the metal.

He always sat with a brace of pistols before him; though a coward when his person was alone in danger, he felt that he could resist any attack when his cash was in jeopardy. The snug appearance of the little room in which he hoarded his treasure attracted the desires of master Jocko, who, besides being stiff with pain, required rest, having been kept from his slumbers longer than usual. He had scaled with ease the plantation wall of the magistrate—for the miser would never have trusted himself near an open window, had he not been fortified against all intruders, save such as now presented itself—and on seeing the before-mentioned light, he doubtless supposed that some good Samaritan was waiting up for the very purpose of giving him shelter; and without further ceremony, therefore, sprang through the casement, and, alighting upon the table, drew in his legs, like a tailor, shouldered the bludgeon that he still held, and, placing the lantern before him, commenced grinning and chattering to attract his host's attention.

Up started Sir Balaam, and, with a natural impulse, laid hands upon the nearest money bag. Jocko, not to be behind hand, caught up another, and again did his moneys rattle one against the other, with increased force.

"Villain! housebreaker!" cried the alarmed magistrate. "Know you who I am? Put down that bag, or I'll fire;" and he snatched up a pistol. The well-taught mimic did the same, but by the awkwardness with which he handled it, the pistol went off instantly. "Murder!" roared the justice; and with a desparate effort at courage, he fired. Jocko thought this too warm a welcome by half, so he went the way he came, still clutching his treasure and the lantern, which he now exchanged for the pistol, having a recollection of the cheerfulness it had before cast upon his path. "Stop, stop!" roared the justice. "Hallo! who waits? Thieves! Murder!"

His outcries roused the entire household.

> "Up jump'd the cook and caught hold of her spit;
> Up jump'd the groom and took bridle and bit;
> Up jump'd the gardener and shoulder'd his spade;
> Up jump'd the scullion, the footman, and maid.
> (The two last, by the way, occasioned some scandal,
> By appearing together with only one candle,
> Which gave for unpleasant surmises some handle.)
> Up jump'd the swineherd, and up jump'd the big boy,
> A nondescript under him acting as pig boy;
> Butler, housekeeper, coachman—from bottom to top;
> Everybody jump'd up without parley or stop,
> With the weapon which first in their way chanced to drop—
> Whip, warming-pan, wig-block, mug, musket, and mop."

The alarmed posse would have put laughter into a weeping willow, so ludicrous was the assemblage; and a fancier in holland smocks, flannel petticoats red night caps, and worsted stockings, would have revelled in the display that presented itself. In fact, they were all half-naked, for—

> "———— the truth to express,
> As you'll easily guess,
> They had none of the time to attend much to dress;
> But he or she,
> As the case might be,
> He or she seizes what he or she pleases,
> Breeches or kirtles, and shirts and chemises;
> And thus, one and all, great and small, short and tall,
> Muster'd at once in the magistrate's hall,
> With upstanding locks, starting eyes, shorten'd breath,
> Like the folks in the gallery scene of Macbeth,
> When Macduff is announcing their sovereign's death."

The motley group had neither time to ask questions or receive an explanation.

"Fly!" shouted the magistrate, as soon as his servants appeared. "A glass of grog, and, perhaps, half-a-crown to the man who apprehends him!

No one knew to whom, nor for what, this liberal offer directed their attention, but all guessed it was to some one, or something outside, from the fact of their righ worshipful master pointing to the window as he spoke. Each eye followed the same direction; and though the eye of the fugitive monkey was hidden from them in the darkness, they were enabled to descry the light he carried, and which flickered like a will-o-the-wisp as he moved onwards.

"What is it—a ghost?" yelled the aroused sleepers, turning all manner of hues, as if some maker of fireworks was playing off his vari-coloured fires against their countenances.

"A ghost! No—a highwayman!" shouted their master. "Follow him, every one of you. The man, woman, or child who stops behind, shall be punished as accomplices."

This terrible intimation was sufficient. Out bundled the whole crew through the window—higgledy-piggledy, as they best could. Here a greasy-smocked cook clutched hold of a fat porter by the tail of his shirt, to keep herself from falling; there the dimity petticoat of a squeaking chambermaid was rent in twain by the skrimmage, and her little leg was seen following its slippered foot, as it tripped shivering to the ground. Some pulled, and some hauled; some screamed, and some squalled, until the least nimble of the body became wedged in one compact mass in the framework of the casement—unable either to advance or retrograde.

In vain the justice swore, and pelted with sofa-pillows the piles of rear-ends which faced him; they quivered for fundamental reasons, but made no progress. At length he snatched up a horsewhip, and gave one lashing stripe across the whole. It was a capital idea; they all jerked out at one pop.

The window was low, and the ground soft, otherwise no little damage might have been the consequence. As it was, a good jolting was all they experienced; and, having scrambled to their feet again, they all set forward, their night clothes streaming in the breeze, and making them appear like a moving field of linen that had been spread out to dry, and then carried along by a sudden gust of wind.

Startled by their halloing and hooting, Jocko hopped along as fast as ever. He, no doubt, fancied himself an object of general persecution, for an ape has as much right to the enjoyment of his own opinions as an oyster to be crossed in love. Not, however, to dwell at present upon so metaphysical a question, we will follow him to the end of his adventures. He flew along, closely followed by his pursuers; and the disasters they met through one tumbling over the other, and similar casualties, completely renewed the scene that had occured when our hero committed his robbery on the Marquis de Vauxrien; and all the guests followed in such ludicrous confusion. In fine, it appeared as if the beginning and end of this notorious adventure was to be marked with tear-away scamperings and hurry scurry. There was this difference, however; the adventures of Jocko were concluded on foot, while those of him who had set the affair going, were concluded on horseback.

The monkey continued to be dodged and hunted entirely through the park until his career was stopped by a broad stream that bounded the grounds. His natural instinct made him pause, and he ran along the margin of the brook for some yards, until he came to a plank, used by the servants in crossing to the public portion of the estate. Jocko was too good a rope dancer to doubt his footing, and away he went unscared, and as merrily as ever. His followers, on witnessing his momentary stoppage, had fancied that they had tired him out, and bellowing with renewed violence, they dashed forward at increased speed. But woeful was the result, for souse they went into the water, every night-cap of them, and such was the noise created by the accident, that to the day of their deaths, they retained the appellation of the "Coldstream Runners" from all who heard of it.

Jocko continued his flight, but was now exhausted; his active hops became a hobble. He had thrown aside his lantern, but still maintained his clutch upon the gold; and this he was abandoning, claw by claw, when he came in sight of a cottage, from which a man, his wife, and several children were making their exit. The ape ran up to them for protection, but his strength could no longer sustain him, and, dropping his booty at the feet of the cottager, he fell down by his side.

The man was at first dismayed, and would have retreated, had not the jingling of the gold caught his ear. He picked up the bag, and had scarcely done so, when the hallooing of those who had managed to flounder across the stream was once more heard. It fell upon the ear of Jocko; with one more effort he regained his feet; plunged into a wood that flanked the house and, to use the language of the nursery book, "never was heard of more."

No. 36.

The last incident had accidentally the effect of adding greatly to the fame of Sixteen-string Jack. It happened that the labourer who had thus become enriched by the pranks of the monkey, was an honest leaseholder, whom the miserly magistrate had long striven to drive off his estates. He had first impoverished, and then sued him for debt, and having issued mesne process, was about to thrust him into the Newcastle jail. Some friendly voice had, however, warned the poor man of his danger, and he resolved, in consequence, to decamp with his family before morning. The scene was a distressing one; he addressed his home as if it could hear his plaints, and was just bewailing his poverty, when Jocko flung upwards of a hundred guineas at his feet. The man was sensible enough to keep his counsel concerning the matter; he gave up his lease the next day, on consideration of an acquittal for his debt, and departed for another part of the kingdom. Here he no longer laid a restraint upon his tongue, and whenever the famous ride of Sixteen-string Jack, from Richmond to the north, became the subject of conversation, he always related, with feelings of gratitude, the benevolent act which he conceived the highwayman had performed; and thus, without any cost, our hero earned a character for liberality, little inferior to that achieved by Turpin himself.

Jack heard of this, and also of the race that had been run. He was in perfect extacies, for he thought that Clayton had done it all, and, of course, acted the most brilliant part in the whole farce. "Who would have thought," exclaimed he to himself, "that that funny rascal would display so much pluck as well as humour? Such tact too! Why, his plundering the old miser, and relieving his oppressed tenant, will bring me as much fame as the ride itself! How the devil he accomplished it I can't fathom!"

Meanwhile, honest Kit was reposing upon the laurels which he had only half earned. After quitting his house, he had walked leisurely into Newcastle, and managed to ascertain that the mayor had received his mission by means of Daft Willy's broom. Late as it was, scouts were despatched in every direction, and by morning all the colliers and keelmen, the sleepers of Gateshead, and the wakers of Newcastle, and above all, the miserly magistrate and his well-ducked servants, learned that Sixteen-string Jack had been moving amongst them, and actually accomplished his ride. The whole district was in a ferment; Clayton mixed with his quondam pursuers, and heightened the excitement by spreading the most marvellous tales concerning Jack. He often declared, in after times, that it vos the funniest fun vot ever vos, to hear the lies they told vith their mouths, and took it in at their precious long ears; and he vowed that he should never have gone through the adventure half so well if the showman had not put his monkey up.

He remained, committing a thousand waggeries, at Newcastle, until he was summoned to join his comrade; and thus ended this premeditated and famous stratagem.

We will now follow the fortunes of Jack.

CHAPTER XXVIII.

A VISIT—A BIT OF CHAFF—CAPTURE OF OUR HERO.

Jack had no sooner got his brave pals once more around him, by which time, throughout the whole of Great Britain, nothing was talked of but the supposed wonderful ride, than he set his wits to works how he was to replenish the exchequer, which by heavy expenses of late had been considerably reduced. For a time he sat, head upon elbow, pondering deeply, for, hemmed in as he was on all sides, every avenue hitherto open to him was closed, his increasing popularity having in fact rendered every step he might take fraught with perils and dangers.

Even whilst pondering, the door was thrown open, and Toby, the immortal landlord, stepped before him.

"Toby, my stunner!"

"Jack my tulip!"

Was all that passed between them for a few seconds, for so absorbed were both in the delight of again meeting, that neither could utter a word for a few minutes.

"Well, Toby, my true-hearted, my own blue-bell," said Jack, at length, "What's in the wind?"

"Danger!" answered Toby, seriously and earnestly.

"Oh, that all," said Jack, with a laugh, free-and-easy, if not entirely hearty, "why damme, I've had that fellow for breakfast, lunch, dinner, tea, and supper, for God only knows how many months past, methought you might have brought me better news—something stirring I mean—something that my heart could leap at, and my mare jump at, that's all I wished."

"John!" exclaimed Toby.

If there be one single individual reader of ours in the world, who, accustomed all his life long to the name of Jack, and finds that name so linked and tied to all that love him — the single exclamation of the word, "John," from the lips of a chosen and prized friend, is sufficient to raise in his mind the emotion that something is wrong.

"John! that's a lovely way to address a fellow, who, like Jack Sheppard of old, ought to be christened 'Jack,' if he was'nt; what's in the wind I say again, I neither understand nor like my new name."

"Hell shiver me, and you needn't ought to, for Jack's the lad of all lads, but slice my wizen, what do you think has happened?"

"Can't tell," said Jack, carelessly.

"Nor guess?" queried Toby.

"No, nor guess," responded Jack.

"Then, Jack—it cuts me to the blessed vitals to reweal it, but you are peached upon—sold—betrayed."

"Betrayed!" exclaimed Jack, starting to his feet, and instinctively feeling for his weapon, "by whom?"

"By one who, clever as he thinks himself, will never live to spend the blood-money he has reaped by the peach—never! we have all sworn it on our solemn davies.'

"But who is the man?" questioned Jack, almost frenzied from impatience, "tell me his name."

"By vun, Jack, as ve have all on us alvays known as a black-hearted scoundrel, but never had no idea tha he vas such a notorious villain as to go and peach. Vhy, blessed if it aint Night-owl Oliver what's been and gone and done it!"

"Ha!" exclaimed Jack, "I never liked that fellow from the first. He carries scoundrel in his face. At the first robbery of the marquis he envied me the command which the unanimous voice of the gang conferred upon me."

"I knows he did," said Toby, "and 'twas like his precious impudence, for, he lead a band like that! vy, bless my stars, I might as reasonably expect to put out the moon with a pair of snuffers! It vorn't to be done, my out-and-outer, 'xcept by you, and when you took it in hand, vy, blow me! 'twas done to perfection! Now, blow me, ve're done, and all through that atrocious villin."

"Done! may Old Nick admire me if I am! no, no, trust me; Jack Rann is not the man to say die, till he's dead. I've baffled them before, old fellow, and I will again, and mark me, if I fail not in my aim, I will bitterly revenge the treachery of Night-owl Oliver."

"By all means do, and sleep me, but he'd be better in the hangman's hands than in ours. But, so help me Newgate, Jack, what noise is that?"

"There is some one at the door," said Jack. "Hist! and, by our Lady, they are endeavouring to force an entrance."

"Oh, Jack," exclaimed Toby, in sincere grief, "in endeavouring to save you I have scragged you—fool that I was to come—they must have traced me here."

"Never mind, old fellow," said Jack, "if it turns out for the worst, it was still done for the best, let that be your consolation. Quiet a moment, I will open the casement and reconnoitre."

"Not so," said Toby, seizing a nightcap that happened to be at hand, and drawing it upon his head, "I'll just shove my pimple out, and see what they are arter."

Toby did so, and listened attentively. He suddenly withdrew his head, exclaiming, as he did so—

"Can you climb up a chimbley?"

Spite of the danger by which he was surrounded, Jack could not forbear a smile.

"Why, damme, Toby, what do you take me for, do you think I am a sweep?"

"No, Jack, I doesn't, but if there ain't any other outlet—why I very much fears it's your only chance for life."

"Then I must give it up, for, tolerably expert at most things, I am sadly deficient in the art of chimney-sweeping. But hark at those fellows outside; hang me if they are not battering the door in.

"So they are, the precious lambs," said Toby, "bless their precious hearts, nothing would afford me such exquisite happiness as seeing on 'em all hanging in a string, like a rope of inguns. That's right, hammer away— that cove knocking now is old Badger, Sir John Fielding's head tipstaff, I know the ring of the blessed metal. Well, they'll certainly batter in that blessed door, so perhaps I'd better speak to them." and, acting upon this suggestion, Toby thrust his cap-covered head outside of the window, and, in a particularly bland tone of voice, inquired if there was anybody there.

"Yes!" was the reply, thundered forth by the head constable, "and I command you to open your door."

"What, at this time of night," said Toby. "Go away with you, do, or I'll call the watch."

"Open your door, I say!" again shouted the officer.

"It gives me pain, my wenerable, to refuse such a respectable elderly gent., but I really must decline. This is a well conducted establishment, and we don't do it; besides, there arn't nobody up; we're all on us snug in bed a snoring."

"I charge you, in the King's name, to open the door."

"Oh, in the King's name, does ye? Well, how is his most gracious majesty?"

"I'll have no evasion," said the officer, losing all patience at the delay.

"No ewasion! I really should think you wouldn't, for its a commodity as we don't sell here, at any price."

"Cease your foolery. We have a warrant for the apprehension of one John Rann, for felony, and, unless you instantly open your doors—"

"Don't put yourself in a passion, my good fellow, I can't think of such a thing. Felony? why, whatever does it mean? Rann—crikey, what a funny name!" I wish you was gone away, and not here, disturbing respectable people from their first sleep."

"Force the door," said the officer to his men, "we may stand parleying with this fool until our prisoner escapes."

In obedience to their superior's orders, the constables set to work, and, having obtained possession of a log of wood, they commenced using it as a battering-ram, to break down the door.

"Oh, if that's what you mean, I'd better come down at once; but I must confess it is the most ungentlemanly conduct as ever I heard on." Toby looked at Jack with an inquiring glance, as if anxious to know what was to be done.

"Open the door," said our hero, "for it is certain unless we do, they will open it for us. Nothing remains but a fight for it. I wish to heaven I had my pistols here; but, so-so, here is a poker—a lovely and effective weapon—so they may now look out for a broken sconce."

Toby descended at his master's bidding, and, withdrawing the bolts and bars, the officers rushed in pell mell, two remaining at the door to seize any attempting to escape. They rushed up stairs, and from the stairs into the room where our hero was waiting their approach, with flashing eyes and most threatening aspect.

"On him, my men," shouted the constable, but the bravest held back, awed by Jack's intimidating glance.

"Ah, that's right," said Jack, with a sneer of significant and scornful bitterness. "Twelve to one is fair play when dogs are the assailants, and a timid one the oppressed; but come on, you see I fear you not, indeed, am waiting your assault."

"John Rann," said the constable, "in the king's name I command you to surrender. Resistance can avail you nothing, so, for your own good, drop that weapon; we have come armed and prepared at every hazard to effect your capture: and if you succumb not to the might and majesty of the law, I must do my duty by main force, for dead or alive—so goes my mandate—I must lodge you in the king's goal of Newgate."

"The long odds are against me, that's a fact," muttered Jack, between his clenched teeth. "Toby, my friend, where are you ?"

"Here," responded Toby, entering the room with a frying-pan in his hand, with which he facetiously tapped the heads of the constable's assistants that chanced to come too near him, "here I is ready and villing to cook the goose of any single von on 'em—now come on," and Toby flourished the frying-pan in the most threatening manner, and, in his flourishing, gave the unhappy constable such accidentally-done-for-the-purpose knocks, that our hero, forgetting his danger, laughed outright; which peal of merriment causing Toby to turn his head, he was instantly seized, and his weapon was wrested from him.

"That just serves you right," said Jack, laughingly; then, throwing the poker into a corner, he advanced, with open hand and smiling face, to the constable, saying, "forgive me, my dear fellow, for detaining you so long. I did but jest, for such have been the misrepresentations of late regarding me, that it was my firm intention to have surrendered myself into the hands of Sir Charles Fielding to-morrow morning, which, although it would have saved you some trouble, would, nevertheless, have been the means of losing you the five hundred pounds reward offered for one John Rann, alias Sixteen-string Jack. Now I, confessing myself to be John Rann, cannot, nevertheless, lay claim to the latter glorious appellation, but still I am your prisoner, and I doubt not his majesty's justices will do you justice, by rewarding you with five hundred pounds for your vigilence, and I have, on the other hand, no doubt he will immediately do a second act of justice by discharging me."

To paint the most astonished face in that assembly was a moral impossibility. The officer looked as if he had really serious doubts whether he had obtained possession of the right man or not, as would also appear to be the opinion of his confederates, for they all appeared greviously disposed to think the five hundred pounds reward was about to slip through their grasping and avaricious fingers, which doubt one of the officers expressed in the following classic words :—

"D——n my eyes !"—a curse so commonly spoken, yet so shockingly impious in its tendency, that a popular author has justly remarked, were the wicked wish to be realised in but one out of every hundred times it is spoken, it would render " blindness as common as the measles." Not content with once uttering it, the fellow repeated the oath, finishing with the words, "what a cursed infernal do, if ve've got the wrong covey."

"We can werry soon make sure of that, for if I arn't got a description of that ere robbery of the squire's, near Bath, with a description of the Sixteen-stringer, blow me!" said another officer, pulling a newspaper from his pocket, and quietly taking a seat, read the following report from a Bath paper:—

"DARING OUTRAGE AND BURGLARY!

"SIXTEEN-STRING JACK NEAR THE CITY OF BATH!!

"UNPRECEDENTED EFFRONTERY!!!

"This notorious, venturesome, and almost supernatural burglar, has paid the citizens of Bath a visit at last, which, as well as the short space of time allowed to us, and the hurried manner in which the account has reached us, we are enabled to give as follows:

"It seems that, shortly after twelve o'clock, the premises of Mr. Giles, the rich landowner and merchant, were broken open by this notorious ruffian and his gang, and property to an immense value extracted therefrom. But what adds to the impudence and astonishment of the robbery is, that the robber actually entered a lady's bed-room, while she was asleep, took a valuable miniature set in diamonds from a table drawer, leaving in its place a diamond ring worth three hundred guineas, and then actually sitting down and writing the lady an apology, and promising to restore the picture whenever he should meet with the original. Mr. Giles was bound by ropes to the balustrades of the staircase, and his life repeatedly threatened by the robbers. Several of the city watch, who had a most desperate encounter with the gang, were dreadfully bruised, and otherwise maltreated. But a tale of unprecedented romance remains to be told! This very Sixteen-string Jack, whom all the kingdom has been hunting after, turns out to be a countryman of our own; his name is John Rann, and his parents reside at a village called Bathwick, near Bath. This identification cannot fail to bring the villain at once to speedy retributive justice.—Bath Journal, November 12, 1777.

"POSTSCRIPT.—We stop the press to add that Sixteen-string Jack is a stout, well-made, fine fresh-coloured young man, twenty-five years of age, about five feet ten inches in height, (and not eight feet, as has been frequently erroneously reported of him), with blue eyes, fine regular teeth, brown curly hair, a nose rather inclined to aquiline, has the remains of a scar on his left cheek, and generally assumes the disguise of a wealthy country farmer. He is a most melodious singer, and is noted for his courtesy and politeness, especially to ladies, in all his felonious practices."

"Stout, fine made, fresh coloured young man, very good looking, five feet ten in height—you are the very man, sir, as I live!"

"I wish I was," said Jack, shrugging his shoulders, "I should be a precious sight better off than I am, but, however, if you are contented in my being the illustrious individual, I am quite content to perform the part of his representative, so perhaps you'll do me the favour to send for a coach at once, for I am anxious to be in bed, even though that bed be in Newgate."

The officer was so much gratified in the prize he had gained, that he willingly acquiesced. The coach was got, and that night was spent by Sixteen-string Jack in Newgate.

CHAPTER XXIX.

JACK'S COMMITTAL FOR TRIAL—A SCENE IN COURT—VISITS IN NEWGATE—AN ESCAPE.

THE next morning our hero was taken before the Lord Mayor—Lord Dashfield, Mr. Malcolm, Sir John Fielding, and other noted personages sharing the bench with the head magistrate. The Mansion House was crowded to suffocation, the majority of the personages present being well-dressed ladies, who had paid enormous prices for their seats, in order to catch a glimpse of the darling hero of the day, Sixteen-string Jack, who had obtained a name as notorious for gallantry towards the fair sex, as it was for daring on the road.

As our hero entered the dock, bowing, as he did so, politely to the bench, a murmur of admiration passed like an electric shock throughout the assembly—so imposing, so beautiful was his appearance.

The murmur stilled, a dead silence reigned, broken only by the occasional sobs of some few women, who were more tender-hearted than their compeers, and whose kindly sympathies were awakened, not only by the appearance of the gallant and exquisitely handsome fellow before them, but also by the dreadful fate that hung hovering over him.

Silence being proclaimed, the charge was entered upon. Innumerable witnesses were called, who each and all swore they had been severally robbed, under different circumstances and in different localities, by a person calling himself Sixteen-string Jack, yet, strange to relate, so excellently had Jack manoeuvred, not one could swear to his identity, and a hum of approbation was already on the rise in the court, for all considered the innocence of the prisoner established, when the Earl of Dashfield was seen to leave his seat, and to make his way to the seat occupied by the Lord Mayor. A whisper passed between them—an ominous whisper! for the Lord Mayor, in tones stern and decisive, informed the court the identity of our hero was established, and that he was in reality that scourge and pest of the country, called Sixteen-string Jack. His lordship finished his oration by committing our hero for trial at the Central Criminal Court.

As Jack rose to accompany the officer who attended him, preparatory to leaving the Mansion House for the prison, for the first time during the long examination, his eyes and those of the Earl of Dashfield met. On the latter, unmitigated hatred and malevolence was visible, whilst Jack expressed nothing but cool contempt. As he was leaving the box, a small bouquet was handed to him; it was composed wholly of myrtle and violets—the type of undying love and friendship. Jack glanced around, to catch the eyes of the generous donor, but in vain. She was too thickly veiled for that; but, bowing with graceful politeness and unfeigned gratitude, he pressed the sweet gift fervently to his bosom and lips; as he did so, a piece of paper fell fluttering to the ground. The officer in whose charge he was, would, with over afficiousness, have made himself possessor of it, but Rann, with a dexterity that use had made habitual to him, favoured the fellow with a jerk of his foot (completely tripping the officer off his legs), by such a back fall as he had not felt before for many and many a day—and we doubt much if he had in the course of his life.

A shout was raised at this reproof that made the house ring again; all, with one exception, and that was, Lord Dashfield, glorying in the presence of mind of the man, who, under such trying circumstances, had still nerve sufficient to punish impertinence. Thinking it an attempt at escape one or two officious constables sprang forward to seize our hero. Jack put them calmly back as though they had been so many schoolboys, then, leaning his hands upon the dock-rail, with his face towards the bench, he read the note, which contained these words:—

"Jack—I will be true to you until death, if you will but let me share your heart again. God knows I have loved you, and to this love may be attributed the care that is breaking my heart—the anguish that is maddening my brain. I have a favour to ask; if a lady, calling herself your sister, applies at the prison, leave orders that she be admitted. It will be myself, you own unhappy,
"ELINOR ROCHE."

Jack had barely finished the perusal before the Lord Mayor, starting to his feet, exclaimed—

"Officer, seize that paper. I demand to see it!"

In an instant it was torn into a hundred pieces, and, dashing it violently towards the bench, Jack said, coolly, "It is at your service, my lord."

He was then removed in a coach, which was followed by an immense concourse of persons, from the Mansion House to Newgate, at which place we will now imagine ourselves, in company with our hero and Toby—in the cell of the former.

"That notrocious willain Oliver, to go and peach," said Toby, blubberingly.

"'Tis the worm's nature to crawl; nestle with the serpent, and be sure he stings you," said Jack, in reply.

"Exactly; vot do you expect from a pig but a grunt? I never had no opinion of them long 'uns; they make tall men as they builds high houses, they runs 'em up cheap, and don't put much stuff in 'em; blast 'em, say I, vith all my heart," exclaimed Toby.

"Let us forget him," said Jack; "you and Kit Clayton have followed my fortunes; through good or ill, you were still the same."

"Vell, vot o' that?" said Toby, "I loved you—that is to say, if one man can love another—and now, captain, ven I, vagabond as I am, stands free and you, on the contrary, quite the reverse, curse me if I wouldn't be hanged instead o' you !—not as I'm at all partial to that there style of rope dancing, though; hang it, not a bit of it, thank you."

"Toby, my tulip, you have a buoyant spirit, cherish it; time will pass away, and I shall be nothing; you will forget me—do not speak—not quite forget me, for in our moods of mirth fond thoughts will come. Now, mark me, Toby, I see it now, that the world is very likely to close upon me for ever, that there is no bread but that of industry, all else is poisoned and valueless."

"Well, pison me if I don't think so," said Toby.

"Hunger alone excuses theft; but he who robs to pamper his vices is a wretch, and deserves to suffer, even though it it be at the gallows," said Jack Rann.

"Don't talk in that notrocious style," said Toby, "you makes one quite moloncholic like. Hang it! captain, I thought as how you was a cove as had a precious sight too much pluck to give up so."

"Because I speak a word of truth, do you count me as having given up?

not so my friend, although these cursed thick and dismal walls are enough to give a cove of stronger nerve than myself the blues."

"And so they are cuss 'em! Now, for my own part, the only side of any prison, as ever I seed yet, that I could feel at all partial to, has always been the outside, but, Jack my rattler, what I come to inquire arter, is this, and its the 'tickler wish of the gang, to know what's to be done for your expense."

"Defence, I presume you mean, Toby. Well, as escape, without coming to trial seems impossible, and as regards that, I've viewed every outlet in this cell, that offered room for a bird to escape from, with a keen eye. I think you cannot do better than engage an advocate for me. With an able one at my back, I feel sure, from the nature of the evidence being so conflicting and contradictory, that I shall escape."

"Shall! the cheek of the word; by heaven you must! At all events, Jack, my tulip, all that can be done in the shape of wit and money to save you shall be done, rely on that, old fellow, and if we could only drag you from this willanous durance by main force, it would be the proudest and happiest moment of our lives, but we can't save you, Jack; but there is one comfort remaining to us, old codger."

"And that is ?" questioned our hero, as the other paused.

"We will have a bitter and b—— vengeance on the head of your base betrayer."

"Say not so," said Jack, earnestly, "for God's sake. If I fall, Toby, my own true friend, let me fall alone. I had a vision of my grave last night in my dream—a grave, too, covered with flowers, indeed Toby—forgive this sentimental folly—but I awoke, with tears in my eyes, and with sorrow in my heart, that I had awoke alive."

"Vell," said Toby, forsaking the energy he had displayed—an energy, that, removing all his rough peculiarities, had exhibited him as a true-hearted and kind-hearted man. "Vell, cuss me! my Sixteen-stringer—my glorious captain—if I have ever done you the discredit to believe anything this side of Tyburn, or, even that it itself could have made your bold heart flutter; but, now, vy, damme, Jack, you don't seem yourself at all. Rely on us, Jack, we will release you from these cursed grey walls if we level them to the ground, stone by stone, we are determined—we are sworn to do it."

Jack smiled as he answered,

"Toby, my brave fellow, however strong your hearts may be to effect my release, believe me, my dear fellow, it is not practicable—were your number quadrupled a dozen times, it could not be done."

"Vether or no, ve've made up our minds to try it, that's a fact, and what we make up our minds to is done, Jack, my nonpareil, vether its possible or impossible."

"That it has been done I verily believe, Toby, my friend, but in this case, believe me, an attempt can only be followed by failure."

"Vell, then good luck to us, ve'll fail! And jolly glad to do it, too; ve are so circumvented about, its quite a treat to die for a good fellow like you."

"None of your blarney," said Jack, "if I cannot meet my doom with a firm front and an undaunted heart, why, Toby, my hearty, I'll call you in to play the man for me."

"And that you'll never do, Jack, gallant heart that you are," said Toby, with tears in his eyes, and with an earnestness of tone altogether unusual to him, "for the death that judge and jury will doom you to, is one you would save a mangy dog from! Ve know this, Jack," said Toby, falling again into his old style of talking, "Ve know it, and, knowing it, are the more determined to save you, since you von't prove a alibi nohow, not even to save your own precious neck."

After this short speech for him, of extra duration, Tobias drew a long sigh, of extra length and breadth of tone—and, gazing with much thoughtfulness at our hero for a few moments, he observed, with a sigh :—

"Night owl Oliver is the man that did the dirty peaching, but he arn't the worst after all. Do you remember that yokel you gave the lovely spat in the mouth to, vhen ve played the undertaker to sich perfection?"

"What, Luke Jones!" exclaimed Rann.

"That's him," said Toby, "he's the fellow that's been and gone, and chucked all our precious fat into the fire. He is the man who prevailed upon the villain, Oliver, to betray you and the gang."

"My better deadly curse upon him," said Jack, in bitter wrath. "Why, Toby, had it not been for his machinations, and those of his infernal master, Heaven knows I should not now have been here. Luke first instructed me in the art of deceit, by making me an accomplice in his poaching expeditions —expedition I should have said, for, on my very first excursion with him, I was waylaid and betrayed."

"Vell, old fellow," said Toby, assuming a gaiety he was far from feeling in his heart, "if its any satisfaction for you to know it, he and Oliver, and the cussed old earl himself, yes, and the squire too, if he shows his ugly mug near London, are all booked for the woody—yes Jack, if the worserest should come to the worst, and the king should fancy he couldn't do well although stretching your wind-pipe, so help me ten men and a boy, Jack, we'll scrag, or pison, or stab each and all on 'em, that is to say, if there is any faith in cold steel or arsenic."

"How often am I to tell you, I neither need or wish violence to be done upon my account?" asked Jack.

"You needn't tell me any oftener, thank ye," said Toby, "for vether you vish or not, if you are booked for the leafless tree, they are all booked for the vorms, and it will as sartinly fall upon 'em in a promiscuous vay, vhen they least expect it, or desire it, as yours vill fall upon you, when your times come—and, talking about time, puts me in mind, Jack, that my spell is vorn out, for here comes the cussed walking lock and key, to show me door."

"And its a blessing for you my brave Toby, he is about to show you the outside, for according to my poor taste and fancy, it is decidedly the preferable side to the in."

"Vat a very bad taste you have got, Jack, to be shure—vy von ud fancy such a jail-bird as the vorld now reckons you, that like a tame canary you wouldn't feel at home any vhere else but in your cage. But here comes old turnkey, so quiet is the word." Then, as the officer of the prison thrust his head in the doorway, he chanted—

"Vell, old straight hair, vy you look as if you'd been voke up in a fright; vot's the matter vith you, eh?"

"Oh, there ain't nothing the matter with me; all I got to say is, your time's up, and so you'd better be off."

"Here's cheek!" said Toby, turning to our hero, appealingly, and from him to the turnkey, with unusual ferocity, " be civil my tulip, or I'm d—d if I'll go at all."

"Werry good," said the turnkey, rattling his keys, as he moved towards the door, " ve've lots of accommodation for you, sir, but I must find you a separate bed, so perhaps you'll follow. I'll ask the governor were the spare bed lies—I know we have got one or two, for the matter of that."

"Don't distress yourself, my dear fellow," said Tobias. I'll endeavour to get a bed for myself, but vot's your charge my dear feller."

Oh! for the matter of that, ve don't charge not nothing here—our lodgings is all free, gratis, for nothing at all."

"Then they are too cheap to be good, that's all I can say," said Toby, " and so I must, for this once, decline it. Well, Jack, my brave fellow, time is up, you see; the die is cast, I must wanish, but what message must I take to the kids—kind love, and a kiss all round, eh?" said Toby.

"Give my best respects to all the brave fellows, and tell them you left me in good health, and brave spirits, with a hoping, wishful heart for another moonlight flit with them over Hounslow Heath. Tell them this, my sterling true old comrade, and as I wring your hand in fervent friendship, and gratitude, so grasp you all their brave palms for me."

"I will—I will," said Toby, a tear of sentimentality stealing into his eye " good bye, my dear Jack, good bye."

"Farewell, for the present," said Jack, gaily, "you will call again soon, my dear uncle, will you not," for such had Toby represented himself, for unless the visitors were bound by ties of consanguinity to the prisoners, or had a special order from a magistrate, an interview was never granted.

"I will, my dear nephy," said Toby, with an hypocritical burst of grief, " if the great and good Sir John Fielding, vill only grant me another order."

"Vich I have not the least doubt in the world, he will take particular delight in doing," said the turnkey, "he is such a very good man—what we should do without him, I really don't know, why this crib 'ud be empty, without his aid and assistance. But come along Mr. Wisiter, time's up, and there is a young woman in the lobby, what's been waiting half an hour, with a order in her fist, to see this precious nephy of yours."

"A young woman to see me!" said Jack, " who can she be?"

"Hang me, if I know," answered the jailor, " she calls herself your sister."

"Sister!" Jack was about to exclaim, "I have none," but a significant glance from Toby, silenced the hasty words, ere yet they were spoken.

"If she be my sister," said Jack, "she is a thousand times welcome, and I pray you will admit her at once. Uncle, my kind friend, once more I bid you adieu."

"Good bye, my dear nephy, good bye," said Toby, "I'm off. Fare thee well."

"How sentimental the old cock is getting to be sure," thought Jack. "Well, well, life is but a farce after all, and what would a farce be without a wry face in it? A precious piece of humbug that Toby is, and what a sterling heart he has in that rough bosom of his. Well, God bless him and all of them say I."

As he finished his soliloquy, the grating of the huge key in the lock, announced a visitor, and on the next instant the heavy door swung back upon its hinges, and the jailor thrust in his head, and exclaimed:

"A lady brings an order for admission to you, Muster Rann, may she come in?"

"Most assuredly, my dear fellow," said Jack, with his habitual gallantry, "a lady as a visitor, is at any time and all times a welcome guest."

"Step in marm, much obleeged to you I am sure, for the yellow boy. You'll excuse my locking the door on you, won't you? I wouldn't do it but it is more than my place is worth, to leave it alone."

The lady bowed her veiled head in acquiescence, but spoke not a word, as she advanced into the cell, the door of which was quickly closed behind her, and the ponderous lock, as it went clanging again into the socket, made the dismal galleries echo again.

CHAPTER XXX.

THE LADY VISITOR—THE ESCAPE—THE PURSUIT—A TRAGEDY.

As the lady entered the cell, Jack arose from the stone seat upon which he had been sitting, and bowing politely, as he advanced towards her, begged, in his old cheerful tone, to be informed who, so far forgetting the fear habitual to her sex, had had the courage to penetrate into the felon's dismal cell.

To this speech the lady made no reply, but, sobbing, with unconstrainable agony, she fell forward, fainting, upon our hero's neck. Then losing all power, and all consciousness, she would have fallen from thence heavily upon the stone floor, had not Jack's strong hand sustained and supported her.

"In God's name calm yourself, my dear madam," said Jack, "indeed, it is madness to give this violent vent to your grief, for no good can, by any possibility, accrue from it, and great danger may."

"Harm! how speak you thus of harm, who, standing on eternity's very verge, would have been supposed to have lost all thought and care for this world. Harm! if harm fall but on you, Jack, it would be no pity for any harm, even death itself to fall upon me, for, losing you, I myself am lost, and if I live, live but the life of misery, of the broken-hearted, for the tendons of our hearts, strained and cracked with bitter grief, yet cruelly refuse to snap asunder."

"What! Elinor Roche, my darling," said Jack, folding her to his bosom, and rapturously kissing away the tears that bedewed her eyes, "this is a pleasure unanticipated, yet wonderfully—entrancingly sweet."

"And yet, for me, alas! dear Jack, you, of all the men in the wide world, the only one I ever loved—to see you confined in this accursed cell, chained like a murderer, my God, it is cruel—inhuman—my heart will burst!"

"Tush, tush, my darling," said Jack, soothingly, "be a woman yourself, and let me beseech you to avoid making one of me.. What is past is gone, irrecoverably gone! I am in Newgate! Well, Elinor, it is my meed—I have earned it by robbery—pillage—by desperate crime."

"Alas! alas! that this confession should come from your lips, Jack!" said Elinor, wringing her hands with the anguish, that overpowered her soul and bowed her spirit, hitherto so proud, to the very earth.

"Yet Elinor, bad as I am, and still more as you may think me, one remembrance sits light upon my heart; these hands were never stained with human blood, Elinor; throughout my career of crime I have ever avoided blood-shedding."

"Thank heaven!" cried Elinor, fervently.

"Amen, say I," cried Jack, "were it not for this consolation, no verier coward on the face of the earth could be found to face death; but, having this innocence in my soul, if the fiat goes forth that I must die, I shall mount the steps of Tyburn tree of death with as firm a foot, and with as peaceful a heart, as if I were mounting the old staircase at Dashfield house, to my own happy bed."

"Would that we were there now," said Elinor, with exceeding fervour, "and that you did, in reality, love me, with the ardour you once professed to do."

"That you have had great cause to doubt me, Elinor, I confess, yet, by Heaven—"

"Nay, swear not by Heaven," said Elinor, with a solemnity, sweet and becoming at such a time, "for Heaven knows without an oath, and He knows I loved you as woman only loves, and this love, filling my whole heart, rendered me incapable of resisting your overtures, for so set was my every thought on you, I would have gone to the grave—through fire, but what I would possess you. And now, picture my feelings when I discovered your faithlessness—picture my madness—the hidious thoughts that lashed me on to my revenge! Oh, could you but do this, you would forgive me, you would indeed, the wrong I did you."

"What wrong, sweetheart?" said Jack, drawing the slender form of the lass nearer to him, "you speak in riddles, Elinor."

"Then you are not aware of my duplicity, Jack,—my heartless treachery towards you; but, as Heaven is my judge, I never thought or wished the evil to be so far extended—no, Jack, no!" and again she burst into a passionate flood of tears.

"I tell you what it is," said Jack, "if you don't let me understand what you are blubbering about, I'll be shot if I don't make myself uncommon scarce, by making the jailor show you the door."

"Don't drive me away, Jack," said the girl, vehemently. "Don't force me away, for Heaven's sake, unless you would see me fall a corpse at your feet."

"Don't mention it," said Jack, in a gay tone, "if there is anything in the world I've an horror of, its cold unwholesome bodies. Why, bless you, my charmer, you are as fascinating as ever, and I'll have a kiss at those cherry lips if I die for it." Jack had one, and not content with one, they clung together in a cordial embrace, and mingled soul to soul in one long delicious kiss.

"Good!" exclaimed Jack, drawing a long breath, rendered necessary by over exertion; "and now, old fellow, just tell me what's the matter to-night, and what the devil there is in the wind to render you so infernally miserable."

"Jack," said the girl, gravely, "you remember your parting night at Dashfield's House?"

"I should rather say I did," said Jack, " my eyes, what an unlucky scrape to get into—unhappy young man that I was!—why, he nailed me in the fact, and how the devil he grew so suspicious of me all of a sudden is a mystery to me, for I'll take my oath *I* never told him, and I'm almost equally certain, my lovely mistress and his right noble countess, did not."

"It was I who told him, Jack, said Elinor.

"You!" said Jack, receding from her in astonishment.

"Yes I," she answered "was so eat up with insatiable jealousy, was so maddened, that a love I thought my own was estranged from me by another, that, in my violent rage, I despatched a note to the earl, acquainting him with your presumption, and his wife's infidelity. Bitterly have I repented it since, Jack—yes, oftentimes have I wished my heart had burst ere my tongue had betrayed you, for, by that one act were you driven to crime—crime, the end of which, in a few short days at most, may be the gallows—your paramour, noble in all things but in this base act, paid the penalty of her sin with her life—"

"Elinor, what mean you?" said Jack, with eagerness.

"This," continued Elinor, sadly, "that she died, and that by the hand of her husband."

"Mean you he murdered her?" asked Jack.

"Yes," she replied, "if ever woman was murdered, she was, and by his hands."

"Base, cowardly bloodhound!" exclaimed Jack, in his grief, "and yet why need I rant, I that brought this doom upon her!"

"Say not so Jack, if not quite blameless, you were but guilty in the least degree, and even she should be spoken of in pity's low tones—pity should o'erweigh her crime, for, to be linked to such a libertine as the earl, to feel and know the dishonour almost daily heaped upon her, is enough to drive a woman, be she pure as heaven's own angels, to a wicked course. She was but mortal, and, feeling her wrongs grievously, she acted in revenge, as erring mortals would. For this revenge she paid, alas! a sad and deadly penalty, and let us hope, as the punishment far o'erweighed the crime, she has met in another and a better world, with the forgiveness denied her here upon earth."

"Amen!" said Jack, fervently, "but what of the Earl? I would have tidings of him. I myself rescued from his clutches Miss Malcolm, Lady Dashfield's sweet young friend."

"I know you did, Jack," said Elinor, "and am sufficiently superstitious to believe that a blessing for that good action will for ever rest upon you."

"The pleasure afforded me at the time was a sufficient blessing then, and for ever," said Jack.

"A good action is ever a constant reward in itself. This truth has been stirring in my heart since we parted at the Mansion House, Jack, and to-day I have come to realise it—to make it plain as daylight to my soul. Jack, I have come to SAVE YOU!"

"To save me!" said Jack, springing to his feet. "How, Elinor, how?"

"By proving your love—that shall be salvation to you. Do you still love me, Jack?"

"I do, and always did, fervently, dear Elinor," exclaimed our hero.

"It is enough almost—you are already half saved. Now, if your heart be true, prove it, and be saved quite!"

"How can I prove it?" asked Jack.

"Thus!" she replied, divesting herself of the feathered hat and riding-habit that she wore.

"What caper is this?" said Jack, in undisguised surprise.

"One, if fortune be but propitious, that shall save your life. Do not remonstrate, Jack, the time for that is past—the time for action has come—we are almost of the same stature, and size, so near, at all events, that those sleepy-headed jailors will not distinguish the difference."

"This mystery I cannot unravel, what hidden motive is there here?"

"What hidden motive—oh, man, how blind! The motive is escape from this cell—is life and liberty, Jack—the means are here. Assume my outward garments, and fly!"

Jack staggered as if he had been struck a violent blow. "And leave you here in thraldom," he exclaimed, "No, never!"

"What can they do to me?" she exclaimed, blythely. "The judge may chide—may imprison me, they can't hang me, you know, Jack. A month—a year or two shut up in jail, and never caged bird will sing more gaily than I, for I shall know my mate is on the wing, soaring at liberty."

"Elinor, my brave old darling, this is like your own noble self, but I cannot accept the sacrifice, my heart revolts at it."

"Of your vanity," said Elinor, "if you will not escape I will share your prison with you, of that I am determined. Do you fear the sneering of the gang? Let them say it was unmanly if they choose, but if they breathe such word to me, I will say to them, 'What is there that man may do to shield a woman, that woman may not do to succour him.'"

"I confess life is dear, and with you beside me, dear Elinor, to point to better fortune—I confess it is hard even to have fear of dying so young. I feel my doom is dreadful."

"Then flee from it whilst the means are yet at hand, and leaving these walls, commence life anew, Jack. Forsake the evil company that, like a festering sore, pollutes, as it crawls, its slimy path around thee. Forsake vice for virtue, and when I leave this place—which, in a few short days may chance to be, we will leave England for America, and commencing a new life in the new world, may yet live and prosper."

"You draw a picture I long to be realised," said Jack; "but to leave you here to suffer—I know not what—for me, Elinor, I cannnot—will not do it."

"On my knees, my dear Jack, let me beseech you to give over this mad fastidiousness. With the host of enemies you have about you, with the earl, the squire, Oliver, Luke Jones, craving for your blood, and all willing to bear false witness that it may be shed, I tell you, if put upon your trial, your doom is inevitable."

"I feel it so," said Jack, with a shudder.

"Then listen to the voice of reason—ha! already the turnkey's heavy footsteps approach, another instant and it will be too late!"

And, half maddened with terror, with the quickness of thought she wrapped her ample habit around, placed her feathered hat upon his head—thrust her handkerchief into his hand, that he might hide his features, and dragged him by main force to the cell door. The door opened—

"Now, marm, I'se sorry to disturb you, but time's up," said the turnkey, gallantly extending his arm, as he spoke, to assist the supposed young lady up the steps.

Jack had no time now for hesitation—he accepted the offered arm, and walking carefully, that the jingling of his irons might not betray him, he passed in safety from the prison into the street.

*   *   *   *   *   *   *

On leaving Newgate, Jack, by short and quick steps, and an uncertain mode of walking, endeavoured to imitate the action of a woman at that exercise, and, with his usual ability, he succeeded to perfection. It was now getting twilight, and the darkening night rendered still the darker, it would almost seem, from the dismal oil-lamps that endeavoured to illuminate it, favoured his escape. He crossed the Old Bailey, and turning down Fleet-lane, he made for Fleet Market, which then occupied the space now known as Farringdon-street; turning into a low tavern in this place, to get a glass of brandy, he well nigh discovered himself, for a party of bacchanals rolled in their uprorious merriments against him with considerable voilence, his bonnet, but lightly thrown upon his head, was dashed to the ground, and the jingle of his irons at the same moment gave ominous token to those who heard the clattering sound, that the person so gaily habited in riding costume before them was no lady, but an escaped prisoner. Uttering a yell, as the sound of the discovery met their ears, some dozen or so, in drunken glee, rushed upon on hero, to effect his capture, for the reward bestowed by the authorities for captured criminals was then considerable.

Jack's heart beat with feelings of hope and fear, as they advanced towards him; hope for his late escape from the thraldom of Newgate's dismal walls, despair at again being thrust ignominously back again. But even in the momentary space of time allotted for these thoughts, the gaze of the crowd glared nearer and fiercer upon him.

Comprehending at a glance the perilous nature of his situation, that violence against the force by which he was opposed would avail him nothing, and knowing from past experience how one daring action has oftentimes won over a crowd, he determined to state who he was, and trust to their generosity; and wisely was this resolve taken, as the sequel verified.

A brawny butcher elbowed his way through the crowd, and placing his hand heavily on Jack's shoulder, exclaimed:

"What, ho, my whipper-snapper—my gay young prison bird, you have nabbed it have you?"

"Hands off, my hearty, or you may catch a hit in your mouth that may spoil your supper. And Jack gathering up his energies sent the butcher backwards with such force, that, staggering, he slipped to the ground—a roar of laughter greeted his fall. Taking advantage of this merriment, and the uproar that arose from it, to throw aside his womanish disguise, Jack stood revealed to them in his glorious and celebrated costume of SIXTEEN STRING JACK, the dashing and courageous knight of the road.

"Now, gentlemen," he said, "you see before you Jack Rann, the highwayman, who, having by the aid of female dress, escaped from Newgate, has sought refuge here, and places his safety in your honour."

A loud and unanimous burst of applause greeted this speech, happily worded as it was to suit their rough but honest natures, and so zealously did the butcher respond to the admiration thus suddenly awakened, that, flying towards our hero, he grasped his hand, and swore by every oath in his memory (which, by-the-bye, was a goodly catalogue), "to defend him whilst there was a drop of blood in his heart."

Jack, responding to the butcher's pressure with a hearty shake of the wrist, said—

"Nay, do not misjudge me, my friends, I did not come here to seek protection, for Jack Rann could always protect himself."

"So you could, Jack!" shouted the now enraptured throng.

"I came here, knowing from my own feelings as an Englishman, that anything in the guise of a woman, is a being to expect our respectful behaviour in all cases, likewise, one who should and could command our assistance if she needed it. But, coming as I did amongst you a strange being, even though clad in woman's dress, what reason had I to expect anything from such strange but honest fellows, but a welcome, such as my rough friend, the butcher here, gave me? None whatever, my dear fellows; and now, in throwing aside the fictitious habiliments, I also throw myself upon your mercy and bounty. I am Jack Rann, for whose head, dead or alive, a heavy reward has been offered. I am Jack Rann, who you have but to drag to Newgate—but a few steps hence—and gold galore shall be your reward. What! even now, do none of you advance to seize me? What fear you? I am unarmed, and even if I were, I declare by heaven I would not use them, for so sick am I of this cowardly traitor's heart that encompasses me about, that if there be a man amongst you who has heart enough to betray me—in God's name let him go and do it."

"If he values his life a straw's end, let him stop, say I," thundered the butcher, "for if he moves a peg, I'll cut his liver out!" and, drawing from his leathern belt a formidable knife, used for slaughtering swine, he held it in a style by far too ferocious and threatening to be pleasant, and one withal, so professionally cool, that the lookers on read in his cool but determined eye, the thoughts of one, who, speaking words, would have made but little matter of realising them.

The landlord seeing how matters stood, and feeling rather honoured than otherwise by our hero's preference for this house, which, in his own mind he had already determined to call *Sixteen string Jack's Arms*, sprang over the bar, and standing by the side of our hero, spoke the following ever-to-be-remembered words: first, we must premise, having taken the precaution to fasten the door against any new comers.

"Mr. Sixteen-strings," said he, bowing to our hero, which Jack returned.

"Mr. Bob, the butcher," to which Mr. Bob replied. "Vell, old frizzle-vig, vot's in the vind?"

"Gemmen and ladies," continued the landlord, which, being then as now a figure of speech, or rather, the powerful figure in a speech, was almost pardonable, but, considering the old landlord had but a specimen of the genus feminine in his possession, or in the house, and that a canary that wouldn't sing, duty compels us to make a note of the errata. But to the speech, as we before reported, he commenced "gemmen and ladies," and we now proceed to give *verbatim et literatim*, the outpourings of the worthy publican, who commenced his harangue after the style of a certain notorious character well known to Shaksperian readers, which we hope includes the whole civilised world.

"What is it that I sees afore me? Is it a dagg-har in his hand? Drop it, Bob, and do come to me, for there the noble Jack Rann stands, and all round and round about us, jolly coves is to be seen. Devil a von on 'em vould betray him, for 'twould be a *gallows* shame."

"So it would, I'm afraid," said Rann, with a laugh, "but drive on, my worthy."

"Vot's our duty now tovards him? Arn't it to succour, cheer, and save? O' course it is, and shall we suffer him for to fall in a felon's grave? Not a bit on it, my hearties. Its all gammon, precious stuff! Instead of betraying him, ve vill keep him—drop that knife, you precious muff."

The last remark was made to Bob, who still kept flourishing the knife after the hazardous fashion Tom Barry occasionally twirls his shillaleigh at Batty's.

"Jack Rann having hooked it from Newgate wall—arn't it our duty to keep him well? If there's a man here wot would betray him, devil take him if he's a man at all, and may he speedily go to h——. That's my wish, you knows I means it. Now, my lads, be good as gold, Jack Rann's a cove wot's free and generous; Jack Rann, the highwayman, brave and bold! And a brave welcome we will give him—a welcome worthy of him, kids; so patter away, and get the grub out, he shall eat, and drink, and swill, and shall stop to resurrection, and be welcome if he will."

"Thank you," said Jack, "but I have an appointment for an hour or so elsewhere, and will gladly be off with your kind permission. Regale these fellows in my absense, and let them rely on it, they will never regret having befriended Jack Rann. Here are five guineas towards an entertainment for them, and I have five more for any gallant fellow who will cleave these fetters from my legs, and yet another five for any friend among ye who will give me a hat, and change coats with me this night."

"Keep your guineas in your pocket, friend Jack—excuse my familiarity, but I will manage it all for you without expense, for God only knows the time may come when the guineas you have may be serviceable to you; so keep them I beseech you; I will free you from your irons, and if the suit I have on is of any service to you, get into them at once—I'll peel without a murmur."

"Friend, I accept your offer, for I feel I cannot adopt a safer diguise than that of a butcher."

"Too ral, loo-ral, I'm as happy as a prince—here goes," and regardless of the lookers on, the good-hearted butcher commenced at once to divest himself of his habiliments. Jack donned them as fast as the other cast them aside, and, in less than three minutes, stood fully equipped in a butcher's attire, and decidedly well armed.

Before they would allow him to depart, they pledged him in a portly bowl of punch, and so warmed and exhilerated did they feel by its effects, that several offered to form a body-guard, and escort our hero in safety, wheresoever or withersoever he desired—but as this Jack at once foresaw would be the means of drawing suspicion upon them—a climax decidedly to be avoided, lest a recognition might result from it, he determined to run the gauntlet alone. Bidding them, therefore, adieu at last, he struck into the labyrinth of streets, which then extended from the Fleet to Temple Bar. Pursuing his way along the Strand, he took a near cut across the fields to the city of Westminster, in those halcyon days, counted almost a days march by the good citizens of London.

Whilst walking rapidly, he suddenly came upon three men, whom he at once recognised without difficulty, to be the officer who had last apprehended him, and in the other two he at once discovered his betrayers, Luke Jones and Night-owl Oliver.

"Good night measters," he said, as he joined, and imitating the tones and manners of a bumpkin, "dark beant it and dismal loike, mayhap you wouldn't have no dejection to allow me to 'company you, it will be more social loike."

"What are you frightened you booby?" said Oliver, "what courageous fellows these yokels are."

"I beant frightened, o' you, old black muzzle, though you're almost enuff to frighten the devil himself with that black mug o' thine, but feeling lonesome loike, I thought as how company were preferable loike. But howsomdever, if you have any dejection, I can drop behind you knows, I beant the man to dip my nose unbidden into any man's porridge."

"Come along my brave fellow," said the tipstaff, "you are heartily welcome to our company, but our friend here is somewhat ruffled in his temper, a friend of his having managed to escape from Newgate a short time since."

"And he be surly over that, well I never knew the loike, why if freend o' mine was to escape so fash, I should be ready to stand on my head, and whistle "o' be joyful," I should be so enormous glad."

"But if the boot was on the other leg, and it was enemy who had escaped, and by that enemy's escape you were too lose five hundred pounds, how should you feel then?"

"Feel is it? like a fool I guess, ready to eat my own calf's head wi' spoite, but lawk a mercy you don't mean to go for to say that any one has escaped, what the king has set five hundred pounds on? Why the loike was never heerd on—why who can he be?"

"It could be no other than the man it is, for none other would have had the audacity to have done it. It is Jack Rann," replied the officer, " or Sixteen-string Jack, as he is called, who has again evaded the ends of the law."

"Do you mean to say he be got quite clear off?"

"I do," answered the officer, " but knowing his haunts as we do, there is but little fear but we shall have him again speedily."

"Got clear off! Ho, ho, ho!" laughed Jack, loud and long, " little Jack escaped agin, how glad I be, surely!"

"Glad!" echoed Luke and Oliver together, as they turned their scowling glances upon the supposed butcher, " What do you mean by being glad? Don't you know its against the law, and that you are liable yourself to be taken up as an accomplice?"

"Don't put yourselves out, my beauties," said Jack, with an expression of so much contempt and satire, that Oliver's brow crimsoned, and his fist clenched involuntarily, at the insulting words of mockery. " You are such a perfect angel to look at—a regular beauty without paint, it's a thousand pities to twist and contort your handsome muzzle, for if von of them ere booksellers at the sign of the Book and Gridiron in Paternoster Row, only had your likeness on their title pages, they'd make their fortins, that's a fact, for vouldn't everybody rush to buy the portrait of a handsome man?"

"If I have any of your chaff, Mr. Butcher, I'll spoil your beauty for you; so you'd better put the kybosh on that red rag of yourn."

"I'm afeard I've got into bad company," said Jack, appealing to the officer, " why he actually patters flash—how very vulgar, low, and priggish."

Oliver uttered a brutal oath, and lifting his huge hand as though he would have smote our hero to the ground, if he dared, muttered between his clenched teeth an oath that he would pull him up.

"Pull me up, will you?" reiterated our hero in a taunting tone, " vell do, for you can't knock me down, that's a fact, for you ain't got the power in your elbow. Why, big as you are, you walking lump of blacking, I'd tip you such a stunner as 'ud make you spin like a peg top."

"Come, come, no quarreling," said the officer, authoritatively. I can't and won't allow it."

"Well, what did he go for to call me an accomplice for?" asked Jack, with well assumed indignation, " I arn't no thief, I arn't and if he was to pull me up, he'd very soon be glad to put me down again."

"He was only threatening of you said the officer, in a pacifying tone, " so drop it, do you hear? As for you," he continued, turning to Oliver, " I am ashamed that you, knowing the important business we are on, can find time to pick a quarrel with an inoffensive man."

This speech of the runner so galled Oliver to the quick, that, fixing his teeth upon his under-lip, he bit it till the blood came, but, by a sudden and determined effort, he mastered his indignation, and maintained a sullen silence until they came upon the rear of Toby's hostelrie. Jack still kept in their company, like a true fellow, as he was, for he felt his safety was less at stake than those of his brave companions, within that doomed house.

"Which do you say is the room?" asked the officer, in a whisper which Jack's quick ears, however, did not fail to catch.

Oliver, pointing to a window, replied, "It is there."

"But to get there?" queried the officer.

"Pass in at the front door; the first turning in the passage brings you to the bar, pass boldly through the bar, into the bar parlour, and there, if you nab not him, you are certain to pounce upon some of his infernal gang."

"You still decline to accompany us then," said the officer.

"Do you think I want my throat cut?" answered Oliver, surlily. "I told you I would not go in. By God I would rather venture into a lion's den than there, for one, equally with the other, would be certain death," and spite of his dogged and daring manner, the traitor shuddered visibly.

"Then wait you outside, and you too, Jones; I am known to the majority of them, and I don't believe they would harm me; beside, seeing I am alone, I might perhaps prevail upon one or two of them to come with me peaceably, for the asses might flatter themselves there is the chance of an escape; to prevent which, however, look well to the priming of your pistols."

"Like a fool," said Oliver, "I have forgotten mine, but I have a knife here that has done me good service before," and he bared the blade of a formidable clasp knife, as he spoke, "and would doubtless do its work again, should it come to a tussel."

"You have pistols, Jones?" inquired the runner.

"I have," replied Jones, with fiendish eagerness, "and all I ask you is to show me a chance of using them."

"That, mayhap, you may have presently, but whilst I think of it, where's the butcher?"

"He slunk off a few minutes ago," replied Oliver; who little knew that our hero lay crouched to the ground within the shadow of the building, an eager listener to their conversation.

"I am almost glad he is gone," said the officer, "for the less seen lurking about here the better for our plans. On second thought, I am not so certain but it might be the better for you also to make yourself invisible, it would be less likely to draw the attention of passers-by, suppose for instance you hide in this shed, you can easily emerge on hearing my signal."

"What will that be?" enquired Jones.

"A low whistle," replied the officer, "three times repeated, on hearing which, come forth at once, and now my lads to your posts, and I will hie me at once to mine."

Jones proceeded at once to the shed, which composed a wing of the old houses, and entering, as if he had been bidden, he threw the door after him Quick as lightning, the thought struck Jack, that the door was fastened on the outside by an iron staple, and as Oliver moved forward to watch the officer's entrance into the house, Jack sprang noiselessly to his feet, and shooting the bolt into the staple prepared for it, Luke Jones was securely caged within.

"Bravo!" chuckled Jack to himself, "friend Luke you have a safe abiding place till the morning, with logs of wood for bed and pillows—if you wake not with sore bones, may I never wake again!"

Jack crept back to his old position, but suddenly remembering a spot where he could see without being seen, he took the circuit of the building, and finding a corner situated advantageously for his purpose, he stood completely opposite to Night-owl Oliver, although entirely hidden from view.

Whilst the traitor and victim were thus employed, we will follow the career of the adventurous officer.

Gaining admittance to the house, after some little delay, he, following Oliver's directions, found himself in the presence of Toby, and one or two others whom he did not know, but to whom, unfortunately for him, his professional features were perfectly familiar. One of them, nudging Toby, who was comfortably dozing in his easy chair, that worthy yawned once or twice, then suddenly opening his eyes to an enormous width, he became aware of the runner.

"Holla, Mr. Barnes," which was the name of the officer, "What's in the wind, that I have the pleasure of your company?"

"A little business that's all," said Barnes, with a knowing smile, "but as I like to manage all my affairs in as comfortable a style as possible, suppose you order me a glass of whiskey-punch and we'll discuss the matter easily."

"Werry good," said Toby, then summoning an assistant, the steaming beverage, with the accompaniment of a long pipe—a regular yard of clay, and no mistake—was placed before Mr. Barnes, who, with a few vigorous puffs, soon gave a tinge to the room, as though it had been impregnated with a black fog.

"Well," said Toby, admiringly, "that is the werry thing I likes to see, a man enjoy his pipe, vy vot a smoker you is to be sure. Strike me sensible, but you does do your bacca in a business like style."

"I does, I know," said the flattered officer, "and always did. Well Toby," said Barnes, after a pause, "I have called to ask a particular favour."

"Give it a name," said Toby, "and if its in the house, consider it done."

"I am pretty certain it is *in the house*," said Barnes, laying a peculiar stress on the latter words, "the fact is," and he ahem'd and coughed, "I want a few moments' conversation with Mr. John Rann."

"Jack Rann," said Toby, with a hearty laugh, "why Barnes, what a funny dog you is. Why you have called at the wrong shop, why didn't you knock at Newgate as you came along?"

"I did," answered Barnes, "and found he had left those lodgings without giving a moment's notice to the landlord, for your's."

"What!" exclaimed Toby, with startling amazement, "why, what do you mean?"

"Exactly what I say, and that is, Jack Rann has escaped from Newgate in the disguise of a woman, and has left the fool, whose dress he borrowed, in prison in his stead, and there she'll lay until she rots—the fool!—unless we find him, which," he said, altering his tone, "it strikes me, won't be long, for we have tracked him to this place; ah, you needn't look so surprised Toby, by God it's a fact! So, perhaps, stowing all chaff and nonsense—for we had quite enough of your witticisms the other night at Rann's lodgings—you will deliver him at once into my custody?"

"Deliver him into your custody. If he *was* here, I tell you plainly I'd see you d——d first, but as he ain't here, you may go to the devil, for anything I care, to search, and be blowed, old cockalorum.'

"You'll repent this insolence, sirrah!" said Barnes, rising, his face crimsoned with passion, "the house is surrounded by my men, who only need my signal to raze this cursed place to the ground."

"Give them the signal, by all manner of means," said Toby, "I ain't afraid of you, if all Bow-street was here, so you needn't look so fierce Mr. Thiefcatcher, for I know, if you pull my old house to the ground, either you or your master, the king, must build me a new one, so pull away, I'm quite willing."

"This is worse than madness," said the officer, sternly, "you have Sixteen-string Jack hid here, and unless you deliver him up to me I will indict you for keeping a rendezvous for theives and bad characters."

"Do you call me a thief, you murthering vagabond," said O'Brien, who, followed by Sheppard and Wide Awake, now entered the room, and caught the latter words of the thieftaker's speech, "by the sowl of Moses, i'll bate that thick skull of thine with this cudgel, till I make it as soft as mealy praties."

The officer, well armed as he was, smiled scornfully at the threat, and his eye suddenly alighting on Wide Awake, he sprang forward to seize him, crying, as he did so, in a triumphant tone.

"What ho! I've nabbed the jackal, the lion cannot be far off!"

"Not so fast, Barnes, my boy," said Wide Awake, "no catchee no havee, you know. What do you want me for ? Show your warrant, can't you ?"

"I can," said the officer, flourishing it triumphantly, "under the hand and seal of Sir John Fielding, a warrant for the apprehensson of one Colledge, alias Wide Awake, for highway robbery and burglary."

"That's me, sure enough," said Colledge, "but feeling so much flattered by his worship's excellent name, 'Wide Awake,' I really cannot at the present belie my name, so you will excuse, I am sure, my giving you the slip!"

"If you stir a step from where you stand," said Barnes, scowling vindictively towards Wide Awake, and drawing forth a pistol as he spoke, "I'll drive a bullet through your skull."

Wide Awake grew pale as death—his breath grew thick and heavy, and he seemed for the moment paralysed by fear. This emotion lasted but an instant though, as, bending his glance upon his adversary, he muttered through his clenched teeth—

"That is your game, is it, the stake's life or death ; well, then, come on."

He suddenly threw himself backward; the officer as suddenly fired! When the smoke disappeared, Wide Awake was gone. The officer's quick eyes caught a glimpse of a person under the bed, which we have before mentioned elsewhere, stood in the room. The next moment the sound of the trap-door, as it sprang back to it's place, fell upon the ear. With the instinctiveness of his crafty race, allied only to that of the ferocious and determined blood-hound, the officer dashed under the bed.

A moment's silence, and all in that room stood gazing on each other with faces of deathly paleness, with suspended breath, like men anticipating a horrible catastrophe.

What sound is that breaking the stillness of the time, that calls forth a groan from every mortal listening?

It was the fall of a human body, a wailing sound of human agony, and all was hushed—hushed in death!

A few minutes sped on; Wide Awake re-appeared—his hair disordered—his eyes bloodshot—his whole frame quivering with the agony of his guilty soul—his whole body tottering, from the scene of horror and death of which he had been an eye-witness, and in which he had been a guilty participator

"Wide Awake, in God's name tell me, what have you done."

"Murder!" shrieked, rather than spoke, the unhappy man, "but he brought his doom upon himself, and forced the crime upon me. Give me water for the love of God—I am choking!"

He drained the goblet they extended to him at a draught.

Seemingly revived, he said: "He was close upon my track—so close that nothing could save but the WELL, the fear of death was on me, I unchained the lid, it fell, and he fell too," said Colledge, with a shudder that ran through the assembly, "striking his head upon the well's edge, a brainless corpse into the dark waters."

"If that bullet had gone through your skull," said Shepherd, pointing to an indentation on the wall, "it would have been cold gruel for you, and that Mr. Barnes intended it should there can be no doubt. I therefore consider you, friend Wide Awake, not guilty of murder, but what he would have been guilty of had he shot you, and that is—justifiable homicide."

Sheppard's straightforward and simple speech was received with applause and somewhat quieted down by the soothing words of his friend, Wide Awake took a seat among them, and as they believed the statement of Barnes, that the house was surrounded by constables, the conversation turned upon what excuse could be made for the disappearance of the officer, and how the body was to be disposed of; that, they were fully aware, for the time, would be an impenetrable mystery, but they feared a future day would come, when the hideous contents of the well might stand revealed to mortal eye.

Leaving them to their cogitations, we will rejoin Jack Rann.

Our hero still continued on the alert, watching every movement of Oliver with the eye of an eagle. Time went, and save and excepting the report of the shot which fell distinctly upon his ear, there seemed no more commotion than if the thiefcatcher had remained without the house. Jack was growing decidedly impatient, when the sound of horses' hoofs, advancing towards the house, caused him to look up, and doing so, he beheld, to his infinite joy, his beloved companions in arms, Clayton and Jared Steele.

As they passed him, disguising his voice as well as he was able, he touched his hat and asked permission to hold their horses.

"Get out of the way my fine fellow, our horses are too well trained to need a loon like you to hold them."

"Well, looking at them a second time," said Jack, in his natural voice

"I should say there is but little fear of their bolting—unless its bolting their grub when they get it."

Both Clayton and Jared sprang from their saddles, as the old familiar and well-loved voice fell upon their ears, and each seizing him by the arm, they drew him under a lamp, and anxiously scanned his features; a simultaneous cry of joy came from their lips, and Clayton was so enraptured he fairly hugged him to his bosom.

"Oh, Jack, my stunner, my noble out an'outer, are you real flesh and blood, or only a ghost?"

"Something more than a vision, I trust," said Jack, as he wrung Kit's hand heartily, then extending it to Steele, "Well, Jared, my good fellow, have you no welcome for me?"

"My heart leaps with joy at the sight of you, and I feel so unexpectedly happy like, I am quite a woman, look at my glistening eyes."

"Crying, by Jove!" said Jack.

"Yes," said Jared, "but thank Heaven they are tears of joy—but Jack, my noble friend, what miracle is this?"

"No miracle Jared, but a service from an angel in the shape of woman, who, loving more fondly than wisely, insisted upon my assuming her clothes, whilst she remained in prison in lieu of me."

"She has the courage of a noble woman," said Jared. "and that she may never repent her devotion I sincerely hope."

"There is no fear of that, Steele, if they dragged her to Tyburn, in dying for me, I verily believe she would die bravely and undauntedly, yea, even happily. But hist, lads; in the delight of this meeting I forgot a little necessary caution—we are watched, Barnes, the Bow-street runner, and the two villains who betrayed me, are over here."

Clayton drew out his pistols, and looked to the priming, "Where are they, Jack? I'll make short work of the lot."

"Gently, Barnes is inside, Luke Jones, an old country friend of mine, is in the outhouse, securely fastened in, and consequently helpless, and out of harm's way—the third, Night-owl Oliver, is standing over in yon dark corner, his lynx-like eyes are glaring on me, even whilst I speak."

Clayton sprang forward to seize him, but when he reached the spot indicated by Jack's outstretched finger, the villain was gone. Kit looked eagerly round, but the look was fruitless.

"He has made himself scarce, and it is well for him he has done so. Now, friend Jack, it will never do for you to loiter here, there is danger in it."

"Can you point out a spot that is not fraught with danger, to one proscribed and hunted like myself. All places are alike to me, for there is danger in every place."

"Point out a place," repeated Clayton, thoughtfully, "no, Jack, hang me if I can."

"I can," said Jared, calmly.

"What is your proposition?" asked Jack.

"That you take Clayton's horse, and ride back with me to Barnet, they are but a couple of hacks that we hired there. A few miles further on, my father and his gang of gipsies, lie encamped; they are sworn fellows and true, and if you can put up with their rough usage for a time, no safer hiding place could be found for you on English ground. There you may rest in peace and security, until the storm blows over, or you have an opportunity of reaching a foreign land."

"It is a capital thought, by Jove," said Clayton, enthusiastically, "and worthy of the bright little head that dictated it."

"I feel it so," said Jack, gratefully.

"Then let us at once to horse, you have a capital disguise, no better could be found in England. It is growing fast towards night, and we have a long ride before us."

"I should like just one word with Toby."

"Not a sentance, not a syllable, it would be most impolitic and unwise, never fear, but he has heard of your escape, and glories in it, heart and soul."

"If he ain't heard on it, poor unenlightened wretch," said Clayton, "and now old fellow, I won't detain you, good bye, success go with you."

Returning his parting words cheerily, Jack and Jared turned their horses heads towards the road leading to Barnet.

CHAPTER XXIX.

JACK AMONG THE GIPSEYS—FINDS A HORSE THAT COMPENSATES HIM FOR THE TEMPORARY LOSS OF OLD SUE—TREACHERY AGAIN, AN ANECDOTE OF WHAT LED TO IT—A RACE FOR LIFE.

JACK found the gipseys as Steele had described, a free-hearted, jovial, rollicking set, for many days he lived in their company, and saw nothing but happiness, their life so very changeful and hilarious with its occasional exigences, all had its charms for Jack. To the majority of the gang Jack speedily became a great favourite, but amongst them were not lacking two or three who considered him an interloper. Their meaning was not expressed in words, but their sullen looks and equivocal answers betrayed them. Although Jack had not the slightest suspicion, yet it was to the thoughtful Jared a source of considerable uneasiness, so much so that during his temporary absence he had engaged a lad named Zekiel to watch and report their movements.

About this time Jack received a visit from Clayton and Sheppard, who, having an engagement a few miles from thence—which engagement was neither more or less than a burglary, by-the-bye—they had visited the encampment, with the view of spending a day or so with their old pal. Jack was of course delighted to see them, and joining with ardour in their views, was all heart to join them in the expedition; there was one obstacle, however, and that, what appeared an insurmountable one, he neither had a horse, or the means of purchasing one, and without this desideratum—for then safety would lay in their speed—his services would tend to injury, rather than good.

Happening to hear the gipsey talking of a noted little mare, close at hand, whom one of the gang, the boy Zekiel, had occasionally borrowed for a marauding expedition, Jack went in search of her stable, and, with his usual luck, found it.

She had been browsing in the paddock, when Jack crouched beneath the window of her stable, but being plentifully gifted with the lady-like gift of curiosity, she had approached and rested her nose upon his shoulder to see what he was about; and, by way of intimating her presence, uttered a snort. Jack, in admiration at her beauty, gently patted her side, and exclaimed :—" Hallo, sweetheart !"

His good-tempered tone and action appeared to make a most favourable impression upon the amiable young stranger, who was not only superior to the prevalent coquetry of her sex, but actually made the tenderest advances, by rubbing her lips against his hand. Encouraged by the action, Jack drew the lips apart and found that she was not yet four years old, and as he playfully touched her with his whip, and stepped back a pace or two to admire her movements, he further found that, for fire and action she surpassed every animal he had ever beheld, excepting of course his own mare Sue.

Rann was an enthusiast in horses; he was a thorough judge, and viewed them with the eye of an artist. Every thought of whatever evil might be hatching against him in the tent, and he had been warned by Jared there was mischief afoot, vanished as he fixed his admiring gaze upon the surpassing animal before him, and he dwelt upon each attraction, as a lover upon the charms of a mistress.

It seemed as if Araby, Turkey, and Barbary had united to bestow their respective excellencies on one steed. Her finely-formed head was small and slender, with a broad flat forehead, and narrow pricked ears of the utmost delicacy. Her eyes, particularly the pupils, were unusually large and prominent, and as brilliant as two suns; her nose was long and arched, and the thin lips of her delicately split mouth were as rosy as a girl's. Her clean, finely-drawn throat and arched neck terminated in a chest of the utmost amplitude, and withers sharpened and elevated in exact proportion with the shoulders.

The trunk had been formed in the mould of grace, and was in such beautiful condition, that the firm flesh swelled on each side of the curved and elastic spine, and formed, as it were, a natural cushion of velvet. In the hind quarters she was equally perfect, being characterised by enormous breadth of loin, shortness and fulness of flank, and roundness and plumpness of crupper, which, while possessing that slight degree of elevation that has been found so essential to the just finish of a racer's qualities, was yet confined within the line of strict beauty. The admiration became thus divided between the excellent muscular condition of the haunches, and the superiority of their formation. The tail was firm and thick at the dock, and at least a yard long; the thighs were ample and fleshy, and the knee-joints large; from that to the fetlock the distance was short, exact, and proportioned, for nature seemed to have formed the extraordinary creature by the nicest rules of calculation. The hough was broadly displayed, with the tendon Achilles standing finely out, like a rope of twisted cat-gut; while, from each prominent fetlock, waved tufts of hair as long and silky as a lady's ringlets. Broad, well-sized pasterns; elevated coronet; hoofs, solid as oak, black as coal, and shining as ebony, high instep round quarters, broad projecting heels, a small thin frog, and a thick concave sole, completed the individual beauties of an animal, which Sixteen-string Jack had never seen equalled.

Like a child viewing a first-rate toy, Jack's delight knew no bounds; he could have hugged the animal for her beauty, and actually laughed aloud with excitement. The steed answered with a neigh, and darted off to the edge of the paddock, then frisked back like a kitten at play. "Was ever such a beauty?" said the highwayman, filliping the side of her chest with the tips of his fingers, and causing her to rear on her hind legs like a well-educated dog at an exhibition. "Is that it, my lady?" continued Rann. "Well, if you are inclined for dancing, allow me to ask the honour of your hand?" and, in the spirit of fun, he pointed out his foot as if he had been born and bred a dancing master, and extended his arms like a Taglioni. At that moment a sudden movement, made simultaneously by Kit and Sheppard, who had approached unnoticed, arrested the attention of our hero, and he instinctively grasped his riding whip as he saw them coming towards him.

"Down, down on your face, captain," whispered Kit; "the Philistines are upon us."

Jack stayed not to question, but threw himself upon the ground, and in an instant the mare did the like, as if she considered the action a new feature in the game they had been playing. Down, at the same moment also, did Clayton and his companion fling themselves close against the shed, in the shadow of the horse, and scarce had they done so, ere they heard the door on the other side opened, followed by the sound of footsteps.

"Remember!" said a voice, which they knew to be that of Night-owl Oliver, "my name musn't be breathed in the affair. I don't want the gang to know who blowed upon them; nor do I, for my own sake, wish to throw any light upon my own whereabouts. All I want is to get that infernal young bully out of the way, for my mind wont be easy, nor my honour satisfied, till I see him dancing upon the invisible tight-rope, at Tyburn."

"And I am to have another ten guineas the moment I return?" asked a second voice, to which Sixteen-string Jack was a stranger.

"Yes, if you don't make a bungle of the matter," returned Oliver. "You must see the Lord Mayor himself, mind, and give him the packet, without a soul knowing a word about it, or else all will go wrong. You say you can get there and back without being missed?"

"I can, and many a good night's work have I done in the same way. Why, ever since she was housed in this paddock for the winter, I've had six night's work a week out of her; and yet she keeps her condition so well hat the farm people don't suspect a word about it. Last night only, I visited twenty hen-roosts a mile apart, over harassing ground, and yet she came in as fresh as a daisy."

"Does she go swiftly?" asked Oliver.

"Like the wind," said the other, whom Jack rightly surmised to be one of the gipseys. "I've known her, when on her mettle, to cover twenty-five feet of ground at a single stroke, and I wouldn't mind backing her to do a mile a minute."

"Well, take care they don't find you out at your tricks, that's all," said Oliver. "Is she ready for use now?"

"I'd just strapped the saddle-girth when you came up."

"Well, get into the saddle as soon as you like. She must henceforward become your own property, for you'll not be able to get back before daylight, even if the mare could do the distance; and, when once missed, the look out will be too sharp to make return safe."

"It'll be running a plaguy risk, though!" resumed the gipsey. "However, it's worth one's while, so I'm off. But stay, I must first put out the fire, and remove the other signs of our meeting."

"I shall leave you to do that alone, then, for it's infernally chilly standing here," said Oliver, "come, Steele," continued he, "what say you to a pipe and a tankard, Long Jemmy and myself have a capital move in view, and it may be worth your while to join us."

"With all my heart," said a voice, which, by its huskiness appeared to proceed from an older person than the first gipsey.—"Times have been d—d bad this winter, and I don't care what game I play to mend them.' These words were followed by a confused murmur of mingled adieus, encouragements, and admonitions, and, eventually, the sound of retreating footsteps announced that the conspirators had separated. Jack and his companions, however, still lay perdue where they had first concealed themselves and distinctly heard a man moving about inside the stable, as if busied in arranging it in order. Having completed his task, he came out humming a gay air, and, making his way to the end of the building opposite the door, made his approach to the grey mare, without any idea of what was in store for him. Jack looked, it was Zekiel.

He was a well made, handsome youth of about eighteen, with ivory teeth, jet black eyes, ebony hair, and mahogany complexion. Jack could not forbear admiring him, but no sooner did he touch the bridle, to assist the mare in rising, than all thoughts of admiration vanished, and the three highwaymen sprung to their feet. Jack's hand was on the gipsey's throat in an instant.

"We mean you no hurt," cried Rann, "but a word, except in answer to us, and you are dumb for ever."

"Ask the young gentleman, who is no doubt a very respectable member, of society," said Kit, "where he has stowed his package to my lord mayor. Kim, dub it up, young mulberry-wash, or I'll take that bit of acquiline of yours between my finger and my thumb, and proceed with all possible expedition to do vot vill greatly annoy your tender susceptibilities."

"Leave him to me," said Rann. "The lad shall not be ill-used unless he deserves it. And now compose yourself, my nobby one, and tell us your name."

"Zekiel Steele," answered the gipsey, in a more careless than disconcerted tone.

"Steele—a very good name for a thief," returned Jack.

"I'm no thief," said the man; "I'm only a poor gipsey chap."

"Stop, stop, stop! Don't go quite so fast." interrupted our hero. "It can be proved on the evidence of these gentlemen and myself that you had saddled and bridled a mare, not your own property, for the purpose of taking it to London; and we have only to give this in detail before the nearest magistrate, and to add that we found the animal in your possesion, to get you hanged out of the way, or to have you sent across the herring-pond at least."

The gipsey scratched his head, and looked like one in a dilemma.

"Reyther perplexing, e'n't it?" said Kit.

"Not at all," answered the gipsey; "I have that about me which will form my excuse, and bring me into favour instead of disgrace with the justice."

"And what is that?" asked our hero.

"A clue to the discovery of Sixteen-string Jack," answered the quick-witted gipsey, fixing his laughing eye, full of meaning, upon Rann.

"Yes, yes; we know all about that." interrupted Sheppard; "but give it up, you young scoundrel, or I'll crack your pate for you."

"Gently, gently," said Rann, "unless I mistake, he's inclined to serve us without having his pate cracked," then, turning to the gipsey, he added, "will you favour me with a view of these papers? I promise to return them if we cannot come to an agreement."

Zekiel made no answer, save by silently taking from his bosom a clumsily folded packet, and handing it to our hero. Jack tore it open, and found it to be an ambiguously worded intimation of his and his comrades' whereabouts, and asking for assistance to capture them.

Jack felt as if he could have brained the treacherous villain; but suppressing his indignation, he turned to the gipsey, and said—"You were to have twenty guineas for this job?" Steele nodded, and Rann resumed—

"What would you take to leave it alone?"

"Service under Sixteen-string Jack himself," answered the gipsey, again fixing his penetrating eye full of confidence and meaning upon our hero. Rann returned the glance, and that single interchange of looks appeared to lay open the souls of each, and to establish a bond of faith between them. Distrust and evil intent vanished on the instant, and Jack, without any hesitation, stretched out his hand.

"I see you know me, and take you at your word," he said, "I have confidence in you, for I am certain no relative of Jared Steele can be a traitor."

"Vell, I'm blessed!" shouted Kit with astonishment. "Is the wictim a going to make friends with his own betrayer?"

"Reyther perplexing, e'n't it?" said Gabriel, laughingly echoing Kit's former words. Kit would have answered by a rap on the head, had not Sheppard, who readily understood the true footing of matters, interposed by shaking hands with the gipsey, and welcoming him as a brother of the turf

"You are a lad of spirit, I see," added the young highwayman, "and I have no doubt possess a head-piece that will carry us out of many a scrape."

"I'll do my best," returned the other. "And now I advise that we shift our position. Oliver and my father will be coming back to see why I have not departed, and the meeting might be awkward. It's more than likely that even now they are waiting in the road to see me pass."

"Suppose I take your place?" said Jack. "The moon is getting behind a cloud, and at the pace I shall go, they will scarcely be able to distinguish the change."

"As you please, noble captain," said the sagacious gipsey, "but be careful of the animal you bestride, and reverence it."

"I do," said Jack, "for she's the greatest beauty I ever saw, and has been making love to me for the last ten minutes."

With these words he placed his hand upon the jetty mane of the mare, and vaulted with one spring into the saddle. The animal seemed sensible of the burden she bore, and reared and pranced as though proud of it. Jack patted her kindly, but he could scarce restrain her impatience to dart forward, and as she curvetted and caracoled like a mad thing, she champed the bit until it was impearled with foam. Rejoiced at these tokens of spirit, our hero resolved no longer to curb it; he, therefore, exclaimed, "Now, then," and slackened the rein at once. In an instant she was off like lightning; she took the fence round her paddock with an easy leap, and, flashing like a firefly over the ground, soon attained the high-road, where Jack beheld Oliver and his companions, as had been anticipated.

Sixteen-stringed Jack hesitated for an instant how to act; but prudence suggested that he had better ride on, without appearing to notice any one, and only, if addressed before passing them, to hold any conference. The complete occultation of the moon behind a dense mass of vapour favoured his design, as it involved the earth in darkness, and rendered all recognition difficult, if not impossible. Crouching close to the saddle, therefore, in order that the difference in size between him and the gipsey might not be too manifest, he patted the noble neck of his magnificent courser, and whispering a word of encouragement in her ear, urged her to a still fleeter pace than she had before taken. Already had she gained the hedge that separated the fallows from the high road—already was this leaped, with the ditch beyond it—and already was she darting full speed past the waylayers, when Oliver and Long Jemmy, who was with him, caught the bridle on each side and the former exclaimed "Stop!"

The sudden check almost threw Rann from his saddle, but recovering himself in time, he twitched the bridle from the hands of his detainers, and putting his mare into a quick walk, said in an under-tone, "Hush! don't you know me? it is I—Zekiel Steele."

"Oh, I know you fast enough," answered Oliver; "and was coming back if I hadn't heard you galloping over the ground. You've been a most infernal time a coming."

Jack replied that he had been picking a stone out of his horse's foot—disguising his voice as he spoke—and then urged the necessity of speeding onwards, lest daylight should cause the mare he rode to be recognised.

"I shall take that chance myself, young shaver," resumed Oliver. "The old man tells me you are not to be trusted, and that you are one o' them milk-hearted fellers as 'ud rather screen a cove than blow upon him. I thought you were in a mighty hurry to get the job into your own hands, and to keep the old chap from getting a word in edgeways."

"Father knows nothing about it, and is only savage that his old bones wouldn't let him take the journey himself," retorted Jack, slyly touching the mare into a trot; but Oliver was too much on the alert to be so easily escaped, and, again checking the animal, exclaimed:—

"Come, come, younker, no larking with me! I tell you I shall take second thoughts and look after my own business; so dismount directly, d'ye hear?"

"Don't bawl so, or you'll bring the cottagers upon us," returned Rann. "I do hear, and am not such a fool as to be choused out of twenty guineas after a bargain has been struck, and so I tell you."

"Pooh! you've got ten, and you may keep 'em, only hand me back the parcel. Come, give it up, or, d—m me, I'll make you!"

Jack knew too well the danger of compliance as well as that of a direct refusal, to give either; but he steered a middle course, by pouring forth professions of fidelity, and persisting in asserting his intention of duly fulfilling his mission. The ruffian, however, cut him short with an imprecation, and roared:—

"Stash your palaver, will you, and do as I order! I stand no nonsense, so do it at once."

"I tell you I won't," said Jack, now perceiving the inutility of further parley—"and to give you a bit of my mind I don't like you half well enough to put myself out of the way for you, so take your hold from the reins, or I'll turn back and pitch your parcel into the fire."

"Don't be a fool, boy;" cried a voice, which Jack knew to be that of old Steele the gipsey. "Remember, we are in good master Oliver's power."

"You may be, but I am not," observed our hero, carelessly; his imitation of Zekiel's manner becoming more perfect with increase of practice.

"Well," ejaculated the old man in a coaxing tone, though he trembled with terror, "but you wouldn't like to see your old father split upon, would you—would you boy?"

"No fear of that," returned the highwayman, beginning to grow weary of the part he was acting:—"if he don't stow his jaw and behave himself I'll split upon him!"

"You!" reiterated Oliver, contemptuously, "why what do you know of me to split about?"

Jack bent his head towards Oliver's ear, and, in a low voice, exclaimed, "Your robberies and burglaries!"

Oliver was thunder struck. He even recoiled from Jack's side, and let go of his mare's bridle. But though his muscular frame was convulsed in every joint, his terrors did not deprive him of that instinct towards self-preservation which is so inherent in all animated nature. "Steele!" he shouted, though scarce able to articulate, "the whelp knows too much for us. Knock him off his beast and throttle him."

Jack laughed, for he had already learned to despise dangers; but at the same time he twisted the thong of his whip round his fingers, and grasping the narrow end of its handle, he brandished the butt-end, exclaiming—"The old man knows better! Let me pass unmolested, or by heavens I will shed your blood!"

"Ha!" resumed Oliver, drawing a pistol from his ample side pocket; "Jemmy look to your barker. And you, fool, down to the ground, or I fire!"

With these words, he for a third time approached Jack; but the highwayman disapproved of such advances, and consequently gave the mare a hint to evade them. The animal took it, like a sensible slut as she was, and once more sprung forward like a pebble from the sling, kicking old Steele to the ground as she did so. With a deep curse, Oliver and Jemmy raised their weapons, and fired at the same instant; but Jack stooped till his locks blended with the mare's mane, and the balls whistled harmlessly over his head. He then raised himself in his stirrups, and exclaimed in his own peculiar voice, " so much for good intentions! and now, dogs, be off; or you will find Jack with the sixteen strings has already made this part of the country too hot to hold you!" With these words, he touched the animal's side with the spur, and in one instant became lost in the darkness.

Thankful at heart for the narrow escape he had had, and determined no more to trust himself in the hands of Jared's father, who, it was self-evident, had for lucre been readily bought over to Oliver's views, he put the brave horse forward at her quickest speed towards a neighbouring village, where he knew he should meet Sheppard and Clayton, on their road to crack the crib, as has been already hinted. Their greeting was a hearty one, and whilst vowing vengeance on the head of Oliver, they were loud in their admiration of the honesty of Jared's brother and the dexterity of Jack Rann.

"How the devil Oliver could have discovered your retreat is a mystery to me," said Sheppard, and so it was in truth to all of them, but a mystery involving so rich a joke that we cannot forbear solving it for the reader's benefit.

Jack, whilst alone among the gipsies, frequently indulged his roving inclinations to such an extent, as to find himself wandering happily some five miles or so from the encampment. It happened one fine morning, he had rather exceeded that distance on a pilgrimage towards London; chancing to look up, he discried in the distance two fellows, who, from their flash attire and rolicking way, he at once made up his mind to be "row-de-dowdy boys," that is, two gemmen of the metropolitan schools, whose genius had learnt them the art of picking pockets of wipes and so forth, and then despising such inert unaspiring vagabonds, as left them to that low and inglorious occupation, to starve or go to the devil in any other way that they pleased.

"So, so," thought Jack to himself, " two humble brothers of the handkerchief fool school, or my eyes deceive me, hang it, but I'll draw their wipes if it be possible, for the fun of the thing."

It so chanced the two individuals were impressed with the same ideas, with the simple exception that they did it for the profit of the thing; for one observed to the other:—

"Look alive, my rhinoceros, here is such a dashing fellow a walking down the road."

"So there is, I declare," said the other vagabond. "Lord, how I should like to pick his pocket."

"Lord, how I should like to catch you at it," thought Jack, but, advancing towards them, merely said, "Good morning to you, gentlemen."

"Oh! good morning, sir," said both the fellows in a breath, "let me hope I have the honour of seeing you well."

"Perfectly well, I thank you," said Jack, who, at that instant, felt his handkerchief leaving his pocket; "but I tell you what, sir," he said, turning fiercely to the fellow who had taken it, "That wasn't at all well done."

"Wh-what wasn't well done?" stammered the fellow.

"That handkerchief rig," said Jack, with a wink as knowing as a wink could be by any possibility in any man's eye.

"Hankicher rig—what hankicher rig?" said the fellow, in pretended astonishment. "I can't make out what you are hammering at; I don't know nothing about a hankicher rig."

"I tell you it wasn't well done by any means," said Jack, "you clumsy-fisted knave, I not only felt it go, but actually saw it go."

"The devil you did," said the fellow.

"Yes," said Rann, "and that is more than you saw when I took yours," and he exhibited, as he spoke, to the prigs' astonished gaze, the fellow's own handkerchief.

The other vagabond instantly burst into a roar of laughter. "Ha, ha, ha!" he shouted, "Capital, the neatest trick I ever heard on, but 'tis well, sir you didn't try the rig on me, else 'twould have been a complete failure."

"Would it," said Jack, quickly, "don't boast—clever men never boast, for their talent is sure to be appreciated without—there, what think you of that?" and he dangled the second thief's handkerchief before his astonished eyes.

"Why, you must be the devil," shouted the fellow.

"Or Sixteen-string Jack," chimed in the second.

"What if I am him?"

"'Twill be the proudest moment of our lives," said the fellows, "the jolliest of meetings."

"Well, I am he," said Rann, "and here, gentlemen, as I never prey upon pals, are your handkerchiefs."

"Thank you," said the prigs, and the one who had extracted our hero's, commenced rummaging in his capacious pockets for Rann's, to return it to him.

"Don't distress yourself," said Jack, with a laugh, "it has already returned to its owner. Gentlemen, your road runs one way—mine, the other. I have the pleasure of wishing you a very good morning, and jovial success to trade."

Jack returned to the camp; the fellows, after making the country too hot to hold them, to London, and growing grandiloquent one night in their cups, they gave vent to the admiration excited in their breasts by their meeting with Jack Rann. Oliver was in the room, and minutely questioned them as to the locality of the gipsey band, and concluding rightly and at once, our hero was screened by the gang over whom Steele reigned, and having in other days detrimental knowledge of the old man, he determined to use such knowledge at once, intending by threats, to force the puerile old man to betray the trust confided in him by his son.

With what success has already been shown.

CHAPTER XXX.

CONSULTATION OF THE GANG—THE DETERMINATION—THE FIRE—THE VICTIM.

WE left the gang after the unhappy castastrophe ot the officer's death, in solemn consultation as to the means to be adopted for the disposal of the corpse. Amongst a variety of suggestions, some of them positively too horrible for repitition, it was finally proposed by Sheppard, that the ghastly remains of the unfortunate man should be destroyed by fire.

To this startling proposition for several minutes no answer was returned. At length, Toby, weighing well every word as he uttered them, said—

"Live in this house longer, I cannot. No, no, the crib must be for ever done up. My life would be one of unceasing horror—one continuous scene of misery, if I were compelled to live in a house where blood had been shed; I will, therefore, take your advice, Sheppard, and destroy the remains of the deed by fire, at the same time I will light so glorious a funeral pile to the poor wretch's memory, that all london shall be lit up with it. Since I cannot inhabit the old place myself I am determined no other man shall, for I'll burn its old timbers to the ground."

"Why, you don't mean to say as how you contemplates firing the house. Why, Toby, my tulip, you'd break your heart over such a sacrifice of property."

"I have a great respect," said Toby, pathetically, as he glanced round the place, "for the old shed, it's a fact, for arn't I passed hundreds of happy hours in it, but that ain't at all likely to be of any manner of use to us, and its precious old tell-tale timbers, if they were investigated, might chance to reveal a secret that might endanger all our precious necks. It's a very hard task, two hundred guineas did I give for this 'ere wooden tenement, and now I am going to consign it to blazes. Two hundred pounds is a good strong dose to loose at one unhappy go, but what's two hundred to the value of a human life? why, it's a flea-bite, it aren't nothing; so I'll do it. Don't speak, nobody, now—it's no use trying to persuade me to alter my mind, I can't—won't—shan't, I'll burn the house to the ground, so you coves had, some of you, better look sharp, for, in less than an hour the sky will have a red look about it, awful to behold."

"The old place will burn like a match," said O'Brian, "and it's myself would propose a convenient way of destroying our little secrets, which would not be wholesome to be exposed, nohow. Now I tell you the caper; we must light the fire down below, then wont the flames arise—for the old timber will burn like a bunch of matches, and with the aid of the trifle of whiskey on the establishment, it's bright eyes will be wanted to find a single inch remaining of the old house at home to morrow morning."

"It shall be done," exclaimed Toby, and he immediately led the way below. The corpse of the unfortunate officer was dragged from the well, and, wrapped in an old tarpaulin, was placed upon a pile of combustible materials that had been scraped together for the purpose—collecting all the valuables on the premises at all portable, Toby threw them into a cart, and drove with all speed to the Jew's, in Pedlar's Acre, with them, then seating himself at the front window of the house, he gazed earnestly in the direction of Westminster. He was not doomed to be disappointed—the awful rays of a terrible fire were speedily visible, and the startled exclamations of alarmed citizens, as they hurried in the direction of the conflagration, broke the stillness of the night. Toby was by this time joined by the rest of the gang, who reported the fact that the fire was burning bravely, the truth of which was plainly borne out by the sky, for such was the awful brilliancy of the scene that the very sky itself seemed a mass of turbulent fire.

Luke Jones paid the penalty of his treachery with his life; fastened in the shed by our hero, he had lain impatiently waiting Barnes' signal and muttering many blasphemous curses on the officer's supposed tardiness. Finally losing all patience, he rushed to the door to release himself from the place. To his intense mortification, he found he was entrapped. Many bitter maledictions did he utter on the dead man's head. Amidst this burst of rage a sound fell upon his ear and curdled his heart's blood with horror. " Fire! fire!" As the words shouted by the anxious populace fell upon his ears, so loud was the roaring and crackling of the flames, it swallowed every other sound. Presently the imminent danger of his situation became more apparent, for already was one side of the outhouse a mass of living flame.

Uttering a cry of anguish as the flames came in, Luke flew to the far-end of the building and raised a series of cries for help. It was in vain, the roaring of the flames drowned his voice, while their intensity speedily became fearfully appalling. More than once he essayed to escape from the horrible fate by which he was surrounded. It was all in vain; the mighty flames hemmed him in on all sides, until, at length, from the intense heat, the clothes upon his body burst forth in flames. Uttering a yell of agony and despair, Luke fell helplessly into the gulf of fire. A charred and blackened mass, scarcely with one distinguishing feature of a human being, was all that remained the following day of Luke Jones.

* * * * * *

We will now rejoin our hero, whom we left in company with Clayton and Sheppard, and who were now concocting a scheme for the robbery of a rich old jeweller, of the name of Bradley.

"If the haul but turn out as I hope and expect it will," said Clayton " rely upon it our fortunes are made. Why, by all accounts this old fool of a Bradley is rolling in riches."

" We will speedily share them with him," said Jack, gleefully, " and now, old fellow, I tell you my plans. From information I managed to glean of the servant-girl, I flatter myself I can, without much difficulty, find my way into the house by scaling the window; once in, I will concoct a plan by which you can join me. Let our nags be in readiness, for, as Night-owl Oliver is on our track, immediately the goods are ours it may be necessary to ride like the devil, and turn the gimcracks at once into money. It is getting dusk now, so I'll make for the house, and in half an hour will have everything ready for you."

By the side of the jeweller's house, which was, in every respect strongly guarded, and firmly secured with bolts and bars, there was an iron tubing, or water spout. As soon as an opportunity arose that he could commence operations in safety, he set about the ascent of this said pipe, and by its means, reached the first floor window. Into this room, at the imminent peril of his neck, Jack managed to creep, and now only awaited the arrival of his pals. At length they came, and Jack flew to the window with joyful eagerness, and unlatched the casement without loss of time.

"In what quarier is the wind?" whispered he; that being the password agreed upon.

"It stands still that it may carry no tales," replied Sheppard, and as the answer satisfied Jack that all was right, he threw out a rope, which he had employed himself in knotting for the purpose, and in a few seconds, Kit and Sheppard stood within the apartment.

It should be explained that Jack's chamber was situated in the back part of the premises, over a low warehouse, and that, consequently, the approach of the housebreakers had been made under unusual circumstances of security, a dwarf wall being their only impediment; whilst their passage up the rope was, of course, performed without chance of discovery, as ever window overlooking the feat had been closed up for hours. So favourable a beginning put them all in spirits, but Jack did not suffer himself to become unguarded through his elation.

"We stand in great danger," he said, "for the place is so well secured from top to bottom, that, without the utmost caution, we shall be caught in some trap, or touch some wire connected with an alarm bell, that will betray our presence at once."

"Something like walking in a rabbit warren, or a preserve snared for poachers," exclaimed Kit Clayton; "however, I suppose you know the whereabouts of these hidden dangers."

"Not so well as I could wish, but I don't fear; and now let me impress one thing upon all: touch nothing but what I myself point out to you."

"I mean nothing unpleasant, captain," said Clayton; "but as an affair like this will cause more noise than anything we have yet done, we shall have to lie quiet for the best part of a year after it, and that would be impossible, without the booty was sufficient to keep us during that period."

"The most grasping fence in Petticoat-lane would give us a thousand pounds for what we shall carry away with us; so calm your disquietude on that head," said Rann. "And now to work: on with your vizors! and give me mine—my cloak too. Sheppard, give me your assistance. Hark! was that the watch?"

"That I'll swear it en't," said Kit, "for I made him as swipey as a drayman's apron about an hour back, and left him snoozing in his box."

"That was well done; and now come on, boys. Let 'No violence' be our motto."

"Werry good," said Kit.

They now proceeded to work. Jack led his companions to the warehouse beneath, and was, on entering, encountered by a large watch dog, that was nightly left at liberty to roam the premises. A word, however, changed his quick bark of defiance into a whine of recognition, and Jack ordered him to lie still. This danger averted, the gang fell to work, and the floor was quickly strewn with articles of every description and grade of value. They were the silks of China and the laces of France, the watches of Geneva, the gold dust of India, and the gems of every country. Nor was there a deficiency of specie—for in those days the banking system had not obtained to the extent of relieving, each evening, the merchant of all care concerning his cash—and Jack, having the keys of the strong box, was enabled to divide between four and five hundred pounds among his companions.

From the store-room they proceeded to the offices, and then penetrated into the very heart of the dwelling-house. Here the amount of valuables that met the greedy gaze of the plunderers on every side, absolutely astounded them; particularly Kit Clayton, who eyed them with a similar sort of a relish to that with which a horse gazes upon a clover field.

"This blessed jeweller," said he to Jack, "has taken unkimmon pains to send to distant parts for us. How very considerate. He knowed as how we had no means of getting over the herring pond, unless sent there by government, and so he fits out his ships, and has all as we wants brought here for us to pick and choose from. He is one of them 'ere sort of ones who will invite a man to dinner to save him the trouble of purviding for himself."

"Hush!" interrupted Sheppard, who had been employed in wrapping nearly a bale of veils from Brussels round his waist. "What voices were those?"

"Woices! Why there was only von, and that was mine."

"Silence!" cried Rann. "I heard whispering as plainly as I hear myself speak."

This, sternly uttered, hushed every attempt at words, and the whole party listened with beating hearts—each man's right hand resting upon his pistol.

"You must have been mistaken," at length said Clayton. "Not a mouse stirs."

"And yet I could have sworn I was right. We know not who may be lurking outside."

"No one who can be acquainted with our being here," said Clayton.

"For all that," returned Rann, "it may be unsafe to venture out at present. We had better, therefore, remain for an hour or two."

"And how are we to amuse ourselves all that time?" said Kit. "Is there anything in the grubbery line to be had?"

"A good thought," said Jack. "I have supped, but could enjoy a bottle of wine before I go. Let us find the pantry, gentlemen."

"To the pantry by all means," cried Kit.

"Amen," said Sheppard. "It would be uncivil to quit the old gentlemen without drinking his health first."

They betook themselves to the kitchen. Having amused themselves for some time among the edibles, they then drew the corks from sundry bottles, and in a short time were on the high road to happiness.

Having eat and drank to their hearts content, Jack gave the word for home. Sheppard and Clayton both descended in safety with their spoil, and our hero's feet were just upon the ground, when, on glancing round, he found himself surrounded by a posse of constables, who had it appears from the first been an eye-witness of the affair; two of them instantly sprang upon him, but shaking them aside, Jack made his way to where the steeds were standing, and leaped at once into the saddle. Astonished at the unexpected activity, Clayton and Sheppard, neither of them having perceived the officers, exclaimed—

"Hallo, Jack, what's the row?" they had scarcely spoken the word, when a pistol shot sounded loud and near.

"There's something up, lads!" exclaimed Jack, drawing one of his holsters, "we are pursued, and must make a bold front and have a hard fight for it.'

"I shud think so, my kinchens," chimed in Kit, well pleased at the idea of a scramble. Out with your powder-mills, take my word you'll want 'em."

As he uttered these words, Clayton trotted forward towards the approaching horseman, but had not got more than a hundred yards, when a second pistol shot rung loudly in their ears, and at the same instant he fell from his horse—the bullet had shattered his shoulder blade.

"By God! poor Clayton's down," exclaimed Jack, in a tone of rage and surprise—"forward, my covy, or the traps will nab him."

Sticking spurs into his horse, Jack dashed forward, and was followed in this by Sheppard, and, just as they reached their fellow companion, they beheld a troop of horsemen coming galloping up, followed by a large concourse of farming men and peasants, armed with pitchforks and bludgeons. They made a general halt, and hemmed in Clayton, as he lay on the ground.

"Here's Sixteen-stringed Jack!—we've cotched him," roared out an officer who was mounted on horseback, "secure him, boys; and remember, there's five hundred guineas reward."

"By God there's a young army!" said Jack, when he saw the mob surround his companion, "'twill be madness to attempt to rescue him as he is now; that must be reserved for some future time. Cut it my covy, fake away."

Suiting his action to the word, Jack leaped his mare over a high hedge, took a narrow dark lane that presented itself to his front, and putting his horse to its full speed, flew away like lightning on the wings of the night Sheppard followed his leader's example, and scrambling away over field, moor, hedge and break, was soon out of sight, leaving poor Clayton in the hands of the Philistines.

On they went at the top of their speed, and on thundering after them came their pursuers. Jack had no difficulty whatever in outstripping them, but on Sheppard, who was mounted on an inferior animal, they gained rapidly.

"This will never do, Sheppard," muttered Jack, "they will nab you, by God! take that lane to the right, I will maintain the road and decoy them from pursuit of you."

On flew Sheppard at Jack's bidding, whilst Jack, curbing the fiery animal he bestrode, waited for the approaching horsemen; this delay was within an ace of having a fatal termination, for the foremost officer, who was considerably in advance of his companions, levelled his pistol, and fired with an aim so correct, that the ball struck Jack's steed in the right eye, and penetrating the noble animal—with a wail of anguish, it fell dead.

The officer was close upon Jack, who, seized with a fit of daring, and half maddened by the death of the horse, he had no backwardness in determining at once to attack the officer. It would be a rare thing, he thought, to spread the terror of his name, by overpowering on foot a mounted man. Added to this, he recollected that he was without a horse, and he consequently resolved to supply himself with one at the stranger's expense.

His resolution formed, he boldly turned into the road, and, grasping the bridle of the approaching horse close by the bit, endeavoured to throw him upon his haunches, and thus dismount his master without trouble. The horseman was, however, too well experienced in the menage to be thus easily unseated, and, though the animal he bestrode, did rear and struggle, the rider maintained possession of his saddle with infinite dexterity, and also inflicted a heavy blow on Jack's temple with his riding whip. An infliction of this sort always has one of two contrary effects: it either paralyzes or stimulates, and in this instance the latter was the case. Jack felt not the blow, nor the blood that followed; but he felt something boiling in his veins that urged him on. Again his powerfully nerved arm stiffened as it was extended, and again he caused the horse to retreat with sudden action. Following this with a heavily dealt blow on the chest of the rider, Jack now succeeded in throwing him full length to the ground, and with an oath, he flung himself upon him.

They struggled desperately, and several times rolled over each other, until at length they had shifted their position a distance of several yards, and they came close against a milestone. Jack's adversary was a powerful man, and our hero felt that he would be overcome, unless, by some great effort, he gained an advantage. The coming in contact with the milestone at once afforded him this, for the stranger's head was close to it, and Jack, grasping his hair on each side, was about to stun him with a blow against the unconscious stone, when, at that moment, the other men appeared, and Jack refrained from dealing the blow.

The stranger, who, a moment before, had expected his brains to be dashed out, viewed this change with astonishment, but had, at the same time, sufficient presence of mind to take advantage of it. He sprung to his feet, and regaining his whip, again struck Jack, and was repeating his blows hard and fast, when the clattering shuffle of a horse's feet, accompanied by a loud "halloo," made him fancy that a comrade of the robber was near, and without thinking of his own horse, he "girded up his loins, and fled."

The traveller, who had so timely appeared, had witnessed part of the attack, with the subsequent flight of the assailant; and he naturally took a different view of the case than the right one, by imagining that Jack was the molested man, and the other the robber; he consequently accelerated the speed at which he was riding, and would have run down the supposed highwayman, but for the darkness in which the fugitive was speedily lost. Deeming further pursuit a loss of time, he reined round his horse, and moved towards the spot where Jack was still prostrate from the stunning effect of the blows he had received.

"Why, how is this?" exclaimed his preserver. "What brought you to this pass? and whom were you struggling with?"

"With Sixteen-string Jack," answered our hero, with the greatest effrontery imaginable, and as much presence of mind as if he had premeditated the lie before the encounter; "he knocked me off my horse, and would have stripped me of everything, had it not been for you."

"And he on foot?" exclaimed the stranger. "Why, the fellow has the courage of a lion; my admiration for him increases with every fresh feat he performs. But come, you require attention—where is your horse; for I will not leave you until I set you on your road.

Jack answered that it was no doubt browsing by the roadside, a supposition that proved to be correct; and, with perfect coolness, he mounted the animal as if he had been its lawful master.

Having all the valuable booty about his person, Jack made at once for London, first taking the precaution to procure another disguise, this done he started at once for Petticoat-lane, and was speedily on the barter with a celebrated Jew fence there, who, not content with the goods at less than half their value, kept protesting—

"Can't give a farthing more, my dear boy; as sure as you've got sixteen strings to your name, I can't afford it."

"Stuff, Peter, why, you know very well these diamonds and jewels will make your fortune—never was there such a blessed haul since the days of Pharoah, when your people bolted with all the gold and silver they could lay their hands on, and walked through the Red Sea. Come, five hundred on the nail, I don't mind notes, and a watch or two, from you."

"Oh, Jack, Jack, you have a conscience—why, don't you know that there will be a careful watch on all goods in this line for a month to come; and if we don't get 'em safe under the hatches of some East Indiaman before twelve o'clock to-day, we must keep 'em close in fear of the traps, for the next three months."

"Bah! you're as hard mouthed as an exciseman," replied Jack to his Jew friend. "Well, if we are to do business, what is your price!"

Two "hundred, not a rap more."

"Curse you for a sinner; here, snatch up these trifles, and give us the chinks for another hundred," said Jack, throwing several watches and pairs of silver mounted pistols on a table before him.

The Jew slowly handled them, turned them over and over, cast a knowing leer up at Jack, and then drawing an old dirty black leather pocket book from his breeches pocket, he unrolled it, and counting out a bundle of notes, and a handful of guineas, he pushed them towards our hero, and pocketing the watches and pistols, exclaimed, "there I know I shall lose by the job, but you're a good customer, so I suppose I must humour you."

"Ah, ah, Master Peter, you're always going to the workhouse; but I don't think you're any nearer than you were twenty years ago; but so as these are righteous, I suppose I musn't grumble."

"Ah, ah," responded the Jew, "you know very well that I've paid a good price, and shall have a job to clear my profits."

"Pitch that to guffins," replied Jack, laughing, as, gathering up the notes and gold, he departed.

This conversation was held between our hero and old Peter, a notorious Jew receiver, who had lived in a cellar, in Petticoat lane, for the last forty years; but as he never allowed a single article of the purchased property to enter his premises, he managed, by crafty dealings, and sometimes an untruth to evade justice, and drive a glorious trade with the cheap merchants o France and Holland, who were ever ready to purchase his stock.

"Well, I think I may make this job wind up my fortune," muttered old Peter to himself, as he dwelt upon the swag he had purchased of Rann and his gang. "A thousand! ah, let me see; why, if I don't make a clean fifteen hundred by it I shall grumble. I must cut this Mr. Sixteen-string Jack; he is too venturesome. I'm sure he'll get grabbed at last, and swing high at Tyburn; and then it might be unpleasant for me; especially as I have given him two forged fifties—bah! he is too eager to find that out. Yes, yes; I must wash my hands of him, and I think of retiring from this dangerous trade.

Thus ruminating, the Jew went on his way to get his purchase shipped before daybreak.

CHAPTER XXXI.

MISS MALCOLM FINDS A LOVER, WHO IS NEVERTHELESS NOT EXACTLY TO HER MIND, AND OUR HERO FINDS AN OPPORTUNITY OF EXERTING HIS GALLANTRY, FROM THE CONSEQUENCES OF WHICH HE INVOLVES HIMSELF IN AN AWKWARD DILEMMA.

MISS MALCOLM, who from her first interview with our hero, has beheld in him one whom her whole heart could love, had viewed with thoughts of distraction and feelings of poignant anguish, the sinful and dangerous career our hero had chosen, and often with all the fervency of a young and truthful heart, had she bent her knee before high Heaven to sue for pardon for him.

Not only the heiress of considerable wealth, but also the possessor of rare personal beauty, and every feminine accomplishment; it became a matte of no wonder that Mr. Malcolm's house was literally besieged by would-b suitors, and aspirants for the lady's hand and fortune. But so enraptured was she with our hero—so earnestly, so devotedly attached to him, even in the dark tide by which he was beset, she turned a deaf ear to all their protestations, vows, and prayers. Nor could her mother's persuasive tongue, or earnest and tearful advices, win her loved and lovely daughter from the object on which she had fixed her guileless heart. No, the more the danger that surrounded him, the more she clung to the darling hero of her soul—the stronger the obloquy heaped upon him the stronger grew her excuses for his conduct—the more powerful grew her love for him. It seemed that the disgrace and ignomy which he so recklessly risked, had no power to steel her heart against him. She was in heart his unalterably—

for weal or woe, for happiness, for ignominy, for a happy life, or a miserable death!

Of her suitors, one in particular essayed more than the others to wean her from her untoward passion, and own her for his bride. He was the Hon. George Dashfield, a captain in the King's 1st Regiment of Cavalry, and heir, after the Earl of Dashfield, to the estates and titles of that name. It was he who, having information of the earl's villanous and lustful wishes after the fair Miss Malcolm, and having, moreover, had the good fortune to ascertain the time and route for the intended abduction, had sought out Clayton, at the Jew's place, in Pedlar's Acre, and, by the lavish dispensation of his gold, had won the services of that worthy, and those of our hero, which ended, as the reader has already been informed, in the glorious rescue of Miss Malcolm, by our brave hero, and the no less glorious discomfiture of the villanous old Earl.

It was a glorious sunset on the afternoon in question, as Miss Malcolm was seated at the drawing-room window of her father's country mansion at Clapham—one of those calm, peaceful evenings, when thoughts of past happy hours, of absent, lost, or departed friends, steals over our mind with a soft and soothing tendency, and when our thoughts blend with a salutary shading, as we view, with half regret, the past, or view, with only half a heart of hope, the future; salutary, inasmuch as it tells us of the mutability of human happiness, and carries the mind to that holier and better place, whence true happiness alone flows.

As she gazed upon the scene before her, rapidly becoming indistinct in the gathering twilight, a few hot tears, awakened by her unhappy thoughts of Jack Rann, dropped upon the book she had been perusing. Even whilst indulging in this mournful reverie, and with the pearly tears yet wet upon her matchless cheeks, the door of the room was noiselessly opened, and her father and the captain came unperceived upon her.

"Still in tears, my beloved Isabel," said the father, with parental tenderness, "why do you indulge in this absurd, this unavailable grief, for a vagabond, who, setting at defiance the laws of God and man, has deservedly forfeited his life to the outraged laws of the King? Believe me, my dear child, it is sinful in the extreme. Think you, were he but an honest man, I would exercise any control over your actions—think you I would raise any objection, even to your linking your fate to his in wedlock? No, my darling, could I be but convinced it would, in the least, conduce to to your happiness, my consent should at once be given; but now, when I see my once happy child bringing herself to an early grave, for the sake of a highwayman, whose neck may be encircled with a halter in a few days, whose life must, eventually, be forfeited, in spite of his almost miraculous escapes, in spite of his undoubted courage, I feel cut to the heart—"

"For God's sake speak not so, father, even the prospect of his suffering the dreadful doom at which you hint, fills my heart with agony. Can nothing be done for him—is there no country but England in which he can spend the remainder of his unhappy life in peace, and in spots where he and his crimes could remain alike unknown? Oh, Captain Dashfield," she said, turning appealingly to her suitor, "cannot you advise me—cannot you avert the doom that now hangs over him?"

"If his fate remained in my hands, lady, answered the young officer, "his salvation should at once be accorded, for I believe him to have been driven to this desperate career. I believe him to have been more sinned against than sinning—but, alas! I am powerless, I lack the means, not the will."

"You have spoken to me of love," said Isabel, in deep tones of emotion, "and, believe me, I feel flattered by the offer of your noble heart: yet, spite of all my father's counsellings, spite of my own innate conviction of your worth, and his unworthiness, my heart still yearns to see him who was my saviour from a fate worse than death, removed from the pale of danger to that of safety.''

"I would it were in my power to change your wishes to realities, believe me, no moment's hesitation should prevent its consummation; but, alas! I am powerless. And yet I have sometimes thought, had I but speech with him, I could turn his thoughts into another channel, could succour, could save him."

"Oh, thank you—thank you a thousand times, for even those words of hope. Promise me, my own dear friend, you will leave no stone unturned, no means untried to effect this desirable end."

"Well," exclaimed the captain, a smile of joy pervading his handsome face. "Well, lady, I will give the prosecution of this scheme immediate and untiring attention, and, should I succeed in freeing your darling hero from the trammels that surround him, should I succeed in placing him in another clime, where he he may re-commence life, and, by the rectitude of his future days, recompense for the follies and crimes of those that are past, may I then, lady, hope to find favour in your eyes?"

"Well done, Fred!" exclaimed Mr. Malcolm, "you are, at last, on the highway of success, you have found the true way to Isabella's heart—there is nothing in the world women admire so much as generosity, and, if it be in your power to save this Rann—of which I, also, should be right glad—believe me, my dear young friend, Isabel will not have the heart longer to refuse you. Go it, old fellow, the citadel is half won, raise the storming ladders, and carry it by a *coup de main!*" But let me run away, or I shall prove a regular Marplot in disturbing your *tete-a-tete*," and the merry old gentleman hurried from the room.

"My dear Isabella," said Dashfield, when they were alone, " believe me, I would not thus ungenerously urge my claim, but I have beheld with pain the inroads this unceasing care has made in a constitution ever so delicate. Believe me, my dear girl, my love is no evanescent love—from boyhood upwards, your image has been enshrined in my heart—the joy of having you for my own dear little wife has been, and is, and ever will be, the highest soaring point of my ambition. This secret would have remained buried in my heart, had an honourable man, and a gentleman, won and obtained possession of your hand and heart; but, seeing with pain—as none could fail to see—that the rich gift of invaluable love has been heedlessly thrown away upon a person most unworthy, I waived the false point of etiquette which had hitherto kept us apart, and, taking the liberty of an old friend, sought your society, in the humble hope that my presence, even if it could not relieve, might yet ameliorate your sorrow. From the transit of being a casual visitor to that of being a constant, and, I hope, not unwelcome one, I learnt the admiration of you, that had so long been struggling in my heart, was nearer akin to deep, sincere, and lasting love than even I myself had been aware of. Under its influence I proposed for your hand, having first obtained your father's sanction ; courteously, yet firmly, you rejected me ; undaunted by one rebuff, I still kept on, for I had a good cause at heart, and was determined to win you. After a lapse of time I again proposed to meet with a denial, and, further, to hear tidings that cut me to the very soul, for, from your candour, I learnt your heart was irrevocably given to another. Cursing my procrastination, to which I imputed my failure, in my agony I sought counsel of my uncle, the Earl of Dashfield, and from him I learnt, scarcely more to my intense astonishment than to my unfeigned agony, that the invaluable prize which the gift of your love would convey on whomsoever it was bestowed, was literally thrown away upon a notorious highwayman. Cut to the heart, it was many a day ere I could think calmly of the matter, but when I again recovered my reasoning faculties, I vowed, as a friend, to us every means in my power to prevent so unhallowed an alliance, for I could not conceive it possible that you could be aware of the nature and character of the man you were so blindly loving. As time kept on his beaten track, my unhappy young rival continued his headlong course to destruction. In your sunken eyes, and attenuated form, I, at length, had sad evidence that his follies and his crimes were not only unknown to you, but they were, in reality, undermining your health, and bringing you to a premature grave, determined to awaken you, if possible, to a sense of what was due to yourself—to save you from the misery so thickly hanging around—I presented myself a third time, with a tale of love, in the hope of dispelling some of the gloom that environed you, and, tell me, sweet Isabella, is my third mission, like its predecessors, doomed to be a failure?"

"As heaven is my judge, no," answered Isabella, frankly extending her hand to the gallant young soldier. "I am so conscious of your merits—so thankful for your unceasing kindnesses, I cannot find it in my heart to let them go unrequited. If you will but place poor Rann in safety, Frederick, and can content yourself with the poor half that remains of this broken heart, I am yours—"

"Oh, joy! am I indeed so blessed," exclaimed young Dashfield, rapturously folding the lovely girl to his heart.

"If I bring you but half a heart and be in safety; yet, in unceasing devotion, in unalterable love, in inflexible duty, you shall never live to miss or regret the part I had unwittingly given to another. No, Frederick, what remains of me, firmly and irrevocably, heart and soul, shall be your own."

"My own angel! my own darling wife, I implicitly believe you, and will be well content with the heaven of love in store for me, but my darling girl I beseech you, tell me when shall the happy day be?"

"When Rann is removed from danger—then if God be willing and yourself in the same mind, you will meet with no objection in Isabella Malcolm."

Almost beside himself with joy, Captain Dashfield vowed again and again to save our hero, and uttered a thousand incoherent senseless nothings, finally, his delight extending beyond all bounds, he rushed from the room, and finding Mr. and Mrs. Malcolm, completely electrified them both, by not only unbosoming him himself to them, but by actually, in his transports, taking them to his bosom, by bestowing so vigourous a hug upon them both that the worthy couple were a good half-hour recovering the breath he had completely squeezed out of their blessed bodies.

Moderating his transports at length, he sufficiently calmed himself to proceed to the drawing-room, and propose to Miss Malcolm their first appearance in public together. It so happened, a new opera was produced that evening at Drury Lane Theatre, upon which occasion a celebrated Italian songstress was to make her first appearance in England,

The royal family had expressed their intention of being present, and with such a combination of talent and rank, as had seldom been seen, even in the walls of "Old Drury." To this place of amusement, after some persuasion, Isabella was induced to go by her importunate lover, and having dressed, the now happy pair, at an early hour in the evening set out for that far famed place of amusement, in a carriage and pair. Whilst they are proceeding to the theatre, we will return to our hero.

Having disposed of the fruits of the burglary at Bradley's, to the advantage which he had, Jack instantly hied to a respectable tailor, who, for the accomodation of the more needy of the aristocracy, kept a goodly supply o gentlemen's clothing, ready-made, upon the establishment. Having chosen a superb suit of gentlemanly attire, and having purchased a sword, Jack was soon metamorphosed into a swell of the first water. Stepping from the clothier's with all the swagger of a man about town, Jack took his way undauntedly down the Strand, ruminating on what his next move should be on the great drama of human life. Whilst chin deep in thought, he suddenly found himself in violent contact with a fellow foot passenger. Contenting himself by merely consigning the unfortunate pedestrian's eyes to eternal darkness, with the characteristic politeness of gentlemen of that enlightened age, he was proceeding onwards at an increased pace, and, if possible, with an increased swagger, when he suddenly felt a hand gently glide into his pocket, which, with the quickness of thought, he seized, and held fast there. Turning upon his assailant, he grasped him by the throat, and, dragging him under a lamp, peered anxiously into his face. A burst of laughter was the result of his investigation, as, in the prig's features, he recognised the never-to-be-forgotten face of Wide-Awake.

"Hallo, my venerable," said Jack, " what game do you call this ?"

"A dose of cold steel if you don't ungrip my throat," said Colledge, savagely, and in a voice rendered unnaturally bass by the pressure on his wind-pipe.

"No, thank you," said Jack, lacking his hold, "my appetite's not keen enough to relish that for supper. What, Wide-Awake, my flower," said Jack, in his own voice, " don't you know me ?"

The changes that crowded into Wide-Awake's face in that interval, would have beat a phantasmargoia to a shadow.

"What, captain," he stammered, " is it you ?"

"It is, old fellow," answered Jack ; " but let's aside, I've a trifle to ask you," and, stepping into a tavern, Jack called for a private dinner, and a bottle of sherry, and they were soon deep in their revelations, Jack learning, for the first time, of the destruction of Toby's house, and the death of the officer, and likewise of the horrible fate of Luke Jones. Whilst, on the other hand, Wide-Awake was speedily in possession of the knowledge of Night-owl Oliver's treachery, Old Steele's fallibility, and the fatal shot that had lodged poor Clayton in the county prison. Almost the first inquiry Jack made was for Elinor Roche.

"What, you mean the girl what hocussed the turnkeys, don't you?"

Rann answered in the affirmative.

"Oh, she's a brick, she is," said Colledge, "all up the back. I tell you what, its my opinion," continued that interesting youth, with extraordinary sagacity, "that she's an out-an-outer—a regular screamer. Why, what do think, the big-wigs actually offered her her liberty, if she'd blow as to your whereabouts, devil a bit, she was as close as a miser's clenched fists, and that's the closest thing I can fancy, so when they found they couldn't get her to patter on the strength of promises, they took her to the press-yard, and tried by torture to worm the secret from her."

"My God!" exclaimed Rann, with sincere emotion.

"Its a fact," said Wide-Awake, seriously, "they half killed her—I might have said, three parts and not lied, but not a word could they get from her. Oh, she is a wonderful woman—blow me if I wouldn't keep a gal myself if I could only get hold of such a piece as she is," said Wide-Awake, with profound admiration.

"And what further punishment did she undergo?"

"None," answered Colledge, "her dose was plenty strong enough I should think, as it was. After the torture they let her go. She was taken to the workhouse, but getting better soon, she left that and now is—blow me if I know where."

Jack heaved a sigh, as he listened to this narrative, for the devotion of Elinor had filled his heart with love for her.

"Well, Wide-Awake," he said, after a pause, "and where were you steering to when I so unexpectedly run foul of you?"

"Oh, I was going to hear this ere new singer, at Drury—there's a glorious company there to-night, the king, and princes, and dukes, and duchesses, and marquisses and marquisesses, and his royal highness the devil only knows who."

"We shall be too late for a seat, I suppose," said Rann, " as I should like to go myself."

"Too late for a seat, what nonsense," said Wide-Awake, rising, "if you only do as I do, I'll warrant to get a seat."

"What notable scheme is that?" inquired Rann.

"Why, I tell you how I work the oracle, I go right to the top, make a noise with one voice, shout out, ' chuck him over,' in another, and pretending to be thrown over, I jump on somebody's back, roll myself up in a ball, like a hedgehog, and roll right over their heads till I come to a good pitching place, then down I drop. My eyes! it's such a lark; don't I make 'em tuck in their twopennies!"

"It strikes me very forcibly I should make you tuck in yours," said Jack, ' if you were to roll over me ; but, however, it's a long time since I've been 'to a theatre, so, for this once, I'll treat myself to Old Drury."

"Wherry good," said Wide Awake, " as old Toby would say—by the by, that antique friend or yours has gone quite mouldy, 'melancholy mad, since the crib's broke up, and I'm half afraid the old wenerable piece of antiquity contemplates turning honest."

Drury-lane was reached at last, and Rann and Wide Awake entered the boxes.

No sooner were they fairly seated, which feat, in consequence of the crowded state of the house, was not accomplished without some difficulty, and only then by the aid of a large fee, than Jack's piercing eye took the circle of the crowded house.

" So, so," thought Jack, as he glanced at the royal box' " the Prince of Wales and his two royal brothers, and, in the same box hang me if there isn't my exquisite friend Beau Brummel—let me remember, the fellow owes me something for a wager that he would not be robbed. Well, well, he's able to owe, I warrant, if not to pay me, so, being the safe side of the hedge, I'll even let that pass."

Beau Brummell, the accomplished and refined companion of George the Fourth, was lounging at his ease in the box. Of this illustrious personage a hundred excellent things have been said—so rich, in fact, that we cannot help recapitulating a few of them here.

A great deal has been said of Beau Nash and his witticisms; but, certainly, there was never anything of his, which was at all equal to the oracular sentences of Mr. Brummell. Of all the *beaux* that ever flourished—at least, of all that ever flourished on the same score—exemplary of waistcoat, and having authoritative boots from which there was no appeal; he appears to have been the only one who made a proper and perfect union of the coxcombical and ingenious. Other men may have been as scientific on the subject of bibs, in a draper-like point of view; and others may have said as good things, which had none of the colouring, or rising out of the consciousness of fashionable pre-eminence. But to proceed to our anecdotes :—

1.—Mr. Brummell having once fallen out of favour with an illustrious personage, (the Prince Regent), was of course to be *cut*, as the phrase is, when met in public. Riding one day with a friend, who happened to be otherwise regarded, and encountering the personage in question, who spoke to the friend without noticing Mr. Brummell, he affected the air of one who waits aloof while a stranger is present; and then, when the great man was moving off, said to his companion, loud enough for the other to hear, and placidly adjusting his bibs, " Eh! who is our fat friend ?"

2. Having taken it into his head, at one time, to eat no vegetables, and being asked by a lady if he had never eaten any in his life, he said, " Yes, madam, I once ate a pea."

3.—Being met limping, in Bond-street, and asked what was the matter, he said, he had hurt his leg, and the worst of it was, it was his favourite leg.

4.—Somebody inquiring where he was going to dine next day, was told that he really did not know: "they put me in my coach, and take me somewhere."

5.—He pronounced of a fashionable tailor that "he made a good coat, an exceedingly good coat—all but the collar: nobody could achieve a good collar but Jenkins."

6.—Having borrowed some money of a city beau, whom he "patronised" in return, he was one day asked to repay it; upon which he thus complained to a friend: "Do you know what has happened?" "No." "Why, do you know, there is that fellow, Tomkins, who lent me five hundred pounds, has had the freedom to ask me for it; and yet I had called the creature—'Tom,' and let myself dine with him."

7.—"You have a cold, Mr. Brummell," observed a sympathising group. "Why, do you know," said he, "that on the Brighton road, the other day, that infidel Weston, (his valet,) put me into a room with a damp stranger."

8.—Being asked if he liked port, he said, with an air of difficult recollection, "Port! port! oh, aye, P-o-r-t! the hot intoxicating liquor so much drank by the lower orders!"

9.—Going to a rout, where he had not been invited, or rather, perhaps, where the host wished to mortify him, and attempted it, he turned round to him, and with a happy mixture of indifference and surprise, asked his *name*. "Johnson," was the answer. "Jauhnson," said Brummell, recollecting and pretending to feel for a card; "Oh! the name, I remember, was Thaun son, (Thompson,) and, Jauhnson and Thaunson, you know—Jauhnson and Thaunson, are really so much the same kind of thing!"

10.—A beggar petitioned him for charity, "Even if it was only a farthing." "Fellow," said Mr. Brummell, softening the disdain of the appellation in the gentleness of his tones, "I don't know the coin."

11.—Having thought himself invited to somebody's country seat, and being given to understand, after one night's lodging, that he was in error, he told an unconscious friend in town, who asked him what sort of a place it was, "that it was an exceedingly good place for stopping one night in."

12.—Speaking lightly of a man, and wishing to convey his *maximum* of contemptuous feeling about him, he said, "He is a fellow, now, that would send his plate up twice for soup!"

13.—It was his opinion that port, and not porter, should be taken with cheese. "A gentleman," said he, "never *malts* with his cheese—he always *ports*."

14—It being supposed that he once failed in a matrimonial speculation, somebody condoled with him; upon which he smiled, with an air of better knowledge on that point, and said, with a sort of indifferent feel of his neckcloth, "Why, sir, the truth is, I had great reluctance in cutting the connexion; but what could I do? (Here he looked deploring and conclusive). Sir, I discovered that the wretch positively ate—cabbage."

15.—Upon receiving some affront from an illustrious personage, he said, "that it was rather too good; by gad, I have half a mind to cut the young one and bring old GEORGE into fashion."

16.—When he went visiting, he is reported to have taken with him an elaborate dressing apparatus, including a silver basin. "For," said he, "it is impossible to spit in clay."

17.—On being asked by a friend, during an unseasonable summer, if he had ever seen such a one? "Yes," replied he, "last winter."

18.—On a reference being made to him as to what sum would be sufficient to meet the annual expenditure for clothes, he said, "that with a a moderate degree of prudence and economy, he thought it might be managed for eight hundred pounds per annum!"

19.—He told a friend that he was reforming his way of life. "For instance," said he, "I sup early; I take a—a—little lobster, an apricot puff, or so, and some burnt champagne about twelve—and my man gets me to bed —by three."

No. 43.

At this instant Miss Malcolm and her lover entered a private box, directly opposite to the one in which Colledge and our hero were sitting, Wide-Awake instantly drew Jack's attention towards them.

"Look opposite, there's a spicy bit of muslin, she is the handsomest woman in the theatre, by jingo, and look if her champeron isn't Clayton's military friend, strike me sensible."

As Jack gazed upon Miss Malcolm to whose fair cheek the excitement of the gay scene had lent a pleasing glow, Jack thought he had never gazed upon a more superb beauty, and as the reminiscences of his meeting with the amiable girl flashed across his memory, a blush of shame lit up his face even to the very temples.

She has soon forgotten me," thought Jack, as a pang of anguish shot through his heart. "Well, fool that I am, how could I expect she would retain in her memory one disgraced, and cursed, and banned as I am." Then giving way to the more generous impulses of his heart, he added, " and God be thanked, she has forgotten me, for the gallant fellow by her side is right noble in birth and blood, and right worthy of her, and it ought rather to be a consolation, and a joy to me, that she has risen triumphant over her love for my vagabond self, since in him she has gained so desirable a companionship, well," said the brave fellow, fervently, "the only harm I wish them, is, that God may preserve and bless them both."

"I say, Jack," observed Wide-Awake, "look at that old buffer in the dress circle, doing the gallant to those young ladies, did you ever see such a gay young scoundrel in your life?" Jack gazed in the direction of Wide-Awake's outstretched finger, and to his surprise beheld in the gallant old buck indicated by Colledge, no less a personage than the Earl of Dashfield.

"All my old friends are here," he whispered to Wide-Awake, "that gay old rascal there was originally my master."

"The devil, he was," said Wide-Awake, surprised in his turn, "what a blessed young cupid he is, ain't he? I say Jack, ain't you anxious to make his acquaintance, suppose I inform him Mr. John Rann, alias Jack with the Sixteen-strings, is in a private, anxiously anticipating the pleasure of shaking his daddle."

"No thank you," said Jack, "I'll content myself by keeping an eye upon his movements, do you the same Colledge, my boy."

"Oh, you want him looked after, do you?" asked Wide-Awake.

Jack nodded assentingly.

"Werry good," continued the young hero, "I wont take my blessed peepers off him, but will watch him as narrowly as a hungry cat would a plump young mouse. Crikey, look at him now, ain't he doing the deeply interesting—oh, no, not at all! What a profitable lesson I should learn to be sure from that delicious juvenile—in the art of love making. Blow me, after this I shall be able to turn lovyer, myself. But soft, the curtain rises, and the play begins."

The curtain rose at the moment, disclosing the first scene in the new opera, and the cantatrice, whose fame has spread o'er Europe, appeared at the footlights. The dead silence which preceeded her appearance was broken by three enthusiastic rounds of applause, which suddenly ceased, as the melody of her rich and powerful voice reverberated through the vast building, so consummate was her acting, so melodious the tone of her truly wonderful voice, that the whole audience seemed suddenly transfixed with wonder at the sweet and bewitching power of the young songstress, who had so suddenly appeared amongst them, destined by the magic of her rare gifts to win their very hearts away. The scene ended, the curtain fell, and silence again reigned in the theatre, broken only by the voices of the enraptured throng, as they, in unqualified terms, loudly expressed their admiration.

Rann again gazed upon the Earl this time to perceive his hyena-like face, fixed in deadly ferocity upon Miss Malcolm and her companion. The look of demoniacal hatred gave place to a smile, if possible, yet still more loathsome, so bitter, so malign was it, Rann absolutely shuddered as he beheld the look of exultation, for, in the Earl's changing features he at once read treachery and mischief.

"That old villain is concocting some damnable plot," he whispered to Wide-Awake. "Watch him narrowly, as you value my friendship, and if he stirs from the box do you follow him."

"What mischief is he hatching, an old reptile?" asked Wide-Awake. "I caught his eye fixed upon yon fair lady's face; think you an ill-wind lurks in that quarter."

"I do," answered Rann, in tones deep and earnest, the more to impress Wide-Awake with the necessity for active vigilance; "he has for years had a longing tooth in that direction, and no crime, even that of murder itself, would prevent the old villain's carrying out his designs, if it were at all practicable."

"I'll look after him, never fear," said Wide-Awake, "although, in the company she is in, strike me if I see much danger. My noble captain opposite has the pluck and strength and courage of twenty such old dotards as he is."

"I am aware of it," said Rann, "but we have received proof an hundred times in our own profession, how strength can be outmatched by cunning, and yon hoary villain is as treacherous and subtle as he is lecherous, and, if he succeed, the victory will not be his so much by force of merit as by force of craft. See, he has already risen to take his departure—look to him, Wide-Awake, and prove yourself worthy of your name and trust, and you shall receive a brave reward, for I would rather sacrifice the last guinea I had in the world—my very life itself—before a hair of that dear girl's head should be injured. Look, he is leaving the box, follow him."

"I am gone," said Wide-Awake, whose whole nature gloried in an expedition by which he could oblige his captain, "his own shadow shall not dog him with more fidelity than I will," and Colledge, as he finished the utterance of the words, sprang from the box, and was gone in pursuit of the earl, who, by that time, had left the box.

The subsequent entertainment, delicious and attractive as it was, in every respect, had no charm for Rann—there was an undefinable dread of some coming evil, yet, what, he could not imagine or divine, gnawing at his heart. This oppressive feeling was further heightened in the course of an hour, by a messenger, who entered the box wherein Captain Dashfield was seated, and delivered a missive. What the purport of the note was, Rann could not, by any living possibility be supposed to know, but he was further strengthened in his opinion that some infernal scheme of treachery was on foot, from the fact that the captain rose, and, after whispering a few words to his lovely companion, he left the box, with the servant, leaving Miss Malcolm totally unprotected. Another hour passed, yet neither the earl, the captain, or Wide-Awake returned, and Jack's growing excitement almost reached the pitch of madness. Presently the same servant, at whose instigation the officer had left, returned, and delivering a message to Miss Malcolm, the young lady, suddenly becoming deadly pale, as if afflicted by some painful intelligence, also hurried from the theatre. Jack seized his sword, which he had stood in a corner, and instantly followed her, but when he reached the street, he found, to his intense sorrow, she was gone.

There was a crowd about the doorway bending over an object on the ground. Jack elbowed his way into the midst, and beheld his faithful aide-de-camp, Wide-Awake, stretched bleeding upon the pavement. Almost frenzied by the sight, and the conflicting circumstances that surrounded, Jack besought of Wide-Awake an explanation.

"I did my best," said poor Colledge, resting his bleeding head upon his hand, "did my best to prevent it, but they was too much for me, Jack—they cut me to the ground."

"And the lady," screamed Jack, "what of her?"

"The old man has got her, Jack—they forced her into a carriage, and drove off up Bow-street. Oh! Jack, I am fainting—dying!" and as the last word escaped from his pallid lips, poor Wide-Awake sank back insensible.

"Look to him, somebody, for God's sake—here is money," and Jack pressed a handful of gold into the first hand he came to, which chanced, for the wonder, to be an honest one, "take him to yonder hotel—run for a doctor, somebody; for more than life depends upon my speed."

"Get you gone, then," said the man, "I will see this young man is well bestowed, and that every care is taken of him," said the man, who held possession of the gold.

"Thanks—a thousand times," said Jack, wringing the man's hand in heartfelt gratitude, then, bounding onward like an arrow from a bow, Jack took his course towards the earl's house in Piccadilly. Such was the speed at which he went, that but few minutes were occupied in the transit, and, pale and breathless from rage and excitement, he seized the handle of the bell, and favoured the porter of the lodge with a peal so sonorous, that the worthy man in question sprang to his feet as if influenced by a magnetic shock. In an instant he threw open the door, and in stammering tones, and teeth chattering with fear, he inquired Jack's business.

"It is with the earl!" exclaimed Jack, as he sprang through the doorway, and hurriedly crossed the court-yard to the house. As he did so, he perceived the earl's carriage being conveyed to the coach-house. Irritated beyond constraint with the fear of being too late, Jack sprang up the marble steps into the hall. Here he was stopped by some half-dozen lacqueys, one of whom, with much politeness, inquired his business.

"It is with the Earl of Dashfield," answered Jack, sternly, "tell me where he is, scoundrel, instantly."

"Oh, yes, certainly," said the fellow, in an accent that was intended to be excessively droll, "my lord is in precisely the position I presume you ought to be—in bed—for you look as if you had been woke up in a desperate fright."

"Tamper not with me, fellow," exclaimed Jack, in a voice that made the flunkey shiver in his pumps. "I would have speech with the earl, and, by heavens, *will*, if I seek out every corner of this accursed edifice."

"Well, my dear impetuous sir—if you must have an audience why you must, but as my lord has laid strict injunctions he should not be disturbed, and as I have too much respect for him to disobey his commands, I have the honour of informing you, with all due deference and politeness, that I'll see you d—d twice over, blast me! before I move one step, either to call him or to take you to him," and the lacquey, who was a very giant to Jack, looked at his compeers for an approving recognition, and they, true to their lick-spittle qualities, were not long in according it.

"What imperance!" lisped one.

"What audacious cheek!" chimed another.

"Bravo, Stoples," said a third.

"Pitch him into the court-yard," suggested a fourth.

"Twist his nose, Stoples," lisped the first again.

Jack was seemingly awakened to his self-importance by this remark, for he instantly caught the speaker's nasal organ between his finger and thumb, and gave it so tremendous a tweak, that the fellow roared with pain. Leaving him, Jack sprang towards the tall flunkey, and administered such a vigorous kick in the breech, that the fellow, from the unwonted impetus, measured his length upon the floor. The others, needing no further proof of his prowess, scampered in all directions. Jack instantly sprang up the marble stairs in the direction where he knew the earl's chamber to lie; on reaching the landing, he was intercepted by other servants, who, hearing the uproar, were hastening to their fellows' assistance.

"How, now, fellow," said one, who was dressed in a plain suit of black, and seemed superior to the others, "so you are the cause of this uproar. What is the meaning of this disturbance? Are you aware you are intruding into a private gentleman's mansion, and are, in fact, making yourself amenable to law for trespass, assault, and battery?"

"I am aware of nothing, sir," said Jack, vehemently, "but that a young lady has been treacherously and forcibly torn from her friends, and conveyed hither, for the worst of purposes; and I am also aware, sir," said Jack, drawing his sword, "that I am here to rescue her, and I will, by heavens, or die in the attempt, therefore if you would prevent bloodshed, give me my way."

"My dear fellow," said the gentleman, mildly, "this is some blunder, the earl has just returned from Drury-lane Theatre somewhat unwell, and quite alone."

"Liar!" cried Jack, in a voice that made the place echo again, "if you attempt to tamper with, or deceive me, by heavens I'll cut your black heart out. You have to deal with no craven, now, fellow," said Jack, glaring at him like an infuriated tiger. "It is I—I, Sixteen-string Jack, who not only demands the lady, but will have her, if I fight to the death."

As our hero thus undauntedly announced his name, the bravest amongst them grew pale from fear, for his feats of intrepidity—his reckless courage—his dashing devilry, had gained him a name to be admired at a distance, and to be feared when at hand.

"If you are he," said the superior servant, "I feel it will be useless to deny the truth. The earl is here, and he has with him a young lady, for what purpose I dare not say, but you may readily guess."

"Tell me what room they are in," cried Rann, impatiently, "that I may fly to her deliverance."

"They are in the earl's chamber," said the man, in a low tone, "but, for God's sake, do not reveal who told you, as it will certainly cost us our places, and, probably, our lives."

"Trust to me, and fear not," said Jack, rushing forward. "I am here to deliver not to involve."

The chamber door reached, Jack found, to his despair, it was locked. At that instant a low moan of anguish from the interior burst upon his ear. Lashed to madness by the sound, Jack dashed himself violently against the door, the fastenings were insufficient to resist the heavy pressure, and the door flew open.

Sword in hand Jack dashed into the apartment. Rudely thrown upon the sumptuous bed lay the lovely form of Miss Malcolm; whilst gloating over his victim with a look really horrible from the lust and licentiousness depicted therein, stood the earl. So entranced was he in the contemplation of his prize—so enwrapt was his imagination in the enjoyment in which he was about villain-like to revel, that he neither heard or heeded Jack's entrance, although it was, in good truth, noisy enough almost to have awoke the dead. He was not suffered long, however, to remain in this unconscious happiness; in an instant, Jack's voice, threatening and sonorous, broke upon his ear, as he exclaimed, in startling tones:—

"Villain! what, again caught then at your damnable tricks. So, so, old man, if you have but injured an hair of this dear girl's head, by heavens I'll wipe the stain out in your heart's best blood."

"What scoundrel are you, that you dare thrust yourself armed and unbidden into my presence? Answer me, I say, or I'll summon my servants and bid them whip you with your own sword—or break your accursed intruding neck down the stairs they ought never have allowed you to ascend."

"They dared not prevent me," said Jack, calmly, "and were their number trebled, even then they would not dare to execute your behest."

"We will see that," said the earl, advancing to the door, but Jack, interposing his person, bid him, in tones of thunder—"Stop!"

"Help, help, help," screamed the earl.

Jack seized the earl by the throat with one hand, whilst, with the other, he brought the sword to within a few inches of my lord's heart.

"By He who made me," cried Jack, "if you cease not that uproar I'll stop your mouth for ever. Get you in yon corner, hound as you are, and stir not on your life until I bid you."

"You bid me!" said the earl, brightening up, for he caught glimpses of his servants hovering round, "and who in the devil's name are you, that you command me in my own house."

"These features ought to be familiar to you, my Lord of Dashfield," said our hero, with a derisive smile, "read them again, are they now unfamiliar to you?"

"Audacious devil that you are, I know you now. Now you scoundrels there," he shouted to his servants, "call in the constabulary, we have captured Jack Rann the highwayman, there's five hundred pounds reward for the man who captures him."

"And for the man who attempts to capture me, my lord, there is certain death—I warn you all, I am a desperate man, and my good sword, come life or death, shall stand my friend, if you urge me in my desperate need. As for you, Lord Dashfield, if you would have the assistance of the officers you are free to depart and summons them, but mark me," and Jack levelled his finger at him with a warning gesture, "I go not to the scaffold alone, no, no, when Jack Rann the highwayman is arrested for robbery—let the Lord of Dashfield, the *murderer*, tremble for his guilty soul, for the officers will be on his track for the murder of his unhappy wife."

Trembling with excessive fear, the earl's knees positively shook together, whilst a cold perspiration, like the damp and clammy dew of death, stood upon his forehead.

"Who says I murdered her?" he groaned rather than spoke, whilst his eyes glared with fearful suspicion around.

"One who is a living witness of the fact," responded Rann, "hast ever heard the name of Elinor Roche?"

"I saw it reported in the newspaper the other day," replied the earl, spitefully, "that the wench had undergone the punishment of the press to make her confess thy whereabouts—coward—dispicable coward that thou art, to leave a woman as hostage for your own black crimes. Rann, I defy you! The accusation is false, no magistrate would listen to it, coming from such vile lips as thine and her's."

"Grant it even so," said Rann unmoved, "there is yet a positive—a damning testimony of your guilt—"

"And that," stammered the earl.

"Is the body of the countess, buried at midnight without your sanction or knowledge. Well may your lips blanch—well may your guilty conscience be apparent in your very face! the reproduction of that body with the murderer's mark upon the throat—the unmistakeable signs of a bloody, brutal, and cowardly murder, with the living testimony which you brave so daringly, would irrevocably seal your doom. If the prospect of Tyburn's fatal tree be fearful to me, how much more appalling ought it to be so to you old man, who will go to it steeped in blood?"

"Mercy! mercy!" implored the earl, as he sank, a shivering heap of wretchedness and fear, into a corner.

A faint groan from Miss Malcolm, who was now awakening from the state of insensibility into which she had fallen, arrested Jack's attention.

"Villain! bloodless, merciless, soulless villain!" exclaimed Rann, "is not this sight enough to clothe your eyes in eternal darkness, you, who have dared again to lay impious hands upon the person of this dear girl?—out of my sight, hound that you are, lest my more indignant nature rise and prompt my just sword to do her justice. Yet, stop! I, who witnessed your unholy triumph, will now witness your ignoble defeat. Miss Malcolm," he exclaimed, raising her gently from the bed, "awake, arouse yourself, I beseech you."

She staggered to her feet, and gazed around with painful astonishment.

"Where am I?" she murmured, "what does this mean?" then as her eye wandered to the crouching form of the earl, she started back, as though a viper lay in her path, and, in tones of heart-breaking agony, besought heaven to save her.

"Heaven has heard your prayer, lady," said Jack, with much feeling "and has made me the humble instrument of His goodness."

"And you will protect me—you will defend me?"

"I will, lady," answered Rann, "to the death."

"Then do remove me from this horrible place, from that bad, wicked man, oh, heaven! why is this punishment again fallen upon me?"

"Be comforted, Miss Malcolm, all will yet be well; there are none who dare attempt to molest us, and I will escort you in safety to your father."

"Thanks, kind sir, my heart will ever hold grateful remembrance of your timely generosity; as for you, sir," she said, turning to the earl, "think not again to escape with impunity. Silence sealed my lips over your first outrage, for I held too much love in my heart for poor Lady Dashfield to wound her by a recital of her husband's villanous conduct. But your second outrageous proceeding has o'erstept all bounds, and this time, black-hearted scoundrel that you are, fear not, but you shall be publicly disgraced, and publicly punished."

"Be it so, madam," said the earl, his face pale to the very lips with passion, "I fear not the ordeal, since the public may learn the fact that Miss Malcolm is the mistress of a knight of the road. The prized companion of a nortorious thief. Glorious news for my nephew, too, will it not be to know he is rivalled in his love by that scape-gallows, Sixteen-string Jack, the footpad."

"Silence, villain," exclaimed Jack, nor dare add insult to injury. That, as Sixteen-string Jack, the world has felt some loss, and I have reaped same unenviable notoriety, I candidly confess, yet spite of all, disgraced, lost, abandoned, as I am, Jack Rann has too much manliness in him to debauch the child of friends, and, too much honour in him to steep his hands in the blood of a woman."

MISS MALCOLM.

"And can it indeed be Mr. Rann who has again saved me?" exclaimed Miss Malcolm, bursting into tears; oh! sir, what wondrous miracle is this?"

"No miracle, my dear Miss Malcolm," answered Jack, smiling, "only a simple matter of fact which I will explain more fully anon. In the meantime let us decamp, the sight of that man is obnoxious, and the breath of this perfumed air is redolent with crime. My Lord Dashfield, you will please excuse our abrupt departure. I need not ask you to hold us in your heart, for that I already feel assured you will do. I leave you now with no punishment excepting what your own guilty conscience and bad passion have heaped upon you. As this lady will seek protection under the vengeful wing of the law, I should seriously advise you to consult your safety, or you may chance find, England somewhat unpleasantly warm for your delicate constitution. I absolutely must demand at your hands—this much—that you do confess yourself a traitorous black-hearted villain—a scoundrel, who deserves to have his ears slit, and be put in the pillory, as a mark for all the offal and filth of London. That you are the representative of a nobleman, without a spark of true nobility in your carcase; the effigy of a man, with the body of a beast, and the heart of a villian; and further, that you do humbly and sincerely upon your bended knees apologise to Miss Malcolm for the outrage, the insult, and the injury you have this day heaped upon her, and moreover, you shall summon your whole household to be eye witnesses of the fact, that they may reap a lesson from your disgrace, and learn how despicably mean, man in his baser qualities may reduce himself."

"I will perish rather than do it," said the earl.

"Not so, my lord, you will do this first, and perish afterwards. Come sir," he said to the head servant, "summon the household, his lordship desires publicly to apologise for his duplicity—get you gone, sir, and obey my mandate, or you and I may perchance quarrel."

The man looked first from his lord to Sixteen-string Jack. In the face of the former he read everything it was possible for the human face to express of the mean and despicable—in that of the latter he perceived, plainly traced, a will that would not be thwarted—of a determination that would not brook opposition, and from this he drew a reasonable inference that it would be better even to chance the loss of his situation than run the risk of a personal conflict with Jack Rann. He therefore obeyed the latter's bidding, and, in a few moments, the whole household were gathered in the room in silent consternation to witness the degradation of a master whom they served, yet heartily hated while they did so.

"These persons comprise the whole of the establishment, do they?"

"They do," was the reply.

"Very good. Now my lord, you will commence the task of justice assigned you, by confessing yourself to be a disgrace to human nature, a blot upon manhood, an old man, whose grey hairs, instead of honour, are a disgrace to him. Come, sir, begin."

"Curse you—curse you," muttered the earl, "I will die first."

"I will have reparation, and if you will concede to the terms I have proposed, you will not trouble me to find means of disgracing you after a still more disgraceful fashion, come sir."

"Cowards, knaves, scoundrels!" exclaimed the earl, as he gazed upon his servants, "to suffer me to be taunted by a villain like that; upon him one and all, and cut him to the ground."

But the servants budged not a foot—Jack's glaring eyes, equally as much as the unsheathed sword in his hand, awed them into passive obedience of his will.

"For the last time I ask you, will or will you not obey my bidding?" said Jack to the earl.

"No, no, no!" shrieked the culprit.

"Be it so, then," said Jack. He advanced to the group of wonderin servants, and took from the hands of one of them, a massive riding whip, with a particularly thick and rigly thong. Jack handed his sword to Miss Malcolm, and, advancing to the earl, he seized him by the collar and speedily stripped his coat from his back. Then grasping the whip tightly by the handle, he applied the thong with such vigour to the sides back and legs of the unfortunate earl, that he danced and screamed with agony. Disregarding his cries and appeals for mercy, Jack stuck to the practice until his vigorous arm began to tire, when, spite of the remonstrances of Miss Malcolm, who, pitying the sufferings of the earl, besought our hero to desist, Jack threw all his remaining strength into a dozen finishing cuts, and then mercifully allowed the earl to roll from his grasp, writhing like an eel in his agony, and completely black in the face.

Taking the sword from Miss Malcolm, he turned to the group and said:—

"You have been eye witnesses of that scoundrel's punishment, ask your own consciences whether he has received a tithe part of what he deserved."

"No, he has not," said several voices.

"The sore bones he will carry about with him for many a day to come, may have a salutary tendency in teaching him, that right must not always be trespassed upon with impunity even by the mighty. I have now to request at your hands free egress from this mansion for myself and this fair lady. If it be freely accorded, as in justice it ought, I have sufficient in this purse," which he threw at their feet, "to give you all an opportunity of drinking the health of Sixteen-string Jack, but if the least movement be made to interrupt myself or this lady, even to the brushing of her dress as she passes, my sword shall find a home in the heart of the man who does it."

Seeing that, they drew aside with respectful politeness; Jack confidently sheathed his weapon, and extending his arm to Miss Malcolm, they passed unmolested from the room and from the house.

CHAPTER XXXII.

THE ESCORT HOME—CONGRATULATIONS—THE SURPRISE—THE FLIGHT—A LEAP INTO THE THAMES.

ON reaching the street, Jack's first care was to hire a hackney-coach, which he ordered to be driven to Mr. Malcolm's country residence. It was to both a delicious ride—so absorbed were both in delightful reminiscences and pleasurable feeling, that they almost felt disappointed when the vehicle stopped at Mr. Malcolm's mansion.

The anxious parents were already on the look out for their beloved child, for, filled with all sorts of wild imaginings at her delay, (Captain Dashfield having returned without her) they had been in an agony at her unaccountable absence; it was, therefore, with emotions of purest delight that they greeted her on her return, and Isabella, unable longer to restrain the pent-up feelings of her overcharged heart, threw herself upon her mother's bosom, and sobbed aloud. "My darling child," cried the fond mother, "what has happened—what can be the matter?"

"Oh, mother, I have had such an escape—thanks to the noble gallantry of this dear gentleman—such an escape, that my heart is like to burst almost at the thought."

"Tush, tush, child," cried the old man, "moderate your grief, child, all is well, you are at home safe and sound, and there is that brave fellow, Captain Dashfield, over head, impatiently awaiting an interview. Bless my soul, I quite forgot the coachman, what a shame to keep the poor man waiting to be sure—let me go and settle with him, and I'll be back in an instant."

"Excuse me, my dear sir," said Jack, with a smile, "but I have urgent business in town to-night—or rather, morning—and shall require his services in that direction; if you will permit me, I will at once take leave of Miss Malcolm, and then take my departure."

"Oh, certainly sir," said old Malcolm, somewhat glad that our hero was going, if the truth must be told, for he had set his heart on a wedding between his daughter and Captain Dashfield, and feared even the slightest interposition might prejudice his wishes, "take your leave of the ladies by all manner of means, sir, I will desire the coachman to wait."

To do the good old gentleman justice, he had certainly not the remotest idea of the important service rendered his daughter by our hero.

"My dear Miss Malcolm," said Jack, at which familiarity both father and mother stared most mightily, " permit me to wish you a good night, and a speedy recovery from the events and annoyances of this memorable—"

"Memorable, indeed, my own dear friend," replied Isabel, with charming simplicity, " how can I ever reward your timely, praiseworthy, and noble devotion."

" By dismissing from your thoughts, dear Isabella—"

" Eh, what?" grunted the father.

" Miss Malcolm, I beg pardon," said Jack, with a smile, as he corrected himself, " by blotting from your memory all recollections of this night, since the reminiscences so awakened are more tinged with sorrow than joy."

"Say not so, Mr. Rann," said Isabel, with much feeling, "believe me, while there is yet life in this poor heart, it will ever throb in fervent gratitude to you."

"Eh, what?" grunted old Malcolm again. "What's your name, sir? Excuse me, you know."

"Certainly," said Jack, "my name is Rann, sir."

"Eh, what?" exclaimed the old gentleman, quite aghast with surprise. Jack repeated the word for his especial benefit.

"Rann, eh? Curious coincidence—not Jack Rann I hope!"

"The very same, sir," answered Jack.

"The devil!" then, drawing a long breath, he went on.

"So you are that scoundrel, Jack Rann, the highwayman, are you?"

"I am," answered Jack.

"Then all I can say is, sir," said the impetuous old man, "I'll not allow my house to be an harbour for thieves, so the sooner you leave it, the better I shall like it, and mayhap the better for your safety."

"I have no fear of that," said Jack calmly.

"Then you would have, if you were not an audacious devil, so I tell you to your head, sir."

"You think so," said Jack in the same calm tone.

"I *know* so," reiterated Mr. Malcolm, and further know, sir, it is my duty, as an honest citizen of England, to give you into custody of the officers of the peace, but as you come peaceably, I scorn to take unfair advantage of you. But nevertheless, sir, I bid you leave my house, sir, begone sirrah begone !"

"Don't distress yourself old gentleman, I'm going," said Jack."

"You'd best be going, whilst your shoes are good."

Then, seemingly inspired by a fresh idea, he turned to his daughter, who was pained beyond measure at this unexpected proceeding.

"Bella my dear, examine your pockets, perhaps the villain has robbed you."

Our hero's face crimsoned to the temples at this insulting supposition.

"You judge me hardly, sir," said Jack, gravely, "and believe me, however culpable my conduct may have been, I do not think myself deserving of this insult at your hands. But it is the way of the world, sir: a world composed of unfeeling hearts, and unforgiving spirits—and so, like many a martyr of a better order, I must bow resignedly to my fate. Farewell, sir, never fear, Jack Rann's shadow shall never again darken this honest door of yours."

Jack turned to Miss Malcolm.

"Farewell, dear lady, may heaven bless, preserve, and cherish you. May the choicest gifts this life can afford be yours, and happiness eternal crown the closing of your life."

As Jack spoke these words in a tone full of tenderness and pathos, the true-hearted girl, unable to restrain the tide of gratitude that swelled her heart, threw herself upon our hero's breast and sobbed convulsively.

"Oh, Jack, my own dear, true friend, do not leave me thus—he spoke in ignorance—he did not, could not mean what he said," then turning appealingly to her father, she poured forth in broken sentences, the recital of the earl's villany, her own dire danger, and the dreadful fate from which she had been rescued by the undaunted bravery of our hero. In an instant the scene was changed. The look of scorn and disdain with which Mr. Malcolm had regarded Jack Rann gave way to a gush of grateful tears, and the old gentleman, in tones of fervour, besought our hero's pardon for the injustice and insult he had heaped upon him.

It was no sooner asked than instantly accorded, and as Jack extended his hand gaily and frankly to him, Mr. Malcolm's delight transgressed all bounds of decorum.

"What an old ass I am! What a brave dear fellow you are! Mother, come down on your knees and thank the saviour of your child," then rushing to the staircase, he shouted to the captain, who, in a state of nervous excitement more easily imagined than described, was pacing the drawing-room overhead.

"Captain Dashfield, I say—why the devil don't you come down—here's Mr. Jack Rann, the highwayman, come to see us—and he's brought home Isabel, come along you dog do, I'm as happy as a prince."

The captain did not need the injunction to be twice repeated, but almost instantly entered the room. He was somewhat startled to be sure, at beholding Miss Malcolm rushing in other arms than his own, and a feeling of jealousy was struggling for the mastery in his bosom, but that was as quickly dispelled as it was awakened, as Jack, with a candour that knew no deceit, and with a smile of unalloyed pleasure illumining his handsome countenance, stepped frankly forward with extended hand.

"Captain, I have robbed you of a glorious treat, inasmuch as I have been instrumental in saving this lady from the hands of an old villain. This pleasurable task by right should have been yours, but since I have returned her safe and sound to your arms, look you, that you hold no jealousy in your heart towards me for the act."

"Jealousy, my dear fellow," exclaimed young Dashfield, enthusiastically, "I owe you an eternal debt of gratitude, my dear fellow, for your noble and gallant services. But I am so enwrapt in mystery—so confused by the incomprehensible events of the last few hours, that I assure you I scarce can explain the extent of my bewilderment."

"That you are scarcely *compos mentis* I must candidly confess," said Jack, with a graceful smile, "or you would not have suffered Miss Malcolm to remain so long in my arms—come sir, take the rich gift heaven vouchsafed you," said Jack, presenting her with a grace at once touching and truthful, "your bosom is the safer abiding place for this fair head. May heaven send it may long support it—may God grant it—may ever he be for her a happy and safe abiding place."

And, uttering these words, Jack Rann, with a tenderness those who knew him best could scarce have credited, placed the dear girl in her lover's arms.

Jack turned to Mr. and Mrs. Malcolm, who were looking on with tearful eyes, and exclaimed in a voice broken with emotion:—

"This scene of happiness is one I shall review with joy to the latest moment of my life."

"God send that the time may be far—far distant," said the old gentleman, with fervour.

"I have but little hope of that," said Jack, with a tinge of melancholy in his tone. "I can perceive too clearly the fate that is in store for me."

"If the powers that be could have their will, friend Rann," said young Dashfield, in a hope inspiring voice, " a dog's death to a certainty would be thine. But if not all-powerful, you have at least in us friends, who have the heart and will to assist you—it only remains for fortune to place the opportunity within our grasp, and, by Jove, I am half inclined to think she is favourably disposed towards us; this eventful night I have a scheme in my head, Jack, for your salvation, of which more anon, but now I am all eagerness to learn the secret of this wonderful deliverance."

"My portion of the narration is a short one. I went to the theatre to wile away an idle hour. The lynx-eyes of a young friend of mine discovered yourself and Miss Malcolm in an opposite box. My own optics led me to discover the Earl of Dashfield. I instructed my aide-de-camp to watch him narrowly, for, from a single glance which he directed towards you, I gleaned there was mischief afloat. I was further strenthened in my suspicion by his leaving the theatre; still further awakened to a sense of impending danger by your absense, and finally convinced by the ultimate withdrawal of Miss Malcolm from the house. I followed her with all speed, but was too late—the plot was successful—she was gone. From my companion, who, by some means, was badly wounded—"

"It was in his gallant endeavour to save me," said Miss Malcolm, with a shudder.

"I learnt," continued Rann, "the lady had been forcibly seized, and also gained intelligence of the route the carriage had taken. My own suspicion did the rest. I flew to Dashfield House—obtained admittance—saved the lady—and read the earl a lesson he will remember to his dying day."

"Most accursed treachery. I read it all now," said Captain Dashfield.

"Then you have certainly the advantage of me," said Jack, "for I cannot imagine how you could by any means, however plausible, been prevailed upon to leave your lady alone and unprotected, in a theatre. It speaks anything but highly of your character for gallantry, sir."

"Appearances I confess are against me, but I think you will admit the realities by which I was surrounded ought satisfactorily to dispose of them. You probably remember a lacquey of the theatre delivering me a missive?"

"I do," said Rann.

"There is the precious missive, sir," said the captain, tendering it to our hero, "give me your opinion upon it."

"As specious a piece of villany—as pretty a piece of treachery, as ever I read," said Jack, as he ran down the document.

"Read it out," said the captain, " I have no secrets from these dear friends, indeed it is due to them as to myself, that the whole truth should be revealed."

"Here goes then," said Jack, swallowing a glass of wine as a preliminary. "Listen all."

"We are all attention," said Mr. Malcolm.

Jack then read the contents of the note which ran in these words:—

"The Earl of Dashfield has been thrown from his horse, and is seriously if not mortally hurt; your instant attendance is required. Hesitate not a moment, or you may be too late, the sufferer is lying at No. —, Duke-street."

"Now, under these circumstances, may I claim forgiveness, dearest Isabel for my seeming discourtesy in leaving you?"

Isabella assented by a slight but significant pressure of the hand.

"You were quite justified in going," said Jack, "that's clear as crystal, but still, captain."

"I am all attention, Mr. Rann."

"Well, then, I must confess I cannot perceive you were justified in staying the time you did."

"It was a matter of necessity, sir, not of choice, inasmuch as I was detained by *force*."

"By force," echoed Jack, "how so?"

"Simply this—when I reached the house, I was ushered, with every appearance of haste up stairs; the party who conducted me left for the purpose of procuring a light, the one she carried having by accident been extinguished."

"By accident, eh," repeated Jack.

"Yes, sir, by accident," said Dashfield, "why do you repeat my words?"

"Why," answered Jack, with a laugh, "because it strikes me there was more desire than accident in the affair.

"You speak truly, sir, I had reasons speedily to believe it was done designedly, for no signs of return became visible, I waited for some time in patience, at length, losing all control, I sprang to the door to effect an egress, imagine my dismay, sir, when I found it locked, and the agonising conviction burst upon me that I had been treacherously entrapped. I shouted, kicked, and thumped, most lustily, but the only answer to my vigorous appeals, were loud and boisterous shouts of laughter, which ever and anon greeted my ears, completely drowning the uproar I made. Driven to desperation, I flew to the window, there was not a chance of escape by that outlet. If one, it was forty-feet from the ground, and death alone could result from such an enterprise. On learning this I redoubled my exertions, and made tenfold more noise than I had hither done. The only answer I received, was shouts of jeering, and derisive laughter from the gang below. Satisfied liberty was not to be gained by an appeal to their good feelings, I tried if the public without would be more on the alert, and dashing the window open, I cried murder, fire, theives, at the top of my lungs. A crowd speedily gathered about the door; alarmed at this, a forbidding fellow came from below with a light, I sprang upon the villain, and verily believe I should have strangled him, if his fellows had not come to his assistance. Finally I forced my way from the house—returning to the theatre, I discovered Miss Malcolm was gone. Supposing she had left for home, indignant at my seeming neglect, I sprang into a cabriolet and drove hither, to learn, to my deep disappointment, she had not returned, for her displeasure was less to be feared than the danger of being exposed to the licentious rabble who nightly prowl the streets of London."

"Did you not also receive a note, Miss Malcolm?" asked Jack.

"I did," answered the young lady, "I have lost the missive, but the purport I well remember, as it was couched in but few words."

"And they were?" queried her father.

"In effects, if not in actual terms, these:—'Captain Dashfield has met with a serious accident, he desires a moment's speech with you. Delay not an instant.' When I reached the lobby, I was instantly hurried by some servants in waiting, into a carriage. I remember a brave youth making strenuous efforts to prevent my entrance, in an instant he fell, covered with blood on the kerb-stone, whilst the carriage was whirled away. More I remember not, excepting that I found, to my unspeakable horror, I was again in the power of Lord Dashfield, from whose evil machinations and wicked intents Mr. Rann's noble undaunted courage, in face of numberless difficulties so wondrously rescued me."

"If there be law and justice to be had in England—that man, earl though he be, and protected, as I grieve to say he is, by the sad example of an impious and licentious court, shall not escape punishment."

"He richly deserves it, and although he is near akin to me, yet will l aid you to the utmost of my power in your efforts to bring him to justice," said Captain Dashfield.

"I accept your proffered aid—but come let us to supper," said Malcolm, in a gayer tone, " we have had enough of troubles and tribulations for one

No. 45.

night—a glorious morn is now breaking, let us crack a bottle of champagne over these joyful reunions, and if we trouble our brain with thinking more, let it be on some expedient whereby we can benefit our brave friend Jack Rann."

They betook themselves to the supper table, and having partook of the good things of this life, proceeded, over the generous juice of the grape, to discuss what was, should, or could be done, to benefit our hero.

"You confess then, Rann," said Mr. Malcolm, "you are tired of the lawless, dangerous career you have been leading?"

"Nay, not exactly so, sir," answered Jack with flashing eyes. "A life on the road has more charms than you wot of, and for a fellow like myself, with no tie to bind him to life, it is just the free, rollicking, dangerous career a young man like myself, with more blood than brains, and more wants than both, would take delight in."

"Could I so far have misinterpreted your meaning then," said Mr. Malcolm, with a disappointed visage ; "did I not understand you to say you would forsake the path of crime, for that of honesty, were but the chance given you ?"

"You did," said Jack.

"Then why this lingering regard for old evil courses and viscious propensities ?"

"Because the love of it has so firm a hold upon me I should lie were I to disown it—God bless you," said Jack, "if you only knew what a delicious life an highwayman's is, hang me if you wouldn't go on the road yourself."

"Not I," said Mr. Malcolm, seriously.

"I tell you, you would," said Jack, on whom the wine was taking an exhilarating effect. "Come, now, I'll give you an illustration. Fancy yourself as I have often been, without a stiver in my purse—with a crew of creditors driving you for money at your back. What's to be done? You argue —your worldly property consists of a brace of barbers."

"Brace of barkers," echoed Mrs. Malcolm, "but you must confess it is very wrong of gentlemen in difficulties to think of keeping two dogs, surely one might suffice."

Jack greeted this economical interposition with an unrestrained burst of laughter.

"I see nothing to laugh at," said the simple old lady. "I consider two dogs an extravagant number for a poor man, who has no ostensible means of feeding his own belly, let alone theirs ; poor dumb things."

Jack gave vent at this till his sides fairly ached.

"Excuse me, man, but upon my soul it is such an exceedingly good joke, I must pay it one respect, ha, ha, ha !"

"Barkers, Mrs. Malcolm," whispered the captain to the lady, "does not mean dogs."

"What on earth does it mean?" said the lady, impatiently. "Dogs are the only things in Natural History that I am aware of that bark—except parrots. I remember a lady who had a parrot that barked once, perhaps, its parrots."

"No, madam," said the captain, unable himself to restrain a smile, "it is merely a technical term for pistols."

"Pistols! pistols!" exclaimed Mrs. Malcolm, letting the words off as though she was positively firing the weapons, "what on earth do people want to give things such incredulous, outlandish names for, I can't conceive for the life of me."

"My dear madam, it's only a funny way that we've got. But to my illustration—you look at your barkers—pistols I mean, and begin to think what they were made for—begin to examine them, perhaps, and from examining them, load them. The thought then strikes you, you have a beautiful little mare, who is never more in her glory than when she has her master athwart her back—this brings you again ruminating upon your empty pockets. They must be filled—that's certain—but how? How? pistol points—the horse leads it—once across his back at a glorious gallop, your blood rises to extacy. Softly, who have we coming here? A couple of travellers, riding in company for safety's sake. The probability of their full pouches brings again unpleasantly to your mind the dilapidated state of your own inexpressibles, with their pockets to let. To think is to do it. A stroke of the spur, and your gallant mare is upon them like a whirlwind. Pistol in hand—stand and deliver in your mouth—trembling for their lives, forth comes their money bags. The caitiffs ride off, well pleased they have escaped with whole skins, whilst you, with heavy pockets and a lightened heart, gallop to town, and right jolly is the highwayman's life till the money grows short again. Why, it's so jovial a life, a poet has actually embodied it in verse. Come, I'll tip you a stave or two—and throwing himself back in his chair, Jack Rann gave vent to the following song:—

THE ROBBER'S LIFE.

On the stream of the world, the robber's life
   Is borne on the blithest wave;
How it bounds into life in a gladsome strife,
   How it laughs in its hiding cave.

At his maiden's lattice he stays the rein,
   How still is his courser proud!
But still as the wind when it hangs o'er the main,
   In the breast of the boding cloud.

With the champed bit, arched crest,
   And the eye of a listening deer,
Like valour, fretful most in rest,
   Least chafed when in career.

Fit slave to a lord when all else refuse,
   To save in his deperate need;
By my troth! I think one whom the world pursues
   Has a right to a gallant steed.

Away my beloved—I hear their feet!
　　I blow thee a kiss, my fair,
And I promise to bring you when next we meet
　　A braid for thy bonny hair,

Hurrah for the booty!—my steed, hurrah:
　　Through bush, through brake, go we;
And the coy moon smiles on our merry way,
　　Like my own love—timidly.

The parson, he rides with a jingling pouch,
　　How it blabs of the rifled poor!
The courtier, he rolls in a gilded coach,
　　How it smacks of a sinecure.

The lawyer revolves in his whirling chaise,
　　Sweet thoughts of a mischief done:
And the lady knoweth the card she plays,
　　In counting her guineas won.

Oh, lady! what, holloa, ye sinless men!
　　My claim ye can scarce refuse;
For when honest folks live on their neighbours, then
　　They encroach on the robber's dues.

The lady changed cheek like a bashful maid,
　　The lawyer talked wondrous fair,
The parson blasphemed, and the courtier prayed,
　　And the robber bore off his share.

Hurrah for the revel! my steed, hurrah!
　　Through bush, through brake, go we;
It is ever a virtue when others pay,
　　To ruffle it merrily.

Oh! there never was life like the robber's, so
　　Jolly, and bold, and free:
And its end—why a cheer from the crowd below,
　　And a leap from a leafless tree.

" And if that is my end," said Jack, " why need we go to grieve? It will save a wondrous sum in doctor's fees, and is the shortest cut to heaven I know of. So hang me, I'll spin my gay career to the end, and when the time comes to snap my thread of life, let it be done by an hempen neckcloth."

" Your heedless way of talking makes me shudder, Jack," said Miss Malcolm, " pray for heaven's sake cease."

" You have drawn a brilliant picture of a highwayman's life, but believe me, Rann, it does not near approach in happiness the life led by an honest man," said Dashfield. " Come, Jack, I must change your opinions, must yet win you to a life of industry and the path of rectitude. Now tell me truly Jack, had you the opportunity, would you not exchange your reckless life for one of quietude, ease, and comfort?"

"I am afraid I couldn't, I am naturally of a restless disposition, and without excitement I should die of *ennui*."

"But is there not various kinds of excitement, and think you another cannot be equally as inviting and profitable now, as that which has a tendency to demoralizing acts, and vicious tendencies?"

"There may be," said Jack, carelessly, "and is, I have no doubt, but the only one I have run against in my gay career, is that which you characterise as one of vicious tendencies."

"What think you, Jack, of the life of an emigrant?" Miss Malcolm suggested.

"It is the very life for you, Jack," shouted the sanguine young officer, "the very life of all others to bring your natural free disposition into full play. Why, in America, Jack, freed from all the trammels of European manners, you might build yourself a house, wander, gun in hand, over miles and miles of forest ground literally swarming with game, and without fear of an ugly encounter with a gamekeeper, or an action for trespass. Might fish in your own lake, grow your own corn, and become at once, like Selkirk of old, and exclaim with him: 'I am monarch of all I survey. My right there is none to dispute.' The dangers by which you might first be surrounded too, would give zest to a vigorous disposition, such as yours. Fancy the glow of triumph that would thrill through your frame, as with unerring aim you brought your bear or wolf to the ground. Fancy the glorious superiority displayed in curbing the wild passions of the Indians, who would worship your feats of daring and intrepidity, as they would the actions of a god, and their admiration once gained, the aggressive spirit once quelled, you would not find in the world more steadfast friends, more faithful allies, were you to search the wide world throughout, than these would prove themselves. There also Jack, in a new world, apart and severed from all the temptations that destroyed you in the old one, you may yet learn to take pride in life, by perseverance and energy, might win yourself a new glorious name, might live long, an honour to yourself and a blessing to your fellow-men, and descending full of years to the grave, might be borne thither by surrounding hearts, regretting the loss they had sustained in the destruction of your prized companionship."

"Such, indeed, would be a glorious destiny, but it is beyond my reach, so why tempt me with fallacious hopes."

"Tell me truly, Jack, as you value your happiness, here and hereafter—as you value our esteem and friendship, if this destiny was placed within your grasp—would you accept it?"

"As God is my judge I would." responded our hero, solemnly.

"Then you are saved, Jack—art saved! There is a vessel chartered to sail from Liverpool, within a week from this time. I will engage a berth in her for you, will ship you a full complement of provisions, ploughs, harrows, and every agricultural implement necessary to establish a first-rate farm, and further, I will place in your hands five hundred pounds, for the purchase of land. That sum in the new world will enable you to purchase a tract of ground, that shall in extent exceed the utmost limits of your ambition, say Jack, shall this be a bargain—will you agree to it?'

"Agree to it," exclaimed Jack, rapturously, "could any sane man refuse so generous, so unexpected an offer. Sir, I accept your proposition with heartfelt gratitude, here is my hand on it."

"Bravo Jack," said Mr. Malcolm, tears of joy flashing in his eyes. "Go, my brave boy—God will sustain you in your good resolve, and still further to aid you in your endeavours, I have here five hundred pounds, which I also devote to your services," and the old gentleman pushed, as he spoke, a pocket-book towards our hero.

Unable to restrain his excessive gratitude, which this princely generosity caused to flow beyond measure, Jack gave vent to his feelings, and sobbed aloud.

They did not disturb him in his transports, being satisfied they would calm and allay his excited feelings, nor were they wrong in their conjecture, for, in a few minutes, Jack had sufficiently recovered to speak calmly on the subject.

"How deeply grateful I am for this kindness, my heart is too full to allow my tongue to speak. But if I accept the aid of this money," said Jack, "it must be upon my own conditions."

"And they are?" asked Mr. Malcolm."

"That immediately I can earn the means, I may be allowed to repay it."

"We can have no possible objection to that, Rann," said Mr. Malcolm, who at once perceived it would be an inducement for Jack to persevere. "What say you, Dashfield?"

"I wished mine to have been a voluntary gift," replied the young officer, "accepted as a present from a friend, who values the heavy obligation under which he lays, but if Rann insists upon returning it—"

"And I do," said Jack, firmly.

"Then I will offer no impediment to your will, and only hope, for your own sake more than mine even, the money may be speedily returned to us, since it will be a gratifying proof you are pursuing your new avocation of industry with energy and perseverance."

"Rely on me for that," said Jack; "and now I must still further impose upon your kindness."

"You have but to name your wants, and if it lays in our power consider them executed."

"I have been thinking," said Rann, "a life in the back wood will be one almost too solitary for a chap who has ever been used to society, and plenty of it. I, therefore, propose, with your permission, to take out a helpmate for me, in the shape of a—a wife."

"An excellent thought," said old Malcolm, "do so, by all manner of means, but have you chosen the lady fair?"

"I have," answered Rann. "She is a noble and devoted girl, and one I am assured who loves me right fondly. Her name is Elinor Roche, sir—she was follow-servant with me at Dashfield House, and is the same girl who underwent the torture for me in the press-yard at Newgate."

"You have made a right worthy selection," said the captain, "and I sincerely hope you may have cause ever to rejoice at it. Is there anything further?"

"Yes," answered Rann, "I am afraid I cannot even now let you off without still further encroachments. There are two beloved companions of mine, whom I cannot reconcile myself to leave behind, one of them Steele by name."

"And *steal* by nature—I have heard of him," said the captain, "and should advise you, Jack, to cut his company."

"You know him not, or you would argue differently," said Jack, warmly, "a more generous-hearted fellow never lived, and for faith, honesty, and truth, sir, certain it is, he is as true as the name he bears."

"You are of course the best judge," said Dashfield, "all I meant to observe, was that the trifle I have heard of him, does not greatly redound to his honour. Who is your other companion?"

"One of whom you have a slight acquaintance, it is no other than young Wide-Awake, the lad who was wounded this evening.'

"Whenever that young imp of mischief leaves the country, Jack, it will be for his country's good," said the captain.

Jack responded with an assenting smile.

"Well," he said, "having settled the preliminaries, and as daylight is now far advancing, you will perhaps allow me to withdraw."

"Of this proposal they would not hear a word, being fully determined to have his company till morning, when the captain proposed that Jack should accompany him to the shipping agents, and that the passage money should be paid.

The ladies, who had long since shown symptoms of weariness, now rose to take their departure, and our hero was in the act of bidding them "good night," when a loud and authoritative knock at the door arrested their attention. They listened with breathless eagerness until the knock was repeated. The servants having long since retired to rest, the captain seized a lamp, and advancing to the casement, peered forth, and, in answer to his challenge—

"Who is there?" a voice answered,

"Open your door in the King's name."

"By heavens, Jack is betrayed," said the captain, in terror, "the house is surrounded with soldiery. "What is to be done?"

"Trapped, eh?" said Jack, coolly; "well, I must run for it, then, that's all—what a lucky thing it is I didn't start a few minutes since, I should have run slap in their blessed arms. Is there no outlet at the back whereby I can escape?"

"None," replied Mr. Malcolm, who actually shivered with dismay, whilst the two ladies, at the ill-tidings, were white and motionless as marble.

"What a nuisance it is there coming at this unseasonable hour," said Jack, with perfect equanimity. "Just as we had settled everything too, to give them a long farewell. Well, there is no help for it, I suppose—fate is fate."

During this short period the clamour without increased to a perfect din.

"They are battering in the door," said the captain, then, turning appealingly to Jack, he said, "can you suggest nothing?"

"Yes," said Jack, "let them in."

"Let them in," was repeated by white and trembling lips.

"Yes," said Jack, "it is the only chance; the fellows are doubtless provided with a secret warrant—thanks to the advice of the earl, who doubtless sent them hither—and they are bound to execute their missive and will; never fear. Let me advise you, ladies, to retire; you, also, Mr. Malcolm, would be best in bed, lest the unpleasant charge of having aided and abetted a highwayman against the officers of the king should be brought against you. Leave me and the captain to deal with them."

"There is a whole platoon of them," exclaimed Mr. Malcolm, in despair, "my God what shall we do, you will be killed."

"Not a bit of it," said Jack, encouragingly, "I have faced dangers not a whit less desperate than this, and yet have escaped scatheless. I tell you I bear a charmed life, so fear not for me, I have made up my mind to escape and will."

"But how?" queried each alternately.

"By force of conrage," said Jack, "which is a thing your Bow-street officers, with all their sagacity, cannot understand, let the captain open the door, the eager fools will at once rush in, and I will take the liberty at the same time of rushing out. Don't you see? they'll fire at me of course, and miss me of course. Pray get to bed. Dangerous as it may seem, it is my only chance of safety, if you love me do not mar that, which, if you hesitate, your hardiness most certainly will do."

Thus entreated, they shook hands in solemn silence with our hero, and Isabella unable to restrain the poignant feelings of anguish, fell back insensible, and in that state was conveyed to her apartment.

It may easily be imagined, during this interval the officers without were not idle. They distributed the soldiers in such directions that every avenue was strictly guarded, whilst they themselves continued battering the door with unexampled zeal.

"Now captain follow me—make no noise, carry no light to attract their aim, throw the door wide open, and trust to my celerity for the rest."

The captain implicitly followed Jack's directions, and presently, to the assailing parties' astonishment, the door stood widely open. Supposing it was from the effects of their blows upon it, they uttered a shout of joy and rushed in. The first tripped over Jack's foot, which was dexterously extended for the purpose, and some half-dozen more falling over their leader's body, lay a struggling mass upon the floor, collaring one another, in the confusion, until they were half strangled, each one congratulating himself on the hope that they had succeeded in capturing our hero.

Gathering up his energies, Jack lept over the prostrate bodies into the road. Knocking down a sentinel as he went. True to the directions he had received, another of the soldiers, as Jack leaped by a terrific bound the garden rails, levelled his piece, and fired. An inch lower and Jack's life and our history were alike ended. The bullet passed through his hat!

On, on, like a startled stag, went Jack, and the hue and cry of his daring escape having been raised, on came a troop of soldiers dashing after him.

It was in truth a gallant race, but far too rapid and impetuous to last long. Jack, although an admirable runner, was at length so fatigued out that his knees knocked together and his heart beat with such fearful rapidity, it seemed like to burst the strings that held it.

Still to hesitate were death, for the sound of his pursuers as they came thundering on behind him was wafted to his ears with fearful distinctness.

"If they persue me to the town, my capture is inevitable," thought Jack, "for the cursed uproar they create will bring the whole place upon me.

God help me, am I to perish thus miserably—is there no shelter at hand? Yes!" he exclaimed aloud as he was struck by a sudden glimpse of hope—the Jew's house is not a mile hence—once there I should be safe—I'll do it, I'll do it, or burst my heart in the attempt."

This resolution nerved our hero again to the task, and forward he sprang with renewed vigour.

It was a hard flight—a mighty struggle was that race for life—and Jack, although he fagged fearfully at last, still kept gallantly on. Brave heart, keep up.

The Jew's house was in sight, another struggle—mightier than any that preceded it, and it was reached.

By a miracle the door was open, the Jew was already up. As Jack crossed the threshold, Saint Paul's bell came booming over the waters—it was four o'clock.

"Mine Got! vhot is the meaning of this?" stammered the Jew, as Jack unceremoniously entered the house; "by Got, ash I live, 'tis Mister Rann."

"It is," murmured the panting Jack; "shut the door, Jew, the bloodhounds are at my heels—I am pursued."

The Jew instinctively flew to the door, and locked and barred it; this done, he assisted our exhausted hero up stairs, and, having administered to him a bumping glass of Hollands, our hero speedily became sufficiently recovered to explain the cause of his arrival.

Toby, who had since the destruction of his own habitation taken up a temporary lodging with Moses, was soon awakened, and instantly flew to greet our hero, although his only covering was his shirt.

"Oh, Jack, my darling!" he exclaimed, as he hugged our hero in his arms; "and is it indeed your own self, my blessed darling boy—what blessed wind has blown you here?"

"An ill wind, I am afraid, my old friend," answered Jack. "I am huned for my life, old fellow."

"Why, you really look like it—why, you seem all out of breath like."

"I have had a narrow escape," said Jack. "Escape, did I say," he added, with a better laugh, "let me not boast too soon, for hark! my pursuers have traced me hither—they are now at the door."

This fact soon became evident from the uproar at the outside of the building.

Toby went to reconoitre "Why, Jack my tulip," he said, "There is a whole regiment of soldiers—your caged, by jingo. But they shall not have you, my boy—no they shall wade through my heart's blood first."

Then turning fiercely round, he exclaimed. "Where's the Jew?"

"Gone to admit them, perhaps," said Jack, "he knows escape is impossible, so, perchance, thinks he may as well have his share of the reward offered for me."

"If that be true, black death shall be the portion of the unbelieving dog!" said Toby, with bitter emphasis.

"Hush!"

It was true, as the clattering of ascending feet upon the staircase plainly testified.

"Toby," said Jack, in the tones of a man who has made up his mind to a desperate deed. "I must not, will not be taken alive," flying to the window, which opened upon the river, he threw it open, " what depth of water is there?"

"Ten feet," answered Toby; "farewell, old fellow—may God bless you! Here they come."

At this instant a dozen soldiers dashed into the room.

"What cheer, old fellow," said Jack, to the foremost, "you would capture Jack Rann, would you?"

"I would and have," said the man, "I have followed you thus far, and now will follow you to the end."

"Come on, then," said Jack, and saying these words, before a arm could be raised to prevent him, he sprang through the casement, into the rushing river.

As he fell a loud voice gave the command " fire!" and a peal of musketry rent the air with its thunder, from the pieces of a group of soldiers stationed on the bank.

The waters closed over the body—a stream of crimson rose to the surface—the soldiers watched with breathless eagerness—but there was no re-appearance, and turning away with looks of exultation, they uttered:

"So perisheth Sixteen-String Jack."

Whether this supposition was correct remains yet to be seen.

CHAPTER XXXIII.

THE DEATH OF TOBY AND THE JEW—OF JACK, AND HIS NARROW ESCAPE—HIS VISIT TO CLAYTON.

SUPPRESSED and startled by this unexpected denouement, the soldiers gazed upon the river until the smoke from their pieces had cleared away, and as no trace of our hero's re-appearance became visible, they, at the command of their officer, shouldered their firelocks, and, with disappointed visages, took their way back to their barracks, spreading a report as they went of the death of Jack Rann.

Tired—with a dastardly hope of reward—the old Jew hobbled into the room, where a small party of the soldiery still remained, and, seemingly unconscious in his grasping eagerness of the presence of Toby, he went to the officer, and said:—

You will not forget me, will you, good sir—remember, I gave you every information, and every advantage, that lay in my power."

" Forget you! no!" exclaimed the officer, gazing, with intense disgust, at the grovelling face that was upturned to his own. "I shall not forget you, neither will I forget to report, in the proper quarter, sir, that your house is a receptacle for thieves; and my firm conviction is, that you are an infamous promoter of crime."

With these parting words, the officer, bidding his men follow him, turned on his heels and took his departure, leaving the Jew, instead of overjoyed with triumph, a prey to the most miserable apprehensions.

Toby, who had remained a silent but not an unmoved spectator of the scene, and firmly believing with the others that poor Jack had fallen a victim to the volley of musketry, immediately the men were removed beyond hearing, sprang upon the Jew, and, seizing him by the throat, he dashed him violently to the ground.

"Viper! so you would betray him, would you—would sacrifice to your paltry love of gain the noble fellow, who periled his life and soul to enrich you?"

"Mercy!" shrieked the Israelite, in abject terror, "they would have found him, Toby—they had found him; and I thought that you and I, Toby—you and I—might as well have our share of the reward."

"Liar! base b—— liar," shouted Toby, well you knew I would not receive blood-money, especially *his*. Curse you, for a grovelling hound as you are. Not content with reaping the cream of all his robberies—not content with gathering the profit of his daring life, you must even sell his body to his enemies—cowardly, unmanly wretch—base, unfeeling, unnatural hound —you're very sight is an hatred to me, and I could kill you for your accursed ingratitude, with as little compunction as I would a mangy hound who had bitten me."

"Mercy! mercy!" gasped the Jew.

"You plead in vain, villain. I cannot find mercy for you. No! there should not be, and there shall not be any mercy for the betrayer of Jack Rann. Down on your knees, Jew, and pray for mercy at the hands of your God, for your hour has come—you, too, shall die."

Stunned and appalled by the dreadful fate by which he was threatened, the Jew uttered some incorent sounds, and then awaking from his lethergy he redoubled the protestations of his innocence, and made the most pathetic appeals for mercy.

"Such mercy as you would have shown Jack Rann shall be yours, none other," said Toby, with all the fixed determination of a deadly and unmoveable resolve.

"You will not kill me, Toby," whined the Jew, "oh, mine dear good friend, tink of the many years we have known one anoder—tink of the friends we have been—the confidence we have had in each other, Toby, tink of this."

"I do think of it, and to see you changed like this in the end, makes me hate, detest, and abhor you. It shows me how dangerous a companionship I have been indulging in—it tells me, not only is poor Jack to perish under your accursed cupidity, but having the secrets and the whereabouts of a dozen men in your hands, their lives would also be sacrificed, should such sacrifice tend to the safety of your own worthless neck and the aggrandizement of your own fortunes."

"Oh, tink not so badly of me," implored the Jew, "tink of the past; how often I might have betrayed you and never did."

"And had not the same halter been woven for your neck that was to encircle ours, you would have done so long ago, even as you would do now, villain, if allowed to run your black career."

"Oh, no, no, I swear no. I will be faithful."

"How often have you sworn to be faithful to us already, how often have you declared you would rather die the death of the gallows than betray a pal, and yet, see the first opportunity that arises, you are as eager as any bloodhound for your prey, must even sacrifice the life of the gallant Jack Rann."

"But I would not again, I swear I would not."

"You would, again and again, thou lying accursed Jew, were the opportunity to arise, and not sufficient would it be that poor Jack and I be destroyed for your ill ends, but Clayton, Sheppard, O'Brien, Wide-Awake, and every member of our once powerful and happy gang, would be brought to Tyburn Tree, that you might live gloating over the riches such destruction would bring you. I see it plainly now, Jew. If you would sacrifice one you would sacrifice all, and therefore I will kill you that they may be saved.

Again and again did the Jew frantically implore Toby to forego his dreadful purpose, but the irrevocably "No," again burst forth.

Terrible and unnatural as it may appear, Toby had in reality determined that the Jew should die, and having in the destruction of his old home and by the death of our hero, whom he loved with parental tenderness, lost every tie that bound him to life, he had also resolved the forthcoming night should witness his own end.

The death of the Jew he considered less as a crime, than as an imperative duty. The rules of the gang, to the fulfilment of each tenet of which every man was bound by oaths, specified that he who was found guilty of an act directly or indirectly involving the life or liberty of a member, should be adjudged a traitor and should perish by death, completely absolved him in his own opinion of any crime of murder that might otherwise cling to him.

The hours flew by, and night drew on apace, and yet the Jew was living yet, upon his knees, imploring for life.

"Waste not thy time in useless petitions," said Toby, "I have said that thou must die—and die thou must. Your time grows short, seek mercy of your God. In half an hour St. Paul's will strike twelve—the first stroke of its bell shall ring thy death knell; its last stroke mine."

But the Jew, heeding not his words, still poured supplication upon supplication for pardon. His shrieks, his cries, his vows, and imploring gestures, the anguish that rent his very soul, the tears that bedewed the very ground were listened to, but were unheeded. Toby was unmovable—his determination was inflexible—his intent deadly.

Hus !

Already the chimes of some of the multitude of churches that environed them gave tokens of the approaching hour. With breathless attention Toby listened for the sound of St. Paul's.

It came at length, booming like thunder over the sleeping city.

As the sound broke upon his ear, Toby advanced, and seized the Jew in his arms as though he were an infant. The window he had already thrown open. From excessive terror, which the fear of death had inspired, the Jew had fainted.

Toby gazed for an instant upon the rushing waters before him. As he did so, the twelfth stroke of St. Paul's fell upon his ears.

"May God have mercy upon our guilty souls, and forgive me what I am about to do."

This was Toby's last prayer.

Uttering it, he sprang into the river with the Jew in his arms, crying, as he did so, "Jack, I come to thee!"

There was a loud splash as the heavy bodies met the stream, and that was all. The rest was hushed in death, and the stream sped on as tranquilly as though it had never been disturbed.

Ten days after, two bodies were discovered floating in Blackwall reach. They were those of the suicide and his victim. Incredible as it appears, so tenacious was Toby's hold of the Jew, that they were still locked in each other's arms.

An inquest was held on the bodies, which were both buried in one grave.

* * * * * * *

Our hero was a most excellent swimmer, and, therefore, finding himself battling with the cold waters of the Thames, he swam so rapidly with the tide, under water, that he managed to remove himself, without coming to the surface for breath, a sufficient distance, to be out of the sight of the soldiery. Unable longer to remain below, he ventured to the surface for breath, inhaling a goodly volume of which, he again dived, and again sped forward with amazing celerity, occasionally coming to the surface to inflate his lungs, and then disappearing again. He swam after this manner until he reached Blackfriars Stairs, where an opportunity was afforded him of landing; but, fearing apprehension, he gathered up his energies, and, by the aid of the tide, which was running rapidly down, he still kept on.

London Bridge at length was reached. By this time his arm, which had been struck by a bullet, and hence the appearance of blood on the surface of the water at Westminster, began to grow stiff and to fail him, whilst he himself, although a vigorous swimmer, from loss of blood, excitement, and over exertion, felt a deadly feeling of faintness creeping over him. He nevertheless had sufficient presence of mind to keep himself afloat, and the tide rapidly bore him onward, until the Tower was past.

At this critical moment, and in the instant when he was sinking from utter exhaustion, some men, who were gazing over the bulwarks of a collier, caught a glimpse of his white face as he was swept rapidly past. To jump into the boat alongside was the work of an instant, and the brave fellows sped after the body with a vigour which life and death alone could lend to their arms. In a few minutes they were upon it, had rescued it, and were now bearing it back in all the triumph of glorious humanity, back to their vessel.

Once on board, the rude men proceeded instantly to apply such restoratives as they had learnt in their dangerous career were beneficial. Hot water being in readiness, our hero was thrown into a warm bath, whilst a jorum of hot brandy and water was poured down his throat. Under this treatment, and by the aid of hot flannels, which were applied to his body, our hero was speedily recovered sufficiently to thank his preservers for the timely aid they had rendered him, which had saved him from inevitable destruction.

When his apparel was dried, and, by the influence of the brandy which had been so freely administered to him, he began to feel his energy return, he attempted to rise from the couch whereon he had been laid. The simple action was sufficient to arouse him to a sense of the painful, if not dangerous wounds he had received. His arm was so swollen, and so desperately painful withal, that the exertion he had made caused him to fall back in a fainting condition.

The eagle-like glance from the eye of the captain of the vessel at once convinced that worthy that our hero had escaped other injury beside that of drowning, and on examining his patient, he discovered near the shoulder the unmistakeable marks of a desperate gun-shot wound.

"Why, mate," he said, kindly, "thou hast been shot as well as drowned, where on airth didst thou get in this dreadful scrimmage. Tell'e the truth, lad, thou art among friends who would rather aid than harm thee."

"I am he whom the world calls Sixteen-string Jack," said our hero, in tones faint from excessive weariness, "you can perhaps guess the rest."

"I can, lad," answered the captain, bluntly, "I can see thou hast had a narrow escape from the hands of the Philistines. I have heard many marvellous tales of thy exploits, Jack; there has been a rare hullabaloo over thee, lad; but I never heard thou either robbed the poor widow or her fatherless children; what thou hast taken, thou hast taken from the rich, and I glory in thee for it, Jack, and, by God, so long as ye like to stop here, thou art right welcome to make the old ship thine home, and, for the present at least, thou'lt find no house so safe a hiding-place. But whiles I talk, thee art suffering." He then turned to his men; "you must keep this affair a secret, lads—if any of you blab, it will be the worse for 'ee. Get thee to shore, Sam," he said to one of them, "and bring a doctor back wid'ee; one we can depend on; we'll cure him, and please God, will save him yet. Save Jack Rann—ay, that would I, as heartily as I would my own broder—dang'un, I glory in un."

The man despatched for a doctor speedily returned bringing with him a skilful member of that fraternity. The bullet was soon extracted and in a few days, thanks to Jack's strong and healthy constitution, the wound healed.

The time limited for the vessel's stay was past and gone, and yet she still remained in the port of London, for the purpose of providing a hiding place for Jack.

From the newspapers, which were brought on board for the purpose, Jack learned, to his intense joy and delight, that it was confidently stated he was dead. In some instances the affair was spoken of with triumph, as though the soldiers had done a deed of great cleverness, and much praise was consequently due to them for it. It was there also openly stated as a fact, that they were indebted for their clue to his whereabouts, from information afforded them by the Earl of Dashfield.

Different papers took different views of the subjects, one in particular, in the course of a long copy of verses "on the life and adventures of glorious Jack Rann," worded him more as a darling hero who had gone to an untimely grave, others again on the other hand acquiesced that his end was an unfitting one, and mourned he had met the fate he had, but they in general wound up their remarks with a facetious hint, that it would have been better for the sake of humanity, and for examples sake likewise, had he met with a dry death, and been hung high and dry at Tyburn.

As Jack conned these paragraphs a smile of exultation lit up his handsome face. The first act he did when he was sufficiently recovered to pen a note, was to despatch a missive to the Malcolms, informing them of his miraculous escape. Their surprise and joy—for they too shared in the general belief of his death—was great and unbounded, and so excessive was their delight, that they instantly sprang into a carriage and hurried off to satisfy themselves that the joyful intelligence was founded on fact.

The meeting was a right joyous one, as may be well imagined, and Mr. Malcolm and the captain, who were both in deep mourning for our hero, were so entranced with joy when they found him, that they actually hugged him in their delight. Their transports of delight over they betook them to a recaptulation of the plan, already discussed, for his emigration to America.

They made the captain of the vessel a present of so weighty a proof of their generosity, that he was induced still further to forego his intention of departing, and arrangements were made with him that he should convey our hero to Liverpool, and not leave him until he had seen him shipped on board the American vessel.

Things having been thus happily arranged, Dashfield took our hero aside and said :

"I am afraid I have some ill-tidings, Jack."

"In God's name, what are they?" asked Jack, eagerly, his hopes falling at the words, "it is ever thus, no sooner does a happy prospect arise before me, than a dark cloud protrudes its dark and unbidden form, and hides the gleam of sunshine—what has happened now—is my hiding place discovered—are the bloodhounds of the law again upon my track?"

"The authorities still retain a firm belief in your death, Jack, and so far you are safe. The intelligence I am the bearer of concerns not you, but one for whom you once had some strong feeling of affection."

"Who can it be?" questioned Jack, "is Elinor Roche ill—dead? Alas! then my brightest hope in life is gone!"

"Not so, Jack—heaven be praised, she is well, and in safety."

"Who is it then—can it be poor Wide-Awake?"

"He, too, has entirely recovered from the injuries he received, and has embraced, with thankful eagerness, the offer I held out to him. It concerns not him, Jack."

"Who is it, then? My sufferings have made me weak and despairing, and, like all invalids, I am full well tested. I pray you keep me not longer in suspense."

"It concerns poor Clayton," answered Dashfield, sorrowfully; "he is ill—desperately ill—I fear unto death."

"Alas, poor Charlie," said Jack, a tear of commiseration falling from his eye as he spoke.

"The pistol-shot wound he received," continued Dashfield, "has, from some cause, and I doubt from the inattention or unskilfulness of the surgeon of the prison, has mortified, and he now lies in a hopeless condition; in fact, beyond recovery. I gleaned these particulars from a newspaper, which informant went further on to state, that he was progressing towards recovery, with slow but certain steps, until the intelligence of your supposed death was conveyed to him, since which period he has drooped perceptibly."

"I am deeply grieved to hear it," said Jack, mournfully, "and can only regret it is not in my power to save him; were it, heaven knows I would exert myself to the uttermost."

"I believe that, Jack," said the captain.

"There is still one thing I can propose and will perform," said Jack, after a thoughtful silence, "before I leave England."

"And that is?" asked young Dashfield, interrogatively.

"I will visit him in his prison. Who knows, if my presence cannot save him, it may still tend to smooth his rugged pathway to the grave."

"The thought is madness, Jack—no, no, the escape you have had is too narrow. I can never consent that you should again thrust yourself in the lion's den."

"Have you not said the report of my death is generally believed?"

"I have," answered Dashfield.

"Where then is there danger? I am entirely unknown in that region, and disarmed of suspicion, by their confidence in my eternal silence, I should pass and repass the portals of the prison in safety."

"Your visit would actually promote suspicion, and they would undoubtedly scan your features closely, and as you have been so elaborately described, detection would be inevitable."

"I neither see it nor fear it. My illness has so reduced me, I am but the skeleton of my former self. I will adopt the disguise of a quiet country gentleman, and, in that garb, my own father would pass me without recognition. Nay, my good friend, deem me not reckless or ungrateful." As Dashfield was about still further to importune him, "I cannot find it in my heart to leave my faithful old friend, my dying comrade, without a word of farewell. Go I must—go I will."

Dashfield saw at once it was impossible to turn our hero from the scheme he had projected, and, with a heavy heart, regretting he had ever mentioned poor Clayton's illness, he hurried aside, and in the bustle of preparation for Jack's departure, endeavoured to forget the cause of his disquietude.

Firm in his resolve, Jack, at daybreak next morning, mounted a horse lent him for the purpose by Dashfield, rode off to the prison that held poor Clayton.

Having obtained the address of a magistrate, who bore a good character for humanity, in the immediate neighbourhood, Jack managed, by representing himself as the prisoner's brother, to obtain an order for admission.

Furnished with this official mandate, he was, on reaching the gaol, ushered at once into the prisoner's cell.

"Alas, poor Clinton! suffering and confinement had indeed done its work. Jack saw, in the attenuated form before him—in the deep-drawn breath—in the glassy eye—sad evidences of the near approach of the wings of terror.

He was so far reduced, so near his end, he did not notice the appearance of our hero, until the ordinary had thrice called his attention to it.

"Clayton," whispered the good old man, in the sufferer's ear, "here is your brother come a long distance to see you ere you die."

"Brother," muttered Clayton, "I had but one, and he died long since—in his infancy. Would I had died too! What pain, what misery I should be saved in this dark and dismal hour."

"The path of sin my unhappy brother chose," said Jack, in low tones to the minister, "has so long kept us estranged from each other, I marvel not he has forgotten me."

"You have indeed had cause to cast him off, young sir, said the minister, with much feeling, "alas, that it should have been so! But, standing as we do now, sir, by his bedside—that bed from which he can never hope to rise again alive—it behoves us to tread lightly upon the painful memories of the past—it behoves us, sir, to raise and fix his thoughts upon another and a better sphere."

"It does," answered Jack, with much emotion, "and may he ever reward you for the interest you have taken in, and for the good you have done my poor brother. I cannot hope to reward you."

"I look to heaven for my reward," said the minister, piously. "I merely cautioned you, young sir, that you might not by any incautious word harrow up the feelings of yonder dying man, for there are some memories, sir, that strew a death-bed with thorns. At such an hour as this, when his life hangs upon a thread, they are to be avoided. There are other recollections also, pure and holy in their nature, that may smoothe and comfort a dying man."

"And those are the words I would pour into his ear," said Jack, "tidings of forgiveness from his broken-hearted mother—a message of peace from his aged father, whose grey hairs he has well nigh brought with sorrow to the tomb. These are the tidings I would impart to him, sir, with others of a private nature, whose message his ears alone are fit to hear."

"My duty teaches me not to pry into any private communication. Speak with him in confidence, I will withdraw until you need my presence." And the minister withdrew.

Jack went to the bedside, and kneeling at his friend's head, he took poor Clayton's burning hand within his own.

"Oh, Charlie," he sobbed, "that it should come to this."

"That voice!" said Clayton, turning himself in his bed, with startled surprise; then, suddenly losing his energy, he said, in the tone of one dead to every hope—

"Methought I heard Jack's voice—brave, gallant Jack Rann. But he is gone from—they are all gone from me—and I have been left to die neglected and forgotten. Yes, poor Jack is dead—dead! And I too am dying, for it has broken my heart."

"Oh, Charlie, my own true, devoted friend! Do you not recognise me? Gaze upon these features—do you not remember them?"

Poor Clayton drew his hand across his dim and fading eyes, then stedfastly gazed upon our hero. For an instant they were illumined with the light of hope—the next they were dark and desolate again. He shook his head, with a despairing gesture, as he muttered—

"They are like—wonderously like; but it is a dream—a delusion—he is dead, dead! and I am dying!"

"It is no phantasy, dear, dear Charlie," said Jack, with increased energy, as his tears fell fast, "It is I, Jack Rann, who now kneels before you."

"What!" exclaimed the dying man, "do I hear aright? Are you not dead? They are indeed Jack Rann's features! Is it my own true friend I see, come to cheer the last dark hours of his poor Clayton?"

"It is I," said Jack, throwing himself into his friend's extended arms.

'God be praised, he has heard my prayer—I die happy!"

And poor Clayton fell back upon his pillow, exhausted.

Fearing the stroke of death had come, Jack hastily summoned the minister.

"His end is rapidly approaching," said the good man—"may God, who died for sinners, have mercy on him, and forgive him his sins!"

"Amen!" responded Jack.

"Jack, my friend," said Clayton, in a tone growing more and more feeble, "I am going, lad—hold my hands—so—thank heaven! I shall now die happy. Tell all our brave boys so! Tell them, my last thoughts on earth were of them."

Then ensued a fearful silence, broken only by the sobs of poor Jack, which burst forth in spite of all his efforts to control them.

"All grows dark, Jack; my heart, how faint it beats," said Clayton, in tones so low they were scarcely audible to Jack, although his ear was lowered to the pallid lips, to catch the remotest sound.

"Lift my head, Jack," said the poor fellow, "this is a blessing unlooked for, to die upon your arm. How faint I grow—how dark it is! Ah, my heart, cease not thy beating yet! How quick the fleeting moments pass!"

Again there was a deep silence.

The sufferer's lips moved, but no sound came from them; whilst upon his marble forehead the damp and clammy dew of death stood in beads.

"All is over," he muttered with great difficulty, "kiss me, Jack."

Jack bent over the suffering form, and pressed his lips to the white ones of the dying man.

"Thanks, thanks!" then, convulsively grasping our hero's hand, convulsively, he murmured, "may God Almighty bless and preserve you—may he—"

The prayer was never finished—ere the closing words could pass his lips, a faint sigh arose from him.

In that sigh, the soul of poor Clayton passed from earth.

From the eyes being closed as if in peaceful slumber, from the pulseless frame, from the cold and clammy hand, Jack knew poor Clayton had passed "to that bourne from whence no traveller ever returns."

CHAPTER XXXIV.

JACK CHANGES HIS STATE FROM SINGLE BLESSEDNESS TO HAPPY MATRIMONY—THE VOYAGE TO LIVERPOOL—HIS DEPARTURE FOR AMERICA, AND WHAT FOLLOWED THEREON.

JACK stayed in the country until the remains of poor Clayton had been peaceably lain in their last resting place—the grave. He then betook himself to London.

Right joyous were the greetings lavished upon him on his return, each of his good friends striving to outvie each other in their goodness and kindness to him.

To his intense delight he found Miss Malcolm was on board the vessel, and to his still further gratification, found that it was the intention of the amiable family to accompany him as far as Liverpool on his journey.

Young Wide-Awake was also on board, and their meeting, and the happy prospect now before them, made their interview one of the most joyous description.

Old Malcolm, his eyes glistening with pleasure, turned to Jack as he pledged him in a bumper, and winking significantly at Captain Dashfield as he spoke, said—

"But Rann, what of your matrimonial scheme, have you not forgotten it and the lady?"

"Not so," answered Jack, colouring slightly; I am as firm in that resolve as ever."

"And you mean to say you have a desire to discover the lady's whereabouts?"

"I have," answered Jack.

"And could I produce the lady here by a simple act of magic, what then, think you that your matrimonial inclinations will still hold good?"

"I swear to you," said Jack, solemnly, "far from retracting my words, were but the opportunity afforded me, I would marry her to-morrow."

"Marriage is a serious step to take," said the good old gentleman, smilingly, "have you calculated the extra expense, and extra duties that would devolve upon you if saddled with a wife?"

"I have weighed and considered all, sir," responded Jack, and am firmly convinced the extra duty would not only be a pleasureable one but a profitable one likewise."

"And the duties involved in matrimony, do not always end here, Jack

In a few years, you know, you may have a group of children clustering round you, think you you would like to hear the sound of father?"

"It would be the delight of my heart, sir!" exclaimed Jack.

"And you think then, notwithstanding your fickle and wayward heart, notwithstanding the unnatural ferocity for which your enemies have given you credit, you would not be found wanting in love for your spouse, or in parental tenderness for your children."

"No, no," said Jack; "vile and unfeeling as I may have been, I am not so bad—not so unnatural as that."

"That being the case," said Mr. Malcolm, happily, "nothing now remains but to effect a joyful re-union. Isabella, my love, perhaps you can prevail upon the lady and gentleman in the next cabin to favor us with their company for a few minutes."

Isabella rose to fulfil this behest, whilst Jack's heart fluttered with a trepidation he had never felt or known before.

The foldingdoor, which separated the two cabins, were thrown open, revealing, to Jack's astonished gaze, a lady in immaculate white—the enchanting emblem of purity and innocence—with a wreath of orange blossoms encircling her temples.

The other was a venerable grey-haired man, habited in the sacred vestments of a minister of the church of God.

Speechless from astonishment, and the various emotions of joy which filled his heart to overflowing, Jack rose to his feet and staggered forward to greet her. The veil now thrust aside revealed the beloved features of Elinor.

White as parian marble the flush, which excitement had caused to visit her fair face, made her look bewilderingly beautiful.

"Elinor, my own darling!" exclaimed our hero, springing forward, and catching her in his arms, "this hour of happiness repays all,"

"It does," she murmured, in tones of touching cadence, as she sank upon his breast, pouring forth a flood of delicious tears that sprang from the fountain of a heart now overcharged with joy.

"And do you indeed love me?"

"I do, heart and soul," answered Jack, rapturously.

"And do not regret this act, that binds me to you for ever."

"Regret it!" cried Jack, enthusiastically, "far from it, I am delighted with it."

"Then heaven has indeed blessed me with much happiness," said Elinor, so overcome with emotion that she turned aside.

"I propose," said Mr. Malcolm, at this juncture, "that we get the ceremony over at once."

The minister expressing his assent to this suggestion, the bride and bridegroom were placed in their position, Captain Dashfield giving away the bride, and Mr. Malcolm officiating as clerk.

And the beautiful marriage ceremony of England lost not a jot of solemnity from being performed within the walls of that old ship, than they would, had they been intoned within the consecrated walls of a church.

The ceremony ended, the priest, in a manner at once fervent and affectionate, blessed the newly-wedded pair—an act of spontaneous kindness peculiarly impressed at that solemn manner.

The clerk's solemn "amen" having died away, the good minister, after partaking slightly of a sumptuous luncheon that was provided, took his departure.

A few minutes later the ship was shifted from her moorings, and was drifting towards the broad Atlantic.

Night came on, glorious in all the bright transparency of a harvest moon; and, as Jack, surrounded by his loving friends, was seated upon the deck, the head of his beautiful wife resting upon his shoulder, there was a feeling of happiness, unalloyed by grief, so pure and so delicious that kings might have envied him.

Liverpool at length was reached; the hour of parting was rapidly approaching.

It was not without many tears, and many protestations of undying attachment on both sides, that they took their departure.

The solemn word, "farewell," at length was spoken—spoken in grief and tears on the part of the Malcolms, for the consciousness was at their hearts, that it would be years, and it might be that they would never again gaze upon the beautiful and interesting pair before them.

"God bless you, Jack," said Mr. Malcolm.

"Health and prosperity, my dear friend," said Dashfield.

"My heart is too full for speech," said Miss Malcolm, in tones of touching tenderness, "but my heart's best affections are with thee—my prayers shall follow you."

"Thanks, our thanks, all!" exclaimed Jack, gaily, "mourn not for me, let us rather rejoice that this good fortune has been reserved for me. In the land to which I am going, I shall carry with me an untainted name. I pledge now my honest word, I will make every exertion, an honest man could and should make, to retrieve the unhappy past."

"Bravo, Jack," said Mr. Malcolm, "I have a whole world of confidence in you."

"And I," echoed Dashfield and Isabella, simultaneously.

Farewell was spoken for the last time.

The time had come—at last the signal for sailing was given—visitors had departed for shore—and the emigrant ship, spreading her white sails, moved majestically over the broad waters of the Atlantic.

There is something extremely affecting in the departure of an emigrant ship—something awful, and that causes a shudder to thrill instinctively through one's frame. This feeling of dread is beautifully embodied in the following verses:—

"Thou semblance of the Angel, Death,
With thy dark dismal shrouding wings,
Whose fluttering seems to catch the breath,
The very latest breath that wrings
The soul from body, thou art there,
Like Hope half-soothing wild despair!

> In thee is promise that thou'lt bring
>   A change of season to the mind
> Of those who *chance* a distant spring
>   From the dull wintry waste behind!
> Yet—what's the wintry waste they leave?
> Alas! all hearts with theirs must grieve!
>
> They quit their Native Land for life,
>   A land they'll weep for when away,
> Sister and Brother—Husband—Wife
>   May never meet another day!
> The living Death of absence, quite
> Obscures the gloom of endless night!
>
> Perchance to some, hope will be true,
>   And lead them on to riches—fame—
> But all they loved, and all they knew
>   In early days, just like a name
> Upon a tombstone will appear,
> And mem'ry vainly wish them near.
>
> Some may return with power to bless
>   The weeping wretches left behind—
> And see that home all loneliness,
>   Where they expected them to find;
> The son for mother look in vain,
> Then seek the wide—wide world again.
>
> The signal's given—away to shore—
>   Break ties of every dearest kind!—
> One parting kiss—one look—one more
>   Farewell to those now left behind!
> Divorcer Ocean! thou dost make
> Many a gentle heart to ache.
>
> Oh! Emigration! thou'rt the curse
>   Of our once happy nation's race!
> Cannot our Fatherland still nurse
>   It's offspring, without taking place
> Of dislocated men to make
> More cause for thy disturbing sake!
>
> Thou art an enemy to peace,
>   Thy restless hope but ends in grief—
> When comforts in the mother cease
>   How can we hope step-dame's relief?
> Better to bear the ills we have,
> Than seek in foreign climes a grave."

A few of the relatives of the emigrants were gathered in a little knot on the quay, taking a last look at those they loved, and whom they felt they had parted from for ever.

The uplifted arm—the waving kerchief, were answered from the ship; it was the last signal; the last mark of recognition that passed between friend and friend, mother and child, brother and sister. There were some stout hearts aboard, that tried to raise a cheer (such a cheer it was) to testify that they left their Fatherland without regret: that they had hopes of finding, in the distant strange land, that prosperity which had been promised them and which they had never tasted in their own.

But many, and by far the greater number, as they gazed upon the fast receding land, felt they were leaving their home, their friends, and all, and they knew not for what. Watching the land of their fathers they were, as it fast disappeared to the gaze, with feelings akin to the sensation of bending over the couch of a dying friend, and seeing the life's breath, each moment growing weaker, expire. At last, all sight of land was lost, and the knowledge of it was like death to their hearts—so wretched, so deserted, so solitary, they felt on that waste of water.

There was here and there a happy face, though, beside those of Elinor and Jack's; one fine handsome young woman, whose rich cashmere shawl gathered tightly around, showed to advantage her graceful form, was administering all the comfort her kind generous soul could suggest to a man and his wife, who had three or four children clustering about them, and whose faces bore marks of the strong veneration they had for the land that gave them birth— cheering words they must have been, of hope and happiness yet in store, to have chased away the heavy marks of care, and called forth in their stead the smile of true light-heartedness. It took but very few hours to alter the aspect of things; they felt they had embarked in a speculation whose proof would award them either good or ill. All their faith had been exhausted on the old land, and so they laid in a new stock for the one to which they were bound—well foreseeing, that if hope and contentment would not avail them, despair and apathy would act worse still.

'Tis the place of all others for a thoroughly selfish man, is an emigrant ship. If the failing was not cured before the journey be completed, he must be incorrigible indeed. It is astonishing how ready all become to assist the other.

But with Jack all was hope and sunshine, although he could not divest himself of a certain feeling of awe, approaching to reverence, that still remained in his breast for the land of his birth.

When the newly wedded pair retired to their cabin for the night, it was with a feeling of blissful hope.

* * * * *

Two days had elapsed, and it was night upon the fathomless sea. The heat throughout the day had been intense—there had not been air sufficient for many hours to fill the sluggish sails, and the becalmed vessel lay inert, like a log upon the dark waters.

Jack and his beloved wife, with Wide-Awake, had mounted to the deck, for the air below was insupportable—it was so dense—so suffocating.

"Shall we lay long thus, think you?" asked Jack, of an old seaman.

"Seest thou that light to south'ard?" replied the mariner.

"I do," answered our hero, as he gazed upon the lurid light in the direction indicated.

"There is a storm brewing there, sir, a reg'lar whistler, or may I never whistle again, old Boreas is at his work, and we shall have wind enough in an hour to make up for the calm we have had."

"You apprehend a hurricane," said Jack, concernedly, as he gazed upon the blanching cheeks of his beloved Elinor. "I hope no immediate danger is at hand."

"As to a hurricane I can't say so much, sir, but I guess we shall have a tolerable sharp gale. But we have sea-room, thank God, and a tight built craft beneath our feet, so please the fate, we'll scud gaily through it; keep your eye to windward, sir, you'll see some stirring changes in that quarter yet."

Jack did so, and instead of the strange lit sky, of such peculiar brilliancy it had arrested universal attention, he beheld an unmixed canopy of lead-like blackness, from whose dark wings ever and anon the lightning shot forth pointed and forked flame, leaving, after its transitory flashes, the scene still blacker and more threatening than before. The reverberation of the awful thunder, heretofore confined to a distant roar, now made the heavens echo with the mighty outbursts, the lightning flashed so vividly now, that the eye shrank from the blinding glare, the wind, that had been freshening, now blew in such violent and fitful gusts that made the very timbers creak again, and made the good ship plunge and rear, like a mighty sea horse in its agony, and as the lightning flashed, and the thunder crashed, and the wind howled on, suddenly from the murky sky came torrents of heavy rain, so fierce, so fast, so deluging, they were fain to seek shelter down below.

As midnight drew on, the storm increased to a fearful pitch, and despising all power of control, the ship, in the war of elements, dashed on at a terrific pace; one by one are the masts gone by the board, and now amidst the terrific fury of the gale, she rolled unmanageable, a perfect wreck.

> "Again the weather threatened—again blew a gale.
> And in the fore and after hold
> Water appeared; yet, though the people knew
> All this, the most were patient, and some bold:
> Until the chains and leathers were worn through
> Of all the pumps—a wreck complete she rolled
> At mercy of the waves, whose mercies are
> Like human beings, during civil war!"

Then fear, despairing heart-rending fear took possession of the boldest spirits, for the water-logged vessel in her heavy pitchings threatened each instant to go down. The scene below was terrible beyond description, here whole families crouched together, as though society could keep off the king of terrors—others, conscience stricken, were on their knees in prayer—others attempting to drown their fear in intoxicating drinks, but the more they drank the greater grew their despair, for their frames seemed invulnerable to the firey liquors.

> "Some cursed the day on which they saw the sun,
> And gnashed their teeth, and howling, tore their hair."

Jack, with the calmness of a brave man, was upon deck, and assisting to the uttermost the brave mariners, when help was useful; when the hour for it was past, and when at length nothing remained but the will of God for calming the mighty tempest to save them, Jack went below to soothe the fears of his affrighted wife, and from his courageous and undaunted bearing, many of his fellow-passengers bore up, and faced with fortitude the end of the tempest. Alas, that end was fated to be death, for the water gained so fast upon the vessel, their only chance of escape from inevitable death lay in a refuge to the boats.

When this dire fatality was known, the most lamentable confusion was the result—the fear-maddened passengers, rushing upon the water-laden deck, drowned the thunder of the storm, by their appalling shrieks of fear, and futile cries for help.

While they were thus engaged in useless lamentations, our hero and the turdy mariners were busily employed providing for their safety.

>   "—— booms, hencoops, spars,
> And all things for a chance had been cast loose,
> That still could keep afloat the struggling tars ;
> For yet they strove, although of no great use."
>
> *   *   *   *   *
>
> "The boats put off, o'ercrowded with their crews,
> She gave a heel—and then a lurch to port,
> And going down head foremost, sunk in short.
> Then rose from sea to sky the wild farewell ;
> Then shriek'd the timid, and stood still the brave,
> And some leap'd overboard with dreadful yell,
> As eager to anticipate their grave ;
> And the sea yawn'd around her like a bell,
> And down she suck'd with her the whirling waves,
> Like one who grapples with his enemy,
> And strives to strangle him before he dies.
> At first, one universal shriek, there rushed,
> Louder than the loud ocean, like a crash
> Of echoing thunder ; and then all was hush'd,
> Save the wild wind, and the remorseless dash
> Of billows ; but at intervals there gush'd,
> Accompanied by a convulsive plash—
> A solitary shriek—the bubbling cry
> Of some strong swimmer in his agony."

One boat, overcrowded by the eager passengers, had gone down headlong—another, containing the captain and the crew, had pushed from the vessel, leaving our hero, and those who remained behind with him, victims to the tempest.

Firm and undaunted in this trying moment stood the noble Jack Rann ; as the last boat receded from their gaze in the pitchy darkness of that night of horror, all hope would seem to have been at an end for the despairing souls left behind. Not so with Jack—a stout and vigorous swimmer—for whilst he had life he had hope. Clasping Elinor to his bosom, he pressed her fervently to his manly heart, and then, bidding her to be brave and bold, he bound her to his body, and dashed into the boiling surge.

The hissing waters lifted him to their surface—a gleam of lightning by a merciful dispensation of the Almighty, showed him the capsized boat, floating keel uppermost. Give way, brave hearts ; striking boldly towards it went Jack—it was reached, and, by an effort almost miraculous, he succeeded in getting astride it. Here was comparative safety. Another gleam of lightning revealed poor Wide-Awake struggling but a few yards from him.

"Elinor, my life—my love !" exclaimed Jack, to the noble girl ; "hold on for the love of God, our poor friend is perishing. Dost hear me, my own wife ?"

"I do," she answered. "Save him, Jack, if it be possible, save him."

The rope that bound them together was loosened by Jack's nervous hands, and, uttering a blessing, he dropped into the ocean, and made gallantly for the direction in which he had last beheld poor Colledge. "A gleam of light," cried Jack, in despair. As if in obedience to his command, the vivid lightning illumined the very spot he desired—but the waters were tenantless—his aid had come too late—poor Wide-Awake had disappeared for ever.

With black despair at his heart, Jack made again desperately for the boat—thanks to Elinor's outstretched arm—he reached it.

The whole of that night found them clinging, with all the tenacity of despair, to its slimy side.

As morning broke, the spirit of the storm seemed appeased, and the light of day again fell upon the waters. To their infinite joy, they discovered they had been wrecked near the land.

Casting his eyes to seaward, Rann could discover no sign of life. The wreck of the ship was still plunging recklessly to and fro upon the boiling waves, but there was no sign of boat or life upon the agitated waters—they alone, of that mighty ship and numerous crew, seemed to have escaped; as the awful conviction forced itself upon their hearts, a silent but fervent prayer of gratitude arose therefrom, and, clasping each other in a fond embrace, they gave thanks for their miraculous preservation in a flood of grateful tears.

The land, barren and unfertile as it seemed, had never before realised so perfect an approach to the joyous land of promise as that. They gazed upon it until their poor eyes fairly gleamed with delight—it lay but a few yards off, and yet to reach it was the task.

Faint and exhausted as he was, Jack had still nerve and courage to try; bidding Elinor cling to him, a behest she performed throughout that dread and direful night with unexampled courage, he betook himself boldly to the water, and set off rapidly for the land.

> "At last with swimming, wading, scrambling, he
> Rolled on the beach, half senseless from the sea.
> There, breathless, with his digging nails, he clung
> Fast to the sand, lest the returning wave,
> From whose reluctant roar his life he wrung,
> Should suck him back to her insatiate grave.
> And there he lay, full length, where he was flung,
> Before the entrance of a cliff worn cave,
> With just enough of life to feel its pains,
> And deem that it was saved perhaps in vain.
> How long in this damp trance he lay
> He knew not, for the earth was gone for him—
> And time had nothing more of night or day
> For his congealing blood and senses dim.
> And how this heavy faintness passed away
> He knew not, till each painful pulse and limb,
> And tingling vein, seemed throbbing back to life,
> For death, though vanquish'd, still retired with strife."

With a sense of desolation, and pain, and weariness, almost insupportable, the rescued pair after having, at the instigation of Elinor, on their bent knees returned thanks to their Creator, crawled, as well as their cut and stiffened limbs would permit them, up the shelving coast.

The land fairly reached at last, Jack anxiously gazed around, and, descrying a house in the distance, they made off for it.

They found to their delight, from the inmates, they were on English ground, the vessel having in the tempest been driven back. They were both penniless, but the English fisherman and his wife, poor though they were, cordially welcomed them, and set before them the best provisions their humble cottage afforded.

Here Jack and Elinor stayed until their strength was somewhat recruited. It then became time to see about removing themselves from that place, for to remain longer a burthen upon the hands of the industrious people who had freely and hospitably entertained them, was as much against their nature as leaving them without some sort of remuneration.

As for our hero the only article of apparel he had at all valuable, were his trousers, which were of course indispensables, and not to be disposed of on any account. Elinor's wardrobe was also extremely limited, in this emergency she drew her wedding ring and keeper from her finger; she felt sincerely hurt at parting with the valuables she clung to with a sacred and holy love, inasmuch as they were the pledges of her union with our hero, but there was no resource. A purchaser was speedily found for them, the majority of the money was presented to the cottagers, as a reward for their kindness, whilst the residue was reserved by Elinor to pay her expenses to London by the waggon.

CHAPTER XXXV.

JACK MEETS WITH A VARIETY OF ADVENTURES, AND COMMITS HIS LAST ROBBERY UPON THE ROAD.

HAVING seen Elinor safely stowed in the waggon for London, which completely swallowed their last crown, Jack set out with a manly heart for the metropolis himself on foot. A chest of clothes having fortunately been washed ashore he selected from its contents a suit of clothes, which save and excepting that they fitted him rather too much, were the very articles he wanted.

The first twenty miles of his long journey were accomplished in a short space of time, and without any event of sufficient importance to be here narrated. It was drawing on towards night as he finished the distance, and feeling somewhat fatigued, for the day had been an excessively sultry one, he turned himself towards the first hostel that presented itself, which he entered with confidence, although he had not a stiver in his purse, and having called for a tankard of ale and some edibles, was speedily profitably occupied reducing one and demolishing the other. This done, Jack took his pipe and strolled forth on a green abutting the house, where a troop of young men were employed in racing, leaping, and other athletic sports.

"Look at George Springer there, hang me if he don't run like a greyhound, and jump like an antelope," said the host, who had taken his station beside our hero, "there's a jump now, didst ever see the like?"

"See the like, yes, man," answered Jack, " and performed it scores of times."

"You have," said the astonished tapster, "well, I must confess thee are well shapen enow for that matter, but don't thee know that George Springer be the only man in the county who can do it."

"Pshaw, man," said Jack, with well assumed indifference, the feat is easy enough."

"Easy be it, ecod!" cried the landlord. "I should just like to see thee do it. George, lad," he shouted to the successful leaper, "here be a man here what can do the trick."

"Is there," said George, who, having up to that time outrivalled all competition, was anxious to preserve, unsullied, his reputation of prince of jumpers of the county. "I'll try a bout with him, landlord," then, turning to Jack, he said "strip man, if thou leapest that barrier, I'll stand a goulden guinea, and a flagon of ale all round—if I don't, blast me."

"Done," said Jack, to whom the prospect of the guinea seemed a God-send in the terribly dilapidated state of his finances. "I'll win your money if I can—should I miss, I'll even take the thumping fall I shall get as a just reward for my temerity."

"I'll bet thee a pound note thee don't do it," roared another.

"Done," said Jack, with unexampled confidence ; " is there any other gentleman in this assembly that has any money to lose—now's the time—rely upon it, gentlemen, you'll never have a better opportunity."

"These bragging fellows are always curs," thought the landlord, who was a warm admirer of Springer's prowess, and a staunch supporter of that agile young gentleman. "I'll bet you the price of the supper you have had, that you don't do it."

"Throw in a bed for the night as well, and its a bet," said Jack.

The landlord nodded assent, and smiled in anticipation of an easy victory.

Our hero walked to the barrier, and found it on a level with the bridge of his nose. He then returned to the starting place, and, throwing aside his heavy boots and his cumbersome coat, he declared himself ready for the encounter. In an instant the self-elected stewards of the place were busily occupied clearing the course—one stood aside with a handkerchief in his hand, to give the signal.

Amidst a breathless silence Jack started, and, springing upward with desperate energy, he cleared the barrier at a bound, and alighted on his feet as calm and collected as if he had walked the distance. A hundred huzzas rent the air with their plaudits, and testified that the honest yeomen succumbed to the agility of the stranger. With a jealousy, mean and disgraceful, Springer attempted to cover his defeat by a further venture, instead of generously confessing he had found a companion worthy as himself; he, therefore, had the barrier raised some three or four inches, although it had before stood at the maximum height of his own skill, and, then, tauntingly challenged our hero to leap it with him. This offer Jack declined, unless some stake was raised to defray the victor for his extra exertion. Nowise backward in anything wherein sport was concerned, a subscription was at once set on foot, and a purse of five guineas was placed upon the standard, as a reward for the lucky individual who should first find a safe alightment upon the ground. A greater contrast could not well be than was thereupon exhibited between Springer and our hero—the first was all excitement and exertion, leaping continually from the ground to get his legs in plastic order. Jack, on the other hand, stood calmly and composed, gazing upon the scene with folded arms, as though the easiest matter in the world lay before him.

Again were the busy attendants in bustling eagerness with their preparations, the grass was carefully raked, that no undue advantage might be gained by either, a scratch or starting place was beaten in the meadow, and again the signaliser, handkerchief in hand, stood at his post, to set the competitors going.

"One, two!" he cried, the third was to be the signal, but before that could be given, Springer, in his undue eagerness, had overstepped the bounds and was half way to the barrier. With the utmost difficulty they at length managed to restrain his impetuosity, and prevail upon to await the appointed moment.

"One—get ready gentlemen," and there was a movement of intense anxiety among the lookers-on.

"Two!" shouted the man at the post.

"Three!" and the white handkerchief fluttered to the ground, and away, like eagles on the wing, darted the enterprising youths.

Up they sprang, Jack so near the standard that he caught the purse triumphantly in his hand, and bore it, as he came lightly to the ground. As for Springer, he was doomed not only to be vanquished, but also to meet with a terrible rebuff, for his legs catching the barrier in his terrific leap, he had been whirled into the air, and fell, after turning a complete somersault, stunned and senseless upon the sod.

Jack was the first to pick his rival from the ground, from whose mouth blood was oozing, and lifting him in his arms as though he had been an infant, he ran with him into the house. The application of sal-volatile, and a strong dose of brandy soon restored the sufferer to consciousness, the first use he made of which was to fix a look of fiendish hatred upon our hero, and to swear he had been unfairly tripped by him as he was in the act of leaping.

"Dog!" exclaimed Jack, with withering scorn, as he dashed the purse to the ground, "I'll leap you again for it, in the morning, twice the height but what I'll beat you. You, the champion of agility—a pretty champion forsooth; if there is not a man in the county who can beat you, send for me thou dissatisfied lying cur, at any hour, at any height or breadth, or distance, I'll prove thou art a braggart and a cur."

Maddened by these taunting words, Springer sprang upon our hero and struck him. Evil was the hour wherein he did so, for Jack returned the blow with such terrible interest, that his opponent the next instant lay at his feet bathed in blood.

If the lookers on were surprised at Jack's dexterity, they were infinitely more astonished at this unexpected display of strength, for Springer was unapproachable as a boxer for many a mile around. As soon as the latter had somewhat recovered himself, he bent a look of ferocity upon Jack, and muttered between his clenched teeth—" I'll pay you for this to-morrow,"

"As you please," said Jack, contentedly. "I intended to have been on my journey by daybreak to-morrow, but, since it lay in my power to oblige so good-tempered a gentleman as yourself, I will willingly forego my journey a few hours for that pleasure."

"Then you will fight me to-morrow?" said Springer.

"I will," answered Jack, "or any one like you, for any sum you like to name, or for love, if you like. You see, gentlemen, I am exceedingly accommodating."

"I tell you what I'd do, if I were you," said the host.

"What?" questioned the bystanders.

"Since there's a dispute about the purse—which, by the by, though its against Master George—I must say, I believe, was fairly won by the t'other, I should propose, as they have come to blows, and seem to wish for to know which is the best man, that they have a jolly good fight for it."

This proposition was received with loud cheers by the bystanders—cheers, which Jack instantly checked—as, looking round, he said, with dignity:—

"I am no pot-house brawler—neither do I choose to degrade myself to the level of a prize-fighter. I only wish it to be understood that I am quite capable of competing with any person here in any exercise they may please to mention, if such trial be fairly and impartially conducted; and, more, I also consider myself capable of resisting any insult, and imagine that I have done so sufficiently in this case already. I, therefore, tender my hand to this young man, to whom I have no ill will, and beg he will forget the blow I gave him in the impetuosity of the moment." And Jack gallantly extended his hand to his antagonist—which Springer would have accepted in the generous spirit in which it was offered—but the advice of his party deterred him.

"He's a cowardly cur," whispered the landlord, "and you can lick him, George, as easily as you can draw on your glove."

"Cut his bragging feathers for him," suggested another, aloud; he was a burly butcher, and looked as if he could have felled an ox with his tremendous fist.

"Jack scanned the speaker from head to foot.

"Don't give advice to others, greasy, you wouldn't like to follow yourself," he said, quietly:—

"Who do you call greasy?" said the butcher, advancing, in a threatening attitude, to Jack.

"You," answered Jack, unabashed.

"If you say it again, man, by God I'll smart you, you s—y-nose upstart, I will," said the butcher.

"No you won't," said Jack, calmly.

"Won't I," said the butcher, gazing upon Jack, as if he would swallow him, boots and all—with a look meant to be terribly appalling. "Why, you sprat, you mackeral, you maggot!" exclaimed the wrathful butcher, almost at his wits end for a simile.

"If I am a maggot," answered Jack, with a provoking smile, "I've so thick a hide that you can't smash me."

"We'll see about that, your vagrant, we will," said the butcher, tearing off his blue smock with the rapidity of lightning.

"Don't hurry yourself," said Jack, who viewed this bluster with supreme contempt, "you'll flutter your nerves, I'm very patient and can wait."

He was not kept waiting long, however, for no sooner was he free from the perplexing garment, then he aimed a blow at Jack, with such terrific fury, that had it taking effect as intended, it must have brained him on the spot. To the great astonishment of all beholders, however, when the scuffle was ended, it was the butcher who lay upon the ground, and our hero was standing triumphantly over him.

Jack had dexterously avoided the butcher's blow, and, in return, had favoured him with such a buffet behind the ear, that the butcher fell to the ground like a shot, and felt as he lay there, more agony in his head, and more lights dancing in his eyes, than he had seen for many a-day.

They lifted the butcher up, but he was dead beaten, his brain and vision was so confused by the blow and fall that he was incapable of further efforts, either of offence or defence, for that night. So they bore him home, and Jack they triumphantly escorted to the tavern, whistling that soul-inspiring tune, "See the conquering hero comes!"

Jack's last act had installed him a very god amongst them, and those who had previously anticipated his downfall with the greatest glee, were now most vociferous in their commendations, and their praises of his powers. The purse and its contents were handed over to him. Springer frankly confessing himself o'ermatched, since a better man than himself had been forced to succumb, and for the remainder of the evening the song and toast went round, and throughout their hilarious glee, all went merry as a marriage bell.

Jack got to bed at last, and stretching his limbs, was speedily in a sound and refreshing slumber.

He arose early in the morning and after a thorough ablution, proceeded down stairs, a hearty breakfast dispatched, he, stick in hand, sallied forth, intending to continued his journey, but a loud shout from the meadow testified that he was recognised.

He turned, and waving his hand, hallooed out to them a "Good bye!" but they were not to be parted with so easily—a troop of them came galloping after him, and, with good-tempered force, dragged him into the meadow, to make another leap for their amusement.

Jack buckled to the task with right good will, and the loud plaudits that followed his every exertion, testified the warm admiration that he awakened at every fresh feat of agility.

Whilst the sports were proceeding, a new comer arrested attention, he was the squire of the village, and the patron of sports of the district. He too joined warmly in Jack's praise.

"Bravo, old fellow! damme, you leap like a buck; talk about leaping, by the bye, I've got a little mare, that I'll back for pluck, against any of her age and weight in the world. And as for beauty, by Jove, there isn't a horse in Christendom, can touch her."

"I have a little mare, or had," said Jack, "that should leap her for her skin were she here."

"She might try," said the squire, "but, damme, sir, she'd lose. Why, who do you think my mare belonged to?"

"I cannot even guess," said Jack. "She might have been the property of the Prince Regent. Report speaks of him as an excellent criterion in matters appertaining to horse-flesh."

"She belonged to a greater than him," said the squire, with sparkling eyes.

"Greater," said Jack, "that is impossible, since his royal highness is the highest person in the kingdom."

"And so he may be, but, in spite of that, I tell you my mare belonged to a greater, better, and braver man than he. What think you, now, of her having been the property of that mad devil—"

"Who?" said our hero.

"Why, SIXTEEN-STRING JACK!" exclaimed the squire, in a burst of exultation.

"What, brave old Sue!" exclaimed Jack, his eyes filling with tears at the memory of the noble brute. "How I should like to see her."

"Should you?" said the squire, "then, by Jove, you shall."

He called one of the underlings by name, and bid him fetch the animal. The man returned in a few moments, leading the noble animal by the bridle.

At the sight of the spirited and faithful creature, who had been his friend and prized companion in many an hour of peril, Jack's ecstacy knew no bounds. He sprang towards her—his arms encircled her arched neck, and he hugged her with as much delight as if he had found a long lost sweetheart. And Sue, with an instinct almost beyond belief, at the sound of her old master's voice, capered, and showed the most exuberant signs of joy, and by her energetic actions in her frolicsome gambols, speedily broke loose from the hand that essayed to detain her, and sent the lookers on flying in all directions.

"So, so, gently lass," said Jack, and the noble animal, restraining her mischievous gambols, stood as passive and still as an obedient child.

"Well, may the devil admire me," said the squire, " if the man wasn't as dead as a gutted herring, I should swear you were Jack Rann himself. But where in the name of all that's wonderful did you make acquaintance with my little mare?"

"There are some tales in life it would be bad policy in any of us to confess, this is one in mine which you must pardon me if I remain silent upon. It is very evident I know the mare, and that is not all, the noble animal also has some recollection of me."

"That she has, and a most profound affection as ever I witnessed in any animal in my life," said the squire. "If it isn't too impertinent a question, may I ask where you ever groom to her?"

"Do I look like a stable-help, then?" said Jack, with a smile, "upon my soul I am exceedingly flattered."

"No, no, I did not mean that, but, to tell the truth, there is something so extremely mystical in this strange meeting that I—" and the young man stammered, "that, in fact, hang me if I can understand it."

"Its a problem you will not solve without my help," said Jack, "if you puzzle your brains till doomsday; and I have already said I decline to tell, so you may as well relinquish the matter. There is one question I should like to ask—perhaps you would have no objection to answer."

"What is it?" asked the squire.

"Where did you get this animal?"

"Get it! why, I bought it—what the devil does the man mean? Do you think I stole it?"

"I had no such unworthy thought of you in my head, believe me," said Jack; "my object in asking was, that I knew this animal was left by his late master in the care of a man, with a promise that she was never to serve another man, but should be carefully kept and attended until she died."

"Then his late master was cursedly deceived in the character of the man he intrusted him with, for no sooner was Sixteen-string Jack shot and gone to heaven, than this mare was advertised as Jack Rann's steed for sale, for two hundred and fifty guineas. I got scent of the affair through my horse-dealer. I got the rhino together, and, starting off post-haste to town, arrived just in time to buy her. Ain't I a lucky dog?"

"You are," answered Jack, "she is an animal any man in the world might be proud of—see what grace and dignity sit in every joint of her—what fire and spirit in her kindling eye, what speed in her limbs? She is a right royal lady," and Jack patted the gallant animal affectionately, a mark of recognition she acknowledged with a loud and joyful neigh."

"I have heard much of her leaping powers," observed the squire, "and have some few exploits, yet nothing at all to compare to those fame has accorded to her during her servitude with her late bold and gallant master."

"She has deserved every praise ever vented upon her," said Jack, "and had a thousand times more been said of her, still many a spirited action of hers would have gone unrecorded. Would'st have a specimen of dexterity?"

"Nothing would please me better," said the squire, with his eyes sparkling with pleasure.

"Lead her behind that hedge," said Jack, pointing to a fine tall quickset that separated one field from another, "and leave her there."

She showed many signs of uneasiness at being led away from her new found master, but was induced at length to go. As soon as the man returned, Jack gave a low whistle, they listened intently, and presently, borne upon the breeze, came the sound of a gentle neigh. Again Jack whistled, but this time in a somewhat louder key, and again did the mare give token of the acuteness of her hearing powers.

"It is wonderful!" said the delighted squire.

"The best of it is to come," said Jack, "I will now whistle three times."

"And what will be the result?" asked the proprietor of her.

"The height is too great," said the squire, apprehensive lest the animal should be injured, "I would not have her hurt for all the world."

"Never fear," said Jack, "I myself have too much love for the gallant brute to test her beyond her powers."

He whistled three times rapidly.

In an instant the form of brave Sue was seen to clear the hedge in a bold bound, and speeding onward like the wind, she came until she approached her master, and then with an homage she bent her knee that he might the more easily mount. Jack could not resist the temptation, and he leaped into the saddle and away they carolled round the meadow like a brace of mad things inflated with delight.

"Brave old Sue!" muttered Jack, as he stroked her glossy sides, "and is it come to this, must we part old girl?"

The mare gave a bound as if indignant at the very thought.

"By heaven, no!" exclaimed Jack, "I cannot—will not part with thee Thou wert born to serve Jack Rann's destinies, and shall to the last!"

Once athwart the back of his gallant mare, exhilerated by her spirited and daring companionship, Jack Rann felt himself no longer the plodding married man, he had of late been torturing his nature to succumb to. No, no, on the back of such a gallant steed as that, he was once again the prince of highwaymen, the gallant, daring, darling Jack Rann.

"Oh, for a brace of pistols," he muttered, as he gallopped round and round the field, as if to display the paces of the animal, but in reality lost in thought. "And I would not journey on my road to London for nothing. The last of the highwaymen is dead they say, what glorious fun it would be to teach them to the contrary—to show them Jack of the Sixteen-Strings was still alive—alive, ha! ha! ha! and kicking."

Jack gave vent to a burst of boisterous delight at the thoughts these feelings engendered.

"But I have sworn I would leave the road for ever," he thought, then turning it gaily to suit his own purposes, he exclaimed, "and so I will after to-day—to-day! I must have one more gallant adventure, and then, heigho, if you will, for an honest life."

Curbing the boisterous temper of the animal, by a single word from his mouth, Jack cantered up to the admiring throng, and, addressing the squire, said:—

"What think you of Jack Rann's mare now, sir, is she worth your money?"

"Aye, that she is," said the squire, "were it quadrupled—she is a right glorious creature, a lamb in calm, a lion when roused."

"She is a true highwayman's horse," said Jack, with manifest pride, "and she knows it, the jade! don't you, Sue?"

The animal responded to the kindly words with a caper of delight.

"Is she stedfast under fire?" asked the squire.

"She would not give an inch or quiver an eyelid, where an hundred pounder to open its fire upon her," responded Jack. "Fetch me a brace of pistols, and I'll give you a practical illustration of her stedfastness."

The pistols were brought—loaded, and, as the squire handed them to our hero, he sung the words of the song:—

"Sit, slave, for a man whom all else refuse,
To save in his desperate need."

"That's a very noble song you are singing, sir, and true to the very letter. I remember singing it myself once," said Jack; then wheeling his hors rapidly round, he bid them set up a mark, but ere they could do so, a brace of wood pigeons flew across. Bang! bang! went the pistols, and down fell the birds, Jack's unerring aim having brought them to the ground.

Amidst the loud and prolonged shouts of admiration that followed this feat, Jack threw the pistols to a fellow standing by, that they might be reloaded. This done and having had them restored to him, he struck Sue lightly with his hand, and away the obedient animal flew hilarious with delight at again having our hero on her back. Twice, thrice, Jack took the circuit of the meadow at a terrific gallop, then pulling up before the squire, with uplifted hat and triumphant smile, he said:—

"Were Sixteen-String Jack again to appear before you, if his life were in danger, and the speed of his brave Sue could save him, say, would thou refuse him the loan of her?"

"No, by God I wouldn't," cried the squire, enthusiastically.

"You have sworn to it," said Jack, " I could have taken your word, but now I am in duty bound to believe you. Listen one, listen all! You have heard the gallant mare I bestride was the highwayman's own, Jack Rann's own bonnie Sue, you have heard how often she has saved his life, and can imagine how, in his heart, he must have prized her, for her more than human devotion. It is all true, every word of it. As true, as it is I, Jack Rann, who claims his own, and bids you a long farewell."

On receipt of these tidings the squire seemed stunned, but instantly recovering from his astonishment, he bid the men shut the gate of the meadow, in order to entrap our hero.

With a smile of derision, and a shout of scorn, that breathed a word in the ear of Sue, away sped the gallant brute, and, taking the gate in a gallant style, she cleared it at a bound.

Jack reined up on reaching the high road, and, hat in hand, thus accosted the squire:—

"Farewell, sir—a thousand thanks for Sue—trust me, I'll treat her well for your sake. Look your last—we're off, and gone. If any would follow me, come on. I love companionship, and will lead you a right glorious race. Good day, gentlemen all, Jack Rann has his own brave Sue, and now echoes his own cry off—'Hurrah for the road!' "

In a twinkling Jack was off and gone, at a pace that set at defiance all attempts to overtake him. The men looked and wondered at this strange and unexpected finale—the squire stamped and blasphemed—but Jack was beyond their looks or their voices, careering gaily on.

* * * * *

It was a glorious moonlight night, when, under the beautiful and softening influence, every leaf and blade of grass wore a look of silvery radiance, that Jack descried, advancing to him in the distance, the mail coach.

"Egad! I'm in luck's way, that's a fact," thought Jack ; " not only have regained old Sue, but there comes a coach-load of wealthy fools to fill my pockets with good hard cash. What a slice of delicious luck this is, to be sure," and he rubbed his hands with glee. "Perhaps I shall gain enough from these addle-headed travellers to start myself and dear Elinor off to Yankee land again. Here goes for a try, at all events." And Jack, giving the beast an encouraging tap, gallopped on, pistol in hand, to meet the coach.

"Stand and deliver!" fell on their ears, like a burst of unwelcome thunder.

The coachman, at the unwonted and unwelcome sounds, shifted uncomfortably in his seat until he faced our hero, and the guard behind instantly began rumaging for his blunderbuss, but the muzzle of Jack's pistol, levelled direct to the head, made him sit down with a fluttering at heart more potent than agreeable.

"Harkee, fellows," said Jack, authoritatively, " if either of you fellows move hand or foot, it shall be at your peril, for, as I'm a living man, I'll put a bullet into your skull."

"Oh, Lord, don't do that, Mr. High—wayman," said the constable, his teeth chattering, and his knees knocking together with affright. "We won't interfere with you nohow."

The guard being similarly awed by Jack's threats to a state of submission, Jack advanced to the coach window, and in the blandest tones imaginable announced his business, which was the signal for a most confounded confusion, the men groaned and swore—the women screamed and sobbed—whilst cries of rape! fire! murder! rent the air.

"Cease this bawling, fools," said Jack, annoyed at this outbreak, "or there may be murder done in reality. Quick! do you hear? your money, purses, gee-gaws, I am a desperate man, and in no humour for fooling to-night, so shell out at once!"

After this forcible appeal, he received a handful in the shape of well-filled purses. Depositing these in the capacious pockets that adorned his coat, he stretched out his hand for more, but the occupants of the carriage simultaneously declared they had not a stiver to bless themselves.

"Very well," said Jack, at the same time, "you have a watch or so, for which I must trouble you, come, madame, that frying pan of yours must be cumbersome, allow me to ease you of it," and by a dexterious twist, Jack detached it from her side. The old lady went into hysterics at his audacity.

"Now, gentlemen, gentlemen," said Jack, in a tone of the greatest good humour, "do have some little consideration of my time, pass out your watches, I beg, or you will give me the trouble of dismounting and fetching them, a step I feel assured we should have reason to lament."

"Give him your trinkets," said a voice, from within at that moment, "I know the villain's voice, and if I can but get a glance at his face, he shall swing for this."

"And I should know that voice, too," said Jack, who overheard the advice, "and have a desire to see your face, come, sir, favour me with a sight of your frontispiece, nothing is more agreeable than mutual recognition," as Jack spoke these words he thrust in his hand and drew the speaker forward.

The moonbeams fell upon their faces as he did so, and revealed to Jack Rann the well-remembered features of the Earl of Dashfield; and the earl, on his part, gazed upon the face of his enemy, Sixteen-string Jack.

"What, hang dog," said the earl, with a grin of deep and deadly hatred, "the rumour of your death was an artful lie, after all! What oh!" he shouted—"coachman, guard, seize him, it is Jack Rann—curs, cowards!" and the earl knashed his teeth with impotent rage; "set upon him, and capture him, and earn the reward set upon his head!"

"They dare not do it," said Jack. "It is as much beyond their strength as yours, thou venomous old man! But since we have met, tell me, my lord Dashfield, how it comes that I find thee travelling in a common coach in a manner so befitting your high rank and station.

No. 56.

"It is because I have been driven from my house by the accursed Malcolms that you set upon me."

"So, so, then," cried Jack, with a burst of glee, "the great Lord Dashfield has been taught that there are such things as laws in England, that may not be infringed with impunity. It is well done," said Jack, "and I glory in it; much good may the lesson do you."

"You glory in my downfall, Jack Rann," said the earl, knashing his teeth with rage; "and now, hear me, I have sworn to be revenged upon you, and will, if I retrace my way to London on foot. You have heaped injury upon injury upon me—I will retaliate ere long—the noose is already woven for your neck, and I swear by Him who made me, I will not take bit or sup, nor rest in peace, until I have set the bloodhounds of the law again upon your track. The noose is woven, the hemp is spun for your neck, I say, and I will not close my eyes in sleep until my hands have encircled it about your accursed throat. Take that, with my bitterest curse upon you, as a parting benediction."

"A blessing or a curse at your hands, old man, are of equal value—both are incapable of good or evil. That I did you one wrong, I confess; that I deeply grieve and ever have repented me of that wrong, I solemnly swear!" and Jack's voice trembled with emotion as he uttered the words. Checking by a strong effort the feelings thus awakened, Jack continued —

"But what is past is gone for ever—therefore, we can't avert it. I am pressed for cash, my lord, or you would not find me again upon the road—which a few days since I believed I had forsaken for ever, but fate has decreed otherwise, and if she has a hempen neckerchief in store for me, as you have prognosticated, I flatter myself I can face that doom with as much courage, and can meet the king of terrors with as little dread as you will, my Lord of Dashfield, though he may wait upon you on a silken couch. But time flies—and I, having a pressing engagement elsewhere, must be flying too—you have favoured me with your purse, I believe, my lord—'

"I have—curse you!" answered the earl.

"A piece of generosity upon your part, that I appreciate fully, believe me, my lord, it will tend to relieve me of much embarrassment. Perhaps, you have no objection to parting with your watch, watching the varying of time may relieve my journey of much of its tediousness; besides, my lord, you know the adage, that trifling gifts bind long friendships."

"It is yours," said the earl, as he placed it in Jack's hand, "and mark my words, Jack, whenever you part with that watch, you may count the hours, for your days are numbered."

"I thank you for your warning," said Jack, for the sound of approaching horsemen smote upon his ear, "it is fairly given, and shall be strictly watched and guarded. Farewell, my lord—good night, gentle ladies!" and with these parting words, Jack urged Sue upon her way.

* * * * *

The approaching horsemen were a party in pursuit of Jack, headed by the veritable young squire from whom Jack had obtained Sue. They learnt from the occupants of the coach, that our hero, after despoiling its inmates of all their valuables, had cooly cantered away on the road to London. Fired and animated by this intelligence, they put their horses to a gallop, and speedily came so near upon our hero, that they could plainly discern him in the distance as he trotted briskly along. With a loud shout they dashed the rowels of their spurs into the sides of their horses until they bled again, and on they went at a headlong speed.

Alarmed at the uproar, Jack turned in his saddle, and comprehending at a glance how the matters stood, he cheered his own animal on by a cheering word, and speedily extended the distance between them. On went the pursued and on, thundering after him, came the pursuers. The moon, which had hitherto been radiant in her beauty, was now occasionally obscured by clouds. Two hours passed, and still the exciting chase continued. Poor Sue's powers of endurance had been taxed to the uttermost, for already had she borne her master over fifty miles of ground that day, and now began to show symptoms of flagging. Jack watched with painful concern the failing powers of the gallant brute, and viewed her sufferings with more concern than the did the danger of capture, that now so imminently threatened, for the pursuers, having changed horses on the road, were mounted on fresh mettlesome steeds.

"This will never do," argued Jack, "poor old Sue is dead beaten. To continue thus is to render capture certain. To wait, is to throw myself completely into the hands of the Philistines. What's to be done?" If I could but give her a mouthful of water, and let her browse till morning, she would be invigorated, and would easily distance them; it shall be done."

He turned his horse's head into a little mead on the right-hand side of the road, and threading it, found at the other end of it a fine field of clover; with a fervent ejaculation of gratitude he jumped from the noble creature's back, and drawing the bridle from her head, he suffered her to crop the dewy herb at pleasure, whilst he himself, under the sheltering limbs of a far speading oak, threw himself upon the grass to think of the incidents of his eventful life and to concoct schemes for its enjoyment for the future. He lay in this state until, fatigued in mind and body, his eyes involuntarily closed, and he dropped into a sound slumber beside the faithful animal who wandering towards him had affectionately laid herself by his side.

How long he slept he knew not, but he was suddenly startled from his sleep by the sound of voices and the rustling of branches, and looking up, he beheld in the struggling light of morning, that his pursuers had discovered his whereabouts, and were, in fact, upon him.

To leap into the saddle was the work of an instant, and using the bridle, which he had retained in his hand, as a whip, the maddened Sue dashed headlong forward, he knew not, cared not whither.

Jack was unconsciously fast hurrying towards a dreadful chalk cliff, that opened its awful abyss at the end of the field.

His pursuers knew this, and in tones of frantic supplication besought him to "Stop," but lashed to madness by the shouts, still wilder the affrighted Sue dashed on.

A terrible shout of dismay and horror burst from the assembly, for at that instant Sue had leaped from the brink of the cliff, and down, down she went from its dizzy heighth to inevitable destruction.

CHAPTER XXXVI.

JACK PROCEEDS TO LONDON, AS ALSO DOES THE EARL—THE WATCH—JACK'S ARREST.

STUNNED and stupefied by his fall, which could not have been from a lesser height than fifty feet, he lay, for some time, totally unconscious of passing events. Recovering his consciousness at length, his first care was for Sue. But she, alas! was past all help or need of it. Her broken limbs—motionless form—the stream of blood issuing from her mouth—all testified the lamentable fact that the noble animal was dead.

With a tear to her memory, a tribute of love and gratitude which Jack's brave heart could not repress, he sprang to his feet, for the shouting voices overhead convinced him that the danger he had escaped at the price of poor Sue's life was still imminent and close at hand, he plunged into the copse which skirted the valley, and hastened, with almost incredible speed, onward.

The whole of that day and the following night, Jack kept on by a by-road which he had ascertained led to the metropolis. By this time footsore, heart sick, and thoroughly beaten, he sought the shelter which a cottage afforded him. Here he recruited exhausted nature by copious draughts of home-brewed ale, and sundry slices from a portly ham, and, amid the greatest of luxuries, midnight found him comfortably ensconced between the clean and wholesome sheets of the cottage bed.

Jack rose with the lark in the morning, refreshed and invigorated in body and mind, and pressing a guinea upon the honest folks who entertained him, he set out with a brave heart for London. He had not proceeded far before he fell in with a farmer, journeying in the same direction, who proudly offered our hero a seat in the chaise cart he was driving. This offer Jack accepted with alacrity, and they journeyed merrily on until they reached the hill at Highgate, where they saw the magnificent doom of St. Paul's, as rising above the clustering spires around, it towered towards the skies. Stopping to refresh his horse at an hotel at the foot of the celebrated hill, Jack shared a flagon of ale with the honest yeoman, and, shaking him heartily by the hand, set out to travel the short distance remaining on foot. This distance was soon accomplished, and Jack found himself again amidst the busy throng that crowded the streets of the city of the world. He had arranged to meet Elinor at the lodgings previously occupied by her in Fetter-lane, thitherward he bent his steps. To his exceeding joy he found her, although she had only arrived a few hours before him, Jack's good feet having borne him at almost as rapid a rate as the four-horse waggon had conveyed her. Their meeting was one of pure delight, his beloved wife expressing her delight, at again beholding him, with many caresses, and many tears of unfeigned joy.

Here they resided in peace for many days, the resources Jack had derived from the earl and his fellow travellers in the coach, proving amply sufficient for their wants; in addition to which Jack had reserved a sum sufficient to convey them to America, whither they intended to sail by the first ship leaving London for those shores. Jack kept his arrival a profound secret from the Malcolms; he had already received so many favors from them, and felt so full of fervent gratitude for their noble exertions in his behalf, that he was determined not to trouble them with a recital of his misfortunes, but to proceed to the New World with the money he had acquired on the road, determined to strain every nerve, when there, to redeem the past, and to repay them the heavy sum they had advanced him, which he considered as a loan, to be honourably repaid, but which they had given freely, without a wish, thought, or desire, of again beholding it.

Many weeks passed before Jack could learn tidings of any vessel leaving for the desired destination. At length one was advertised to sail from London for New York, on the 30th of November, 1774. Jack instantly collected all his money together, and started to the docks where the ship was lying, at once to engage a berth for himself and wife.

Whilst he was thus engaged, Elinor's landlady entered the apartment with a look of consternation upon her features. Noticing the unusual concern displayed in the open and good-natured countenance of her landlady, Elinor asked instantly what was the matter.

"Oh, my good friend," said the unhappy landlady, wringing her hands, and sobbing convulsively, " that it should come to this! I, who have been a housekeeper five and forty years, and never troubled anybody to call twice or a shilling, oh dear, oh dear."

' My dear woman," said Elinor, "what is the matter? pray compose yourself."

"Oh, never!" said the afflicted landlady, " 1 never dreamt such a thing in the horridest nightmare as ever I had. I am a ruinated and undone woman for ever! The tax collector called for the king's taxes—I couldn't pay him—and, oh lord, my heart will break! the broker is in the house!"

"And I have thoughtlessly allowed myself to get in your debt!" said Elinor, in a tone of regret, " my dear lady," she said, feeling in her pocket for her purse, " what is the amount you require?"

"Five pounds, fourteen, and two pence," answered the woman, with a low curtsey, " and may the heavens bless you, my dear ma'am, for your princely goodness!"

To her deep disappointment and chagrin, Elinor discovered, in giving Jack her purse, she had unwittingly given him every stiver she possessed, and had left herself penniless.

"It is very annoying," she said, with a perplexed and confused look, that I gave my husband this money—every farthing I possessed—it is extremely unfortunate."

"It is, indeed," said the woman, bursting into a sudden gush of tears, "If they are not gone before my husband's return, he'll murder me, I'm sure he will."

Elinor had received painful evidence of the man's extreme brutality towards his unfortunate wife, and felt deeply distressed she should have been the cause, however innocently, of involving her in this trouble. Of Jack's return there was no certainty whatever; it might be immediately, for aught she knew. Suddenly she remembered Jack had confided a watch to her care, and, flying to a drawer in which it was carefully concealed, hastily exclaimed:—

"Let the servant pledge this for the amount wanted, I can easily redeem it when my husband returns."

"You have saved me," exclaimed the grateful woman, and, falling upon her knees, she bedewed Elinor's hands with her grateful tears.

This watch was the earl's!

The girl was despatched to the pawnbroker's, with the watch.

"Well, my little dear," said that great relative of the distressed portion of the human race," what can I do for you this lovely day? A gold watch, jewelled, ah! made by Silver and Co.—number one aught—two aught (1020) engraved on the case; presented to the Earl of Dashfield. By jingo, this is the identical timepiece we have been looking for this month past. Walk round the counter, my dear." The girl obeyed him. "This watch is a great prize, my dear, where did you get it from?"

Alarmed at the equivocal looks bent on her by the pawnbroker, and his inquisitive satellites, the startled girl seized the watch, and would have departed with it, as she came, but they forcibly detained her, and the obliging capitalist bid one of his assistants run to Bow-street, and tell Sir John Fielding that they had captured the watch taken from the Earl of Dashfield.

The man sped on his errand with alacrity, and in a very short space of time, returned with the magistrate and a whole posse of Bow-street runners.

Returning the pawnbroker's bows and cringes with a look of disdain, the magistrate requested if he could be accommodated with a private room, as he did not wish to interrogate the girl in public, the shop being, by that time, swarming with curiosity mongers, who had with manifest pleasure and the greatest zeal followed the worthy magistrate and his subordinates.

"Oh, certainly, Sir John, certainly," said the money lender, with a profound bow, "my parlour is quite at your service," and to the best parlour they were straightway ushered.

"Do not be alarmed, my good girl," said Sir John, who noticed the trepidation of the girl, "we do not for an instant suppose you stole the watch, and all we shall require of you, will be truthful and honest answers to the questions that may be put to you, giving which, no harm may be feared, for no harm can come to you, but if you equivocate or deny the truth, you will be considered *paticeps criminus* with him who committed it, and punished accordingly."

Turning to the pawnbroker he said:—

"The notification served upon you, and upon all others engaged in your trade collectively and individually throughout the metropolis, arose from the following circumstances:—I received a visit from the Earl of Dashfield, who has made himself sufficiently notorious by a prosecution instituted against him for attempted abduction, who swore upon oath, that whilst travelling in the Liverpool mail coach, that vehicle had been stopped by a highwayman, that that highwayman, was none other than the notorious robber, Jack Rann, or Sixteen-String Jack; so that the man, the honest portion of the world had been congratulating themselves by having got rid of by gun-shot wound, or by drowning, was still proved to be at large, to the injury of the king's liege subjects. The deponent further made oath that in addition to moneys, he had been robbed of a gold watch, maker's name Silver, No. 1202, and besought me, as he set great store by the watch, it having been presented to him, to use means for recovering it for him. I do so, so far as lays in my power, by serving notices upon all the pawnbrokers, of the loss of the property, desiring them in case it should be presented as a pledge, that it and the party bringing it were to be detained until I had examined them. Thus far the earl's statement of the robbery is verefied, it only remains for us to find whether the thief is in reality Sixteen-String Jack, of which suggestion I must confess I have the strongest doubts in my own mind, relying as I do on the testimony of the soldiery who saw him perish before their eyes, but whether it be him thus astoundedly come to life again or not, it matters little to us, so that the actual culprit be apprehended and made an example of, to the terror of other evil doers."

Sir John Fielding then commenced an examination of the girl, whose plain unvarnished relation, had the impress of sufficient truth, to meet with general belief.

"This is sufficient," said Sir John Fielding, rising, "all that remains now is to apprehend this mysterious gentleman, who without apparent means of support, contrives to live like a gentleman. Officer, go at once to the Horse Guards, get an order for a dozen infantry, and bring them hither."

Whilst these untoward events were concocting, Elinor and her landlady were in the greatest consternation at the extraordinary length of time the girl was gone. More than once or twice the landlady hurried out in search of her, but returned each time with dismay imprinted upon her features; the girl was nowhere to be seen. She, however, was soon released from her trouble and embarrassment by the return of Jack, who instantly paying her demand, the house was speedily freed of those importunate and unwelcome visitors—the broker and his man.

"Well, Jack," said Elinor, her face beaming with love and tenderness, as she gazed upon our hero, "what news have you for us?"

First-rate," answered Jack, with great glee, "I have been on board the ship; Hope is her name, and right well she deserves it, for she is as hopeful and gallant a barque as ever clave the blue waters of the Atlantic. I have arranged with the captain; have paid him a deposit for the berth, and, wind and weather permitting, we sail for New York on the 30th of November. Hurrah! my dear wife, there is luck in store for us yet."

Hardly had these words of gayful anticipation escaped his lips, before a loud knock at the door caused each to start with surprise.

"Hallo!" said Jack, "who the devil's that, I wonder?" Some more creditors of the old woman, perhaps. Go and see, Ele.; and here, mate," he added, jocularly, "if it should be any one inquiring for me, tell them I am engaged—not to be seen on any account. What ho, my tulips! gaily go the mill!" he added, as another startling rap evinced the impatience of the applicants. "If that door was not of extra sound and seasoned stuff, it would have been smashed to smithereens long before this. Cut and come again, my darlings," said Jack, as an application of the knocker, louder than any that preceded it, sent its echoes through the house.

Elinor descended to the door—for the landlady was absent—and found herself confronted by the pawnbroker and the servant girl—the latter in tears. Of the pawnbroker she had a passing acquaintance, and therefore viewed his appearance without trepidation or alarm. A smile of exceeding great good humour was spread over his crafty face, as he said, with great serenity of manner, "You sent this watch to me, madam?"

"I desired the girl to raise some money upon it, being pressed for a trifling payment at the time," answered Elinor; then glancing at the tear-marked face of the girl, she added, "I hope you did not suspect she came with it without my consent or knowledge."

"Oh, no, certainly not," answered the crafty trader.

"Then I presume the article is not worth the price I desired to be advanced upon it."

"It is worth five times the sum, madam," answered the man of business.

"Indeed," said Elinor, with surprise, "then why did you not at once give her what she asked? But it is of no consequence; my husband having returned, and furnished me with the money, I have no necessity for parting with the property, and will, therefore, take it of you at once."

This gratuitous piece of information was precisely what the pawnbroker desired.

"In an instant, madam—beg pardon—I have a friend waiting without."

He rejoined the magistrate and the soldiery, who were in waiting.

"It is all right, Sir John—It is a double cage, and both birds are in it." He placed the watch in his hand.

Sir John stepped forward, followed by the soldiery.

"Arrest that woman," said Fielding, and Elinor was instantly seized, beckoning the soldiers to advance, he ascended the stairs and entered the room where our hero was sitting.

"John Rann," said Sir John Fielding, in a solemn voice, for in the person before him, he at once recognised the young man who had been placed before him at Bow-street, "you are my prisoner, armed with the warrant of the king, I arrest you on the charge of highway robbery.

"Sir John Fielding," said Jack, in a tone firm and resolute, for he also knew the magistrate, "were the king himself here to back his warrant, I would die ere I would surrender! Back, I say! if you value your life a pin's fee, back with you, for by him who made me, if you advance one single step to seize me, your blood be on your own head—I am a desperate man—"

"I know it, and have provided myself with a desperate remedy." He threw open the door. "Soldiers, do your duty."

They advanced with fixed bayonets and levelled pieces.

Jack saw at once the odds were against him. "Sir John," he said, frankly extending his hand, which the worthy magistrate took and shook heartily, "I am your prisoner, and it gives me some pleasure in this dark hour to confess so, for you are the only man in England worthy of taking me.

"My duty is a painful one, Mr. Rann, said the good man, a tear of commiseration appearing in each eye, "but it must, nevertheless, be fulfilled."

"I know it is," said Jack, adding, with a smile, "and it is with extreme unwillingness upon my part that I give you this trouble, I do assure you."

"I think we can dispense with these soldiers," and Sir John looked at our hero, inquiringly.

"Yes, certainly," said Jack, "they are no friends of mine. I am not ambitious. I need no guard of honour, God knows!"

"And you will accompany me, without attempting to escape?" asked Fielding.

"You have spoken the word, Sir John, I pledge you my honour I will not."

"It is enough. Soldiers, retire to your garrison. They went their way.

Jack's word of honour was given, rather than break which he would have died; for Jack, with all his faults, was an honourable man.

Sir John made Jack's commitment out in the presence of his prisoner, and when Jack had selected some clothes, and other things necessary for himself and wife, they walked arm and arm down Fleet-street, and up Ludgate-hill: Sir John walking by the side, and freely conversing with them, so that they bore the appearance of three friends in social conversation.

They entered Newgate by the governor's private door, who attended upon them from that time up to the day of their trial as if they were respected guests on a visit of ceremony with him.

CHAPTER XXXVII.

THE TRIAL—CONVICTION AND CONDEMNATION.

JACK'S unexpected capture was like a horrible murder at the present day—quite a "God-send" to the newspaper press of the metropolis. Flaring placards, in blood-red letters of a foot long, told the gaping throng of his capture, which was deemed, on the part of Sir John Fielding, one of unexampled sagacity and cunning.

"The age of miracles has not entirely ceased," said one of those profound oracles. "The dead alive! Yes, gentle reader, Jack Rann, or Sixteen-stringed Jack, as he is more extensively known, instead of lying in the depth of Father Thames, as we all believed, has been found on terra firma—alive and well. Thanks to the unexampled sagacity and acuteness of our unrivalled justice, Sir John Fielding, the villain was triumphantly secured, and is now again an inmate of the strong room of Newgate, to prevent his escape from which, turnkeys are continually with him, night and day. He will take his trial on Monday next, and, it is confidently anticipated, will be hanged the week following. Of these startling and thrilling events, we shall have verbatim reports, so readers will act wisely in bespeaking early copies of the paper."

It was through this medium Jack's kind and true friends, the Malcolms, were apprised of his unhappy position. So confident were they in their knowledge of his departure for the New World, they believed at the first this was a piece of chicanery on the part of the newsmongers, to obtain a larger circulation for their papers, but feeling too much interest at heart, young Dashfield, now the happy and accepted suitor of Miss Malcolm, flew to the prison.

Hope died within him on entering the portal, for Jack's well-known voice, in a burst of unconstrained joyous laughter broke upon his ear. So intense were his feelings of grief, as he heard it, that the noble-hearted fellow fell back insensible, so heart-stricken with grief was he at hearing the worst had been realised in regard to poor Jack. The noise occasioned by his fall brought forth the governor, and close upon his heels came Jack.

"Why, Dashfield," he said, his gay tone unchanged, "what blessed wind has blown you hither? This is more than I bargained for. This is a very particular friend of mine," said Jack, to the governor, "may I beg the favour of your parlour for a quiet chat. I have news of some importance to communicate to him?"

"Certainly, Mr. Rann," said the governor, in the most polite and gentlemanly tones. "Any friend of yours is welcome."

"What think you of that, Dashfield, my boy, you are welcome to Newgate? The governor is paying you rather an equivocal compliment—but come along, my fine fellow, accept his hospitality for once," and Jack led Dashfield, who, with faltering steps, followed him into the private apartment allotted him by the governor.

"Jack," said Dashfield, taking our hero's hand, whilst tears of sorrow rose unbidden to his eyes. "It cuts me to the heart to hear you talk thus thoughtlessly—think, for God's sake, of the perilous position in which you stand."

"Will a grieving heart, complaining tongue, or groaning breast, relieve me from these stone walls?" Not a bit of it—I am acting like a philosopher. Dashfield, my boy, what can't be cured must be endured; and, therefore, in the name of all that's jolly, why may I not as well laugh as pine my time away here. Its all fate, my boy! fate who has o'ertopped me at last. I begin to think I was born to be hung, or, curse me, if I shouldn't have been swamped with Wide-Awake, and the other poor devils, who went down in the wreck."

"The wreck!" echoed Dashfield.

"Yes, the wreck," said Jack—"but I forgot you had not heard of the misfortunes I have undergone since I last saw you."

A few moments sufficed to put the young officer in possession of all the circumstances of the loss of the emigrant ship, the facts of which the reader has already become acquainted. Jack related also his subsequent career.

"Pity you I do, from my soul," said Dashfield, when he had made an end. "But oh, Jack, had the promise you had given us—had our unceasing love for you no weight to save you from plunging again in that vortex of crime, from whose dread consequences you have already had so miraculous an escape, I do blame you, and feel most deeply hurt, that you should not have applied to us, who, you must have known, would have felt pleasure in again assisting you. Oh, Jack, you have acted most blameable in this—I can never forgive you for it."

"I acted like an independant fool, as I am," said Jack. "I wanted to make my fortune without your assistance, but the run of luck was against me—old father Time himself seems to have had a spite against me, for hadn't it have been for that accursed watch, I shouldn't have been kicking my heels in Newgate. But don't look so doleful, old fellow—if the worst comes to the worst, why, what's the odds? I can only die once, you know; and, perhaps, its fitting I should leave the world in as public a manner as possible, since, all my life long, I have played so public a part in it. But, I say, I go before the head beaks on Monday—me, and the missus, they've nabbed her, too—just like the selfish brutes ain't it? Wouldn't it be as well if I had a counsel?"

"I have already instructed my solicitor to retain one for you," said Dashfield.

"It will need a long-headed one to get me out of this scrape," said Jack, "but you are a jolly good fellow, Dashfield, and I am grateful to you for your kindness for poor Elinor's sake—as for me—and no matter—I will not distress you by any foreboing—I will escape if I can—that is, if they'll let me, for I am on my parole of honour here, and wouldn't break faith with the governor if I found the door open for me to-morrow morning."

"I sincerely trust in a merciful God that you may leave this dreadful place," said Dashfield. "Believe me, Jack, no stone shall remain unturned that can lead to that most blessed consummation."

"God bless you, old fellow," said Jack, gratefully, wringing the others hand, "I shall never forget your kindness—live long or die speedily, I shall never forget it. But poor Elinor—you will not leave without seeing her, she needs consolation and advice, as to me, I shape my temperament to the wind that blows, and in human life, you may set it down as a grand maxim, there is nothing like despising trouble, and the heavier they grow the less you ought to care for them."

"I will go and see Mrs. Rann at once. I have a message for her from the ladies."

"That's right," said Jack, by-the-bye, Dashfield, how is the ladye fair—when comes the wedding off?"

"Don't talk of that, Jack, whilst you are in this danger, we haven't heart even to think of it. It is at present set aside."

"We'll soon have it on the boards again, old fellow, but go and see Elinor, poor girl, it is sad for her," said Jack, as tears of emotion filled his eyes "so soon a wife, so early a widow."

* * * * *

It is the day of trial and the court-house is literally beseiged by a countless throng, eager to catch a glimpse of the hero, Sixteen-string Jack. Im mense sums were paid by hundreds for the privilege of a seat in court, and in less than five minutes from the opening of the doors, it was crowded to suffocation.

A silence, deep and solemn as the grave, was there, when the judge, in whose hands lay Jack's fate, entered, in his ermine robes, and took his seat upon the bench.

"Bring forth the prisoner."

In an instant, Jack Rann, carefully watched and guarded by two turnkeys, entered the dock. All eyes were turned to him—some glistening with tears of pity—others flashing with admiration. None looked with scorn.

A carnation glow was upon his cheek that made him, eminently handsome as he undoubtedly was, look more than usually beautiful, whilst his unruffled visage, his undaunted carriage, and flashing eye, told of a spirit that the law, in all the majesty of its terrors, had no power to bend or break. Jack bent his head to the judge, then glancing at the thousand inquiring and admiring faces that met his own, he bowed also politely to the visitors.

It was all they wanted to awake the admiration that was struggling for vent within them. Spite of the threatening look of the javelin-men and officers, a loud cheer arose; it was borne on the breeze to the watchers without, and, "Long live Jack Rann, the gallant, brave, and free!" was shouted by ten thousand enthusiastic voices. In vain did the clerk of the court proclaim silence—cheer followed cheer, until the court rang again with the inspiring sound.

The counsel for the prosecution has risen—the trial proceeds. With an eloquence worthy of a better cause than of aiding in the destruction of a fellow-creature, the Attorney-General makes his speech, laying open every crime committed by our hero, and finally proving him to be the blackest villain that ever trod the face of the earth—a wretch so crime-stained that he was not fit to live. Crime after crime had been arraigned against him, so as to render an escape almost impossible.

The robbery of the marquis was the first, although there was abundance of proof they had been actually robbed, and that by a man calling himself Sixteen-streen Jack, yet, thanks to the arguing and cross-examination, hankering, and bullying of Jack's counsel, it fell to the ground; for not a single witness would take upon himself to swear that Jack was the man. Charge after charge fell to the ground, amidst loud bursts of applause, which the officers, spite of their utmost endeavours, found it impossible to repress.

All other charges were dismissed, one only remained—it was the robbery of the earl.

Up to his entrance into the witness-box, Jack's triumphant acquittal seemed an absolute certainty, but the earl's evidence changed the happy aspect of affairs; hope faded, and anon died. The sum and substance of his evidence was this :—

"I was on my road to Liverpool, intending to leave England, in consequence of a prosecution being instituted against me. The coach in which I travelled was stopped by a highwayman. On my solemn oath, the prisoner at the bar was the man. In addition to money, he took from me a watch—the same now produced in court. I retraced my steps to London, and gave information to Sir John Fielding of the robbery, with a description of the watch stolen from me."

Sir John Fielding's evidence went far to complete the fatal chain of evidence. It was in these words :—

"Upon information afforded me by the last witness, I used means to discover the perpetrator of the robbery. I caused a description of the watch to be served upon every pawnbroker in London, with commands that, should the property be offered them, the person should be detained, and I apprised of the circumstances. The property was at length offered as a pledge, I was informed of the circumstance, and, accompanied by a picquet of troops, I went to the prisoner's lodging. The female prisoner—his wife—confessed to having sent the property, and further stated it belonged to her husband; upon this I took them into custody."

This evidence, supported by other witnesses, closed the case for the prosecution.

Jack's counsel defended him right manfully, he urged upon the attention of the jury the fact of the spite that the Earl of Dashfield had confessed he bore against our hero; he pleaded that instigated by this wicked and dishonourable spite, he had concocted an unfounded charge against an innocent and injured man. He called upon the jury to stand one and all manfully in the defence of outraged innocence and justice, he called upon them to brand with the ignominous name of liar, the vindictive old scoundrel who had now left the box covered with infamy, he confidently trusted in them to record the innocence of his client, and return to their homes with the peaceful consolation in their souls, that in performing a sacred duty that they had rescued from the jaws of death, a gallant and noble young man.

A buzz of admiration ran through the court as the advocate took his seat.

The judge briefly summed up, charging the jury to weigh with profound attention the evidence that had been laid before them, to do their duty manfully and fearlessly in the sight of God and man, to deliver a verdict that they could in justice reconcile to their consciences.

The jury stood many minutes in earnest consultation, and then begged to retire.

Terrible was that lapse of time to all within that court—awfully solemn was the deathly stillness that pervaded, faces grew pale with horror, the breath is hushed by sickening fear, the eyes grow dim by dread, suffocation seems to oppress the chest.

But hush! the jury have returned and answered to their names.

The only unmoved person in this trying time, was the heroic Jack, who had not changed colour, or blinked an eye-lid, who now turned his face towards those men upon whose tongues hung his destiny—life or death.

"What say you, gentlemen of the jury, is the prisoner at the bar guilty or not guilty?"

The foreman clears his throat like one who has grown suddenly husky and hoarse, and mutters something in a tone too low for human ears to hear.

Again is the question repeated.

Oh, awful silence! Oh, terrible hesitation.

Again the foreman of the jury attempts to speak, but fails, but essaying at length his lips form the terrible word, GUILTY!

With an undaunted brow, with a smile of courage in this terrible moment, Jack listens to the awful word of his sentence.

"John Rann, you will pass from here to the prison from whence you came, thence to the place of execution, where you will be hanged by the neck, until you are dead, dead, dead, and may the Lord God Almighty have mercy on your soul."

He passes with a firm foot from the dock and is gone.

Sobs and cries of lamentation fill the court with piteous sounds, they are borne without, whispered, below the breath, with tearful eyes and agitated faces go the words, "CONDEMNED TO DIE."

CHAPTER XXXVII.

"LAST SCENE OF ALL THAT ENDS THIS STRANGE EVENTFUL HISTORY."
SHAKSPEARE.

CONDEMNED TO DIE.

IMAGINATION fails in depicting the horror and despair consequent upon these terrible words—"Condemned to die!" The usually hatless idlers went away sad in heart and depressed in spirit, as the death-like token fell upon their ear. All sympathised—all mourned—for Jack, throughout his gay career, had never robbed a poor man's home—had never drained a tear from a widowed eye; and his sad fate, therefore, deserved some token of their kind and pitying remembrance.

Prepared, as it were, for his fate—for in his own mind he had summoned up the impossibility of escape against such a tide of evidence—he left the bar, without betraying, in the slightest degree, any emotion of fear, dread, or astonishment. This extraordinary nerve and unflinching behaviour sustained him to the direful end. The minister prayed, preached, and besought, with all the energy of a fanatic, in order to bend, what he termed, our hero's stubborn spirit. But Jack stood proof against all, save and excepting those truthful narrations of Him who died that sinners might be saved—to those he listened with an open, believing, and prayerful heart.

Captain Dashfield was the first to visit and console him after his sentence. In his hopeful and friendly zeal, he raised an anticipation of escape in Jack's mind that was, alas! never to be realised.

"My dear Jack," he said, the joyous light of hope beaming from his eyes, 'you can form no conception of what an immense interest people are taking in your welfare. A petition is on foot, and already some five hundred names have been added to the scroll, praying the king's most excellent majesty to extend his royal clemency to yourself. Under such a pressure of solicitations from the best and noblest of his citizens, I am sure he cannot refuse."

"Could he see with your eyes," said Jack, with a smile, "his royal pardon would not be withheld one single minute. But since he is allowed to have a mind of his own, and that somewhat an eccentric one, he may, perhaps, consider the petition an unworthy one, and, consigning that to the flame, may, with the same breath, consign me to Tyburn. Be that as it may, old fellow, and should the worst come to the worst, believe me, I shall gaze upon the Tree with resignation—even like unto the man, who, purchasing a coffin long before his decease, so familiarised himself with the king of terrors, that he could rest in his shroud with as much quietude at heart as he could in his bed. Placing all faith in Him who died for sinners' forgiveness, I can meet my fate firmly and undauntedly. And why should I fear death? Where my hand stained in blood to the wrist, He might have terrors for me calculated to make me quake with fear—but, thank heaven, it is for no murder I am about to suffer—no, no, that pang is saved me, and for the rest, why should I care?"

"If they hang you, Jack, it will be cold-blooded murder in reality," said Dashfield, "but they cannot—shall not do it—a thought has struck me—I will go to Brummell, he is a friend of mine, and in good favour with the regent. I will beseech of him to prevail upon the king to pardon you. Brummell, with all his extravagant follies, is a good man, and a Christian at heart, and will not turn a deaf ear to my supplication. What think you of the idea, Jack?"

"It is a right glorious one, a word from Brummell is worth twenty petitions, and his heart leaped with renewed hope. "But when can you see him, I am all impatience to ascertain the end of this new hope."

"I will seek him at once, Jack," answered Dashfield, "so for the present, farewell."

He arose, and at once went in quest of Brummell, who with Major Hanger and other nobilities of the day, were killing time at *ecarte*. To his honour be it recorded, Brummell's ear was always open to a petition for mercy, and he listened to Dashfield's statement with a willing and attentive ear.

"By Jove, I must see George about this—so gallant a fellow must not die—shall not die—I give you my word upon it, sir, go and comfort him with this assurance, if such an intrepid fellow can be by any possibility supposed for one single instant in want of comfort. But supposing I get the royal pardon for him, it can only be on condition of abandoning the road, tho 'fore God, he is the pleasantest highwayman I ever dealt with. Myself and Major Hanger had the felicity of being robbed by him once. I was tied to a tree, back 'gainst bark—Hanger there, found himself in a soft bed of a ditch hard by, ha, ha, ha! the drolest adventure that ever befel any man in existence. But get you gone in peace, sir, the man shall be saved—young George and myself are not on the best of terms, but he will not refuse his old friend, Brummy, a trifle like that."

"You will forgive my being importunate," said Dashfield, "but since the life of a dear friend is at stake, let me beseech you to write at once. I will myself be the bearer of the missive to Carlton House."

"As you will, sir. It shall be done," and calling for pen, ink, and paper, Brummell at once indited the following characteristic words:—

"In H M.'s gaol of Newgate lies John Rann, against whom sentence of death has been recorded. The said John Rann promises to abstain from all evil courses for the future, if pardoned. Please pardon the said John Rann, and oblige. Thine,   BRUMMELL.

"There," said Brummell, folding up the document, "there is salvation for your friend."

"I earnestly hope so," said Dashfield.

No. 52.

"Hope, my dear fellow, it has resolved itself into a certainty. Give that to the Prince Regent, he will at once give you a pardon."

"May God bless you for your noble generosity," said Dashfield, when Brummell, stopping his thanks with a wave of the hand, bid him be gone.

Dashfield flew to Carlton House—the prince was from home. A guinea fee gained him admittance to the valet de chambre of England's heir, who, for this remuneration, promised to lay the important note upon the regent's dressing-case. Satisfied he had secured the safety of our hero, Dashfield flew back to the prison, and from thence to the Malcolms, reporting as he went that Jack was saved.

Alas! delusive hopes! Brummell, for his sarcasm upon the regent, was in bad odour at Court, and his royal highness, in his petty malice, would not condescend to notice the late favourite's letter, but thrusting it unread into the fire, he said:—

"Another begging letter from that fellow, Brummell, I'll warrant—that," as he burnt it, "is the only answer he will ever get from me."

Day by day, as the order for execution was deferred, hopes grew stronger —vain hope. One morning the governor and ordinary entered Jack's cell— the former carried a mandate, signed by the royal hand, and sealed by the royal seal—It was the death warrant. In obedience to the usual custom, it was formally read to Jack by the governor.

"It is enough, sir," he said, "I am well content."

From that hour until the day of execution, the ordinary was a constant visitor with Jack.

Spite of all the despairing circumstances that environed him, Jack still maintained his unflinching spirit, and gay temper. Under the influence of this tide of hilarious glee, he was found on one occasion entertaining seven young ladies, who had honoured his cell with their presence; and, during this period conversation never flagged, but the laugh was as light, and the heart was as joyous as ever. Rare Jack Rann!

* * * *

The morning of the 30th of November, 1774, broke gloriously over the bustling city, and a brilliant ray of sunlight fell upon the thousands of faces watching round Newgate, for the day whereon our hero was to expiate his crimes by his life, had arrived, and oh! sad difference to the same whereon he had hoped to have left England for America. A death-like silence now reigned throughout the countless assembly: the prison door is opened, a voice shouts "He comes!" and instantly ten thousand voices in a deafening cheer greet our hero as he nimbly ascends the steps into the cart destined to convey him to the fatal tree at Tyburn. Their uproarious conduct—their joyful exclamations, their cheering cries—were such as to be more befitting attendance on the chariot wheels of a conqueror going to receive reward for his valour, than on the last step of a malefactor destined to die a fearful death.

On rolls the ponderous vehicle, almost filled with bouquets thrown by fair ladies from their balconies to the darling hero of the day, and the mo gathering strength as it progresses, presents a countless sea of human heads to the beholder.

St. Giles's is reached at length, and forth from the tavern celebrated for many ages past as the last resting place for malefactors on the road to death, comes the steaming bowl of St. Giles—whose hands are these that bears it—what young man is that apeing the landlord. There was no mistake, his jetty ringlets and laughing black eyes—it was Jarad Steele, the gipsey.

"What ho! Jack, my stunner, take thy draught, man, at St. Giles's, and let it be a right hearty one, 'twill warm thy heart for the fray."

"I am already prepared for that, Jared, my good friend," answered Jack, with a smile, then taking the bowl from Steele's outstretched hands, he drank long life and happiness to the surrounding throng, a cheer arose in return that made the welkin ring, and made the military close round the carriage, fearful lest the people in their enthusiasm should attempt the rescue of our hero.

"Jared, my friend, this happiness is beyond my most sanguine expectations—your hand, old fellow, I longed once again to feel its firm and honest grip, before mine grew cold and motionless for ever."

"Did'st think I had deserted thee, friend Jack—no, by heavens, I only longed for a dark hour like this to show you how firm a friend you have in Jared Steele—a word in your ear, my boy," and Jared whispered a something in our hero's ear that caused the latter to start with surprise, it was but momentary though, the emotion speedily subsided.

"Jared, my truthful loving friend, I thank you from the bottom of my heart for this unlooked for proof of your devotedness, but as you love me, listen to my last prayer—heed my last words! This must not—cannot be, mine alone shall be the only blood shed this day. I am resigned to my fate, and am prepared to meet it."

"I tell you, old friend, we are prepared to save you, and more, are determined to do it. Look around; cannot you discern amidst the sea of faces some old familiar countenance you were wont to be familiar with? I tell you there are a hundred of us armed to the teeth, sworn upon our souls to save or die by you."

"And by my soul," answered Jack solemnly, "I will not accept the proffered aid—I will abide my doom—nay, if you hesitate, I announce the attempt that is to be made to the soldiers."

"That would only be a twice told tale, for I have already peached," said a voice like the hiss of a snake in their ears, they turned simultaneously and confronted the dark and vindictive face of Night Owl Oliver.

"I swore I would see thee hanged, thou upstart cur," said Oliver, with hellish glee, "and curse you, but I will."

"Accursed villain!" exclaimed Jared, "take that for thy treachery," and drawing a pistol from his breast he levelled it at Oliver, but before he could fire, Jack struck the weapon from his grasp.

"Jared if you love me, draw your men off—escape is impossible, fresh military are arriving in every direction."

"Thou black-hearted malicious hound, you shall bitterly rue this," said Jared to Oliver, "by the God who made me, you shall," and Jared raised his hand impressively to heaven as he swore to the dreadful oath.

"Suffer me to die in peace—this brawl disgusts me," said Jack, "leave him unmolested, Jared, he will bring a better death upon himself, I can see it in his hang-dog countenance the while I speak. Farewell, my brave friend."

"Farewell," answered Jared, as choking with sobs the brave fellow in obedience to our hero's last wish took his departure and signalled his men off the ground.

On proceeded the sad procession—passing one house a white kerchief was waved. It was Miss Malcolm, who with superhuman courage had come to gaze upon him who had won and held her virgin love. It was but a glance she had of our hero, for the next moment, uttering a heart rending shriek of despair, she fell back insensible.

Tyburn is reached, and the fatal tree looms forebodingly in the distance. It is reached, and the cart is placed beneath the fatal beam.

Every head uncovered—every eye moistened—every heart full to bursting with grief, as they gaze upon the devoted young man, in all the pride and bloom of manly beauty, so soon to perish ignominiously before their eyes.

Oh, God! that such scenes should be.

"Hush! silence! the prisoner speaks," shouts a voice, and then sobs are hushed, and a death-like silence prevails.

"Friends," said Jack Rann, in a calm and collected voice, and with a look of confidence wonderfully at variance with the agitated faces around him, "you have come to see a brave man die. May his fate be a warning to you—may his last words sink deep into your hearts, and be a warning to save you from sin and destruction. Young men, to you, I, one of the race of highwaymen, more particularly address myself. Listen to my words as to a voice coming from the grave—for, in a few moments, the tongue now addressing you will be silenced for ever. I beseech you to be honest, for honesty is the sure road to happiness ; without it there can be no peace of mind—no real joy upon earth. Turn you away from the path of sin—it is the path of misery, leading to death. Be sober, drink fetters the soul, weakens the mind, destroys the body. These are the last counsels of Sixteen-string Jack—follow them, and God will bless you throughout your road of life, Had I followed them, I should not now be standing doomed to die a dog's death on this tree—but if only one of you take warning, I shall not have lived or have died in vain.

After a few moments Jack Rann ceased to exist. His wife, who we left in Newgate, was afterwards liberated, but the awful climax of her matrimonial career had such an effect on her health, that but a brief space intervened between the execution of her husband and her own death.

THE END.

Steal not this Book my honest friend
for fear the Gallows should be your end
and when I die the Lord +shew—

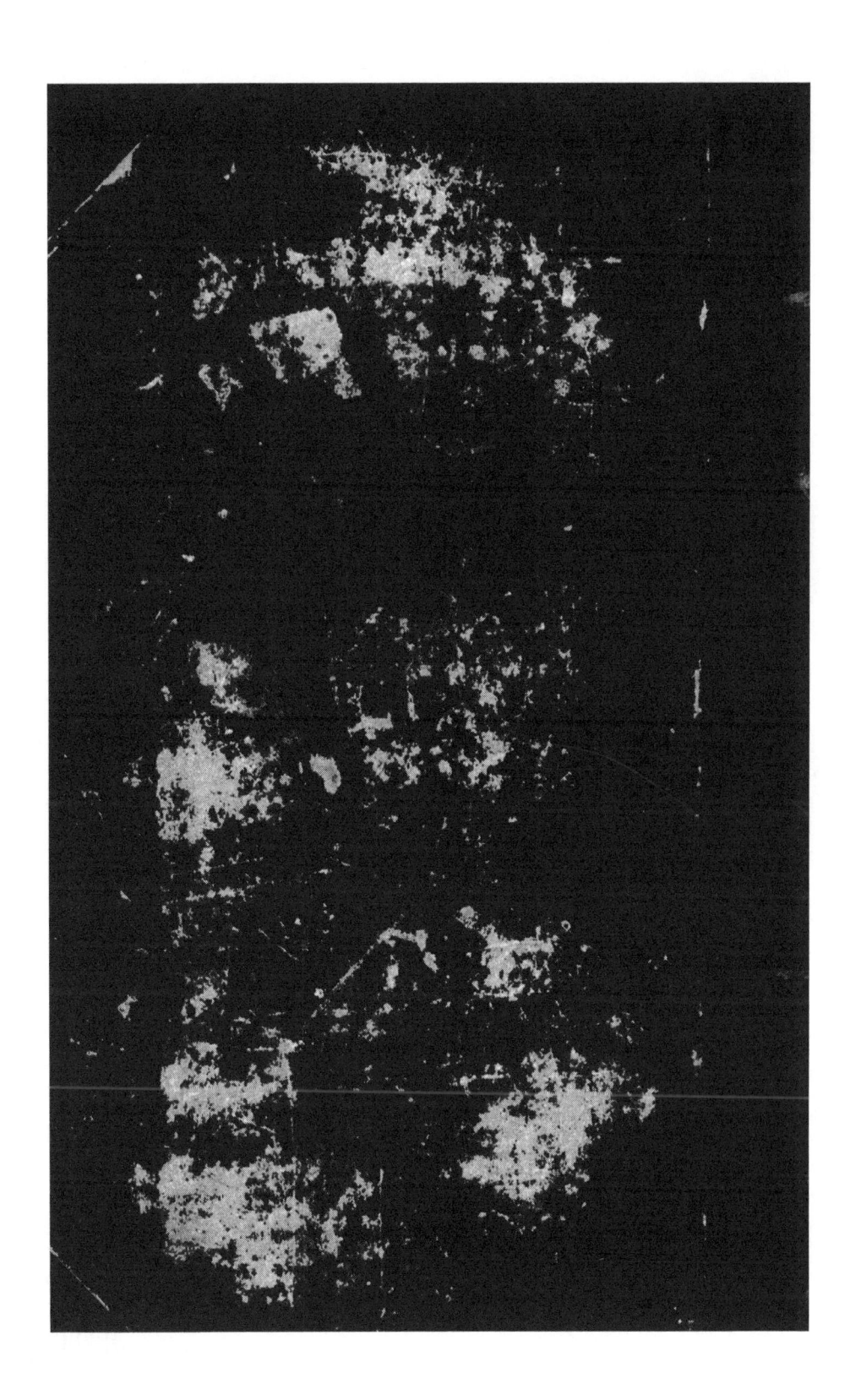

Ingram Content Group UK Ltd.
Milton Keynes UK
UKHW031835060323
418105UK00011B/1214